Roll of the Fallen

Trevor Harkin

2009

War Memorial Park Publications

City of Coventry

Roll of the Fallen

The Great War

First Edition 2009

This book is sold subject to the conditions that it shall not, by way of trade or otherwise, be lent, re-sold, hired out or otherwise circulated without the publisher's prior consent.
All rights reserved.

No part of this publication may be reproduced or transmitted in any form or by any means electronic or mechanical, including photographic or recording, or any information retrieval system, without the permission in writing from the publishers.
Copyright © Trevor Harkin 2009

Published by War Memorial Park Publications

For a copy of this publication e-mail trevorharkin@btinternet.com

In association with

Printed on Recycled Paper

Printed on a RICOH Pro C900 at The RICOH Arena Printroom, Coventry.

In Memory of

those who fought and fell in

The Great War

Preface

In 2004 on a visit to the War Memorial Park I noted the details of a memorial plaque dedicated to a Private F. Grant. Having researched my own family tree, I researched Private Grant's details via the Commonwealth War Grave Commission and on subsequent visits to the War Memorial Park noted the names on all the plaques. I added all these details to a web page and launched www.warmemorialpark.co.uk.

Local appeals were made and relatives of the deceased came forward with information, this enthusiasm combined with the number of hits the website received inspired me to research further. It was during research into *'Bablake School and the Great War'*, and *'War Memorial Park'* that I realized a number of men were missing from the original Roll of the Fallen printed in 1927. The release of the Roll coincided with the dedication of the cenotaph by Field Marshall Earl Haig and contained the names of 2,587 fallen men. Copies were made available at the time for purchase by the family and friends of the Fallen. After publication a further thirteen names were added in an amendment.

This 2009 Edition adds further details to the biographies of the Fallen with the addition of photos where applicable.

Trevor Harkin

Acknowledgments

Researching and compiling this book would not have been possible without the support of my wife, Emma and children Molly and Toby allowing me to indulge in this passion.

The Commonwealth War Grave Commission (CWGC) Head Office in particular Maureen Annetts was fundamental in helping with the complex searches and background information whilst their UK Office assisted with grave location in the UK. The work of the equivalent bodies in Australia and Canada also needs to be recognized. Information on the men with an Australian or Canadian connection have been uploaded to the relevant web pages. For those commemorated in Tyne Cot Cemetery, research has been shared with the Passchendaele project.

The men commemorated enlisted with a number of different Regiments and thanks need to be expressed to the following curators and archivists.

Alastair Massie from the National Army Museum, Jacqueline Minchinton from Northampton County Council, Matthew Buck, Curator Kings Regiment Liverpool Museums, Bryan Johnson Curator of the Warwickshire Yeomanry Museum, David Baynham and Stephanie Bennett from the Royal Regiment of Fusiliers (Royal Warwickshire), Mike Marr and Dino Lemonofides, Oxfordshire and Buckinghamshire Light Infantry Museum, Mick Wilkes from the Worcestershire and Sherwood Foresters` Regiment, Celia Green and Martin Everett from the Royal Regiment of Wales Museum, Colonel (Retd) I. H. McCausland of Royal Green Jackets, Alan Readman, West Sussex Records Office, Major (Retd) T. W. Stipling and Barry Yelland Duke of Cornwall's Light Infantry Museum, Tony Sprason, Lancashire Fusiliers' Museum, Martin Everett and Brian Owen, Regimental Museum of the Royal Welsh, Major C. M. J Deedes, Light Infantry Office, Geoffrey J. Crump, Cheshire Military Museum, Louis Scully, Worcestershire Regiment, Rachel Holmes, Royal Hampshire Regiment Museum, Major Douglas Farrington, Lancashire Regiment, Lieutenant Colonel George Latham, Seaforth Highlanders, and finally Stuart Eastwood, Border Regiment.

Thanks also to the following individuals and institutions who assisted. Dr. Robin Darwall-Smith, Magdalen College, Presidents and Fellows of Magdalen College, Mr. Michael Riordan, St. John's and the Queen's Colleges, Jackie Tarrant-Barton, Old Etonian Association, Julie Wakefield, Museum of the Royal Pharmaceutical Society, Alan Nutt, Chairman, Coventry No 3 Branch (GEC) Royal British Legion, Valerie Bedford and David Fletcher, Tank Museum, Rolls Royce Heritage Trust, Parkside Branch, Miss Anna Sander, Lonsdale Curator of Archives and Manuscripts, Balliol College, Jo Draper, Lyme Regis Museum, John Moreland and Rusty MacLean, Rugby School, Vicky Harrison, York Minster, Rob Phillips, King Henry VIII School Library, Terry Patchett, Bablake School, John Devereaux, King's Liverpool Regiment John Burton & Vince Taylor, Bedworth Historical Society, Damien Kimberley, Archive Researcher, Coventry's Transport Museum, David Read, Soldiers of Gloucestershire Museum and Nigel Lutt, Bedfordshire and Luton Archives and Records Section.

In the research, I came across a number of individuals who are working on projects which have relevance to those commemorated. In particular, information has been shared with the following and I thank them for their input and permission to use pictures and material. Rob Phillips, King Henry VIII School, Terry Reeves, Local War Memorials, Patrick Casey, Clifton Rugby Club, Andrew and Liz McDonald, Second Lieutenant Cheshire, Mandy Breculli, Foleshill Congregational Church, Stephen Pearson, Western Front Association, Stockport, Alex Revell for information on those killed in the RAF, Rod Evans for information on the men with a Birmingham connection, Kevan Darby on men with the 9th Bn., Royal Warwickshire, Susan Tall, Kenilworth Men, Steve Morse, 9th Bn. Sherwood Foresters, Alan Tucker for information on men with the Royal Warwickshire Regiment, Rev. Michael Edward, Senior Minister, Salem Baptist Church, Roger Davis, Ian O'Hara and Father Paul Burch, St. Thomas the Apostle Church, Longford, Melvyn Pack, Fromelles Men, Malcolm Cooper, The Great War Society, Terry Carter Birmingham Pals Battalion, Robin Trigger, Ryton Memorial, and Chris Baker webmaster and author of the Long, Long Trail: The story of the British Army in the Great War.

The records maintained by Andrew Beechey, Coventry Local Studies Library and the City Archives have been essential in adding information to the details of the fallen and those who served and their permission to use pictures and photographs is gratefully acknowledged as well of the assistance of staff.

Thanks to the following for publicity, Sheila Adams from *'The Earlsdon Echo'*, Tom Cooke, BBC CWR, Cheryl Liddle, Coventry University Alumni Association, Cathy Clapison, Coventry Council, Mike and Vivien Mattocks from the Coventry Family History Society, The Coventry Telegraph, Mercia FM, Warwickshire Life, Marion Thomas for displaying a poster in the café in the park and Christopher Jones from Kundert & Co. Solicitors for association with this project.

Neil Clark for access to his pictorial databases on officers who died in the Great War. Mick Baker for donating an entire series of *'The Great War...I Was There'*. Diana Fisher for the indexing work on local service men, Kay Dunkley, Coventry Family History Society, Brian Cornelius, Tim Parsons, David Hughes and Roydon Buckler for an insight into medal collecting and Lee Lindon for access to his medals and ephemera on Coventry men. Nigel Hoare for access to his WW1 books, Alexander Hoare for assistance with promotional materials, Dave Lewis from Culture and Leisure and Mark Percival, GIS Manager, Coventry City Council and Ron Herdman former Chairman, Friends of the War Memorial Park.

In numerous cases I have been contacted directly by the families of the Fallen and I thank them for their assistance. Colin Irving (Gunner Herbert Charles Collingbourne), Rebecca Baker (Gunner Alfred George Middleton), Robert Clarke (Lance Corporal Victor Leslie Clarke), Father Michael Gamble (Private William Stagg), Daphne Plummer (Private Arthur Lewin Marshall Bull), Terry Patchett (Trooper William Ivens Patchett), Jill and Trevor Paginton (Lance Corporal Sydney James Riley), Maxine Spencer (Private Eric Keppell Purnell), Andrew Bell (Private Walter Frank Francis), Mrs Julie Stevenson (Private Lawrence Cecil Cox), Lynne and Nigel Page (Gunner Frederick George Page), Mr R. Barnett (Sapper William Joseph Barnett), Mrs Vera Bench (Bench family), Malcolm Bennett (Bench family), Bertram Rawlins (Son of Private Bert Rawlins), Alan Turner (Private William Simmons), Peter Tomlinson (Private Ernest Edward Waring), Mr. Ken Olorenshaw (Private Percy Elliman), Victoria Constance Hutt (Private Bert Hutt), Graham Williams (Private Bertie Hutt), Mr. Richards (Captain Joseph Arthur Richards), Mr. John Greenhill (Second Lieutenant Joseph Arthur Edwards), Damien Kimberley (Private Edward Ernest Kimberley), Richard Parker (Privates George and Leonard Twamely), and R. Chittem (Private John Thomas Chittem), Stan Corrall, (Private Joseph Henry Corrall), Pauline Greenfield (Private Horace Godsell), Diane Fisher (Lance Corporal Walter Athersuch), Jenny Coates (Lance Corporal Leonard Morris), Darren Brown, (The crew of the E18), Dave Lewis (Privates David Charles and Private William Colin Flavell), Madeline Pallett (Second Lieutenant Frederick Charles Vincent), June and John Raven, (Private Ernest Kilpack), and Michael Smith (Private Edward Walter Newbold).

To those who remain anonymous but were cajoled into helping by those mentioned above, I also express my thanks.

The Evidence

Throughout this book various resources have been compiled to build a history of the men who fell from Coventry in the Great War, the main sources of reference were the Soldiers Died in the Great War Database, the original Roll of the Fallen and the Commonwealth War Grave Commision. The Commission's official cut off date for a death to be counted as war related is the 31st August 1921, this date is determined by *'The Termination of the Present War (Definition) Act'*. Some of the men commemorated died after the 31st August 1921, these are not formally documented as war related. About one third of the Commission's records show no details for next of kin. This is because not all the "Final Verification" forms sent to the last known address of a casualty's next of kin were returned.

The Commission were kind enough to search Next of Kin details for Allesley, Ash Green, Binley, Canley, Coundon, Coventry, Earlsdon, Exhall, Foleshill, Keresley, Tile Hill and provide details on local cemeteries including London Road, Windmill Road and those in the districts of Binley, Foleshill, Walsgrave and Stoke.

The *'City of Coventry: Roll of the Fallen'* published in 1927, includes the names of 2,587 soldiers who fell and were either born, employed or resided in Coventry. Detail on each entry varies but typically covers name, rank, regiment, former regiment, address, birth details, occupation and in some cases employer. It is estimated that over 35,000 soldiers from Coventry served during the Great War. The original Roll of the Fallen referred to a memorial in the Cathedral Church of St. Michaels which was probably lost during the air raids of World War 2.

Local memorials have also been consulted to understand where the men worked, lived, worshipped and are commemorated. Sadly some of these are no longer in existence and photographs were used. Church Memorials included St. John's Church, St. Barbara's Church, Queens Road Church, St. Michael's Church, St. Paul's Church, Holy Trinity, St. James Church, Central Methodist Hall, St. Thomas (Keresley), St. Thomas the Apostle (Longford), Roll of Honour, Salem Baptist Church and Wesleyan Church (Stoney Stanton Road). Works, School and Social Club memorials included Triumph and Gloria Works, Coventry Chain, Iliffe & Sons Ltd, Post Office, Coventry Corporation Memorials (Gas Department, Education, Finance, Electricity etc), British Thompson Houston, Dunlop Memorial, Earlsdon Working Mens Club, Barras Green Working Mens Club, Bablake School, King Henry VIII School and plaques in the War Memorial Park.

District memorials included Ryton, Walsgrave, Wolston, Radford, Baginton and Exhall.

The Coventry Graphic, The Midland Daily Telegraph, The Coventry Herald, Bedworth Echo and Foleshill News and The Coventry Chronicle, Rudge Record, Siddeley Deasy Works Magazine: The Employees Quarterly, The Wheatleyan (Bablake School Magazine), The Coventrian (King Henry VIII School Magazine), Bablake School Roll of Honour, The Link (Coventry Chain) Magazine, The Limit, White & Poppe Magazine, The Original Roll of Honour 1927, St. Thomas Parish Magazine, Coventry Corporation: Roll of Honour. The Great War and Siddeley Deasy Motor Co. Ltd Roll of Honour were all consulted. Other sources have been consulted: *'Canadian Overseas Expeditionary Force Attestation Papers'*, *'The National Archives of Australia'*, and the UK National Archives.

Museum and local councils have also started their own databases and material has been taken from these sources. In numerous cases I have been contacted by members of the family and the information was received gratefully. It is important to note, however, that the cross- referencing of material has indicated anomalies, in particular order of forenames, middle names, rank, spelling, address etc. In the case of names I have gone with the majority. *'The London Gazette'* has been used for citations and dates of commission. Each piece of evidence from the above sources adds to the picture of those commemorated. Original records should be consulted if required or further information is sought.

Coventry and the Great War

From the assassination of Archduke Franz Ferdinand on 28th June 1914, it took only five weeks for Europe to slide from a state of peace to a state of war. Britain was bound by treaty to aid Belgium and thus declared war against Germany on the 4th August 1914. The War would take more then four years to end with the signing of the Armistice on the 11th November, 1918. To mark the end of the war, the 19th July, 1919 was declared as the date for a Celebration of Peace and events were held nationally to mark the occasion. The events in Coventry started on the 18th July, 1919 at 8.00pm with massed singing with over 4,000 boys from the Elementary Schools and ended at 7.00pm on the 19th July, 1919 with singing from 4,000 girls from the Elementary Schools.

To mark the occasion an Official Programme priced 4d was published and the following by H. C. Wilkins extracted.

From the outbreak to the close of this gigantic struggle, the city was a microcosm of War. Large ordnance had been made here for some years before 1914, and representatives of the Government purchased other munitions in the city as early as 'War Sunday' (August 2nd). From that time till after the Armistice was signed (November 11th, 1918) the production of War material went on. It was not until the closing week of July that the public realized the probability of War – not generally indeed, till the last day. Notices to reserves and to sailors and soldiers on furlough in the city to report at depots and stations were served during one night, and the men departed quietly by early trains next morning.

Crowds of people left Coventry for their holidays and the 7th battalion Warwickshire Territorial's for annual camp at Rhyl- so little was the real international situation understood. On Sunday British Cabinet Councils were held, English newspapers appeared morning, afternoon and night; sermons and prayers in the churches took note of ' a time of unparalleled anxiety'. The Bank Holiday following was rather a time of scuttling back home than of enjoyment of people at distant places. Tuesday found banks still closed, with intimation that they would open on Friday. The British Government delivered it's ultimatum to Germany. The die was cast. In the succeeding days of that terrible week the people returned home in thousands; the Territorial's came back to be sent to Weymouth for duty: Colonel Wyley called for volunteers to raise a second battalion and men quickly responded. It was a time of much outward excitement, but the citizens were calm about the duty of Great Britain in the crisis. A Recruiting Office was at once set up in the Masonic Hall and young men lined up in their thousands. It is estimated COVENTRY SENT AN ARMY OF OVER 35,000 TO THE COLOURS. Even boys left their employments in the early days of the war to volunteer for a share in the work. Many over stated their age in order to enlist.

Committees for all kinds of War Work, including the relief of men, women and children whose relatives were in the fighting forces were quickly called into existence. Red Cross work was organized, funds for prisoners of war and others were opened, and most liberally supported during the whole period of hostilities. Everybody who could help, did so. Clergymen went as Chaplains in Navy and Army, others to work in factories; some doctors took duty in the field and at Home Stations, and those who remained here shared the work of absent colleagues; layman took war duty at soldiers camps and elsewhere. There were large bodies of citizens who did voluntary work connected with recruiting, tribunals, pensions and billeting. The work was undertaken in addition to normal working hours and over 4,000,000 hours were worked during a period of a little over eighteen months. By the middle of August England became the asylum of Belgians driven from their homes, and Coventry took in some hundreds. The refugees first of all lodged at Whitley Abbey under the care of a local committee. Their 'token of gratitude' is a morale slab on the staircase of St. Mary's Hall. The prices of almost all necessities of life rapidly increased and there was soon a grave shortage.

The Navy and Army, through the War Department spent over £40,500, 000 in Coventry. The city was an arsenal for four and a half years. The Ministry of Munitions was formed in May, 1915 and extensive orders for munitions were placed in Coventry. We produced big ordnance, quick firing guns, aeroplanes and parts, machine tools, shells, small arm munitions, motor vehicles of all kinds, cycles, tanks, ambulance trailers, aircraft engines, magnetos, gun and submarine parts, bombs, incendiary bullets, drop forgings and the National Filling Factory supply the following remarkable figures; Fuses filled 19,940,000; Grenades filled 9,880,000; Detonators filled 31,060,000. Aerodromes and flying grounds were made. Night work was as persistent as day labour. In almost all factories, funds for the relief of the dependents of those who were serving, were commenced and over £100,000 had been subscribed when hostilities ceased.

It was not enough of course, to build and equip factories for making appliances of war; they had to filled with workers. The labour forces of the country were organized through the Employment Exchanges and 30,000 men, women and girls were drafted into Coventry. Six hundred houses were quickly put up on Stoke Heath, in Holbrook's Lane five hundred wooden cottages, but these tenements were not nearly sufficient, so there was official billeting of lodgers. Dwellings were more then full. The fact that work was done by some people in the day, and by others in the night, helped to render the domestic situation less acute than it otherwise may have been. Beds, like the piece of furniture at Goldsmith's Village Inn, 'contrived a debt to pay' – they were used both day and night. (Special legislation of the time arrested rise of house rents and landlord's powers in vacating tenancies!). Over sixteen thousand people came to Coventry, daily by railway train, and went out at evening or morning; Birmingham, Leamington, Warwick, Rugby. Bedworth, Nuneaton and Atherstone and all the villages round about, had their Coventry workers.

The people who temporarily lived in the city, and many of whom had no real homes in which to rest out of working hours, crowded the darkened streets and houses of amusement and paraded the town thoroughfares and suburban roads. It was a weird sight to see policemen on point duty wearing (red) electric lights in their helmets.

Ariel warfare did not seriously affect Coventry. No actual damage took place here through air raids, but the city was the object of at least two attacks. Precautions were taken in the mobilization of special constables with a motor cyclist corps, and many warnings had to be given to the public to screen windows and to keep indoors. On January 31st, 1917, German raiders skirted the City and passed to South Staffordshire, were much damage was done. The dropping of bombs twenty miles away was distinctly heard in Coventry. On April, 12th , 1918 the raiders dropped bombs in the grounds of Whitley Abbey and on Baginton Sewage Farm. The guns at Keresley and Wyken Grange came into action, and the powerful searchlights were used. Aeroplanes were send up from Radford Ground to meet the raiders, who, however, passed to the south west and avoided conclusions.

There were three Royal visits tot he City during the War- King George V came in 1915; the Queen and Princess Mary in 1917; and Princess Victoria in 1917. His Majesty reviewed the 29th Division at Knightlow Hill in March, 1915.

It was a new experience for the English People to be rationed for necessities of life, but that was one of the unavoidable incidents of the war. Supplies of all sorts were very short in the winter of 1917 -1918 and always dear in price. But food rationing, which came during the Autumn of 1917, stopped the queues outside shops which had been so distressing and experience to the women folk. We were rationed too, for coal, gas, and electric light. It is a tale of brave days and an epic to be told for generations to come. Public restaurants were set up in St. Mary's Hall kitchen and in Ford Street.

Women did work hitherto undertaken by men only. There were policewoman and post women and telegraph messenger girls, there were tram women; shops and public schools were nearly all staffed by women; women railway porters, farm workers, drivers, shop porters etc.

It is not possible within the limits of only a few pages to mark more then the scant record of the great work in Coventry and Warwickshire Hospital and the Coventry Division of the V.A.D. 21 Warwickshire. The hospital had 140 civilian beds at the outbreak of war; and at the end there were 160 civil and180 military beds. The hospital treated 2,497 wounded soldiers; Courtaulds V.A.D 1,246; Hill Crest V.A.D over 1,000.

Seventeen convoys came to Coventry. The motor transport attached to VAD21 Warwickshire dealt with the transport of wounded soldiers for the whole of Warwickshire; there were 45 members who removed 6,250 cases and covered, 17,250 miles.

Original Foreword

At the start of 1924, the mammoth task of compiling the 'Roll of the Fallen' was given to the City Librarian, Charles Nowell. The details from the initial pages of the Roll of the Fallen are replicated below:

For the purpose of compiling this roll the term "Coventry men" has been held to include those born in Coventry, together with those who at any time lived or were employed in the City. The following details have been inserted wherever possible: name, Rank, regiment or Ship; Place and date of birth; residence and occupation; date of enlistment; date of death and place of burial; details of service decorations awarded. This record was compiled at the invitation of the City Council of Coventry, by Charles Nowell, City Librarian and printed by W. W. Curtis Ltd, Cheylesmore Press, Coventry, September, 1927.

Foreword
The citizens of Coventry as a lasting tribute to those who fell in the Great War 1914 –1918, have provided (by subscription) the War Memorial and the beautiful Park in which it is erected. In the Memorial itself, is placed this Roll of the Fallen, so that those who follow may be ever reminded of the sacrifice they so nobly made, together with the consequent grief borne by those who mourned them.

Although great care has been taken in the compilation of this record, it cannot possibly be a complete roll of those who fell, and arrangements have been made to include any additional names, which may be received later, in the official copy to be enshrined in the Memorial, and in those copies available for public inspection in St. Mary's Hall and in the Gulson Library.

This civic roll of honour, therefore is record of 2,587 Coventry men who fell in the great war of 1914-1918 a record of men who gave us their all for us. How our hearts throb with emotion at the price paid, yet with what pride do we recall devotion, their valour, their sacrifice even unto death; perpetuating the glorious traditions characteristic of the British nation wherever liberty and freedom has been assailed.

What of the future and the inheritances placed in our care and custody by these brave heroes ?, "never again", should be our watchword. It should be the duty of those who are their successors to work and labour, with all earnestness, to make the future happier, more peaceful and more joyful.

So may our destiny be along the surer paths of Peace, may we be spared the terrors and sufferings of war endured by those we lovingly cherish and ever remember. May their memories and sacrifices be the precursor of an everlasting Peace and the brotherhood of mankind.

Coventry has taken a prominent part in many events which have shaped the history of England, but no chapter of its annals is finer then that containing this glorious but tragic record. Therefore let those who follow after see that its glory remains undimmed, and that this sacrifice is ever held in proud and grateful remembrance

> *Their glorious name shall be adored,*
> *Great with love and great their worth;*
> *Their fame shall purify the earth,*
> *And honour be their dear Reward.*
>
> *Alderman Fred Lee, Mayor*

'The Coventry Herald' stated "The Roll of the Fallen, is witness indeed to the share of Coventry in the grim struggle which saw many thousands leave the city to take part in the war. It is a grievous loss – no less the 2,587 men in their prime, having years of usefulness before them, to whom, in numerous instances no doubt, life was very precious and widening in all its allure: plenty of sons whose parents have never ceased to mourn them, not a few heads of families whose widows and children still feel the loss".

Roll of the Fallen

ABBEY, Sergeant, Alfred. 840648, D Battery, 307th Brigade, Royal Field Artillery. Killed in action, 13th August, 1917. Born 7th December, 1887 at Northampton. Resided at 80, Coventry Street, Upper Stoke. Enlisted Coventry, 1915. Gas Fitter, Coventry Gas Works Ltd. Commemorated St. John's Church and Gas Department Memorial, Coventry Corporation. Leaves a widow and two children. Grave Ref. III. E. 13. White House Cemetery, St. Jean-Les-Ypres, Belgium.

ABEL, Private, Frederick Cecil. 50938, 9th Bn., Cheshire Regiment formerly Royal Warwickshire Regiment. Died of wounds received at Messines Ridge, 20th June, 1917. Age 19. Son of Sidney and Mary Eliza Abel of 92, Widdrington Road, Coventry. Born 5th February, 1898, at Hassocks, Sussex. Enlisted October, 1916 at Coventry. Loom Builder. Brother of Pioneer Sidney Arthur Abel. Commemorated War Memorial Park. Grave Ref. 213. 6. 29. (Screen Wall). Kensal Green (All Soul's) Cemetery, London.

ABEL, Pioneer, Sidney Arthur. 130193, 1st Bn., Special Brigade, Royal Engineers formerly Middlesex Regiment. Died of wounds (gas) on the Somme, 26th June, 1916 when a shell burst a pipe through which asphyxiating gas was being discharged, died a few hours later. Age 20. Son of Sidney and Eliza Mary Abel, of Coventry. Born 8th February, 1896 at Brighton. Resided at 92, Widdrington Road, Coventry. Enlisted December, 1915. Brass Finisher. Brother of Private Frederick Cecil Abel. Commemorated War Memorial Park. Grave Ref. 1. B. 45. Louvencourt Military Cemetery, Somme, France.

ABROOK, Lance Corporal, Ernest Albert. 33032, 1st Bn., Royal Berkshire Regiment formerly 17292, Royal Warwickshire Regiment. Killed in action, 10th September, 1917. Age 37. Son of Tom and Elizabeth Abrook, of Ryde, Isle of Wight. Born Ryde, Hants. Enlisted Coventry. Grave Ref. I. A. 31. Beuvry Communal Cemetery Extension, France.

ADAMS, Captain, Arthur Joseph. 1st Bn., Royal Warwickshire Regiment. Killed in action, 30th August, 1918 druing an attack on Cambrai. Born 22nd January, 1885 at Coventry. Resided at London. Enlisted September, 1914 in a Public Schools Bn. Commissioned with 3rd Bn., Royal Warwickshire and badly wounded 2nd July, 1916. Send to France, April, 1918 with the 1st Bn. Solicitor. Practised at 25, Bedford Row, W. C., and Coventry. Commemorated Bablake School Memorial. Son of Mr. W. H. Adams, 28, Allesley Old Road. Leaves a widow and two children. Brother of Second Lieutenant Fredererick Adams, RFC. Grave Ref. VI. E. 1. Vis-En-Artois British Cemetery, Haucourt, France.

ADAMS, Gunner, Charles Ernest. 183957, 25th Battery, 35th Brigade, Royal Field Artillery. Killed in action, Ypres, 20th October, 1917. Age 30. Son of Charles and Rose Adams, of 104, Queen's Walk, Peterborough. Husband of Amy Ethel Adams of 50, Northfield Road, Coventry. Born 27th January, 1887, at Peterborough. Enlisted November, 1916 at Coventry. Memorial Ref. Panel 4 to 6 and 162. Tyne Cot Memorial, Zonnebeke, West-Vlaanderen, Belgium.

ADAMS, Private, Eric. 9350, 2nd Bn., South Staffordshire Regiment. Died of wounds, 17th May, 1915. Born at Moseley, Worcestershire. Resided at Coventry. Storekeeper, Coventry Corporation Gas Department. Commemorated Gas Department Memorial, Coventry Corporation. Grave Ref. III. D. 15. Bethune Town Cemetery, France.

ADAMS, Second Lieutenant, Frederick. 53rd Squadron, Royal Flying Corps and General List. Shot down over the German lines near Messines, 12th May, 1917. Age 28. Son of W. H. and E. Adams of Coventry. Born 24th October, 1888 at Coventry. Resided at Coventry. Mechanic. Reburied in 1924. Commemorated Bablake School Memorial. Brother of Captain Arthur Joseph Adams. Son of Mr. W. H. Adams, 28, Allesley Old Road. Grave Ref. I. H. 20. Oosttaverne Wood Cemetery, Heuvelland, West-Vlaanderen, Belgium.

ADAMS, Private, Frederick William. 12500, 76th Coy., Machine Gun Corps. Reported to have been shot by a sniper and died instantaneously, 26th September 1917. Born 19th March, 1982 at Coventry. Resided at 49, Stanley Street, Great Heath. Enlisted December, 1916 at Coventry. Employed W. H. Grant and Son, Foreman, Textiles. Leaves a widow. Grave Ref. L II. C. 8. Poelcapelle British Cemetery, Belgium.

ADAMS, Private, John (also known as Jack). 2406, B Company, 1st/7th Bn., Royal Warwickshire Regiment. Killed in action, near Messines 9th May, 1915 struck by a shell. Brother of Mr. F. A. Adams, of 10, Thomas Street, Butts, Coventry. Born 19th March, 1892 at Coventry. Resided at back of 2, Moat Street. Enlisted September, 1914 at Coventry. Fiancé of Miss Hilda Harris of 34, Weston Street. Commemorated War Memorial Park and Siddeley Roll of Honour. Grave Ref. V. C. 8. La Plus Douve Farm Cemetery, Comines-Warneton, Hainaut, Belgium.

ADAMS, Private, John. 8094, 2nd Bn., Welsh Regiment. Killed in action, 6th November, 1914. Age 28. Son of Caleb and Sarah Ann Adams. Husband of Elizabeth Abigail Adams, of 376, Longford Road, Exhall, Coventry. Commemorated Saint Thomas the Apostle, Longford. Born Rowley Regis, Staffs. Enlisted Mountain Ash. Memorial Ref. Panel 37. Ypres (Menin Gate) Memorial, Ieper, West-Vlaanderen, Belgium.

ADAMSON, Second Lieutenant, George. 12th Bn., Highland Light Infantry. Died, leading his men, Battle of Loos, 25th September, 1915. Age 22. Only son of John (Surveyor, Customs and Excise, Coventry) and Dorothy Adamson, of 10, Ashley Gardens, Tunbridge Wells formerly of Southwood, Styechale Avenue. Born 27th January, 1893 at Gargunnock, Stirlingshire. Resided at Coventry from 1906 until 1911, educated King Henry VIII School, then undergraduate at St. John's College, Oxford. Enlisted September, 1914. Commemorated King Henry VIII School. Received commission, 27th November, 1914. Memorial Ref. Panel 108 to 112. Loos Memorial, Pas de Calais, France.

ADCOCK, Captain, Harold Meredyth. "D" Coy., 10th Bn., Lancashire Fusiliers. Killed in action, 5th July, 1916. Age 25. Son of Charles and Alice Margaret Adcock, of 15, Charleville Mansions, Barons Court, West Kensington, London. Educated at Ellesmere College, Shropshire (Member O. R. C.) Christ's College, Cambridge (Medieval and Modern Languages Tripos, 1912, Member O.T.C.). Schoolmaster at Real Gymnasium, Frankfurt-an-der-Oder, Prussia, and later at Bablake School Coventry. Officer Commanding, Cadet Corps at Bablake. Gazetted, September, 1914 to the Lancashire Fusiliers. Born 23rd August, 1890 at Horsham, Sussex. Resided in Meriden Street. Commemorated St. John's Church and Bablake School Memorial. Memorial Ref. Pier and Face 3 C and 3 D. Thiepval Memorial, Somme, France. (Possibly buried in Sheeter Wood near Pozieres).

ADDISON, Sergeant, Charles. 528059, 14th Bn., London Regiment (London Scottish) formerly 3349, Gordon Highlanders. Killed in action, 31st August, 1918. Age 34. Husband of Marion Addison, of 39, Grafton Street, Coventry. Born at Aberdeen. Resided Aberdeen. Grave Ref. Sp. Mem. B. 4. H. A. C. Cemetery, Ecoust-St. Mein, Pas de Calais, France.

ADKINS, Private, Charles. 3194, 7th Reserve Bn., Royal Warwickshire Regiment. Died, home, 8th March, 1916. Age 38. Son of Mark and Elizabeth Adkins, of Coventry. Served in the North West Frontier Expedition, 1908. Enlisted Coventry. Grave Ref. 163. 145. Coventry (London Road) Cemetery.

ADKINS, Private, Charles Edwin. 267733, 2nd/6th Bn., Royal Warwickshire Regiment. Killed in action, 27th May, 1918. Age 34. Son of Mr. and Mrs. Edward Adkins, of Fillongley. Husband of Ada Mabel Adkins, of Didgley Cottage, Fillongley, Coventry. Employed at Coventry. Enlisted Nuneaton. Grave Ref. 4/5. Isbergues Communal Cemetery, Pas de Calais, France.

ADKINS, Driver, George Henry. T/293322, 3rd Div. Train, Royal Army Service Corps. Died of wounds, received at Cambrai, 30th September, 1918. Age 30. Son of Mr. and Mrs. A. C. Adkins, of Coventry. Husband of L. A. Adkins, of 29, Spon End, Coventry. Born 10th March, 1888 in Day's Lane. Enlisted June, 1916 at Coventry. Horse Driver. Grave Ref. XIV. B. 16. Grevillers British Cemetery, Pas de Calais, France.

ADKINS, Ordinary Seaman, Thomas Frederick. J/21941, HMS Bulwark, Royal Navy. Killed, 26th October, 1914 with internal explosion of vessel. Age 18. Resided Stoneleigh. Memorial Ref. Panel 3. Portsmouth Naval Memorial.

ADLER, Private, Edward. 266855, 2nd/7th Bn., Royal Warwickshire Regiment. Killed in action, 3rd December, 1917. Born 10th November, 1894 in Bradford Street. Resided at 57, Freehold Street. Enlisted in 1916 at Coventry. Driver. Memorial Ref. Panel 3. Cambrai Memorial, Louveral, France.

ADMANS, Lance Corporal, Walter George. 13092, 1st Bn., Coldstream Guards. Died of wounds, received in the Battle of Hooge, 10th August, 1915 in hospital at Calais. Son of Walter George and Ida Admans of Sunny Side Cottage, Donnington, Newbury, Berkshire. Born at Hampstead, Middlesex. Resided in Avon Street, Barras Green. Enlisted October, 1914 at Coventry. Employed by Johnson and Mason. Leaves a widow and two children. Grave Ref. A. 3. 1. Calais Southern Cemetery, France.

ADSETT, Private, Thomas. 291455, C Company, 13th Bn., Gloucestershire Regiment formerly 5654, Royal Warwickshire Regiment. Died whilst prisoner of war (France), 31st October, 1918 captured 26th April. Born 3rd November, 1898, at 9c. 4h. Well Street. Resided in Union Street. Brother of Miss W. Adsett who resided at 13c. 4h. Well Street, Coventry. Enlisted June, 1916, Coventry. Grave Ref. 136. Erquelinnes Communal Cemetery, Belgium.

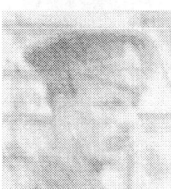

AGER, Private, John Alfred. 28471, 11th Bn., Royal Berkshire Regiment formerly 24504, Hampshire Regiment. Wounded at Marne, 29th July, 1916 and died 13th August, 1916. Born 14th October, 1886, at 2c. 4h. Chauntry Place. Resided at 8c. 5h. Cox Street. Employed Sherbourne Works, Lower Ford Street as a Polisher. Grave Ref. Div. 3. D. 7. Ste. Marie Cemetery, Le Havre, France.

AGUTTER, Ordinary Seaman, Frederick George. J/55479, H.M. Brig 'I', Royal Navy. Lost in submarine action, 14th December, 1917. Memorial Ref. Special Memorial Malta (Capuccini) Naval Cemetery. Alternative commemoration – buried in Pantellaria Communal Cemetery.

AITKEN, Corporal, Alfred. 17511, Oxfordshire and Buckinghamshire Light Infantry. Died of wounds, 16th April, 1917. Shot in the leg by a sniper whilst in France, and died after leg amputation in Bristol Southern Hospital. Age 26. Son of Mrs. Aitken, of 16 White's Row, Warwick Road, Kenilworth. Born Kenilworth. Enlisted Coventry. Resided Kenilworth. Grave Ref. C. 395. Kenilworth Cemetery.

AITKEN, Private, Charles Henry. 18443, 5th Bn., Oxfordshire and Buckinghamshire Light Infantry. Killed in action, 25th September, 1915. Age 29. Husband of Amy Aitken, of 14, Althorpe Street, Leamington Spa. Born Leamington. Enlisted Coventry. Memorial Ref. Panel 37 and 39. Ypres (Menin Gate) Memorial, Belgium.

AKERMAN, Private, Fred A. 12350, 2nd Bn., Irish Guards. Killed in action, 14th April, 1918. Aged 35. Husband of Elsie Wilson (formerly Akerman), of Beech House, Saunders Avenue, Bedworth. Born in Loughborough. Enlisted in Coventry. Memorial Ref. Addenda Panel. Ploegsteert Memorial.

AKERS, Private, Fredrick Alexander. 17774, 2nd Bn., Coldstream Guards. Killed in action on the Somme, 18th November, 1916. Born 4th May, 1890 at 25, George Street. Resided at 81, Freehold Street. Enlisted January 1916 at Coventry. Engineer (drop forgings). Memorial Ref. Pier and Face 7D and 8D, Thiepval Memorial, France.

ALBROW, Private, Herbert. 307642, 1st/8th Bn., Royal Warwickshire Regiment. Killed in action, 27th August, 1916. Age 21. Son of Mrs. Elizabeth Louisa Albrow, of 13, Huntingdon Road, Earlsdon, Coventry. Born 3rd March, 1896 at Coventry. Resided at 1, Matlock Road. Enlisted September, 1915 at Coventry. Fitter's Assistant, Daimler Works. Memorial Ref. Pier and Face 9 A 9 B and 10 B. Thiepval Memorial, Somme, France.

ALDRIDGE, Private, Caleb. 37884, 2nd/5th Bn., Gloucestershire Regiment. Died, 19th April, 1918. Son of Caleb and Alice Aldridge, of 136, Nicholls Street, Hillfields, Coventry. Husband of Sarah Jane Aldridge, of 4/116, Cromwell Street, Nechells, Birmingham. Born Darlaston, Staffordshire. Enlisted Nechells, Birmingham. Memorial Ref. Panel 60 to 64. Loos Memorial, Pas de Calais, France.

ALFORD, Private, Harry. 1962, 2nd Bn., Royal Warwickshire Regiment. Killed in action, La Bassee, 19th December, 1914. Born at Stoke, Coventry. Resided at Rowe Farm, Clay Lane, Stoke. Enlisted Coventry. Memorial Ref. Panel 2 and 3. Ploegsteert Memorial, Belgium.

ALGAR, Private, Charles. 18705, 1st Bn., Somerset Light Infantry. Killed in action, 24th October, 1918. Age 34. Son of Mrs. L. Algar, of 645, New George Street, Coventry. Born at Banbury. Employed at Coventry. Enlisted Coventry. Grave Ref. C. 18. Verchain British Cemetery, Verchain-Maugre, Nord, France.

ALLCHIN, Lance Sergeant, Joseph Edward. 3/3581, 1st Bn., King's Own Yorkshire Light Infantry. Died as a result of a compound fracture of the foot and dysentery, Bombay Presidency General Hospital, Alexandria, Egypt on the 15th January, 1916. Born in 1884, at Burton-on-Trent. Resided at 47, Stoney Stanton Road. Employed in Brass Shop at Daimler Ltd. Enlisted, April 1915 at Coventry. Son of George Thomas Allchin. Grave Ref. C. 57. Alexandria (Chatby) Military and War Memorial Cemetery.

ALLCHURCH, Private, Thomas Herbert. 45196, 1/6th Bn., Northumberland Fusiliers, formerly 9816, Army Cyclist Corps. Died, 2nd April, 1918. Born 6th August, 1889 at Worcester. Resided at Coventry. Accountant Clerk. Commemorated Queen's Road Memorial and Bablake School Memorial. Enlisted October, 1914 at London. Memorial Ref. Panel 16 to 18. Pozieres Memorial, France.

ALLCOAT, Lance Corporal, Arthur Victor. 17262, 8th Bn., Somerset Light Infantry. Killed in action, 23rd April, 1917. Age 23. Son of Joseph and Emma Allcoat, of Coventry Road, Wolvey, Warwickshire. Born 12th April, 1894, at Wolvey. Resided at Wolvey. Employed by the Hillman Motor Company. Enlisted August 1914 at Nuneaton. Memorial Ref. Bay 4. Arras Memorial, Pas de Calais, France.

ALLEN, Lance Corporal. South Wales Borderers. Died 1915.

ALLEN, Major, Harry. 8th Bn., Gloucestershire Regiment. Died of wounds, received at Cambrai, 16th January, 1918. Born 13th May, 1870, at Newport Pagnell. Resided at 27, Queen Mary's Road. Employed by Courtaulds Ltd. Enlisted September, 1914. Commemorated War Memorial Park. Grave Ref. VIII. D. 20. Rocquigny-Equancourt Road British Cemetery, Manancourt, France.

ALLEN, Corporal, Henry James Olaf, DCM. 320171, 6th Bn., City of London Regiment. Killed in action, 7th June, 1917. Age 20. Son of Thomas Allen and of Caroline Allen, of 10, Paradise Place, High Street, Marleybone, London. Born at Melton Mowbray, Leicestershire. Resided at Holbron (formerly Coventry). Enlisted London. Memorial Ref. Panel 57. Ypres (Menin Gate) Memorial, Belgium.

ALLEN, Driver, Leslie. 223712, 49th Div. Ammunition Col., Royal Field Artillery formerly R/X/4/23419, Royal Army Service Corps. Died 13th September, 1918. Age 20. Born at Tottenham. Son of Frederick and Rose Allen, of 53, Temple Road, Cowley, Oxford. Enlisted Coventry. Grave Ref. VI. H. 2. Duisans British Cemetery, Etrun, France.

ALLEN, Private, Richard. 16633, 14th Bn., Royal Warwickshire Regiment. Died of wounds, received at Arras, 15th June, 1917. Age 27. Son of Richard and Emma Allen, of Crescent Avenue, Stoke, Coventry. Born 31st January, 1890, at Coventry. Resided at Coventry. Carpenter. Enlisted February, 1916 at Coventry. Commemorated St. Michael's Church. Grave Ref. IV. J. 49. Duisans British Cemetery, Etrun, Pas de Calais, France.

ALLEN, Gunner, Robert. 20844, 49th Siege Battery, Royal Garrison Artillery. Killed in action, by a high explosive shell, 6th September, 1917. Born 6th October, 1885 at Birmingham. Resided at 15, George Street, Coventry. Employed by Courtaulds Ltd. Enlisted August, 1914 at Birmingham. Completed 14 years, Army Service. Leaves a widow. Grave Ref. II. A. 14. White House Cemetery, St. Jean-Les-Ypres, Belgium.

ALLEN, Air Mechanic 3rd Class, Sam. 148539, 3rd Flying School, Royal Air Force. Died at home from influenza, 17th November, 1918 whilst stationed at Stechford. Age 30. Resided 4c. 8h. Brewery Street, Coventry. Left a widow and three children. Grave Ref. 211. 129. Coventry (London Road) Cemetery.

ALLEN, Private, Walter Rowland. 23951, 1st Bn., Royal Warwickshire Regiment. Killed in action, 5th July, 1917. Born Coventry. Resided Ryton-on-Dunsmore, Coventry. Machinist. Enlisted Coventry. Commemorated Ryton Memorial. Grave Ref. II. A. 18. Crump Trench British Cemetery, Fampoux, France.

ALLEN, Lance Corporal, William Alan, MM. 266110, 2/7th Bn., Royal Warwickshire Regiment. Killed in action, 23rd March, 1918. Born 18th August, 1893, at Birmingham. Resided at 18, Charterhouse Road, Coventry. Fitter. Enlisted October, 1914 at Coventry. On 18th May, 1917, he was awarded the Military Medal and Divisional Commander's Parchment for although not being the member of any Lewis Gun team, he voluntarily took charge of a recovered gun and used it with great effect at an attack on the village of Fresnoy-le-Petit, at times carrying both the gun and the ammunition single-handed. Memorial Ref. Panel 18 and 19. Pozieres Memorial, France.

ALLEN, Corporal, William John. 3660, 2/7th Bn., Royal Warwickshire Regiment. Died of wounds, 16th July, 1916. Age 32. Son of William and Sarah Allen, of Bedworth. Husband of Amy Allen, of Sandpit, Bulkington. Born Bedworth. Enlisted Coventry. Formerly worked Charity Colliery. Grave Ref. II. C. 8. Laventie Military Cemetery, La Gorgue, France.

ALLETT, Private, Arthur. 13048, 6th Bn., Lincolnshire Regiment. Died at Gallipoli, 15th August, 1915. Age 32. Son of William Allett. Husband of Kitty Bell (formerly Allett), of 49, Silverton Road, Coventry. Born at Geddington, Kettering or Great Easton, Leicestershire. Resided at Coventry. Grave Ref. J. 103. Alexandria (Chatby) Military And War Memorial Cemetery, Egypt.

ALLIBONE, Private, Bertie Walwyn. 10191, 7th Bn., Northamptonshire Regiment. Killed in action, 16th July, 1916. Age 24. Son of John Allibone, of 29, Highfield Road, Coventry. Born 17th March, 1892, at Barby, Northants. Resided at 29, Highland Road. Labourer. Enlisted December, 1914 at Rugby. Memorial Ref. Panel 43 and 45. Ypres (Menin Gate) Memorial, Ieper, West-Vlaanderen, Belgium.

ALLIBONE, Private, Henry James Sidney Green. 266607, 1/7th Bn., Royal Warwickshire Regiment. Died, 30th October, 1918. Age 28. Employed at Coventry. Enlisted Coventry. Grave Ref. 7. C. 3. Montecchio Precalcino Communal Cemetery Extension, Italy.

ALLSO, Lance Corporal, Percival Allen. 252, 16th Bn., Royal Warwickshire Regiment. Killed in action, 27th July, 1916. Born Stratford, Essex. Resided at Stratford. Member of Valuation Staff, Coventry. Enlisted Birmingham. Memorial Ref. Pier and Face 9A 9B and 10B, Thiepval Memorial, Somme, France.

ALLSOP, Private, Samuel Herbert. 45851, 13th Coy., Machine Gun Corps (Infantry) formerly 19182, Royal Warwickshire Regiment. Killed in action, 13th September, 1916. Brother of Mr. J. T. Alsop, of The Scaddaws, Hartshorne, Burton-on-Trent. Born Linton, Derby. Enlisted Coventry. Memorial Ref. Pier and Face 5 C and 12 C. Thiepval Memorial, Somme, France.

ALLTON, Private, Joseph. 22397, 15th Bn., Royal Warwickshire Regiment. Killed in action, 8th May, 1917. Age 25. Son of Thomas and Maria Allton, of 14, Woodlands Road, Bedworth. Born 21st June, 1892 at Bedworth. Resided at 14, Woodlands, Bedworth. Cycle Mechanic, Coventry Challenge Cycle Works Ltd. Enlisted October, 1916 at Warwick. Memorial Ref. Bay 3. Arras Memorial, France.

ALLTON, Private, William. 15280, 1st Bn., Royal Warwickshire Regiment. Killed in action, 21st June, 1916. Age 18. Born 2nd May, 1898 at Bedworth. Son of Thomas and Maria Allton. Resided at 14, Woodlands Road, Bedworth. Employed Newdigate Colliery, Packing Case Maker. Enlisted October, 1915 at Nuneaton. Grave Ref. II. B. 18. Auchonvillers Military Cemetery, France.

AMEY, Private, William. 438, 1st Bn., Royal Warwickshire Regiment. Killed in action, 25th April, 1915. Born Grafton-Under-Wood, Kettering. Enlisted Coventry. Resided Kettering. Memorial Ref. Panel 8. Ypres (Menin Gate) Memorial, Belgium.

AMOS, Private, Charles Henry. 1614, 9th Bn., Royal Warwickshire Regiment. Died at Amara, Mesopotamia of malaria, 13th July, 1916. Born 9th January, 1897 at Willenhall, Staffordshire. Resided at 16, Adelaide Street. Turner. Enlisted in 1914 at Coventry. Grave Ref. IX. G. 11. Amara War Cemetery, Iraq.

AMOS, Private, Frank. 55852, 17th Bn., Welsh Regiment. Killed in action, 4th January, 1918. Born Slapton, Northants. Enlisted Coventry. Resided Northampton. Grave Ref. Sp. Mem. 2. St. Leger British Cemetery, France.

AMOS, Private, Frank. S/10071, 8th Bn., Black Watch (Royal Highlanders), formerly 94243, Royal Field Artillery. Killed in action, 8th October, 1915. Born Walsgrave. Enlisted Coventry. Resided Binley/Brinklow. Grave Ref. C. 12. Blauwepoort Farm Cemetery, Belgium.

ANCOTT, Private, John William. 23939, 7th Bn., Duke of Cornwall's Light Infantry. Killed in action, 16th August, 1917. Age 23. Son of Joseph and Elizabeth Ancott, Hartshill, Atherstone, Warwickshire. Born Nuneaton. Enlisted Coventry. Resided Atherstone. Memorial Ref. Panel 80 to 82 and 163A. Tyne Cot Memorial, Belgium.

ANDERSON, Captain, David Wilson, MC and Bar. 6th Bn., London Regiment. Killed in action, 8th August, 1918. Age 28. Son of Mrs. Amelia Anderson, of 26, Maule St., Carnoustie, Forfarshire. Dentist, Coventry. Commemorated Wolston Memorial. Grave Ref. XVIII. B. 8. Villers-Bretonneux Military Cemetery, France.

ANDERSON, Private, Roland Brookes. 2998, 1/7th Bn., Royal Warwickshire Regiment. Killed in action, 15th July, 1916. Born 22nd October, 1894 at Coventry. Resided at Coventry. Clerk. Enlisted October, 1914 at Coventry. Memorial Ref. Pier and Face 9A 9B and 10B. Thiepval Memorial, Somme, France.

ANDERTON, Private, Harry. 8530, Royal Scots. Served as Powers. Killed in action, 3rd May, 1917. Born Atherstone. Enlisted Coventry. Resided Atherstone. Commemorated Coventry Chain Memorial. Memorial Ref. Arras Memorial, France.

ANDREWS, Corporal, Frank Septimus. 11463, 9th Bn., Royal Fusiliers. Died at Cambrai, 30th November, 1917. Born 24th March, 1890 at Isham, Northants. Resided at Coventry. Grocer's Assistant. Enlisted June, 1916 at Coventry. Memorial Ref. Panel 3 and 4, Cambrai Memorial, Louverval, France.

ANDREWS, Lance Corporal, George. 9810, 1st Bn., Royal Warwickshire Regiment. Killed at Ypres, 12th October, 1916. Born in 1879, at Washwood Heath, Birmingham. Resided at Coventry. Wheelmaker. Enlisted November, 1914, Coventry. Commemorated St. John's Church. Enlisted Coventry. Memorial Ref. Pier and Face 9A 9B and 10B. Thiepval Memorial, France.

ANDREWS, Lance Corporal, Harmond William. 21820, 12th Bn., Hampshire Regiment. Died, 30th September, 1917. Age 27. Son of William Andrews, of Belle Vue, Rayleigh Road, Basingstoke, Hants. Husband of Lillian Sinclair (formerly Andrews), of 47, Henderson Road, Eastney, Portsmouth. Born Portsmouth. Enlisted Coventry. Resided Bangor, Carnarvon. Grave Ref. 1214. Salonika (Lembet Road) Military Cemetery, Greece.

ANSTEY, Private, William Thomas. 11163, 5th Bn., Oxfordshire and Buckinghamshire Light Infantry. Killed in trenches, 16th October, 1915. Age 34. Son of William Anstey, of 21, Hertford Place, Butts, Coventry. Born 4th November, 1882 in Lamb Street. Resided in 25, East Street. Dealer. Enlisted August, 1914, Coventry. Had served seven years with the 1st Bn., Royal Warwicks. Memorial Ref. Panel 37 and 39. Ypres (Menin Gate) Memorial, Ieper, West-Vlaanderen, Belgium.

ANTROBUS, Private, Alfred Percy. 15/1643, 15th Bn., Royal Warwickshire Regiment. Killed in action, 4th June, 1916. Age 18. Son of Alfred and Sarah Antrobus of 51, Doncaster Road, Scunthorpe. Born Allesley. Enlisted Birmingham. Resided Maxstoke, Warwicks. Grave Ref. I. D. 24. Faubourg D'Amiens Cemetery, Arras, France.

ARCH, Private, James Jacob. 38960, 2/6th Bn., Lancashire Fusiliers formerly 270443, Royal Army Service Corps. Killed in action, 21st March, 1918. Born and enlisted in Coventry. Memorial Ref. Panel 32 to 34. Pozieres Memorial, France.

ARCHER, Private, John James. 41768, 8th Bn., Royal Inniskilling Fusiliers. Killed in action, 16th August, 1917. Age 19. Son of James and Emma Archer. Resided at Foleshill. Enlisted Coventry. Memorial Ref. Panel 70 to 72. Tyne Cot Memorial, Belgium.

ARIES, Sergeant, Wallace. 207954, 11th Bn., The Queen's (Royal West Surrey Regiment) formerly 202154, Oxfordshire and Buckinghamshire Light Infantry. Killed in action, 10th October, 1918. Born Chipping Norton. Employed by Coventry Corporation, City Engineer's Department. Resided Chipping Norton. Enlisted Oxford. Commemorated City Engineer's Department Memorial, Coventry Corporation. Grave Ref. V. G. 3. Les Baraques Military Cemetery, Sangatte, France.

ARIS, Lance Corporal, Mark. 11043, 5th Bn., Oxfordshire and Buckinghamshire Light Infantry. Killed in action, 6th August, 1915. Born Wittie, Leics. Enlisted Rugby. Memorial Ref. Panel 37 and 39. Ypres (Menin Gate) Memorial, Belgium.

ARMITAGE, Private, Richard. 202818, 8th Bn., Border Regiment. Killed in action, 14th June, 1917. Age 18. Son of Isaac and Elizabeth Ann Armitage, of 14, Common Way, Stoke Heath, Coventry. Born in 1899 at Workington, Cumberland. Enlisted Workington. Memorial Ref. Panel 35. Ypres (Menin Gate) Memorial, Ieper, West-Vlaanderen, Belgium.

ARMSTRONG, Sergeant, Tom. 5801, 10th Bn., Royal Warwickshire Regiment. Killed by sniper, Givenchy, 16th December, 1915. Born 23rd December, 1884 at Newcastle upon Tyne. Resided at back of 5, St. Peter's Street. Vertical Miller. Enlisted September, 1914. (Formerly known around Coventry as Boxer, Tom Harvey). Enlisted Coventry. Grave Ref. II. H. 1. St. Vaast Post Military Cemetery, Richebourg-L'Avoue, France.

ARNOLD, Gunner, Ernest George. 238697, 'A' Bty., 210th Bde., Royal Field Artillery. Killed in action, 4th April, 1918. Son of Mr. J. Arnold of High Street, Coleshill, Birmingham. Born at Foleshill. Enlisted Sutton. Resided Birmingham. Grave Ref. VI. D. 2. Bienvillers Military Cemetery, France.

ARNOLD, Private, Herbert Edward. G/125002, 44th Bn., Royal Fusiliers. Died of acute bronchitis at Dunkirk, 22nd January, 1919 in a demobilization camp. Age 34. Long Service and Good Conduct Medal. Husband of M. J. Arnold, of 17, East Street, Coventry. Born 10th December, 1885 in Chauntry Place. Resided at 109, East Street. Fitter, Humber Works. Enlisted January, 1915. Leaves widow and two children. Grave Ref. IV. E. 8. Dunkirk Town Cemetery, Nord, France.

ARNOLD, Acting Sergeant, William S. (Alias Picker, the true family name). 38770, 402nd Bty, Royal Horse Artillery. Killed in action, 23rd July, 1917. Born at London. Resided at Coventry. Grave Ref. I. F. 23. Canada Farm Cemetery, Belgium.

ARTHUR, Private, A. Employed at Coventry. Died of wounds 1917.

ASH, Private, Sydney. 41919, 2nd Bn., Worcestershire Regiment formerly 24286, Royal Warwickshire Regiment. Killed in action, 12th April, 1918. Age 18. Son of Mr. and Mrs. E. Ash, of 285, Munition Cottages, Holbrooks Lane, Foleshill, Coventry. Born 22nd December, 1898, in Boston Place. Resided at 29, Station Street West. Turner, Rover Works. Grave Ref. V. D. 18. Wulverghem-Lindenhoek Road Military Cemetery, Heuvelland, West-Vlaanderen, Belgium.

ASHBY, Private, William. 33129, 6th Bn., Oxfordshire and Buckinghamshire Light Infantry formerly 7954, Royal Warwickshire Regiment. Killed in action, 20th September, 1917. Born at Coventry. Resided at 37, Lower Wellington Street. Cycle Mechanic. Enlisted April, 1916 at Coventry. Memorial Ref. Panel 96 to 98. Tyne Cot Memorial, Belgium.

ASHFIELD, Private, Samuel George. 1939, 1st /7th Bn., Royal Warwickshire Regiment. Killed in action, 14th July, 1916 at Pozieres about 150 yards into No Man's Land. Age 20. Son of Mrs. S. A. Ashfield, of 14, College Square, Silver Street, Coventry. Born 12th January, 1896, at Burnt Post. Resided at 11, College Square, Cook Street. Filer, Rudge Works. Enlisted August, 1914. Memorial Ref. Pier and Face 9A 9B and 10B. Thiepval Memorial, Somme, France.

ASHFORD, Private, Charles. 27472, 4th Bn., South Wales Borderers. Killed Mesopotamia, 30th April, 1917. Age 29. Son of Frederick Richard and Agnes Emily Ashford. Born 31st January, 1888, at Newport, Monmouthshire. Resided at 51, Hastings Road. Cashier. Enlisted December, 1915, Coventry. Memorial Ref. Panel 16 and 62. Basra Memorial, Iraq.

ASHMALL, Private, Alfred Josiah. 38350, 16th Bn., Royal Warwickshire Regiment. Killed in action, 23rd August, 1918. Age 21. Son of George and Florrie Ashmall. Husband of Ethel Wilson (formerly Ashmall), of 12, Camden Street, Stoke, Coventry formerly 72, Arden Street, Earlsdon. Born 13th September, 1896 at Coventry. Resided at 73, Berkeley Road South. Tool Maker, Alfred Herberts, The Butts. Enlisted November, 1917 at Coventry. Memorial Ref. Panel 3. Vis-En-Artois Memorial, Pas de Calais, France.

ASHMORE, Lance Corporal, Alfred Lewis. 11306, 1st Bn., Worcestershire Regiment. Died as prisoner of war (Germany), 12th August, 1918. Born at Angmering, Sussex. Enlisted London. Grave Ref. B. 7. Glageon Communal Cemetery. France.

ASHTON, Private, Harold. 63104, 113th Coy., Machine Gun Corps formerly 5855, London Regiment. Died of wounds, 30th April, 1917. Age 25. Son of Thomas James and Ruth Ashton, of 22, Wellington Street, Coventry. Born 11th April, 1892 at Coventry. Resided at Coventry. Clerk. Enlisted May, 1916 at Coventry. Grave Ref. 3. C. 5. Ferme-Olivier Cemetery, Ieper, West-Vlaanderen, Belgium.

ASHWORTH, Private, Roland. 34956, 2/7th Bn., Lancashire Fusiliers. Killed in action, 13th November, 1917. Age 20. Son of Mrs. Elizabeth Ashworth, of 118, Manchester Road, Castleton, Lancs. Born Castleton, Lancs. Enlisted Coventry. Resided Rochdale, Lancs. Memorial Ref. Panel 54 to 60 and 163A. Tyne Cot Memorial, Belgium.

ASKEW, Private, Wilfred Robert. CH/2211(S), 2nd R.M. Battalion. Royal Naval Division, Royal Marine Light Infantry. 26th October, 1917. Age 23. Son of Mr. and Mrs. Robert Askew, of 68, Lythalls Lane, Foleshill, Coventry. Born 11th April, 1894, at Stoneleigh. Fitter. Grave Ref. XVI. E. 6. Poelcapelle British Cemetery, Langemark-Poelkapelle, Belgium.

ASQUITH, Gunner, Albert. 3413, 47th Div. Ammunition Col., Royal Field Artillery. Died of accidental injuries at hospital, 18th October, 1916 received in motor lorry accident. Age 23. Son of Alfred and Sarah Ann Asquith, of 83, Stoney Stanton Road, Coventry. Born 2nd May, 1893, at Bradford. Resided at Coventry. Fitter, previously at Rover. Enlisted June, 1915. Grave Ref. G. 8. Beauval Communal Cemetery, Somme, France.

ASTILL, Private, William Nathan. 15118, 2nd Bn., Royal Welsh Fusiliers. Killed in action, 8th February, 1916. Age 21. Son of David and Hannah Astill, of 3, Henley Road, Bell Green, Foleshill, Coventry. Enlisted Warwick. Grave Ref. K. 16. Cambrin Churchyard Extension, Pas de Calais, France.

ASTON, Gunner, Frank. 183886, 40th Bty. 40th Bde., Royal Field Artillery. Died of wounds (gassed) 2nd July, 1918. Age 24. Son of Tom and Julia Aston. Husband of Alice Aston, of Humber Road, Stoke, Coventry. Born 4th December, 1893, at Coventry. Resided at 41, St. George's Road. Builder's Estimating Clerk. Enlisted November, 1916 at Coventry. Brother of Corporal Harry Aston. Grave Ref. IV. A. 16. Tourgeville Military Cemetery, Calvados, France.

ASTON, Corporal, Harry. L/1777, 9th (Queen's Royal) Lancers. Died of wounds at home from injuries received at Mons, 25th November, 1914 died at Fazakeley Hospital following operation for abscess of the liver. Age 24. Born 18th March, 1890 at Coventry. Resided at 22, Colchester Street. Soldier, spent six years in the Army. Brother of Gunner Frank Aston. Commemorated Bablake School Memorial. Grave Ref. 11. 3. Coventry (London Road) Cemetery.

ASTON, Private, Henry Amos. 266556, 10th Bn., Royal Warwickshire Regiment. Killed in action, 22nd March, 1918. Enlisted Coventry. Resided Warwick. Memorial Ref. Bay 3. Arras Memorial, France.

ASTON, Private, William Thomas. 13509, 6th Bn., East Yorkshire Regiment. Killed in action, 9th August, 1915. Son of Richard and Jane Aston, of 29, Binley Avenue, Binley, Coventry. Born Worcester. Enlisted Sheffield. Resided Worcester. Memorial Ref. Panel 51 to 54. Helles Memorial, Turkey.

ATHERSUCH, Lance Corporal, Walter. 265352, 2nd /7th Bn., Royal Warwickshire Regiment. Killed in action, 21st March, 1918. Age 20. Son of William and Mary Athersuch, of 14, Wright Street, Coventry. Born in All Saint's Parish, Coventry. Employed by Coventry Chain Company Ltd. Enlisted Coventry. Commemorated Coventry Chain Memorial. Memorial Ref. Panel 18 and 19. Pozieres Memorial, Somme, France.

ATKIN, Corporal, Johnson. 99068, 214th Army Troops Coy., Royal Engineers. Accidentally killed 15th May, 1916, injuries received in accident, Flesselles, France. Age 37. Son of William and Harriet Atkin, of Bridlington. Husband of Violet Atkin, of 26, Narrow Lane, Coventry. Born 3rd February, 1879 at Bridlington, Yorks. Resided at 29, Mason Road. Bricklayer. Enlisted May, 1915 at Coventry. Commemorated Gas Department Memorial, Coventry Corporation. Grave Ref. E. 7. Villers-Bocage Communal Cemetery Extension, Somme, France.

ATKINS, Private, Albert. 2334, 1st Bn., Royal Warwickshire Regiment. Killed in action, 25th April, 1915. Born 9th February, 1891 in Mill Street. Son of George and Emma Atkins, of Coventry. Resided at 16, Queen Street. Soldier. Employed Messrs. Phillips and Marriott. Enlisted Coventry. Grave Ref. V. B. 1. Oosttaverne Wood Cemetery, Belgium.

ATKINS, Private, Alick. 31887, 1st Bn., Worcestershire Regiment. Died of wounds, 10th February 1917. Age 33. Son of George and Emma Atkins, of Coventry. Born 2nd March, 1886 at Coventry. Resided in Bishop Street. Horse Driver, Rob and Eales Electric Light Works. Enlisted 1915 at Coventry. Commemorated Holy Trinity Church. Leaves a widow and four children. Grave Ref. II. D. 6A. Wimereux Communal Cemetery, Pas de Calais, France.

ATKINS, Lance Corporal, Arthur. 241633, 1/6th Bn., Royal Warwickshire Regiment. Killed in action, 1st April, 1917. Born 1st June, 1885 in Swan Street. Resided at 6, Sparkbrook Street. Greengrocer's Assistant. Enlisted Coventry. Grave Ref. I. J. 4. Epehy Wood Farm Cemetery, Epehy, France.

ATKINS, Corporal, Arthur Shoebridge. 2763, 40th Bn., Australian Infantry. Killed in action, 6th October, 1917. Age 39. Born at Hobart, Tasmania. Son of Charles James and Kate Elizabeth Atkins. Husband of Annie Scott Atkins, of 48, Fairlight St., Manly, New South Wales. Born Coventry. Enlisted 18th May, 1916. Grave Ref. XXXV. D. 7. Tyne Cot Cemetery, Belgium.

ATKINS, Lance Corporal, Charles. 30924, 1st Bn., East Lancashire Regiment formerly 64227, Royal Horse Artillery. Killed in action, 8th September, 1918. Born Coventry. Resided Birmingham. Enlisted Portsmouth. Grave Ref E. 29. Y Farm Military Cemetery, Bois-Grenier, France.

ATKINS, Lance Corporal, Harold Samuel. 34642, 2nd Bn., Royal Warwickshire Regiment formerly 4599, Worcestershire Regiment. Killed in action, 27th October, 1917. Brother of Fred Atkins, of 43, Seagrave Road, Coventry. Born Kidderminster. Enlisted Kidderminster. Grave Ref. VI. E. 5. Hooge Crater Cemetery, Ieper, West-Vlaanderen, Belgium.

ATKINS, John H. Commemorated Wolston Memorial.

ATKINS, Rifleman, John Sheasby. Z/905, 4th Bn., Rifle Brigade. Killed in action, France, 15th March, 1915. Age 20. Son of Mr. & Mrs. W. Atkins, of Stretton-on-Dunsmore, Rugby. Employed by Humber Ltd. Enlisted Rugby. Born Stretton-on-Dunsmore. Memorial Ref. Panel 46 – 58 and 50, Ypres (Menin Gate) Memorial, Belgium.

ATKINS, Private, Lewis William Henry. 11012, 1st Bn., Coldstream Guards. Died, 22nd December, 1914. Age 20. Son of Jerry and Harriett Atkins, of Goodyears Road, Exhall, Coventry. Born Tibshelf, Derby. Enlisted Nuneaton. Resided Exhall. Memorial Ref. Panels 2 and 3. Le Touret Memorial, Pas de Calais, France.

ATKINS, Private, Reginald George. G/23927, 5th Bn., Middlesex Regiment. Accidentally killed 23rd July, 1916. Age 23. Son of George Frederick and Harriett Jane Atkins, of 18, Alexander Cottages, Shakespeare, Huntingdon. Born at Coventry. Resided at Huntingdon. Grave Ref. RR. 35. Huntingdon (Priory Road) Cemetery, Huntingdon.

ATKINS, Acting Sergeant, Walter J. 9717, 1st Bn., Royal Welsh Fusiliers. Killed in action, 25th September, 1915. Age 27. Son of Thomas and Eliza Atkins. Resided at 4c. 2h. Leicester Street. Enlisted August, 1914 at Coventry. Cycle Mechanic employed by the Challenge Cycle & Motor Co. Ltd. Born Wolston. Commemorated Wolston Memorial. Appeal made by Miss A. Harris, 40 Hood Street, Coventry. Memorial Ref. Panel 50 to 52. Loos Memorial, France.

ATKINS, Private, Walter. 2258, 1st Bn., Royal Warwickshire Regiment. Killed in action, 23rd October, 1916. Born in 1893, in All Saints Parish, Coventry. Employed by Messrs. Calcott Bros. Resided 14, Herbert Row, Gulson Road, Coventry. Enlisted Coventry. Memorial Ref. Pier and Face 9A 9B and 10B. Thiepval Memorial, France.

ATKINS, Gunner, Walter William. 206148, Machine Gun Corps (Heavy Branch) formerly 32027, Machine Gun Corps. Died at Military Hospital, Bovington Camp, 9th February, 1917. Son of Mr. W. Atkins, of 57, Henley Road, Bell Green, Coventry. Born 4th August 1895, at 57, Henley Road, Bell Green. Resided at 57, Henley Road, Bell Green. Engineer. Enlisted March, 1916 at Coventry. Commemorated War Memorial Park. Grave Ref. Foleshill Congregational Burial Ground, Coventry.

ATKINS, Private, Wilfred. 16867, 10th Bn., Royal Warwickshire Regiment. Died of wounds, 28th September, 1917. Age 25. Son of Mr. and Mrs. S. Atkins, of Kidderminster. Born 15th October, 1892. Resided at 20, Harefield Road. Wages Clerk. Enlisted in 1916 at Coventry. Grave Ref. I. C. 17. Outtersteene Communal Cemetery Extension, Bailleul, France.

ATKINS, Lance Corporal, William Henry. 6940, 2nd Bn., Worcestershire Regiment. Killed in action, at Loos, 25th September, 1915. Born 9th June, 1882, at Rowley, Staffordshire. Resided at 12, Swanswell Terrace. Polisher. Reservist. Enlisted Worcester. Served eight years in India. Leaves a widow and one child. Memorial Ref. Panel 64 and 65. Loos Memorial, France.

ATKINS, Private, William Joseph. 2317, 52nd Coy., Mechanical Transport, Army Service Corps. Died of tuberculosis, 24th November, 1916 after being discharged. Husband of Rose Atkins of 55, Sir Thomas White's Road, Coventry. Born in 1890. Resided at 27, Thomas Street. Fitter. Enlisted September, 1914. Employed Rover Co. Ltd. Leaves a widow and one child. Grave Ref. 53. 93. Coventry (London Road) Cemetery.

ATTENBOROUGH, Private, Arthur. 9719, 2nd Bn., Royal Warwickshire Regiment. Killed in action, 3rd September, 1916. Age 31. Son of I. I. A. Attenborough, of 91, Druid St., Hinckley. Husband of Mary A. L. Jeffcote (formerly Attenborough), of 22, Mansion Street, Hinckley, Leicestershire. Born Nuneaton. Enlisted Coventry. Resided Hinckley. Memorial Ref. Pier and Face 9 A 9 B and 10 B. Thiepval Memorial, France.

ATTWOOD, Private, Alfred George. 17221, 6th Bn., Oxfordshire and Buckinghamshire Light Infantry. Killed in action, 3rd September, 1916. Age 28. Son of Alfred and Jane Attwood, of 60, Marston Street, Oxford. Husband of Winifred E. Attwood, of 71, Widdington Road, Coventry. Born Basingstoke. Enlisted Oxford. Memorial Ref. Pier and Face 10 A and 10 D. Thiepval Memorial, Somme, France.

ATTWOOD, Private, Arthur. G/7559, 3rd Bn., Middlesex Regiment. Killed in action, 30th September, 1915. Age 20. Son of James and Mary Attwood, of 3, Hazel View, Darley Dale, Derbyshire. Born Peak Forest, Derbyshire. Enlisted Coventry. Resided Hackney, Matlock. Memorial Ref. Panel 99 to 100. Loos Memorial, France.

AUSTIN, Private, Albert. 9986, 10th Bn., Royal Warwickshire Regiment. Killed in action, 28th April, 1916. Age 28. Son of Henry Austin. Husband of Harriet Elizabeth Ruth Austin, of 20, Barset, Road, Nunhead, London. Born Woodstock, Oxon. Enlisted Coventry. Resided Steeple Aston, Oxon. Grave Ref. II. F. 22. Rue-Du-Bacquerot No.1 Military Cemetery, Laventie, France.

AUSTIN, Private, Harry. 266487, 2/7th Bn., Royal Warwickshire Regiment. Killed in action, 19th July, 1916. Appeal by Mrs. F. Smith, 51, Cromwell Street, Red Lane, Coventry. Enlisted Coventry. Memorial Ref. Panel 22 to 25. Loos Memorial, France.

AUSTIN, Rifleman, William. R/1428, 1st Bn., King's Royal Rifle Corps. Died of wounds, 27th July, 1916. Age 28. Son of George Austin, of 46, King St., Burton-on-Trent. Husband of Florence Austin, of 94, Beech Street, Burton-on-Trent. Born 14th November, 1888 at Burton-on-Trent. Resided at Coventry. Porter Goods Guards (Railway). Enlisted June, 1915 at Coventry. Memorial Ref. Pier and Face 13 A and 13 B. Thiepval Memorial, Somme, France.

AVERNS, Private, Noel Raymond. PS/10210, 7th Bn., Royal Fusiliers. Died of wounds, 19th November, 1916. Age 19. Son of Ernest Lloyd Averns and Mary Louisa Averns, of 38, Shaftesbury Road, Coventry. Born 8th December, 1896 at Brussels. Resided at Earlsdon. Teacher. Enlisted December, 1915. Commemorated St. Barbara's Church and Bablake School Memorial. Grave Ref. O. II. B. 1. St. Sever Cemetery Extension, Rouen, Seine-Maritime, France.

AVERNS, Private, Raymond Frederick John. 17772, 6th Bn., Queen's Own (Royal West Kent Regiment) formerly 3327, Royal Fusiliers. Died (France) whilst a prisoner of war, 30th July 1918. Age 22. Son of Raymond Herbert and Laura Dean Averns of 12, Lydgate Road, Coventry. Born 9th June, 1896 at Coventry. Resided at 12, Lydgate Road. Undergraduate, Cambridge University. Enlisted June, 1916 at Coventry. Husband of Florence Austin, of 94, Beech Street, Burton-on-Trent. Commemorated Radford Memorial, St. John's Church and Bablake School Memorial. Grave Ref. A. 78. Conde-Sur-L'escaut Communal Cemetery, Nord, France.

AVES, Corporal, John Frederick Thomas. 7779, 1st Bn., Lincolnshire Regiment. Killed in action, 1st November, 1914. Age 25. Son of John and Mary Ann Emma Aves, of 5, Dalton Square, Hertford Place, The Butts, Coventry. Born 21st September, 1888, in Hearsall Lane. Resided at 5, Dalton Square, Butts. Soldier. Enlisted London. Memorial Ref. Panel 21. Ypres (Menin Gate) Memorial, Ieper, West-Vlaanderen, Belgium. (possibly buried in Ypres Cemetery).

AVIS, Private, Arthur John. 92, 54th (1st /1st East Anglian) Casualty Clearing Station. Royal Army Medical Corps. Died at sea, 13th August, 1915. Born in 1890. Resided at Coventry. Enlisted Ipswich. Clerk. Memorial Ref. Panel 199 and 200 or 236 to 239 and 328. Helles Memorial, Turkey.

AVISON, Gunner, Arthur-Denham. 1969, 1st Coy., Machine Gun Corps (Motors). Killed in action, 15th April, 1918. Age 33. Son of William Johnson Avison and Clara Annice Avison. Husband of Evelyn Margaret Avison, of 5, Stanley Terrace, Blue Bell Lane, Huyton, Liverpool. Born Barnsley. Enlisted Coventry. Resided Liverpool. Grave Ref. I. D. 1. Mont Noir Military Cemetery, St. Jans-Cappel, France.

AYRES, Private, Thomas. 4599, 1/7th Bn., Royal Warwickshire Regiment. Killed in action, 25th July, 1916. Born 23rd March, 1896, at 13c. 14h. Far Gosford Street. Resided in Swan Lane. Apprenticed W. W. Curtis Ltd., Printer. Enlisted November, 1915 at Coventry. Memorial Ref. Pier and Face 9A 9B and 10B. Thiepval Memorial, France.

BACON, Private, George Colin. 50745, 1st Bn., Somerset Light Infantry. Killed in action, 24th October, 1918. Son of J. and M. Bacon, of Henley Green, Coventry. Husband of Lillian Bacon, of Hunters Close, Dean Row, Wilmslow, Cheshire. Born 30th June, 1897, at Henley Green, Foleshill. Resided at 188a, Bell Green Road. Fitter's Apprentice. Enlisted Coventry. Grave Ref. A. 21. Verchain British Cemetery, Verchain-Maugre, Nord, France

BADGER, Mechanic, William Josiah. 302919, HMS Invincible, Royal Navy. Killed in action, at Battle of Jutland, 31st May, 1916. Age 32. Son of Josiah and Agnes Badger, of Rugby. Husband of Dorcas May Badger, of Wolston, Coventry. Memorial Ref. 15. Portsmouth Naval Memorial, Hampshire.

BAGLIN, Lance Corporal, George. 3516, 2nd Bn., Royal Warwickshire Regiment. Killed in action, 21st March, 1917. Age 21. Born 3rd February, 1896, at 13, Aylesford Street. Resided at 78, Mulliner Street. Millwright, Humber Works. Enlisted 18th August, 1914 at Coventry. Grave Ref. F1. Ervillers Military Cemetery, France.

BAGNELL, Private, Thomas. 1932, 1/6th Bn., North Staffordshire Regiment. Died of wounds, home, 2nd October, 1916. Age 39. Son of Thomas and Sarah Bagnall. Born at Walton-on the- Hill, Staffordshire. Resided at Coventry. Grave Ref. East of Church, Castle Church (St. Mary) Churchyard.

BAILEY, Corporal, Alfred. 597, 3rd Bn., 1st Australian Brigade. Killed in action, Dardanelles, 25th April, 1915. Born 19th, June, 1886 at Coventry. Emigrated and resided at Sydney, Australia. Government Engineer, Petersham, Sydney. Apprenticeship served Alfred Herbert Ltd. Enlisted August, 1914. Commemorated Bablake School Memorial. Only son of Mrs. Thomas Bailey, Samson and Lion, Swanswell Terrace. Engaged to Miss Ida Bellchambers. Of Petersham, Sydney. Memorial Ref. 19. Lone Pine Memorial, Turkey.

BAILEY, Sergeant, Christopher. 3224, 2/7th Bn., Royal Warwickshire Regiment. Killed in action, 19th July, 1916. Last seen with ten of his men in the German trenches. Son of George and Caroline Bailey of 111, Broomfield Road. Husband of Flora Mildred Sline (formerly Bailey), of 3, Atherton Road, Forest Gate, London. Born 2nd March, 1890 at Coventry. Resided at 48, Sir Thomas White Road, Coventry. Clerk. Enlisted October, 1915, Coventry. Employed Middlemore and Lamplugh and later Coventry Chain. Commemorated Coventry Chain Memorial. Memorial Ref. Panel 22 to 25. Loos Memorial, France.

BAILEY, Private, Ernest Alfred. 251728, 5th Bn., Essex Regiment. Killed in action, 26th March, 1917. Born Coventry, 1882. Enlisted Coventry. Resided Coventry. Memorial Ref. Panel 33 to 39. Jerusalem Memorial, Israel.

BAILEY, Sapper, Ernest William. 170895, 218th Field Coy., Royal Engineers. Killed in action, 8th July, 1917. Age 29. Son of Sarah Bailey. Husband of Edith Jane Bailey, of 65, Lily Road, South Yardley, Birmingham. Born Bordesley, Warwickshire. Enlisted Coventry. Resided Hampton-in-Arden, Warwickshire. Grave Ref. I. D. 27. Coxyde Military Cemetery, Belgium.

BAILEY, Private, Frank Lambert. 27316, 6th (Wiltshire Yeomanry) Bn., Wiltshire Regiment. Killed in action, 23rd March, 1918. Born Bodycott, Oxon. Enlisted Coventry. Resided Bodicote, Oxon. Memorial Ref. Bay 7. Arras Memorial, France.

BAILEY, Sergeant, Frederick George. 265740, 1/7th Bn., Royal Warwickshire Regiment. Killed in action, 8th October, 1917. Age 26. Son of George H. P. and Helena M. Bailey, of High Street, Great Wakering, Essex. Born Great Wakering, Essex. Enlisted Coventry. Resided Leamington. Memorial Ref. Panel 23 to 28 and 163A. Tyne Cot Memorial, Belgium.

BAILEY, Private, George Henry. 10761, 1st Bn., Coldstream Guards. Died, 29th October, 1914. Born Matlock Bank, Derby. Enlisted Coventry. Memorial Ref. Panel 11. Ypres (Menin Gate) Memorial, Belgium.

BAILEY, Private, Herbert William. 16915, 14th Bn., Royal Warwickshire Regiment. Killed in action, 3rd September, 1916. Age 26. Son of William Thomas and Elizabeth Bailey. Born Oakham, Rutland. Enlisted Coventry. Resided Northampton. Memorial Ref. Pier and Face 9 A 9 B and 10 B. Thiepval Memorial, Somme, France.

BAILEY, Private, John. 12139, 2nd Bn., Royal Warwickshire Regiment. Killed in action, 25th March, 1916 by the bursting of a shell attached to a bombing party. Age 24. Son of David and Sarah Ann Bailey, of 27, Wootton Street, Bedworth. Born Longford. Employed Longford Brick and Tile Co. Enlisted Nuneaton. Grave Ref. E. 10. Point 110 New Military Cemetery, France.

BAILEY, W. G. This name appeared on the memorial to the memory of members of the Independent Order of Oddfellows in the Cathedral Church of St. Michael. Possibly the brother of Mr. Thomas Bailey who was drowned on the Lusitania.

BAILEY, Lance Corporal, Walter S. 276864, 1st/7th Bn., Argyll and Sutherland Highlanders. Killed in action, 23rd March, 1918. Born Coventry. Enlisted Coventry. Resided Chiswick, London. Commemorated Central Methodist Hall and Bablake School Memorial. Memorial Ref. Bay 9. Arras Memorial, France.

BAILLIE, Lieutenant, Humphrey John, MC. 2nd Bn., Dorsetshire Regiment. Killed in action, 2nd March, 1916. Age 23. Son of the Reverend William Gordon Baillie and Mary Harriet Baillie of Sutton Mead, Mortonhampstead, Devon. Born Newham-on-Severn, Glos. Employed by Matterson, Huxley and Watson, Ltd. Awarded Military Cross for gallantry at Ahwaz. Grave Ref. N. 6. Kut War Cemetery, Iraq.

BAINES, Sapper, Cyril Johnson. 41380, 66th Field Coy., Royal Engineers. Killed in action, Gallipoli, 9th August, 1915. Born Oakham, Rutland. Enlisted Coventry. Memorial Ref. Panel 23 to 25 or 325 to 328. Helles Memorial, Turkey.

BAKER, Alfred. Commemorated Holy Trinity Church.

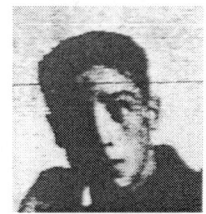

BAKER, Private, Alfred. 18722, 5th Bn., Oxfordshire and Buckinghamshire Light Infantry. Killed in action, Loos, 25th September, 1915. Age 16. Born 31st October, 1898 at Birmingham. Resided at 17, Henrietta Street. Employed Britannia Foundry as a Moulder. Enlisted May, 1915, Coventry. Memorial Ref. Panel 37 and 39. Ypres (Menin Gate) Memorial, Belgium.

BAKER, Private, Alfred Charles. 41820, "C" Coy., 3rd Bn., Worcestershire Regiment formerly 6613, Royal Warwickshire Regiment. Killed in action, 27th May, 1918. Age 20. Son of William and Laura Ellen Baker, of 5 Court, 3 House, Far Gosford Street, Coventry. Born 20th August, 1898 at Coventry. Resided at 5c. 3h. Far Gosford Street. Turner. Enlisted in 1916 at Coventry. Commemorated War Memorial Park. Memorial Ref. Soissons Memorial, Aisne, France.

BAKER, Private, Edward Harold. 35223, 19th Bn., Royal Warwickshire Regiment. Killed in action, 27th September, 1918. Age 19. Son of Edward Thomas and Sarah Ann Baker, of Knightcote, Leamington Spa. Born Leamington. Enlisted Coventry. Memorial Ref. Panel 3. Vis-en-Artois Memorial, France.

BAKER (Alias Virgin true family name), Corporal, George. G/4099, 2nd Bn., Royal West Surrey Regiment. Died 25th September, 1915. Age 26. Son of George and Sibina Elizabeth Virgin, of 41, Vale Road, Bushey, Herts. Born at Coventry. Resided at Coventry. Enlisted Guildford, Surrey. Memorial Ref. Loos Memorial, France.

BAKER, Private, Harry. 19667, 1st Bn., Wiltshire Regiment formerly 16705, Oxfordshire and Buckinghamshire Light Infantry. Killed in action, 16th June, 1915. Age 24. Resided at 140, Radford. Cycle Mechanic, Challenge Cycle Works. Enlisted December, 1914, Coventry. Born at Coventry. Resided at Birmingham. Commemorated Radford Memorial. Leaves a widow and one child. Memorial Ref. Panel 53. Ypres (Menin Gate) Memorial, Belgium.

BAKER, Private, Samuel. 266453, 1/7th Bn., Royal Warwickshire Regiment. Killed in action, 20th April, 1917. Enlisted Coventry. Resided Derby. Memorial Ref. Pier and Face 9 A 9 B and 10 B. Thiepval Memorial, France.

BALDOCK, Corporal, Joseph. 206133, Machine Gun Corps attached "F" Bn., Tank Corps. Killed in action, 31st July, 1917 volunteered to leave his machine when it was in a shell hole and under heavy fire, he was killed instantly. Age 21. Son of Mrs. Young, of 86, Villiers Street, Stoke, Coventry. Husband of Cissie May Baldock, of 6, Brooklands, Lightwood Road, Buxton. Born 1st November, 1896 at Nuneaton. Resided at 86, Villiers Street. Commemorated St. Michael's Church. Employed Coventry Plating Co. Ltd. Enlisted Coventry. Memorial Ref. Panel 56. Ypres (Menin Gate) Memorial, Ieper, West-Vlaanderen, Belgium.

BALE, Rifleman, Oliver. 22636, 2nd Bn., King's Royal Rifle Corps. Died, home, 23rd November, 1922. Born 13th January, 1888 in Albert Street. Resided at 14, Castle Street, Mechanic. Enlisted, May 1916. Grave Ref. Coventry (London Road) Cemetery.

BALL, Private, Arthur. 201464, 1st /4th Bn., Welsh Regiment formerly 16822, Gloucestershire Regiment. Killed in action, 27th March, 1917. Age 22. Son of William Ball, of The Outwoods, Great Packington, Coventry. Enlisted Birmingham. Memorial Ref. Panels 30 to 32. Jerusalem Memorial, Israel.

BALL, Private, Bertie. M2/033301, Army Service Corps. Died, Home, 4th March 1915. Age 24. Son of Mr. and Mrs. John Ball, of Kingstone Lisle, Wantage, Berks. Born Westcott, Bucks. Enlisted Coventry. Resided Montague, Berks. Grave Ref. II. 24. 4. Midsomer Norton (St. John the Baptist) Church Cemetery.

BALL, Private, Ernest. 331274, 18th Bn., Royal Warwickshire Regiment. Died at Ranelagh Road, Military Hospital, Ipswich, 2nd July, 1917 as a result of injuries received in bayonet practice. Age 18. Born Coventry. Resided Hillfields. Employed Triumph Works. Enlisted Coventry. Commemorated Triumph and Gloria Memorial. Grave Ref. D. 28. 34. Ipswich Cemetery.

BALL, Private, H. J. 51083, Princess Patricia's Canadian Light Infantry, (Eastern Ontario Regiment). Killed in action by a shell, 8th May, 1915. Only son of the Reverend J. Ball of Earlsdon. Emigrated in 1907. Employed in a laboratory in Alberta. Age 29. Memorial Ref. Panel 10. Ypres (Menin Gate) Memorial, Belgium.

BALL, J. Commemorated Wesleyan Church.

BALL, John. Commemorated Walsgrave-On-Sowe Memorial.

BALL, John. Commemorated Saint Thomas the Apostle, Longford.

BALL, Corporal, Jonah. 8566, 9th Bn., Royal Warwickshire Regiment. Killed in action, Mesopotamia, 25th June, 1916. Born Wombridge, Wellington, Salop. Enlisted Coventry. Resided Wellington. Grave Ref. XV. H. 5. Amara War Cemetery, Iraq.

BALLARD, Corporal, Henry Herbert. 265501, 1/7th Bn., Royal Warwickshire Regiment. Killed in action, 27th August, 1917. Born St. Paul's, Warwick. Enlisted Coventry. Resided Warwick. Memorial Ref. Panel 23 to 28 and 163A. Tyne Cot Memorial, Belgium.

BALLARD, Gunner, Joseph. 66473, 30th Heavy Artillery Group, Royal Garrison Artillery. Killed in action, 20th June, 1918. Born 17th September, 1883 at Foleshill. Resided at 20c. 5h. Much Park Street. Store Keeper. Commemorated Triumph & Gloria Memorial. Enlisted Coventry. Grave Ref. III. A. 11. La Targette British Cemetery, Neuville-St. Vaast, France.

BALLARD, Private, Thomas John. 241729, 15th Bn., Royal Warwickshire Regiment. Died of wounds, 28th May, 1918. Age 32. Husband of Mrs. S. Ballard, of Coventry. Born in 1886 at Coventry. Grave Ref. 2. G. 5. Tannay British Cemetery, Thiennes, Nord, France.

BALLINGTON, Sergeant, William. 99072, 214th Army Troops Coy., Royal Engineers. Died of wounds, 22nd September, 1917, mortally wounded by a bomb from an enemy aeroplane and died in hospital. Age 32. Son of Herbert and Annie Ballington. Husband of Lily Lavinia Ballington, of 20, Faulkner Street, Blackley, Manchester. Born at Derby. Resided at Coventry. Body Finisher, Humber Ltd. Enlisted May, 1915 at Coventry. Grave Ref. VII. D. 9. Dozinghem Military Cemetery, Belgium.

BAMBER. Employed by Rover Company Ltd. Killed in action.

BANKES, Captain, Edward Nugent. 3rd Bn. attd. 2nd Bn., Royal Dublin Fusiliers. Died, 26th April, 1915 wounded day before at St.Julien.. Age 39. Youngest son of Henry Hyde Nugent Bankes and the Hon. Mrs. Nugent Bankes. Husband of Lettice A. Bankes, of "Meriden Hall," Coventry. Served in the South African Campaign with Lumsden's Horse and Dorset Imperial Yeomanry, subsequently in the 2nd Dragoon Guards (Queen's Bays). Educated Charterhouse. Born 3rd October, 1875. Queens Medal and five clasps, South Africa. Memorial Ref. Panel 44 and 46. Ypres (Menin Gate) Memorial, Ieper, West-Vlaanderen, Belgium.

BANKS, Lance Corporal, William George. 12229, 9th Bn., Devonshire Regiment. Killed in action, 30th September, 1915. Age 20. Son of William and Louie Banks. Born at Kentford, Surrey. Resided at Coventry. Enlisted Nuneaton. Memorial Ref. Panel 35 to 37. Loos Memorial, France.

BANNARD, Lance Sergeant, Bertie Charles. 265657, 1/7th Bn., Royal Warwickshire Regiment. Killed in action, 13th August, 1917. Age 27. Brother of Mr. E. G. Bannard, of 6, Little Virginia, Kenilworth. Born St. Nicholas, Kenilworth. Enlisted Coventry. Resided Kenilworth. Employed as a Polisher at the Daimler Works. Memorial Ref. Panel 8. Ypres (Menin Gate) Memorial, Belgium.

BANNISTER, Private, John. 5493, 3rd Bn., Coldstream Guards. Killed in action, 15th September, 1916. Born Burton, Staffs. Enlisted Coventry. Resided Maltby near Rotherham. Memorial Ref. Pier and Face 7 D and 8 D. Thiepval Memorial, Somme, France.

BANNISTER, Private, Walter. 3755, 2/7th Bn., Royal Warwickshire Regiment. Died of wounds, 20th July, 1916. Age 29. Husband of L. Hollingworth (formerly Bannister), of 72, Bedford Street, Leamington Spa. Born 21st April, 1887, at Burton-upon-Trent. Resided at 69, Highfield Road. Gas Fitter, Coventry Gas Works. Enlisted in 1914, Coventry. Leaves a widow and one child. Commemorated Gas Department Memorial, Coventry Corporation. Grave Ref. XI. A.32. Merville Communal Cemetery, France.

BARBER, D. Educated at Bablake School. Commemorated Bablake School Memorial.

BARBER, G. N. Educated at Bablake School. Commemorated Bablake School Memorial.

BARBER, Lance Corporal, Joseph Newton. 41040, 1st Bn., Royal Dublin Fusiliers formerly 296758, Army Service Corps. Died of pneumonia while a Prisoner of War at a German Hospital, 17th October, 1918. Age 32. Son of George and Harriett Barber. Husband of Gertrude Mary Barber, of "Beechwood", Westwood Road, Tile Hill, Coventry. Born 26th March, 1886, at 5, Cope Street. Resided at 56, Mickleton Road. Wholesale Grocer. Enlisted February, 1917, Coventry. Commemorated Queens Road Memorial and War Memorial Park. Leaves a widow and one child. Grave Ref. C. 13. La Louviere Town Cemetery, La Louviere, Hainaut, Belgium.

BARFORD, Lieutenant, Kenneth Purnell. 2nd Sqdn., Royal Flying Corps. Reported missing, Somme area, 27th March, 1918. Shot down in a low sortie in the Albert area. Age 19. Son of Henry Widowson Barford and Mary Barford, of The Bungalow, Kenilworth Road, Coventry. Born 1899 at Coventry. Resided at Coventry. Student. Commemorated King Henry VIII School and War Memorial Park. Memorial Ref. Arras Flying Services Memorial, Pas de Calais, France.

BARKER, Private, Edward Vernon. 27998, 10th Bn., Royal Warwickshire Regiment. Killed in action, 22nd March, 1918. Born Barston, Warwicks. Enlisted Coventry. Resided Kenilworth. Memorial Ref. Bay 3. Arras Memorial, France.

BARKER, Sergeant, George Edward. 9455, 1st Bn., King's Shropshire Light Infantry. Killed in action, 23rd October, 1914 whilst defending the front line trenches at Armentieres. Educated at Bablake School. Commemorated Fillongley Memorial and Bablake School Memorial. Born Adelaide, South Australia. Enlisted Coleshill. Brother of Sergeant Henry Barker. Memorial Ref. Panel 8. Ploegsteert Memorial, Belgium.

BARKER, Sergeant, Henry. 8291, 1st Bn., Kings Shropshire Light Infantry formerly 8947, Royal Engineers. Killed in action, 23rd October, 1914 whilst defending the front line trenches at Armentieres. Educated at Bablake School. Born at Coventry. Enlisted Coventry. Resided Whittington, near Lichfield. Commemorated Fillongley Memorial and Bablake School Memorial. Brother of Sergeant George Edward Barker. Memorial Ref. Panel 8. Ploegsteert Memorial, Belgium.

BARKER, Private, James. 16833, 14th Bn., Royal Warwickshire Regiment. Killed in action, 12th September, 1916. Born 4th December, 1894, at Coventry. Resided in Well Street. Enlisted January, 1916, Coventry. Labourer. Memorial Ref. Pier and Face 9A 9B and 10B. Thiepval Memorial, France.

BARKER, Pioneer, Luke. 162444, Depot, Royal Engineers. Died home, 27th June, 1917. Age 41. Husband of Amy Barker, of 5, Earlsdon Street, Coventry. Born in 1876 at Sutton-in-Ashfield, Notts. Enlisted December, 1915, Coventry. Commemorated Earlsdon Working Mens Club and St. Barbara's Church. Grave Ref. 188. 3. Coventry (London Road) Cemetery.

BARKER, Private, Thomas Henry. 227029, 1st Bn., Royal Berkshire Regiment formerly 2533, Royal Warwickshire Regiment. Killed in action, 21st August, 1918. Age 25. Son of Arthur F. and Amelia Barker, of 8, Lord Street, Chapel Fields, Coventry. Born 3rd February, 1895, at Coventry. Enlisted September, 1914, Coventry. Moulder. Commemorated Queens Road Memorial and War Memorial Park. Grave Ref. XX. E. 5. Bienvillers Military Cemetery, Pas de Calais, France.

BARKER, Private, William. 30065, 10th Bn., Royal Warwickshire Regiment. Died of wounds, 15th December, 1917. Born at Wolston. Employed at Coventry. Enlisted Coventry. Commemorated Wolston Memorial. Grave Ref. VII. B. 1. Rocquigny-Equancourt Road British Cemetery, Manancourt, France.

BARLOW, Private, Henry. 14894, 11th Bn., Royal Warwickshire Regiment. Killed in action, 11th August, 1916. Born Tamworth. Enlisted Coventry. Grave Ref. VI. K. 17. Flatiron Copse Cemetery, Mametz, France.

BARLOW, Private, Henry. 266144, 2/7th Bn., Royal Warwickshire Regiment. Killed in action, 19th July, 1916. Age 20. Resided 24, Co-Operative Street, Alderman's Green. Enlisted Coventry. Commemorated Saint Thomas the Apostle, Longford. Memorial Ref. Panel 22 to 25. Loos Memorial, France.

BARLOW, Acting Lance Corporal, Herbert. 206120, 3rd Coy., A Bn., Machine Gun Corps (Heavy Branch) formerly 1768, Machine Gun Corps. Died of wounds, 7th June, 1917. Age 26. Son of Walter and Annie Barlow, of 37, Station Road, Pilsley, Chesterfield. Born Pikley, Derby. Enlisted Coventry. Grave Ref. XIII. C. A. Lijssenthoek Military Cemetery, Belgium.

BARNACLE, Private, Alfred Victor. 202093, 1st /4th Bn., Leicestershire Regiment. Killed in action, 21st April, 1917. Age 32. Son of Mr. and Mrs. J. Barnacle, of Much Park Street, Coventry. Husband of Emma Jane Barnacle, of 42, Syston Street, Leicester. Born in 1885 at Coventry. Enlisted Leicester. Grave Ref. II. A. 2. Mazingarbe Communal Cemetery Extension, Pas de Calais, France.

BARNACLE, Driver, Charles. 119035, 21st Div. Ammunition Col., Royal Field Artillery. Killed in action, Ypres, 2nd October, 1917. Age 20. Son of Frank and Esther Barnacle, of 3 Court, 5 House, Walsgrave Road, Coventry. Born 21st September, 1897 at Birmingham. Resided at 5, Atkins Square, Walsgrave Road. Enlisted November, 1915, Coventry. Fitter, Hillman's Motor Co., Coventry. Memorial Ref. Panel 4 to 6 and 162. Tyne Cot Memorial, Zonnebeke, West-Vlaanderen, Belgium.

BARNARD, Private, Samuel. 9070, 1st Bn., Royal Munster Fusiliers. Died of wounds, 21st November, 1917. Age 28. Son of Henry Barnard, of 85, Stoke Road, Gosport, Portsmouth. Billeted Coventry. Born Gosport. Enlisted Gosport. Resided Gosport. Grave Ref. II. D. 12. Bucquoy Road Cemetery, Ficheux, France.

BARNBY, Private, Francis Richard. 11167, 6th Bn., Oxfordshire and Buckinghamshire Light Infantry. Killed in action, 3rd September, 1916. Born at Hull. Resided at Hull. Enlisted Coventry. Formerly employed at Coventry. Memorial Ref. Pier and Face 10A and 10 D. Thiepval Memorial, France.

BARNES, Private, Frank. 10518, 11th Coy., Machine Gun Corps formerly 22253, Northants Regt. Killed in action, 4th October, 1917. Born Northampton. Enlisted Coventry. Resided Warwick. Memorial Ref. Panel 154 to 159 and 163A. Tyne Cot Memorial, Belgium.

BARNES, Lance Corporal, Harry Cecil. 6/386, 6th Bn., Royal Warwickshire Regiment. Died of pneumonia, 5th July, 1921. Age 18. Son of Thomas Charles and Eleanor Jane Barnes, of 26, The Gardens, Dulwich, London. Grave Ref. 227. 137. Coventry (London Road) Cemetery.

BARNES, Sergeant, Harvey. 9676, 7th Bn., South Staffordshire Regiment. Killed in action, 9th August, 1915. Age 45. Son of John and Harriet Barnes, of Droitwich, Worcester. Husband of Mary Barnes, of 129, Corporation Cottages, Holbrook Lane, Foleshill, Coventry. Born Droitwich. Enlisted Litchfield. Resided Sheffield. Memorial Ref. Panel 134 to 136. Helles Memorial, Turkey.

BARNES, Gunner, Richard. 16224, "C" Bty. 70th Bde., Royal Field Artillery. Killed in action, by a shell, 21st March, 1918. Age 28. Son of Mr. and Mrs. Richard Barnes, of 37, Albion Street, Coventry. Born 15th August, 1889, at Birmingham. Iron Polisher, Rover Co. Enlisted September, 1914 at Coventry. Commemorated War Memorial Park. Employed Rover Co. Ltd. Grave Ref. VII. B. 6. Faubourg D'Amiens Cemetery, Arras, Pas de Calais, France.

BARNETT, Private, Harry. 9016, Royal Welsh Fusiliers. Killed in action, 19th October, 1914. Age 28. Husband of Amy Phyllis Barnett, of 6, Spring Lane, Kenilworth. Born St. John's, Kenilworth. Enlisted Coventry. Memorial Ref. Panel 22. Ypres (Menin Gate) Memorial, Belgium.

BARNETT, Private, Henry. 9614, 1st Bn., Royal Warwickshire Regiment. Killed in action, 18th December, 1914. Husband of Mrs. A. Barnett, of 36, Littlefield, Stoke Heath, Coventry. Born in 1882 in Junction Street. Resided at 9, Broad Street. Enlisted Coventry. Employed by Swift of Coventry Ltd. Reservist. Grave Ref. I. B. 12. Prowse Point Military Cemetery, Comines-Warneton, Hainaut, Belgium.

BARNETT, Private, Stephen. 3367, 2nd /7th Bn., Royal Warwickshire Regiment. Reported missing, presumed killed, 19th July, 1916. Age 36. Son of Mrs. Barnett, of 10 Court, 4 House, Cox Street, Coventry. Born 8th February, 1880 at Coventry. Enlisted Coventry. Brazier. Memorial Ref. Panel 22 to 25. Loos Memorial, Pas de Calais, France.

BARNETT, Sapper, William Joseph. 99028, 234th Field Coy., Royal Engineers. Reported, missing, presumed killed, 31st July, 1917. Age 22. Son of Joseph Henry and Ellen Barnett, of 49, Newland Road, Coventry. Born 27th April, 1895 at 40, King William Street. Resided at 40, King William Street. Bricklayer. Enlisted Coventry. Commemorated War Memorial Park. Memorial Ref. Panel 9. Ypres (Menin Gate) Memorial, Ieper, West-Vlaanderen, Belgium.

BARNSDALL, Acting Lance Corporal, Raymond Frank. M2/033353, 688 Mechanical Transport, Coy., Royal Army Service Corps. Died, Balkans, 3rd November, 1918. Age 34. Son of Mr. E. Barnsdall. Born at Cricklewood, London. Born Wigston, Leics. Enlisted Coventry. Resided Hendon. Grave Ref. G. 8. Skopje British Cemetery, The former Yugoslavia Republic of Macedonia.

BARNSLEY, Private, Sydney. 3772, 9th Bn., Lancashire Fusiliers. Died of wounds, Gallipoli, 8th August, 1915. Born Coventry. Memorial Ref. Panel 58 to 72 or 218 to 219. Helles Memorial, Turkey.

BARNWELL, Private, Arthur. 16439, C Coy., 2nd Bn., South Staffordshire Regiment. Killed in action, 9th August, 1916. Resided vicinity of Corley Moor and Fillongley. Memorial Ref. Pier and Face 7B. Thiepval Memorial, Somme, France.

BARNWELL, Private, John. 33046, 1st Bn., Royal Berkshire Regiment. Killed in action, 23rd March 1918. Age 27. Husband of Mrs. Lillian Blasdale (formerly Barnwell), of Court, 15 House, Spon End, Coventry. Born Coventry. Enlisted Coventry. Memorial Ref. Bay 7. Arras Memorial, Pas de Calais, France.

BARR, Rifleman, Joseph. S/11273, 5th Bn., Rifle Brigade. Died of wounds, 9th April, 1920. Age 34. Husband of Emily Emma Barr, of 7, Barras Heath Hostels, Swan Lane, Coventry. Born at Coventry. Grave Ref. 242. 33. Coventry (London Road) Cemetery.

BARR, Private, John Davis. 48551, 5th Bn., Royal Berkshire Regiment formerly 40379, Somerset Light Infantry. Killed in action, 26th August, 1918. Age 19. Son of James J. Barr of 97, Clarendon Street, Leamington. Born Leamington. Resided at Leamington. Enlisted Leamington. Employed by Rotheram & Sons Ltd. Grave Ref. III. H. 16. Peronne Road Cemetery, Maricourt, France.

BARRETT, Private, Frederick Henry. DM2/206859, 905th Motor Transport Coy., Army Service Corps. Lost in HMT Transylvania, killed whilst bound for Egypt (hit by submarine), 4th May, 1917. Age 32. Son of S. A. and W. Barrett. Husband of R. M. Barrett, of "Annandale," 17, Meriden Street, Coventry. Born 20th August, 1884 at Northampton. Resided at 26, Fleet Street. Enlisted August, 1916 at Coventry. Florist and Fruiterer. Commemorated St. John's Church and War Memorial Park. Grave Ref. D. 3. Savona Town Cemetery, Italy.

BARRETT, Engine Room Artificer 4th Class, Montague Herbert. M/12359, HMS Defence, Royal Navy. Killed in action, Battle of Jutland, 31st May, 1916. Born 31st May, 1894. Resided 170, Stoney Stanton Road. Employed Coventry Ordnance Works. Enlisted March, 1915. Parents resided Dorsetshire. Memorial Ref. 14. Plymouth Naval Memorial.

BARRY, Private, Kenneth. SPTS/4774, 23rd Bn., Royal Fusiliers. Killed in action, Deville Wood, Battle of the Somme, 27th July, 1916. Age 20. Son of 0. W. and Amy E. Barry, of 83, Grafton Street, Coventry. Born in 1896, at Coventry. Resided at Manchester. Student, Textiles, Manchester University. Enlisted February, 1916, Manchester. Commemorated Bablake School Memorial and War Memorial Park. Memorial Ref. Pier and Face 8 C 9 A and 16 A. Thiepval Memorial, Somme, France.

BARRY, Private, Michael. 7861, 1st Bn., Royal Munster Fusilier. Age 24. Killed in action, 12th May, 1915. Son of Mary and Patrick Barry. Resided Cork. Enlisted Tralee, Kerry. Born St. Anne's, Kerry. Billeted in Coventry. Memorial Ref. Panel 185 to 190. Helles Memorial, Turkey.

BARTLETT, Private, Albert. 377, 18th Bn., Australian Infantry. Killed in action, Mereaucourt Wood, 28th August, 1918. Age 23. Son of Francis S. L. and Alice Bartlett, of 43, Aldbourne Road, Coventry. Born at West Bromwich, England. Born 22nd November, 1894. Resided at Coventry until 1914 when he emigrated to Australia. Boundary Rider. Enlisted May 1915. Commemorated War Memorial Park. Grave Ref. II. E. 3. Assevillers New British Cemetery, Somme, France.

BARTLETT, Private, Henry. 9749, 1st Bn., Northamptonshire Regiment formerly Royal Army Medical Corps. Killed at Loos, 25th September, 1915. Born 23rd August, 1891 at Coventry. Resided at Northampton previously 80, Paynes Lane. Fitter. Enlisted December, 1914. Employed Rudge, Turnery Department. Commemorated War Memorial Park. Father J. Bartlett employed Rudge. Memorial Ref. Panel 91 to 93. Loos Memorial, France.

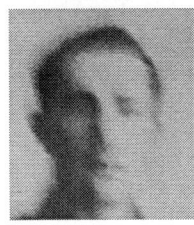
BARTLETT, Private, John. 266302, 10th Bn., Royal Warwickshire Regiment. Died of wounds, 7th November, 1918. Son of Mrs. E. Bartlett, of 14, King Richard Street, Coventry. Born 10th March, 1898 at Hillfields. Resided at Coventry. Fitter. Enlisted December, 1915 at Coventry. Commemorated War Memorial Park. Grave Ref. II. G. 16. Awoingt British Cemetery, Nord, France.

BARTLETT, Lance Corporal, John Charles. 8738, 2nd Bn., Oxfordshire and Buckinghamshire Light Infantry. Killed in action, 1st August, 1916. Age 26. Son of John Henry and Annie Bartlett, of 74, Stanley Road, Earlsdon, Coventry. Born at Banbury. Resided at Coventry. Enlisted Oxford. Memorial Ref. Pier and Face 10 A and 10 D. Thiepval Memorial, Somme, France.

BARTLETT, Acting Bombardier, William. 32575, 118th Bty., Royal Field Artillery Died of wounds, Home, 8th June, 1915. Age 29. Son of Richard and Sarah Bartlett, of The Moat Farm, Bedworth. Born Sudborough, Northampton. Enlisted Coventry. Memorial Ref. Gen. 7337 (Screen Wall). Tottenham Cemetery.

BARTLETT, Private, William Arthur. 265381, 1st /7th Bn., Royal Warwickshire Regiment. Died of wounds, 12th August, 1918. Age 21. Son of Thomas and Emma Bewley Bartlett, of Coventry. Born 7th July, 1897, at 17, Cox Street. Resided at 44, Much Park Street. House Decorator. Enlisted August, 1914 at Coventry. Grave Ref. 1. B. 9. Cavalletto British Cemetery, Italy.

BARTON, Lance Corporal, Herbert John, 28263, 1st Bn., Hampshire Regiment. Killed in action, 8th June, 1918. Age 19. Son of John and Elizabeth Barton, of White Stitch, Meriden, Coventry. Native of Great Packington, Warwickshire. Enlisted Coventry. Grave Ref. D. 16. Gonnehem British Cemetery, Pas de Calais, France.

BARWELL, Private, William. 20153, 2nd Bn., The Duke of Cornwall's Light Infantry formerly 11104, Royal Warwickshire Regiment. Age 45. Died Salonika, 7th July, 1916. Son of Elijah and Ann Caroline Barwell. Born Brackley, Northampton. Resided at Coventry. Enlisted Birmingham. Grave Ref. 1381. Mikra British Cemetery, Kalamaria, Greece.

BARWICK, Private, Edward Sidney. 20206, 11th Bn., Royal Warwickshire Regiment. Died of severe wounds, 14th April, 1917 in the 11th General Hospital. Born at Wiveliscombe, Somerset. Resided at 18, Winchester Street, Coventry. Employed Mr. Phillips, The Grange. Enlisted Coventry. Grave Ref. XXII. H. 9a. Etaples Military Cemetery, France.

BASELEY, Private, Arthur James. 3413, 2nd /7th Bn., Royal Warwickshire Regiment. Died of wounds 12th January, 1917. Severe wounds received on the Somme, 10th January, 1917. Age 21. Son of Emily and Joseph Duckett (step-father), of 6, Keresley Heath, Coventry. Born in 1896, at 6, Keresley Heath. Resided at 6, Keresley Heath. Gardener. Enlisted November, 1914, Coventry. Commemorated St. Thomas Memorial. Grave Ref. VII. B. 12. Contay British Cemetery, Contay, Somme, France.

BASKETTS, Private, George. 1712, 2/6th Bn., Royal Warwickshire Regiment. Killed in action, 21st March, 1918. Born in St. John's Parish. Husband of Mrs. F. Basketts. Resided at 3c. 3h., St. John's Street. Cycle Finisher, Premier Cycle Co. Ltd. Enlisted 21st August, 1914 at Coventry. Leaves a widow and two children. Memorial Ref. Panel 18 and 19. Pozieres Memorial, France.

BASTOCK, Private, Jack. 45021, 1st Bn., Royal Inniskilling Fusiliers formerly Devonshire Regiment. Died of wounds, 15th October, 1918. Age 19. Son of Edwin and Mary Bastock, of Lutterworth End. Born 1st February, 1899 at Cubbington. Resided at Lutterworth End, Cubbington. Labourer, Coventry Swaging Company. Enlisted March, 1917. Grave Ref. IV.D. 4. Duhallow ADS Cemetery, Belgium.

BATCHELOR, Private, Ernest Edward. 1301, 2nd Bn., Royal Warwickshire Regiment. Killed in action, 16th May, 1915. Son of William and Eliza Gertrude Batchelor, of Ebenezer Cottage, Tachbrook Road, Whitnash, Leamington Spa. Born Whitnash, Warwicks. Enlisted Coventry. Resided Leamington. Memorial Ref. Panel 6. Le Touret Memorial, France.

BATCHELOR, H. Commemorated St. Barbara's Memorial.

BATCHELOR, Private, Thomas Henry. 35003, 5th Bn., Royal Berkshire Regiment. Died of wounds, 25th December, 1917. Age 37. Son of Thomas and Ann Batchelor, of Napton, Warwickshire. Born Napton, Warwick. Enlisted Coventry. Grave Ref. XVI. A. 27. Cologne Southern Cemetery, Germany.

BATCHELOR, Private, William Leonard. 271012, 10th Bn., East Kent Regiment formerly 2568, West Kent Yeomanry. Palestine, 6th, November, 1917. Age 29. Son of William and Mary Batchelor. Husband of Kathleen M. Spreckley (formerly Batchelor) of 15, Nottingham Road, Melton Mowbray. Born in Sydney, Australia. Resided at Peckham Rye (Surrey) formerly Coventry. Grave Ref. M.57. Beersheba War Cemetery, Israel.

BATES, Driver, Arthur, Royal Army Service Corps. Died home, 10th August, 1921. Born 18th January, 1874, at Cannock Chase, Derbyshire. Resided at 8, Church End. Labourer. Enlisted September, 1914. Grave Ref. Stoke (St. Michaels) Churchyard, Coventry.

BATES, Lance Corporal, Arthur. 412, 1st Bn., Royal Warwickshire Regiment. Killed in action, 13th October, 1914. Born in St. Peter's Parish, Coventry. Resided Coventry. Enlisted Warwick. Grave Ref. II.N. 341 (Buried near this spot), Meteren Military Cemetery, France.

BATES, Lance Corporal, Arthur. 6918, 2nd Bn., Royal Irish Regiment. Killed in action, 4th May, 1915. Born in Coventry. Enlisted Birmingham. Grave Ref. XXVII. A. 4. New Irish Farm Cemetery, Belgium.

BATES, Private, Arthur Thomas. 7176, 34th Mobile Section, Royal Army Veterinary Corps. Died of dysentery, Salonica, 7th November, 1916. Son of James and Maud Bates, of Coventry. Husband of Florence Bates, of 249, Stoney Stanton Road, Coventry. Age 34. Born 5th February, 1881 at Birmingham. Resided at 26, Lincoln Street. Mechanic,(Shoeing Smith). Enlisted March, 1915 at Coventry. Grave Ref. 663. Salonica Anglo French Military Cemetery, Lembet Road, Greece.

BATES, Private, Charles Ernest. 306781, 2nd Bn., Royal Warwickshire Regiment. Killed in action, Ypres, 9th October, 1917. Age 40. Son of Mrs. Ann Bates, of 86, Spon End, Coventry. Born 21st May, 1878 at Radford near Leamington Spa. Resided at 86, Spon End. Carter. Enlisted March, 1916 at Coventry. Memorial Ref. Panel 23 to 28 and 163A. Tyne Cot Memorial, Zonnebeke, West-Vlaanderen, Belgium.

BATES, Private, Frank. 265218, 2nd Bn., Royal Warwickshire Regiment. Died of wounds, received in action, 12th October, 1917. Age 27. Brother of Mr. H. Bates, of 4/10, Cow Lane, Coventry. Born 2nd March, 1890, at 18, Junction Street. Resided in 45, Cromwell Street. Silk Spinner, Courtaulds Ltd. Enlisted August, 1914. Commemorated War Memorial Park. Grave Ref. I. P. 17. Godewaersvelde British Cemetery, Nord, France.

BATES, Private, Harold. 3435, 2nd /7th Bn., Royal Warwickshire Regiment. Killed in action, 19th July, 1916. Age 27. Son of Henry Bates, of 72, Fitton Street, Nuneaton. Husband of Annie Sedgley (formerly Bates), of 127, Corporation Cottages, Holbrook Lane, Coventry. Enlisted Coventry. Memorial Ref. Panel 22 to 25. Loos Memorial, Pas de Calais, France.

BATES, Private, Herbert. 2433, 1st Bn., Royal Warwickshire Regiment. Killed in action, 29th October, 1914. Age 21. Son of Walter Arthur Bass. Born 15th May, 1893 at 19, Freeth Street. Resided at 66, Paynes Lane. Soldier. Enlisted Warwick. Grave Ref. La Ferte-Sous-Jouarre Memorial, France.

BATES, Private, John William. 235067, 2/4th Bn., Gloucestershire Regiment. Died, 3rd December, 1917. Age 25. Son of Charley and Flora Bates, of 163, Cranbury Road, Eastleigh. Won a Silver Cup for rifle shooting at Arras. Born Coventry. Enlisted Southampton. Memorial Ref. Panel 6. Cambrai Memorial, Louverval, France.

BATES, Sergeant, Oliver. 2506, "A" Coy. 1st /7th Bn., Royal Warwickshire Regiment. Died of wounds, 6th August, 1916 at Calais General Hospital having been taken there by hospital ship and had right leg amputated. Age 25. Son of Oliver and Clara Bates, of 63, Beaconsfield Road, Stoke, Coventry. Born 26th July, 1891 in St. Michael's Parish. Printer. Enlisted September, 1914 at Coventry. Commemorated St. Michaels Memorial and War Memorial Park. Employed Messrs Caldicott and Felthams. Grave Ref. E. 4. 2. Calais Southern Cemetery, Pas de Calais, France

BATES, Private, Thomas Harold. 16878, 1st Bn., Coldstream Guards. Killed in action, 28th March, 1918. Age 23. Father of Dorothy Iris Bates, of 95, King George's Avenue, Little Heath, Foleshill, Coventry. Born in 1985 at Banbury. Resided at Coventry. Moulder. Enlisted Coventry. Grave Ref. IV. H 30. Bucquoy Road Cemetery, Ficheux, Pas de Calais, France.

BATES, Corporal, Thomas Healy. 9074, 1st Bn., Royal Warwickshire Regiment. Killed in action, 31st March, 1918. Age 27. Son of Thomas Charles and Martha Bates, of Ryton-on-Dunsmore, Coventry. Enlisted November, 1914 at Coventry. Employed Binley Colliery. Commemorated Ryton Memorial. Grave Ref. XVII. H. 26. Cabaret-Rouge British Cemetery, Souchez, Pas de Calais, France.

BATES, Private, Thomas Herbert. 15813, 14th Bn., Royal Warwickshire Regiment. Killed in action, 3rd September, 1916. Son of Mrs. Bates, of 1, Prices Place, Brook Street, Leamington. Born Coventry. Enlisted Leamington. Memorial Ref. Pier and Face 9A 9B and 10B. Thiepval Memorial, France.

BATES, Private, William. 9517, 1/5th Bn., Leicestershire Regiment. Killed in action, 11th October, 1918. Born St. Michael's, Coventry. Enlisted Leicester. Resided Coventry. Grave Ref. IV. C. 20. Busigny Communal Cemetery Extension, France.

BATES, Private, William Henry. 4978, 22nd Bn., Australian Infantry. Killed in action, by a shell, 5th October 1917. Age 22. Son of George and Harriet Bates, of 45, Kingfield Street, Coventry. Born in 1895. Resided at 45, King Fields. Former Humber Employee. Born Coventry. Enlisted 17th February, 1916. Grave Ref. EE. 65. Buffs Road Cemetery, Ieper, West-Vlaanderen, Belgium.

BATTY, Gunner, Sidney. 72311, Division Ammunition Col., (Attached New Zealand and Australian Division), Royal Field Artillery. Died, Egypt, 25th April, 1915. Age 20. Son of Joseph and Louisa Batty. Born Coventry. Enlisted Birmingham. Grave Ref. A. 16. Port Said War Memorial Cemetery, Egypt.

BAUGHAN, Private, Henry. 23124, 1st Bn., Royal Warwickshire Regiment. Killed in action, 30th August, 1918. Age 30. Son of Harry and Annie Baughan, of Tan Yard, Tile Hill, Coventry. Born Berkswell. Resided Berkswell. Enlisted Coventry. Memorial Ref. Panel 3. Vis-En-Artois Memorial, Pas de Calais, France.

BAUSOR, Private, Norman Samuel. 41833, "B" Coy., 5th Bn., Royal Berkshire Regiment formerly 3856, Berkshire Yeomanry. Died of wounds, received at Aveluy Wood, 27th March, 1918 near Albert. Age 19. Son of John and Lydia Bausor, of "Duntroon", 6, Queen Victoria Road, Coventry. Born 27th November, 1898, at Coventry. Resided at Coventry. Butcher's Assistant. Enlisted February, 1917 at Coventry. Commemorated St. John's Church, King Henry VIII School and War Memorial Park. Grave Ref. II. L. 14. Bouzincourt Ridge Cemetery, Albert, Somme, France.

BAXTER, Gunner, Arthur. 139428, 154th Heavy Bty., Royal Garrison Artillery formerly 17705, Royal Warwickshire Regiment. Died of wounds (gas), 15th August, 1917. Age 19. Son of Mrs. Emma Baxter, of 12, Waterloo Street, Hillfields, Coventry. Born 12th June, 1898, at 57, King William Street. Resided at 12, Waterloo Street. Employed Triumph Works, Tool Room as a Turner. Enlisted 27th March, 1916 in Coventry with Royal Warwickshire Regiment transferred December, 1916. Commemorated War Memorial Park. Grave Ref. I. B. 54. Outtersteene Communal Cemetery Extension, Bailleul, Nord, France.

BAXTER, Gunner, Arthur Gordon. 2346, Machine Gun Corps (Motors). Died, Home, 10th October, 1915. Age 21. Son of John George and Clara Baxter, of Wanstead. His brother Leonard Arthur Baxter also fell. Born Wanstead. Enlisted Coventry. Resided Folkestone. Grave Ref. 48. 55556. City Of London Cemetery and Crematorium, Manor Park.

BAXTER, Private, Frank. 43984, 5th Bn., Royal Berkshire Regiment. Killed in action, 27th September, 1918. Born 14th March, 1899, at Wolstanton, Staffordshire. Resided at 32, Cross Road, Foleshill. Apprentice, Toolroom. Enlisted Coventry. Memorial Ref. Panel 7. Vis-En-Artois Memorial, France.

BAXTER, Private, Frederick. 5487, 10th Bn., Royal Warwickshire Regiment. Died of wounds, 5th February, 1916. Born Rugby. Enlisted Coventry. Grave Ref. G. 16. Rugby (Clifton Road) Cemetery.

BAXTER, Private, George. 303241, 2/7th Bn., Manchester Regiment. Killed 21st March, 1918. Born at Milton, Northants. Formerly member of Co-operative Prize Choir. Enlisted Manchester. Resided Flixton, Lancashire. Memorial Ref. Panel 64 to 67. Pozieres Memorial, France.

BAYLISS, Private, Alfred William. 31199, 2nd Bn., Royal Welsh Fusiliers formerly 87419, Royal Field Artillery. Killed in action, Givenchy, 22nd June, 1916 when buried during the explosion of a mine. Age 19. Only son of William Edward Bayliss, of 39, Terry Road, Coventry. Born 22nd December, 1896, at King's Norton. Educated Frederick Bird School. Clerk. Enlisted May, 1915. Grave Ref. II. A. 23. Gorre British And Indian Cemetery, Pas de Calais, France.

BAYLISS, Captain, Percival Baron. 5th Bn., Tank Corps. Killed in action, 3rd October, 1918. Age 21. Son of Thomas and Sabina Elizabeth Bayliss of Sherbourne, Esme Road, Sparkill, Birmingham. Born Coventry. Memorial Ref. Panel 11. Vis-En-Artois Memorial, France.

BAYLISS, Lance Sergeant, Thomas Talbot. 6506, 1st Bn., Coldstream Guards. Killed in action, 9th October, 1917. Born 2nd, July, 1889, in Cromwell Street. Resided at 179, Stoney Stanton Road. Soldier. Enlisted Coventry. Memorial Ref. Panel 9 to 10. Tyne Cot Memorial, Belgium.

BEACHAM, Sapper, Harry. 224766, 126th Field Company, Royal Engineers. Killed in action, 24th March, 1918. Born 27th July, 1885 at Allesley. Resided at Berkswell. Carpenter and joiner. Enlisted Coventry. Memorial Ref. Panel 10 to 13. Pozieres Memorial, France.

BEACHAM, Private, William Charles. 50545, 2nd Bn., Royal Berkshire Regiment formerly 39954, Royal Warwickshire Regiment. Killed in action, 27th April, 1918 at Villiers Bretonneux. Age 18. Son of William and Emma Beacham, of Raglan House, Old Road, Allesley, Coventry. Born in 1900 at Allesley. Resided at Allesley. Carpenter. Enlisted in 1917 at Coventry. Commemorated Bablake School Memorial. Grave Ref. II. P. 14. Adelaide Cemetery, Villers-Bretonneux, Somme, France.

BEAL, Private, Ernest. 2401, 1st /7th Bn., Royal Warwickshire Regiment. Died of wounds, Foncquevillers, 23 March, 1916 when seriously injured during a heavy bombardment. Age 19. Son of William and Nellie Beal, of 147, Narrow Lane, Coventry. Born 3rd, November, 1896 at Coalville, Leicestershire. Resided at 147, Narrow Lane. Turner, Humber Ltd. Enlisted September, 1914 at Coventry. Commemorated St. Paul's Church. Grave Ref. I. C. 8. Foncquevillers Military Cemetery, Pas de Calais, France.

BEALE, Private, Joseph Robert. 20001, 6th Bn., Dorsetshire Regiment formerly 2363, Royal Warwickshire Regiment. Died of wounds, 10th October, 1917. Born Nuneaton. Enlisted Coventry. Resided Nuneaton. Grave Ref. VII. C. 44. Mendinghem Military Cemetery, Belgium.

BEALES, Gunner, Archibald George. 249183, "C" Bty. 285th Bde., Royal Field Artillery. Killed in action, 30th September, 1918. Age 38. Son of Archibald George Beales, of 2, Chauntry Place, Coventry. Born 23rd August, 1886 at Military Barracks, Athlone. Resided at 2, Chauntry Place. Haulier. Enlisted April, 1917, Coventry. Commemorated Holy Trinity Panels. Grave Ref. II. F. 13. Naves Communal Cemetery Extension, Nord, France.

BEALES, Private, William. 16391, 1st Bn., Royal Warwickshire Regiment. Killed in action near Arras, 17th April, 1917. Age 20. Born 27th November, 1896, at 2, Chauntry Place. Resided at 2, Chauntry Place. Machinist, Calcott Bros., Gosford Street. Enlisted November, 1915 at Coventry. Commemorated Holy Trinity Panels. Grave Ref. Special Memorial (Grave destroyed by shell fire) B. 7. Sunken Road Cemetery, Fampoux, France.

BEASLEY, Lance Corporal, Harry. 226139, 182nd Trench Mortar Battery, 2/7th Bn., Royal Warwickshire Regiment. Killed in action, 21st March, 1918. Mother Mrs. T. W. Beasley, Walsgrave on Sowe. Commemorated on the Walsgrave-On-Sowe Memorial. Enlisted Coventry. Memorial Ref. Panel 18 and 19. Pozieres Memorial, France.

BEASLEY, Private, Joseph. 11323, 7th Bn., Leicestershire Regiment. Killed in action, 29th October, 1915. Born Longford. Enlisted Nuneaton. Grave Ref. I. A. 13. Albert Communal Cemetery Extension, France.

BEASLEY, Gunner, Walter. 65920, B Battery, 77th Brigade, Royal Field Artillery. Killed in action, 11th July, 1917. Born in 1893, at Longford. Resided at Grange Road, Longford. Employed by Courtaulds Ltd. Enlisted Coventry. Husband of Mrs. Beasley (nee Colling), 2 Woodshires Road and married Salem Baptist Church. Commemorated Saint Thomas the Apostle, Longford and Roll of Honour, Salem Baptist Church. Grave Ref. I. B.15. Gwalia Cemetery, Belgium.

BEAUFOY, Company Sergeant Major, Arthur. 14559, 8th Bn., Royal Berkshire Regiment. Killed in action, 23rd October, 1916. Born 20th June, 1888, in Arthur Street. Resided in West Street. Machinist. Enlisted August, 1914 at Coventry. Grave Ref. II. A. 1. Le Cateau Military Cemetery, France.

BEAUFOY, Private, Benjamin. 1122, 2nd Bn., Royal Warwickshire Regiment. Killed in action, 7th November, 1914. Age 25. Son of Mr. W. and Mrs. L. Beaufoy, of 23, Bryan Road, Coventry. Husband of Daisy Boland (formerly Beaufoy), of 90, Str Molo Marina, Sliema, Malta. Born 29th September, 1891, in Stoney Stanton Road. Resided in Harnall Lane East. Machinist. Memorial Ref. Panel 8. Ypres (Menin Gate) Memorial, Ieper, West-Vlaanderen, Belgium.

BEAUFOY, Private, Horace. 17/1529, 17th Bn., West Yorkshire Regiment (Prince of Wales's Own). Killed in action, 30th July, 1916. Age 18. Son of Mrs. Emily Beaufoy of 3, St. Agnes Lane, Coventry. Born in 1897 at Coventry. Resided at 3, St. Agnes Lane. Enlisted Leeds. Twice wounded. Commemorated Holy Trinity Panels. Memorial Ref. Pier and Face 2A 2 C and 2 D. Thiepval Memorial, Somme, France.

BEAUFOY, Private, Reginald Thomas. 45073, 1st Bn., Norfolk Regiment. Killed in action, 8th November, 1918. Age 20. Born at Great Heath. Son of Mr. and Mrs. Thomas Beaufoy, of "St. Keyne," Queen Mary's Road, Coventry. Born 18th September, 1898, in Lockhurst Lane. Resided in Queen Mary's Road. Grinder. Enlisted June, 1918 at Coventry. Commemorated Bablake School Memorial and War Memorial Park. Grave Ref. In South Corner. Bachant Communal Cemetery, Nord, France.

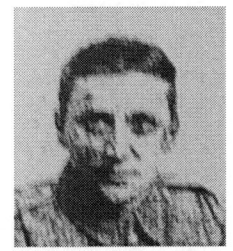
BEAUMONT, Private, Ernest Charles. 4544, 1/7th Bn., Royal Warwickshire Regiment. Killed in action, Beaumont Hamel, 19th July, 1916. Born in 1887, in Well Street. Resided at 4c. 10h. Castle Street. Polisher. Enlisted November, 1915 at Coventry. Commemorated Post Office Memorial. Grave Ref. I. F.6. Bapaume Post Military Cemetery, Albert, France.

BEAUMONT, Private, William. 16029, 8th Bn., Duke of Wellington's (West Riding Regiment). Killed in action, by a shell which penetrated the dug out whilst he slept, 14th June, 1917. Age 29. Son of Oliver and Mary Jane Beaumont, of Huddersfield. Husband of Ethel Mary Judd (formerly Beaumont), of 21, Hertford Place, Butts, Coventry. Born 23rd October, 1888 at Huddersfield. Resided at 13, Junction Street. Moulder, Messrs Matterson, Huxley & Watson Ltd. Enlisted February, 1915 at Coventry. Leaves a widow and one child. Grave Ref. II. C. 5. R.E. Farm Cemetery, Heuvelland, West-Vlaanderen, Belgium.

BECK, Private, Arthur. 1909, 2nd Bn., Royal Warwickshire Regiment. Killed in action, 25th September, 1915. Born 23rd January, 1884 at Coventry. Resided at 29c. 8h. Gosford Street. Fitter. Enlisted August, 1914, Coventry. Memorial Ref. Panel 22 to 25. Loos Memorial, France.

BECK, Lance Corporal, Frank. 1964, 1st Bn., Royal Warwickshire Regiment. Killed in action, Battle of the Somme, 2nd July, 1916. Age 34. Son of Jeremiah Beck. Husband of Mrs. F. Beck, of 6 House, 23 Court, Gosford Street, Coventry. Born 4th February, 1882 in All Saint's Parish. Resided at 23c. 6h. Gosford Street. Machinist. Enlisted August, 1914. Memorial Ref. Pier and Face 9 A 9 B and 10 B. Thiepval Memorial, Somme, France.

BECK, Private, George Edward. 55677, 10th Bn., Northumberland Fusiliers, formerly 898, Army Service Corps. Killed in action, 27th October, 1918. Age 28. Son of Harry and Herriott Eliza Beck, of Erdington, Birmingham. Only brother of Lawrence A. Beck. Born at Coventry. Grave Ref. 3. B. 11. Tezze British Cemetery, Italy.

BECK, Private, Joseph Arthur. 2764, 9th Bn., Royal Warwickshire Regiment. Died, Mesopotamia, 1st September, 1918. Age 41. Son of Thomas and Ann Elizabeth Beck, of 4, Cook Street, Coventry. Born 11th July, 1878 at 9c. 11h. Well Street. Resided at 27, Henry Street. Labourer. Enlisted August, 1914 at Coventry. Memorial Ref. Panel 2. Column 1. Tehran Memorial, Iran. (Buried at Baku)

BECKETT, 2nd Corporal, Ernest Edward, MM. 312621, 1st Signal Coy., Royal Engineers formerly 121081, Royal Field Artillery. Died of wounds, Boulogne, 4th September, 1918. Age 25. Son of Edward and Charlotte Beckett of 78, King George's Avenue, Foleshill, Coventry. Born 19th February, 1894, at Chatham. Resided at Coventry. Clerk. Enlisted November, 1914 at Coventry. Awarded the Military Medal in December, 1917 for conspicuous gallantry and devotion to duty whilst in charge of a forward visual station where he had under his charge a party of ten attached signalers. He remained on duty for 48 hours continuously, sending several very important messages back by lamp, and during the greater part of this time his station was subject to very heavy fire. Grave Ref. III. B. 17. Terlincthun British Cemetery, Wimille, Pas de Calais, France.

BEDDOES, Private, George. 41920, 2nd Bn., Worcestershire Regiment formerly 23491, Royal Warwickshire Regiment. Killed in action, 17th April, 1918. Born Ironbridge, Salop. Enlisted Coventry. Resided Ironbridge. Memorial Ref. Panel 5. Ploegsteert Memorial, Belgium.

BEDFORD, Private, Charles Ernest. 16822, 14th Bn., Royal Warwickshire Regiment. Killed in action, 30th July, 1916. Born Leicester. Enlisted Coventry. Memorial Ref. Pier and Face 9A 9B and 10B. Thiepval Memorial, Somme, France.

BEDNALL, Private, William. 2554, 2nd Bn., Royal Warwickshire Regiment. Killed in action, 18th December, 1914. Born Coventry. Resided at Coventry. Enlisted Warwick. Memorial Ref. Panel 2 and 3. Ploegsteert Memorial, Belgium.

BEDNELL, L. Commemorated St. John's Church.

BEE, Private, Frederick William. 265928, 2/7th Bn., Sherwood Foresters (Notts and Derby Regiment). Killed in action, 27th September, 1917. Born at Radford, Nottinghamshire. Resided at 98, Chandos Street. Grave Ref. VI. H. 4. Tyne Cot Cemetery, Belgium.

BEECH, Sapper, Betram. WR/262580, 259th Light Railway Operating Company, Corps of Royal Engineers. Died, 4th September, 1918. Age 22. Son of Mrs. Mary Beech of Cotes Heath, Eccleshall, Staffs. Born 6th September, 1895 at Bowsey Wood, Staffordshire. Resided at 27, Station Road West, Longford or Cotes Heath, Staffordshire. Enlisted Staffordshire. Plate layer. Grave Ref. IV. D. 21. Abbeville Communal Cemetery Extension, France.

BEECH, Lieutenant, Rowland Auriol James. A Squadron, 16th (The Queen's) Lancers. Killed in action near Ypres, 21st February, 1915 rushing forward to throw bombs. Age 26. Eldest son of Colonel R. J. Beech and Mrs. Beech, of Brandon Hall, Coventry. Born 22nd August, 1888. Educated Eton and Sandhurst. Grave Ref. G. 2. Ypres Town Cemetery, Ieper, West-Vlaanderen, Belgium.

BEECH, Rifleman, William Herbert. B/203079, 9th Bn., Rifle Brigade formerly R/16859, King's Royal Rifle Corps. Killed in action 15th September, 1916. Age 18. Son of William H. and L. Beech, of 29, St. Michael's Road, Stoke, Coventry. Born 3rd July, 1897, at 19c. 7h. Gosford Street. Resided at 19c. 7h. Gosford Street. Enlisted November, 1915 at Coventry. Fitter, Radiator Company Ltd. Grave Ref. III. L. 1. Delville Wood Cemetery, Longueval, Somme, France.

BEESLEY, Lance Corporal, Victor George William. 11609, 2nd Bn., Duke of Cornwall's Light Infantry. Killed in action, 14th March, 1915. Born in 1895, at Banbury. Resided at Coventry. Enlisted August, 1914, London. Labourer. Memorial Ref. Panel 20. Ypres (Menin Gate) Memorial, Belgium.

BEESLEY, Private, William Henry. 306782, 2/8th Bn., Royal Warwickshire Regiment. Killed in action, Pozieres, 27th August, 1916. Born 3rd December, 1877, at Conway Buildings, Spon End. Resided at 9, Spon End. Enlisted June, 1916 at Coventry. Watch Case Engraver also workman, Coventry Corporation. Commemorated Gas Department Memorial, Coventry Corporation. Grave Ref. IV. E. 35. Pozieres British Cemetery, Ovillers-La-Boiselle, France.

BELCHER, Private, Harry Walter. 6538, 2nd Bn., South Staffordshire Regiment. Killed in action, Givenchy, 10th March, 1915. Age 33. Son of John and Lucy Belcher, of Oliver Street, Birmingham. Husband of Ellen Scriven (formerly Belcher), of 40, The Orchard, Alveley, Bridgnorth, Salop. Born 23rd January, 1881, at Birmingham. Resided at 42, Smith Street. Enlisted Birmingham. Reservist. Labourer. Commemorated Wesleyan Church. Memorial Ref. Panel 21 and 22. Le Touret Memorial, France.

BELL, Private, George, 241592, 1st /6th Bn., Royal Warwickshire Regiment. Killed in action, 1st April, 1917. Age 32. Husband of Harriett E. Bell, of 49, Raglan Street, Coventry. Born 22nd November, 1885, in Little Park Street. Resided at 49, Raglan Street. Packer, Triumph Works. Commemorated Triumph and Gloria Memorial and War Memorial Park. Parents resided St. John Street. Enlisted Coventry. Grave Ref. I. T. 2. Epehy Wood Farm Cemetery, Epehy, Somme, France.

BELL, Private, John William. 10685, 2nd Bn., Duke of Wellington's (West Riding Regiment). Killed in action, 7th March, 1915. Age 22. Son of William Bell, of Foleshill, Coventry. Husband of Rosa Susannah Elizabeth Bell. Born Branston, Lincs. Enlisted Keighley, Yorks. Resided Seaton Delaval, Newcastle-on-Tyne. Grave Ref. Sp. Mem. C. 12. Tuileries British Cemetery, Ieper, West-Vlaanderen, Belgium.

BELLIS, Armourer's Crew, William Francis. M/20240, HMS Glory I, Royal Navy. Died of influenza, 7th November, 1918. Age 21. Son of William Henry and Elizabeth Bellis, of 188, Swan Lane, Coventry. Born 5th December, 1896 at 6c. 2h. Bond Street. Resided at 49, Rudge Road. Enlisted February, 1916. Fitter. Grave Ref. Sp. Mem. A1. Murmansk New British Cemetery, Russian Federation.

BELTON, Able Seaman, John. 5003A, HM Mercantile Fleet Auxiliary, Lady Cory Wright. Drowned in English Channel, 26th March, 1918. Son of John and Honor Belton, of 5, Lower Merchants Road, Galway. Born 4th April, 1895, at Galway. Resided at Colony Cottages. Sailor. Memorial Ref. 31. Portsmouth Naval Memorial.

BENCH, Sergeant, Charles William. 6266, 1st Bn., Royal Warwickshire Regiment. Killed in action, Ypres, 23rd July, 1917 whilst manning the parapet. Born 1st January, 1879 at Warwick. Resided at 93, Broad Street. Son of Joseph and Elizabeth Bench, of 93, Broad Street, Coventry. Enlisted August, 1914. Spinner. Grave Ref. I. B. 9. Crump Trench British Cemetery, Fampoux, France.

BENCH, Sergeant, Ernest William. 950, 2nd Bn., Royal Warwickshire Regiment. Killed in action, Loos, 25th September, 1915. Age 26. Son of Joseph and Elizabeth Bench, of 93, Broad Street, Coventry. Born 5th January, 1889 at Warwick. Resided at 93, Broad Street. Grave Ref. I. B. 8. Cabaret-Rouge British Cemetery, Souchez, Pas de Calais, France.

BENCH, Sergeant, Joseph. 1558, 1st Bn., Royal Warwickshire Regiment. Killed in action, 11th April, 1917. Born 21st December, 1891 at Warwick. Resided at 26 Station Street East. Soldier. Son of Joseph and Elizabeth Bench, of 93, Broad Street, Coventry. Memorial Ref. Arras Memorial, France.

BENCH, Private, Thomas. 260264, 2/8th Bn., Worcestershire Regiment. Killed in action, 15th November, 1917. Born 27th June, 1880 at Warwick. Resided at Warwick (home in Coventry). Enlisted in 1917. House Decorator. Grave Ref. IV. B. 2. Browns Copse Cemetery, Roeux, France.

BENCH, Private, William Thomas. 22111, 57th Coy., Machine Guns Corps (Infantry) formerly 2804, Royal Warwickshire Regiment. Killed in action, 16th May, 1917. Born 12th April, 1893. Resided at Coventry. Enlisted August, 1915 at Coventry. Railway Goods Porter. Memorial Ref. Panel 56. Ypres Menin Gate, Belgium.

BENFIELD, Private, Bertram. 41336, 1st Bn., Duke of Cornwall's Light Infantry formerly 8/18433, T. Res. Bn. Died of wounds, 16th April, 1918. Age 19. Son of Ernest George and Mary Ann Benfield, of North End, nr. Leamington. Enlisted Coventry. Grave Ref. II. C. 26. Aire Communal Cemetery, France.

BENNETT, Company Sergeant Major, Alfred. 6426, 1st Bn., Royal Munster Fusiliers. Killed in action, 26th April, 1915 wounds received to stomach and heart leading a charge on a village. Born Ballyseedy, Kerry. Enlisted Tralee. Resided Tralee. Billeted Coventry. Memorial Ref. Panel 185 to 190. Helles Memorial, Turkey.

BENNETT, H. Commemorated St. John's Church.

BENNETT, Harry. Killed in action. Name on Roll of Honour in Cathedral Church of St. Michael.

BENNETT, Gunner, Horace Frederick. 936, 4th (South Midland) Bde., Royal Field Artillery. Died at home, of injuries received in an accident, Colchester, 1st February, 1916. Born 12th February, 1892 at 26c. 4h. Spon Street. Resided at 36, Sherbourne Street. Water Meter Fitter. Enlisted April, 1915 at Coventry. Commemorated Water Department Memorial, Coventry Corporation. Grave Ref. 183. 109. Coventry (London Road) Cemetery.

BENNETT, Private, Percy John. 24055, 2nd Bn., Royal Warwickshire Regiment. Died of wounds, Abbeville, 19th October, 1917. Age 31. Third son of William and Ann Bennett of Weston, Warwickshire. Husband of Elizabeth Bennett of Emscote. Born 6th August, 1886 at Wappenbury, Warwickshire. Resided at 44, Hill Street, Emscote, Warwick. Labourer, Maudslay Motor Co. Enlisted February, 1917 at Coventry. Grave Ref. III. D. 11. Abbeville Communal Cemetery, France.

BENNY, Private, Richard. 266525, 1/7th Bn., Royal Warwickshire Regiment. Killed in action, 4th October, 1917. Born in 1894 at Foleshill. Resided at 14, Ash Grove, Stoney Stanton Road. Driller. Enlisted in 1916 at Coventry. Memorial Ref. Panel 23 to 28 and 163A, Tyne Cot Memorial, Belgium.

BENSON, Lance Corporal, Alfred. 16/1438, 16th Bn., Royal Warwickshire Regiment. Killed in action, 16th April, 1917. Age 33. Husband of Hannah Benson of 33, Allcock Street, Deritend, Birmingham. Born at Coventry. Resided at Bordesley Green, Birmingham. Enlisted Birmingham. Memorial Ref. Bay 3. Arras Memorial, France.

BENSON, Private, Fergus John. 3123, 2/7th Bn., Royal Warwickshire Regiment. Killed in action, Ypres, 27th November, 1916. Age 20. Son of Mr. W. H. Benson of 13, Charles Street, Wolverhampton. Native of Stretton-under-Fosse. Born 21st February, 1896 in All Saint's Lane. Resided at Stretton-under-Fosse. Employed by the Dunlop Rim and Wheel Company, Ltd. Enlisted October, 1914 at Coventry. Grave Ref. VII. D. 14. Warlencourt British Cemetery, France.

BENSON, Lance Corporal, William Eli. 9482, C Company, 1st Bn., Royal Warwickshire Regiment. Killed in action, 25th April, 1915. Age 33. Son of William and Ellen Benson, 4c. 2h. Cox Street, Coventry. Husband of Elizabeth Benson of 134, Broomfield Road, Coventry. Born in 1882 at Coventry. Enlisted Coventry. Memorial Ref. Panel 8. Ypres (Menin Gate) Memorial, Ieper, West-Vlaanderen, Belgium.

BENTLEY, Private, Alfred Garnett. PS/11198, 4th Bn., Royal Fusiliers (City of London Regiment). Killed in action, 1st December, 1917. Age 39. Son of Thomas and Emma Bentley, of Liverpool. Husband of Winifred Kate Bentley, of 72, Broadway, Coventry. Born 23rd May, 1879 at Liverpool. Enlisted June, 1916. Schoolmaster, Elementary School. Commemorated Education Department Memorial, Coventry Corporation and War Memorial Park. Enlisted Coventry. Grave Ref. II. C. 34. Favreuil British Cemetery, Pas de Calais, France.

BERESFORD, Lance Corporal, William. 3851, 1st /7th Bn., Royal Warwickshire Regiment. Died of wounds in hospital, 15th February, 1916 after the bursting of a shell injured in the left side by shrapnel. Age 22. Son of Samuel and Elizabeth Beresford, of Coventry. Born 3rd April, 1893 at Coventry. Resided at 12, Victoria Place, Far Gosford Street. Enameller, Humber Works Ltd. Enlisted January, 1915 at Coventry. Grave Ref. 1. C. 32. Louvencourt Military Cemetery, Somme, France.

BERRY, Private, Arthur Edwin. 16579, 1st Bn., Royal Warwickshire Regiment. Killed in action, Passchendaele, 4th October, 1917. Age 23. Son of George W. and Mary Berry, of 22, Perkins Street, Coventry. Born 28th April, 1894 at 7, George Street. Resided at 22, Perkins Street. Enlisted February, 1916, Warwick. Clerk. Commemorated War Memorial Park. Memorial Ref. Panel 23 to 28 and 163A. Tyne Cot Memorial, Zonnebeke, West-Vlaanderen, Belgium.

BERRY, Private, Frederick. 20901, 1/6th Bn., Royal Warwickshire Regiment. Died of wounds, 10th December, 1916. Age 34. Husband of Prudence Berry. Born at Radford. Resided at Offchurch, Warwick. Grave Ref. C. 3. Martinpuich British Cemetery, France.

BETHELL, Captain, Thomas Henry. D Company, 2nd /7th Bn., Royal Warwickshire Regiment. Killed in action, near Pozieres, 19th July, 1916. Shot down whilst gallantry leading an attack on the Germans second line of trenches, received a wound in the head. Age 31. Son of Thomas Burnet and Annie Jane Bethell, of 5, The Quadrant, Coventry. Born 24th January, 1885 at Coventry. Resided at Coventry. Barrister at law. Memorial Ref. Panel 2 and 3. Ploegsteert Memorial, Comines-Warneton, Hainaut, Belgium.

BETTERIDGE, Private, Albert. 33020, 1st Bn., Royal Berkshire Regiment. Killed in action, near Arras, 10th March, 1917. Age 19. Son of Mrs. Amelia Betteridge of 2, Whitehouse Lane, Church Street, Chipping Norton. Born in 1887 at Chipping Norton. Resided at 7, Brookville Terrace. Machinist, Deasy Works. Enlisted May, 1916 at Coventry. Memorial Ref. Pier and Face 11 D. Thiepval Memorial, France.

BETTERIDGE, Private, Arthur John. 6297, 62nd Coy, Machine Gun Corps (Infantry) formerly R/14015, King's Royal Rifle Corps. Died of wounds, 21st September, 1917. Age 42. Husband of Rosa M. Betteridge of 57, Deakins Road, Hay Mills, Birmingham. Born at King's Norton. Employed at Coventry. Enlisted Coventry. Grave Ref. I. E. 32. Godewaersvelde British Cemetery, France.

BICKNELL, Private, Leonard Leslie. 19700, 2nd/7th Bn., Royal Warwickshire Regiment. Died of wounds, Poperinghe, 2nd September, 1917 after being injured on his first visit to trenches, 19th August, 1917. Age 19. Born 27th January, 1898 at 32, Moor Street, Earlsdon. Resided 16, Hollis Road. Enlisted Coventry. Grocers assistant. Commemorated War Memorial Park. Grave Ref. XVIII. F. 9. Lijssenthoek Military Cemetery, Belgium.

BIDDLE, Private, Albert Edward, MM. 85656, 148th Company, Machine Gun Corps (Infantry) formerly 8324, Royal Warwickshire Regiment. Killed in action, 9th October, 1917. Age 23. Son of Edith Lewis, of George Cottages, Kenilworth Road, Berkswell, Coventry. Enlisted Coventry. Gazetted for Military Medal, 17th September, 1917. Memorial Ref. Panel 154 to 159 and 163A. Tyne Cot Memorial, Zonnebeke, West-Vlaanderen, Belgium.

BIDDLE, Corporal, George. 27369, 115th Company, Machine Gun Corps (Infantry). Killed in action, 7th July, 1916. Age 24. (served as Phillips). Son of George and Louisa Biddle, of 10, Grange Terrace, Walsgrave Road, Wyken, Coventry. Born at Courthouse Green, Foleshill. Resided at Coventry. Miner. Enlisted September, 1914. Memorial Ref. Pier and Face 5 C and 12 C. Thiepval Memorial, Somme, France.

BIGGS, Corporal, George Cyril. 1625, 1/7th Bn., Royal Warwickshire Regiment. Killed in action, 14th July, 1916. Aged 21. Son of George Robert and Ada Mary Biggs of 52, High Street, Nuneaton. Educated at Bablake School. Commemorated Bablake School Memorial. Memorial Ref. Pier and Face 9A 9B and 10B. Thiepval Memorial, Somme, France.

BILLING, Sapper, Frank. 250010, 56th Div. Signal Coy., Royal Engineers. Killed in action, 14th October, 1918. Age 23. Son of Fred and Sarah Billing, of Whoberley Hall, Coventry. Born 27th August, 1895 at Wyken. Resided at Coventry. Bank Clerk. Enlisted January, 1916 at Coventry. Commemorated King Henry VIII School. Grave Ref. II. D. 24. Dadizeele New British Cemetery, Moorslede, West-Vlaanderen, Belgium.

BILLINGHAM, Lance Corporal, Clarence. 9029, 10th Bn., Royal Warwickshire Regiment. Died of wounds, 14th June, 1917. Age 20. Son of Alfred and Emily Billingham, of Adstone, Towcester, Northants. Native of Adstone. Born Adstone, Towcester, Northants. Enlisted Coventry. Resided Adstone. Commemorated Stoke St. Michaels Memorial. Grave Ref. XXII. K. 26A. Etaples Military Cemetery, France.

BIRCH, Private, Donald Sydney. 2931, 1/7th Bn., Royal Warwickshire Regiment. Killed in action, 18th February, 1916. Age 22. Son of Joseph and Mary Birch, of 27, Guild Street, Stratford-on-Avon. Enlisted Coventry. Resided Stratford-on-Avon. Grave Ref. I. D. 18. Foncquevillers Military Cemetery, France.

BIRCH, Corporal, Herbert Leslie. 240627, 1st /6th Bn., North Staffordshire Regiment. Killed in action, 1st July, 1916. Age 21. Son of John William and Elizabeth Birch, of 4, Steeplefield Road, Radford, Coventry. Memorial Ref. Pier and Face 14 B and 14 C. Thiepval Memorial, Somme, France.

BIRCH, Private, Walter. 30032, 2nd Bn., Royal Warwickshire Regiment. Killed in action, Battle of the Somme, 3rd September, 1916. Born 24th May, 1886 at Coventry. Resided at Coventry. Electrician. Enlisted March, 1916 at Coventry. Grave Ref. 5. H. 1. London Cemetery and Extension, Longueval, France

BIRCH, Sapper, William Edward. 151315, 253rd Tunn. Coy., Royal Engineers, formerly 6212, Duke of Cornwall's Light Infantry (Royal Engineers). Killed in action, 1st July, 1916. Born Birmingham. Resided Coventry. Enlisted Nuneaton. Labourer, employed by Coventry Corporation, Electricity Department. Commemorated Electricity Department Memorial, Coventry Corporation. Memorial Ref. Pier and Face 8A and 8D. Thiepval Memorial, France.

BIRD, Private, Harry. 971, 1st Bn., Royal Warwickshire Regiment. Killed in action, 12th April, 1918. Born at Darlaston, Staffordshire. Resided at Coventry. Memorial Ref. Panel 2 and 3. Ploegsteert Memorial, Belgium.

BIRD, Private, Harry Elijah. 5242, 1st Bn., Worcestershire Regiment. Died of wounds, 21st August, 1915. Age 38. Son in law of Mrs. Mary Maguire of College Hill, Templemore, Co. Tipperary. Native of Birmingham. Served in the South African Campaign. Born 7th June, 1879 at Stourbridge. Resided in Swanswell Street. Employed as conductor, local trams then as a polisher, Rover Works. Reservist. Commemorated St. John's Church. Grave Ref. III. A. 8. Sailly-Sur-La-Lys Canadian Cemetery, France.

BIRD, Lance Corporal, James. 15535, 7th Bn., Royal Berkshire Regiment. Killed in action, Salonika, 13th March, 1917. Born High Broughton, Lancs. Enlisted Coventry. Resided Bedworth. Grave Ref. F. 1349. Karasouli Military Cemetery, Greece.

BIRD, Lieutenant, John Greville Hobart. 2nd Bn., Royal West Surrey Regiment. Killed in action, Ypres, 26th October, 1914. Sent to defend a trench at a spot with severe enemy fire and whilst trying to go to the aid of one of his men was hit and died instantaneously. Age 25. Born 11th November, 1888 at Wolverhampton. Educated at King Henry VIII School and Oundle, previous to joining regular Army in January, 1914, was a Tea-Planter in Ceylon. Commemorated King Henry VIII School. Memorial Ref. Panel 11 – 13 and 14. Ypres (Menin Gate) Belgium.

BIRD, Private, Joseph. 29547, 14th Bn., Worcestershire Regiment. Killed in action, Langemarck, 9th October, 1917. Born at Coventry. Resided at 40, Eden Street. Enlisted Coventry. Grave Ref. C. 40. Ruisseau Farm Cemetery, Belgium.

BIRD, Private, Joseph. 30299, C Company, 6th Bn., Somerset Light Infantry formerly 202965, Wiltshire Regiment. Killed in action 21st March, 1918. Born 4th November, 1886 at Court House Green. Resided at 1, Lynton Road. Miner. Enlisted May, 1917 at Coventry. Memorial Ref. Panel 25 and 26. Pozieres Memorial, France.

BIRD, Private, Thomas. 16577, 1st Bn., Royal Fusiliers formerly 9th Reserve Cavalry. Killed in action, 21st June, 1917. Age 21. Son of Henry and Jane Bird of 28, Coventry Road, Hay Mill, Birmingham. Born at Coventry. Resided at Birmingham. Memorial Ref. Panel 6 and 8. Ypres (Menin Gate) Memorial, Belgium.

BIRDSEY, Lance Corporal, Herbert Fred. 2539, 1/7th Bn., Royal Warwickshire Regiment. Killed in action, 14th July, 1916. Age 32. Son of Matthew and Hannah M. Birdsey of 100, Sutton Road, Watford. Born 26th September, 1883 at Watford. Resided at 34, Melbourne Road, Coventry with his sister, Mrs. Whitehorn. Painter, Coventry Chain. Commemorated Coventry Chain Memorial. Enlisted August, 1914 at Coventry. Memorial Ref. Pier and Face 9A 9B and 10 B. Thiepval Memorial, France.

BIRT, Pioneer, Frank. Royal Engineers. Died, home, 21st October, 1917. Born 29th May, 1870 at Painswick, Gloucester. Resided Coventry. Builder's labourer. Enlisted November, 1914. Grave Ref. Buried Coventry.

BISHOP, Private, Frederick John. 15318, 11th Bn., Royal Warwickshire Regiment. Killed in action, near Albert, 9th August, 1916. Age 20. Son of Mr. and Mrs. J. Bishop, of 81, Cambridge Street, Coventry. Born 17th February, 1896 at Hastings. Resided at 81, Cambridge Street. Labourer, Smith's Stamping Works. Enlisted October, 1915 at Coventry. Memorial Ref. Pier and Face 9 A 9 B and 10 B. Thiepval Memorial, Somme, France.

BISHOP, Sergeant, William Francis. 13570, 10th Bn., Worcestershire Regiment. Killed in action, 6th July, 1917. Age 22. Born Harvington, Worcs. Enlisted Coventry. Resided Harvington. Son of William and Sarah Ann Bishop, of Malt House Cottage, Harvington, Evesham, Worcs. Memorial Ref. Panel 34. Ypres (Menin Gate) Memorial, Belgium.

BISSELL, Gunner, Harry. Royal Garrison Artillery. Died at home, due to the effects of being gassed, 16th September, 1918. Born 14th February, 1880 at Radford. Resided at Radford. Polisher. Reservist. Grave Ref. Coventry (Radford, St. Nicholas) Churchyard.

BISSICKS, 2nd Lieutenant, Francis. 48th Squadron, Royal Flying Corps. Killed 2nd January, 1917. Age 27. Son of Henry James and Agnes Bissicks of 20, Fairmount Road, Brixton, London. Born at Vincennes, France. Resided at Foleshill. Grave Ref. Sec F. Grave 321. Bristol (Canford) Cemetery.

BLABY, Private, John. 26607 formerly 20401, Royal Berkshire Regiment. Killed in action, 23rd April, 1917. Age 31. Son of Mrs. Alice Blaby of Coddesford, Brackley, Northants. Born Coddesford, Oxford. Resided Coventry. Enlisted Warwick. Grave Ref. VI. D. 10. La Chauderie Military Cemetery, Vimy, France.

BLACK, Private, John. 200839, 1/4th Bn., Royal Sussex Regiment. Died of wounds, Palestine, 21st August, 1917. Born 7th January, 1895 in Peel Street. Son of Mr. J. Black of 33, Northfield Road, Coventry. Resided at Shoreham. Shop Assistant, previously employed Co-Operative Society, Victoria Street, Hillfields Branch. Enlisted in 1915. Grave Ref. A. 232. Deir El Belah War Cemetery, Israel.

BLACKMOOR, Private, Joseph. 2356, 1st Bn., Royal Warwickshire Regiment. Killed in action, 13th October, 1914. Age 22. Son of John and Mary Blackmoor, of 121, George Street, Gun Hill, Arley, Coventry. Enlisted Nuneaton. Grave Ref. III. F. 711. (Buried near this spot). Meteren Military Cemetery, Nord, France.

BLACKSHAW, Rifleman, Arthur John. B/203081, 3rd Bn., Rifle Brigade formerly R/17079 Kings Royal Rifle Corps. Killed by shell-fire, 27th March, 1918. Born 28th September, 1896 in Little Church Street. Only son. Resided at 72, King William Street with his parents. Enlisted at Coventry on the 25th November, 1915. Educated Trinity Schools. Coventry Chain, Tool maker. Commemorated Coventry Chain Memorial and War Memorial Park. Grave Ref. Panel 81 to 84. Pozieres Memorial, France.

BLACKWELL, Private, George. 8442, 2nd Bn., South Lancashire Regiment. Killed in action, 20th September, 1914. Age 28. Son of Frederick and Rebecca Jane Blackwell, of School Lane, Walsgrave-on-Sowe, Coventry. Born Harbury. Resided Coventry. Commemorated Walsgrave-on-Sowe Memorial. Enlisted Warwick. Employed Filler, Binley Colliery previously a groom. Engaged to a Mrs. Griffin of Milverton. Memorial Ref. La Ferte-Sous-Jouarre Memorial, Seine-et-Marne, France.

BLAKE, Trooper, Charles Patrick. 3rd Bn., King's Own Hussars. Died, home, from consumption, 8th March, 1917. Born 27th June, 1890 in Stoney Stanton Road. Resided at 58, Eagle Street. Soldier served for 11 years. Grave Ref. Coventry (London Road) Cemetery.

BLAKE, Private, Percival William. Essex Regiment. Died, Home 8th May, 1918. Born 13th May, 1883 at Leamington. Resided in Canada. Prospector. Enlisted in 1914. Grave Ref. Coventry (London Road) Cemetery.

BLAKEMORE, Private, James. 13832, 8th Bn., South Staffordshire Regiment. Killed in action, 23rd April, 1917. Age 33. Son of John and Mary Blakemore, of 21, Ransome Road, Arley, Coventry. Born at Blakenhall, Staffordshire. Resided at Arley. Employed Coventry. Memorial Ref. Bay 6. Arras Memorial, Pas de Calais, France.

BLAKEMORE, Private, Martin. 1608, 1st Bn., Royal Warwickshire Regiment. Killed in action, 12th October, 1916. Age 22. Son of John and Mary Blakemore, of 29, Ransome Road, Arley, Coventry. Memorial Ref. Pier and Face 9 A 9 B and 10 B. Thiepval Memorial, Somme, France.

BLAMIRE, Private, Reginald. 42502, 1st Bn., Royal Warwickshire Regiment. Died, 9th November, 1918. Born Hampton-in-Arden. Enlisted Coventry. Resided Hampton-in-Arden. Grave Ref. D. 25. Preseau Communal Cemetery Extension, France.

BLAZEBY, Private, Sydney. 39707, 57th Field Ambulance, Royal Army Medical Corps. Killed in action, 9th June, 1918. Age 32. Son of John and Sarah Blazeby, of 43, Ashby St., Queen's Rd., Norwich. Born Lakenham, Norfolk. Enlisted Coventry. Resided Norwich. Grave Ref. VII. H. 5. Marfaux British Cemetery, France.

BLOOR, Sergeant, Harold Bertram. 55071, 34th Bn., Machine Gun Corps (Infantry) formerly 27616, Worcestershire Regiment. Died of wounds, 11th August, 1918. Age 18. Son of Richard and Ada Alice Westwood (formerly Bloor), of 3/22, Guest St., Hockley, Birmingham. Born Birmingham. Enlisted Coventry. Grave Ref. Q. IV. F. 9. St. Sever Cemetery Extension, Rouen, France.

BLORE, Private, James. 6433, 1/5th Bn., Royal Warwickshire Regiment. Died of wounds, Dernancourt, 27th November, 1916. Enlisted Warwick, May, 1916. Born 1st November, 1892 at Derby. Resided at 93, Somerset Road. Weaver. Grave Ref. IV. D. 36. Dernancourt Communal Cemetery Extension, France.

BLOWER, Gunner, Albert. 1111, Royal Field Artillery. Died, Home, 4th May, 1916. Son of William Blowers of 7, Brandon Street, Leicester. Husband of Leah Lister (Formerly Blowers) of 118, The Fairway, Saffron Lane, Leicester. Enlisted Coventry. Grave Ref. 00. 228. Leicester (Gilroes) Cemetery.

BLOWER, Private, Arthur. 33512, 6th Bn., Leicestershire Regiment. Died of wounds, 9th October, 1917. Age 28. Husband of Violet H. Blower, of 28, Wright Street, Coventry. Native of Hinckley. Grave Ref. I. F. 47. Godewaersvelde British Cemetery, Nord, France.

BLOXHAM, Private, George. 15622, 1st Bn., Royal Warwickshire Regiment. Died of wounds, 19th April, 1918. Born at Foleshill. Employed by Messrs. Mills and Company. Enlisted Coventry. Grave Ref. I. C. 18. Pernes British Cemetery, France.

BLOXHAM, Private, Henry. 19705, Wiltshire Regiment formerly Oxfordshire and Buckinghamshire Light Infantry. Died, Home, 3rd September, 1918. Born at Ryton-on-Dunsmore. Resided at Ryton-on-Dunsmore. Employed at Coventry. Commemorated Ryton Memorial. Grave Ref. In East Part. Ryton-on-Dunsmore (St. Leonard) Churchyard.

BLOXHAM, J. Duke of Cornwall's Light Infantry. Resided Ryton. Commemorated Ryton Memorial.

BLOXHAM, Private, Thomas William. 14580, C Coy., 8th Bn., Royal Berkshire Regiment. Killed in action, 25th September, 1915. Born 28th November, 1890 in 58, St. John Street. Resided at 23c. 7h. Much Park Street. Machinist. Enlisted September, 1914 at Coventry. He leaves a widow and two children. Memorial Ref. Panel 93 to 95. Loos Memorial, France.

BLOXHAM, Gunner, Vincent Arthur. 840237, "D" Battery, 240th Brigade, Royal Field Artillery (South Midland Howitzers). Died of wounds, Boulogne, 18th September, 1917. Age 21. Son of George and Alice Bloxham, of Coventry. Born 19th April, 1896 in Moor Street. Resided at 68, Stanway Road. Enlisted Coventry, August, 1914. Clerk. Commemorated Bablake School Memorial and War Memorial Park. Grave Ref. VI. A. 33. Wimereux Communal Cemetery, Pas de Calais, France.

BLUNDELL, Lance Corporal, Cecil. Duke of Cornwall's Light Infantry. Died, home, 2nd March, 1920. Born 27th December, 1898 at 62, Well Street. Resided at 8, Herberts Row, Gulson Road. Employed by Coventry Swaging Company, Ltd. Enlisted May, 1917. Grave Ref. Coventry (London Road) Cemetery.

BLUNT, Boy 1st Class, Horace. J/38096, HMS Defence, Royal Navy. Killed in action, Battle of Jutland, 31st May, 1916. Age 16. Son of John T. and Matilda Blunt, of 34, Highland Road, Earlsdon, Coventry. Born 26th July, 1899 at Northampton. Resided at Coventry. Employed Telegraph Boy, Coventry Railway Station. Enlisted April, 1915. Memorial Ref. 13. Plymouth Naval Memorial, Devon.

BLYTHE, Private, Arthur Herbert. 8293, 18th (Queen Mary's Own) Hussars. Killed in action, St. Julien near Ypres, 13th May, 1915. Age 25. Husband of Caroline Blythe of Mansion Buildings, Bishop's Itchington, Leamington. Mother and father resided 183, Melbourne Road. Commemorated Iliffe & Sons Ltd Memorial. Born Birmingham. Resided Coventry. Enlisted Worcester. Memorial Ref. Panel 5. Ypres (Menin Gate) Memorial, Belgium.

BLYTHE, Air Mechanic 3rd Class, Harry. 189606, 2nd Aircraft Depot, Royal Air Force. Died, home, 23rd October, 1918. Employed at Coventry. Grave Ref. 187. 179. Coventry (London Road) Cemetery.

BLYTHE, Corporal, John (also known as Jack). 58511, 24th Div. Ammunition Column, No. 4 Section, Royal Field Artillery. Died of injuries received in railway accident, Calais, 25th September, 1917. Age 26. Son of Mr. And Mrs. J. Blythe of 5, Berry, Street, Coventry. Born 3rd January, 1892, at Coventry. Resided at 5, Berry Street. Enlisted January, 1915 at Coventry. Painter and Decorator. Commemorated War Memorial Park. Grave Ref. I. B. 2. Les Baraques Military Cemetery, Sangatte, France.

BOAK, Lance Corporal, William Wallace. 95641, 251st Tunnelling Coy., Royal Engineers. Killed in action, 29th May, 1916. Age 28. Son of Wallace and Mary Boak, of Wrexham, North Wales. Husband of Eva McCoy (formerly Boak), of 31, Crescent Avenue, Stoke, Coventry. Grave Ref. CC. 4. Cambrin Military Cemetery, Pas de Calais, France.

BODIN, Lance Corporal ,Walter. 2912, 1st/7th Bn., Royal Warwickshire Regiment .Died of wounds, 4th September, 1916 received in action, 19th August. Died fighting side by side with his brother, Bert. Son of Mrs. Allen (late Mrs. Bodin) of 129, Stoney Stanton Road, Coventry formerly 28, George Street. Born 1st December, 1894, at Dudley. Resided at 28, George Street. Enlisted Coventry, October, 1914. Apprentice-printer, Messrs Caldicott and Feltham. Commemorated War Memorial Park. Grave Ref. Plot X. Row B. Grave 8a. Etaples Military Cemetery, France.

BOILES, Private, Frank. 45852, 95th Coy., Machine Gun Corps. Killed in action 29th September, 1916. Son of Albert Henry and Ellen Boiles of 4, Springfield Terrace, Harbury, Leamington. Commemorated St. Thomas Memorial. Grave Ref. I. K. 17. Grove Town Cemetery, Meaulte, France.

BOLTON, Corporal, Allen. 3/2954, 15th Bn., Royal Warwickshire Regiment. Killed in action, Ginchy, 24th September, 1916. Age 18. Son of Allen and Selina Bolton of 48, King Street, Leamington Spa. Born 22nd April, 1898 at 1c. 2h. London Road. Resided at Leamington. Cycle Enameller. Enlisted August, 1914. Memorial Ref. Pier and Face 9A 9B and 10B. Thiepval Memorial, France.

BOLTON, Private, Ernest James. 10221, 3rd Bn., Coldstream Guards. Killed in action, St. Julien, 5th February, 1915. Age 20. Son of Mr. and Mrs. G. M. Bolton, of 60, East Street, Coventry. Born 20th June, 1894 in Dale Street. Soldier. Employed Hillman Motor Company Ltd. Enlisted Coventry. Memorial Ref. Panels 2 and 3. Le Touret Memorial, Pas de Calais, France.

BOLTON, Gunner, John Fraser. Royal Field Artillery. Died, home, 26th December, 1924. Born 1st January, 1894 at Sheffield. Resided at 17a, Cobden Street. Fitter. Enlisted August, 1914. Grave Ref. Foleshill Cemetery.

BOLTON, Private, Robert. 9084, 11th Bn., Royal Warwickshire Regiment. Killed in action, 13th August, 1916. Born Sunbury-on-Thames, Middx. Enlisted Coventry. Grave Ref. VI. B. 35. St. Sever Cemetery Extension, Rouen, France.

BOND, Private, Joseph. 10752, 1st Bn., Coldstream Guards. Died of wounds, 21st November, 1914. Age 19. Son of Joseph H. and K. Bond, of 32, Crossman Street, Sherwood, Nottingham. Born St. Barnabas, Derby. Enlisted Coventry. Resided Derby. Grave Ref. I. M. 38. Poperinghe Old Military Cemetery, Belgium.

BOND, Gunner, Patrick. 60868, 29th Div. Ammunition Col., Royal Field Artillery. Died, 1st February, 1916. Age 22. Son of Patrick and Lizzie Bond, of Ireland. Husband of Margaret Bond, of 12, Bulls Head Lane, Coventry.Born Cappamore, Co. Limerick. Enlisted Limerick. Grave Ref. 71. Salonika (Lembet Road) Military Cemetery, Greece.

BONES, Lieutenant, Arthur Meyrick. 1st Bn., King's African Rifles. Killed in action, 28th October, 1917 at N'gomeni. Born 28th April, 1893 at Coventry. Resided in South Africa. Employed South African Constabulary. Enlisted August, 1914. Born 28th April, 1893. Son of Arthur Anderson Bones and Ellen Bones. Educated Masonic School, Bushey and afterwards King Henry VIII. Previously employed Triumph. Commemorated Triumph & Gloria Memorial and King Henry VIII School. Grave Ref. IV. B. 3. Iringa Cemetery, Tanzania.

BONHAM, Leading Signalman, Edward, 230299, HMS Torrent, Royal Navy. Killed by mine explosion in North Sea, 23rd December, 1917. Age 29. Son of Walter and Mary Ann Bonham, of Coventry. Born in 1888. Resided at 93, Brook Street. Memorial Ref. 21. Plymouth Naval Memorial, Devon.

BONHAM, Private, Harold George. 6645, 20th Bn., London Regiment. transf. to (409500) 883rd Area Employment Coy. attd. O.C. Troops Office., Labour Corps formerly 23128 Somerset Light Infantry. Died of pneumonia, 20th October, 1918. Age 27. Son of Alfred and Fannie Bonham, of "Bangor," Friars Road, Coventry. Born 8th August 1891 at Coventry. Resided at Coventry. Enlisted March 1916 at Coventry. Clerk Gas Office. Commemorated Bablake School Memorial, War Memorial Park and Gas Department Memorial, Coventry Corporation. Grave Ref. Div. 62. V. L. 14. Ste. Marie Cemetery, Le Havre, Seine-Maritime, France.

BOOKER, Private, Samuel Thomas. 66283, 1st /2nd Welch Field Amb., Royal Army Medical Corps. Died of influenza, Tel El Kebir, 6th January, 1919. Age 39. Son of Isaac and Ann Booker. Husband of Elizabeth Booker, of 71, Hamilton Road, Stoke, Coventry. Born 29th April, 1879 at Walsall. Motor Trimmer's Assistant. Enlisted August, 1915. Grave Ref. 25. Tel El Kebir War Memorial Cemetery, Egypt.

BOON, Second Lieutenant, Arthur. Royal Flying Corps. 29th March, 1917. Age 22. Son of James and Mercy Boon, of Temple Road, Buxton, Derbyshire. Born at Stockport. Grave Ref. 141. 175. Coventry (London Road) Cemetery.

BOOTH, Company Quartermaster Sergeant, Frank, DCM. 25030, 2nd Bn., Machine Gun Corps (Infantry) formerly Oxfordshire and Buckinghamshire Light Infantry. Killed in action 10th September, 1918. Age 27. Son of John Walter and Blanche Booth of 103, King's Road, King's Heath, Birmingham. Born in St. John's Parish. Grave Ref. I. J. 22. Vaulx Hill Cemetery, France.

BOOTH, Gunner, Thomas Wilkinson. 135538, 115th Bty. 25th Bde., Royal Field Artillery. Killed in action, 5th October, 1918. Age 25. Son of Thomas Wilkinson Booth, of Outwoods Farm, Great Packington, Coventry. Born at Aston Cliff. Employed at Coventry. Enlisted Coventry. Grave Ref. D. 4. Berthaucourt Communal Cemetery, Pontru, Aisne, France.

BOOTH, Private, William (Real family name, Faulkner served as Booth). 26934, 1st Bn., Worcestershire Regiment. Killed in action, 29th July 1917. Age 17. Son of Alfred Edward and Mary Ann Faulkner of 2, Camden Street, Derby. Enlisted Blandford, Dorset. Resided Coventry. Memorial Ref. Panel 34. Ypres (Menin Gate) Memorial, Belgium.

BOSMAN, Rifleman, William Frederick. 52338, 15th Bn., Royal Irish Rifles formerly 37888, Royal Warwick Regiment. Killed in action, 22nd October, 1918. Enlisted Warwick. Resided Coventry. Born 24th July, 1897 at 10, Palmer Lane. Resided at 18, Cash's Lane. Driller. Grave Ref. VIII. A. 8. Harlebeke New British Cemetery, Belgium.

BOSTOCK, Private, George. 36356, 149th Coy., Machine Gun Corps (Infantry). Killed in action, 26th October, 1917. Age 22. Son of Arthur and Sarah Bostock, of Coventry Road, Brandon, Coventry. Born 28th December, 1894 at Brandon. Resided at Brandon. Grocer's Assistant. Enlisted February, 1916 at Coventry. Memorial Ref. Panel 154 to 159 and 163A. Tyne Cot Memorial, Zonnebeke, West-Vlaanderen, Belgium.

BOSTOCK, Private, Jack. 45021, 1st Bn., Royal Inniskilling Fusiliers formerly 70959, Devon Regiment. Died of wounds, 15th October, 1918. Age 19. Son of Edwin and Mary Bostock of Lutterworth End, Cubbington. Born Cubbington. Enlisted Coventry. Grave Ref. IV. D. 4. Duhallow A.D.S. Cemetery, Belgium.

BOSWELL, Private Walter Howard. 6739, 2nd Bn., Royal Welch Fusiliers. Killed in action, La Bassee, 20th September, 1915. Age 32. Son of Joseph Boswell. Born 10th February, 1883 at Birmingham. Resided at 50, Bradford Street. Reservist. Grave Ref. A. 8. Cambrin Churchyard Extension, France.

BOSWELL, Private, William. 23310, 11th Bn., Leicestershire Regiment. Died of wounds, 1st June, 1917. Age 19. Son of George Henry and Elizabeth Boswell, of Coventry, previously West Bromwich, Staffs. Born 1898 in Birmingham. Resided at Foleshill. Employed Daimler Company Ltd. Grave Ref. VI. E. 67. Bethune Town Cemetery, Pas De Calais, France.

BOSWORTH, Sapper, Charles. 158231, 257th Tunnel Coy., Royal Engineers. Killed in action, 9th April, 1917. Born Church Gresley, Derbyshire. Enlisted Coventry. Grave Ref. III. B. 1. Rue-Du-Bacquerot No.1 Military Cemetery, Laventie, France.

BOSWORTH, Trooper, Herbert. 3360, 1st Life Guards. Killed in action, 2nd September, 1916. Age 21. Son of John and Annie Bosworth of 14, Silver Street, Kettering. Resided in Gordon Street. Repairer, Rudge Works. Enlisted October, 1914 at Coventry. Memorial Ref. Pier and Face 1A. Thiepval Memorial, France.

BOSWORTH, Private, Walter. 1365, 1st Bn., Royal Warwickshire Regiment. Killed in action, 25th April, 1915. Resided in Eden Street. Memorial Ref. Panel 8. Ypres (Menin Gate) Memorial, Belgium.

BOTT, Private, William Henry. 20520, 10th Bn., Royal Warwickshire Regiment. Died of wounds, Cambrai, 13th April, 1918. Age 41. Son of Caroline Bott, of Coventry. Enlisted Warwick. Resided at 7c. 6h. Spon End. Polisher. Enlisted July, 1916. Born 2nd October, 1876 at 86, Spon End. Grave Ref. X. C. 13A. Wimereux Communal Cemetery, Pas de Calais, France.

BOTTERILL, Private, Albert William. 7956, 2nd Bn., Coldstream Guards. Killed in action, 18th March, 1918. Age 29. Husband of Alice May Botterill, of Church Cottage, Clifton, Rugby. Born Newbold, Warwick. Enlisted Coventry. Resided Rugby. Grave Ref. C. 8. Fampoux British Cemetery, France.

BOTTRILL, Bombardier, John William. 59007, A Bty., 100th Brigade, Royal Field Artillery. Died of wounds, Salonika, 4th March, 1917. Age 32. Husband of Mrs. S. Bottrill of 6, Ashby Square, Loughborough. Born at Oakham, Rutland. Enlisted Coventry. Resided Coventry. Grave Ref. 946. Salonika (Lembet Road) Military Cemetery, Greece.

BOTTRILL, Private, Raymond George. DM2/190435, 272nd Motor Transport. Royal Army Service Corps, Died 10th February, 1919. Born 17th August, 1896 at Walsgrave-on-Sowe. Resided at Walsgrave-on-Sowe. Fitter. Enlisted July, 1916. Grave Ref. C. 3. Maubeuge (Sous-Le-Bois) Cemetery, France.

BOULSTRIDGE, Private, Harold Thomas. 13396, 1st Bn., Coldstream Guards. Died of wounds, Ypres, 10th October, 1917 in a field hospital. Age 24. Brother of Arthur J. Boulstridge, of 4, Cash's Lane, Coventry. Born 19th March, 1893 at Leicester. Resided at Coventry. Enlisted August, 1914 at Coventry. Employed Clerk, Messrs. Smith and Son, Printers. Grave Ref. I. B. 4. Solferino Farm Cemetery, Ieper, West-Vlaanderen, Belgium.

BOURNE, Private, Augustus. 30050, A Coy., 9th Bn., Royal Warwickshire Regiment. Died of wounds, Mesopotamia, 1st September, 1918. Age 29. Son of Albert and Ann Bourne, of 73, Grove Cottage, Hawkesbury, Warwickshire. Born Leicester. Enlisted Coventry. Resided Hawkesbury. Commemorated Saint Thomas the Apostle, Longford. Memorial Ref. Panel 2. Column 2. Tehran Memorial, Iran.

BOURNE, Private, George Daniel. 17196, 5th Bn., Oxfordshire and Buckinghamshire Light Infantry. Killed in action, Arras, 30th July, 1916. Son of Mr. and Mrs. J. H. Bourne. Born 10th January, 1891 in Grey Friars Lane. Resided at 65, Godiva Street. Sheet Metal Worker, Blakemore's, Godiva Street. Enlisted January, 1915 at Coventry. Husband of Mrs. F. G. Bourne of 47, St. John's Street. Leaves a widow and two children. Memorial Ref. Bay 6 and 7. Arras Memorial, France.

BOURNE, Driver, Joseph Henry. 59008, Royal Field Artillery. Died of injuries received in accident, 4th March 1915. Born 23rd March, 1878 at 3 Grey Friars Lane. Resided at 22, Warwick Lane. Barman. Enlisted January, 1915 at Coventry. Grave Ref. 199. 20. Coventry (London Road) Cemetery.

BOULSFIELD. Private, Sidney Robert. 2446, B Coy., 1st Bn., Royal Warwickshire Regiment. Killed in action, 26th April, 1915. Age 19. Son of George and Sarah Jane Boulsfield, of the Lawn's Cottage, Lutterworth Road, Nuneaton. Born at Coventry. Resided at Nuneaton. Memorial Ref. Panel 8. Ypres (Menin Gate) Memorial, Belgium.

BOWDEN, Private, Walter. P. 27825, 14th Bn., Gloucestershire Regiment. Killed in action, 29th July, 1916. Age 32. Son of William H. Bowden of Churchill Farm, Churchill, Axminster, Devon. Resided in Coventry. Memorial Ref. Pier and Face 5A and 5B. Thiepval Memorial, France.

BOWEN, Private, Arthur Samuel. 50587, 14th Bn., Royal Warwickshire Regiment. Died of wounds, 29th May 1918. Age 18. Son of Mr. and Mrs. Bowen, of 48, Court, 15, House, Spon Street, Coventry. Born 11th November, 1899 at 21c. Spon Street. Resided at 48c. 15h. Spon Street. Cycle Hand. Commemorated St. John's Church. Enlisted Coventry. Grave Ref. Row A. Grave 16. Thiennes British Cemetery, Nord, France.

BOWEN, Private, Percy Edgar. 1774, A Squadron, Leicestershire Yeomanry. Died of wounds, 13th May, 1915. Employed by Humber Ltd. Born Hinckley. Resided Hinckley. Enlisted Hinckley. Memorial Ref. Panel 5. Ypres (Menin Gate) Memorial, Belgium.

BOWER, Lieutenant, W. C. E. Royal Army Medical Corps attached 1st Bn., Newfoundland Regiment. Killed in action, 19th October, 1916. Husband of Mrs. M. M. Hopkinson (formerly Bower), of Court End, Adderbury, Banbury, Oxon formerly The Lion House, Allesley. Grave Ref. VI. C. 1. Guards' Cemetery, Lesboeufs, France.

BOWERS, Private, Thomas. 268138, 2/7th Bn., Royal Warwickshire Regiment. Died, 18th November, 1918. Age 26. Son of Thomas Bowers, of 76, Jubilee Cottages, Great Wratting, Haverhill, Suffolk. Born Haverhill, Suffolk. Enlisted Coventry. Grave Ref. IX. A. 10B. Mont Huon Military Cemetery, Le Treport, France.

BOWLER, Private, Frank Brotherhood. 40136, 1st Bn., Royal Dublin Fusiliers, formerly 33563, Leicestershire Regiment. Killed in action, 24th April, 1917. Born Coventry. Enlisted Coalville. Resided Coventry. Memorial Ref Bay 9. Arras Memorial, France.

BOWNS, Private, Harry. 32661, 8th Bn., York and Lancaster Regiment. Killed in action, 7th June 1917. Age 22. Son of Joseph Bowns and Lucy Bowns, of 5, Grange Terrace, Walsgrave Road, Wyken. Husband of Amy E. Bowns, of 15, Wyken Terrace, Walsgrave Road, Coventry. Born September, 1895 at Binley. Wheelwright's Labourer, Coventry Ordnance Works Ltd. Enlisted October, 1916 at Coventry. Memorial Ref. Panel 36 and 55. Ypres (Menin Gate) Memorial, Ieper, West-Vlaanderen, Belgium.

BOWNS, Lance Corporal, John. 16174, 8th Bn., Oxfordshire and Buckinghamshire Light Infantry. Killed in action, Salonika, 24th April, 1917. Age 25. Son of Joseph and Lucy Bowns, of 5, Grange Terrace, Walsgrave Road, Wyken, Coventry. Born Keresley. Employed Wyken Colliery. Enlisted Coventry. Resided Wyken. Memorial Ref. Doiran Memorial, Greece.

BOWNS, Private, Thomas Henry. 266446, 7th Bn., Royal Warwickshire Regiment. Died of wounds 5th July, 1917. Aged 19. Resided Bedworth. Enlisted Coventry. Grave Ref L. N. 42. Bedworth Cemetery.

BOWRON, Private, Alfred Charles. 14720, 2nd Bn., Worcestershire Regiment. Killed in action, 16th May, 1915. Age 19. Son of George and Keziah Bowron, of 5, Station Street East, Coventry. Born at Foleshill. Enlisted Coventry. Memorial Ref. Panel 17 and 18. Le Touret Memorial, Pas de Calais, France.

BOYCOTT, Private, George. 61135, Welsh Regiment. Drowned, 21st September, 1919. Age 20. Son of William and Elizabeth Boycott, of 180, Broomfield Road, Coventry. Grave Ref. E. 158. Pembroke Dock Military Cemetery, Pembrokeshire.

BOYES, Sapper, William Edwin. 4/1404, New Zealand Engineers. 17th December, 1918. Son of Edwin Boyes, of Holly Cottage, Allesley, Coventry. Born at Warwick, England. Served on Western Front, 1916-18. Grave Ref. C.1.39. Wanganui (Aramoho) Cemetery, Wanganui District, New Zealand.

BOYNTON, Private, John Henry. 242272, 2/6th Bn., Royal Warwickshire Regiment. Killed in action, 26th March, 1918. Born West Hartlepool, Durham. Enlisted Coventry. Resided Warwick. Grave Ref. I. J. 25. St. Souplet British Cemetery, France.

BRADBURY, Private, Arthur Ernest, 266630, 10th Bn., Royal Warwickshire Regiment. Died of wounds, 30th May 1918. Age 30. Son of John and Lucy May Bradbury, of 4, Lime Terrace, Lockhurst Lane, Coventry. Born 11th January, 1886 at Willenhall. Labourer. Enlisted November, 1915 at Coventry. Memorial Ref. Soissons Memorial, Aisne, France.

BRADBURY, Cyril. Killed in action. Name on Roll of Honour in Cathedral Church of St. Michael.

 **BRADLEY**, Private, Frederick. 32328, (Signaller), 1st Bn., East Lancashire Regiment formerly 2/4th Bn., East Kent Regiment. Died of wounds, 8th October, 1917 in hospital. Age 30. Son of Frederick and Emma Bradley, of 275, Goodman Street, Burton-on-Trent. Husband of Fanny Bradley (now Hadwick), of 13, Booth's Fields, Little Heath, Foleshill, Warwickshire. Born 14th March, 1887 at Burton-on-Trent. Employed Courtaulds. Enlisted Coventry. Grave Ref. XXX. A. 5A. Etaples Military Cemetery, Pas De Calais, France.

BRADLEY, Geoffrey. Killed in action. Name on Roll of Honour in Cathedral Church of St. Michael.

BRADLEY, Private, George. 10971, 1st Bn., Royal Warwickshire Regiment. Killed in action, 2nd November, 1915. Born 27th January, 1882 at Walsall. Resided at 15c. Well Street. Annealer. Enlisted February, 1915 at Coventry. Grave Ref. III. D. 3. Sucrerie Military Cemetery, Colincamps, France.

BRADLEY, Gunner, Thomas Ernest. 74892, 59th Siege Bty., Royal Garrison Artillery. Killed in action, 4th October, 1918. Brother of Mr. H. A. Bradley, of 76, Harnall Lane, East Coventry. Born Bradford. Enlisted Doncaster. Grave Ref. II. A. 18. Sains-Les-Marquion British Cemetery, Pas de Calais, France.

BRADSHAW, Corporal, John Welch. 265706, 1/7th Bn., Royal Warwickshire Regiment. Killed in action, 4th October, 1917 by a sniper. Age 32. Born St. John's, Kenilworth. Enlisted Coventry. Resided Ingleside, Warwick Road, Kenilworth. Memorial Ref. Panel 23 to 28 and 163A. Tyne Cot Memorial, Belgium.

BRADSHAW, Private, Lewis. 1858, 1st Bn., Royal Warwickshire Regiment. Killed in action, 25th April, 1915. Age 38. Son of William and Anne Elizabeth Bradshaw, of Harborough Magna, Warwickshire. Born Harborough Magna, Rugby. Enlisted Coventry. Memorial Ref. Panel 8. Ypres (Menin Gate) Memorial, Belgium.

 **BRAIDLEY**, Corporal, George. 43100, 1st Bn., Royal Dublin Fusiliers. Died of wounds, caused by a shell bursting in the dug out, Ypres, 17th July, 1917. Age 23. Son of John and Martha Braidley, of 113, Grange Road, Longford, Coventry. Born 1st August, 1893 at Mapplewell, Yorkshire. Resided at 147, Grange Road. Foleshill. Mechanic, Courtaulds Ltd. Enlisted 1st September, 1914. Commemorated Saint Thomas the Apostle, Longford. Grave Ref. III. B. 17. Bard Cottage Cemetery, Ieper, West-Vlaanderen, Belgium.

BRAIN, Private, Albert. 1088, A Coy., 2nd Bn., Royal Warwickshire Regiment. Killed in action, 21st November, 1914. Age 22. Son of Mrs. J. Hoare, of 56, Calthorpe Street, Banbury, Oxon. Born Banbury, Oxon. Enlisted Coventry. Resided Banbury. Memorial Ref. Panel 2 and 3. Ploegsteert Memorial, Belgium

 **BRAIN**, Lance Corporal, Thomas. 1327, 2nd/4th Bn., Oxfordshire and Buckinghamshire Light Infantry. Died of wounds at No. 7 Casualty Clearing Station, Merville, 7th October, 1916 after suffering compound fracture of the right thigh on the 6th October, 1916. Age 23. Son of Henry and Avery Brain of 15, Town's End, Neithrope, Banbury. Born at Neithrope. Resided at 20, Moat Street. Rim Puncher, Wheel Building Department, Rudge Works. Enlisted in 1914. Grave Ref. I. A. 21. Merville Communal Cemetery Extension, France.

BRAITHWAITE, Aircraftman 2nd Class, Percy. 269150, 24th Sqdn., Royal Air Force. Accidentally killed 12th July, 1920. Age 19. Son of George William and Ethel Braithwaite, of 14, King Edward Road, Coventry. Grave Ref. 20. 143. Coventry (St. Paul's) Cemetery.

BRAMHAM, Private, George Henry. 17294, 2nd Bn., Hampshire Regiment formerly 10037, Oxfordshire and Buckinghamshire Light Infantry. Killed in action, Gallipoli, 6th August, 1915. Born Burton-on-Trent. Enlisted Coventry. Resided Burton-on-Trent. Grave Ref. I. D. 17. Twelve Tree Copse Cemetery, Turkey.

BRANDETH, Private, Albert. 1994, 1st/5th Bn., Cheshire Regiment. Killed in action, 17th June, 1916. Born at Macclesfield. Resided in Coventry. Grave Ref. II. C. 3. Hebuterne Military Cemetery, France.

BRASSE, Sergeant, Horace Joseph. 10541, "B" Bty. 58th Bde., Royal Field Artillery. Died of wounds, Gallipoli, 15th August, 1915. Age 25. Husband of May Guest (formerly Brasse), of 4, Summerland Row, The Butts, Coventry. Born 25th March, 1889 at Northampton. Machinist. Enlisted September, 1914 at Coventry. Enlisted Coventry. Grave Ref. III. D. 8. Hill 10 Cemetery, Turkey.

BRASSINGTON, Private, Harry, (formerly known as Harry Pontoon). 2118, 1st Bn., Royal Warwickshire Regiment. Killed in action, 13th October, 1914. Son of George and Sarah Jane Pouton (nee Hudson), of 24, Cow Lane, Coventry. Born 11th November, 1888 at 10c. 8h., West Orchard. Resided in Butcher Row formerly Bond Street. Soldier. Enlisted Coventry. Grave Ref. I. N. 334. (Buried near this spot). Meteren Military Cemetery, Nord, France.

BRAY, Gunner, Ernest Edward Charles. 19368, 56th Siege Bty., Royal Garrison Artillery. Killed in action, 6th October, 1916. Age 29. Son of Frederick James and Emily Ann Bray. Born at Bristol. Resided at 423, Foleshill Road with his sister, Mrs. T. G. A. Robertson. Employed Courtaulds and previous Coventry Chain Co. Grave Ref. VI. H. 7. Serre Road Cemetery No.1, France.

BREE, Private, Harry. 18700, 1st Bn., Somerset Light Infantry. Killed in action, 24th October, 1918. Age 36. Son of John and Sarah Ann Bree, of Daventry, Northants. Husband of Florrie Bree, of 117, Wyley Road, Coventry. Born 1st May, 1882 at Daventry. Resided at 117, Wyley Road. Coach Painter. Enlisted May, 1918 at Coventry. Commemorated Radford Memorial. Grave Ref. A. 17. Verchain British Cemetery, Verchain-Maugre, Nord, France.

BREESE, Corporal, Harold. 305808, 1/8th Bn., Royal Warwickshire Regiment. Killed in action, 16th August, 1917. Born at Aston, Birmingham. Name on Roll in St. Thomas's Church. Grave Ref. Panel 23 to 28 and 163A. Tyne Cot Memorial, Belgium.

BRENNAN, Private, John Francis Patrick. 42985, 5th Bn., Royal Berkshire Regiment. Died of wounds, 15th October, 1918. Age 19. Son of John and Charlotte Brennan, of 45, Bond St., Coventry. Born Coventry. Enlisted Coventry. Born 5th March, 1898 in Thomas Street, Butts. Resided at 43, Bond Street. Engineer. Enlisted February, 1918 at Coventry. Grave Ref. III. B. 27. Houchin British Cemetery, Pas de Calais, France.

BRENNAN, Lance Corporal, Michael William, (served as Williams). 7512, 1st Bn., Duke of Cornwall's Light Infantry. Killed in action, Battle of the Somme, 23rd July, 1916. Age 18. Husband of Mrs. T. A. Marlow of 934, 7th Street, South Lethbridge, Alberta, Canada. Born 13th June, 1885 at Birmingham. Resided at Alberta, Canada, (home previously in Coventry). Postman. Reservist. Memorial Ref. Pier and Face 6B. Thiepval Memorial, France.

BREWER, Corporal, Alfred (Albert) Edward. 2877, 1/7th Bn., Royal Warwickshire Regiment. Killed in action, 25th July, 1916. Age 26. Son of Joseph and Louisa Brewer, previously of Campden Road, Ipswich. Husband of Ruth Catherine Brewer of 55, Alston Road, Ipswich. Born 23rd November, 1889 at Ipswich. Resided at 14, Kensington Road. Photographer, Mr. E. W. Appleby. Member of Warwick Lane, Wesleyan Church. Enlisted Coventry. Memorial Ref. Pier and Face 9A 9B and 10B. Thiepval Memorial, France.

BREWERTON, Sergeant, Arthur Robert. 4153, 1/6th Bn., South Staffordshire Regiment. Killed in action, 1st July 1916. Age 18. Son of Robert and Alice Brewerton of III, Church Road, Bradmore, Wolverhampton. Born at Coventry. Enlisted Wolverhampton. Memorial Ref. Pier and Face 7B. Thiepval Memorial, Somme, France.

BREWIN, Private, Alfred. 12006, 8th Bn., Leicestershire Regiment. Died of wounds, 19th July, 1916. Husband of Melina Walker (formerly Brewin), of 166, Leicester Causeway, Coventry. Born Melton Mowbray. Enlisted Melton Mowbray. Grave Ref. II. B. 52. Heilly Station Cemetery, Mericourt-L'abbe, Somme, France.

BRICKNELL, Company Sergeant Major, George MM. 10088, D Coy., 8th Service Bn., South Staffordshire Regiment. Killed in action, 12th October, 1917 by the explosion of a large shell. Age 37. Son of Charles and Mary Ann Bricknell of Lower Ladies Hill, Kenilworth. Husband of Emma Bricknell of 29, Warwick Road, Kenilworth. Born Hockley, Warwickshire. Enlisted Warwick. Employed by Rover Company Ltd. Awarded Military Medal for carrying a message under heavy fire. Memorial Ref. Panel 90 to 92 and 162 to 162A. Tyne Cot Memorial, Belgium.

BRIDCUTT, Gunner, Arthur Elijah. 40822, Royal Field Artillery attached Royal Garrison Artillery. Killed in action, North Russia, 11th August, 1919. Age 23. Son of John and Esther Bridcutt, of Roke Benson, Oxon. (buried Troitza Chyd.). Born Benson, Oxford. Enlisted Coventry. Resided Benson. Memorial Ref. Sp. Mem. B12. Archangel Allied Cemetery, Russian Federation.

BRIDGE, Private 2nd Class, Walter Joseph. 98568, 10th Balloon Sect., Royal Air Force. Killed in action, by a shell, Artois, 5th September, 1918. Age 39. Husband of Johanna Bridge, of 45, Station Street West, Foleshill, Coventry. Born 13th April, 1879 at 43, Nelson Street. Chargehand, Courtaulds Ltd. Enlisted 8th October, 1917. Grave Ref. II. C. 25. Vis-En-Artois British Cemetery, Haucourt, Pas de Calais, France.

BRIGHT, Lance Sergeant, Albert Edward, DCM, MM. 10719, 4th Bn., Coldstream Guards. Died of wounds, 14th April, 1918. Age 23. Son of Alfred and S. Bright of 13, Ventnor Road, Hockley, Birmingham. Born in St. Michael's Parish, Coventry. Distinguished Conduct Medal award, gazetted 3rd June, 1918. Grave Ref. XXI. D. 20. Cabaret Rouge British Cemetery, Souchez, France.

BRIND, Private, John. 1533, "A" Coy., 2nd Bn., Royal Warwickshire Regiment. Died of wounds to the neck and legs (received in France), 19th November, 1914 at Leeds Infirmary. Age 25. Son of Mr. and Mrs. John Brind, of Swindon. Husband of Emma Brind, of 216, Lockhurst Lane, Coventry. Born at Fairford, Glos. Enlisted Coventry. Grave Ref. Screen Wall. W. 429. Leeds (Lawns Wood) Cemetery, Yorkshire.

BRINDLE, Private, Harry, DCM. 18232, 11th Bn., Royal Fusiliers. Killed in action, 23rd March, 1918. Born Coventry. Enlisted Coventry. Resided Coventry. Distinguished Conduct Medal award, gazetted 3rd June, 1918. Memorial Ref. Panel 19 to 21. Pozieres Memorial, France.

BRINE, Private, Albert. 16403, 1st Bn., Hampshire Regiment formerly 13083, Oxfordshire and Buckinghamshire Light Infantry. Died of wounds, Home, 8th August, 1915. Born St. Oswald's, Manchester. Enlisted Coventry. Resided Moston, Manchester. Grave Ref. B. N.C. 222. Manchester (Philips Park) Cemetery

BRINKWORTH, Private, Charles F. 201707, 1/5th Bn., King's Own Scottish Borderers. Killed in action, Egypt, 19th April, 1917. Age 36. Husband of Margaret Brinkworth of 35, Bank Street, Troon. Born Coventry. Enlisted Glasgow. Resided at Troon, Ayr. Memorial Ref. Panels 23 and 24. Jerusalem Memorial.

BRISLIN, Private, John. 2587, 1st /7th Bn., Royal Warwickshire Regiment. Killed in action, 10th May, 1915. Age 22. Son of John and Hannah Brislin, of Coventry. Born 24th December, 1892 at Coventry. Resided at 22, Hartlepool Road. Fitter, Triumph Works. Enlisted September, 1914 at Coventry. Commemorated Triumph & Gloria Memorial. Employed Triumph works. Grave Ref. V. A. 8. La Plus Douve Farm Cemetery, Comines-Warneton, Hainaut, Belgium

BRITTAIN, Private, George. 16731, 15th Bn., Royal Warwickshire Regiment. Killed in action, Battle of the Somme, 3rd September, 1916. Born 8th June, 1893 at Newhall Green, Fillongley. Resided at 43, Cox Street. Labourer. Enlisted January, 1916 at Coventry. Memorial Ref. Pier and Face 9A 9B and 10B. Thiepval Memorial, France.

BRITTAIN, Private, Harry Amos. 16760, 14th Bn., Royal Warwickshire Regiment. Posted as missing, killed in action, 3rd June, 1917. Age 25. Son of Amos and Elizabeth Brittain, of 16, Lincoln Street, Coventry. Born 16th November, 1891 at Allesley. Resided at 16, Lincoln Street. Groom. Enlisted Coventry. Grave Ref. V. D. 22. Orchard Dump Cemetery, Arleux-En-Gohelle, Pas de Calais, France.

BROADBENT, Private, Albert. 13167, 6th Bn., Oxfordshire and Buckinghamshire Light Infantry. Killed in action, France, 22nd July, 1916. Age 21. Son of John and Isabella Broadbent of West Smethwick, Staffs. Born at Smethwick, Staffordshire. Resided at Foleshill. Grave Ref. I. L. 39. Rue-Petillion Military Cemetery, Fleurbaix, France.

BROADWAY, Private, A. 14205, Royal Warwickshire Regiment formerly 15321 Royal Berkshire Regiment. Died at home, 9th November, 1918. Enlisted Coventry. Resided Bedford. Grave Ref. 12. 128. Coventry (St. Paul's) Cemetery.

BRODERICK, Private, John Alfred. SPTS/4621, 23rd Bn., Royal Fusiliers. Killed in action, 13th November, 1916. Age 20. Son of Alfred and Elizabeth Broderick, of Old Milverton, Warwick. Born Old Milverton. Enlisted Coventry. Resided Old Milverton. Commemorated Dunlop Memorial. Grave Ref. B . 43. Redan Ridge Cemetery No.1, Beaumont-Hamel, France.

BROMAGE, Private, Arthur Edward. 58101, 3rd Bn., Royal Warwickshire Regiment. Died Home, 9th August, 1918. Husband of Elizabeth Selina Bromage of 60, Parkes Street, Warwick. Born Coventry. Enlisted Warwick. Grave Ref. L. G. 23. Dover (St. James's) Cemetery.

BROMLEY, Private, William. 10656, 5th Bn., Oxfordshire and Buckinghamshire Light Infantry. Died of wounds, 13th July, 1915. Born Leicester. Enlisted Coventry. Resided Shirebrook, Notts. Grave Ref. I. B. 4. Poperinghe New Military Cemetery, Belgium.

BROOK, Private, Arthur. 7934, 1st Bn., Border Regiment. Killed in action, Gallipoli, 21st August, 1915. Born Coventry. Resided at 6, Junction Street. Employed by Rotheram and Sons Ltd. Reservist. Enlisted Coventry. Memorial Ref. Panel 119 to 125 or 222 and 223. Helles Memorial, Turkey.

BROOKES, Rifleman, Alfred Leonard. R/33936, 2nd Bn., King's Royal Rifle Corps formerly 28184, Gloucestershire Regiment. Died of wounds, 10th July, 1917. Age 21. Son of Mr. A. and Mrs. L. Brookes, of Fisher Road, Foleshill, Coventry. Husband of Mrs. W. E. Brookes, of 8, Jeynes Buildings, Oldbury Road, Tewkesbury. Born 1896 at Tewkesbury. Enlisted Tewkesbury. Memorial Ref. Nieuport Memorial, Nieupoort, West-Vlaanderen, Belgium.

BROOKES, Sergeant, Edward. 1168, 1st/7th Bn., Royal Warwickshire Regiment. Died from wounds, Wulverghem, Belgium, 11th May, 1915, reported to have been shot in the side, at 1.00 am when returning from patrol after sentry reported someone in the lines, died an hour later. Age 36. Husband of Florence Amelia Brookes, of 46, Craners Road, Coventry. Born 1st May, 1879 at Willenhall. Resided in Alma Street. Fitter. Enlisted August, 1914, Coventry. Employed Handlebar Shop, Brake Fitting, Rudge Whitworth Works. Brother of Lewis Brookes. Grave Ref. V. B. 4. La Plus Douve Farm Cemetery, Comines-Warneton, Hainaut, Belgium.

BROOKES, Sapper, Henry Oliver. 99011, 214th Army Troops Coy., Royal Engineers. Died of wounds, 22nd September, 1917. Age 23. Son of Henry and Prudence Brookes, of Mill House, Whitley, Coventry. Born 16th March, 1894 at Whitley Abbey Farm, Coventry. Enlisted Coventry. Resided at 24, Crabmill Lane, Foleshill. Bricklayer. Enlisted May, 1915. Grave Ref. VII. D. 3. Dozinghem Military Cemetery, Poperinge, West-Vlaanderen, Belgium.

BROOMHEAD, Sergeant, William. S/8665, 8/10th Bn., Gordon Highlanders. Killed in action, 17th September, 1916. Age 23. Son of Mr. and Mrs. J. Broomhead of Ingleside, Hardwick Square, Buxton. Born Coventry. Enlisted Buxton. Memorial Ref. Pier and Face 15B and 15C. Thiepval Memorial, Somme, France.

BROMWICH, Gunner, Edgar John Henry. 128351, "V" 5th Trench Mortar Bty., Royal Field Artillery. Died of wounds, 24th April, 1917. Age 21. Son of Mr. A. H. and Mrs. R. A. Bromwich, of 10, Chessher Street, Hinckley, Leicestershire. Born Hinckley. Enlisted Coventry. Grave Ref. I. C. 13. Quatre-Vents Military Cemetery, Estree-Cauchy, France.

BROOKMAN, Sergeant, Henry Edward. 1742, "C" Bty., 110th Bde., Royal Field Artillery. Died of wounds, 4th June, 1917. Age 20. Son of Henry E. and Ellen Brookman, of 20, Clive Road, Belvedere, Kent. Born Fulham. Enlisted Coventry. Grave Ref. II. A. 6. Westhof Farm Cemetery, Belgium.

BROUGH, W. Employed by Humber Ltd.

BROUNHILL, Private, Clifford. 44185, 2nd Bn., Suffolk Regiment formerly M/303307 Army Service Corps. Killed in action, 2nd August, 1918. Age 21. Son of Harry and Ellen Brounhill, of Birmingham. Born at Birmingham. Resided at Coventry. Enlisted Grove Park, Kent. Grave Ref. III. F. 6. Sandpits British Cemetery, Fouquereuil, France.

BROWETT, Captain, Arnold Leslie Thackhall. 2/7th Bn., Royal Warwickshire Regiment. Killed in action, Neuve Chapelle, 6th July, 1916. Born 22nd August, 1885 at Coventry. Resided at Corley. Educated Rugby School. Solicitor, Messrs Browetts Solicitors, Bayley Lane. Enlisted August, 1914. Son of Mr. William Thackall Browett. Husband of Mrs. Gladys Browett (nee Barton). Educated Rugby School. Leaves a widow and two girls. Grave Ref. I. B. 17. Pont-Du-Hem Military Cemetery, La Gorgue, France.

BROWN, Private, Alfred James. 24585, 2nd /5th Bn., Royal Warwickshire Regiment. Died of wounds, received at Cambrai, in a casualty clearing station, 6th December, 1917. Age 33. Son of James and Rose Brown, of Coventry. Husband of Caroline Elizabeth Brown, of 36, Lockhurst Lane, Foleshill, Coventry. Born 20th December, 1884 at Shotteswell, near Banbury. Baker, Mr. W. J. Stafford, 146, Lockhurst Lane. Enlisted 26th March, 1917, Coventry. Grave Ref. VIII. B. 19. Rocquigny-Equancourt Road British Cemetery, Manancourt, Somme, France.

BROWN, Private, Archibald James. 29771, 14th Bn., Worcestershire Regiment. Killed in action, 14th November, 1916. Age 33. Son of Alexander and Elizabeth Brown. Born Leeds. Enlisted Coventry. Resided Leeds. Memorial Ref. Pier and Face 5 A and 6 C. Thiepval Memorial, Somme, France.

BROWN, Rifleman, Arnold. 302082, 5th Bn., London Rifle Brigade. Killed in action, Battle of the Somme, 9th October, 1916. Student of Bristol College. Three months student minister at Queen's Road Baptist Church. Commemorated Queen's Road Memorial. Enlisted November, 1915. Born Hornsey. Enlisted London. Resided Hornsey. Youngest son of Dr. Charles Brown, Baptist Minister. Memorial Ref. Pier and Face 9D. Thiepval Memorial, France.

BROWN, Private, Arthur. 9955, 1st Bn., Royal Warwickshire Regiment. Killed in action, 13th October, 1914. Born Littlethorpe, Narborough. Enlisted Coventry. Resided Littlethorpe. Grave Ref. II. K. 274. Meteren Military Cemetery, France.

BROWN, Private, Bertram. 266558, 1st /7th Bn., Royal Warwickshire Regiment. Killed in action, 11th August, 1917. Age 29. Son of John Everard Brown and Emma Brown, of 42, Blythe Road, Coventry. Born 19th July, 1888 at Coventry. Resided at 143, George Street. Blacksmith's Striker. Enlisted 1916, Coventry. Memorial Ref. Panel 8. Ypres (Menin Gate) Memorial, Ieper, West-Vlaanderen, Belgium.

BROWN, Pioneer, Charles. WR/282058, Railway Operating Dept., Royal Engineers. Died 25th November, 1918. Age 26. Husband of Lizzie Brown, of 129, Bell Green Road, Foleshill, Coventry. Born 23rd January, 1892 at Cowley. Resided at 141, Cross Road. Millwright. Enlisted 1916. Grave Ref. VI. H. 8. Les Baraques Military Cemetery, Sangatte, Pas de Calais, France.

BROWN, Private, Charles Davis. 12011, 1st Bn., Grenadier Guards. Died of wounds, 9th December, 1916. Age 29. Son of Joseph and Mary Brown, of Grove Park, Chiswick, London. Constable in the Coventry City Police Force. Born 6th December, 1887 at Grove Park, Chiswick Resided at 219, Walsgrave Road. Reservist. Enlisted London. Commemorated Police Force Memorial, Coventry Corporation. Grave Ref. O. III. C. 3. St. Sever Cemetery Extension, Rouen, Seine-Maritime, France.

BROWN, Gunner, Christopher. 44780, 37th Anti-Aircraft Coy., Royal Garrison Artillery. Died Home, 5th November, 1918. Born October, 1891 at Bell Green. Resided in College Square, Cook Street. Butcher. Enlisted August, 1914 at Coventry. Grave Ref. Special Memorial. Scunthorpe Parish Churchyard.

BROWN, Driver, David Cliffe. 39661, 43rd Bn., Royal Field Artillery. Lost on HMS Hampshire, 5th June, 1916. Brother of Mr. J. Brown of 7, King George's Avenue, Little Heath. Served in India. Joined the army, 1904. Memorial Ref. Hollybrook Memorial, Southampton.

BROWN, Sergeant, Ernest. 265999, 1/7th Bn., Royal Warwickshire Regiment. Killed in action, 18th April, 1917. Born in 1879. Resided at 23, Bradford Street, Coventry. Bricklayer. Enlisted October, 1914 at Coventry. Memorial Ref. Pier and Face 9A 9B and 10B. Thiepval Memorial, France.

BROWN, Lance Corporal, Frank Llewellyn John. 3285, 2nd /7th Bn., Royal Warwickshire Regiment. Died of wounds, 30th September, 1916. Age 19. Son of Arthur and Mary Ann Brown, of Brighton House, Brighton Street, Coventry. Born 24th December, 1897 at 9, Hood Street. Resided at Brighton House, Brighton Street. Fitter. Enlisted November, 1914, Coventry. Commemorated Triumph & Gloria Memorial Grave Ref. B. 31. Douai Communal Cemetery, Nord, France.

BROWN, Private, Frederick, MM. 10852, 2nd Bn., Royal Warwickshire Regiment. Died of wounds, 4th May, 1917. Born at Sutton, Surrey. Resided Coventry. Grave Ref. I. E. 16. Achiet-Le Grand Communal Cemetery Extension, France.

BROWN, Second Lieutenant, Harold Masters, MC. 5th Bn., Royal Berkshire Regiment. Died of wounds, 9th July, 1916. Wounds received 2nd July, 1916. Age 27. Son of William and Keziah Harriett Brown of Slinfold, Sussex. BSc (Hons). Teacher, Bablake School. Commemorated Bablake School Memorial. Awarded Military Cross on the 2nd July, 1916 for conspicuous gallantry when he led his company into an attack with great dash. Wounded in five places. Born Slinfold, 31st July, 1888. Grave Ref. I. A. 35. Etaples Military Cemetery, France.

BROWN, Private, Herbert. Army Service Corps. Invalided home. Died 10th November 1914 at a railway near Green Lane Bridge suffering from enteric fever. Age 25. Resided Pridmore Road. Car tester, repairer, Rover Works. Grave Ref. Buried Coventry.

BROWN, Private, Herbert. 266318, 2/7th Bn., Royal Warwickshire Regiment attached 143rd Bn., Machine Gun Corps (Infantry). Killed in action, 14th July, 1916. Age 20. Son of Mr. And Mrs. H. Brown. Born Coventry. Enlisted Coventry. Memorial Ref. Pier and 9A 9B and 10B. Thiepval Memorial, France.

BROWN, Lance Corporal, Horace Harry. 8421, A Coy., 3rd Platoon, 2/6th Bn., Royal Warwickshire Regiment. Died of wounds, 31st March, 1918. Age 24. Son of Thomas and Sarah Ann Brown of Mount Pleasant, Walsgrave. Born 12th August, 1893 at Walsgrave on Sowe. Resided at Walsgrave on Sowe. Commemorated Walsgrave-On-Sowe Memorial. Driller. Enlisted August, 1914 at Coventry. Memorial Ref. Panel 18 and 19. Pozieres Memorial, France.

BROWN, Private, J. Ambrose. 13274, 2nd Bn., The Queen's (Royal West Surrey Regiment). Killed in action, 2nd April, 1917. Age 19. Son of Ambrose Brown, of 44, Northfield Road, Coventry. Born at Melbourne, Australia. Resided at Berkhampstead (formerly Coventry). Enlisted Berkhampstead. Grave Ref. I. A. 27. Croisilles British Cemetery, Pas de Calais, France.

BROWN, Private, James. 14th Bn., Worcestershire Regiment. Killed in action, Beaumont Hamel, 13th November, 1916. Resided Coventry. Sheet Metal Worker. Enlisted April, 1916.

BROWN, Lance Bombardier, John Henry. 278492, 10th Coy., Royal Garrison Artillery. Died Cork, 27th October, 1918. Born 6th March, 1890 at Northampton. Resided at 2, Bishop Street. Labourer. Enlisted October, 1914 at Coventry. Grave Ref. 7. 45. Coventry (London Road) Cemetery.

BROWN, Private, Robert. CMT/2321, M. T., Army Service Corps. Died, Home 11th November, 1914. Age 24. Husband of Susanna Lane (formerly Brown), of 2 Court, 1 House, Warwick Lane, Coventry. Born at St. John's, Warwick. Enlisted Coventry. Reservist. Grave Ref. 12. 132. Coventry (London Road) Cemetery.

BROWN, Private, Walter. 267961, 1/8th Bn., Liverpool Regiment. Killed in action, 10th September, 1917. Born at Coventry. Resided at Liverpool. Enlisted Liverpool. Memorial Ref. Panel 31 to 34 and 162 and 162A and 163A. Tyne Cot Memorial, Belgium.

BROWN, Air Mechanic 2nd Class, William. 129531, 2nd Northern Aircraft Repair Depot, Royal Air Force formerly Royal Engineers. Died of septic pneumonia, Leeds Hospital, 21st June, 1918 following an injury to his left hand which resulted in blood poisoning. Age 25. Husband of Annie Brown, of 15, Junction Street, Coventry. Born 4th August, 1893 at Woolwich. Resided at 11, Hertford Place. Employed as a wheel builder in the RAF formerly Fitter, Tool Making Department, Rudge Works. Enlisted June, 1915. Grave Ref. 198. 52. Coventry (London Road) Cemetery.

BROWN, Gunner, William Edwin. 16243, "D" Bty., 235th Bde., Royal Field Artillery. Killed in action, 7th May, 1918. Age 25. Son of Thomas P. and Elizabeth Ann Brown, of Canley Gates, Coventry. Born Coventry. Enlisted Coventry. Grave Ref. A. 5. Bavelincourt Communal Cemetery, Somme, France.

BROWNLOW, Private, Albert. 4792, 1st Bn., Royal Warwickshire Regiment. Killed in action, 30th August, 1918. Born in 1888 in Birmingham. Resided at 60, Gordon Street. Setter Up, Press Department, Rudge Works. Enlisted in 1914, sent home for munitions work after being gassed, recalled, 2nd April, 1918. Born Peterborough. Enlisted Birmingham. Grave Ref. I. E. 45. Vis-En-Artois Cemetery, Haucourt, France.

BRUCE, Major, Jonathon Maxwell. 107th Indian Pioneers. Killed in action, 24th November, 1914. Age 41. Eldest son of R. T. Bruce, C.I.E. Husband of Mabel W. Bruce of Kenilworth, Seymour Road, Hampton Wick, Kingston on Thames. Commemorated St. Thomas Parish Magazine, Roll of Honour. Grave Ref. I. A. 14. Bethune Town Cemetery, France.

BRUNTON, Private, Thomas Arthur. 4434, 2/7th Bn., Royal Warwickshire Regiment. Killed in action, Somme, 14th June, 1916. Age 22. Son of Walter and Mary Jane Brunton, of Dewsbury, Yorks. Born 12th June, 1894 at Dewbury. Resided at 107, Far Gosford Street. Capstan Hand. Enlisted June, 1915 at Coventry. Grave Ref. I. H. 2. Rue-du-Bacquerot No. 1. Military Cemetery, Laventie, France.

BRUSHETT, Sergeant, Harold. 1948, 41st Trench Mortar Bty., Royal Artillery. Died of wounds, France, 28th December, 1916. Age 28. Son of George Sidney and Sarah Brushett. Native of Kidderminster, Worcestershire. Born at Kidderminster. Resided at 134, Elmsdale Avenue, Foleshill. Employed Coventry Chain Company Ltd. Enlisted Coventry. Commemorated Coventry Chain Memorial. Grave Ref. X. C. 42A. Lijssenthoek Military Cemetery, Belgium.

BRYAN, Company Sergeant Major, Richard Hammond, DCM. 242363, 2/6th Bn., Royal Warwickshire Regiment. Killed in action, 27th July, 1918. Age 42. Husband of Harriet Ann Bryan, of 7, Madeley Street, Crewe, Cheshire. Born at St. Thomas's, Dublin. Resided at Coventry. Enlisted Crewe. Awarded Distinguished Conduct Medal, 17th April, 1918 for conspicuous gallantry and devotion to duty. During an attack when all his company officers had become casualties, he took command and rallied his men with admirable coolness. Totally indifferent to danger, he walked about within twenty yards of the enemy position under intense machine gun fire and eventually withdrew the company in a most skilful manner. He has on all occasions displayed great coolness and devotion to duty. Grave Ref. IV. A. 7. Berlin South-Western Cemetery, Germany. (Moved from original burial, 1924- 1925).

BUBB, Sergeant, Thomas William. 22644, 61st Bn., Machine Gun Corps (Infantry) formerly 2072, Royal Warwickshire Regiment. Killed in action, St. Quentin, 21st March, 1918. Born 8th December, 1885 at Hunscote, Warwickshire. Resided at 29, Broomfield Road. Miner. Enlisted August, 1914. Enlisted Nuneaton. Grave Ref. VI. E. 16. Grand-Seraucourt British Cemetery, France.

BUCK, Lance Corporal, Henry George. 32918, 6th Bn., Oxfordshire and Buckinghamshire Light Infantry. Killed in action, 22nd November, 1917 formerly 17702, Royal Warwickshire Regiment. Born Warwick. Enlisted Coventry. Resided Attleborough. Memorial Ref. Panel 7. Cambrai Memorial, Louverval, France.

BUCKINGHAM, Private, Albert Edward. 42677, D Coy, 10th Bn., Royal Warwickshire Regiment. Killed in action, 25th September, 1918. Age 32. Husband of Elsie K. Buckingham, of 186, Barrows Road, Sparkhill, Birmingham. Born at Hampstead, London. Resided at Summerfield, Clarendon Road, Kenilworth. Lorry Driver. Enlisted Coventry. Commemorated Water Department Memorial, Coventry Corporation. Grave Ref. IV. H. 12. Le Touret Military Cemetery, Richebourg-L'avoue, France.

BUCKINGHAM, Private, C. SS/17601, 25th Labour Coy., Army Service Corps. 3rd July, 1916. Enlisted Coventry. Grave Ref. 189. Salonika (Lembet Road) Military Cemetery, Greece.

BUCKINGHAM, Private, Edgar Herbert. 37766, 2nd/7th Bn., Royal Warwickshire Regiment. Killed Calonne near Merville, 14th April, 1918. Born 27th May, 1898 at Coventry. Born Coventry. Enlisted Cheltenham, May 1916. Commemorated Central Methodist Hall, St. Barbara's Memorial, Bablake School Memorial and War Memorial Park. Resided Coventry. Confectioner. Enlisted May, 1916. Memorial Ref. Panel 2 and 3. Ploegsteert Memorial.

BUCKLAND, Private, Henry. 34032, 1st Bn., Duke of Cornwall's Light Infantry formerly 20179, Royal Warwickshire Regiment. Killed in action, 2nd October, 1917. Age 42. Son of William Buckland, of 23, Chester Street, Coventry. Born 16th July, 1875 at 35, Norfolk Street. Resided at 23, Chester Street. Enlisted Coventry. Gold watch case maker. Commemorated St. John's Church, Bablake School Memorial and War Memorial Park. Grave Ref. V. O. 3. Meteren Military Cemetery, Nord, France.

BUCKLEY, Second Lieutenant, Edmund Maurice. 7th Bn., Royal Welsh Fusiliers. Died of wounds (received in Gallipoli) on board the Clan Macgillivray, 12th August, 1915. Wounds received the previous day at Suvla Bay. Age 29. Son of Sir Edmund Bart Buckley and of Lady Buckley, of 2, Marine Parade, Barmouth, previously of Maesllan, Barmouth, N. Wales. Born 1st December, 1886. Resided at Westgate, Stoke Park. Educated at Manchester University. In Charge of Motor Cycle Repair Department, Humber Ltd. Enlisted August, 1914. Grave Ref. K. 19. Lancashire Landing Cemetery, Turkey.

BUCKLEY, Private, James Frederick. 22192, 7th Bn., Gloucestershire Regiment formerly 21904, Reserve Cavalry. Died, Amara, Mesopotamia, 2nd March, 1917. Age 22. Son of William and Alice Buckley, of 89, Chandos Street, Coventry. Born 2nd January, 1895 at 17, Clarence Street. Resided at 89, Chandos Street. Milk Vendor. Enlisted September, 1914, Warwick. Grave Ref. XIII. D. 3. Amara War Cemetery, Iraq.

BUCKSEY, Rifleman, Frederick. 6320, 1st Bn., Rifle Brigade. Killed in action, St. Marguerits, 13th September, 1914. Born in 1879 at Fulham. Resided at 288, Longford Road. Labourer. Reservist. Born Fulham, Middlesex. Enlisted London. Commemorated Saint Thomas the Apostle, Longford. Grave Ref. III. E. 4. Vauxbuin French National Cemetery, France.

BULL, Driver, Albert Edward. 10356, 18th Div. Ammunition Col., Royal Field Artillery. Died Stourbridge, 17th February, 1919. Age 31. Son of Thomas and Louisa Bull, of 52, School Lane, Radford Semele. Born 31st March, 1887 at Chesterton, Warwickshire. Resided at 49, Warwick Street. Railway Goods Porter. Enlisted August, 1914. Grave Ref. Radford Semele (St. Nicholas) Church, Leamington.

BULL, Private, Arthur Lewin Marshall, 34656, 2nd Bn., Oxfordshire and Buckinghamshire Light Infantry. Died of wounds, 5th October, 1918. Age 19. Son of Richard and Frances Greenway of Coventry. Born 19th June 1899, at Dartford, Kent. Resided at 13, Arden Street. Enlisted July 1917 at Coventry. Planer. Commemorated St. Barbara's Church and War Memorial Park. Grave Ref. VIII. K. 14A. Mont Huon Military Cemetery, Le Treport, Seine-Maritime, France.

BULL, Private, George. 17190, 2nd Bn., Hampshire Regiment formerly 3/16547 Oxfordshire and Buckinghamshire Light Infantry. Killed in action, Gallipoli, 6th August, 1915. Born in St. Michael's Parish. Commemorated St. John's Church. Enlisted Coventry. Memorial Ref. Panel 125-134 or 223-226 228-229 & 328. Helles Memorial, Turkey.

BULL, Driver, Henry Harold. 61994, 29th Div. Ammunition Col., Royal Artillery. Died at sea, 23rd October, 1915. Age 20. Son of Mr. H. S. and Mrs. C. Bull, of 12, Granville Square, St. Pancras, London. Born at Coventry. Enlisted Leeds. Memorial Ref. Mikra Memorial, Greece.

BULL, Rifleman, Percy. R/727, 4th Bn., King's Royal Rifle Corps. Killed in action, 3rd October, 1918. Age 26. Son of Charles and Rachel Bull, of 101, Emscote Road, Warwick. Born 14th February, 1892 at Coventry. Resided at Coventry. Parcel Porter (Railway). Enlisted September, 1914, Nuneaton. Memorial Ref. Panel 9. Vis-En-Artois Memorial, France.

BULLOCK, Private, George. 55477, 10th Bn., Welch Regiment attached attd. 114th Coy., Machine Gun Corps formerly 21381, Oxfordshire and Buckinghamshire Light Infantry. Died of wounds, 11th September, 1917. Age 33. Son of Shradk Bullock. Husband of Margaret Wilkinson (formerly Bullock), of 4, Moreton Place, Castle Street, Coventry. Native of Banbury, Oxon. Born at North Newington, Banbury. Resided at 4, Moreton Place, Castle Street. Carter. Enlisted November, 1915, Coventry. Grave Ref. VI. B. 17. Dozinghem Military Cemetery, Westvleteren, Belgium.

BULLOCK, Second Lieutenant, Henry Acton Linton BA. 7th Bn., Royal Warwickshire Regiment. Killed in action near Pozieres, 14th July, 1916. Born 6th January, 1885 at Coventry. Resided at Coventry. Educated St. John's College, Oxford. Solicitor. Enlisted May, 1915. Commemorated St. John's Church, King Henry VIII School and War Memorial Park. Eldest son of Mr. F. A. Bullock. Memorial Ref . Pier and Face 9 A 9 B and 10 B. Thiepval Memorial (buried near Pozieres).

BULLOCK, Corporal, R, MM. 18736, , 9th Bn., King's Own Yorkshire Light Infantry. Killed in action, 7th November, 1918. Husband of L. Bullock, of 296, Munition Cottages, Holbrook Lane, Foleshill, Coventry. Born West Bromwich. Enlisted Wath-on-Dearne. Grave Ref. II. B. 3. Dourlers Communal Cemetery Extension, Nord, France.

BUNCE, Second Lieutenant, George Owen. 2nd Bn., South Wales Borderers. Killed in action, Dardanelles, 9th May, 1915. Age 31. Second son of William Bunce. Husband of Clara Bunce, of 12, Marle Hill Parade, Cheltenham. Born 12th December, 1883 at Aldershot. Received Queens Medal and two clasps, South africe. Enlisted April, 1900. Left a widow and two children. Memorial Ref. Panel 80 to 84 or 219 and 220.Helles Memorial, Turkey.

BUNKER, Private, Frederick Alfred. 16769, 9th Bn., Royal Warwickshire Regiment. Killed in action, 25th January, 1917. Born Luton. Enlisted Coventry. Grave Ref. XIX. J. 1. Amara War Cemetery, Iraq.

BUNKER, Private, Harold. 266069, 2nd /7th Bn., Royal Warwickshire Regiment. Killed in action, 18th April, 1918. Age 20. Son of Mr. and Mrs. Bunker, of 127, Stoney, Stanton Road, Coventry. Born Coventry. Enlisted Coventry. Grave Ref. II. D. 5. St. Venant-Robecq Road British Cemetery, Robecq, Pas de Calais, France.

BUNKER, Lance Sergeant, Raymond Ernest. 9748, 6th Bn., King's Shropshire Light Infantry formerly 9591, Royal Warwickshire Regiment. Killed in action Mericourt, near Arras, 3rd October, 1918. Age 34. Brother of Thomas Bunker, of 127, Stoney Stanton Road, Coventry. Born 2nd July, 1884 at Lower Clopton, Mickleton, Gloucestershire. Resided at Coventry. Labourer. Enlisted August, 1914 at Coventry. Memorial Ref. Panel 8. Vis-En-Artois Memorial, Pas de Calais, France.

BUNNEY, Private, Arthur George. 266712, 1st /7th Bn., Royal Warwickshire Regiment. Died of wounds, 21st April 1917. Son of Mrs. C. Clarke, of 82, Princess Street, Foleshill, Coventry. Born 13th April, 1894 in Nicholas Street. Resided at The Hollies, Wolston. Engineer. Enlisted in 1915, Leamington. Commemorated Wolston Memorial. Employed Bleumel Bros Ltd. Grave Ref. II. G. 17. Templeux-Le-Guerard British Cemetery, Somme, France.

BUNSTER, Pioneer, William John. WR/336046, Inland Waterways and Docks, Royal Engineers. Died at home, 30th October 1918. Age 37. Husband of Florence Ada Aston (formerly Bunster), of 97, Munition Cottages, Holbrook's Lane, Foleshill, Coventry. Born in London. Enlisted Leamington. Resided Coventry. Grave Ref. B. F. 25. Wareham Cemetery, Dorset.

BURBRIDGE, Acting corporal, David John. M2/117262, Army Service Corps attd. 4th Light Armoured Motor Bty. Died East Africa, 23rd April, 1917. Age 30. Son of Joseph Henry and Ellen Mary Burbridge. Husband of E. K. Burbridge, of Garfield, Thame, Oxon. Born Horsham. Enlisted Coventry. Resided Thame, Oxon. Grave Ref. 2. E. 6. Dar Es Salaam War Cemetery, Tanzania.

BURDETT, Private, Thomas. 204401, 1st Bn., Somerset Light Infantry formerly 2261, Somerset Yeomanry. Died of wounds, 30th March, 1918. Age 28. Son of Thomas and Mary Ann Burdett, of Banbury. Husband of Harriett Drakeford (formerly Burdett), of Exhall, Coventry. Born 29th May, 1889 at Hawkesbury Stop, Longford. Resided at 163, Grange Road, Longford. Tram Driver. Enlisted September, 1916. Commemorated Transport Department Memorial, Coventry Corporation. Grave Ref. V. F. 75. Duisans British Cemetery, Etrun, Pas de Calais, France.

BURDIN, Lieutenant, Frank Amesbury. 2nd Bn., Royal Warwickshire Regiment. Killed in action, 16th May, 1915. Reported to have been shot through the heart whilst leading his platoon by a sniper. Age 27. Son of Harry and Mary Jane Burdin, of 120, Foleshill Road, Coventry. Born 24th December, 1887 at Watford. Resided Coventry. Mechanic, Rover Works. Enlisted August, 1914. Grave Ref. II. F. 15. Le Touret Military Cemetery, Richebourg-L'avoue, Pas de Calais, France.

BURGESS, Second Lieutenant, Phillip Gulson. 8th Bn., Royal Berkshire Regiment. Died of wounds, whilst prisoner of war, St. Clothilde, Douai, 13th October, 1915. Age 24. Son of John Gulson Burgess and Jessie Anne Burgess, of Belsize House, Worthing, Sussex. Born 4th April, 1891. Engineer. Enlisted August, 1914. Grave Ref. D. 4. Douai Communal Cemetery, France.

BURGUM, Gunner, Josiah. 1843, Machine Gun Corps (Motors) attd. 1st/2nd King's African Rifles. Killed in action, 17th October, 1917. Age 21. Son of John Dean Burgum and Mary Burgum, of 79, Lorne Street, Farnworth, Lancs. Born Great Lever. Enlisted Coventry. Resided Moses Gate. Grave Ref. 6. K. 4. Dar Es Salaam War Cemetery, Tanzania.

BURKE, Private, Michael. 8277, 1st Bn., King's Liverpool Regiment. Killed in action, 16th May, 1915. Age 29. Son of Patrick and Margaret Burke. Resided Coventry. Labourer, employed Coventry Corporation Gas Department. Born Widnes. Enlisted Warrington. Commemorated Gas Department Memorial, Coventry Corporation. Memorial Ref. Panels 6 to 8. Le Touret Memorial, France.

BURLEY, Private, Michael. 9536, 1st Bn., Royal Munster Fusiliers. Killed in action, 25th April, 1915. Age 22. Son of Peter and Mary Burley, of Cornmarket, Ennis, Co. Clare. Enlisted Ennis. Born Ennis. Billeted in Earlsdon. Memorial Ref. Panel 185 to 190. Helles Memorial, Turkey.

BURNETT, Private, Samuel. 10637, 1st Bn., Royal Warwickshire Regiment. Killed in action, Arras, 3rd May 1917. Age 26. Son of Mr. S. and Mrs. C. Burnett, of 15, Chapel Street, Coventry. Husband of Mrs. Burnett of 1c. 5h. Chapel Street, Coventry. Born 7th September, 1891 in Chapel Street. Resided in Chapel Street. Iron Polisher, Coventry Chain. Commemorated Coventry Chain Memorial and Holy Trinity Panels. Enlisted January, 1915 at Coventry. Memorial Ref. Bay 3. Arras Memorial, Pas de Calais, France

BURNS, Private, Thomas. 36863, 1st Bn., Northumberland Fusiliers formerly Army Service Corps. Killed in action, 20th November, 1917. Age 23. Son of John and Sarah Burns. Born 17th January, 1894 at 40, Bradford Street. Resided 40, Bradford Street. Machinist. Enlisted April, 1915, Rugby. Memorial Ref. Bay 2 and 3. Arras Memorial, France.

BURR, Sergeant, Leonard Oliver. 305359, 1st /8th Bn., Royal Warwickshire Regiment. Killed in action, 1st July 1916. Age 24. Son of Henry and Annie Burr, of Wenlock Road, Aston, Birmingham. Husband of Florence Jane Witherspoon (formerly Burr), of 96, Vine Street, Coventry. Born London. Enlisted Birmingham. Memorial Ref. Pier and Face 9 A 9 B and 10 B. Thiepval Memorial, Somme, France.

BURROWS, Private, Alfred. 9762, 1st Bn., Royal Warwickshire Regiment. Killed in action, Meteren, 13th October 1914. Age 35. Son of William and Alice Burrows, of 11, Norfolk Street, Coventry. Born 19th December, 1879 at Coventry. Resided at 23, Stanton Street. Cycle Finisher. Reservist. Enlisted Coventry. Commemorated St. John's Church and War Memorial Park. Grave Ref. III. F. 712. (Buried near this spot). Meteren Military Cemetery, Nord, France.

BURROWS, Private, Basil. M4/160000, M.T., Royal Army Service Corps. Died, home, 18th February, 1919. Age 33. Son of Daniel and Rhoda Burrows, of Coventry. Husband of Rosina Burrows, of Balsall Street, Balsall Common, Coventry. Commemorated Queen's Road Church. Grave Ref. 110. 103. Coventry (London Road) Cemetery.

BURROWS, Lance Corporal, Ernest John. 3609, 2/7th Bn., Royal Warwickshire Regiment. Killed in action, 6th June, 1916. Born Chapel End, Warwick. Enlisted Coventry. Resided Walsgrave. Commemorated Walsgrave-On-Sowe Memorial. Grave Ref. M. 7. Cambrin Churchyard Extension, France.

BURROWS, Private, George. 10505, 4th Bn., Royal Fusiliers. Killed in action, St. Eloi, 22nd May, 1915. Age 24. Son of William and Annie Burrows, of Northampton. Born at Northampton. Resided at 7, Gambles Buildings, Foleshill. Enlisted Aldershot. Grave Ref. XIV. E. 22. Voormezeele Enclosure No.3, Belgium.

BURROWS, Private, Richard. 14472, 9th Bn., Worcestershire Regiment. Died of wounds at sea, 1st June, 1916. Age 24. Son of William and Annie Burrows, of Northampton. Born at Birmingham. Resided at 149, Villiers Street, Stoke, Coventry. Enlisted Aldershot. Grave Ref. XIV. E. 22. Voormezeele Enclosure No.3, Belgium.

BURTON, Private, Charles Silvester. 28657, 10th Bn., Royal Warwickshire Regiment. Killed in action, Beaumetz, 23rd March, 1918. Born Minworth, Warwickshire. Enlisted Warwick. Resided Coventry. Born 24th August, 1878 at Minworth, Warwickshire. Resided Little Park Street, Cycle Hand. Enlisted November, 1916, Warwick. Memorial Ref. Bay 3. Arras Memorial, France.

BURTON, Sergeant, John Watson. 2416, 1/7th Bn., Royal Warwickshire Regiment. Killed in action 26th June, 1916. Age 24. Son of Thomas and Louisa Jane Burton, of 6, Starley Road, Coventry. Born 18th July, 1892 at Coventry. Resided Coventry. Tailor. Enlisted September, 1914 at Coventry. Commemorated Bablake School Memorial. Grave Ref. I. E. 4. Heburtne Military Cemetery, France.

BURTON, Private, Joseph Charles. 71326, 4th Bn. Royal Fusiliers formerly Durham Light Infantry. Died of wounds, Frevent, France, 30th March, 1918. Born 25th April, 1886 at Coventry. Resided at 12, Little Church Street. Artificial Silk Spinner, Courtaulds Ltd. Enlisted September, 1916 at Coventry. Leaves a widow and two children. Grave Ref. A. 6. St. Hilaire Cemetery Extension, Frevent, France.

BURTON, Lance Corporal, William, DCM. 10685, 1st Bn., Leicestershire Regiment. Killed in action Battle of the Somme, 15th September, 1916. Born in 1893 at Aylestone, Leicestershire. Resided at 17, Mulliner Street. Employed by Albion Drop Forgings. Enlisted August, 1914. DCM awarded August, 1915. Eldest son of Mr. And Mrs. W. Burton of 71, Mulliner Street. Memorial Ref. Pier and Face 2 C and 3 A. Thiepval Memorial, France.

BUSBY, Second Lieutenant, Elijah Wilfred Thornycroft. Tank Corps. Died, Home 6th March, 1919. Born 6th June, 1896 at Coventry. Resided at 54, Hamilton Road. Engineer. Enlisted in 1914. Grave Ref. Coventry (London Road) Cemetery.

BUSBY, Corporal, George Smith. 307750, 1/8th Bn., Royal Warwickshire Regiment. Died of wounds, 24th October, 1918. Born Monk's Kirby. Enlisted Coventry. Resided Brockhurst. Age 34. Son of William and Mary Ann Busby, of Brockhurst, Lutterworth, Rugby. Grave Ref. I. A. 14. Premont British Cemetery, France.

BUTCHER, Private, Arthur. 63173, 16th Bn., South Lancashire Regiment formerly 9555, Royal Welsh Fusiliers. Died, home, 23rd June, 1918. Born Smethwick. Enlisted Coventry. Memorial Ref. Screen Wall (South). V. C. 12. Liverpool (Anfield) Cemetery.

BUTCHER, Private, Thomas, 29889, 10th (Prince of Wales's Own Royal) Hussars. Died of wounds, 9th March, 1918. Age 27. Husband of Florence A. Butcher, of 2, Trentham Road, Coventry. Born Stony Stratford. Enlisted Coventry. Resided Coventry. Grave Ref. V. C. 12. Tincourt New British Cemetery, Somme, France.

BUTLER, 1st Class Stoker, Albert Edward. SS/111999, HMS Niger, Royal Navy. Killed Straits of Dover, 11th November, 1914. Born 10th September, 1893 at Harrow. Resided at 33a Gosford Street. Joined the Navy aged 18. Memorial Ref. 4. Portsmouth Naval Memorial.

BUTLER, Trooper, C. Hussars. Commemorated Dunlop Memorial.

BUTLER, Private, Charles Ernest. 17180, 1st Bn., Coldstream Guards. Age 23. Killed in action, 27th September, 1918. Born Bicester. Enlisted Coventry. Resided Rothersthorpe. Age 23. Son of Mr. W. H. and Mrs. A. Butler, of Dunkley Row, Rothersthorpe, Northampton. Grave Ref. II. D. 10. Sanders Keep Military Cemetery, Graincourt-Les-Havrincourt, France.

BUTLER, Sapper, Ernest William. 217560, 35th Div. Signal Coy., Royal Engineers. Killed in action, 27th March, 1918. Born at Great Bridge, Staffordshire. Employed Coventry. Enlisted Coventry. Memorial Ref. Henencourt Wood Cemetery Memorial and Ribemont Communal Cemetery Extension, Somme, France.

BUTLER, Private, John, 14480, 8th Bn., Royal Berkshire Regiment. Killed in action, 24th June 1917. Killed by a shell, bursting over the dug out. Age 24. Son of William Butler, of 53, Coronation Road, Coventry. Born 21st September, 1892 in Gilbert Place, Brook Street. Enlisted Rugby, 22nd August, 1914. Resided Albert Street, Coventry. Machinist, Singer Works. Commemorated War Memorial Park. Memorial Ref. Nieuport Memorial, Nieuwpoort, West-Vlaanderen, Belgium.

BUTLIN, Rifleman, Roland Bertie. R/1150, 11th Bn., King's Royal Rifle Corps. Killed in action, 10th July, 1916. Age 21. Son of Jesse and Agnes Butlin, of Warwick Street, Wolston, Coventry. Born in 1895, Coventry. Enlisted Rugby. Resided Coventry. Commemorated Wolston Memorial and Queen's Road Church. Grave Ref. S. 5. Potijze Burial Ground Cemetery, Ieper, West-Vlaanderen, Belgium.

CADDEN, Private, Herbert. 265870, 2nd /7th Bn., Royal Warwickshire Regiment. Killed in action, 9th April, 1917. Husband of Mrs. M. L. Cadden, of 42, Freeth Street, Coventry. Employed Swift Co. Ltd. Enlisted October, 14th 1914. Leaves a widow and children. Grave Ref. IV. C. 7. Chapelle British Cemetery, Holnon, Aisne, France.

CAFFREY, Private, George Arthur. 201266, 7th Bn., Tank Corps formerly 2286, Machine Gun Corps. Killed in action, 2nd September, 1918. Age 24. Son of George and Minnie Caffrey, of Old Maengwyn, Machynlleth, Mont. Born Machyullath, Montgomery. Enlisted Coventry. Grave Ref. II. C. 15. Vaulx Hill Cemetery, France.

CALDICOTT, Captain, Alan. 10th Bn., The Loyal North Lancashire Regiment attached 1st/2nd, King's African Rifles formerly Public Schools Battalion. Killed in action, 7th December, 1916. Born in 1887. Resided at 4, Spencer Road, Coventry. Educated at Lindley Lodge near Nuneaton and Bradfield College. Enlisted September, 1914. Employed by W. D. and H. O. Wills, Ltd, of Bristol. Only son of Mr. and Mrs. R. B. Caldicott. Commemorated War Memorial Park. Grave Ref. 2. B. 15. Dar Es Sallam War Cemetery, Tanzania.

CALDICOTT, Gunner, Frederick Walter. 614034, 15th Warwick Bde., Royal Horse Artillery. Killed in action, 9th April, 1917. Age 25. Son of Frederick C. and Hannah Caldicott, of 3, Warwick Avenue, Earlsdon, Coventry formerly The Lawn, Foleshill Road. Commemorated Queen's Road Church and Bablake School Memorial. Memorial. Grave Ref. B. 1. Beaurains Road Cemetery, Beaurains, Pas de Calais, France.

CALDICOTT, Major, R. B. Died 1st June, 1918. Age 59. Employed textile trade. Retired 1897. Recruiting Officer. Lost a son in the Army, Captain Alan Caldicott. Grave Ref. Coventry (London Road) Cemetery.

CALLOW, Private, Louis. 12166, 11th Bn., Hampshire Regiment formerly 7087, Royal Warwickshire Regiment. Killed in action, 9th September, 1916. Age 19. Son of John and Sarah Ann Callow, of Meriden, Coventry. Born Meriden. Enlisted Coventry. Resided Meriden. Memorial Ref. Pier and Face 7 C and 7 B. Thiepval Memorial, Somme, France.

CALLOWAY, Private, Arthur James. 3469, 2nd /7th Bn., Royal Warwickshire Regiment. Died of wounds, 21st July 1916, received 19th July, 1916. Age 19. Son of William and Mary Ann Calloway, of Walsgrave-on-Sowe, Coventry. Born Coventry. Enlisted November, 1914, Coventry. Commemorated Walsgrave-On-Sowe Memorial. Grave Ref. I. C. 30. Laventie Military Cemetery, La Gorgue, Nord, France.

CAMWELL, Private, Horace. 27331, 6th (Wiltshire Yeomanry) Bn., Wiltshire Regiment. Killed in action, 23rd March, 1918. Born Coventry. Enlisted Warwick. Resided Coventry. Memorial Ref. Bay 7. Arras Memorial, France.

CANNING, Private, William John. 1277, 1st Bn., Royal Warwickshire Regiment. Killed in action, 5th April, 1916. Age 24. Son of Mr. and Mrs. W. Canning, of 19, Vecqueray Street, Coventry. Born St. Michael's, Coventry. Enlisted Warwick. Resided Coventry. Grave Ref. III. A. 9. Bienvillers Military Cemetery, France.

CANNON, Sergeant, Patrick. 20617, 14th Bn., Gloucestershire Regiment. Died of wounds, 24th May, 1917. Born Bermondsey, London. Enlisted Coventry. Grave Ref. B. 1. Nesle Communal Cemetery, France.

CANTRILL, Private, Herbert Victor. 2688544, Depot, Canadian Army Service Corps. Died of pneumonia, 11th October, 1918 at sea. Age 26. Son of Henry and Annie Cantrill, of Foleshill. Educated Red Lane Elementary and Bablake School. Previously employed an auto mechanic and chauffeur and resided 226 Stoney Stanton Road. Commemorated Bablake School Memorial. Grave Ref. H. 34. Coventry (Windmill Road) Cemetery.

CANTRILL, Wireman 2nd Class, James Horace. M/11612, HMS Pheasant, Royal Navy. Killed by mine explosion off Orkneys, 1st March, 1917. Age 19. Son of John Pearson Cantrill and Elizabeth Cantrill, of 172, Cross Road, Great Heath, Coventry. Commemorated War Memorial Park. Memorial Ref. 22. Plymouth Naval Memorial.

CAPEL, Harry. Commemorated Saint Thomas the Apostle, Longford.

CAPENER, Rifleman, Reginald. 5286, 2nd Bn., Rifle Brigade. Killed in action, 9th May, 1915. Age 18. Brother of Mrs. Lucy Allinson, of 56, Brandwood Road, King's Heath, Birmingham. Born Stockingford. Enlisted Birmingham. Resided Coventry. Memorial Ref. Panel 10. Ploegsteert Memorial, Belgium.

CAREY, A. Commemorated Triumph & Gloria Memorial.

CARPENTER, Private, Albert Henry. 16666, 11th Bn., Royal Warwickshire Regiment. Killed in action, Passchendaele, 8th October 1917. Age 27. Son of Mr. and Mrs. J. M. Carpenter, of 537, Foleshill Road, Coventry. Born 15th September, 1890 at Great Heath. Stationer. Enlisted February, 1916. Grave Ref. LXIV. A. 10. Tyne Cot Cemetery, Zonnebeke, West-Vlaanderen, Belgium.

CARPENTER, Rifleman, Charles Arthur. Z/825, 1st Bn., Rifle Brigade. Killed in action, 13th May, 1915. Born 3rd November, 1889 at Cubbington. Resided at Cubbington. Railway Carter. Enlisted September, 1914, Rugby. Grave Ref. LIV. A. 1. Poelcapelle British Cemetery, Belgium.

CARPENTER, Rifleman, Ernest Alfred. Z/820, 4th Bn., Rifle Brigade. Killed in action, 11th June, 1915. Age 24. Son of William Carpenter, of Penn's Cottages, Cubbington, Leamington Spa. Born 12th August, 1891 at Cubbington. Resided at Cubbington. Labourer. Enlisted September, 1914. Grave Ref. II. F. 5. Houplines Communal Cemetery Extension, France.

CARPENTER, Private, Francis William. 4161, "B" Coy., 1/7th Bn., Royal Warwickshire Regiment. Died of wounds received on the Somme, 28th June, 1916. Age 31. Son of Joseph and Ellen Jane Carpenter, of Penn's Cottages, Cubbington, Leamington Spa. Born 23rd May, 1885 at Cubbington. Resided Coventry. Enlisted March, 1915, Coventry. Grave Ref. B. 18. Beauval Communal Cemetery, France.

CARPENTER, Private George. 201717, 2/4th Bn., Royal Berkshire Regiment. Died 7th October, 1916. Born Coventry. Enlisted Reading. Resided Coventry. Memorial Ref. Panel 93 to 95. Loos Memorial, France.

CARPENTER, Private, Sidney. 307851, 13th Bn., Liverpool Regiment. Killed in action, 28th March, 1918. Age 42. Son of John and Harriet Carpenter, of 20, Pemberton Street, Old Trafford, Manchester. Born Foleshill. Resided Manchester. Grave Ref. VI. 0. 2. Bucquoy Road Cemetery, Ficheux, France.

CARR, Private, Frederick Walter. 16451, "A" Coy. 1st Bn., Royal Warwickshire Regiment. Killed in action, 25th June, 1916. Age 21. Son of Frederick W. and Edith J. Carr, of Coventry. Born Coventry. Enlisted Coventry. Grave Ref. II. B. 18. Auchonvillers Military Cemetery, Somme, France.

CARROLL, Corporal, John James (Michael). 2039, 1/7th Bn., Royal Warwickshire Regiment. Died of wounds, 11th May, 1915. Born 25th November, 1886 at Holy Trinity, Coventry. Resided at 31, Booth Fields, Little Heath, Foleshill. Moulder. Enlisted August, 1914, Coventry. Commemorated Coventry Chain Memorial. Leaves a widow. Grave Ref. II. A. 75. Bailleul Communal Cemetery Extension (Nord), France.

CARTER, Corporal, Bert. 27952, B Company, 81 Platoon, 1st Bn., Royal Warwickshire Regiment. Died of wounds, 3rd May, 1917. Age 21. Youngest son of Mrs. Mary Jane Carter, and Mr. F. W. Carter of 94, Vine Street, Coventry. Born 6th February, 1895 at Raglan Street, Coventry. Enlisted September, 1914 at Coventry. Book Binder, Messrs. Parbury Bros., Grove Street Memorial Ref. Bay 3. Arras Memorial, Pas de Calais, France.

CARTER, Corporal, Charles John. 16230, A" Bty. 108th Bde., Royal Field Artillery. Killed in action, Ypres, 22nd February, 1916. Born 3rd September, 1892 at Walsgrave on Sowe. Enlisted Coventry. Resided Radford. Clerk, Coventry Ordnance Works. Enlisted August, 1914. Leaves a widow and one child. Member of Webster Street, Baptist Church. Grave Ref. I. H. 25. Menin Road South Military Cemetery, Belgium.

CARTER, Private, F A. G/81837, Middlesex Regiment. transf. to (159767), Labour Corps. Died at home, 24th November 1918. Age 32. Son of Mrs. Amelia Carter, of 51, Tyrolean Square, Cobholm, Great Yarmouth. Husband of Eliza Carter. Grave Ref. 12. 144. Coventry (St. Paul's) Cemetery.

CARTER, Second Lieutenant, Gerald Francis. 7th Bn., King's Royal Rifle Corps. Died of wounds, 30th July, 1915 after leading a bombing party at Hooge. Name on Roll of Honour in Cathedral Church of St. Michael. Undergraduate St. John's College, Oxford. Only son of Alfred Henry Carter of The Lindens, Abingdon. Memorial Ref. Panel 51 and 53. Ypres (Menin Gate) Memorial, Belgium. (Buried Sanctuary Wood)

CARTER, Private, Harold. 1701, 1st Bn., Royal Warwickshire Regiment. Killed in action, 1st July, 1916. Born 7th February, 1892. Resided at Coventry. Railway Goods Porter. Born Long Itchington. Enlisted August, 1914, Warwick. Memorial Ref. Pier and Face 9A 9B and 10B. Thiepval Memorial, France.

CARTER, Henry. Resided at Foleshill. Killed in action, March, 1918.

CARTER, Private, Herbert Harry. G/51913, 17th Bn., Royal Fusiliers. Killed in action near Oppy Wood, 28th April, 1917. Age 28. Son of Henry and Mary Ann Carter, of Rectory Cottage, Exhall, Coventry. Born 22nd September, 1888 at Great Malvern. Enlisted Janaury, 1916 at Bedworth. Resided Rectory Cottage, Exhall. Enlisted January, 1916. Memorial Ref. Bay 3. Arras Memorial, Pas de Calais, France.

CARTER, Sapper, Richard. 193293, 251st Tunnelling Coy., Royal Engineers. Died (gassed) 25th March, 1918. Age 33. Husband of Mrs. Emma Carter, of 9, Grove Street, Coventry. Born 7th February, 1885 at Chipping Norton. Resided at 46, Gosford Street. Miner, Binley Colliery. Enlisted August, 1914. Leaves a wife and two children. Grave Ref. N. 31. Cambrin Military Cemetery, Pas de Calais, France.

CARTER, Lance Corporal, William. DM2/154392, E Siege Park, Army Service Corps. Killed in action, 25th April, 1918. Age 22. Eldest son of William and Hannah Mary Carter, of Church Street, Barford, Warwick. Born Derby. Enlisted Coventry. Resided Barford, Warwick. Grave Ref. XXVII. H. 6. Lijssenthoek Military Cemetery, Belgium.

CARTY, Second Lieutenant, William George. 13th Bn., attached 10th Bn., Royal Warwickshire Regiment. Killed in action, 25th March, 1916. Age 25. Son of William James and Lucy Carty, of 8, Guy's Cliffe Terrace, Warwick. Born 30th December, 1890. Resided at Coventry. Bank Clerk. Enlisted October, 1914. Grave Ref. II. F. 15. Rue-Du-Bacquerot No.1 Military Cemetery, Laventie, France.

CARVELL, Private, Edmund Harry. 10442, 1st Bn., Royal Warwickshire Regiment. Killed in action, 30th April, 1918. Age 29. Son of Charlotte Carvell, of I, Union Row, Brunswick Street, Leamington. Native of Leamington. Born St. Michael's Parish, Coventry. Resided at Leamington. Grave Ref. LXVI. A. 30. Etaples Military Cemetery, France.

CASH, Lieutenant, Geoffrey George Edwin. 6th Bn. attd. 8th Bn., The Loyal North Lancashire Regiment. Killed in action near Thiepval, 27th August, 1916. Age 21. Son of Sidney and Elsie Cash, of The Moat House, Keresley, Coventry. Educated at Marlborough College and Magdalen College, Oxford. Born 1st January 1885 at Coventry. Enlisted August 1914. Commemorated War Memorial Park and St. Thomas Memorial. Grave Ref. VI. G. 20. A.I.F. Burial Ground, Flers, Somme, France.

CASHMORE, Private, Ernest. 9898, 2nd Bn., Oxfordshire and Buckinghamshire Light Infantry. Killed in action, 16th May, 1915. Age 21. Son of Mrs. Mary Ann Cashmore, of 46, Harley Street, Stoke, Coventry. Born 15th May, 1891 at 17, White Friars Street, Coventry. Enlisted Coventry. Soldier. Memorial Ref. Panel 26. Le Touret Memorial, Pas de Calais, France.

CASHMORE, Company Sergeant Major, George, MM. 266361, 2/7th Bn., Royal Warwickshire Regiment. Died of wounds, 22nd March, 1918. Born 19th June, 1891 at West Bromwich. Resided at 72, King George's Avenue, Foleshill formerly 5, Chauntry Place. Employed by Courtaulds Ltd. Enlisted 27th January, 1915, Coventry. Commemorated Holy Trinity Panels. Military Medal awarded for good conduct of holding a battle line on Welsh Ridge, east of Villers Pluich. Official statement: He organized and led bombing parties throughout the afternoon on 5th December, 1917, during the many attacks on our trenches whilst the situation was very critical. His conduct was very fine and his example of coolness had a good effect upon the men. Leaves a widow and one child. Grave Ref. P. IX. O. 2B. St. Sever Cemetery Extension, Rouen, France.

CASHMORE, Private, Joseph. 66, 1st Bn., Royal Warwickshire Regiment. Died of wounds, Boulogne, 25th April, 1915. Born at Coventry. Resided 14c. 6h. Much Park Street. Reservist. Had been wounded several times. Enlisted Coventry. Grave Ref. VIII. B. 6. Boulogne Eastern Cemetery, France.

CASTLE, Private, Fred. 10015, 1st Bn., Coldstream Guards. Died of wounds, 29th October, 1914. Age 23. Son of John and Mary Elizabeth Castle, of Longborough, Moreton-in-the-Marsh, Glos. Two other brothers also fell. Born Longborough, Gloucs. Enlisted Coventry. Resided Morton-in-Marsh, Gloucester. Grave Ref. II. B. 11. Ypres Town Cemetery, Belgium.

CASWELL, Private, Arthur Edward. 18724, 2nd Bn., Coldstream Guards. Killed in action, Passchendaele, 31st July, 1917. Age 34. Son of John and Edith Annie Caswell. Husband of Agnes Mary Caswell, of Dean Cottage, Allesley, Coventry. Born 18th May, 1883 at Handsworth, Birmingham. Commemorated Iliffe and Sons Memorial. Clerk. Enlisted Coventry. Memorial Ref. Panel 11. Ypres (Menin Gate) Memorial, Ieper, West-Vlaanderen, Belgium.

CASWELL, Private, Wilfred. 12628, 9th Bn., Royal Warwickshire Regiment. Died Mesopotamia, 1st July, 1917. Age 32. Husband of A. Caswell of 2, Gilbert Street, Coventry. Native of Gloucester. Born 21st November, 1884 at Gloucester. Labourer. Enlisted June, 1915 at Coventry. Grave Ref. D. 150. Alexandria (Hadra) War Memorial Cemetery, Egypt.

CATER, Private, Edgar Percival. 21790, 5th Bn., Oxfordshire and Buckinghamshire Light Infantry. Killed in action, 24th August, 1916. Age 20. Son of J. Cater, of Bedworth, Nuneaton. Husband of Elsie May Cater, of 10, Hayes Lane, Exhall, Coventry. Born Wyken. Resided Collycroft. Grave Ref. X. G. 6. Delville Wood Cemetery, Longueval, Somme, France.

CAWLEY, Lance Sergeant, Thomas. 19733, 16th Bn., Royal Scots. Killed in action, 3rd August, 1916. Born Sligo, Ireland. Enlisted Edinburgh. Resided Coventry. Memorial Ref. Pier and Face 6 D and 7 D. Thiepval Memorial, France.

CEMM, Lance Sergeant, Howard. 266864, 2/5th Bn., Royal Warwickshire Regiment. Died of wounds, (whilst prisoner of war), 19th January, 1918. Born 4th January, 1891 at Sparkhill, Birmingham. Resided at 415, Foleshill Road. Coach Trimmer. Enlisted Coventry. Grave Ref. V. C. 17. Le Cateau Military Cemetery, France.

CHADWICK, Corporal, John. 206114, Machine Gun Corps (Heavy Branch) formerly 1240, 9 Coy. "C" Bn. Machine Gun Corps. Killed in action, 20th April, 1917. Age 31. Son of Arthur and Elizabeth Chadwick, of 89, Albion Street, Leeds. Born Leeds. Enlisted Coventry. Grave Ref. IV. B. 5. Faubourg D'Amiens Cemetery, Arras, France.

CHADWICK, Sergeant, Thomas Braithwaite. 80087, 6th Armoured Car Coy., Machine Gun Corps (Motors) attached Dunster Force. Killed in action, Baku, Mesopotamia, 26th August, 1918. Age 26. Son of Benjamin and Alice Chadwick. Husband of Winifred May Chadwick, of 41, Thomas Street, Coventry. Born 10th April, 1894 at Ulverston. Resided at 13, Gun Lane, Stoke Heath. Turner and Fitter. Enlisted March, 1918 at Coventry. Memorial Ref. Panel 42. Basra Memorial, Iraq.

CHAMBERLAIN, Private, Charles Henry. 3312, 9th Bn., Royal Warwickshire Regiment. Killed in action, Mesopotamia, 29th March, 1917. Born Temple, Balsall Heath. Enlisted Coventry. Resided Burton Green. Memorial Ref. Panel 9. Basra Memorial, Iraq.

CHAMBERLAIN, Private, Ernest Edward. 241575, 1/6th Bn., Royal Warwickshire Regiment. Killed in action, 27th August, 1917. Age 30. Son of Charles and Mary Chamberlain, of High Street, Coleshill, Birmingham. Born at Foleshill. Memorial Ref. Panel 23 to 28 and 163A. Tyne Cot Memorial, Belgium.

CHAMBERS, Gunner, Edward Ralph. 3049, 108th Heavy Battery, Royal Garrison Artillery. Died, 14th September, 1914. Age 37. Son of Mr. and Mrs. Chambers, of Spilsby, Lincs. Husband of Alice Elizabeth Chambers, of 40, Winn Street, Lincoln. Born St. James, Lincs. Enlisted Coventry. Resided Lincoln. Memorial Ref. La Ferte-Sous-Jouarre Memorial, France.

CHAMBERS, Gunner, Ernest. 11019, "D" Bty. 58th Bde., Royal Field Artillery. Died of wounds, at sea, 7th October, 1915. Age 19. Son of Ernest and Kate Chambers, of Rookery Cottages, Church Lawford, Rugby. Born Coventry. Commemorated Wolston Memorial. Enlisted Coventry. Memorial Ref. Panel 21 and 22. Helles Memorial, Turkey.

CHAMBERS, Lance Corporal, George. 265487, 1/7th Bn., Royal Warwickshire Regiment attd. Signal Sect. H.Q. 112th Infantry Bde. Killed in action, 15th May, 1918. Age 33. Son of Mrs. M. Soden, of 1, Moss Street, Leamington Spa. Born St. Nicholas, Warwick. Enlisted Coventry. Resided Leamington. Grave Ref. E. 19. Couin New British Cemetery, France.

CHAPLIN, Private, Sydney. 12901, 6th Bn., Oxfordshire and Buckinghamshire Light Infantry. Died of wounds, 18th August, 1916 after having one of his amputated. Age 23. Son of William Henry and Maria Chaplin. Born 9th June, 1893 at Coventry. Enlisted Warwick. Resided 78, Lockhurst Lane, Coventry. Employed Daimler Company Ltd. Grave Ref. IV. E. 19. Doullens Communal Cemetery Extension No.1, France.

CHAPMAN, Private, Horace. 24551, 2/6th Bn., Royal Warwickshire Regiment. Killed 3rd December, 1917. Born 22nd April, 1898 at Glascote, Warwickshire. Resided at 9, Swan Lane. Employed Courtaulds Ltd. Enlisted March, 1917 at Coventry. Memorial Ref. Panel 3. Cambrai Memorial, Louverval, France.

CHAPMAN, Corporal, Robert. 2383, 1/7th Bn., Royal Warwickshire Regiment. Died, 8th July, 1916. Age 27. Son of Alex. and Margaret Chapman, of 43, Wathen Road, Leamington Spa, Warwickshire. Native of Aberdeen. Born St. Clemens, Aberdeen. Enlisted Coventry. Resided Leamington. Grave Ref. I. D. 14. Couin British Cemetery, France.

CHAPMAN, Private, Robert. 9693, 1st Bn., Coldstream Guards. Died of wounds, 30th September, 1915. Born St. John's, Warwick. Enlisted Coventry. Resided Leamington. Grave Ref. I. D. 39. Noeux-Les-Mines Communal Cemetery, France.

CHAPMAN, Lance Corporal, Thomas. 13949, 6th Bn., Oxfordshire and Buckinghamshire Light Infantry. Killed in action, 7th October, 1916. Age 28. Son of William and Caroline Chapman, of Moulton, Northants. Born Moulton, Northants. Enlisted Coventry, Resided Yardley, Northants. Memorial Ref. Pier and Face 10 A and 10 D. Thiepval Memorial, Somme, France.

CHAPPLE, Private, Ronald Charles Eric. 206129, Machine Gun Corps (Heavy Branch) formerly 2439, Machine Gun Corps (Heavy Branch). Killed in action, 16th September, 1916. Son of Charles and Gertrude E. Chapple, of 9, Egham Street, Canton, Cardiff. Born Southampton. Enlisted Coventry. Grave Ref. Pier and Face 5 C and 12 C. Thiepval Memorial, Somme, France.

CHARLEY, Rifleman, Arthur James. R/16032, 8th Bn., King's Royal Rifle Corps. Died of wounds, 3rd May, 1917. Born 13th June, 1895 at 62, King William Street, Coventry. Resided 17, Queen Street. Painter and Decorator. Enlisted October, 1915, Coventry. Memorial Ref. Bay 7. Arras Memorial, France.

CHARLEY, Private, David William, MM. 14572, 8th Bn., Royal Berkshire Regiment. Killed in action, 13th July, 1916. Born Coventry. Enlisted September, 1914. Resided 7, Little Church Street, Coventry. Decoration of Military Medal given for bravery when the Prussian Guard tried to break through the line , Private Charley gave the alarm. Leaves a widow and five children. Employed Messrs Joy and Co., Brooklyn Road. Memorial Ref. Pier and Face 11D. Thiepval Memorial, France.

CHARLEY, H. Commemorated Coventry Chain Memorial.

CHARLWOOD, Private, James Helme. 265155, 1st /7th Bn., Royal Warwickshire Regiment. Died of wounds, 15th August, 1917. Age 20. Brother of Mrs. Ames, of 67, Highland Road, Earlsdon, Coventry. Born 29th October, 1896 in St. Michael's Parish. Resided at 36c. 3h. Much Park Street. Moulder. Enlisted August, 1914 at Coventry. Grave Ref. III. G. 15. Dozinghem Military Cemetery, Poperinge, West-Vlaanderen, Belgium.

CHARLWOOD, Private, John Helme. 2352, 1st Bn., Royal Warwickshire Regiment. Killed in action, St. Julien Wood, Ypres, 25th April, 1915. Age 20. Son of John Helme Charlwood. Born St. Michael's Parish, Coventry. Enlisted Warwick. Resided 1, Much Park Street, Coventry. Memorial Ref. Panel 8. Ypres (Menin Gate) Memorial, Belgium.

CHARNLEY, Private, George William. M2/119538, 706th Coy., Army Service Corps. Died of wounds, Balkans, 19th August, 1916. Age 39. Husband of Caroline Charnley, of 3, Ashton Street, Merefield, Rochdale. Born Bolton, Lancs. Enlisted Coventry. Resided Rochdale. Grave Ref. 1612. Mikra British Cemetery, Kalamaria, Greece.

CHATLAND, Private, Joseph Oliver. 204099, 3rd Bn., Worcestershire Regiment. Killed in action, 12th June, 1918. Age 27. Son of Mr. and Mrs. J. M. Chatland, of Coventry. Husband of Mrs. Nellie Chatland, of 140, Bolton Road, Small Heath, Birmingham. Born Coventry. Enlisted Birmingham. Resided Birmingham. Grave Ref. XI. A. 13. Cologne Southern Cemetery, Koln(Cologne), Nordrhein-Westfal, Germany.

CHATLAND, Private, William George. 229, 1st Bn., Royal Warwickshire Regiment. Killed in action, Ypres, 25th April, 1915. Age 28. Son of George and Sophia Chatland, of 30, Adelaide Street, Coventry. Born 25th June, 1886 at Little Church Street, Coventry. Enlisted Coventry. Resided at 110, Broad Street. Machinist, Messrs Calcott Bros. Memorial Ref. Panel 8. Ypres (Menin Gate) Memorial, Ieper, West-Vlaanderen, Belgium.

CHATTAWAY, Private, George Henry. 268224, 1/7th Bn., Royal Warwickshire Regiment formerly 3411, Warwick Yeomanry. Killed in action, Laventie, 2nd March, 1917. Born in 1894, Bridlington, Yorkshire. Enlisted Warwick. Resided 18, Duke Street, Coventry. Fitter, Rover Works. Enlisted November, 1915. Grave Ref. V. F. 5. Assevillers New British Cemetery, France.

CHATTAWAY, Driver, Herbert Alexander. 840576, "A" Bty. 307th Bde., Royal Field Artillery. Died of wounds, in hospital, 14th August 1917. Age 19. Son of Alfred and Sarah Chattaway, of Gosford Street, Coventry. Born 26th April, 1898 at 3, Bridge Cottages, Far Gosford Street, Coventry. Enlisted Coventry. Resided 21c. 3h. Gosford Street. Driller, Messrs Hollick and Pratt. Enlisted February, 1915. Grave Ref. V. D. 13. Brandhoek New Military Cemetery, Ieper, West-Vlaanderen, Belgium.

CHATTAWAY, Private, Louis. PLY/16262, 2nd R.M. Bn. R.N. Div., Royal Marine Light Infantry. 28th April, 1917. Age 21. Son of William and Harriet Chattaway, of 18, Raglan Street, Coventry. Memorial Ref. Bay 1. Arras Memorial, Pas de Calais, France.

CHATTAWAY, Phillip. Killed in action. Name on Roll of Honour in Cathedral Church of St. Michael. Possibly Second Lieutenant Phillip Spencer Chattaway. 6th Bn., Cheshire Regiment. Killed in action, 14th October, 1916. Age 20. Son of Frederick Daniel and Elizabeth Chattaway, of 151, Woodstock Road, Oxford. Scholar of Eton and Christ Church. Grave Ref. VIII. A. 7. Lonsdale Cemetery, Authuile, France.

CHATWIN, Lance Corporal, Alfred. 265148, "B" Coy. 2nd /7th Bn., Royal Warwickshire Regiment. Killed in action, Fromelles, 19th July, 1916. Age 20. Son of William and Caroline Chatwin, of 55, Leicester Street, Coventry. Born 22nd January, 1896 at 4c. 1h. Leicester Street. Resided at 55, Leicester Street. Enameller, Messrs Mills and Fulford. Enlisted, 1914. Memorial Ref. Panel 22 to 25. Loos Memorial, Pas de Calais, France.

CHECKLEY, Private Arthur. 266693, 11th Bn., Royal Warwickshire Regiment. Killed in action, near Arras, 23rd April, 1917. Born 6th June, 1884, at 63, Edgwick Road. Resided at 63, Edgwick Road, Foleshill, Coventry. Enlisted December, 1914. Bricklayer. Commemorated War Memorial Park. Memorial Ref. Arras Memorial. Pas de Calais, France.

CHECKLING, Private, Sidney. 60452, 13th Bn., Devonshire Regiment. transf. to (145041), Labour Corps, Died of phthisis, 31st March, 1919. Age 35. Husband of Harriett E. Hill (formerly Checkling), of Back 23, Weston Street, Coventry. Born at Coventry. Grave Ref. Screen Wall. C. 1. "C." 174. Birmingham (Brandwood End) Cemetery.

CHEESMAN, Sergeant, Howard George. 10441, 2nd Bn., South Wales Borderers. Killed in action, 28th June, 1915. Age 25. B Son of Mr. and Mrs. A. Cheesman, of 38, Gordon Road, Gillingham, Kent. Born Bearstead, Kent. Enlisted Chatham. Billeted Coventry. Memorial Ref. Panel 80 to 84 or 219 and 220. Helles Memorial, Turkey.

CHESHIRE, Second Lieutenant, Raymond Russell. 1st /8th Bn., Royal Warwickshire Regiment. Killed in action, St. Julien, 4th October, 1917. Age 19. Second son of William Woodward Cheshire (retired schoolmaster) and Emma Mary Cheshire, of "Rayleigh." 96, Earlsdon Avenue, Coventry. . Born 6th April 1898, at Handsworth, Birmingham. Resided at Coventry. Enlisted 1916 in the Birmingham O.T.C. Auctioneer's Articled pupil. Educated Commercial School and King Edward High School, Birmingham. Commemorated War Memorial Park. Memorial Ref. Panel 23 to 28 and 163A. Tyne Cot Memorial, Zonnebeke, West-Vlaanderen, Belgium.

CHESTER, W.L. Post Office

CHINN, Private, F. E. DM2/137771, 626th M.T. Coy., Royal Army Service Corps. Died of influenza, 6th December, 1918. Age 22. Son of Mr. F. and Mrs. A. Chinn, of 8, Adkins Square, Walsgrave Road, Coventry. Employed Coventry. Grave Ref. VII. F. 9. Dar Es Salaam (Upanga Road) Cemetery, Tanzania.

CHISHOLM, Private, John Robert. 9733, 2nd Bn., Royal Welsh Fusiliers. Killed in action, during a bombardment, 2nd January, 1916 whilst attending a wounded comrade. Age 25. Son of Mrs. S. A. Wilkins, of 6, Bramble Street, Coventry. Born 26th November, 1890 at 128, Far Gosford Street. Resided at 40, Godiva Street. Printer, British Photo Engraving Co. Ltd. Grave Ref. J. 41. Cambrin Churchyard Extension, Pas de Calais, France.

CHITTEM, Private, John Thomas. 15001, 3rd Bn., Worcestershire Regiment. Killed in action, 6th October, 1916. Age 26. Son of John Chittem. Husband of Elizabeth Chittem, of 68, Parliamentary Road, Glasgow. Born 9th July, 1889 at Coventry. Resided at 30c. 7h. Gosford Street. Cycle Finisher. Enlisted 1914, Coventry. Grave Ref. B. 6. Grandcourt Road Cemetery, Grandcourt, France.

CHITTEM, Private, William. 19760, 9th Bn., Royal Warwickshire Regiment. Died, Mesopotamia 21st September, 1918. Age 38. Husband of M. J. Chittem. of 52. Hill Street, Coventry. Born Coventry. Enlisted Coventry. Employed Coventry Gear Case Ltd. Memorial Ref. Panel 2. Column 2. Tehran Memorial, Iran.

CHRISTIE, Gunner, Hugh. 107646, 409th Siege Battery, Royal Garrison Artillery. Killed in action, 17th September, 1917. Born at Linlithgow. Resided Coventry. Grave Ref. IX. G. 13. Vlamertinghe New Military Cemetery, Belgium.

CLAES, Soldier, Jules Cesar. Belgian Army. Died, 9th November 1918. Grave Ref. Grave 177.168. Coventry (London Road) Cemetery.

CLAPP, Private, James. 4443, 10th Bn., Royal Warwickshire Regiment. Killed in action, 26th September, 1918. Born 26th March, 1897 at 356, Radford Road. Enlisted Nuneaton. Resided 356, Radford Road, Coventry. Fitter. Enlisted September, 1914. Commemorated Radford Memorial. Grave Ref. V. A. 11. Guards Cemetery, Windy Corner, Cuinchy, France.

CLARK, B. Employed by Rover Company Ltd. Killed in action.

CLARK, Private, Joseph. 131643, 34th Bn., Machine Gun Corps (Infantry) formerly 40027, Somerset Light Infantry. Died, 18th October, 1918. Age 19. Son of Robert Clark, of Atherstone. Born Atherstone. Enlisted Coventry. Resided Atherstone. Grave Ref. Sp. Mem. Terlincthun British Cemetery, Wimille, France.

CLARK, Private, Joseph. L/7939, 1st Bn., The Queen's (Royal West Surrey Regiment). Killed in action, 31st October, 1914. Born Southwark, Surrey. Enlisted Guildford, Surrey. Resided Coventry. Grave Ref. XX. F. 18. Hooge Crater Cemetery, Belgium.

CLARKE, Lance Sergeant, Alfred Henry. 6253, 1st Bn., Royal Welsh Fusiliers. Killed in action, 30th October, 1914. Age 32. Son of John and Elizabeth Clarke, of Wolston, Warwickshire. Husband of Florence Mabel Elizabeth Spink (formerly Clarke), of 30, Ford Street, Coventry. Employed Messrs Courtaulds Ltd. Leaves a widow and two children. Memorial Ref. Panel 22. Ypres (Menin Gate) Memorial, Ieper, West-Vlaanderen, Belgium.

CLARKE, Private, Albert William. 52283, 2nd Bn., Worcestershire Regiment. Killed in action, 4th July, 1918. Age 19. Son of Albert John and Sarah Alice Clarke, of "The Beeches," Lichfield Road, Four Oaks, Sutton Coldfield, Birmingham. Born Allesley, Coventry. Born Coventry. Enlisted Birmingham. Resided Sutton Coldfield Grave Ref. XI. F. 5. Nine Elms British Cemetery, Poperinge, West-Vlaanderen, Belgium.

CLARKE, Private, Arthur. 36597, 11th Bn., Northumberland Fusiliers. Killed in action, 15th June, 1918. Age 27. Son of Henry and Eliza Clarke, of 13, Waterloo Street, Coventry. Grave Ref. Plot 2. Row E. Grave 5. Magnaboschi British Cemetery, Italy.

CLARKE, Private, Cecil Leonard. 63291, 183 Coy., No. 2. Section, Machine Gun Corps (Infantry) formerly 20969, Royal Warwickshire Regiment. Killed in action, 10th December, 1917. Missing since 3rd December, 1917. Resided 21, Rudge Road, Coventry. Employed Dunlop Works. Born Clarendon. Enlisted Coventry. Commemorated Wesleyan Church and Dunlop Memorial. Memorial Ref. Pier and Face 5C and 12. Thiepval Memorial, Somme, France.

CLARKE, Private, David. 23555, 1st Bn., Coldstream Guards formerly 2942, Household Bn. 16th October, 1918. Age 32. Son of David and Mary Ann Millar Clarke of Coventry, Husband of Eleanor Vosper (formerly Clarke), of 38, Gresham Street, Coventry. Born 23rd January, 1886 at 5, Leicester Street. Resided at 18, Clement Street. Enlisted May 1917, Coventry. Plumber. Commemorated War Memorial Park and Siddeley Deasy Roll of Honour. Grave Ref. III. C. 19. Romeries Communal Cemetery Extension, Nord, France.

CLARKE, Sergeant, Edward, MM. 8533, 33rd Trench Mortar Battery, 7th Bn., Border Regiment. Killed in action, by machine gun fire, 26th August, 1918. Resided Ryton-on-Dunsmore. Awarded Military Medal, 1918; During an attack Sergeant Clarke by his coolness and utter disregard of personal danger, was instrumental in ensuring the working of four guns engaged in barrage fire. Though under heavy fire the whole time, he walked from one gun position to another, supervising and cheering on the teams and setting a fine example of courage and coolness to all. Sergeant Clarke had only been in the reserve nine months when war broke out. Employed Messrs Mills and Fulford, Stoney Stanton Road, Coventry. Commemorated Ryton Memorial. Born at Ryton-on-Dunsmore. Resided at 23, Eagle Street. Reservist. Enlisted Coventry. Grave Ref. I. VH. 29. Warlencourt British Cemetery, France.

CLARKE, Private, Frank. 12740, 1st Bn., Worcestershire Regiment. Killed in action, 9th January, 1915. Age 23. Second son of Walter and Sarah Clarke, of 19, Smith Street, Coventry previously of Dyer Arms, Spon End. Born Coventry. Enlisted Coventry. Memorial Ref. Panel 17 and 18. Le Touret Memorial, Pas de Calais, France.

CLARKE, Private, George. 178026, Machine Gun Corps (Infantry). Died, Home, 29th October, 1918. Age 30. Son of Charles and Elizabeth Rachel Clarke. Husband of Rose Clara Clarke, of Norton, Daventry, Northants. Born Ashton, Northants. Enlisted Coventry. Resided Weedon, Northants. Grave Ref. Right of Main Path. Norton (All Saints) Churchyard.

CLARKE, Gunner, Harry. 297176, 109th Heavy Bty., Royal Garrison Artillery formerly 8915, 156th Oxford Heavy Battery, Royal Garrison Artillery. Killed in action, 3rd June, 1917. Age 21. Son of Caroline and Harry Clarke, of 68, Adelaide Street, Coventry. Employed Godiva Cycle Co. Ltd. Commemorated Bablake School Memorial and Triumph & Gloria Memorial. Born Birmingham. Enlisted Coventry. Grave Ref. VII. E. 7. Vlamertinghe Military Cemetery, Ieper, West-Vlaanderen, Belgium.

CLARKE, Private, Henry. 16829, 14th Bn., Royal Warwickshire Regiment. Killed in action, 3rd September, 1916. Age 23. Son of James and Rebecca Clarke, of 42, Bright Street, Coventry. Born Coventry. Enlisted Coventry Grave Ref. 9. F. 42. London Cemetery and Extension, Longueval, Somme, France.

CLARKE, Private, Herbert. 29208, 119th Coy., Machine Gun Corps (Infantry) formerly 15650, Royal Warwickshire Regiment. Died of wounds, 19th July, 1917. Age 19. Son of James and Charlotte Clarke, of 604, Stoney Stanton Road, Coventry. Born Coventry. Enlisted Nuneaton. Resided Coventry. Grave Ref. I. C. 2. Rocquigny-Equancourt Road British Cemetery, Manancourt, Somme, France.

CLARKE, Private, Herbert. Royal Warwickshire Regiment. Died, home, 9th March, 1922. Bprn 4th April, 1880 in Riley Street. Resided back of 37, Castle Street. Polisher. Enlisted November, 1914. Grave Ref. Buried Coventry.

CLARKE, Private, Herbert Mark. 1319, 2nd Bn., Royal Warwickshire Regiment. Died of wounds to the thigh, whilst a prisoner of war, 26th October, 1914. Born St. Thomas, Coventry. Enlisted Coventry. Employed Coventry Repetition Co. Ltd previously employed Telegraph Messenger, Post Office. Resided 33, Monk's Road. Grave Ref. VIII. J. 35. Cabaret-Rouge British Cemetery, Souchez, France.

CLARKE, Private, John Alfred. 4648, 2/7th Bn., Royal Warwickshire Regiment. Killed in action, 19th July, 1916. Age 36. Husband of Edith Bessie Clarke. Employed Deasy Motor Works. Born Kenilworth. Enlisted Coventry. Commemorated War Memorial Park. Memorial Ref. Panel 22 to 25. Loos Memorial, France.

CLARKE, Private, James. 21516, 3rd Bn., Royal Warwickshire Regiment. Died, home, 6th March, 1917. Born Foleshill. Enlisted Warwick. Resided Exhall. Grave Ref. In North-West Part. Grave Ref. Exhall (St. Giles) Churchyard.

CLARKE, Private, John William. 7536, "D" Coy. 1st Bn., Royal Warwickshire Regiment. Killed in action, 25th April 1915. Husband of Alice A. Clarke, of 60, Mulliner Street, Coventry. Native of Leicester. Also served in India. Born Alford, Lincolnshire. Enlisted Warwick. Resided Coventry. Memorial Ref. Panel 8. Ypres (Menin Gate) Memorial, Ieper, West-Vlaanderen, Belgium.

CLARKE, Private, Joseph James. 19561, 1st Bn., Coldstream Guards. Killed in action, 22nd August, 1918. Age 20. Son of Mrs. Esther Clarke, of Priory Row, Wolston, Coventry. Commemorated Wolston Memorial. Memorial Ref. Panel 3. Vis-En-Artois Memorial, Pas de Calais, France.

CLARKE, Private, Leonard. 8193, 2nd Bn., Northamptonshire Regiment. Killed in action, 8th July, 1916. Age 32. Son of Benjamin Clarke, of 63, Tyrrell Street, Leicester. Born Coventry. Enlisted Warwick. Memorial Ref. Pier and Face 11 A and 11 D. Thiepval Memorial, France.

CLARKE, Private, Leonard Crick. 43861, 8th Bn., King's Own Yorkshire Light Infantry formerly 164044, Royal Horse and Royal Field Artillery. Killed in action, 27th May, 1917. Age 36. Son of Jacob and Charlotte Clarke. Husband of Harriet Lillian Clarke, of 102, Purser Road, Northampton. Born St. Giles, Northampton. Enlisted Coventry. Grave Ref. Sp. Mem. 22. Railway Dugouts Burial Ground, Belgium.

CLARKE, Lance Corporal, Levi. 10552, 3rd Bn., Coldstream Guards. Killed in action, 15th September, 1916. Born Swanwell, Bucks. Enlisted Coventry. Grave Ref. XIII. M. 10. Guards' Cemetery, Lesboeufs, France.

CLARKE, Private, Percy. 17907, 14th Bn., Royal Warwickshire Regiment. Killed in action, 10th June, 1917. Born Coventry. Enlisted Coventry. Husband of Mrs. P. Clarke, 16c. 2h. Much Park Street. Employed Smiths Stamping Works. Grave Ref. VIII. G. 39. Orchard Dump Cemetery, Arleux-En-Gohelle, France.

CLARKE, P. Commemorated Triumph and Gloria Memorial.

CLARKE, Private, Reginald John James. L/14992, 2nd Bn., Royal Fusiliers. Killed in action, Gallipoli, 25th April, 1915. Age 25. Nephew of Bessie Henly, of 10, Heath Road, Harrow, Middx. Born Coventry. Enlisted London. Resided Hounslow. Memorial Ref. Panel 37 to 41 or 328. Helles Memorial, Turkey.

CLARKE, Private, Thomas. 10474, 3rd Bn., Coldstream Guards. Died of wounds, 11th July, 1917. Age 23. Son of William and Maria Clarke. Native of Little Eaton, nr. Derby. Born Little Eaton, Derby. Enlisted Coventry. Resided Little Eaton, Derby. Grave Ref. XXII. M. 15. Etaples Military Cemetery, France.

CLARKE, Lance Corporal, Victor Leslie. 266061, 2nd/7th Bn., Royal Warwickshire Regiment. attd. 182nd Trench Mortar Bty. Died of wounds, 3rd July 1918 received 26th June, 1918. Age 24. Youngest son of John and Mary Jane Clarke, of 66, Villa Terrace, Radford, nr. Coventry. Born 7th April 1894, at 64a, Radford. Resided at 66, Villa Terrace, Radford. Enlisted November, 1914. Assembler, British Thompson Houston Works, Lower Ford Street. Commemorated Bablake School Memorial and War Memorial Park. Grave Ref. III. G. 15. Aire Communal Cemetery, Pas de Calais, France.

CLARKE, Private, William Tutton. 10243, 2nd Bn., South Wales Borderers. Killed in action, 8th May 1915. Age 24. Son of George Clarke, of 39, Lyne Road, Newport, Mon. Husband of Minnie Clarke, of 9, South Street, Coventry. Memorial Ref. Panel 80 to 84 or 219 and 220. Helles Memorial, Turkey.

CLEAVER, Private, Albert Ernest. 18877, 15th Bn., Royal Warwickshire Regiment. Killed in action, 26th October, 1917. Age 19. Son of Fredrick Charles and Annie Cleaver, of 40, Kingfields, Coventry. Born Coventry. Enlisted Coventry. Memorial Ref Panel 23 to 28 and 163A. Tyne Cot Memorial, Zonnebeke, West-Vlaanderen, Belgium

CLEAVER, Private, James. 445873, 8th Bn., Royal Berkshire Regiment. Killed in action, 23rd October, 1918. Born Congerstone, Leicestershire. Enlisted Leamington. Resided Coventry. Grave Ref. V. F. 15. Le Cateau Military Cemetery, France.

CLEAVER, Private, Joseph Turton. 4302, 1st/7th Bn., Royal Warwickshire Regiment. Killed in action, 1st July, 1916. Age 31. Son of Samuel and Ellen Cleaver, of 7, Providence Place, Much Park Street, Coventry. Employed Calcott's as a charge hand. Enlisted Coventry. Memorial Ref. Pier and Face 9 A 9 B and 10 B. Thiepval Memorial, Somme, France.

CLEAVER, Private, Walter Thomas. 36674, 8th Bn., Gloucestershire Regiment formerly 19161, Royal Warwickshire Regiment. Died, 30th May, 1918. Age 22. Son of James and Elizabeth Cleaver, of Shilton, Coventry. Born Yelvertoft, Warwicks. Enlisted Nuneaton. Resided Shilton. Memorial Ref. Soissons Memorial, Aisne, France.

CLEGG, Private, William, 7854, 1st Bn., Duke of Cornwall's Light Infantry. Killed in action, 21st October, 1914. Age 31. Son of G. W. and L. Clegg, of Coventry. Husband of Annie J. Clegg, of Connor Downs, Hayle, Cornwall. Born Gwithian, Hayle, Cornwall. Enlisted Phillack, Hayle. Resided Coventry. Memorial Ref. Panel 19. Le Touret Memorial, Pas de Calais, France.

CLEMENTS, Private, George. 22421, 14th Bn., Royal Warwickshire Regiment. Killed in action, 27th June, 1917. Born Coventry. Enlisted Coventry. Husband of Mrs. E. Clements, 40, Howard Street, Coventry. Employed Ordnance Works. Leaves a widow and two children. Grave Ref. IX. A. 44. Orchard Dump Cemetery, Arleux-En-Gohelle, France.

CLEMENTS, Private, Herbert William. M2/097969, No. 1 G. H. Q., Reserve M.T. Coy., Army Service Corps. Died of wounds, 9th October, 1918. Born Witney, Oxon. Enlisted Coventry. Resided Witney. Grave Ref. VII. E. 12. Tincourt New British Cemetery, France.

CLEVERLEY, Private, Harvey. 912, 1st Bn., Seaforth Highlanders. Died of wounds, 24th May 1915 in hospital at Bristol. Previously bayoneted through the arm and shoulder in the Battle of Neuve Chapelle. Age 25. (Served as Cox). Son of J. and Ann Cleverley. Born at Coventry. Grave Ref. Screen Wall. 3. 665. Bristol (Arnos Vale) Cemetery, Gloucestershire.

CLEVERLEY, Private, William Harvey Thomas. 3913, 2nd Bn., Royal Warwickshire Regiment. Killed in action, 12th March, 1915. Son of J. and Ann Cleverley. Born Coventry. Enlisted Birmingham. Memorial Ref. Panel 6. Le Touret Memorial, France.

CLEWS, Private, Arthur Ernest. 24570, 2nd /7th Bn., Royal Warwickshire Regiment. Died of wounds, 20th May 1918 at the 2/1 Midland Field Ambulance Station. Age 18. Son of George and Mary Ann Clews, of Coventry. Born Coventry. Enlisted Coventry. Commemorated St. John's Church. Employed Daimler Foundry. Resided with sister, Mrs. F. Mills, 5 Summer Row, Spon Street. Grave Ref. III. B. 18. St. Venant-Robecq Road British Cemetery, Robecq, Pas de Calais, France.

CLEWS, Private, Frank. 22503, 1st Bn., Duke of Cornwall's Light Infantry. Killed in action, 23rd July, 1916. Age 24. Son of Mrs. Louisa Clews, of 29, Lower Nelson Street, Coventry formerly resided Spon End. Employed Singer. Enlisted 21st June, 1915 at Coventry. Born St. John, Coventry. Grave Ref. XXXI. G. 6. Delville Wood Cemetery, Longueval, Somme, France.

CLEWS, Private, John. 44004, 9th Bn., King's Own Yorkshire Light Infantry formerly 164645 Royal Horse Artillery & Royal Field Artillery. Killed in action, Arras, 9th April, 1917. Age 30. Son of John and Ann Clews, of Chapel End, Atherstone. Husband of Hannah Clews, of 199, Heath End, Chilvers Coton, Nuneaton. Born 30th June, 1887, at Stockingford. Resided in Lewis Road, Foleshill. Enlisted October, 1916 at Coventry. Insurance Agent. Commemorated War Memorial Park. Grave Ref. D. 16. Cojeul British Cemetery, St. Martin-Sur-Cojeul near Arras, France.

CLEWS, Private, Leonard. 265907, 1st /7th Bn., Royal Warwickshire Regiment. Killed in action, 11th August, 1917. Age 21. Son of Charles and Alice Clews, of 155, North Street, Upper Stoke, Coventry. Born Coventry. Enlisted Coventry. Memorial Ref. Panel 8. Ypres (Menin Gate) Memorial, Ieper, West-Vlaanderen, Belgium.

CLIFFORD, Corporal, Albert Henry. 14742, B Coy., 6th Platoon, 8th Bn., Royal Berkshire Regiment. Killed in action, 13th October, 1915. Age 30. Son of Mrs. Ellen Clifford, of 27, Church Road, Rainbow Hill, Worcester. Husband of Margaret Clifford, of 82, Nicholls Street, Hillfields, Coventry. Enlisted September, 1914 at Coventry. Born Broad Heath, Worcs. Employed Phoenix Foundry, Godiva Street, Coventry. Memorial Ref. Panel 93 to 95. Loos Memorial, Pas de Calais, France.

CLIFFORD, Private, George. 4714, 10th Bn., Royal Warwickshire Regiment. Killed in action, 27th February, 1916 reported to have been shot whilst trying to fire at a German sniper over the parapet. Born St. Mark's, Coventry. Enlisted Warwick, August, 1914. Resided 8, Rood Lane, Coventry. Grave Ref. I. F. 10. Rue-Du-Bacquerot No.1 Military Cemetery, Laventie, France.

CLIFFORD, Private, John Robert. 28601, 15th Bn., Royal Warwickshire Regiment. Killed in action, 26th August, 1918. Age 27. Son of John and M. Clifford, of Beeston, Notts. Husband of Phaebe Elizabeth Magdalen Clifford, of Coventry. Enlisted Coventry. Born Beeston. Memorial Ref. Panel 3. Vis-En-Artois Memorial, Pas de Calais, France.

CLIFFORD, Lance Corporal, John William. 16619, 5th Bn., Oxfordshire and Buckinghamshire Light Infantry. Killed in action, 3rd May, 1917. Enlisted Coventry. Memorial Ref. Bay 6 and 7. Arras Memorial, France

CLIFFT, Sapper, Harold. 32441, 2nd Field Squadron, Royal Engineers. Killed in action, 23rd March, 1918. Enlisted Coventry. Resided Kenilworth. Grave Ref. III. J. 2. Grand-Seraucourt British Cemetery, France.

COATES, Private, Frank. 33160, 6th Bn., Oxfordshire and Buckinghamshire Light Infantry formerly 19580, Royal Warwickshire Regiment. Killed in action, 20th September, 1917. Age 19. Son of Augustus and Charlotte Coates, of 198, Broad Street, Foleshill, Coventry. Born Coventry. Enlisted Coventry. Memorial Ref. Panel 96 to 98. Tyne Cot Memorial, Zonnebeke, West-Vlaanderen, Belgium.

COATES, Private Frederick Arthur. 36338, 2nd Bn., Wiltshire Regiment. Killed in action, 1st June, 1918. Born Coventry. Enlisted Birmingham. Resided Birmingham. Grave Ref. I. B. 5. Chambrecy British Cemetery, France.

COATES, Private, R. 201798, 5th Bn., Royal Warwickshire Regiment. Died 29th January, 1919. Grave Ref. 136. 142. Coventry (London Road) Cemetery.

COCKER, Corporal, Henry. 206109, 10 Coy., D Bn., Machine Gun Corps (Heavy Battery). Killed in action, 10th April, 1917. Enlisted Coventry. Memorial Ref. Beaurains Road Cem. No. 2 Mem., Panel 5. London Cemetery, Neuville-Vitasse, France.

COCKERELL, Second Lieutenant, Donal Chessum. A Coy., 5th Bn., London Regiment. Killed in action, 6th November, 1918. Age 22. Son of Charles of Harrington's Mineral Water Company Ltd. and Edith Mary Cockerell of Roseneath, Burges Road, Thorpe Bay, Essex. Native of Southend on Sea. Commemorated Iliffe & Sons Ltd Memorial. Grave Ref. I. A. 9. Angreau Communal Cemetery, Belgium.

COCKERILL, Private, George. 4581, 1st Bn., Royal Warwickshire Regiment. Killed in action, 7th July, 1915. Enlisted Coventry. Resided Loughborough. Memorial Ref. Panel 8. Ypres (Menin Gate) Memorial, Belgium.

COGGINS, Private, Charles Edward. 265082, 2nd Bn., Royal Warwickshire Regiment. Killed in action, 26th October, 1917. Age 27. Husband of Lucy M. G. Coggins, of 207, Henley Road, Bell Green, Foleshill, Coventry. Commemorated Walsgrave-on- Sowe Memorial. Born Warmington. Enlisted Coventry. Memorial Ref. Panel 23 to 28 and 163A. Tyne Cot Memorial, Zonnebeke, West-Vlaanderen, Belgium.

COLE, Private, Ambrose. 310082, Warwickshire Yeomanry. Died, Egypt, 27th May, 1918. Drowned at sea, on board, Leasowe Castle. Born St. Michaels, Coventry. Enlisted Warwick. Resided Coventry. Educated Bablake School. Commemorated Bablake School Memorial. Memorial Ref. Chatby Memorial.

COLE, Private, Edward David. 265550, 2/7th Bn., Royal Warwickshire Regiment. Killed in action, 5th December, 1917. Born Rowley's Green, Coventry. Enlisted Coventry. Memorial Ref. Panel 3. Cambrai Memorial, Louverval, France.

COLE, Private, Frank. 81683, 5th Bn., Machine Gun Corps (Infantry) formerly 21514, Royal Warwickshire Regiment. Killed in action, 21st August, 1918. Enlisted Coventry. Age 26. Son of Francis and Louisa Cole, of Great Everdon, Daventry, Northants. Grave Ref. IV. F. 12. Queens Cemetery, Bucquoy, France.

COLEMAN, Lance Corporal, George Betram. 11059, 11th Bn., Royal Warwickshire Regiment. Killed in action by a sniper, 10th April, 1917. Age 23. Son of Mrs. Sarah Coles, of Rookery Cottage, Church Lawford, Rugby. Employed by Mr. C. Whiteman, Raglan Street, Coventry formerly Lord Craven's Estate. Born Priors Hardwick. Enlisted Coventry. Resided Old Lodge Farm, Binley. Memorial Ref. Bay 3. Arras Memorial, France.

COLEMAN, Private, James. 3808, 11th Bn., Royal Warwickshire Regiment. Died, 9th April, 1916. Age 34. Born Longton, Staffs. Son of John Coleman, of Longton, Staffs. Enlisted Coventry. Grave Ref. St. Joseph's. Q. IOA. Sheffield (St. Michael's) Roman Catholic Cemetery.

COLEMAN, Private, James Stephen. G/62997, 13th Bn., Royal Fusiliers formerly 192912, Army Service Corps. Killed in action, 4th October, 1917. Age 20. Son of James and Frances Coleman, of 19, Ludgate Street, The Leys, Tamworth, Staffs. Born Tamworth. Enlisted Coventry. Resided Coventry. Grave Ref. VI. A. 4. Hooge Crater Cemetery, Belgium.

COLEMAN, Private, Thomas. 26822, 12th Bn., Duke of Cornwall's Light Infantry formerly 20466, Royal Berkshire. Died, 4th October, 1916. Son of John Hillary and Emma Coleman. Native of Leamington Spa, Born Leamington. Enlisted Coventry. Grave Ref. II. F. 30. La Neuville British Cemetery, Corbie, France.

COLES, Private, James. 11653, 9th Bn., Royal Warwickshire Regiment. Died, 23rd May, 1916. Age 24. Husband of Amy Ash (formerly Coles), of Exhall Green, Exhall, Coventry. Born Blana, Mon. Enlisted Nuneaton. Commemorated Saint Thomas the Apostle, Longford. Memorial Ref. Panel 9. Basra Memorial, Iraq.

COLES, Private, Harry. 7754, 2/5th Bn., Norfolk Regiment attached 189383, 242nd Employment Coy., Labour Corps formerly 4230, Royal Warwickshire Regiment. Died of wounds, 29th September, 1917. Enlisted Coventry. Father of William H. Coles, of 18, Bedford Road, Rushden, Northants. Grave Ref. I. C. 51. Duhallow A.D.S. Cemetery, Belgium.

COLLACOTT, Thomas. Commemorated Queens Road Memorial.

COLLEDGE, Petty Officer, William Edward. HMS Pembroke. Died, home, 13th February, 1922. Born 7th August, 1884 at Pailton near Rugby. Resided at 97, Dorset Road. Body Maker. Enlisted October, 1914. Grave Ref. Radford Cemetery.

COLLEGE, Private, Archer. 24649, 2/8th Bn., Royal Warwickshire Regiment. Killed in action, 3rd September, 1917. Age 29. Son of Thomas College. Husband of Susan Eliza College, of Church Lawford, Rugby. Born Brinklow. Enlisted Coventry. Memorial Ref. Panel 23 to 28 and 163A. Tyne Cot Memorial, Belgium.

COLLETT, Private, Christopher William. 9673, 9th Bn., Royal Warwickshire Regiment. Died, Mesopotamia, 15th May, 1918. Age 21. Son of Christopher and Rachel Collett, of 36, Fair Green, Diss, Norfolk. Born Diss, Norfolk. Enlisted Coventry. Resided Diss. Grave Ref. XVI. L. 7. Baghdad (North Gate) War Cemetery, Iraq.

COLLETT, Private, Joseph. 26885, 10th Bn., Duke of Cornwall's Light Infantry formerly 20636, Royal Berkshire Regiment. Killed in action, 25th March, 1918. Born Coventry. Enlisted Coventry. Memorial Ref. Bay 6. Arras Memorial, France.

COLLETT, Private, Percy James. 10677, "A" Coy., 2nd Bn., South Wales Borderers. Died of wounds, 6th May, 1918. Age 27. Foster son of Mrs. E. Harris, of 26, Sparkbrook Street, Coventry. Born Marleybone, London. Enlisted Stratford. Grave Ref. I. B. 5. Berlin South-Western Cemetery, Berlin, Brandenburg, Germany.

COLLETT, Private, Sydney. 18137, Royal Warwickshire Regiment. Died, 28th January, 1917. Age 20. Son of Mr. S. and Mrs. C. Collett, of Block 2, Cook Street, Coventry. Born Coventry. Enlisted Warwick. Resided Coventry. Grave Ref. 180. 149. Coventry (London Road) Cemetery.

COLLIER, Gunner, Bernard. 177209, 156th Siege Bty., Royal Garrison Artillery. 23rd January, 1919. Age 27. Husband of Sarah Ann Duggan (formerly Collier), of 50, Oliver Street, Coventry. Grave Ref. 957. Ashby-De-La-Zouch Cemetery, Leicestershire.

COLLINGBOURNE, Gunner, Herbert Charles. 360, 1st (Warwick) Bty., Royal Horse Artillery. Died of wounds, St. Omer Hospital, 4th January, 1916 from injures caused by the bursting of a high explosive shell. Age 23. Son of David Charles and Sarah Jane Collingbourne, of 52, St. Nicholas Street, Coventry. Born 9th May, 1892 at 6, Colchester Street. Resided at 41 King Edward Road. Enlisted Leamington, 1914. Telegraphist and sorter, Post Office. Commemorated Post Office Memorial, Bablake School Memorial and War Memorial Park. Grave Ref. II. B. 7. Longuenesse (st. Omer) Souvenir Cemetery, Pas de Calais, France.

COLLINS, Corporal, Alfred. 203973, 2/4th Bn., Oxfordshire and Buckinghamshire Light Infantry. Killed in action, 22nd August, 1917. Born Berkswell. Enlisted Coventry. Resided Berkswell. Memorial Ref. Panel 96 to 98. Tyne Cot Memorial, Belgium.

COLLINS, Private, Arthur Ernest. 22935, 1st Bn., Northamptonshire Regiment. Died of wounds, 22nd November, 1917. Age 23. Son of Alfred and Mary Ann Collins, of Hannington, Northampton. Enlisted Coventry. Grave Ref. VI. H. 21. Wimereux Communal Cemetery, France.

COLLINS, Private, Frederick. 15797, 2nd Bn., Royal Warwickshire Regiment. Killed in action, 1st October, 1917. Age 31. Son of Mrs. Ellen Elizabeth Allibon, of 1/24, Le Corte Street, Coventry. Born Foleshill. Enlisted Coventry. Memorial Ref. Panel 23 to 28 and 163A. Tyne Cot Memorial, Zonnebeke, West-Vlaanderen, Belgium.

COLLINS, Private, Joseph. 159355, 56th Bn., Machine Gun Corps (Infantry) formerly 34973, Royal Berkshire Regiment. Died of wounds, 18th September, 1918. Born Bloxham, Oxon. Enlisted Coventry. Grave Ref. IV. B. 41. Aubigny Communal Cemetery Extension, France.

COLLYER, Sapper, J. P. 541814, Canadian Engineers. Died, home, 15th December, 1916. Commemorated St. John's Church. Grave Ref. 74. 52. Coventry (London Road) Cemetery.

COLPMAN, Private, Frank. 42540, 2nd Bn., Worcestershire Regiment formerly 20896, Oxfordshire and Buckinghamshire Light Infantry. Killed in action, 21st May, 1917. Born Coventry. Enlisted Coventry. Memorial Ref. Bay 6. Arras Memorial, France.

COLSTON, Private, Ernest James. G/18188, 7th Bn., Queen's Own (Royal West Kent Regiment) formerly PS/11558, Royal Fusiliers. Killed in action, 29th September, 1916. Age 25. Son of James Ellington Colston, of 204, Longford Road, Longford, Coventry. Husband of Emily Louisa Colston, of 4, Canonsleigh Crescent, Leigh-on-Sea, Essex. Born London, Middx. Enlisted Coventry. Resided Coventry. Commemorated Saint Thomas the Apostle, Longford. Memorial Ref. Pier and Face 11 C. Thiepval Memorial, Somme, France.

COLTMAN, Private, Arthur Albert George. 43233, 1st Bn., Royal Berkshire Regiment. Killed in action, 29th September, 1918. Age 24. Son of Mr. and Mrs. A. E. Coltman, of 62, Queen Victoria Road, Coventry. Husband of Florence May Coltman, of 120, George Street, Coventry. Born Coventry. Enlisted Leamington. Resided Coventry. Grave Ref. II. C. 2. Flesquieres Hill British Cemetery, Nord, France.

COLVER, Private, Frank. 10131, 1st Bn., Sherwood Foresters (Notts and Derby Regiment). Killed in action, 4th March, 1917. Age 29. Son of Thomas and Emma Colver. Born Wigston, Leicestershire. Enlisted Derby. Resided Coventry. Memorial Ref. Pier and Face 10C 10D and 11A. Thiepval Memorial, France.

COLVILLE, Rifleman, Samuel. 49330, 1st Bn., Rifle Brigade formerly 22354, 3rd Bn., Royal Irish Rifles. Killed in action, 20th October, 1918. Born Belfast. Enlisted Belfast. Resided Coventry. Grave Ref. A. 3. Haspres Coppice Cemetery, Haspres, France.

COMPTON, Lance Corporal, James Henry. 33629, 8th Bn., Gloucestershire Regiment. Died of wounds, 29th March, 1918. Age 28. Husband of G. M. Compton, of 202, Melbourne Road, Coventry. Born Coventry. Enlisted Coventry. Leaves a wife and one child. Employed Messrs. Curtis and Beamish. Grave Ref. II. C. 27. Abbeville Communal Cemetery Extension, Somme, France.

CONNOLLY, Private, James. 49350, 20th Bn., Royal Fusiliers formerly PS/8468, Royal Fusiliers. Died, Home 7th May, 1917. Age 19. Son of Michael and Helen Connolly, of 13, Carmelite Road, Coventry. Born Haywood, Lancashire. Enlisted Coventry. Resided Coventry. Educated Bablake School. Commemorated Bablake School Memorial. Grave Ref. 212. 20. Coventry (London Road) Cemetery.

CONWAY, Private, Wilfred Bernard. 25070, 2/5th Bn., West Riding Regiment. Killed in action, 20th October, 1918. Commemorated Wolston Memorial. Enlisted Rugby. Born Tatchbrook, Warwicks. Grave Ref. C. 54. Quievy Communal Cemetery Extension, France.

COOK, Lieutenant, B. E. Royal Engineers. Died of pneumonia contracted on active service, 7th November, 1918. Age 23. Son of William H. B. and Lillian Ethel Cook, of Brentwood, Stoke Green, Coventry. Husband of Maude Ritch Cook, of "Bengal," Bath Road, Devizes. Born at Higher Broughton, Manchester. Grave Ref. S. 3. Devizes Cemetery, Wiltshire.

COOK, Private, Ernest Charles. 2847, A Coy., 1/7th Bn., Royal Warwickshire Regiment. Killed in action, 16th October, 1915. Born Moreton-in-the-Marsh, Glos. Enlisted Coventry. Grave Ref. I. D. 40. Foncquevillers Military Cemetery, France.

COOK, Gravenall. Commemorated Holy Trinity Panels.

COOK, Private, Thomas Alfred. 70756, 4th Section, 10th Coy., Machine Gun Corps (Infantry) formerly 2321, Royal Warwickshire Regiment. Killed in action, 12th April, 1917. Age 24. Son of Thomas and Alice Cook. Brother of Miss. A. Cook, 24, Sparkbrook Street, Coventry. Born Kensington. Enlisted Warwick. Resided Evesham. Formerly resided Kenilworth. Memorial Ref. Sp. Mem. B6. Point-Du-Jour Military Cemetery, Athies, France.

COOKE, Bombardier, Arthur Gilbert. 135535, D Bty., 122 Bde., Royal Field Artillery. Killed in action, 18th November, 1914. Age 27. Son of Frank and Alice Cooke, of Halifax. Husband of Elsie M. Cooke, of Halifax, Yorks. Born Halifax, Yorks. Enlisted Coventry. Grave Ref. II. L. 7. Poperinghe New Military Cemetery, Belgium.

COOKE, Private, Herbert. 1st Bn., Royal Welsh Fusiliers formerly 6th Bn., Royal Warwickshire Regiment. Killed in action, 21st October, 1914. Enlisted 1904.

COOKE, Sergeant, Irvine. 265430, A Coy., 1/7th Bn., Royal Warwickshire Regiment formerly 1860, Mon, Regiment. Killed in action, 4th October, 1917. Age 24. Commemorated Iliffe & Sons Ltd Memorial. Son of Alfred and Florence R. K. Cooke, of 13, Prince Street, Queen's Square, Bristol. Born Bristol. Enlisted Newport. Resided Bristol. Grave Ref. X. D. 19. Cement House Cemetery, Belgium.

COOKE, Private, John. 15355, 4th Bn., Worcestershire Regiment. Killed in action, Gallipoli, 12th May, 1915. Age 35. Son of Mr. and Mrs. J. Cooke of 54, Villa Lane, Radford. Born Radford, Coventry. Employed Rover Co. Ltd. Commemorated Radford Memorial. Enlisted 1st September, 1914. Memorial Ref. Panel 104 to 113. Helles Memorial, Turkey

COOKE, Corporal, Percy. 14526, 7th Bn., Leicestershire Regiment. Killed in action, 8th October, 1918. Born Coventry. Enlisted Leicester. Memorial Ref. Panel 5. Vis-En-Artois Memorial, France.

COOKE, Lance Corporal, Stanley Waterton. 9674, 9th Bn., Royal Warwickshire Regiment. Died, Mesopotamia, 28th November, 1915. Born Meriden. Enlisted Coventry. Resided Meriden. Commemorated St. Thomas Memorial. Memorial Ref. Panel 9. Basra Memorial, Iraq.

COOKE, S. Commemorated Coventry Chain Memorial.

COOKE, Private, William Fredrick. 2469, "A" Coy., 1st /7th Bn., Royal Warwickshire Regiment. Died of wounds, 17th March 1916 just after midnight after being struck by fragments from a rifle grenade. Age 21. Son of Thomas William and Eleanor Eliza Cooke, of 13, Lord Street, Chapelfields, Coventry. Born October 1894, at St. Stevens, Hounslow. Resided at 13, Lord Street. Enlisted August 1914 at Coventry. Apprentice (Engineering) to Coventry Chain Company. Commemorated Coventry Chain Memorial, Queen's Road Church and War Memorial Park. Grave Ref. I. D. 15. Foncquevillers Military Cemetery, Pas de Calais, France.

COOKE, Private, William Herbert. 6659, 1st/20th Bn., London Regiment formerly 4829 East Kent Regiment. Killed in action, 1st October, 1916. Born 4th February, 1886 at Bond Street. Resided at 42, Bond Street. Enlisted Coventry. Meter repairer. Commemorated St. John's Church and War Memorial Park. Memorial Ref. Pier and Face 9D 9C 13C and 12C. Thiepval Memorial, France.

COOKSEY, Second Lieutenant, Wilfred Maurice. "B" Special Coy., Royal Engineers. Died of wounds, 13th April 1917. Age 27. Son of John Hudson Cooksey, Mining Engineer, of West Bromwich and Handsworth, and Phebe Cooksey, of New Vale, Balsall Common, Nr. Coventry. Grave Ref. I. H. 64. Barlin Communal Cemetery Extension, Pas de Calais, France.

COOMBS, Lance Corporal, Albert. 9777, 8th Bn., King's Own (Royal Lancaster Regiment). Died of wounds, 11th May, 1916. Born Coventry. Enlisted Coventry. Grave Ref. II. D. 46. Bailleul Communal Cemetery Extension (Nord), France.

COOME, Member, Agnes Hilda. 10879, Women's Royal Air Force. 19th December, 1918. Grave Ref. 225. 136. Coventry (London Road) Cemetery.

COOPER, Corporal, Edward. 202195, 2nd /6th Bn., Royal Warwickshire Regiment. Killed in action, 18th April, 1918. Son of Mr. J. Cooper, of 57, Monks Road, Coventry. Born Huntingdon. Enlisted Coventry. Grave Ref. I. E. 20. St. Venant-Robecq Road British Cemetery, Robecq, Pas de Calais, France.

COOPER, Private, Frank. 2831, 1st /1st Warwickshire Yeomanry. Died, Egypt, 19th April, 1916 whilst on outpost duty. Age 16. Son of Frank and Elizabeth Cooper, of 2 Court, 2 House, Gosford Street, Coventry. Native of Loughborough. Enlisted Warwick. Grave Ref. A. 31. Kantara War Memorial Cemetery, Egypt.

COOPER, Private, George. 9459, 1st Bn., Oxfordshire and Buckinghamshire Light Infantry. Died, Mesopotamia, 27th November, 1916. Son of John Cooper of South Street, Steeple Aston, Oxon. Born Radford, Warwick. Enlisted Coventry. Grave Ref. XXI. K. 14. Baghdad (North Gate) War Cemetery, Iraq.

COOPER, Corporal, Hector Cecil. 261828, 2nd Bn., Tank Corps formerly 2812, Machine Gun Corps. Killed in action, 21st September, 1918. Enlisted Coventry. Memorial Ref. Panel 11. Vis-en-Artois Memorial, France.

COOPER, Private, Herbert. 5736, 1st Bn., Border Regiment. Killed in action, Gallipoli, 28th April, 1915. Nephew of Sarah Oswin, of 5 Court, 3 House, Gosford Street, Coventry. Born Coventry. Enlisted Garstang, Lancashire. Resided Coventry. Memorial Ref. Panel 119 to 125 or 222 and 223. Helles Memorial, Turkey

COOPER, Private, Reginald C. 301898, 2nd Bn., Royal Scots. Killed in action, 26th September, 1917. Born Derby. Enlisted Coventry. Resided Derby. Memorial Ref. Panel 11 to 14 and 162. Tyne Cot Memorial, Belgium.

COOPER, Gunner, W. H. 16307, 92nd Brigade, Royal Field Artillery. Died, home, 30th November, 1918. Age 34. Son of Thomas and Emma Cooper, of Coventry. Grave Ref. 183. 117. Coventry (London Road) Cemetery.

COPE, Sergeant, Walter. 11335, 7th Bn., Leicestershire Regiment. Killed in action, 26th October, 1915. Aged 35. His comrades stated he was using a catapult to throw grenades into the German trenches and it must of gone off before he was ready. Enlisted 2nd September, 1914 in Nuneaton. Born in Wilnecote, Warwickshire. Resided Warwick. Employed at the sinking operation at the Warwickshire Coal Company, new colliery at Keresley formerly Criff Clara and at Newdigate Colliery. Leaves a wife and five children. Grave Ref. I. A. 65. Bienvillers Military Cemetery, France.

COPSON, Corporal, Harry Beeton. 275002, Royal Warwickshire Regiment. transf. to (23209), Labour Corps. Died, home, 27th October, 1919. Age 41. Son of Isaac and Harriet Copson. Husband of Emily Maria Copson (nee Pratt), of "Beatonia," 23, Beresford Avenue, Coventry. Born at Atherstone. Grave Ref. Old Ground. 322. Atherstone Cemetery, Warwickshire.

COPSON, Private, Jonathon. 4242, Royal Warwickshire Regiment. Died of wounds, 31st July, 1916. Enlisted Coventry. Resided Exhall. Grave Ref. B. 48. Coventry (Windmill Road) Cemetery.

CORBETT, Private, Frederick. 6673, 2nd Bn., Royal Welsh Fusiliers. Died of wounds, 22nd September, 1915. Age 40. Son of Mr. and Mrs. Corbett of 480, Garrison Lane, Small Heath, Birmingham. Born Aston, Birmingham. Enlisted Coventry. Grave Ref. IV. D. 84. Bethune Town Cemetery, France.

CORBEY, Private, Ernest. 307616, 1/8th Bn., Royal Warwickshire Regiment. Killed in action, 27th August, 1916. Born Coventry. Enlisted Rugby. Memorial Ref. Pier and Face 9A 9B and 10B. Thiepval Memorial, France.

CORBISHLEY, Lance Corporal, Thomas, MM. M2/097930, Mechanical Transport, Army Service Corps attached 153rd Siege Bty., Royal Garrison Artillery. Died, 2nd November, 1918. Age 26. Son of Charles and Mary Edith Corbishley of 71, Howard Road, Leicester. Born Congleton, Cheshire. Enlisted Coventry. Resided Leicester. Gazetted for Military Medal, 11th November, 1916. Grave Ref. S. II. BB. 13. St. Sever Cemetery Extension, Rouen, France.

CORDIN, Private, William Alfred. 5154, 1st /6th Bn., Royal Warwickshire Regiment. Killed in action, 17th August, 1916. Age 21. Son of William Cordin, of 6, Market Street, Longford, Coventry. Born Wigan. Enlisted Warwick. Commemorated Saint Thomas the Apostle, Longford. Memorial Ref. Pier and Face 9 A 9 B and 10 B. Thiepval Memorial, Somme, France.

CORNELL, Private, Arthur F. G/26810, 21st Bn., Middlesex Regiment. Killed in action, 24th March, 1918. Son of Mrs. Jane Cornell of II, Lowfield Road, West Hampstead. Commemorated Iliffe & Sons Ltd. Born Cherry Hinton, Cambs. Enlisted Harlesden. Memorial Bay 7. Arras Memorial, France.

CORNHILL, Private, Herbert Charles. 267924, 8th Bn., Royal Warwickshire Regiment. Killed in action, 22nd April, 1918. Age 42. Husband of Margaret Ann Cornhill of 55, Alma Road, St. Kilda, Melbourne. Born Broxburne, Herts. Enlisted Coventry. Grave Ref. Screen Wall. 6. 718. Bristol (Arnos Vale) Cemetery.

CORNS, Rifleman, John. 48443, 13th Bn., Rifle Brigade formerly 40408, King's Own Yorkshire Light Infantry. Killed in action, 13th September, 1918. Born Wombourn, Staffordshire. Enlisted Lichfield. Resided Coventry. Memorial Ref. Panel 10. Vis-En- Artois Memorial, France.

CORRALL, Private, Joseph Henry. 266062, 2/6th Bn., Royal Warwickshire Regiment. Died of wounds, 1st April, 1918. Born Coventry. Enlisted Coventry. Grave Ref. IV. B. 39. Premont British Cemetery, France.

COTON, Driver, Joseph. 143000, A Battery, 84th Brigade, Royal Field Artillery. Killed in action, 9th December, 1917. Brother of Mrs. Charles Gupwell of Brandon. Enlisted 1915. Grave Ref. III. D. 4. Duhallow A.D.S. Cemetery, Belgium.

COTTERELL, Private, Thomas. 12979, 8th Bn., South Staffordshire Regiment. Killed in action, 11th May, 1916. Born Coventry. Enlisted Birmingham. Grave Ref. I. A. 23. Cite Bonjean Military Cemetery, Armentieres, France.

COTTERRELL, Private, Reginald Elvan, PO/2543(S), 1st R.M. Bn. R.N. Div., Royal Marine Light Infantry. 8th October, 1918. Son of William and Fanny Cotterrell, of Lower Wyche, Malvern, Worcs. Husband of Beatrice E. Ryder (formerly Cotterrell), of "Ingle Nook," 77, Maudslay Road, Earlsdon, Coventry. Memorial Ref. Panel 1. Vis-En-Artois Memorial, Pas de Calais, France.

COTTON, Private, Frederick. 2350, 1st Bn., Royal Warwickshire Regiment. Died of wounds, 2nd July, 1915. Born St. Paul's, Walsall, Staffs. Enlisted Warwick. Resided Coventry. Memorial Ref. Panel 8. Ypres (Menin Gate) Memorial, Belgium.

COTTON, Private, Harry. 27786, 1st Bn., Bedfordshire Regiment. Died of wounds, 17th April 1918. Age 27. Son of Tom and Mary Ann Cotton, of Coventry. Born Coventry. Enlisted Bedford. Resided St. Albans. Grave Ref. 1. B. 3. Tannay British Cemetery, Thiennes, Nord, France.

COTTRELL, Private, Alfred. 9846, 3rd Bn., Welsh Regiment. Died of wounds, Home, 6th November, 1914. Age 26. Husband of Florence Beatrice Marshall (formerly Cottrell) of 130, Eldon Road, Canton, Cardiff. Born Birmingham. Enlisted Coventry. Resided Canton, Cardiff. Grave Ref. Screen Wall. 1. C. B. 1068. Greenwich Cemetery.

COULSON, Private, Thomas William. 266508, 1/5th Bn., Royal Warwickshire Regiment. Died of wounds, 10th September, 1918. Age 20. Son of Frederick and Elizabeth Coulson of Littlethorpe, Leicester. Enlisted Coventry. Resided Littlethorpe, Leicester. Grave Ref. I. D. 11. Cavalletto British Cemetery, Italy.

COURT, Private, Arthur Leonard. 242717, 1/6th Bn., Royal Warwickshire Regiment. Killed in action, 4th October, 1917. Age 22. Son of Mr. O. G. and Mrs. M. A. Court of 22, Church Street, Stratford on Avon. Born Stratford-on-Avon. Enlisted Coventry. Resided Stratford-on-Avon. Grave Ref. V. F. 22. Tyne Cot Cemetery, Belgium.

COURT, Private, Joseph. 12558, 1st Bn., Coldstream Guards. Killed in action, 18th October, 1915. Age 27. Son of Joseph Court, of Oak House, Hob Lane, Berkswell, Coventry. Born Haseley, Warwick. Enlisted Coventry. Resided Berkswell. Memorial Ref. Panel 7 and 8. Loos Memorial, Pas de Calais, France

COURTS, Pioneer, Amos Harry. 170795, A Special Coy., Royal Engineers. Killed in action, 4th August, 1917. Age 28. Husband of Sarah Lillian Courts, of 65, Park Road, Bedworth, Nuneaton. Born Longford. Enlisted London. Teacher, Elementary School, Coventry. Resided Coventry. Commemorated Education Department Memorial, Coventry Corporation and Bablake School Memorial. Grave Ref. IV. A. 5. Medinghem Military Cemetery, Belgium.

COWD, Chaplain 4th Class, The Rev. Arthur Martin, Army Chaplains' Department. attd. 81st Field Amb. Died, 22nd December, 1918. Age 28. Son of Mr. Arthur G. Cowd, and Mrs. Ellen Cowd of 8, Kirby Road, Earlsdon, Coventry. Grave Ref. III. B. 57. Mazargues War Cemetery, Marseilles, Bouches-du-Rhone, France.

COWE, Private, Henry. M2/079419, Mechanical Transport, Army Service Corps. Died, 30th June, 1918. Age 24. Son of William and Euphernia Cowe of Muirhouse, Stow, Midlothian. Born Melrose, Scotland. Enlisted Coventry. Resided Crookstonheriot. Grave Ref. V. D. 9. Pernes British Cemetery, France.

COX, Private, Charles William. 7117, 6th Dragoon Guards (Carabineers). Died of wounds, 3rd May, 1915. Age 28. Son of Edwin and Isabel Cox, of 4, Lawford Villas, Eastwood Lane, Westcliff-on-Sea. Husband of Mabel Cox, of 10, Paradise Street, Coventry. Grave Ref. VIII. B. 28. Boulogne Eastern Cemetery, Pas de Calais, France.

COX, Private, Francis Daulman, 5243, 22nd Sqdn., Royal Flying Corps and 28th Bn., London Regiment (Artists' Rifles), Died of wounds, 26th November, 1916 in Canadian General Hospital after being wounded in aerial action, 17th November, 1916. Age 24. Son of Walter James and Mary Jane Cox, of 4, Coundon Street, Coventry. Native of Coventry. Born in 1892. Resided at 4 Coundon Street. Enlisted London. Educated Bablake School. Commemorated Bablake School Memorial and War Memorial Park. Grave Ref. XX. C. 8. Etaples Military Cemetery, Pas de Calais, France.

COX, Second Lieutenant, Francis Henry Cox. 1st Bn., Royal Warwickshire Regiment. Killed in action, 23rd October, 1916 near Lesboeufs by a shell. Educated Bablake School. Commemorated Bablake School Memorial. Memorial Ref. Pier and Face 9 A 9 B and 10 B. Thiepval Memorial, Somme, France.

COX, Lance Corporal, Frank. M2/079979, 708th Motor Transport Coy, Army Service Corps. Died, Balkans, 22nd October, 1918. Age 29. Son of Walter and Emma Cox. Husband of Elizabeth J. B. Cox of 7, Pine Street, Blackburn. Born Blackburn, Lancs. Enlisted Coventry. Resided Blackburn. Commemorated Holy Trinity Panels. Grave Ref. J. 3. Skopje British Cemetery, Macedonia.

COX, Gunner, George Frederick, 158513, 128th Heavy Bty., Royal Garrison Artillery. Killed in action, 21st March, 1918. Age 28. Husband of F. E. M. Cox, of 9, Latham Road, Coventry. Born London. Enlisted Coventry. Memorial Ref. Panel 10. Pozieres Memorial, Somme, France.

COX, Private, Harry. 94219, 16th Bn., Royal Welsh Fusiliers formerly 60846, Monmouthshire Regiment. Died of wounds, 10th November, 1918. Age 19. Son of Mr. H. and Mrs. E. J. Cox, of 30, Valley Road, Ebbw Vale, Monmouth. Born Coventry. Enlisted Newport. Resided Ebbwvale, Monmouth. Grave Ref. XB. 6. B. Mont Huon Military Cemetery, Le Treport, France.

COX, Sergeant, Harry. 5207, 1st Bn., Rifle Brigade. Died of wounds, Home, 16th August, 1915. Shot in the leg and died after having his leg amputated. Age 20. Son of Theresa Cox. Born Hatton, Warwick. Enlisted Coventry. Resided Kenilworth. Grave Ref. Kenilworth Cemetery.

COX, Private, Herbert William. 37914, 10th Bn., East Yorkshire Regiment. Killed in action, 14th August, 1918. Age 34. Son of Mr. and Mrs. J. C. Cox. Born Barrow-on-Soar, Leics. Enlisted Coventry. Memorial Ref. Panel 4. Ploegsteert Memorial, Belgium.

COX, Private, Lawrence Cecil. 4515, "B" Coy. 1st /7th Bn., Royal Warwickshire Regiment. Killed in action, 14th July, 1916. Age 25. Son of Lavinia Cox, of 4,Finchley's Buildings, King William Street, Coventry, and Richard Cox. Husband of Gertrude Muriel Cox, of 4, Inchley's Buildings, King William Street, Coventry. Born 6th May, 1891, at Nuneaton. Resided at Pridmore Road. Enlisted Coventry, October 1915. Co-Operative Stores Manager. Commemorated War Memorial Park. Memorial Ref. Pier and Face 9 A 9 B and 10 B. Thiepval Memorial, Somme, France. (Possibly buried at Ovillers).

COX, Rifleman, Walter William. 5539, 3rd Bn., Rifle Brigade. Killed in action, 2nd February, 1916. Born Coventry. Enlisted Bury St. Edmunds, Suffolk. Resided Coveney, Cambridge. Grave Ref. I. E. 3. Menin Road South Military Cemetery, Belgium.

COYNE, Private, William. 10890, 8th Bn., South Staffordshire Regiment. Died of wounds, 24th December, 1915. Age 22. Son of Mr. and Mrs. Coyne, of 12 Court, 10 House, Newsummer Street, Birmingham. Born Coventry. Enlisted Birmingham. Grave Ref. VI. A. 3. Etaples Military Cemetery, France.

COZENS, Private, Alfred Henry. 15250, 10th Bn., East Yorkshire Regiment. Killed in action, 15th July, 1916. Age 34. Son of Mr. and Mrs. J. C. Cox. Born Norwich. Enlisted Coventry. Memorial Ref. Panel 4. Ploegstreet Memorial, Belgium.

CRACKNELL, Private, James. 4080, A Coy, 1st Bn., Royal Warwickshire Regiment. Killed in action, 26th April, 1915. Age 37. Son of Edwin and Martha Cracknell. Born Birmingham. Enlisted Coventry. Memorial Ref. Panel 8. Ypres (Menin Gate) Memorial, Belgium.

CRAMP, Private, Edward James. 5111, 1/6th Bn., Royal Warwickshire Regiment. Killed in action, 25th August, 1916. Born Coventry. Enlisted Coventry. Memorial Ref. Pier and Face 9A 9B and 10B. Thiepval Memorial, France.

CRAMP, Gunner, Reginald. 830578, 306th Bde., Royal Field Artillery. Died of wounds, Rouen Hospital, 2nd April, 1917 due to pneumonia after receiving wounds in action. Age 23. Son of Edward and Mrs. E. J. Cramp, of 273, Swan Lane, Coventry. Born Coventry. Enlisted Coventry. Employed Triumph works. Grave Ref. O. III. E. 6. St. Sever Cemetery Extension, Rouen, Seine-Maritime, France.

CRAMP, Lance Sergeant, Walter Ernest. 25895, 14th Bn., Worcestershire Regiment. Died of wounds, 3rd May, 1917. Age 24. Son of John and Annie Cramp. Husband of Alice Beatrice Cramp, of Wilden Lane, Stourport, Worcestershire. Native of Coventry. Grave Ref. XVIII. G. 14A. Etaples Military Cemetery, Pas de Calais, France.

CRAMP, Private, William. 157, 1st Bn., Royal Warwickshire Regiment. Killed in action 13th October, 1914. Age 29. Son of William and Mary Cramp. Husband of Lucy Wheatley (formerly Cramp), of Little Boyton, Foleshill, Coventry. Commemorated Saint Thomas the Apostle, Longford. Grave Ref. IV. A. 554. (Buried near this spot.). Meteren Military Cemetery, Nord, France.

CRAN, Private, William Ernest. 9627, 2nd Bn., South Wales Borderers. Died of wounds, at sea, 7th June, 1915. Born Kensington. Enlisted London. Billeted Coventry. Memorial Ref. Panel 80 to 84 or 219 and 220. Helles Memorial, Turkey.

CRANER, Sergeant, Frank. 68046, 117th Bty. 26th Bde., Royal Field Artillery. Killed in action, 9th November, 1917. Age 26. Son of Thomas and Mary Ann Craner, of 74, Station Street, Foleshill, Coventry. Born Coventry. Enlisted Warwick. Grave Ref. XI. D. 7. Vlamertinghe New Military Cemetery, Ieper, West-Vlaanderen, Belgium.

CRANER, Cook's Mate, Victor. M/10421, HMS Bristol, Royal Navy. Died of pneumonia, 13th May, 1919. Age 24. Son of Thomas and Mary Ann Craner, of 74, Station Street, East Foleshill, Coventry. Memorial Ref. 32. Portsmouth Naval Memorial.

CRANER, Sergeant, William, MM. 242235, 8th Platoon, B Company, 1/4th Bn., Gloucestershire Regiment. Died of wounds, 15th October, 1918 injured on the 10th October, 1918 which necessitated leg amputation. Age 23. Born Coventry. Enlisted Coventry. Resided Foleshill. Grave Ref. 1. D. 5. Cavalletto British Cemetery, Italy.

CRAVEN, Lance Sergeant, Henry Smith. G/3896, 6th Bn., The Buffs (East Kent Regiment). Killed in action, Givenchy, 6th March 1916. Age 24. Son of Arthur Craven, of 27, Spencer Street, Coventry. Born 22nd February, 1892 in St. Peter's Parish. Resided at 27, Spencers Street. Enlisted Canterbury, October 1914. Civil Servant. Commemorated Bablake School Memorial, War Memorial Park and Wesleyan Church. Memorial Ref. Panel 15 to 19. Loos Memorial, Pas de Calais, France.

CRAVEN, Private, Herbert Leo. 10263, 2nd Bn. The Loyal North Lancashire Regiment. Killed in action, East Africa, 4th November, 1914. Born Coventry. Enlisted Blackburn. Grave Ref. Tanga Memorial Cemetery, Tanzania.

CRAWFORD, Private, Thomas John. 9241, 8th Bn., Royal Welsh Fusiliers. Killed in action, 9th April, 1916. Age 28. Husband of Maud Elsie Crawford, of Shilton Lane, Shilton, Coventry. Born Chester. Enlisted Chester. Memorial Ref. Panel 15. Basra Memorial, Iraq.

CREW, Private, George. 20804, 1/6th Bn., Royal Warwickshire Regiment formerly 247, Cyclist Coy. Died of wounds, 4th February, 1917. Born St. James, Bristol. Enlisted Bristol. Resided Coventry. Grave Ref. A. 6. Eclusier Communal Cemetery, Eclusier-Vaux, France.

CRIBDON, Driver, Arthur. 2123, M. T., Army Service Corps. Died of sickness, home, 18th May, 1915. Age 27. Son of William and Elizabeth Kirby (formerly Cribdon), of 391, Stoney Stanton Road, Coventry. Enlisted Witton. Grave Ref. 145. 29. Coventry (London Road) Cemetery.

CRIPPS, Gunner, James. 136191, 290th Siege Bty., Royal Garrison Artillery. 17th September, 1918. Age 18. Son of Mrs. E. Cripps, of 15, Chauntry Place, Coventry. Born Coventry. Enlisted Coventry. Commemorated Holy Trinity Panels. Grave Ref. A. 35. Queant Communal Cemetery British Extension, Pas de Calais, France.

CRISP, Private, Clarence Victor. 12728, 9th Bn., Royal Warwickshire Regiment. Died of wounds, 14th April 1916. Age 22. Son of James and Susannah Crisp, of 148, Munition Cottages, Holbrooks Lane, Foleshill, Coventry. Employed Alfred Herbert's Ltd. Native of Maldon, Essex. Memorial Ref. Panel 9. Basra Memorial, Iraq.

CROFTS, Private, Charles Harry. 13176, 9th Bn., Royal Warwickshire Regiment. Killed in action, 5th April, 1916. Born Burton-on-Trent, Staffs. Enlisted Coventry. Resided Nuneaton. Memorial Ref. Panel 9. Basra Memorial, Iraq.

CROFTS, Private, Fred. 37920, 12th (West Somerset Yeomanry) Bn. Somerset Light Infantry formerly 1464, Worcestershire Yeomanry. Killed in action, 21st October, 1918. Born Coventry. Enlisted Worcester. Memorial Ref. Panel 3. Ploegsteert Memorial, Belgium.

CROFTS, Private, Walter. 24405, 1st Bn., Worcestershire Regiment. Killed in action, 31st July, 1917. Son of Mr. J. Crofts, of 2 Court, 5 House, Bond Street, Coventry. Born Coventry. Enlisted Worcester. Resided Coventry. Memorial Ref. Panel 34. Ypres (Menin Gate) Memorial, Ieper, West-Vlaanderen, Belgium.

CRONAN, Private, Thomas. 12173, 2nd Bn., Royal Warwickshire Regiment. Killed in action, 14th July, 1916. Commemorated Triumph & Gloria Memorial. Born Coventry. Enlisted Coventry. Resided 21, Vincent Street. Employed Triumph Works. Memorial Ref. Pier and Face 9 A 9 B and 10 B. Thiepval Memorial, France.

CRONIE, Quarter Master Sergeant, Peter James. 92126, 22nd Bn., Tank Corps formerly 117034, Royal Army Service Corps. Died, Home, 30th October, 1918. Age 32. Son of James Cronie. Husband of Lillian Daly(Formerly Cronie) of Louis Villa, Silverdale, Newcastle Born Hanley, Staffs. Enlisted Coventry. Grave Ref. C. E. 1334. Newcastle under Lyne (Silverdale) Cemetery.

CROOK, Lance Corporal, Frederick W. 242287, 2/6th Bn., Royal Warwickshire Regiment. Killed in action, 6th September, 1917. Born Coventry. Enlisted Coventry. Husband of Mrs. E. Crook, 4c. 4h. Cow Lane, Coventry. Employed British Thompson Houston Works, Lower Ford Street. Memorial Ref. Panel 23 to 28 and 163A. Tyne Cot Memorial, Belgium.

CROSSLAND, Private 2nd Class, Charles. 127366, No. 1 Aircraft Acceptance Park, Royal Air Force. Died of pneumonia, 30th June, 1918. Age 30. Son of Charles and Sarah Ann Crossland. Born at Dukinfield. Grave Ref. 198. 59. Coventry (London Road) Cemetery.

CROSSLEY, W. Commemorated Radford Memorial.

CROSTHWAITE, Corporal, Harry. M2/050260, Mechanical Transport, Army Service Corps attached C Siege Park. Killed in action, 7th August, 1918. Age 23. Son of Routledge and Hannah Crosthwaite of Chieveley House, Fence Houses, Co. Durham. Born Fence Houses, Durham. Enlisted Coventry. Resided Fence Houses. Grave Ref. XIV. D. 2. St. Pierre Cemetery, Amiens, France.

CROWSON, Private, Joseph. 14395, 4th Bn., Worcestershire Regiment. Killed in action, Gallipoli, 27th November, 1915. Born Coventry. Enlisted Coventry. Son of Mrs. Stanbridge of 3, Park Side. Employed Daimler Co. Ltd. Memorial Ref. Panel 104 to 113. Helles Memorial, Turkey.

CROWTHER, Private, Harry. 20661, 14th Bn., Gloucestershire Regiment. Died of wounds, 28th July, 1916. Age 23. Son of George and Mrs. M. H. Crowther of 53, London Road, Spalding, Lincolnshire. Born Spalding, Lincs. Enlisted Coventry. Grave Ref. I. H. 7. Corbie Communal Cemetery Extension, France.

CROWTON, Private, Frederick. 33022, 6th Bn., Royal Berkshire Regiment. Died of wounds, home, 26th October, 1917. Wounded by shrapnel in France and passed away at London Military Hospital. Age 19. Son of William Crowton, of 11, Court, 3 House, Well Street, Coventry. Enlisted May 8th, 1916. Employed Mills and Fulford Ltd., Stoney Stanton Road, Coventry. Grave Ref. 193. 13. Coventry (London Road) Cemetery.

CRUTCHLOW, Private, William Joseph. 266116, 1/7th Bn., Royal Warwickshire Regiment. Killed in action, 8th October, 1917. Born Coventry. Enlisted Coventry. Memorial Ref. Panel 23 to 28 and 163A. Tyne Cot Memorial, Belgium.

CUMBERLAND, Gunner, Frank. 840305, C Bty, 86th Bde., Royal Field Artillery. Died of wounds, 23rd October, 1917. Age 22. Son of Oliver and Mary Cumberland of Laburnum Cottages, Carcroft, Doncaster. Born Bulwell, Notts. Enlisted Coventry. Grave Ref. XXII. D. 17. Lijssenthoek Military Cemetery, Belgium.

CURRAN, Private, Joseph. 7379, 2nd Bn., Connaught Rangers. Killed in action, 6th November, 1914. Born Elphin, Co. Roscommon. Enlisted Claremorris. Resided Coventry. Memorial Ref. Panel 42. Ypres (Menin Gate) Memorial, Belgium.

CURREY, Private, John Emerson. 9163, 11th Bn., Royal Warwickshire Regiment. Killed in action, 9th July, 1916. Enlisted Coventry. Resided Foleshill, Coventry. Memorial Ref. Pier and Face 9A 9B and 10B. Thiepval Memorial, Somme, France.

CURTIS, Private, William Guy. 64, 14th Bn., Royal Warwickshire Regiment. Killed in action, 23rd July, 1916. Age 29. Son of Caroline Elizabeth Curtis, of 37, Minstead Road, Gravelly Hill, Birmingham. Husband of Florence Curtis, of 62, Huntingdon Rd., Earlsdon, Coventry. Commemorated St. Barbara's Church. Memorial Ref. Pier and Face 9 A 9 B and 10 B. Thiepval Memorial, Somme, France.

CUSSICK, Private, William. 9557, 2nd Bn., South Wales Borderers. Killed in action, 2nd May, 1915. Born Spring Meadow, Staffs. Enlisted Monmouth. Billeted Coventry. Memorial Ref. Panel 80 to 84 or 219 and 220. Helles Memorial, Turkey.

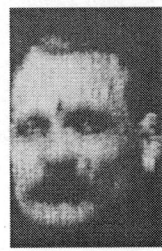
CUTLER, Private, Samuel. 34993, 1st Bn., Royal Berkshire Regiment. Posted as missing since 28th April, 1917. Age 35. Husband of Eliza Cutler, of 66, Red Lane, Coventry. Enlisted December, 1916. Employed Courtaulds. Born Darlaston. Enlisted Coventry. Memorial Ref. Bay 7. Arras Memorial, Pas de Calais, France.

CUTTS, A. Commemorated St. John's Church.

CUTTS, Private, Aaron. 11885, 4th Bn., Worcestershire Regiment. Killed in action, 4th June, 1916. Age 35. Native of Coventry. Son of Matthew and Sarah Ann Cutts, of 15, Barras Lane, Coventry. Born Coventry. Enlisted Nuneaton. Resided Coventry. Grave Ref. II. C. 11. Auchonvillers Military Cemetery, Somme, France.

CUTTS, Private, Arthur. 41727, 1/8th Bn., Royal Inniskilling Fusiliers formerly 23005, Royal Warwickshire Regiment. Killed in action, 16th August, 1917. Born Coventry. Enlisted Birmingham. Resided Coventry. Grave Ref. XII. A. 6. Tyne Cot Cemetery, Belgium.

CUTTS, Private, Frederick. 13551, 5th Bn., Oxfordshire and Buckinghamshire Light Infantry. Killed in action, 30th July, 1915. Born Coventry. Enlisted Coventry. Commemorated St. John's Church. Memorial Ref. Panel 37 and 39. Tyne Cot Memorial, Belgium.

CUTTS, Private, John. 22228, 1st Bn., Gloucestershire Regiment formerly 21349, Cavalry Reserve. Killed in action, 27th August, 1916. Son of Mr. and Mrs. Cutts of Conway Buildings, York Street, Coventry. Employed Mr. Geo. Harris, Earlsdon. Born St. Thomas's, Coventry. Enlisted Nuneaton. Memorial Ref. Pier and Face 5A and 5B. Thiepval Memorial, Somme, France.

DAINTY, Rifleman, Hugh Corbett. (Served as Rifleman, George Franklin). 10614, 3rd Bn., King's Royal Rifle Corps. Died of wounds, 15th June, 1915. Son of John William and Edith Mary Dainty of the Manor House, Collyweston, Stamford. Born Sutton-Mansfield. Enlisted Coventry. Resided Nottingham. Grave Ref. II. A. 7. Etaples Military Cemetery, France.

DALE, Gunner, Frank. 201060, A Bty., 147th Bde., Royal Field Artillery. Died, Home, 8th November, 1918. Age 24. Son of Mrs. Frances Dale, of 8, North Road, Leominster, Herefordshire. Enlisted Coventry. Resided New Bilton, Rugby. Grave Ref. 17. 1. Writtle (All Saints) Churchyard.

DALTON, Private, Matthew Thomas. 35952, 14th Bn., Royal Worcestershire Regiment. Killed in action, 4th February, 1917. Born 26th January, 1890 in Lockhurst Lane, Coventry. Enlisted Coventry. Greengrocer. Commemorated St. Paul's Church. Memorial Ref. Pier and Face 5 A and 6 C. Thiepval Memorial, France.

DALTON, Lance Bombardier, Stanley Stephen. 931098, "D" Bty. 290th Bde., Royal Field Artillery. Killed in action, 24th April, 1918. Age 19. Son of Mr. R. G. Dalton, of 16, Francis Street, Coventry. Born in 1899, St. Pancras, London. Resided at 16, Francis Street. Grave Ref. II. D. 3. Adelaide Cemetery, Villers-Bretonneux, Somme, France.

DALY, Private, Michael. 10149, 1st Bn., Royal Munster Fusiliers. Killed in action, 10th July, 1915 reported to have been shot whilst on sentry duty. Buried in the firing line. Billeted at Coventry. Resided at 89, Kingston Road. Born Cork, Ireland. Memorial Ref. Panel 185 to 190. Helles Memorial, Turkey.

 **DANIELS**, Private, George Albert. 16854, 2nd /5th Bn., Royal Warwickshire Regiment. Killed in action, La Vacquerie, near Cambrai , 3rd December, 1917. Age 25. Son of Harry and Ellen Daniels, of 30, Clements Street, Coventry. Employed at G.P.O. Coventry for 11 years. Born 22nd February, 1892 at Coventry. Resided in 30, Clements Street. Enlisted February 1916. Commemorated Post Office Memorial and War Memorial Park. Postman. Memorial Ref. Panel 3. Cambrai Memorial, Louverval, Nord, France.

DANIELS, Sapper, Henry William. 43864, 86th Field Coy., Royal Engineers. Died of wounds, Gallipoli 20th November, 1915. Age 20. Son of Joseph and Harriett Daniels, of 57, Sackville Street, Coventry. Born 23rd May, 1895 at Burton-on-Trent, Staffs. Enlisted Warwick. Resided Byron Street, Coventry. Grinder. Enlisted September, 1914. Grave Ref. D. VII. 2. Pieta Military Cemetery, Malta.

 **DANKS**, Private, Albert Edward. 31730, 15th Bn., Hampshire Regiment formerly Motor Machine Gun Section and 16343, 2/7th Bn., Royal Warwickshire Regiment. Killed in action, 7th October, 1916. Age 22. Son of William and Sarah Ann Danks, of Ashgreen House, Exhall, Warwickshire. Coal Merchant, Bull and Anchor Inn. Memorial Ref. Pier and Face 7 C and 7 B. Thiepval Memorial, Somme, France.

DANKS, Sergeant, Walter. R/692, 10th Bn., King's Royal Rifle Corps. Killed in action, 3rd September, 1916. Age 31. Son of Frederick and Ann Danks, of 11, Four Oaks Common Road, Sutton Coldfield, Birmingham. Born Coventry. Enlisted Westminster, Middx. Resided Sutton Coldfield. Memorial Ref. Pier and Face 13 A and 13 B. Thiepval Memorial, Somme, France.

DARBY, Lance Corporal, Edward. 25558, 14th Bn., Gloucestershire Regiment. Killed in action, 19th July, 1916. Born Walsall, Staffs. Enlisted Coventry. Memorial Ref. Pier and Face 5A and 5 B. Thiepval Memorial, Somme, France.

 **DARBY**, Private, George Henry. 8771, 1st Bn., Coldstream Guards. Died of wounds, 9th June, 1915 whilst a prisoner of war. Age 25. Son of William Darby. Husband of Emily C. Ford (formerly Darby), of 3, Corporation Cottages, Holbrook Lane, Coventry. Born at Foleshill. Enlisted Coventry. Grave Ref. XV. N. 38. Cabaret-Rouge British Cemetery, Souchez, Pas de Calais, France.

DARBYSHIRE, Private, Thomas William. PLY/2434(S), 1st Royal Marine Bn. Royal Naval Division, Royal Marine Light Infantry. Killed in action Flesquieres, 5th March 1918. Age 26. Son of B. J. and S. J. Darbyshire, of Coventry. Husband of Edith E. Gospill (formerly Darbyshire), of 6, Stanley Street, Foleshill, Coventry. Born 15th March 1891 at Selby, Yorkshire. Enlisted September 1917. Clerk. Commemorated War Memorial Park. Grave Ref. X. A. 29. Rocquigny-Equancourt Road British Cemetery, Manancourt, Somme, France.

D'ARCY, Gunner, Matthew. 70468, 112th Heavy Battery, Royal Garrison Artillery. Killed in action, 5th November, 1917. Resided at Foleshill. Born Danesfort, Co. Kilkenny, Ireland. Enlisted Kilkenny. Grave Ref. VIII. I. 103. Boulogne Eastern Cemetery, France.

DARKE, Private, Percival George. Royal Munster Fusiliers. Died of wounds, Gallipoli, 29th August, 1915. Born 3rd September, 1893 at Bewdley. Resided in Ireland. Buried at sea. Billeted Coventry.

DARLING, Gunner, William James. 1962, Machine Gun Corps (Motors). Killed in action, 23rd March, 1918. Age 36. Father of Miss E. Darling, of 8, Ruddigore Road, New Cross, London. Born Battersea. Enlisted Coventry. Resided Catford. Grave Ref. Buried near this spot. II. A. 5. Delsaux Farm Cemetery, Beugny, France.

DARLISON, Private, Thomas. 43872, 8th Bn., King's Own Yorkshire Light Infantry formerly 5/21859, 6th T. R. Bn,. Killed in action, 15th June, 1918. Age 22. Son of William and Elizabeth Darlison, of Bedworth. Born Bedworth. Enlisted Coventry. Grave Ref. 1. B. 9. Granezza British Cemetery, Italy.

DARLOW, Boy, I B. J/67322(PO), HMS Repulse, Royal Navy. Died, home, 25th October, 1918. Age 18. Son of Mrs. S. Darlow, of 3 Court, 15 House, Hill Street, Coventry. Grave Ref. 220. 76. Coventry (London Road) Cemetery.

DARLOW, Jack. Killed in action. Name on Roll of Honour in Cathedral Church of St. Michael.

DARVILL, Private, Ernest William. 4537, 1/7th Bn., Royal Warwickshire Regiment. Killed in action, Martinpuich, 27th November, 1916. Born 11th October, 1888 at Coundon. Resided at 106, Newcombe Road. Painter. Enlisted November, 1915 at Coventry. Grave Ref. D. 15. Martinpuich Military Cemetery, France.

DARVILL, J. Employed by Rover Company. Killed in action.

DASWELL, Private, Herbert. Royal Warwickshire Regiment. Killed in France, 7th August, 1919. Born in Spon Street. Resided at 6c. 1h. Spon End. Labourer. Enlisted January, 1915.

DAVENPORT, Private, Charles. 3858, 2/7th Bn., Royal Warwickshire Regiment. Killed in action, 28th August, 1916. Age 29. Born 1st March, 1885 in Eden Street, Coventry. Enlisted Coventry. Resided 98, Eden Street, Coventry. Godiva Harrier. Employee Wyken Colliery Co. Ltd, Miner. Memorial Ref. Panel 22 to 25. Loos Memorial, France.

DAVENPORT, Lance Corporal, Frank. 2055, 9th Bn., Royal Warwickshire Regiment. Killed in action, Mesopotamia, 25th January, 1917. Born Pailton, Rugby. Enlisted Coventry. Resided Pailton. Memorial Ref. 9. Basra Memorial, Iraq.

DAVENPORT, Lance Corporal, Henry Charles. 3492, "C" Coy. 2nd /7th Bn., Royal Warwickshire Regiment. Died whilst prisoner of war, 19th July, 1916. Age 21. Son of John and Hannah Davenport, of 52, Hugh Road, Stoke, Coventry. Born 15th June, 1895 at Stoneleigh. Butcher, Mr. T. Powers, Craven Street. Enlisted November, 1914 at Coventry. Memorial Ref. Panel 22 to 25. Loos Memorial, Pas de Calais, France.

DAVENPORT, Rifleman, Thomas Docker. 5/391, 1st Bn., Rifle Brigade . Killed in action, 10th November, 1914. Born Pailton. Enlisted Coventry. Resided Pailton. Memorial Ref. Panel 10. Ploegsteert Memorial, Belgium.

DAVENPORT, Gunner, William Ewart. 1210, D Bty., 306th Bde., Royal Field Artillery. Killed in action, 18th July, 1916. Age 18. Son of Alice S. Davenport, of Harborough Magna, Rugby. Born Harboro Magna, Warwick. Enlisted Coventry. Grave Ref. II. E. 11. Laventie Military Cemetery, La Gorgue, France.

DAVIDSON, Private, James Innes. 86424, 19th Bn., Liverpool Regiment formerly 3907, Queen's Oxford Hussars. Killed in action, 30th March, 1918. Born 1899 at Edinburgh. Enlisted Warwick. Resided Coventry. Employed Triumph Cycle Co. Ltd. Memorial Ref. Panel 21 to 23. Pozieres Memorial, France.

DAVIES, Private Albert Reuben. 12790, 2nd Bn., Northamptonshire Regiment. Killed in action. 9th May, 1915. Age 26. Son of Thomas Davis, of Fosters Booth, Towcester, Northants. Railway Fuelman. Employed by London Midland & Scottish Railway Co. Ltd, Goods Department. Memorial Ref. Panel 7. Ploegsteert Memorial, Belgium.

DAVIES, Rifleman, Arthur Edward. R/16963, 13th Bn., King's Royal Rifle Corps. Killed in action, Mametz Wood, 7th August, 1916. Age 22. Son of Edward and Ada Jane Davies, of 33, Argyll Street, Stoke, Coventry. Born 12th March, 1894 at Fillongley. Resided at Jordan Well. Baker and Confectioner. Enlisted November, 1915 at Coventry. Memorial Ref. Bay 7. Arras Memorial, Pas de Calais, France.

DAVIES, Sergeant, Charles William. 265455, 1/7th Bn., Royal Warwickshire Regiment. Killed in action, 27th August, 1917. Age 26. Husband of Elizabeth Davies, of 26, Lister Street, Attleborough, Nuneaton. Born Milverton, Warwick. Enlisted Coventry. Resided Nuneaton. Grave Ref. X. E. 12. Tyne Cot Cemetery, Belgium.

DAVIES, Private, Cyril. 202140, 1/5th Bn., Royal Warwickshire Regiment. Killed in action, 4th October, 1917. Born Handsworth, Staffs. Enlisted Coventry. Resided Handsworth, Staffs. Memorial Ref. Panel 23 to 28 and 163A. Tyne Cot Memorial, Belgium.

DAVIES, Second Lieutenant, David Claude Graham. 1st Siege Battery, Royal Garrison Artillery. Died of wounds, 15th May, 1915. Age 23. Born in 1892 at Llanrwst. Resided at Rugby. Educated at Bangor University College. Son of Thomas John and Ammie Louisa Davies of Awelon, 15, Holbrook Avenue, Rugby. Charge-hand, Electrical Laboratory, British Thompson Houston Ltd. Former Coventry City player. Grave Ref. II. G. 15. Bethune Town Cemetery, France.

DAVIES, Private, Ernest. 7401. 2nd Bn., South Lancashire Regiment. Killed in action, 24th October, 1914. Born Leamington. Enlisted Coventry. Resided Leamington. Memorial Ref. Panel 23. Le Touret Memorial, France.

DAVIES, Corporal, Herbert. Resided at Earlsdon. Killed in action, August, 1916.

DAVIES, Lance Corporal, John Charles. 41624, 5th Bn., Royal Berkshire Regiment. Killed in action, 22nd September, 1918. Age 20. Son of Harry and Hannah F. Davies, of 56, Lower Wellington Street, Coventry. Commemorated Coventry Chain Memorial. Born Wolverhampton. Enlisted Coventry. Memorial Ref. Panel 7. Vis-En-Artois Memorial, Pas de Calais, France.

DAVIES, Private, Stanley. 9777, 2nd Bn., South Wales Borderers. Died of wounds, 15th May, 1915. Age 27. Husband of Jessie Davies, of 7, Weston Street, Coventry. Born Newbridge, Mon. Enlisted Pontypool. Grave Ref. C. 151. Alexandria (Chatby) Military and War Memorial Cemetery, Egypt.

DAVIS, Private, Carl. 29182, 8th Bn., East Surrey Regiment. Killed in action, 19th May, 1918. Born 4th June, 1900 at Marylebone, Middx. Enlisted Warwick. Resided Coventry. Driller. Memorial Ref. Panel 44 and 45. Pozieres Memorial, France.

DAVIS, Bombardier, Ernest Frank. 51116, 15 Bty., Royal Field Artillery. Killed in action, 31st October, 1914. Born Birmingham. Enlisted Coventry. Mentioned in Despatches. Memorial Ref. Panel 1. Le Touret Memorial, France.

DAVIS, Sergeant, Howard. S/978, 8th Bn., Rifle Brigade. Died of wounds, Hooge, Belgium 31st July, 1915. Age 27. Son of Edwin and Susan M. Davis, of Birmingham. Born in 1888 at Birmingham. Resided at Wylde Green, Birmingham. Clerk. Enlisted August, 1914. Grave Ref. III. A. 5A. Lijssenthoek Military Cemetery, Belgium.

DAVIS, Private, James. 12297, 1st Bn., Hampshire Regiment formerly 5345, Royal Warwickshire Regiment. Killed in action, 28th March, 1918. Born 17th February, 1887 at Cox Street, Coventry. Enlisted Warwick. Resided 9, Priory Street, Coventry. Engineer. Enlisted August, 1914. Memorial Ref. Bay 6. Arras Memorial, France. (Possibly buried Roeux).

DAVIS, Rifleman, James. 8098, 4th Bn., King's Royal Rifle Corps. Died of wounds, 10th May, 1915. Age 26. Son of James and Lucy Davis, of 6/78, Men's Hostels, Holbrook's Lane, Coventry. Born 1899, Coventry. Enlisted Coventry. Memorial Ref. Panel 51 and 53. Ypres (Menin Gate) Memorial, Ieper, West-Vlaanderen, Belgium.

DAVIS, Private, Leonard James. 201064, F Bn., Tank Corps formerly 2628, Machine Gun Corps. Died of wounds, 29th November, 1917. Age 21. Son of George C. and Catherine Davis of 1, Wellington Buildings, Bow, London. Born Leyton, Essex. Enlisted Coventry. Grave Ref. V. B. 6. Rocquigny-Equancourt Road British Cemetery, Manancourt, France.

DAVIS, Private, Percy. 16733, 9th Bn., Royal Warwickshire Regiment. Killed in action, Mesopotamia, 25th January, 1917. Age 26. Son of Thomas and Elizabeth Davis, of 20, Park Street, Attleborough, Nuneaton. Born Coventry. Enlisted Nuneaton. Resided Attleborough. Grave Ref. XIX. J. 4. Amara War Cemetery, Iraq.

DAVIS, Walter. Commemorated Wolston Memorial.

DAVISON, Driver, Ernest. 66763, 10th Bty., Royal Field Artillery. Died, Malta, 27th October, 1915. Born Eccleshall, Staffs. Enlisted Coventry. Grave Ref. A. XVIII. 6. Pieta Military Cemetery, Malta.

DAVISON, Private, Harold. 11193, 13th Bn., Royal Fusiliers. Killed in action, 16th November, 1916. Age 27. Son of Robert and Elizabeth Davison. Husband of Gertrude Davison, of 75, Binley Road, Coventry. Born 14th October, 1899 at Birmingham. Enlisted June, 1916, Coventry. Resided 75, Binley Road, Coventry. Clerk. Memorial Ref. Pier and Face 8 C 9 A and 16 A. Thiepval Memorial, Somme, France.

DAVISON, Private, James Everett. M2/080951, 9th G.H.Q. Reserve M.T. Coy., Army Service Corps. Died, 10th November, 1918. Born South Shields. Enlisted Coventry. Resided South Shields. Grave Ref. I. B. 15. Caudry British Cemetery, France.

DAVOILE, Sapper, Frederick William. 46228, 97th Field Coy., Royal Engineers. Killed in action, 26th June, 1916. Age 28. Son of F. W. Davoile and Mrs. L. M. Davoile, of 8, Waveley Road, Coventry. Born 15th October, 1888 in Vincent Street, Coventry. Enlisted Warwick. Fitter. Enlisted September, 1914. Commemorated St. John's Church. Employed Singer and Co. Grave Ref. B. 5. Ville-Sur-Ancre Communal Cemetery, Somme, France.

DAWN, Private, Albert. 22887, 9th Bn., Royal Warwickshire Regiment. Died Mesopotamia, 14th July, 1917. Born 19th July, 1894 at Nottingham. Resided at 171, Bolingbroke Road, Coventry with his uncle, H. Haddon. Broacher. Enlisted November, 1916 at Coventry. Employed Small Tool Department, Coventry Ordnance Works. Born Beeston, Notts. Resided Beeston. Grave XI. K. 15. Baghdad (North Gate) War Cemetery, Iraq.

DAWSON, Private, Leonard. 266818, 1st /8th Bn., Royal Warwickshire Regiment. Killed in action, 27th August, 1917. Age 19. Son of Mrs. Christina Rose (formerly Dawson), of 7, Princess Street, Foleshill, Coventry. Born in 1898. Enlisted Coventry. Memorial Ref. Panel 23 to 28 and 163A. Tyne Cot Memorial, Zonnebeke, West-Vlaanderen, Belgium.

DAWSON, Petty Officer, Torpedo Instructor, William Henry. HMS Kingfisher. Died, home, 13th January, 1919 from heart failure and bronchitis. Born 13th October, 1868 at Wicklow, Ireland. Resided at 7, Newcombe Road. Electrician, Rudge Works. Reservist. Invalided out of service, 11th September, 1918. Grave Ref. Plymouth.

DAY, Sergeant, Arthur. 6263, 1st Bn., Worcestershire Regiment. Missing, assumed killed between 6th July 1916 – 10th July 1916. Age 34. Son of John and Annie Day, of Belbroughton, Stourbridge, Worcs. Husband of Mary Day, of 97, Kingston Road, Coventry. Born 6th October, 1881 at Belbroughton near Stourbridge. Storekeeper at Siddeley. Reservist. Commemorated War Memorial Park and Siddeley Roll of Honour. Memorial Ref. Pier and Face 5 A and 6 C. Thiepval Memorial, Somme, France.

DAY, Private, Francis Joseph. 20109, 12th Bn., Gloucestershire Regiment. Killed in action, 3rd September, 1916. Age 34. Adopted son of Mr. F. E. Baker, of 3, Crofts Cottages, Albion Street, Coventry. Born Whitechapel, London. Enlisted Bristol. Memorial Ref. Pier and Face 5 A and 5 B. Thiepval Memorial, Somme, France.

DAY, Private, J. 16196, 8th Bn., Oxfordshire and Buckinghamshire Light Infantry. Died, home, 5th May, 1919. Age 33. Son of Mrs. Annie Day, of 59, Clifton Street, Old Hill, Staffs. Husband of Annie Hodgkins (formerly Day) of 11, Aylesford Street, Coventry. Employed Coventry. Grave Ref. 219. 39. Coventry (London Road) Cemetery.

DAY, Private, John. 17189, 2nd Bn., Hampshire Regiment formerly 16546, Oxfordshire and Buckinghamshire Light Infantry. Killed in action, Gallipoli, 6th August, 1915. Born Hugglescott, Leicester. Enlisted Coventry. Resided Nottingham. Memorial Ref. Panel 125-134 or 223-226 228-229 & 328. Helles Memorial, Turkey.

DAY, Private, William. 29267, 3rd Bn., Grenadier Guards. Killed in action, 27th November, 1917. Brother of Mrs. F. Kendrick, of 4, Colledge Road, Holbrook Lane, Coventry. Born 4th August, 1885 at Birdingbury, Warwickshire. Resided at 125, Broad Street. Labourer. Enlisted February, 1917 at Coventry. Memorial Ref. Panel 2. Cambrai Memorial, Louverval, Nord, France.

DAYNES, Private, Frederick Henry. 23679, 2nd Bn., Worcestershire Regiment. Killed in action, Givenchy, 9th December, 1915. Shot by a sniper. Age 20. Son of Mr. and Mrs. R. H. Daynes, of 9, Howard Street, Coventry. Born 21st July, 1895 Plumstead, London. Enlisted January, 1915. Coventry. Machinist, Maudslay Works. Grave Ref. I. C. 18. Woburn Abbey Cemetery, Cuinchy, Pas de Calais, France.

DE HERIZ, Gunner, Cyril Ralph Vane Smith. 614439, 15th (Warwick) Brigade, Royal Horse Artillery. Killed in action, Battle of Arras, 9th April, 1917. Age 31. Son of the Rev. Lionel Forbes Vane Smith de Heriz and Hannah Maria his wife. Born at High Ercall, Salop. Born 1st June, 1885 at Wellington, Salop. Resided at Over Whitacre. Clerk. Enlisted July, 1915. Grave Ref. A. 31. Beaurains Road Cemetery, Beaurains, France.

DE SAIX, Private, John. 43874, 8th Bn., King's Own Yorkshire Light Infantry formerly 183304, Royal Horse and Royal Field Artillery. Killed in action, 29th September, 1917. Born Dublin, Ireland. Enlisted Coventry. Memorial Ref. Panel 108 to 111. Tyne Cot Memorial, Belgium.

DEACEY, Private, John. 10709, 1st Bn., Irish Guards. Killed in action, 30th March, 1918. Born Mayo, Co. Mayo. Enlisted Coventry. Resided Thorne Lane, Co. Mayo. Memorial Ref. Bay 1. Arras Memorial, France.

DEACON, Private, Percival John. 16791, 9th Bn., Royal Warwickshire Regiment. Killed in action, Mesopotamia, 25th January, 1917. Age 25. Son of M. J. and Lizzie Deacon, of 21, Liddle Street, Stoke-on-Trent. Born at Worcester. Born 6th March 1892 at Worcester. Enlisted Birmingham. Resided Coventry. Shop assistant. Enlisted October, 1915. Grave Ref. XIX. J. 6. Amara War Cemetery, Iraq.

DEACON, Private, William. 35265, 16th Bn., (Depot), Royal Warwickshire Regiment. Died 8th October, 1918. Age 19. Son of William and Ann Elizabeth Deacon, of 3, Henry Street, Chilvers Coton. Resided at Chilvers Coton, Nuneaton. Cycle Mechanic. Enlisted February, 1916. Grave Ref. 14. 3. Chilvers Coton (All Saints) Churchyard, Nuneaton.

DEAN, Lance Corporal, Arthur. 13683, 2nd Bn., Oxfordshire and Buckinghamshire Light Infantry. Killed in action, Beaumont Hamel, 13th November, 1916. Born in 1892 at West Bromwich. Resided at 59, Alma Street. Turner and Fitter. Enlisted September, 1914, Coventry. Memorial Ref. Pier and Face 10 A and 10 D. Thiepval Memorial, Somme, France.

DEAN, Private, John. SPTS/4377, 23rd Bn., Royal Fusiliers. Killed in action, St. Laurent Blagny, Arras, 12th April, 1917 by a shell exploding in a trench just behind him. Son of George Dean. Born 17th June, 1897 in Stoney Stanton Road, Coventry. Enlisted Leamington. Resided 12, Swanswell Street, Coventry. Capstan Operator, Messrs Rotheram, Spon Street. Enlisted November, 1915. Commemorated Wesleyan Church. Grave Ref. I. D. 24. Bailleul Road East Cemetery, St. Laurent-Blangy, France.

DEBENHAM, Private, William Bertram, 206155, "D" Coy., Machine Gun Corps (Heavy Branch) formerly 32105, Machine Gun Corps. Killed in action, 15th September, 1916. Age 24. Son of Mrs. Annie Laureen Appleton, of 33, Northumberland Road, Coventry. Born 29th January, 1892 at Berlin (of English Parents brought to England when three weeks old). Employed by Rotheram and Sons Ltd. Enlisted, 1915 at Coventry. Commemorated St. John's Church. Memorial Ref. Pier and Face 5 C and 12 C. Thiepval Memorial, Somme, France.

DEGNAN, Private, Joseph. 10043, 1st Bn., Coldstream Guards. Killed in action, Mons, 25th September, 1914 whilst on outpost duty. Age 23. Son of Michael Henry and Adelaide Degnan, of 50, London Road, Coventry. Born 31st July, 1891 at Derby. Soldier. Enlisted Coventry. Grave Ref. Sp. Mem. 9. Vendresse Churchyard, Aisne, France.

DENNISON, Private, Ernest William. M2/098039, 619th Mechanical Transport Coy., Army Service Corps. Died, Egypt, 22nd May, 1916. Age 33. Son of William and Susannah Dennison, of St. Annes-on-the-Sea, Lancs. Husband of Gertrude Valentina Dennison, of 96, Brookside Road, Golders Green, London. Born Preston. Enlisted Coventry. Resided Blackpool. Grave Ref. F. 70. Cairo War Memorial Cemetery, Egypt.

DENNY, Private, Joseph Thomas. 9510, 1st Bn., Royal Warwickshire Regiment. Killed in action, 12th October, 1916. Born in 1885 in St. Michael's Parish. Resided at 5c. 3h. Brewery Street. Reservist. Enlisted Coventry. Leaves a widow and three children. Employed Daimler Works. Broother of Private Walter Denny Memorial Ref. Pier and Face 9 A 9 B and 10 B. Thiepval Memorial, Somme, France.

DENNY, Private, Walter. 4531, 1/7th Bn., Royal Warwickshire Regiment. Killed in action, 14th July, 1916. Employed at Coventry. Enlisted Coventry. Brother of Private Joseph Denny. Memorial Ref. Pier and Face 9A 9B and 10B. Thiepval Memorial, Somme, France.

DENT, Austin. Killed in action. Name on Roll of Honour in Cathedral Church of St. Michael.

DENTON, Private, Frederick George, 997, 2nd Bn., Royal Warwickshire Regiment. 1st December, 1914. Age 24. Only son of George and Mary Denton, of Arley, Coventry. Born Windsor. Enlisted Nuneaton. Resided Windsor. Grave Ref. 1289. Fort Pitt Military Cemetery, Kent.

DENTON, W. Employed By Rover Co. Ltd. Killed in action.

DENTON, Private, Walter George. 17589, 1st Bn., Duke of Cornwall's Light Infantry. Died of wounds, home, 13th November, 1915. Age 24. Husband of Amy L. Denton, of 11, North Villiers Street, Leamington Spa. Employed By Rover Co. Ltd. Born St. John's, Leamington. Enlisted Leamington. Grave Ref. 68. 73. Leamington (Whitnash Road) Cemetery.

DERRY, Private, John Jordan. 20465, 16th Bn., Royal Warwickshire Regiment. Killed in action, 15th June, 1918. Age 33. Son of John Jordan and Lucy Derry, of Coventry. Born in 1885 at Hednesford, Staffs. Resided at Brinklow, Coventry. Enlisted Coventry. Grave Ref. Plot 3. Row B. Grave 5. Tannay British Cemetery, Thiennes, Nord, France.

DERVIS, Private, Walter George Stephen. 33003, formerly 6185, Royal Warwickshire Regiment. Killed in action, 22nd August, 1917. Born South Hackney, Middx. Enlisted Coventry.

DESBOROUGH, Private, Thomas Henry. 266259, "D" Coy. 2nd /7th Bn., Royal Warwickshire Regiment. Killed in action, 19th July, 1916. Age 21. Son of W. and Georgina Desborough, of 60, Mulliner Street, Coventry. Born 12th September, 1885 at Coventry. Labourer. Commemorated Iliffe and Sons Ltd Memorial. Enlisted January, 1915 at Coventry. Memorial Ref. Panel 22 to 25. Loos Memorial, Pas de Calais, France.

DEVER, Private, John. 265465, 1/7th Bn., Royal Warwickshire Regiment. Killed in action, 27th August, 1917. Age 27. Son of Mr. and Mrs. Patrick Dever, of Barrack Hill, Westport, Co. Mayo. Born Westport, Co. Mayo. Enlisted Coventry. Grave Ref. Enclosure No.4 XIII. E. 7. Bedford House Cemetery, Belgium

DEVINE, Sergeant, Noah. 16251, 2nd Bn., West Riding Regiment formerly 11418, North Staffordshire Regiment. Died of wounds, 9th July, 1916. Son of Elizabeth Devine, of 63, Stanley Street, Burton-on-Trent. Born Coventry. Enlisted Burton-on-Trent. Grave Ref. IV. D. 1. Doullens Communal Cemetery Extension No.1, France.

DEWIS, Sergeant, John Henry. 16842, 1st Bn., Royal Warwickshire Regiment. Killed in action, Pacuat Wood, 15th April, 1918. Born 18th September, 1889 in Freehold Street, Coventry. Resided 63, Northumberland Road. Despatch Clerk. Enlisted February, 1916 at Coventry. Memorial Ref. Panel 2 and 3. Ploegsteert Memorial, Belgium.

DEWIS, Private, Joseph Norman. 9305, 3rd Bn., Coldstream Guards. Killed in action, Battle of the Somme, 15th September, 1916. Born 10th March, 1894 at 13c 4h. Jordan Well, Coventry. Resided at 24, Short Street. Soldier. Enlisted Coventry. Memorial Ref. Pier and Face 7 D and 8 D. Thiepval Memorial, Somme, France.

DEWIS, Private, Walter George Stephen. 33003, 2/4th Bn., Oxfordshire and Buckinghamshire Light Infantry formerly Royal Warwickshire Regiment. Died of wounds, Passchendaele Ridge, Ypres, 22nd August, 1917. Born 2nd July, 1888 at London. Resided at Coventry. Linotype Operator. Commemorated Iliffe and Sons Ltd Memorial. Enlisted in 1916. Memorial Ref. Panel 96 to 98. Tyne Cot Memorial, Belgium.

DICKENS, Private, Frederick Andrew. 12568, 3rd Bn., Coldstream Guards. Killed in action, 15th September, 1916. Born St. Mary's, Northants. Enlisted Coventry. Resided Rushton, Northants. Memorial Ref. Pier and Face 7 D and 8 D. Thiepval Memorial, Somme, France.

DICKERSON, Private, Henry Edward Percy. 325149, 1st Bn., Cambridgeshire Regiment. Killed in action, 14th October, 1916. Age 23. Son of Mrs. Jane Johana Dickerson, of 12, Earl Street, Cambridge. Born at Cambridge. Employed at Coventry. Memorial Ref. Ref. Pier and Face 16 B. Thiepval Memorial, Somme, France.

DIGNAN, Lieutenant, Albert Guy. 7th (South Irish Horse) Bn., Royal Irish Regiment. Killed in action, 23rd March, 1918. Age 23. Son of Charles Coleman Dignan and Angeline Dignan of Ballinagard House, Roscommon. Nephew of Dr. Burke of Coventry. Educated St. Bede's College, Manchester. Memorial Ref. Panel 6. Pozieres Memorial, France

DILNOTT, Driver, John Oliver. 11522, C Bty., 66th Bde., Royal Field Artillery. Death occurred from peritonitis, Mesopotamia, 3rd September, 1917. Born 18th January, 1894 at Coventry. Resided at 53, Raglan Street. Gardener, Mr. Sidney Cash Ltd. Enlisted September, 1914, Coventry. Commemorated Holy Trinity Panels. Grave Ref. XII. C. 4. Baghdad (North Gate) War Cemetery, Iraq.

DILNOTT, Corporal, William Henry. 8821, 1st Bn., Royal Welsh Fusiliers. Killed in action, Fricourt, 30th June, 1916. Age 30. Eldest son of Mr. and Mrs. T. H. Dilnott, of Raglan Street, Coventry. Born 18th December, 1888 at Trinity, Coventry. Resided at 53, Raglan Street. Machinist, Coventry Ordnance Works. Reservist. Commemorated Holy Trinity Panels. Enlisted Coventry. Grave Ref. II. D. 20. Citadel New Military Cemetery, Fricourt, Somme, France.

DILWORTH, Private, Albert Edward. 64401, 16th Bn., Manchester Regiment formerly 45856, Essex Regiment. Killed in action, 25th September, 1918. Age 19. Son of Mrs. T. H. Dilworth, of 5, New Row, Kenilworth. Born Kenilworth. Enlisted Coventry. Resided Kenilworth. Memorial Ref. Panel 120 to 124 and 162 to 162A and 163A. Tyne Cot Memorial, Belgium.

DINGLEY, Private, Albert Bert. 12802, 11th Bn., Royal Warwickshire Regiment. Killed in action, Albert, 13th August, 1916. Born in 1880 at 2, Cook Street. Resided at 2, Cook Street. Haulier. Enlisted Coventry. Memorial Ref. Pier and Face 9 A 9 B and 10 B. Thiepval Memorial, Somme, France.

DINGLEY, Private, John. 16855, 15th Bn., Royal Warwickshire Regiment. Died of wounds, 3rd September, 1916. Age 23. Son of Henry and Elizabeth Dingley, of 19, Stephen Street, Coventry. Born 15th September, 1892 at 23, Upper Well Street, Coventry. Baker. Enlisted February, 1916, Coventry. Commemorated Holy Trinity Panels. Grave Ref. 2. B. 22. Corbie Communal Cemetery Extension, Somme, France.

DIPPER, Private, Arthur William. 5550, 1st Coy., 2nd Bn., Coldstream Guards. Killed in action, La Bassee, 28th February, 1915. Died from the shock of two shells exploding close to his head. Age 31. Son of Frank and Matilda Dipper, of Stretton-on-Dunsmore, Rugby. Born 24th November, 1883 at Stretton on Dunsmore. Resided at Coventry. Bank Messenger. Reservist. Enlisted Coventry. Memorial Ref. Panel 2 and 3. Le Touret Memorial, France. (Possibly buried La Bassee Canal Bridge).

DIXON, Private, Charles. 20322, 7th Bn., Duke of Cornwall's Light Infantry formerly Royal Warwickshire Regiment. Died of wounds, 3rd September, 1916. Born 13th March, 1889 in Henry Street. Resided at 11, Bond Street. Machinist. Commemorated Triumph and Gloria Memorial and Holy Trinity Panels. Enlisted October, 1914 at Coventry. Memorial Ref. Pier and Face 6 B. Thiepval Memorial, Somme, France.

DOBBINS, Private, John Allen. 3000, 2/7th Bn., Royal Warwickshire Regiment. Killed in action, Armentieres, 19th July, 1916 by a shell. Born 16th April, 1897 at Coventry. Resided at 60, Alma Street. Oil and Colour Merchant's Apprentice, Mr. Courts, Cope Street. Enlisted October, 1914, Coventry. Commemorated St. Michael's Church. Grave Ref. VI. B. 2. Aubers Ridge British Cemetery, Aubers, France.

DOBINSON, Lieutenant, Stanley Raine. 10th Bn., attached 1/4th Bn., West Yorkshire Regiment. Educated at King Henry VIII School, 1899 to 1904. Killed in action, April, 1918. Commemorated King Henry VIII School. Memorial Ref. Panel 31 and 32. Pozieres Memorial, France.

DODD, Gunner, Harry. 840635, C Bty., 306th Bde., Royal Field Artillery. Killed in action, 22nd August, 1917. Age 21. Son of Harry and Ada Dodd, of 138, Bulkington Road, Bedworth. Born Bedworth. Enlisted Coventry. Grave Ref. III. G. 16. White House Cemetery, St. Jean-Les-Ypres, Belgium.

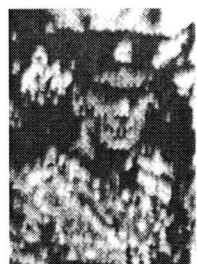

DODSON, Acting Lance Corporal, Alfred Charles. 400988, 2nd Bn., Essex Regiment formerly 7456, Bedfordshire Regiment. Killed in action, 15th August, 1918. Age 32. Son of John and Sophia Dodson, of 15, Crown Walk, St. Ives, Hunts. Husband of Ada Dodson (nee Reeves), of 28, Bowling Green Street, Warwick. Born Swavesey, Cambs. Enlisted Huntingdon. Resided Coventry. Memorial Ref. Panel 85 to 87. Loos Memorial, France.

DODSON, Lieutenant, Frederick Hugh. 12/683, 6th (Hauraki) Coy., Auckland Regiment, New Zealand Expeditionary Force. Killed in action between 25th April, 1915 and 29th April, 1915. Son of Maude Dodson of Courtville. Annexe, Auckland. Aged 23. Educated Bablake School. Commemorated Bablake School Memorial. Memorial Ref. Lone Pine Memorial, Turkey.

DODSWORTH, Lance Corporal, Edmund Francis. 2305, 5th Bn., London Rifle Brigade. Died of wounds, 2nd July, 1916. Age 41. Son of Lt.-Col. Edmund Dodsworth and Ruth Dodsworth. Employed Coventry. Grave Ref. I. B. 10. Doullens Communal Cemetery Extension No.1, France.

DOLBY, Private, John Thomas. 8214, 1st Bn., Royal Munster Fusiliers. Killed in action, 1st May, 1915. Age 33. Son of John Dolby and Catherine, of Kirby Lodge, Melton Mowbray, Leicestershire. Billeted Coventry. Born Melton Mowbray. Enlisted Ilkeston, Derby. Memorial Ref. Panel 185 to 190. Helles Memorial, Turkey.

DOODSON, Private, Ewart. 206130, 12th Coy., D Bn., Machine Gun Corps (Heavy Branch) formerly 2474, Machine Gun Corps. Killed in action, 9th April, 1917. Age 18. Adopted son of Mr. and Mrs. Tyas Wood, of 4, Scout Hill Terrace, Dewsbury, Yorks. Born Elland, Yorks. Enlisted Coventry. Memorial Ref. Bay 10. Arras Memorial, France.

DORMAN, Captain, Edward Crump. 1st Bn., Royal Munster Fusiliers. Killed in action 1st May, 1915. Age 30. Son of John William and Marion Isabelle Dorman of Raffeen, Kinsale, County Cork. Husband of Hilda Penn Dorman of Knockmourne, Conna, Co. Cork. Billeted Coventry. Born 1885. Commissioned November, 1908. Memorial Ref. Panel 185 to 190. Helles Memorial, Turkey.

DOWELL, Private, Sidney William. 19223, 2 Platoon, A Coy., 10th Bn., Royal Warwickshire Regiment. Killed in action, 18th November, 1916. Age 28. Husband of Harriet Caroline Dowell, of 26, Bridge End, Warwick previously 40, Villier Street, Coventry. Parents resided Bubbenhall. Born Bubbenhall. Enlisted Coventry. Employed Courtaulds. Grave Ref. B. 32. Grandcourt Road Cemetery, Grandcourt, France.

DOWNES, Private, John William. 42539, 2nd Bn., West Yorkshire Regiment. Killed in action, 24th June, 1917. Age 25. Son of John and Annie Downes. Husband of F. Downes, of 17/2, South Street, Park, Sheffield. Born Sheffield. Enlisted Coventry. Grave Ref. I. S. 18. Menin Road South Military Cemetery, Belgium.

DOWNSWORTH, Driver, Harry. Royal Field Artillery. Died, Home, 3rd November, 1918. Born 15th March, 1884 at Hull. Resided at Coventry. Fruiterer. Reservist.

DOWSWELL, Private, Herbert, 4504, 1st /7th Bn., Royal Warwickshire Regiment. Killed in action, 14th July, 1916. Age 26. Son of Mrs. Kate Dowswell, of 6 Court, 1 House, Spon End, Coventry. Employed Coventry. Enlisted Coventry. Memorial Ref. Pier and Face 9 A 9 B and 10 B. Thiepval Memorial, Somme, France.

DRAKE, Private, George. 5783, 1st Bn., Royal Munster Fusiliers formerly 8140, Lancers of the line. Died of wounds, Gallipoli, 29th August, 1915. Born Bewdley, Worcs. Enlisted Deptford, Surrey. Resided Coventry. Memorial Ref. Panel 185 to 190. Helles Memorial, Turkey.

DRAKEFORD, Private, John William. PLY/1540(S), 1st Royal Marine Bn., Royal Naval Division, Royal Marine Light Infantry. Killed in action, 26th October, 1917. Born 25th June, 1896 at Foleshill. Resided at 46, Stoney Stanton Road. Coremaker. Enlisted August, 1916. Memorial Ref. Panel 1 and 162A. Tyne Cot Memorial, Belgium.

DRAKELEY, Second Lieutenant, Reginald Kenneth. 9th Bn., Royal Warwickshire Regiment. Died of wounds, Kut-el-Amara, 20th April, 1916. Born 4th February, 1896 at Birmingham. Resided at Wallasley, Cheshire (Formerly Coventry). Police Officer. Educated Bablake School. Enlisted 1914. Commemorated Bablake School Memorial and Saint Thomas the Apostle, Longford. Grave Ref. XXI. D. 1. Amara War Cemetery, Iraq.

DRAKELEY, Rifleman, Thomas. 15/52156, 15th Bn., Royal Irish Rifles formerly 5968, Royal Warwickshire Regiment. Killed in action, 20th October, 1918. Age 36. Son of John and Jane Drakeley. Born at Nuneaton. Born Coventry. Enlisted Nuneaton. Grave Ref. VII. A. 4. Harlebeke New British Cemetery, Belgium.

DRAYTON, Private, Charles Hindon. 19646, 1st Bn, Wiltshire Regiment. formerly 13943, Oxfordshire and Buckinghamshire Light Infantry. Killed in action, 16th June, 1915. Age 19. Son of Mr. and Mrs. Hindon, of 4, Leicester Street, Coventry. Born 7th September, 1895 at Belton, Lincolnshire. Toolmaker, Singer Ltd. Enlisted September, 1914, Coventry. Death reported May, 1916. Memorial Ref. Panel 53. Ypres (Menin Gate) Memorial, Ieper, West-Vlaanderen, Belgium.

DREW, Private (Signaller), James. 16230, 10th Bn., Royal Warwickshire Regiment. Killed in action, 25th March, 1918. Age 22. Son of Eli J. and Emily Drew, of The Common, Kenilworth, Warwickshire. Born 11th February, 1896 at Solihull. Resided at Kenilworth. Clerk. Enlisted January, 1916 at Coventry. Memorial Ref. Bay 3. Arras Memorial, France.

DREWITT, Private, Henry John. 254877, 3rd Bn. Attached 2/2nd Bn., City of London Regiment. Killed in action, 26th August, 1918. Born at Coventry. Resided at Holloway. Memorial Ref. Panel 10. Vis-en-Artois Memorial, France.

DRIVER, Private, Percy James. 14968, 11th Bn., Royal Warwickshire Regiment. Killed in action, 29th April, 1917. Born Tachbrook, Warwicks. Enlisted Coventry. Memorial Ref. Bay 3. Arras Memorial, France.

DRY, Driver, Charles Frederick. 10140, 7th Div. Ammunition Col., Royal Field Artillery. Died of wounds, 4th September, 1916. Born Oxford. Employed Coventry. Enlisted Coventry. Grave Ref. I. B. 12. Dantzig Alley British Cemetery, Mametz, France.

DUFNER, Sergeant, Leonard Bennett. 80120, 6th Light Armoured Motor Bty., Machine Gun Corps (Motors). Killed in action, Mesopotamia, 26th August 1918. Age 21. Son of Herbert John and Elizabeth Dufner of 106, Sir Thomas Whites Road, Coventry. Born 2nd September, 1897 in Clifton Terrace, Lower Ford Street. Enlisted March 1918. Engineer. Commemorated War Memorial Park. Memorial Ref. Panel 42. Basra Memorial, Iraq.

DUGMORE, Private, Harry. 307851, 1/8th Bn., Royal Warwickshire Regiment. Killed in action, 4th October, 1917. Born 24th October, 1896 at Smethwick. Resided at 1, St. Osburg's Road. Coremaker. Commemorated Coventry Chain Memorial. Enlisted in 1916 at Coventry. Memorial Ref. Panel 23 to 28 and 163A. Tyne Cot Memorial, Belgium.

DUMBLETON, Company Sergeant Major, Francis George, DCM. 9656, 10th Bn., Northumberland Fusiliers. Died of wounds, 9th August, 1916. Age 37. Husband of Alice Louisa Dumbleton, of 8, Hazelbank Road, Catford, London. Born Coventry. Enlisted London. Awarded Distinguished Conduct Medal for conspicuous gallantry during an attack when under exceptionally heavy fire, he collected and controlled a disorganised party of men left without an Officer, and attaching himself to another battalion, took part in the attack and the subsequent capture of prisoners. Grave Ref. III. A. 8. Heilly Station Cemetery, Mericourt-L'abbe, France.

DUNKLEY, Sergeant, Frederick. 1211, "A" Bty. 59th Bde., Royal Field Artillery. Killed in action, 24th December, 1916. Age 23. Son of John and Ellen Dunkley. Born at Buckingham. Employed Coventry. Grave Ref. III. T. 12. Pozieres British Cemetery, Ovillers-La Boisselle, France.

DUNN, Private, Joseph. 293172, 1/7th Bn., Cheshire Regiment. Killed in action, Egypt, 3rd November, 1917. Born Limehouse, Middx. Enlisted Coventry. Grave Ref. E. 3. Beersheba War Cemetery, Israel.

DUNN, Private, Oliver, 23862, 10th Bn., Royal Warwickshire Regiment. Died of wounds, 16th August, 1918. Age 33. Son of William and Sarah Ann Dunn, of Foleshill, Coventry. Husband of Alice Dunn. Wounded at Cambrai, 1917. Born 1885, Coventry. Enlisted Coventry. Bricklayer, Electricity Department. Commemorated Electricity Department Memorial, Coventry Corporation. Grave Ref. IV. A. 27. Pernes British Cemetery, Pas de Calais, France.

DUNN, Private, Thomas William. 265603, 1st /7th Bn., Royal Warwickshire Regiment. Died of wounds, Ypres, 5th October, 1917. Age 26. Son of Mr. and Mrs. T. Dunn, of 6, Newdigate Road, Coventry. Born 13th November, 1891 at South Shields. Polisher. Enlisted September, 1914 at Coventry. Employed Rover Co. Ltd. Memorial Ref. Panel 23 to 28 and 163A. Tyne Cot Memorial, Zonnebeke, West-Vlaanderen, Belgium. (Possibly buried at Ypres).

DUNN, Private, W. D. 1/7th Bn., Royal Warwickshire Regiment. Killed in action according to original Roll of Honour. Employed Humber Ltd. Suffered gunshot wound in the head, reported in hospital at Le Havre, 10th March, 1916. Resided 27, Vernon Street.

DURHAM, Private, William Henry. 19020, 1st Bn., Dorsetshire Regiment formerly 17936, Worcestershire Regiment. Died of wounds, 28th April, 1918. Age 20. Son of William and Matilda Durham, of 43, Harnall Lane East, Coventry. Born 26th January, 1898 at 6, St. Agnes Lane, Coventry. Resided at 43, Harnall Lane East. Apprentice Machinist, Alfred Herbert Ltd. Enlisted September, 1914, Coventry. Grave Ref. X. C. 28. Mendinghem British Cemetery, Belgium.

DURRANT, Gunner, Alfred. 58547, 25th Bty. 35th Bde., Royal Field Artillery. Killed in action, 20th October, 1917. Born Coventry. Resided Highcliffe, Hants. Memorial Ref. Panel 4 to 6 and 162. Tyne Cot Memorial, Belgium.

DYER, Private, Arthur George. 34197, 12th Bn., Somerset Light Infantry. Killed in action, 6th November, 1917. Age 21. Son of Edgar and Ella Dyer, of 131, Holyhead Road, Coventry. Native of Highbridge, Somerset. Born 1896 at Highbridge, Somerset. Grave Ref. L. 49. Beersheba War Cemetery, Israel.

DYSON, Driver, Richard. 135537, 256th Bde., Royal Field Artillery. Killed in action, 13th October, 1918. Born Birmingham. Enlisted Coventry. Grave Ref. D. 3. Ramillies British Cemetery, France.

EADON, Private, Henry. 2393, 1st Bn., Royal Warwickshire Regiment. Killed in action, 25th April, 1915. Born Napton, Warwick. Enlisted Coventry. Memorial Ref. Panel 8. Ypres (Menin Gate) Memorial, Belgium.

EAGLES, Private, Alfred Samuel. 4435, 1/7th Bn., Royal Warwickshire Regiment. Killed in action, 14th July, 1916. Age 21. Son of Mr. W. H. and Mrs. F. Jones, of 1 Court, 4 House, Moorsom Street, Hockley, Birmingham. Enlisted Coventry. Resided Birmingham. Memorial Ref. Pier and Face 9 A 9 B and 10 B. Thiepval Memorial, France.

EAGLES, Gunner, William Henry. 75854, 145th Heavy Bty., Royal Garrison Artillery. Killed in action, 28th October, 1917. Age 25. Son of Mr. and Mrs. William Eagles, of Berkswell, Coventry. Born Berkswell. Enlisted Birmingham. Resided Dorylesden, Lancs. Grave Ref. XII. D. 10. The Huts Cemetery, Ieper, West-Vlaanderen, Belgium.

EALES, Private, Charles. 28323, 3rd Bn., Northamptonshire Regiment transferred to 546153, Labour Corps formerly 7089, Northants Regt. Died, home, 7th November, 1918. Age 27. Son of Charles Henry Eales and Catherine Eales, of 19, Harley Street, Stoke, Coventry. Born Bugbrooke, Northants. Enlisted Northampton. Resided Coventry. Grave Ref. 463. I. 17962. Northampton (Towcester Road) Cemetery, Northamptonshire.

EALES, Private, Walter Frederick. 34031, 1st Bn. Duke of Cornwall's Light Infantry formerly 18938, Royal Warwickshire Regiment. Killed in action, 23rd April, 1917. Born 29th September, 1897 at Bugbrooke. Resided at 19, Harley Street. Labourer. Enlisted 1916 at Coventry. Memorial Ref. Bay 6. Arras Memorial, France.

EALES, Private, William Edward. 38654, 1st Bn., Duke of Cornwall's Light Infantry formerly 226955, Royal Army Ordnance Corps. Killed in action, 22nd September, 1918. Age 34. Son of William Henry and Maria Eales. Husband of Helen Eales, of 55, Waverley Road, Kenilworth, Warwickshire. Born at Exeter. Resided Kenilworth. Enlisted Coventry. Memorial Ref. Panel 6. Vis-en-Artois Memorial, France.

EARDLEY, Private, John William. 266713, (4687). 1st /7th Bn., Royal Warwickshire Regiment. Killed in action, 14th July 1916. Age 24. Son of Mrs. W. Eardley, of 33, Albion Street, Coventry. Husband of Ada Milne (formerly Eardley), of 4, Union Street, Coventry. Commemorated Coventry Chain Memorial. Born Coventry. Enlisted Coventry. Leaves a widow and one child. Memorial Ref. Pier and Face 9 A 9 B and 10 B. Thiepval Memorial, Somme, France.

EARLE, Private, George. 33672, 1/1st Bn., Oxfordshire and Buckinghamshire Light Infantry formerly 41285, Royal Berkshire Regiment. Killed in action, Passchendaele, 8th October, 1917. Born 15th September, 1880 at Foleshill. Resided in Boston Place. Weaver. Enlisted May, 1917 at Coventry. Memorial Ref. Panel 96 to 98. Tyne Cot Memorial, Belgium.

EATON, Private, John Frderick. L/11531, 9th (Queen's Royal) Lancers. Killed in action, 21st August, 1918. Age 28. Husband of Mabel Eaton, of 31, Queen Street, Coventry. Born Bethnal Green. Enlisted Whitehall. Resided Dalston. Grave Ref. B. 22. Railway Cutting Cemetery, Courcelles-Le-Comte, Pas de Calais, France.

EATON, Gunner, Percy Allen. 110539, 224th Siege Battery, Royal Garrison Artillery. Killed in action, 30th July, 1917. Born 1884 in Kettering, Northants. Enlisted Birmingham. Resided 21, Victoria Street, Coventry. Pawnbroker's Assistant, Mr. A. Evans. Grave Ref. II. F. 7. Klein-Vierstraat British Cemetery, Belgium.

EAVES, Private, Ernest. 16502, 9th Bn., Royal Warwickshire Regiment. Died, Mesopotamia 14th November, 1916. Age 23. Son of Edward and Mary Ann Eaves, of 14, Sherbourne Street, Coventry. Born 9th February, 1892 at Coventry. Butcher. Enlisted February, 1916, Warwick. Resided Coventry. . Commemorated St. John's Church. Grave Ref. IX. A. 2. Amara War Cemetery, Iraq.

EAVES, Private, Harold. 1778, 1/7th Bn., Royal Warwickshire Regiment. Killed in action, 14th July, 1916. Born Coventry. Enlisted Coventry. Resided at 73, Howard Street. Employed Daimler Co. Ltd. Memorial Ref. Pier and Face 9 A 9 B and 10 B. Thiepval Memorial, Somme, France.

ECCLES, Private, William Christopher. 28656, 1/6th Bn., Royal Warwickshire Regiment. Killed in action, 4th October, 1917. Born in 1885. Resided at 16, Mansell Street. Labourer. Employed Rowland Hill and Sons Ltd. Enlisted Coventry. Memorial Ref. Panel 23 to 28 and 163A. Tyne Cot Memorial, Belgium.

EDMANS, Lance Corporal, Joseph Phillip Hayward, MM. 9779, 5th Bn., Royal Berkshire Regiment. Died of wounds, 5th April, 1918. Age 25. Son of James Heywood Edmans and Alice Maud Edmans, of Hackney, London. Born at Hackney, Middlesex. Resided at Wolston. Employed Coventry. Commemorated Wolston Memorial. Gazetted for Military Medal, 19th November, 1917. Grave Ref. VI. E. 52. Doullens Communal Cemetery Extension No.1, France.

EDMONDSON, F. Employed by Alfred Herbert Ltd.

EDMUNDS, Private, William. 9897, 1st Bn., Royal Welsh Fusiliers. Died of wounds, 13th November, 1914. Born in St. Michael's Parish. Commemorated St. John's Church. Enlisted Coventry. Grave Ref. A. 6. Halluin Communal Cemetery, France.

EDSON, Private, Alfred Sear. 382, 15th Bn., Royal Warwickshire Regiment. Killed in action, 3rd September, 1916. Born Coventry. Enlisted Birmingham. Resided Coventry. Memorial Ref. Pier and Face 9 A 9 B and 10 B. Thiepval Memorial, Somme, France.

EDWARDS, Private, Alfred. 11314, 6th Bn., Oxfordshire and Buckinghamshire Light Infantry. Killed in action, Guillemont Farm, Battle of the Somme, 3rd September, 1916. Age 22. Born 25th February, 1894 at 100, Much Park Street, Coventry. Resided 5c. 10h. Much Park Street, Coventry. Coremaker, Daimler Foundry. Enlisted September, 1914 at Nuneaton. Memorial Ref. Pier and Face 10 A and 10 D. Thiepval Memorial, Somme, France.

EDWARDS, Private, Alfred. 19060, 15th Bn., Royal Warwickshire Regiment. Died of wounds, 2nd July, 1917. Born 8th June, 1898 in York Street, Coventry. Enlisted Coventry. Resided 4, Radford Road with his Uncle and Aunt, Mr. and Mrs. J. Cooke. Machinist, Daimler Works. Enlisted May, 1916. Grave Ref. III. E. 3. Aubigny Communal Cemetery Extension, Aubigny-en-Artois.

EDWARDS, Lance Sergeant, Alfred. F/1379, 13th Bn., Middlesex Regiment. Killed in action, 4th November, 1918. Born 1894 at Coventry. Enlisted Bristol. Resided Southville, Bristol. Professional Footballer. Enlisted 1914. Grave Ref. A. 2. Villers-Pol Communal Cemetery Extension, France.

EDWARDS, Second Lieutenant, Arthur Joseph. 16th Bn., Royal Warwickshire Regiment. Killed in action, Cambrai, 27th September, 1918. Husband of Nora Emily Edwards, of 56, Stanway Road, Coventry. Born 9th June 1891. Resided at Coventry. Enlisted in 1915. Commercial Traveller. Commemorated War Memorial Park. Grave Ref. VI. H. 1. Gouzeaucourt New British Cemetery, Nord, France.

EDWARDS, Private, Francis John. 202313, 2/4th Bn., West Riding Regiment. Died of wounds, 27th December, 1917. Age 23. Son of Elisha and Lily Edwards of 438, Anglesey Road, Burton-on-Trent. Born Burton-on-Trent. Enlisted Coventry. Resided Burton-on-Trent. Grave Ref. P. V. H. 7A. St. Sever Cemetery Extension, Rouen, France.

EDWARDS, Private, Frederick John. 242258, 2/6th Bn., Royal Warwickshire Regiment. Died of wounds, France, 14th April, 1917. Born at Ashow, Warwickshire. Employed Coventry. Enlisted Coventry. Grave Ref. O. VIII. B. 1. St. Sever Cemetery Extension, Rouen, France.

EDWARDS, G.E. Commemorated Iliffe & Sons Ltd.

EDWARDS, Private, Henry. 29128, 2nd Bn., Gloucestershire Regiment. Killed in action, Salonika, 7th December, 1916. Age 23. Son of Mrs. M. Edwards. Husband of A. M. Taylor (formerly Edwards), of 58, Craners Road, Coventry. Born 16th June, 1893 at 27, Leigh Street, Coventry. Carpenter. Enlisted Coventry. Memorial Ref. Doiran Memorial, Greece.

EDWARDS, H. Commemorated Post Office Memorial.

EDWARDS, Gunner, J. Royal Field Artillery. Killed in action, 1916. Commemorated St. Thomas Memorial.

EDWARDS, Private, James. 1096, 2nd Bn., Royal Warwickshire Regiment. Killed in action, 23rd January, 1915. Born in 1889 at Birmingham. Resided at 47, Gosford Street. Well known boxer under 'Mick Edwards'. Employed by Coventry Corporation Electricity Department. Enlisted Coventry. Resided Birmingham. Commemorated Electricity Department Memorial, Coventry Corporation. Grave Ref. IV. C. 12. Ration Farm Military Cemetery, La Chapelle-Darmentieres, France.

EDWARDS, Private, James Henry. 4122, 1st Bn., Royal Warwickshire Regiment. Killed in action, 23rd October, 1916. Born 18th October, 1894 at Hoxton, London. Resided at 20, Dean Street. Storekeeper, Rover Company Ltd. Enlisted 1914 at Coventry. Memorial Ref. Pier and Face 9 A 9 B and 10 B. Thiepval Memorial, Somme, France.

EDWARDS, Private, Jesse. 16828, 9th Bn., Royal Warwickshire Regiment. Died of wounds, Mesopotamia, 15th September, 1918. Born Fenny Compton, Warwicks. Enlisted Coventry. Memorial Ref. 2. 2. Tehran Memorial, Iran.

EDWARDS, Second Lieutenant, John Wesley, MC. 1st /1st , Queen's Own Worcestershire Hussars (Worcester Yeomanry). Killed in action, 8th November, 1917. Age 27. Son of John Wesley Edwards, of 55, Freeman Street, Coventry. Grave Ref. XIX. D. 11. Gaza War Cemetery, Israel.

EDWARDS, Sergeant, Phillip Charles. 52226, 15th Bn., Royal Irish Rifles formerly 2523, Royal Warwickshire Regiment. Killed in action, 26th April, 1918. Age 25. Son of James and Sarah Edwards, of 14, Wedgnock Terrace, The Cape, Warwick. Born Warwick. Enlisted Coventry. Resided Warwick. Grave Ref. A. 12. Cinq Rues British Cemetery, Hazebrouck, France.

EDWARDS, Private, William. 22781, (1st) 10th Bn., Worcestershire Regiment. Died of wounds, Peronne, 5th March, 1917. Age 27. Son of Edmund and Mary Ann Edwards. Born 3rd August, 1887 at 36, Wellington Street. Resided at 17, Highfield Road. Enlisted in 1914, Coventry. Miller. Commemorated War Memorial Park. Grave Ref. I. G. 11. Hem Farm Military Cemetery, Hem-Monacu near Peronne.

EGLESE, Private, Henry Archibald. M2/033362, 406th Mechanical Transport Coy., Royal Army Service Corps attd. II Corps Heavy Artillery. Killed in action, 19th May, 1918. Born 15th May, 1881 at Walworth, London. Enlisted Coventry. Resided at 73, Harnall Lane West. Motor Driver. Enlisted January, 1915. Grave Ref. V. B. 9. Longuenesse (St. Omer) Souvenir Cemetery, France.

EIFFES, Private, George John Henry. 14289, 1st Bn., Royal Fusiliers. Killed in action, 31st July, 1917. Age 22. Son of Jean and Emma Austsa Eiffes of 16, Princess Street, Richmond, Surrey. Enlisted Hounslow. Resided Richmond. Commemorated Iliffe & Sons Ltd. Grave Ref. II. L. 1. Perth Cemetery (China Wall), Belgium.

ELDEN, Private, Percy James. 19613, 10th Bn., Royal Warwickshire Regiment. Killed in action, 20th September, 1918. Age 34. Son of Mrs. Amelia Elden, of Broome, Bungay, Suffolk. Husband of Bridget Jones (formerly Elden), of 5, Tower Cottages, Leicester Street, Coventry. Born 5th April, 1884 at Broome, Norfolk. Bricklayer. Enlisted June, 1916 at Coventry. Memorial Ref. Panel 22 to 25. Loos Memorial, Pas de Calais, France. Possibly buried near Richbourg l'Avoue.

ELIOTT, Captain, Hugh Russell. 3rd Bn., Worcestershire Regiment. Killed in action, 12th October, 1914. Age 41. Son of Maj. Gen. William Russell Eliott. Husband of Constance Mary Eliott (nee Sedgwick), of Elnothington, Hollingbourne, Kent. Formerly Adjutant of the 7th Bn., Royal Warwickshire Regiment at Coventry, 1910 to 1913. Served in the Boer War. Grave Ref. IV. D. 14. Brown's Road Military Cemetery, Festubert, France.

ELKS, Rifleman, Edwin Russell. 13094, 8th Bn., King's Royal Rifle Corps. Killed in action, 3rd May, 1917. Age 15. Son of Edwin John (Lance Corporal, Royal Engineers) and Martha Elks, of 209, Walsgrave Road, Coventry. Born 25th December, 1901 at Burton-on-Trent. Machinist. Enlisted 14 years and 4 months and his mother secured his discharge and he re-enlisted spending his 15th birthday in France. One of the youngest casualties of The Great War. Father was a Lance Corporal in the Royal Engineers. Memorial Ref. Bay 7. Arras Memorial, Pas de Calais, France.

ELL, Private, Leonard. 203189, 2/5th Bn., Sherwood Foresters (Notts and Derby Regiment) formerly 29953, Bedfordshire Regiment. Died of wounds, 28th September, 1917. Born Coventry. Enlisted Watford. Resided Coventry. Grave Ref. VI. F. 7. Dozinghem Military Cemetery, Belgium.

ELLIFFE, Private, William Robert. 8th Bn., Northamptonshire Regiment. Died, home, 2nd February, 1917. Coal Wagoner. Grave Ref. Coventry (London Road) Cemetery.

ELLIMAN, Private, Percy. 2532, 1st/7th Bn., Royal Warwickshire Regiment. Killed in action, Battle of the Somme, 14th July, 1916. Born 28th January, 1888 at Stoke, Coventry. Resided at 31, Moor Street. Enlisted September, 1914. Chain Finisher for Coventry Chain Company. Commemorated Coventry Chain Memorial, St. Barbara's Church, St. John's Church and War Memorial Park. Enlisted Coventry. Leaves a widow and one child. Memorial Ref. Pier and Face 9 A 9 B and 10 B. Thiepval Memorial, Somme, France.

ELLIOTT, Private, Alfred Reginald. CH/1793(S), 1st Royal Marine Bn., Royal Naval Division, Royal Marine Light Infantry. 28th April, 1917. Son of William and Elizabeth Elliott, of 32, Canford Road, Heckford Park, Poole, Dorset. Husband of Hilda Mary Emeline Lane (formerly Elliott), of 9, Cleveland Road, Stoke, Coventry. Memorial Ref. Bay 1. Arras Memorial, Pas de Calais, France.

ELLIOTT, Sergeant, Ernest Clifford. R/1311, 20th Bn., King's Royal Rifle Corps. Killed in action, 28th April, 1918. Age 23. Son of William and Emma Jane Elliott, of 67, Nelson St., Whittington Moor, Chesterfield. Born 30th August, 1896 at Whittington Moor, near Chesterfield. Resided at 28, Highland Road. Toolmaker. Enlisted September, 1914. Educated Bablake School. Commemorated Bablake School Memorial. Grave Ref. IV. A. 32. Chocques Military Cemetery.

ELLIOTT, Private, Francis John. 3300, 9th Bn., Royal Warwickshire Regiment. Killed in action, 10th August, 1915. Age 26. Son of Charles Elliott, of Brook Street, Wolston, Coventry. Commemorated Wolston Memorial. Born Bubbenhall. Enlisted Coventry. Memorial Ref. Panel 35 to 37. Helles Memorial, Turkey.

ELLIOTT, Private, Herbert, 203302, 1st /5th Bn., Royal Warwickshire Regiment. Killed in action, 19th August, 1917. Age 39. Husband of Lucy Elliott, of 2 Court, 2 House, Whitefriars Street, Coventry. Born 1st February, 1879 at Coventry. Brazier, Whitehouse Cycle Works, Friars Road, Coventry. Enlisted 6th July, 1916, Coventry. Memorial Ref. Panel 23 to 28 and 163A. Tyne Cot Memorial, Zonnebeke, West-Vlaanderen, Belgium.

ELLIOTT, Gunner, Samuel James. 48532, 14th Siege Battery, Royal Garrison Artillery. Killed in action, Gallipoli, 17th May, 1915. Age 21. Son of William and Emma Jane Elliott, of 67, Nelson Street, Whittington Moor, Chesterfield. Born 6th March, 1894 at Worksop. Resided at 28, Highland Road. Painter. Enlisted November, 1914 at Coventry. Educated Bablake School. Commemorated Bablake School Memorial. Memorial Ref. Panels 23 or 325. Helles Memorial, Turkey.

ELLIS, Private, Albert Edward. 9513, 3rd Bn., Worcestershire Regiment. Died of wounds, 19th July, 1917. Born Buttevant, Co. Cork. Enlisted Coventry. Resided Coventry. Grave Ref. XXII. M. 7. Etaples Military Cemetery, France.

ELLIS, Rifleman, Albert George. S/11214, 9th Bn., Rifle Brigade formerly 87264, Royal Artillery. Killed in action, 9th August, 1915 by a shell bursting in the trench. Born at Hastings. Resided Much Park Street. Employed by Swift of Coventry Ltd. Enlisted in 1915 at Coventry. Leaves a widow and one child. Memorial Ref. Panel 46 - 48 and 50. Ypres (Menin Gate) Memorial, Belgium.

ELLIS, E. Employed by Rover Company Ltd. Killed in action.

ELLIS, Sapper, Harry. WR/30111, 328th Quarrying Coy., Royal Engineers formerly 17706, Royal Warwickshire Regiment. Died, 12th September, 1918. Age 30. Born Sapcote, Leicester. Enlisted Coventry. Son of Charles and Ada Ellis, of Sapcote, Leicestershire. Grave Ref. V. E. 7A. Les Baraques Military Cemetery, Sangatte, France.

ELLIS, Private, Horace Jesse. Royal Berkshire Regiment. Died home, 12th October 1917. Born 19th March, 1891 at Banbury. Resided at 3c. 7h Bayley Lane. Enlisted March, 1916. Labourer. Commemorated War Memorial Park and Siddeley Deasy Roll of Honour. Grave Ref. Coventry (London Road) Cemetery.

 **ELSON**, Private, A W. 16413, 1st Bn., Hampshire Regiment. Died of wounds, 6th April, 1918. Age 28. Husband of Gertrude Ethel Elson (nee Davies), of 14, Stoney Stanton Road, Coventry. Grave Ref. XXXII. B. 10. Etaples Military Cemetery, Pas de Calais, France.

ELVIS, Private, Frank. West Riding Regiment. Died (Home) wounds received at Mons in 1914, 28th March, 1917. Born 10th November, 1883 at Coventry. Resided at Coventry. Telegraph Messenger. Grave Ref. Handsworth Cemetery.

EMBRA, Albert Edward. 7902, 9th Coy., Machine Gun Corps (Infantry) formerly R/15991, King's Royal Rifle Corps. Killed in action, 1st July, 1916. Born 11th August, 1893. Resided at 630, Foleshill Road. Labourer. Employed Alfred Herbert Ltd. Born Norton, Oxon. Enlisted Coventry. Memorial Ref. Pier and Face 5 C and 12 C. Thiepval Memorial, Somme, France.

EMERY, Gunner, Thomas. 45972, 1st/1st Welch Heavy Bty., Royal Garrison Artillery. Killed in action, 2nd September, 1918. Age 23. Son of Mr. and Mrs. T. Emery, of 122, Sandford Street, Lichfield, Staffs. Born Walsall. Enlisted Coventry. Resided Walsall. Memorial Ref. Panel 3. Vis-En-Artois Memorial, France

ENDALL, Private, Wilfred Reginald. 59382, 1st /8th Bn., Worcestershire Regiment. Died of wounds, 18th November, 1918. Age 19. Son of Joseph and Minnie Endall, of "Elliscombe," Lythall's Lane, Coventry. Native of Marlow, Bucks. Born 3rd April, 1899 at Marlow, Bucks. Enlisted June, 1918, Coventry. Resided Coventry. Mechanic. Grave Ref. S. III. O. 22. St. Sever Cemetery Extension, Rouen, Seine-Maritime, France.

ENGLAND, Private, Ralph. 24714, 3rd Bn., Grenadier Guards. Killed in action, 14th September, 1916. Born 30th January, 1896 at Ratley near Banbury. Resided at 9, Park Side. Grinder. Memorial Ref. Pier and Face 8D. Thiepval Memorial, Somme, France.

ENSOR, Gunner, Francis Arthur. 48566, 706th Bty., Royal Field Artillery. Died, Kut-el-Amara, Mesopotamia, 30th August, 1916. Husband of Edith Ensor, of Taher Building, Parel, Bombay, India. Born 23rd June 1889 at Keresley. Enlisted Coventry. Resided at 76, Brook Street. Turner. Reservist. Grave Ref. XXI. C. 23. Baghdad (North Gate) War Cemetery, Iraq.

ENSOR, Lance Bombardier, Sidney. 86782, 41st Div. Ammunition Col., Royal Field Artillery. Died 11th July, 1918. Resided at Nuneaton. Employed Coventry. Enlisted Coventry. Grave Ref. III. C. 24. Esquelbecq Military Cemetery, France.

ESSEX, Private, Thomas. 28615, 15th Bn., Royal Warwickshire Regiment. Killed in action, 24th August, 1918. Born St. Mary's, Warwick. Enlisted Coventry. Grave Ref. XIV. W. 7. Ovillers Military Cemetery, France.

ESSEX, Private, Thomas William. 37824, 8th Bn., Leicestershire Regiment formerly 3669, East Lancashire and Royal Engineers. Killed in action, 10th October, 1917. Age 33. Son of Thomas William and Alice Essex, of 66, Borough Road, Altrincham. Husband of Rose Essex, of 106, Stamford Park Road, Hale, Altrincham, Cheshire. Born Coventry. Enlisted Altrincham, Cheshire. Resided Hale, Cheshire. Memorial Ref. Panel 50 to 51. Tyne Cot Memorial, Belgium.

 **ESSEX,** Private, Walter Thomas. 28615, 15th Bn. Royal Warwickshire Regiment. Killed in action, 24th August, 1918. Born 25th August, 1887 at Warwick. Resided at 26, Station Street East. Employed the Rover Co. Ltd. Enlisted August, 1914. Grave Ref. 14. W. 7. Ovillers Military Cemetery, Ovillers-la-Boiselle, France.

ETHERIDGE, Private, Walter Charles. 202006, 1/5th Bn., Royal Warwickshire Regiment. Killed in action, 15th June, 1918. Age 23. Son of Mr. and Mrs. W. Etheridge, of Studley, Warwickshire. Born Spernell, Warwickshire. Enlisted Coventry. Resided Fletchamstead, near Coventry. Grave Ref. 2. C. 7. Magnaboschi British Cemetery, Italy.

EVANS, Private, Alfred Louis. 246102, 2nd Bn., Canadian Infantry (Eastern Ontario Regiment). Killed in action, 20th April, 1918. Age 40. Son of Francis Teale Evans and Sarah Evans, of Coventry. Husband of Emily Leah Evans, of Laurentian View, Ottawa, Ontario. Grave Ref. V. C. 2. Roclincourt Military Cemetery, Pas de Calais, France.

EVANS, Private, David. 5208, 1/4th Bn., Royal Berkshire Regiment. Killed in action, 23rd July, 1916. Age 33. Husband of Ellen Lily Evans, of 36, Cumberland Road, Reading, Berks. Born Coventry. Enlisted Reading. Memorial Ref. Pier and Face 11 D. Thiepval Memorial, Somme, France.

EVANS, Lance Corporal, Frederick William. 15859, 11th Bn., Royal Warwickshire Regiment. Killed in action, 13th August, 1916. Age 32. Son of Mr. and Mrs. Thomas Evans, of 106, Bromyard Road, Worcester. Born Tenbury, Worcs. Enlisted Coventry. Memorial Ref. Pier and Face 9 A 9 B and 10 B. Thiepval Memorial, Somme, France.

EVANS, George. Killed in action. Name on Roll of Honour in Holy Trinity Church.

EVANS, Private, John. 2183, 1st Bn., Royal Warwickshire Regiment. Killed in action, 12th October, 1916. Age 25. Son of Edward and Mary E. Evans, of 16, Grange Avenue, Binley, Coventry. Born St. George's, Wolverhampton. Enlisted Nuneaton. Memorial Ref. Pier and Face 9 A 9 B and 10 B. Thiepval Memorial, Somme, France.

EVANS, Lance Corporal, Joseph. CH/19608, 1st Royal Marine Bn., Royal Naval Division, Royal Marine Light Infantry. 26th October, 1917. Age 19. Son of James and Charlotte Evans, of Goodyers End, Exhall, Coventry. Memorial Ref. Panel 1 and 162A. Tyne Cot Memorial, Zonnebeke, West-Vlaanderen, Belgium

EVANS, Cadet, P J. 182002, Royal Air Force. Died, home, 9th September, 1918. Age 18. Son of John Evans, of Balsall Street, Balsall Common, Coventry. Grave Ref. In North-West part. Temple Balsall (St. Mary) Churchyard, Warwickshire.

EVANS, Corporal, Philip John. 2227, C Bn., Machine Gun Corps (Heavy Branch). Killed in action, 4th July, 1917. Age 21. Son of John and Annie Elizabeth Evans. Native Chester. Enlisted Coventry. Grave Ref. I. A. 6. Gwalia Cemetery. Belgium.

EVANS, T. Employed By Rover Company Ltd. Killed in action.

EVANS, Private, William Henry. 63225, 56th Coy., Machine Gun Corps (Infantry) formerly 21202, Royal Warwickshire Regiment. Killed in action, 31st July, 1917. Born Wolverhampton. Enlisted Coventry. Memorial Ref. Panel 56. Ypres (Menin Gate) Memorial, Belgium.

EVERALL, Rifleman, Harold. A/3706, 10th Bn., King's Royal Rifle Corps. Died of wounds, 23rd December, 1915. Age 24. Son of A. John and Jane Everall, of 64, Kingsway, Coventry. Born 1891, Coventry. Enlisted 1914, Warwick. Resided Coventry. Mechanic. Grave Ref. I. D. 70. Sailly-Sur-La-Lys-Canadian Cemetery, Pas de Calais, France.

EVEREST, Private, George Edward. 15110, "C" Coy. 1st Bn., Bedfordshire Regiment. Killed in action, 23rd January, 1916 on mining fatigue. Age 28. Son of William and Susannah Everest, 21, Stanley Street, Foleshill, Coventry. Born at Woolwich. Resided at Coventry. Enlisted St. Albans. Commemorated War Memorial Park. Grave Ref. V. B. 12. Citadel New Military Cemetery, Fricourt, Somme, France.

EVERETT, Private, Albert George. 16431, 9th Bn., Royal Warwickshire Regiment. Died, Mesopotamia, 4th July, 1916. Born 9th April, 1893 at Maldon, Essex. Resided at 380, Foleshill Road. Wood Machinist. Enlisted February, 1916 at Coventry. Grave Ref. VII. A. 5. Amara Cemetery, Iraq.

EVERSDEN, Private, Charles. 307756, 1/8th Bn., Royal Warwickshire Regiment. Killed in action, 23rd October, 1918. Age 36. Son of Joseph Eversden, of Little Brickhill, Bletchley, Bucks. Born Little Buckhill, Notts. Enlisted Nuneaton. Resided Coventry. Grave Ref. D. 30. Pommereuil British Cemetery, France.

EVERSDEN, Private, William. 17458, 10th Bn., Royal Warwickshire Regiment. Died of wounds, 12th November, 1917. Age 33. Son of Joseph Eversden, of Little Brickhill, Bletchley, Bucks. Born Little Brittle, Bucks. Enlisted Nuneaton. Resided Coventry. Grave Ref. VI. A. 3A. Mont Huon Military Cemetery, Le Treport, France.

EVETTS, Gunner, William John. 845269, 48th Trench Mortar Bty., Royal Field Artillery. Killed in action, Ypres, 27th July, 1917. Assumed to be at a dressing station and informed he had been buried by another unit. Age 21. Son of John and Mary Evetts, of 6, Brookville Terrace, London Road, Coventry. Born 12th April 1896 at Coventry. Resided at 6, Brookville Terrace. Enlisted October 1914. Engineer, Maudslay Motor Co. Ltd. Commemorated War Memorial Park. Grave Ref. I. G. 29. La Brique Military Cemetery, No.2, Ieper, West-Vlaanderen, Belgium.

EYKELBOSCH, Private, John. 16405, 11th Bn., Royal Warwickshire Regiment. Died of wounds received in the Battle of the Somme, 19th July, 1916. Age 19. Son of Joseph and Fanny Eykelbosch, of 39, Spencer Street, Coventry. Born 8th October, 1898 at 5, Sovereign Row, Coventry. Resided 5, Sovereign Row. Machinist, Triumph Works. Enlisted January, 1916. Coventry. Commemorated Triumph and Gloria Memorial. Grave Ref. I. J. 14. Albert Communal Cemetery Extension, Somme, France.

FACER, Rifleman, Cornelius. 41914, 7th Bn., Royal Irish Rifles formerly 202563, Northamptonshire Regiment. Killed in action, 8th August, 1917. Son of Elizabeth Facer, 83, St. Edmunds Road, Northampton. Born Northampton. Enlisted Northampton. Resided Coventry. Memorial Ref. Addenda Panel 57 to 60. Ypres (Menin Gate) Memorial, Belgium.

FACER, Lance Corporal, Frederick Pitham. R/1246, 8th Bn., King's Royal Rifle Corps. Killed in action, 3rd July, 1916. Age 24. Son of Mr. and Mrs. Facer, of Old Bilton, Rugby. Husband of Rose Facer, of Rosy Walk, Ryton-on-Dunsmore, Coventry. Born Rugby. Enlisted Rugby. Resided Rainsbrook. Commemorated Ryton Memorial. Grave Ref. I. E. 29. Faubourg D'Amiens Cemetery, Arras, Pas de Calais, France.

FAIRBROTHER, A. H. Died, home. 9th July, 1916. Born 1st April, 1897. Resided at Rugby. Railway Clerk. Enlisted February, 1916.

FALKNER, Private, John Edward Charles Burbidge. 26819, 12th Bn., East Surrey Regiment. Died of wounds, 29th September, 1918. Born 10th October, 1899 at Leamington. Enlisted Grove Park, Kent. Resided 20, Eagle Street, Coventry. Vanman. Enlisted October, 1917. Grave Ref. II. H. 15. Zantvoorde British Cemetery, Belgium.

FARDON, Private, Arthur. 2568, 1/7th Bn., Royal Warwickshire Regiment. Killed in action, Pozieres, 14th July, 1916. Born 14th February, 1891 at 9, Shakespeare Terrace, Stoney Stanton Road. Resided at 38, Somerset Road. Fitter, Standard Motor Works Ltd. Enlisted September, 1914. Grave Ref. I. E. 6. Pozieres British Cemetery, Ovillers-La Boisselle, France.

FARMER, Private, Albert Edward. 16881, 14th Bn., Royal Warwickshire Regiment. Killed in action, near Arras, 25th June, 1917. Age 21. Son of George and Mary Jane Farmer, of 20, Minster Road, Coventry. Born 14th July, 1896 at Leamington. Resided in Minster Road. Clerk. Memorial Ref. Bay 3. Arras Memorial, Pas de Calais, France.

FARMER, Boy 1st Class, Henry Gordon. J/40828, HMS Malaya, Royal Navy. Killed in action, Battle of Jutland, 31st May, 1916. Struck by a shell. Age 16. Son of George and Mary Jane Farmer, of 20, Minster Road, Coventry. Born 10th August, 1899 at Leamington. Resided at 23a Coundon Road. Coremaker. Enlisted June, 1915. Commemorated Bablake School Memorial. Memorial Ref. 13. Plymouth Naval Memorial, Devon.

FARMER, Gunner, Thomas. 73511, 115th Heavy Bty., Royal Garrison Artillery. Killed in action, near Ypres, 1st November, 1917. Son of Mr. W. Farmer, of 2 Court, 5 House, Paynes Lane, Coventry. Born 5th September, 1880 at Coventry. Enlisted April, 1916, Coventry. Resided at 24, East Street. Fitter. Grave Ref. II. C. 9. Minty Farm Cemetery, Langemark-Poelkapelle, West-V., Belgium.

FARNDON, Private, Herbert A. 4275, 2nd Bn., Royal Warwickshire Regiment. Killed in action, by a shell, 20th March, 1916. Son of Thomas and Alice Farndon. Husband of Mrs. E. Farndon, of 85, York Buildings, Bulkington Road, Bedworth. Born in Little Beaton, Warwickshire. Enlisted Nuneaton. Miner employed Exhall Colliery. Leaves a wife and four children. Grave Ref. D. 12. Point 110 New Military Cemetery, France.

FARRELL, Private, Daniel. 8799, 2nd Bn. Royal Welsh Fusiliers. Killed in action, 15th July, 1916. Born Coventry. Enlisted Birmingham. Memorial Ref. Pier and Face 4 A. Thiepval Memorial, Somme, France.

FARRELL, Pioneer, Frank Clifford. 288994, No. 1 Special Coy., Royal Engineers. Killed in action, near Albert, 23rd June, 1918. Age 28. Son of Simpson Farrell and Ada Farrell. Husband of Emily Peggy Farrell, of 12, St. Nicholas Street, Coventry. A member of the Pharmaceutical Society, passed the examination in January, 1915. Born 23rd June 1890 at Derby. Resided at 89 Northfield Road. Enlisted Coventry September, 1917. Assistant Chemist, Mr. Bird, Station Street. Commemorated War Memorial Park. He leaves a widow and a child. Memorial Ref. Panel 10 to 13. Pozieres Memorial, Somme, France.

FARRELL, Able Seaman, Walter John. Bristol Z/3998, B Coy., Hawke Bn., Royal Naval Division, Royal Naval Volunteer Reserve. Died of wounds (gassed), 19th March, 1918. Age 25. Eldest son of John and Florence Farrell, of 20, East Street, Coventry. Born 13th November 1892, at London. Resided at 20, East Street. Enlisted Portsmouth, June, 1916. Blacksmith. Godiva Harrier. Commemorated War Memorial Park. Grave Ref. II. G. 11. Achiet-Le-Grand Communal Cemetery Extension, Pas de Calais, France.

FARREN, Private, Joseph. 265409, 2/7th Bn., Royal Warwickshire Regiment. Killed in action, 19th July, 1916. Born 18th March, 1896 at London. Resided at Coventry. Machinist. Enlisted, 1914. Son of Mr. and Mrs. Farren of 57, Whitefriars Lane, Coventry. Memorial Ref. Panel 22 to 25. Loos Memorial, France.

FARROW, Private, Albert Edward. 442444, 2nd /1st London Field Ambulance, Royal Army Medical Corps. Killed in action, 5th November, 1918. Age 22. Son of William and Eliza Farrow, of Coventry. Born 17th February, 1896 at London. Resided at Coventry. Butcher. Enlisted November, 1914. Grave Ref. A. 11. Sebourg Communal Cemetery, Nord, France.

FAULKNER, Private, Samuel Turner. 301682 (late 5846), 1st /5th Bn., Royal Warwickshire Regiment. Died of pneumonia, 25th January, 1917. Age 30. Son of Isaac Faulkner. Husband of Mary Ellen Faulkner, of 8c. 1h. Jordan Well, Coventry. Born 10th December, 1886. Resided at 8c. 1h. Jordan Well. Labourer, Coventry Chain formerly Tailor, Messrs Goldie Brothers. Enlisted February, 1916. Leaves a wife and one child. Grave Ref. II. B. 25. Abbeville Communal Cemetery Extension, Somme, France.

FAULKNER, Private, William Alfred. 26934. 1st Bn., Worcestershire Regiment. Killed in action, Somme, 29th July, 1917. Age 17. (Served as Booth), Son of Alfred Edward and Mary Ann Faulkner, of 2, Camden Street, Derby. Born 2nd December, 1899 at Derby. Resided at 570, Foleshill Road. Planer. Memorial Ref. Panel 34. Ypres (Menin Gate) Memorial, Belgium.

FAULKS, Private, Leonard. 3261, 1st/7th Bn., Royal Warwickshire Regiment. Killed in action, Battle of the Somme, 11th November, 1916. Born 26th December, 1896 at Foleshill. Resided at 4, Crabmill Lane. Driller, Siddeley Deasy. Commemorated War Memorial Park and Siddeley Roll of Honour. Memorial Ref. Pier and Face 9 A 9 B and 10 B. Thievpal Memorial, Somme, France.

FAWSON, Sergeant, Alfred Leonard, MM. 52386,15th Bn., Royal Irish Rifles formerly 3900, Royal Warwickshire Regiment. Killed in action, 20th October, 1918. Age 30. Son of Mr. and Mrs. Fawson, of 53, Oxford Street, Coventry. Born 1888 in Chauntry Place, Coventry. Enlisted Coventry. Resided in West Street. Wheel Maker. Enlisted January, 1915. Awarded Military Medal, 15th October, 1918 for gallantry in action. Gazetted for Military Medal, 14th May, 1919. Grave Ref. VII. A. 11. Harlebeke New British Cemetery, Harelbeke, West-Vlaanderen, Belgium.

FAWSON, Lance Sergeant, James. 14583, 8th Bn., Royal Berkshire Regiment. Killed in action, Loos, 13th October, 1915. Last seen in communications trench, firing at advancing Germans. Age 24. Son of James and Mary Fawson, of 53, Oxford Street, Coventry. Husband of Lily Fawson, of 44, Spon Street, Coventry. Born 16th March, 1891 at 53, Oxford Street, Coventry. Resided at 22, West Street. Iron Polisher. Enlisted September, 1914, Coventry. Leaves a wife and three children. Memorial Ref. Panel 93 to 95. Loos Memorial, Pas de Calais, France.

FAZAKARLEY, Private, Herbert. 16110, 10th Coy., Machine Gun Corps (Infantry) formerly 9463, Royal Warwickshire Regiment. Killed in action, 10th December, 1916. Born Coventry. Enlisted Worthing. Resided Coventry. Memorial Ref. Pier and Face 5 C and 12 C. Thiepval Memorial, Somme, France.

FEARNALL, Private, William. 6222, 1st Bn., King's Shropshire Light Infantry. Killed in action, 18th September, 1916. Born St. Mary's Bridgnorth. Enlisted Shrewsbury. Resided Binley, Coventry. Memorial Ref. Pier and Face 12A and 12D. Thiepval Memorial, France.

FELL, Corporal, Jack (John). 2826, 3rd Div. Ammunition Col., Royal Field Artillery. Died, 4th November, 1916. Age 33. Son of Thomas and Sarah Fell, late of 9, Church Terrace, Cubbington, Leamington Spa. Served in the South African Campaign. Grave Ref. III. F. 6. Doullens Communal Cemetery Extension No.1, France.

FELL, Private, Reuben. 2841, C Coy., 2nd Bn., Royal Warwickshire Regiment. Killed in action, Battle of the Somme, 3rd September, 1916. Age 42. Son of Thomas Fell. Born 22nd June, 1873 at Coventry. Resided at 16, Peel Street. Labourer, Mr. Middleton, Plasterer previously soldier. Brother of T. Fell of 3, Brewery Street. Brother of Mrs. Jackson, 16, Peel Street. Enlisted August, 1914. Grave Ref. XIV. H. 8. Delville Wood Cemetery, Longueval, France.

FELTHAM, Private, William Henry. 2443, 1st /7th Bn., Royal Warwickshire Regiment. Killed in action, near Arras, 6th September, 1915 by a shell. Age 20. Son of William Henry and Elizabeth Feltham, of Coventry. Born 12th March, 1896 in St. Michael's Parish. Resided at 42, New Buildings. Machinist. Commemorated Holy Trinity Panels and Triumph and Gloria Memorial. Grave Ref. I. D. 28. Foncquevillers Military Cemetery, Pas de Calais, France.

FERN, Sapper, Fredrick Ernest. 86524, 176th Tunn. Coy., Royal Engineers. Killed in action, 25th August, 1915. Age 31. Son of Job and Matilda Fern, of 110, Bell Green Road, Foleshill, Coventry. Born in 1884 at Walsgrave. Enlisted Ashby de la Zouch. Grave Ref. II. B. 3. Guards Cemetery, Windy Corner, Cuinchy, Pas de Calais, France.

FERRAR, Rifleman, Arthur. 304754, 1/5th Bn., London Rifle Brigade. Killed in action, 5th July, 1918. Born at Filey, Yorkshire. Resided at Merton. Formerly employed at Coventry. Commemorated St. Barbara's Church. Memorial Ref. Bay 9. Arras Memorial, France.

FESSEY, Private, John. S/12404, 1st Bn., Gordon Highlanders. Killed in action, 16th June, 1917. Born at Winshill, Derbyshire. Employed at Coventry. Grave Ref. VIII. B. 10. Vis-en-Artois British Cemetery, Haucourt, France.

FIELD, Private, Alonzo Leonard. 2423, 1st Bn., Royal Warwickshire Regiment. Killed in action, whilst sniping, 2nd October, 1915. Age 20. Son of Mr. and Mrs. James Field, of 99, Earl's Road, Nuneaton. Native of Salford, Manchester. Employee of Triumph Cycle Co., Coventry. Born 12th May, 1895 at Salford. Formerly employed by Humber and Mr. Davies, Broadgate. Soldier. Father served with 2/7th Bn., Royal Warwickshire. Grave Ref. III. B.11. Sucrerie Military Cemetery, Colincamps, Somme, France.

FIGG, Private, Frank Percy. G/18196, 7th Bn., Queen's Own (Royal West Kent) Regiment formerly PS/11554, Royal Fusiliers. Killed in action, 30th September, 1916. Born Uxbridge, Middx. Enlisted Coventry. Resided Coventry. Memorial Ref. Pier and Face 11 C. Thiepval Memorial, Somme, France.

FINCH, Private, Charles Albert. 20287, 2/5th Bn., Royal Warwickshire Regiment. Killed in action, 6th September, 1917. Born Coventry. Enlisted Leamington. Grave Ref. VI. H. 5. Tyne Cot Cemetery, Belgium.

FISHER, A. South Staffordshire Regiment. Resided in Perkins Street. Moulder. Enlisted August, 1914.

FISHER, Driver, Ambrose. 216729, 126th Bde. Ammunition Col., Royal Field Artillery formerly Private, R/258222, Royal Army Service Corps, Remounts. Killed in action, 20th July, 1917. Enlisted January, 1917, Coventry. Born 13th September, 1897 at Birmingham. Resided at 4, Cook Street. Machinist, Maudslay Works. Grave Ref. III. G. 21. Vlamertinghe New Military Cemetery, Belgium.

FISHER, Gunner, Charles. 826708, 240th Bde., Royal Field Artillery. Died, Italy, 29th July, 1918. Age 27. Son of Joseph and Fanny Fisher, of Kibworth, Leicestershire. Born Coventry. Enlisted Coventry. Grave Ref. 3. C. 9. Montecchio Precalcino Communal Cemetery Extension, Italy.

FISHER, Private, J. Shropshire Light Infantry. Brother of Mrs. Coates of Keresley.

FISKE, Lance Corporal, H. 14320, B Coy, 7th Platoon, 1st Bn., Royal Warwickshire Regiment. Killed in action, 12th October, 1916. Information requested by Mrs A. Mills, 16, Gresham Street, Coventry. Memorial Ref. Pier and Face 9 A 9 B and 10 B. Thiepval Memorial, Somme, France.

FITCH, Private, Albert Edward. 14709, C Coy., 10th Bn., Hampshire Regiment. Killed in action, Gallipoli, 21st August, 1915. Age 21. Son of John and Sarah Fitch, of 41, Engleton Road, Radford, Coventry. His father and three brothers also served. Born 18th October, 1893 at 43, Cromwell Street. Resided at 20, Arden Street. Stamper. Enlisted November, 1914. Commemorated St. Barbara's Church. Memorial Ref. Panel 125-134 or 223-226 228-229 & 328. Helles Memorial, Turkey.

FITCHETT, Rifleman, Percy. 10728, 2nd Bn., King's Royal Rifle Corps. Died of wounds, Hooge, 31st October, 1914. Born 6th August, 1896 at St. Johns, Coventry. Enlisted Winchester. Resided Coventry. Soldier. Commemorated St. John's Church. Grave Ref. XXVIII. C. 10. New Irish Farm Cemetery, Belgium.

FITZGERALD, Private, Robert. 11325, 1st Bn., Royal Warwickshire Regiment attached attd. 178th Coy., Royal Engineers. Killed in action, 10th October, 1915. Born St. Annes, Belfast. Enlisted Hereford. Resided Coventry. Grave Ref. I. C. 6. Norfolk Cemetery, Becordel-Becourt, France.

FLANAGAN, Private, Ernest James. 3326, 2nd Bn., Royal Warwickshire Regiment. Died of wounds, received in France, died, home, 14th September, 1917. Born 13th February, 1894 at 25, Spon End, St. Michael's, Coventry. Enlisted August, 1914, Warwick. Resided 29, Spon End, Coventry. Fitter, Swift Company. Commemorated St. John's Church. Grave. 188. 188. Coventry (London Road) Cemetery.

FLANAGAN, Private, Frank Reginald. 9680, 9th Bn., Royal Warwickshire Regiment. Killed in action, Gallipoli, 22nd July, 1915. Age 31. Son of Mrs. Flanagan, of 26, Coombe Street, Coventry. Husband of Mrs. A. J. Ansell (formerly Flanagan), of 28, Craners Road, Coventry. Born 31st January, 1884 in St. Peter's Parish. Plate Polisher, Triumph Works. Commemorated Triumph & Gloria Memorial and St. Michael's Church. Enlisted 5th September, 1914. Leaves a widow and child. Memorial Ref. Panel 35 to 37. Helles Memorial, Turkey.

FLANAGAN, Rifleman, Henry Lawrence. 5715, 2nd Bn., King's Royal Rifle Corps. Killed in action, Bethune, 30th December, 1914. Born 25th May, 1886 at Leicester. Resided at 66, Craners Road. Cycle Hand, Auto Machinist Coy. Reservist. Leaves a widow and three children. Memorial Ref. Panel 32 and 33. Le Touret Memorial, France. (Possibly buried Bethune),

FLANDERS, Private, Frank Albert. 955, 2nd Dragoons (Royal Scots Greys). Died of wounds, Poperinghe, 12th November 1917 wounded on 12th March. Age 32. Son of Mr. and Mrs. J. A. Flanders, of Coventry. Born 2nd October, 1884 at Coventry. Enlisted August, 1914. London. Resided 189, Gulson Road, Coventry. Barman. Reservist. Grave Ref. IX. E. 4. Nine Elms British Cemetery, Poperinge, West-Vlaanderen, Belgium.

FLAVELL, Private, David Charles, 242262, "B" Coy. 15th Bn., Royal Warwickshire Regiment. Killed in action, Arras, 26th October, 1917. Age 20. Son of John and Mary Ann Flavell, of 80, Church Road, Bell Green, Foleshill, Coventry. Born 26th March, 1897 at Bell Green, Coventry. Enlisted Coventry. Resided Bell Green, Coventry. Butcher. Memorial Ref. Panel 23 to 28 and 163A. Tyne Cot Memorial, Zonnebeke, West-Vlaanderen, Belgium.

FLAVELL, Corporal, J. G. 10379, 1st Bn., Sherwood Foresters. Killed in action, 25th April, 1918. Born at Kettering, Northants. Resided at Foleshill. Enlisted Nottingham. Grave Ref. II. G. 8. Adelaide Cemetery, Villers-Bretonneux, France.

FLAVELL, Private, William Colin. 24365, 1st Bn., Grenadier Guards. Killed in action, 11th October, 1918. Age 30. Son of John and Mary Ann Flavell, of 80, Church Road, Bell Green, Foleshill, Coventry. Born 15th September, 1888 at Bell Green. Resided at Bell Green. Miner. Enlisted November, 1915. Grave Ref. C. 6. St. Vaast Communal Cemetery Extension, Nord, France.

FLECKNEY, Private, Alfred Martin. 7096, 1st Bn., Northamptonshire Regiment. Died of wounds, 22nd October, 1914. Age 30. Husband of Grace Fleckney, of Cranford St. John, Kettering, Northants. Born 10th October, 1884 at Kettering. Resided at 46, Queen Mary's Road. Tram Driver. Enlisted August, 1914. Leaves a widow and two children. Commemorated Transport Department Memorial, Coventry Corporation. Memorial Ref. Panel 43 and 45. Ypres (Menin Gate) Memorial, Belgium.

FLEMING, Private, Thomas. 16317, 1st Bn., Hampshire Regiment formerly Oxfordshire and Buckinghamshire Light Infantry. Killed in action, Ypres, 9th July, 1915. Born 7th November, 1874 at Birmingham. Resided at 29, Canterbury Street. Fitter. Enlisted November, 1914. Memorial Ref. Panel 35. Ypres (Menin Gate) Memorial, Belgium.

FLEMMING, Private, Alfred. 11919, A Coy., 2nd Bn., Worcestershire Regiment. Died of wounds, (Whilst prisoner of war), 1st November, 1914. Born Coventry. Enlisted Northampton. Resided 62, King William Street. Coventry. Leaves a widow. Memorial Ref. Panel 34. Ypres (Menin Gate) Memorial, Belgium.

FLETCHER, Private, Alfred. 19348, 1st Bn., Royal Warwickshire Regiment. Killed in action, Arras, 11th April, 1917. Resided at 21, Bristol Road. Memorial Ref. Sp. Mem. B. 7. Point-Du-Jour Military Cemetery, Athies, France.

FLETCHER, Second Lieutenant, Charles. 7th Sqdn., Royal Air Force. Died, of wounds, received in aerial combat the previous day, 29th September, 1918. Age 22. Son of Charles Joseph Fletcher and Ann of 60, Summerland Place, The Butts, Coventry. Born 21st March, 1896, at Coventry. Resided at 60, Summerland Place, Butts. Enlisted April 1918. Draughtsman. Commemorated War Memorial Park. Leaves a widow. Grave Ref. III. C. 18. Haringhe (Bandaghem) Military Cemetery, Poperinge, West-Vlaanderen, Belgium.

FLETCHER, Private, George. W/1147, 13th Bn., Cheshire Regiment. Killed in action, 7th July, 1916. Born Coventry. Enlisted Wallasey, Cheshire. Resided Seacombe. Memorial Ref. Pier and Face 3 C and 4 A. Thiepval Memorial, Somme, France.

FLETCHER, M. Commemorated Coventry Chain Memorial.

FLETCHER, Private, William. 4528, 1st Bn., Royal Warwickshire Regiment. Killed in action, 24th May, 1915. Age 21. Son of Benjamin and Edith Fletcher, of Ash Green, Exhall, Coventry. Born Ash Green, Exhall. Enlisted Nuneaton. Memorial Ref. Panel 8. Ypres (Menin Gate) Memorial, Ieper, West-Vlaanderen, Belgium

FLINN, Driver, Edward. 87870, Royal Field Artillery. Died of wounds, 23rd July, 1917. Age 18. Born at Warwick. Resided at Coventry. See Mason true family name.

FLINT, Charles. Killed in action.

FLINT, Corporal, Edward. 43662, 10th Bn., Lincolnshire Regiment formerly Royal Warwickshire Regiment. Killed in action, 25th November, 1916. Age 28. Son of John and Sarah Flint, of St. Neots, Hunts. Husband of Eva Flint, of 10, House, 14 Court, Little Park Street, Coventry. Born 8th July, 1890 at Eynesbury, Hunts. Fitter. Enlisted May, 1915. Commemorated Water Department Memorial, Coventry Corporation. Grave Ref. IV. C. 29. Brewery Orchard Cemetery, Bois-Grenier, Nord, France.

FLINT, Rifleman, John Byran. 8851, 4th Bn., King's Royal Rifle Corps. Died of wounds, home, 1st March, 1919. Son of Mrs. E. S. Flint, of 68, Longford Road, Longford, Coventry. Born 14th June, 1892 in Much Park Street. Cycle Hand. Grave Ref. 110. 2. Coventry (London Road) Cemetery.

FLOCKTON, Private, Albert Victor. 10203, 1st Bn., Coldstream Guards. Killed in action, Rozroy, 6th September, 1914 reported to have been shot in the back. Age 20. Son of Joseph William and Emma Flockton, of 137, Little Heath Road, Foleshill, Coventry. Born 20th March, 1894 at Stratford-upon-Avon. Soldier. Clerk, Orderly Room, Aldershot. Grave Ref. Sp. Mem. Montreuil-Aux-Lions British Cemetery, Aisne, France.

FLORENCE, Private, Tom. 62987, 5th Bn., King's Own Yorkshire Light Infantry formerly 5/220218, T. R. Bn. Killed in action, 2nd September, 1918. Born Coventry. Enlisted Leicester. Grave Ref. III. J. 14. Vaulx Hill Cemetery, France.

FLOWERS, Trooper, Ernest William. 1117, Household Battalion formerly 3748, 2nd Life Guards. Killed in action, 3rd May, 1917. Age 22. Son of Mrs. K. M. Flowers, of Keresley, Coventry. Born Keresley. Enlisted Coventry. Resided Coventry. Commemorated St. Thomas Memorial. Grave Ref. A. 59. Roeux British Cemetery, Pas de Calais, France.

FLOWERS, Private, William Henry. 17323, 11th Bn., Royal Warwickshire Regiment. Killed in action, 28th September 1916. Age 34. Son of John and Harriett Flowers, of 55, Bacon Yard, Little Heath, Foleshill, Coventry. Born 24th May, 1882 in Bishop Street. Resided in Little Heath Road. Labourer. Enlisted March, 1916. Grave Ref. J. 15. Tranchee De Mecknes Cemetery, Aix-Noulette, Pas de Calais, France.

FLOWERS, Rifleman, William John. S/2756, 10th Bn., Rifle Brigade (Prince Consorts Own). Killed in action, 3rd September, 1916. Born Wolston. Enlisted Rugby. Resided Wolston. Commemorated Wolston Memorial. Memorial Ref. Pier and Face 16B and 16C. Thiepval Memorial, France.

FLUDE, Private, Dennis Percy. PLY/17015, 1st Royal Marine Bn., Royal Naval Division, Royal Marine Light Infantry. Died of wounds, 20th November, 1916. Age 19. Son of William and Hannah Flude, of Coventry. Born 8th May, 1897 in Station Street West. Resided at 75, Station Street West. Core Maker. Enlisted August, 1914. Grave Ref. XX. A. 13A. Etaples Military Cemetery, Pas de Calais, France.

FOLLOWS, Private, Christopher, 16382, 2nd Bn., Royal Warwickshire Regiment. Died of wounds, 3rd Ginchy, September, 1916. Age 20. Son of Samuel and Lydia Follows, of 90, Cox Street, Coventry. Born in 1896 at Wolverhampton. Messenger, Town Clerk's Department since 1914. Commemorated Town Clerk's Department Memorial, Coventry Corporation. Enlisted 1916. Memorial Ref. Pier and Face 9 A 9 B and 10 B. Thiepval Memorial, Somme, France.

FOLEY, Lance Sergeant. South Wales Borderers. Killed in action, 1915. Billeted Coventry.

FOLEY, Private, Timothy. 9494, 1st Bn., Royal Munster Fusiliers. Died of wounds, 5th May, 1915. Billeted Coventry. Born Cork. Enlisted Cork. Resided Cork. Grave Ref. E. 81. Alexandria (Chatby) Military Cemetery and War Memorial Cemetery, Egypt.

FORD, Lance Corporal, Leonard William. 146, D Coy., 1st Bn., Royal Warwickshire Regiment. Killed in action, Ypres, 25th April, 1915 wounded in fighting for Hill 60. Born 3rd October, 1886 at Coventry. Resided Coventry. Tinsmith. Born Birmingham. Enlisted Coventry. Grave Ref. XIII. C. 13. New Irish Farm Cemetery, Belgium.

FORD, R. Commemorated Triumph & Gloria Memorial.

FORD, Private, William. 4852, 1/7th Bn., Royal Warwickshire Regiment. Killed in action, 25th July, 1916. Employed at Coventry. Enlisted Coventry. Memorial Ref. Pier and Face 9 A 9 B and 10 B. Thiepval Memorial, Somme, France.

FORD, Private, William Frank. 15399, 9th Bn., West Yorkshire Regiment (Prince of Wales's Own). Killed in action, 9th August, 1915. Age 19. Son of John David and Emma Ford, of 45, Mountford Street, Sparkhill, Birmingham. Brother of Mrs. W. J. Clews of 137, North Street, Coventry. Born Sparkhill. Enlisted Birmingham. Memorial Ref. Panel 47 to 51. Helles Memorial, Turkey.

FORGE, Driver, William. 79328, 16th Bty. 41st Bde., Royal Field Artillery. Killed in action, 14th May, 1916. Age 26. Son of William I. and Annie Forge, of 428, Church Street, Pietermaritzburg, Natal. Native of Ladysmith, Natal. Born 4th February, 1890. Resided at Upper Wellington Street. Machinist. Enlisted August, 1914, Coventry. Commemorated Triumph & Gloria Memorial. Grave Ref. V. C. 20A. Etaples Military Cemetery, France.

FORSYTH, Lieutenant, Samuel Sanford. Royal Field Artillery. Killed in action, Hooge, 23rd September, 1915. Age 30. Son of Col. Frederick Aitken and Mrs. Ellen Sanford Forsyth. Born 31st October, 1884 at Leamington. Resided at Leamington. Educated at Wellington College and Hertford College. Solicitor. Enlisted August, 1914. Mentioned in Despatches. Brother at Coventry. Memorial Ref. Panel 5 and 9. Ypres (Menin Gate) Memorial, Belgium.

FOSTER, Private, Alfred. 203191, 2/6th Bn., Royal Warwickshire Regiment. Killed in action, 21st March, 1918. Born 11th May, 1886 in Much Park Street, Coventry. Enlisted July, 1916, Coventry. Resided at 10, Albion Street. Machinist. Enlisted Memorial Ref. Panel 18 and 19. Pozieres Memorial, France.

FOSTER, Private, Frederick. G/11475, 10th Bn., Royal West Kent Regiment. Killed in action, 16th September, 1916. Age 27. Son of Frederick and Jemima Foster, of Sandhill House, Pembury, Kent. Born at Chart Sutton, Maidstone. Born at Chart, Sutton, Kent. Resided at Hollingbourne. Formerly employed at Coventry. Grave Ref. XIII. F. 8. Caterpillar Valley Cemetery, Longueval, France.

FOSTER, Private, George. 21704, 14th Bn., Gloucestershire Regiment. Died of wounds, to left arm and leg, 22nd August, 1916. Age 51. Son of John and Caroline Foster, of Coventry. Husband of Lucy Foster, of 13, All Saints' Lane, Coventry, Warwickshire. Born 7th July, 1864 at Jordan Well, Coventry. Enlisted 25th July, 1915, Birmingham. Wheelwright, Humber Ltd. Grave Ref. 2. B. 104. Corbie Communal Cemetery Extension, Somme, France.

FOSTER, Private, George William. 13109, 7th Bn., Oxfordshire and Buckinghamshire Light Infantry. Died from malaria, Salonika, 27th September, 1916. Wounded 19th August, 1916. Born Coventry. Enlisted August, 1914 at Coventry. Resided 4, Guild Road. Employed Bricklayer, Mr. Bromley Builder. Grave Ref. 484. Salonika (Lembet Road) Military Cemetery, Greece.

FOSTER, Private, Herbert Henry. 68904, 11th Bn., Royal Welsh Fusiliers formerly T4/235463, Royal Army Service Corps. Killed in action, Serbia, 18th September, 1918. Born 11th January, 1897 at 30, Arthur Street. Resided at 11c. 4h. Much Park Street, Coventry. Plumbers Apprentice. Enlisted February, 1916, Coventry. Grave Ref. III. F. 23. Doiran Military Cemetery, Greece.

FOSTER, J. Employed by Humber Ltd. Killed in action.

FOSTER, Gunner, Wilfred Henson. 181621, 245th Siege Bty., Royal Garrison Artillery. Died Cologne, 4th March, 1919. Born 29th June, 1894 at Wellingborough. Resided at 30, Grantham Street. Coach painter. Enlisted August, 1917. Grave Ref. III. B. 15. Cologne Southern Cemetery, Germany.

FOSTER, Private, William. 9359, 1st Bn., Royal Warwickshire Regiment. Died of wounds, 18th September, 1914. Age 29. Husband of Mrs. E. J. Foster, of 30, Roseland Cottages, Little Heath, Foleshill, Coventry. Born 4th July, 1885 at Birmingham. Tram Conductor, Coventry Tramway. Reservist. Leaves a widow and one child. Commemorated Transport Department Memorial, Coventry Corporation. Memorial Ref. La Ferte-Sous-Jouarre Memorial, Seine-et-Marne, France.

FOX, Private, Edwin. 125114, 328th (Home Service) Field Amb., Royal Army Medical Corps. Died 1st July, 1918. Born 28th November, 1887 at Hunningham. Resided at 3, Cambridge Street. Artificial silk spinner. Enlisted August, 1917. Grave Ref. CE. 685. Grangegorman Military Cemetery, Ireland.

FOX, Sapper, Frederick Beauclere. 46974, 85th Field Coy., Royal Engineers. Died of wounds received at Gallipoli, on board hospital ship, Nevasa, 31st August, 1915. Born at Sleaford, Lincs. Motor Body maker. Enlisted September, 1914. Memorial Ref. Panel 23 to 25 or 325 to 328. Helles Memorial, Turkey.

FOXON, Sergeant, Thomas, MM. Royal Warwickshire Regiment. Died Home, 15th January, 1925. Born 31st July, 1891 at 26, King William Street. Resided at 6, back of 444, Stoney Stanton Road. Fitter. Enlisted March, 1915. Awarded the Military Medal for bravery in the field, 20th August, 1918 and gazetted 11th December, 1918. Grave Ref. Coventry (London Road) Cemetery.

FRANCE, Private, Herbert. G/18195, 7th Bn., Queen's Own (Royal West Kent Regiment) formerly PS/10987, Royal Fusiliers. Died of wounds, 18th October, 1917. Age 22. Son of John and Mary E. France of 19, Birkhead Street, Heckmondwicke, Yorkshire. Born Heckmondwyke, Yorkshire. Enlisted Coventry. Resided Coventry. Grave Ref. VI. E. 3. Wimereux War Cemetery, France.

FRANCIS, F. Commemorated Triumph & Gloria Memorial.

FRANCIS, Sapper, Percy John. 32431, 90th Field Coy., Royal Engineers. Killed in action, Montauban, 3rd July, 1916 whilst working on defences. Age 31. Son of Lewis Henry Francis, of 62, Hugh Road, Stoke, Coventry. Born 7th August, 1886 at 46, Howard Street. Resided at Wolverhampton. Enlisted October, 1914, Wolverhampton. Fitter, Sunbeam Wolverhampton. Enlisted Resided Coventry. Freeman of the City, served apprenticeship with Daimler Co. Ltd. Commemorated War Memorial Park. Grave Ref. II. G. 9. Quarry Cemetery, Montauban, France.

FRANCIS, Private, Walter Frank. 41343, 6th Bn., Dorsetshire Regiment formerly 45055, Royal Army Medical Corps. Died of wounds, 14th October, 1918. Born 17th November at Coventry. Resided at 11, Croft Road. Enlisted November, 1914, Coventry. Turner. Commemorated St. John's Church and War Memorial Park. Grave Ref. XIII. D. 28. Rocquigny-Equancourt Road British Cemetery, Manancourt, France.

FRANKLIN, Private, Alfred. 12413, 1st Bn., Coldstream Guards. Died of wounds, received at Loos, 1st October, 1915. Having saved the lives of several comrades injured comrades in the trenches, shot on return. Age 26. Son of Mr. and Mrs. Benjamin Franklin, of 122, Grange Street, Burton-on-Trent, Staffs. Born 22nd January, 1888 at Burton-on-Trent. Resided Croft Road formerly 24, Ena Road, Coventry with his brother. Labourer formerly employed Coventry Corporation Electricity Works, Motor repair shop. Enlisted Coventry. Resided Burton-on-Trent. Commemorated Electricity Department Memorial, Coventry Corporation. Grave Ref. I. D. 21. Noeux-Les-Mines Communal Cemetery, France.

FRANKLIN, Lance Corporal, Arthur. 8548, 15th Bn., Royal Warwickshire Regiment. Killed in action, Battle of the Somme, 28th August, 1916. Born 11th May, 1895 at Hillfields, Coventry. Resided at 30, Leicester Street. Coach trimmer. Enlisted August, 1914, Coventry. Memorial Ref. Pier and Face 9 A 9 B and 10 B. Somme, France.

FRANKLIN, Rifleman, Ernest. 13925, 1st Bn., Royal Irish Rifles. Killed in action, 25th September, 1915. Born Coventry. Enlisted Drogheda, Co. Louth. Memorial Ref. Panel 9. Ploegsteert Memorial, Belgium.

FRANKLIN, Private, Hollister Clare. 10888, 2nd Bn., Honourable Artillery Company. Died of wounds, 22nd January, 1918. Age 34. Son of Mr. And Mrs. John Hollister Franklin of Cricklade, Wiltshire. Born in 1882, at Malmesbury. Resided at 5, Stoney Road. Enlisted Armoury House, May, 1917. Bank Cashier. Commemorated War Memorial Park. Grave Ref. Plot IV, Row B, Grave 7.Giavera British Cemetery, Arcade, Italy,

FRANKLIN, Private, James. 28567, 10th Bn., Royal Warwickshire Regiment. Killed in action, 20th April, 1918. Age 20. Son of William and Betsy Franklin, of Meriden, Warwickshire. Born at Meriden. Resided Meriden. Employed Coventry. Enlisted Coventry. Grave Ref. XI. D. 9A. Wimereux Communal Cemetery, France.

FRANKLIN, Gunner, John. 113899, Y 4th Trench Mortar Bty., Royal Field Artillery. Killed in action, 29th July, 1917. Age 25. Son of Joseph and Rhoda Franklin of Bourne End Lane, Boxmoor, Herts. Born Coventry. Enlisted Coventry. Memorial Ref. Bay 1. Arras Memorial, France.

FRASER, Private, Donald. 23861, 2nd /7th Bn., Royal Warwickshire Regiment. Killed in action, 20th August, 1918. Age 41. Native of Inverness. Husband of Annie Fraser, of 41, Poplar Road, Earlsdon, Coventry. Born 1st May 1877, at Dunain, Inverness. Enlisted January 1916 at Coventry. Tailor and cutter. Commemorated Earlsdon Working Men's Club, St. Barbara's Church and War Memorial Park. Grave Ref. 5. E. 12. Tannay British Cemetery, Thiennes, Nord, France.

FRASER, Stoker 1st Class, Frederick William, DSM. K/11724, HM Submarine G7, Royal Navy. Killed in loss of vessel in North Sea, 1st November, 1918. Age 24. Son of Lucy Bell (formerly Fraser) and Charles Bell (step-father), of 101, Gosford Street, Coventry. Born 1894. Memorial Ref. 28. Plymouth Naval Memorial, Devon.

FRAZER, Private, William Tom. 15927, 2nd Bn., Grenadier Guards. Died of wounds, 28th September, 1916. Age 22. Son of Francis and Emma Frazer, of 95, Colony Cottages, Holbrook Lane, Foleshill, Coventry. Born St. Nicholas, Newbury. Enlisted Reading. Grave Ref. I. G. 47. Grove Town Cemetery, Meaulte, Somme, France.

FREDERICKSON, Gunner, Henry Ernest. 13173, 38th Trench Mortar Bty., Royal Field Artillery. Died, 24th March, 1918. Enlisted Coventry. Resided Coventry. Grave Ref. III. C. 8. Merville Communal Cemetery Extension, France.

FREEMAN, Private, Arthur Richard. PS2681, 16th Bn., Middlesex Regiment. Killed in action, 1st July, 1916. Born 3rd September, 1876 at Stepney, Middlesex. Enlisted 1915, Woldingham, Surrey. Resided 132, North Street, Coventry. Manufacturing Chemist, Wyley's Wholesale Chemist. Memorial Ref. Pier and Face 12D and 13B. Thiepval Memorial, Somme, France.

FREEMAN, Private, James Spencer. 19667, 1st Dorsetshire Regiment formerly 31718, Bedfordshire Regiment. Died of wounds, 19th April, 1918. Born 3rd November, 1888 at Finedon, Northants. Resided Coventry. Butcher. Enlisted November, 1916, Bishops Stortlford. Commemorated St. Barbara's Church. Grave Ref. P. 9. P. 1A. St. Sever Cemetery Extension, Rouen, France.

FREEMAN, Private, John. 47062, 6th Bn., Royal Inniskilling Fusiliers formerly 33162, Royal Warwickshire Regiment. Died of wounds, Home, 19th October, 1918. Age 33. Son of David and Louisa Freeman, of Blind Lane, Berkswell. Born Berkswell. Enlisted Coventry. Grave Ref. New War Memorial. Berkswell (St. John the Baptist) Churchyard.

FREEMAN, Sergeant, Sidney. 19581, B Coy., 15th Bn., Royal Warwickshire Regiment. Killed in action, 9th May, 1917. Husband of Mrs. Freeman, 34 Mickleton Road, Coventry. Born Wroxton, Oxon. Enlisted Coventry. Memorial Ref. Bay 3. Arras Memorial, France.

FREEMAN, Private, Thomas Alfred. 59383, 1st/8th Bn., Worcestershire Regiment formerly 58249, Royal Warwickshire Regiment. Killed in action, Landrecies, 4th November, 1918. Age 20. Son of Herbert A. and Louise Freeman, of 26, Vine Street, Coventry. Born 15th March, 1898 at 26, Vine Street, Turner. Enlisted June, 1918. Coventry. Enlisted Coventry. Grave Ref. B. 33. Landrecies British Cemetery, Nord, France.

FRENCH, Private, Arthur Edgar. 94062, 1st Bn., The King's (Liverpool Regiment) formerly 37669, Royal Warwick Regiment. Died of wounds, 26th April, 1918. Age 19. Son of Thomas Richard French, of Styvechale, Coventry. Born 1899, Long Itchington, Warwickshire. Enlisted Coventry. Resided Coventry. Commemorated St. James's Church. Grave Ref. I. D. 3. Bagneux British Cemetery, Gezaincourt, Somme, France.

FRENCH, Lance Corporal, Arthur James. 8573, 9th Bn., Royal Warwickshire Regiment. Killed in action, Mesopotamia, 5th April, 1916. Born 15th May, 1894 at Bishops Itchington. Resided Leamington. Railway Goods Porter. Enlisted September, 1914 at Coventry. Memorial Ref. Panel 9. Basra Memorial, Iraq.

FRENCH, Private, Dennis Francis Henry. 15899, 6th Bn., Oxfordshire and Buckinghamshire Light Infantry. Died of wounds in hospital, 24th February, 1916. Injured 21st February, 1916 with serious head wound from enemy machine gun whilst on duty at a listening post. Born 26th February, 1885 at Burton-on-Trent. Resided at 8, Northfield Road. Employed Butcher, London Central Meat Co., Berry Street. Enlisted November, 1914, Coventry. Grave Ref. IV. D. 32. Lijssenthoek Military Cemetery, Belgium.

FRENCH, Private, James. 41185, Depot, The King's (Liverpool Regiment) formerly 137092, Royal Field Artillery. Died home, of wounds received at Arras, 15th May 1917. Age 24. Son of James French, of 10, League Place, Moat Street, Coventry. Born 17th February, 1893 at Glasgow, Lanark. Enlisted May, 1916, Coventry. Resided 1c. 10h. Moat Street, Clerk. Coventry. Grave Ref. 212. 4. Coventry (London Road) Cemetery.

FRENCH, Private, William. T/242998, 7th Bn., The Queen's (Royal West Surrey Regiment). Killed in action, 21st October, 1917. Age 27. Son of William and Ruth French, of Shilton, Coventry. Husband of Gertrude P. E. James (formerly French), of Lapstone. Chipping Campden, Glos. Born Potters Green. Enlisted Coventry. Resided Shelton. Grave Ref. VI. C. 3. Cement House Cemetery, Langemark-Poelkapelle, Belgium.

FRETTER, Private, Henry Walter. 15885, 1st Bn., Grenadier Guards. Killed in action, 23rd December, 1914. Age 25. Son of Mr. and Mrs. Walter Fretter, of 24, Munition Cottages, Foleshill, Coventry. Born Nasby, Northants. Enlisted Norpthampton. Memorial Ref. Panel 1. Ploegsteert Memorial, Comines-Warneton, Hainaut, Belgium.

FRETWELL, Private, William. 19845, 2nd Bn., Wiltshire Regiment formerly 1479, Royal Warwickshire Regiment. Killed in action, 18th October, 1916. Born 19th November, 1894 at Newark, Notts. Son of Mrs. Fretwell, 3, Mason Road, Foleshill. Enlisted Coventry. Resided Coventry. Milling Machinist. Memorial Ref. Pier and Face 13A. Thiepval Memorial, Somme, France.

FRIDAY, Private, James Edward. 4135, 1st Bn., Welsh Guards. Died of wounds, St. Leger, 24th August, 1918. Age 32. Born 19th January, 1886 in Raglan Street, Coventry. Enlisted August, 1917, Coventry. Resided No. 1, back of 23, New Street. Turner. Commemorated Holy Trinity Panels. Grave Ref. B. 4. Moyenneville (Two Tree) Cemetery, France.

FRIEDRICHSEN, Private, Emil James. 51016, 9th Bn., Cheshire Regiment formerly 22546, Royal Berkshire Regiment. Killed in action, 6th June, 1918. Age 25. Husband of Dorothy Jane Weller (formerly Friedrichsen), of 333, Brook Lane, King's Heath, Birmingham. Born Birmingham. Enlisted Coventry. Grave Ref. II. E. 4. Marfaux British Cemetery, France.

FRISBY, Private, Albert Edward. 24293, 15th Bn., Sherwood Foresters (Notts and Derby Regiment). Died of wounds, 22nd July, 1917. Age 18. Son of Mr. J. and Mrs. E. Frisby, of 39, Canal Road, Longford, Coventry. Born. St. Michael's, Lincs. Enlisted Stamford, Lincs. Resided Coventry. Commemorated Saint Thomas the Apostle, Longford. Grave Ref. I. B. 18. Tincourt New British Cemetery, Somme, France.

FRISBY, Private, Edward Hedley. 4338, 1/7th Bn., Royal Warwickshire Regiment. Died of wounds, 1st September, 1916. Death due to an accident while being instructed with a machine gun. Age 26. Son of George and Lucy Letitia Frisby, of 14, Sydney Street, Melton Mowbray, Leics. Born Melton Mowbray, Leicestershire. Resided Radford. Enlisted Coventry. Employed by his brother, Mr. Frisby, Baker, Foleshill Road. Resided Radford, Coventry. Commemorated Holy Trinity Panels. Grave Ref. II. D. 20. Couin British Cemetery, France.

FROST, Private, James. 18052, 14th Bn., Royal Warwickshire Regiment. Died of wounds, 9th May, 1917. Born at Daventry, Northants. Resided at 74, Church Road, Bell Green. Butcher, 607 Stoney Stanton Road. Enlisted 1916, Warwick. Grave Ref. Grave Ref. II. H. 50, Aubigny Communal Cemetery Extension, France.

FROST, Private, Mark. 4295, 19th Bn., Australian Infantry, Australian Imperial Force. Killed in action, 8th October, 1917. Age 32. Son of Matthew and Emily Jane Frost. Husband of Alice L. Frost, of 25, Lord's Road, Leichhardt, New South Wales. Born at Coventry, England. Grave Ref. XIII. B. 9. Passchendaele New British Cemetery, Zonnebeke, West-Vlaanderen, Belgium.

FROST, Private, Sidney. 43470, 2nd Bn., Worcestershire Regiment formerly 57472, Royal Warwickshire Regt. Died of wounds, 11th November, 1918. Born 28th March, 1896 at Lee's Buildings, Stoney Stanton Road, Coventry. Resided Brooklyn Road. Turner. Enlisted June, 1918, Coventry. Grave Ref. I. B. 23. Caudry British Cemetery, France.

FRY, Captain, Alfred Andrew, OBE. 12th Wing, Royal Air Force formerly Monmouthshire Regiment. Died Esher, Surrey, 27th June, 1919. Born in 1870 at Coventry. Soldier. Mentioned in Despatches. Grave Ref. Tier. 12. 4. Esher (Christ Church) Churchyard.

FRY, Private, P. 7813295, Machine Gun Corps (Infantry). Drowned, 4th July, 1921. Age 19. Son of Albert and Mary Fry. Grave Ref. 238. 209. Coventry (London Road) Cemetery.

FULLYLOVE, Lance Corporal, Arthur Herbert. 10526, 2nd Bn., Royal Warwickshire Regiment. Killed in action, 25th September, 1915. Age 26. Son of A. and Eliza Fullylove, of Higham-on-the-Hill, Nuneaton. Born Higham-on-the-Hill, Nuneaton. Enlisted Coventry. Resided Higham-on-the-Hill. Memorial Ref. Panel 22 to 25. Loos Memorial, France.

FULLYLOVE, Private, Walter. 10527, 2nd Bn., Royal Warwickshire Regiment. Killed in action. Born Chapel End, Warwicks. Enlisted Coventry. Resided Caldecote, Warwicks. Memorial Ref. Panel 22 to 25. Loos Memorial, France.

FULWELL, Private, John William. 14561, 7th Bn., Royal Berkshire Regiment. Died of wounds, Salonika 24th September 1918 possibly injured 27th April, 1918. Age 44. Husband of Caroline Fulwell, of 152, Camden St., Parade, Birmingham. Born at Coventry. Grave Ref. III. J. 5. Taranto Town Cemetery Extension, Italy

FULWELL, Private, Leonard. 19655, 1st Bn., Wiltshire Regiment formerly 13556, Oxfordshire and Buckinghamshire Light Infantry. Killed in action, 23rd September, 1915. Born St. John's, Warwick. Enlisted Coventry. Resided Coventry. Employed Premier Motor Co. Ltd. Memorial Ref. Panel 53. Ypres (Menin Gate) Memorial.

FURNISS, Sergeant, Walter, DCM. 1838, 13th Bde., Australian Field Artillery. Killed in action, 8th October, 1918. Age 28. Son of Alfred and Agnes S. E. Furniss, of 29, Ribble Road, Stoke, Coventry, England. Native of Lower Heyford, Hants. Awarded Distinguished Conduct Medal, when on the 24th April, 1918 the battery position was subjected to very heavy shell fire this NCO maintained his gun in action in an efficient manner during the whole time. Gazetted 1st January, 1919. Grave Ref. I. B. 6. Bellicourt British Cemetery, Aisne, France.

FURBOROUGH, Private, Thomas. 307757, 2nd Bn., Royal Warwickshire Regiment. Killed in action, 9th October, 1917. Age 27. Son of Thomas Furborough, of Narborough Road, Cosby. Husband of Rebecca Furborough, of Whetstone Road, Cosby, Leicester. Enlisted Coventry. Resided Ryton, Bulkington. Memorial Ref. Panel 23 to 28 and 163A. Tyne Cot Memorial, Belgium.

FURNIVAL, Lance Corporal, Alfred. 3764, 2nd /7th Bn., Royal Warwickshire Regiment. Killed in action, 20th September, 1916. Died at his post whilst working his Lewis gun. Age 24. Husband of Mrs. Furnival, of 70, Station Street West, Foleshill, Coventry. Born Coventry., Enlisted January, 1915 at Coventry. Resided Foleshill. Employed Exhall Colliery. Grave Ref. III. A. 2. Laventie Military Cemetery, La Gorgue, Nord, France.

FURNIVAL, Able Seaman, Edwin. R/657, Anson Bn., Royal Naval Division. Killed in action, 25th August, 1918. Born 10th August, 1894 at Bedworth. Resided at 16, Stanley Street. Bricklayer. Enlisted 1917. Memorial Ref. Panel 1 and 2. Vis-En-Artois Memorial, France.

FUTRILL, Private, Charles. 5270, 1st Bn., Coldstream Guards. Killed in action, 14th September, 1914. Age 29. Son of George and Fanny Futrill. Husband of Betsy S. A. Futrill, of 14, Pridmore Road, Coventry. Born 25th December, 1884 in Worcestershire. Soldier, previously workman, Coventry Corporation. Enlisted Coventry. Gas Department Memorial, Coventry Corporation. Grave Ref. I. B. 21. Vailly British Cemetery, Aisne, France.

FUTRILL, Lance Corporal, William. 5595, 16th (The Queens) Lancers. Killed in action, 21st February, 1915. Born Worcestershire. Enlisted Coventry. Resided Norwich. Memorial Ref. Panel 5. Ypres (Menin Gate) Memorial, Belgium.

GABBITAS, Private, Charles Edwin. 15937, 11th Bn., Royal Warwickshire Regiment. Died of wounds received in France, 16th August, 1916. Age 22. Son of Edwin and Fanny Gabbitas. Husband of Jessie Gabbitas, of 3, Century Street, Newark. Born at Little Carlton, Newark. Born at Newark, Notts. Resided at 31, Severn Road. Police Constable. Commemorated Police Force Memorial, Coventry Corporation. Grave Ref. Near North-West angle of Church Tower. South Muskham (St. Wilfred) Churchyard.

GADSBY, Walter. 15900, 9th Bn., Devonshire Regiment. Killed in action, 15th March, 1916. Age 29. Born 1884. Son of William and Elizabeth Gadsby, of Branston, Burton-on-Trent. Husband of Lily Gadsby, of 38, Leghorn Road, Harlesden, London. Resided at 4, Bedford Street. Inspector employed Alfred Herbert Ltd. Enlisted March, 1915, Coventry. Grave Ref. I. D. 22. Dartmoor Cemetery, Becordel-Becourt, France.

GAISFORD, Private, William. 2516, 1/7th Bn., Royal Warwickshire Regiment. Killed in action, 20th August, 1916. Age 25. Son of Mrs. Letitia Gaisford, of 5, South Front, Dews Road, Salisbury, Wilts. Born at Fisherson, Wiltshire. Resided 11, Percy Street. Enlisted Coventry. Employed H. Williamson, Watch and Clock manufacturers. Resided Salisbury. Commemorated St. John's Church. Memorial Ref. Pier and Face 9 A 9 B and 10 B. Thiepval Memorial, Somme, France.

GALLOWAY, Able Seaman, F. R/1664, Hood Bn., Royal Naval Div., Royal Naval Volunteer Reserve. Died of wounds, whilst prisoner of war 1st January, 1918. Employed Coventry. Grave Ref. II. 21. Fontaine-Au-Pire Communal Cemetery, France.

GAMBLE, Private, Harry. 13047, 10th Bn., Duke of Wellington's (West Riding Regiment). Died of wounds (gas), 9th January, 1916. Age 19. Son of Henry and Mary Ann Gamble, of 136, Little Heath Road, Foleshill, Coventry. Born Blackburn. Enlisted Skipton, Yorks. Resided Coventry. Grave Ref. C. 51. Old ground. Kelbrooke (St. Mary) Churchyard, Yorkshire.

GANDY, Rifleman, George Henry. Y/826, 2nd Bn., King's Royal Rifle Corps. Killed in action, 25th September, 1915. Born Coventry. Enlisted Birmingham. Memorial Ref. Panels 101 and 102. Loos Memorial, France.

GANDY, Private, James Vivian. M2/130610, Army Service Corps. Died, Home, 5th November, 1918. Age 22. Son of Mrs. Mary Jane Bryden of 14, Oxford Street, Workington. Born Workington. Enlisted Coventry. Resided Workington. Grave Ref. 12. B. 21. Workington (Harrington Road) Cemetery.

GANLEY, Company Sergeant Major, Thomas. 9721, D Coy. 1st Bn., Royal Warwickshire Regiment. Died of wounds, in a French hospital, 23rd December, 1917. Age 32. Son of Thomas and Mary Ann Ganley, of Coventry. Husband of Ellen Ganley, of 9, Clarence Street, Coventry formerly 67, Chandos Street. Born 1885, Coventry. Enlisted Warwick. Resided Coventry. Employed Rex Motor Manufacturing Company Ltd. Reservist. Commemorated Earlsdon Working Men's Club. Grave Ref. V. D. 52. Duisans British Cemetery, Etrun, Pas de Calais, France

GARBUTT, Private, Cyril Maurice. 4917, 16th (The Queens) Lancers. Killed in action, 23rd March, 1918. Born Arkley, Glocs. Resided Headingley. Commemorated War Memorial Park. Memorial Ref. Panel 5. Pozieres Memorial, France.

GARDNER, Gunner, Alfred. 77978, 353rd Siege Bty., Royal Garrison. Died of wounds, 19th October, 1917. Husband of Mrs. M. Meller (formerly Gardner), of Barton-in-the-Beans, Nuneaton. Born Coventry. Enlisted Leicester. Grave Ref. I. O. 46. Godewaersvelde British Cemetery, France.

GARDNER, Private, Alfred. 50535, "C" Coy. 5th Bn. King's Own Yorkshire Light Infantry, formerly M/298275, Royal Army Service Corps. Killed in action, 27th March, 1918. Age 19. Son of Alfred and Alice Elizabeth Gardner, of 29, Comyn Street, Leamington Spa. Born Coventry. Enlisted Coventry. Memorial Ref. Bay 7. Arras Memorial, France.

GARDNER, Air Mechanic 2nd Class, Arthur. 126856, 1st Aeroplane Supply Depot, Royal Air Force. Died 22nd June, 1918. Age 40. Son of Richard and Elizabeth Gardner. Husband of Agnes Gardner, of 76, King Edward Road, Rugby. Born 31st May, 1878 at Brailes near Banbury. Resided Rugby. Carpenter and joiner. Enlisted August, 1916. Grave Ref. I. B. 16. Terlincthun British Cemetery, Wimille, France.

GARDNER, Private, Basil Ronald Leslie. 206105, D Bn., Machine Gun Corps (Heavy Branch) formerly 32210, Machine Gun Corps. Killed in action, 11th April, 1917. Born High Wycombe, Bucks. Enlisted Coventry. Memorial Ref. Bay 10. Arras Memorial, France.

GARDNER, Private, Charles Percy. 266881, C Coy., 2/7th Bn., Royal Warwickshire Regiment. Killed in action, 24th October, 1918. Age 27. Son of William Henry and Mary Jane Gardner of The Midlands, Wylds Lane, Worcester. Born Gloucester. Enlisted Coventry. Grave Ref. B. 15. Canonne Farm British Cemetery, Sommaing, France.

GARDNER, D. Employed Rover Co. Ltd. Killed in action.

GARDNER, Lance Corporal, Ernest. B/3280, 8th Bn., Rifle Brigade. Killed in action, 24th August, 1916. Age 22. Son of Mr. F. and Mrs. E. Gardner, of Canal Side, Ansty, Coventry. Born Birmingham. Resided Birmingham. Memorial Ref. Pier and Face 16 B and 16 C. Thiepval Memorial, Somme, France.

GARDNER, Private, Harry. 17787, 10th Bn., Royal Warwickshire Regiment. Killed in action, 31st May, 1918. Born Banbury, Oxon. Enlisted Coventry. Resided Banbury. Memorial Ref. Soissons Memorial, France.

GARDNER, Lance Corporal, Horace. 17268, 1st Bn., Worcestershire Regiment. Killed in action, 10th August, 1916. Age 23. Son of Albert and Mary Jane Gardner, of Leckenham Road, Astwood Bank, Redditch. Born Redditch. Employed Coventry. Grave Ref. III. M. 18. Vermelles British Cemetery, France.

GARDNER, Private, John. 27691, 14th Bn., Royal Warwickshire Regiment. Killed in action, 21st May, 1917. Age 22. Son of Mrs. M. E. Gardner, of Temple Balsall, Knowle, Birmingham. Enlisted Coventry. Resided Fen End, Warwicks. Grave Ref. II. A. 15. Bois-Carre British Cemetery, Thelus, France.

GARDNER, Private, John Edward, (Known as Jack). 16867, 11th Bn., Royal Warwickshire Regiment. Killed in action, Battle of the Somme, 14th July, 1916. Born 9th July, 1893 at Birmingham. Resided at 217, Walsgrave Road. Eldest son of Mr. and Mrs. J. Gardener. Machinist, Auto Works, Read Street. Enlisted February, 1916 at Coventry. Grave Ref. II. E. 2. Gordon Dump Cemetery, Ovillers-La Boiselle, France.

GARDNER, Private, Percy Charles. 266881, C Coy., 2/7th Bn., Royal Warwickshire Regiment. Killed in action, 24th October, 1918. Age 27. Son of William Henry and Mary Jane Gardner, of The Midlands, Wylds Lane, Worcester. Born 18th November, 1890 at Gloucester. Resided at 15, Mayfield Road. Clerk. Enlisted March, 1916. Grave Ref. B. 15. Canonne Farm British Cemetery, Sommaing, France.

GARDNER, Private, Thomas. 2510, 1/7th Bn., Royal Warwickshire Regiment. Died of wounds received at Battle of the Somme, 25th July, 1916. Born 26th September, 1896 at Grantham, Lincs. Resided at 5c. 8h. Chauntry Place. Wheel Builder. Enlisted September, 1914, Coventry. Commemorated Holy Trinity Panels. Grave Ref. V. B. 22. Warloy-Baillon Communal Cemetery Extension, France.

GARDNER, Private, Thomas Harris. 328046, 2nd /7th Bn., Royal Warwickshire Regiment. Died of wounds, whilst prisoner of war, 11th June, 1918. Age 30. Husband of Mrs. L. M. Gardner, of 67, St. John Street, Coventry. Born Edgehill, Warwicks. Enlisted Warwick. Grave Ref. XII. A. 10. Berlin South-Western Cemetery, Berlin, Brandenburg, Germany.

GARDNER, Private, William. 12903, 6th Bn., Oxfordshire and Buckinghamshire Light Infantry. Killed in action, near Guillemont, 3rd September, 1916. Born 28th June, 1895 at Kenilworth. Resided at 76, Lockhurst Lane. Tool Grinder, White and Poppe Ltd. Enlisted September, 1914. Memorial Ref. Pier and Face 10 A and 10 D. Thiepval Memorial, Somme, France.

GARDNER, Private, William. 5386, 2/6th Bn., Royal Warwickshire Regiment. Killed in action, 21st March, 1918. Born Temple Balsall, Warwicks. Enlisted Coventry. Resided Far Cotton, Northants. Memorial Ref. Panel 18 and 19. Pozieres Memorial, France.

GARDNER, Private, William George Caviar. 874585, 78th Battalion, Canadian Infantry (Manitoba Regiment). Killed in action, Passchendaele, 30th October, 1917. Age 24. Son of George William and Emily Gardner. Born 3rd December, 1891 at 102, Gosford Street. Resided Manitoba, Canada. Farmer. Sister resided 1, Charter House Road. Enlisted February, 1916. Commemorated War Memorial Park. Memorial Ref. Panel 24 - 26 - 28 - 30. Ypres (Menin Gate) Memorial, Belgium.

GARLICK, Private, Albert Ernest. 53078, 3rd Bn., Worcestershire Regiment. Died whilst a Prisoner of War, Soissons, 13th June, 1918. Age 19. Born at Leamington Spa. Son of Ernest Mark and Lucy Garlick, of Hillcrest, Broomfield Place, Coventry. Enlisted Coventry. Resided Coventry. Born 11th October, 1898 at Leamington. Resided at 26, Moor Street. Grocer. Enlisted 1916. Commemorated St. Barbara's Memorial. Grave Ref. II. J. 5. La Ville-Aux-Bois British Cemetery, Aisne, France.

GARLICK, Private, Frederick William. 20909, 1/6th Bn., Royal Warwickshire Regiment. Died of wounds, 8th February, 1917. Age 27. Son of William and Jane Garlick. Husband of Adela May Garlick, of 17, Park Rd., Melton Mowbray. Born Leicester. Resided 17 Stoke Row off Clay Lane. Employed Auto Co. Enlisted Coventry. Grave Ref. II. A. 51. Bray Military Cemetery, France.

GARLICK, Private, Walter. 18338, 11th Bn., Worcestershire Regiment. Killed in action, Salonika, 10th October, 1916. Age 28. Son of Walter and Ann Garlick, of 17, Back Gulson Road, Coventry. Born 16th January, 1893 at Coventry. Wheel Builder, Triumph Ltd. Enlisted September, 1914. Commemorated Triumph & Gloria Memorial. Grave Ref. B. 255. Karasouli Military Cemetery, Greece.

GARNER, Private, David. 20144, 6th Bn., Depot, Wiltshire Regiment formerly 87087, Royal Field Artillery. Died, home, 14th June, 1917. Son of Mr. F. Garner, of II, London Road, Coventry. Born Coventry. Enlisted Coventry. Resided Coventry. Grave Ref. C. CE. 799. Warrington Cemetery, Lancashire.

GARNER, Private, Frederick William. 44062, 4th Bn., South Wales Borderers. Mesopotamia, 10th February, 1917. Age 31. Son of Joseph Henry and Victoria Elisabeth Garner, of 57, White Friar's Street, Coventry. Husband of Alice Docker (formerly Garner) of 44, Little Fields, Stoke Heath, Coventry. Born 1st August 1887, in Vernon Street. Resided at 4c. 4h.,Whitefriars Street. Enlisted Coventry May, 1916. Cycle enameller. Commemorated War Memorial Park. Memorial Ref. Panel 16 and 62. Basra Memorial, Iraq.

GARNER, Private, John Alick. 3062, A Coy., 1st /7th Bn., Royal Warwickshire Regiment. Killed in action, Foncquevillers, 19th March, 1916 during bursting of shell in the doorway of a dugout. Age 19. Son of Reuben and Mary Ann Garner, of 7, George Street, Coventry. Born 10th July, 1897 at Courthouse Green. Universal Grinder, Rudge Whitworth works. Enlisted October, 1914 at Coventry. Grave Ref. I. D. 14. Foncquevillers Military Cemetery, Pas de Calais, France.

GARNESS, Sapper, Samuel. 47072, Royal Engineers attd. 147th Army Bde., Royal Field Artillery. Killed in action, 30th October, 1918. Age 28. Born Birmingham. Resided at 289, Foleshill Road. Son of Samuel Garness, of "Madresfield," Upper Promenade, Colwyn Bay, Denbighshire. Grave Ref. B. 20. Thiant Communal Cemetery, France.

GARRATT, Private, William. 91324, 13th Bn., The King's Liverpool Regiment formerly 330747, Royal Warwickshire Regiment. Killed in action, Beaumont Hamel, 16th April, 1918. Age 17. Son of George and Sarah Garratt, of 49, Mount Street, Coventry. Born 24th July, 1900 in Hertford Place. Resided at 49, Mount Street. Pressworker. Enlisted April, 1915, Coventry. Resided Coventry. Grave Ref. III. C. 6. Chocques Military Cemetery, Pas de Calais, France.

GARRETT, Private, David. 22414, 16th Bn., Royal Warwickshire Regiment. Died of wounds, 23rd December, 1917. Age 22. Son of William and Harriet Garrett, of Hawkesbury Stop Canal Office, Longford, Coventry. Native of Banbury. Employed Coventry. Enlisted Warwick. Resided Longford. Grave Ref. V. D. 11B. Mont Huon Military Cemetery, Le Treport, Seine-Maritime, France.

GARRETT, Private, Edmund Frederick. 16036, 2nd Bn., Oxfordshire and Buckinghamshire Light Infantry. Killed in action by a shell, Loos, 15th October, 1915. Born 26th October, 1886 at Coventry. Enlisted Coventry, November, 1914. Resided Much Park Street, Coventry. Tinsmith, Coventry Radiator Co. Ltd. Grave Ref. B. 16. Quarry Cemetery, Vermelles, France.

GARRETT, Gunner, John. 34489, A Bty., 282nd Brigade, Royal Field Artillery. Killed in action, Poperinghe, 5th September, 1917. Age 31. Son of Mr. and Mrs. George Garrett of Crimscote, Stratford-on-Avon. Husband of Edith Timms. Resided 4, Spring Lane, Kenilworth. Left a wife and two children. Employed Daimler Coventry. Grave Ref. IV. F. 10. Dozinghem Military Cemetery, Belgium.

GARRETT, Private, Samuel Hussleby. 3065, 2/7th Bn., Royal Warwickshire Regiment. Drowned accidentally, Chelmsford, 15th July, 1915. Age 19. He came from Coventry. Born 1st April, 1898 in Vicarage Hill near Rugby. Resided at 18, Broomfield Road. Clerk. Enlisted October, 1914 at Coventry. Commemorated Bablake School Memorial and British Thompson Houston. Grave Ref. 183. 92. Coventry (London Road) Cemetery.

GARRISON, Private, John Samuel. 12002, 9th Bn., Leicestershire Regiment. Killed in action, 14th July, 1916. Born All Saint's, Coventry. Enlisted Nuneaton. Resided 5c. 7h. Far Gosford Street, Coventry. Memorial Ref. Pier and Face 2 C and 3 A. Thiepval Memorial, Somme, France.

GARSIDE, Second Lieutenant, Jack. Royal Air Force formerly 5542, Oxfordshire and Buckinghamshire Light Infantry. Killed while flying (crashed), Brancaster, Norfolk, 18th November 1918. Age 21. Son of George and Sylvia Garside, of 47A, Widdrington Rd., Coventry. Born 19th June 1897 at Cleckheaton, Yorkshire. Resided at Coventry. Enlisted October 1915. Engineer, British Thompson Houston. Commemorated British Thompson Houston and War Memorial Park. Grave Ref. 30. 2. Coventry (London Road) Cemetery.

GASCOIGNE, Private, William Joseph. 6776, 1st Bn., Coldstream Guards. Killed in action, 29th October, 1914. Born Hampton-in-Arden. Enlisted Birmingham. Resided Canley near Coventry. Memorial Ref. Panel 11. Ypres (Menin Gate) Memorial, Belgium.

GASKIN, Petty Officer Stoker, Thomas. 298849(PO), HMS Victory, Royal Navy. 28th August, 1914. Age 34. Son of Jane Ellen and Thomas Gaskin, of 9, London Road, Coventry. Memorial Ref. 530. Portland Royal Naval Cemetery, Dorset.

GARVIE, Acting Engine Room Artificer, George Robert. M/15878, HMS Arabis, Royal Navy. Torpedoed at sea, 11th February, 1916. Born 28th July, 1882 at Hessle. Resided at 18, Holmsdale Road. Engineer. Enlisted October, 1915. Memorial Ref. 14. Plymouth Naval Memorial.

GAYTON, Private, Frank. 265499, 1st /7th Bn., Royal Warwickshire Regiment. Killed in action, Beaumont Hamel, 14th July 1916. Age 21. Son of John and Mary Gayton, of 4, Bull's Head Lane, Stoke, Coventry. Born 24th June, 1894 at Stoke, Coventry. Fitter. Enlisted October, 1914 at Coventry. Friend of Miss. Wise of 52, Latham Road, Earlsdon. Commemorated Stoke St. Michaels Memorial. Memorial Ref. Pier and Face 9 A 9 B and 10 B. Thiepval Memorial, Somme, France.

GEATER, Acting Engine Room Artificer 4th Class, Edward James. M/31978, HMS Victory II, Royal Navy. Died home, 10th September 1918. Age 22. Son of Captain and Mrs. Geater, of 32, Waveley Road, Coventry. Born 23rd July, 1896, at Fort Chambray Gozo, Maltese Islands. Resided at 32, Waveley Road. Enlisted June 1918. Fitter. Commemorated War Memorial Park. Grave Ref. E. 28. 22. Haslar Royal Naval Cemetery, Hampshire.

GEDDES, Corporal, L. Royal Field Artillery. Employed at Coventry. Died whilst prisoner of war in German hands, 1918.

GEE, Private, Alfred. 37312, 1st Bn., Wiltshire Regiment. Killed in action, 27th May, 1918. Age 19. Son of Alfred and Teresa Gee, of 46, Norborough Road, Doncaster. Born Nottingham. Enlisted Coventry. Resided Thorne, Yorks. Memorial Ref. Soissons Memorial, France.

GEORGE, Private, James Joseph. 18049, 14th Bn., Royal Warwickshire Regiment. Killed in action, by a shell, 11th November 1917. Age 32. Son of William and Eliza George, of 24A Pridmore Road, Coventry. Born 1884, Nuneaton. Enlisted April, 1916, Warwick. Resided Coventry. Engineer, Wool Factory, Lockhurst Lane. Memorial Ref. Panel 23 to 28 and 163A. Tyne Cot Memorial, Zonnebeke, West-Vlaanderen, Belgium.

GERETY, Rifleman, Michael. 5868, 1st Bn., Rifle Brigade. Killed in action, Loos, 25th September, 1915. Born 13th October, 1886 at Mullingar, Watermeath, Ireland. Enlisted March, 1915 at Woolwich, Kent. Resided 63, Primrose Hill Street, Coventry. Bricklayer. Grave Ref. K. 5. Mesnil Ridge Cemetery, Mesnil-Martinsart, France.

GETHING, Private, Walter Blagg. 51889, 9th Squadron, Machine Gun Corps (Cavalry) formerly 3312, 3/1st Warwick Yeomanry. Killed in action, 22nd March, 1918. Age 26. Mentioned in Despatches. Son of Walter and Florence Gething, of Lichfield. Husband of Rose Gething, of Lockwood, Saskatchewan, Canada. Born Lichfield, Staffs. Enlisted Warwick. Resided 166, Foleshill Road, Coventry. Employed Daimler. Memorial Ref. Panel 93 and 94. Pozieres Memorial, France.

GHENT, Corporal, Frederick Austin. PLY/1667 (S), 2nd Bn., Royal Naval Division, Royal Marine Light Infantry. Killed in action, 26th October, 1917. Born 28th May, 1883. Resided at 301, Stoney Stanton Road. Hairdresser and Tobacconist, Elite Saloon, near the Ordnance Works. Enlisted 22nd October, 1916. Grave Ref. XVII. B. 10. Poelcapelle British Cemetery, Belgium.

GIBBENS, Wheeler, Reginald Frederick Henry. Royal Field Artillery. Died home, 29th March 1925 due to the effects of gas. Born 2nd February, 1895 at Keresley. Resided at 6, Huntingdon Road. Motor Body Builder. Enlisted September, 1914. Commemorated War Memorial Park. Grave Ref. Coventry (London Road) Cemetery.

GIBBS, Private, Bertie. 42579, 1/8th Bn., Royal Warwickshire Regiment. Died of wounds, 5th November, 1918. Born Wandsworth, London. Enlisted Coventry. Resided Rugby. Grave Ref. II. D. 22. Premont British Cemetery, France.

GIBBS, Cadet, David. 242005, 38th Squadron, Royal Air Force formerly East Kent Regiment. Died, home 8th August, 1918. Age 20. Son of A. P. and Emma Gibbs, of 14, Kimberley Road, Rugby. Born at Moseley, Birmingham. Born in 1899 at Birmingham. Resided at Rugby. Bank Clerk. Enlisted 1914 at Coventry. Grave Ref. B. 487A. Rugby (Clifton Road) Cemetery.

GIBBS, Private, Henry. 16395, 7th Bn., Duke of Cornwall's Light Infantry formerly 6197, Royal Warwickshire Regiment. Died of wounds, 23rd March, 1918. Son of Mr. H. Gibbs, of 48, Red Lane, Coventry. Born 21st August, 1892 at Foleshill. Enlisted September, 1914, Nuneaton. Resided Coventry. Employed Daimler Company Ltd. Grave Ref. III. A. 12. Roye New British Cemetery, Somme, France.

GIBNEY, Lance Sergeant, Patrick Augustine. 632, 1st/1st., Warwickshire Yeomanry. Died of wounds, 10th January, 1917. Resided Coventry. Born Bilston. Enlisted Warwick. Resided Margate. Employed Coventry. Grave Ref. F. 189. Kantara War Memorial Cemetery, Egypt.

GIDLOW, Private, G. W. DM2/163556, Royal Army Service Corps. Mechanical Transport attached 488th Siege Battery Ammunition Column. 17th December, 1919. Husband of A. Gidlow of 16, Cross Princess Street, Tunstall, Stoke on Trent. Commemorated Exhall Memorial. Grave Ref. VII. C. 13. Duisans British Cemetery, Etrun, France.

GIFFFORD, Private, William Henry. 2157, 1st Bn., Royal Warwickshire Regiment. Killed in action, St. Julien, 25th April, 1915. Born 13th April, 1894 in Little Park Street. Resided 30, Webster Street. Machinist. Enlisted Coventry. Memorial Ref. Panel 8. Ypres (Menin Gate) Memorial, Belgium.

GILBERT, Gunner, James Charles. 213413, 354th Siege Bty., Royal Garrison Artillery. 13th November, 1918. Born in 1883. Resided at 18, St. Lawrence Road, Foleshill. Labourer employed by Alfred Herbert Ltd. Enlisted 1918. Grave Ref. S. II. LL. 15. St. Sever Cemetery Extension, Rouen, France.

GILBERT, Private, Joseph Gatcliff. 20369, 11th Bn., Royal Warwickshire Regiment. Died of wounds, 12th May, 1917. Age 23. Husband of C. B. Gilbert of Black Bank, Bedworth. Born Bedworth. Enlisted Coventry. Resided Bedworth. Grave Ref. XVIII. M. 8A. Etaples Military Cemetery, France.

GILBERT, Second Lieutenant, Stanley Claude. 99th Squadron, Royal Air Force. Shot down at Moulins-les-Metz, 26th September, 1918. Born 19th April, 1899 at Chapel Fields Farm, Allesley Old Road. Resided at Crabmill Farm, Crabmill Lane. Motor Engineer. Enlisted, May, 1917. Commemorated King Henry VIII School. Grave Ref. Near north boundary. Ste. Ruffine Communal Cemetery, France .

GILES, Private, Bertie Arthur. 206122, (1883), C Coy., Machine Gun Corps (Heavy Branch) formerly 1883, Machine Gun Corps. Killed in action, 15th September, 1916. Age 18. Son of Thomas and Emma Giles of 79, Bourne Road, Colchester. Born Barking, Essex. Enlisted Coventry. Memorial Ref. Pier and Face 5C and 12C. Thiepval Memorial, Somme, France.

GILES, Lance Corporal, Joseph James. 8521, 1st Bn., Border Regiment. Killed in action, Gallipoli, 11th June 1915. Age 28. Son of Mr. and Mrs. F. A. Giles, of 32, Alma Street, Coventry previously of Kidderminster. 8 years, 10 months' Service. Born 31st August, 1887 at Kidderminster. Resided at 31, Stratford Street. Soldier. Enlisted Coventry. Grave Ref. XI. D. 19. Geogheghan. Twelve Tree Copse Cemetery, Turkey.

GILES, Private, Stephen Walter. 1400, 4th Bn., Royal Warwickshire Regiment. transf. to (281683) 634th Home Service Employment Coy., Labour Corps. Died, home, 15th February, 1918, gassed at Loos. Age 22. Son of Mr. and Mrs. Giles, of 32, Alma Street, Coventry. Born 12th September, 1895 at Bewdley, Worcs. Plumber. Enlisted 1914 at Coventry. Grave Ref. 201. 19. Coventry (London Road) Cemetery.

GILKS, Private, Albert. 37967, 11th Bn., Royal Warwickshire Regiment. Died, 27th January, 1918. Age 19. Son of Samuel and Maria Gilks of Finley Hill Cottages, Hatton. Born Kineton, Warwicks. Enlisted Coventry. Resided Kenilworth. Grave Ref. P. VI. G. 11B. St. Sever Cemetery Extension, Rouen, France.

GILL, Sapper, Frederick Matthew. 48223, 93rd Field Coy., Royal Engineers. Died of wounds, (Gassed), 17th February, 1918. Age 31. Son of Fredrick Gill, of Newcastle-on-Tyne. Born 21st June, 1887 at Newcastle-on-Tyne. Resided at 27, Smith Street. Engineer. Enlisted August, 1914 at Coventry. Grave Ref. X. B. 25. Rocquigny-Equancourt Road British Cemetery, Manancourt, France.

GILL, Private, Frederick William. 330744, 15th Bn., Royal Warwickshire Regiment. Killed in action, 10th October, 1917. Age 20. Youngest son of Frank and Catherine Gill, of 88, Godiva Street, Coventry. Born 14th April, 1897 at 13c. 2h. St John's Street. Engineer's Labourer, Rover Works. Enlisted December, 1915. Grave Ref. I. K. 48. Voormezeele Enclosures No.1 and No.2, Ieper, West-Vlaanderen, Belgium

GILL, Private, Thomas Henry. 202979, 1/4th Bn., Wiltshire Regiment. Died of wounds, Egypt, 6th June, 1918. Enlisted Coventry. Resided Coventry. Commemorated Saint Thomas the Apostle, Longford. Grave Ref. S. 35. Ramleh War Cemetery, Israel.

GILLAM, Private, Albert E. 25169, 8th Bn., East Surrey Regiment. Killed in action, 1st December, 1917 hit by a piece of a shell whilst in a working party. Age 28. Son of John C. and Mrs. Alice Gillam of Duns Tew, Deddington, Oxford. Resided Mill End, Kenilworth. Employed Courtaulds, formerly Gardener, Wilton House. Grave Ref. II. B. 23. Bleuet Farm Cemetery, Belgium.

GILLESPIE, Rifleman, Horace John. S/24440, 11th Bn., Rifle Brigade. Died of wounds, 15th June, 1917. Age 24. Son of Alexander and Alice Ingledew (formerly Gillespie), of 23, Mill Street, Coventry. Born in London. Memorial Ref. 213. 7. 28. (Screen Wall.). Kensal Green (All Souls') Cemetery, London.

GILLESPIE, J. North Staffordshire Regiment. Died of wounds, 1917. Employed Coventry.

GILLETT, Gunner, Sydney George. 78311, 337th Siege Bty., Royal Garrison Artillery. Killed in action, 30th September, 1917. Age 21. Son of Albert Henry and Jane Gillett of Chapel Lane, Wychbold, Droitwich. Born Humbury, Worcester. Enlisted Coventry. Resided Wychbold, Worcester. Grave Ref. I. K. 9. Voormezeele Enclosures No.1 and No.2. Belgium.

GILLIVER, Private, Ernest. 3203, 1/7th Bn., Royal Warwickshire Regiment. Killed in action, 14th July, 1916. Enlisted Coventry. Resided Nuneaton. Memorial Ref. Pier and Face 9A 9B and 10B. Thiepval Memorial, Somme, France.

GILMORE, Sapper, John. 23458, 5th Signal Coy., Royal Engineers. Died of influenza, 28th October, 1918 whilst a prisoner of war. Age 30. Son of Andrew and Mary Gilmore, of 30, Stanley Street, Foleshill, Coventry. Native of Birr. Kings Co. Grave Ref. IX. G. 9. Cologne Southern Cemetery, Koln(Cologne), Nordrhein-Westfal, Germany.

GITTINS, Private, Charles Anthony. 240065, 2/6th Bn., Royal Warwickshire Regiment. Killed in action, 26th August, 1917. Born Coventry. Enlisted Birmingham. Resided Coventry. Memorial Ref. Panel 23 to 28 and 163A. Tyne Cot Memorial, Belgium.

GLANVILLE, Sergeant, Frank Edgar. 13731, 99th Coy., Machine Gun Corps (Infantry) formerly Gloucestershire Regiment. Killed in action, Battle of the Somme, 27th July, 1916. Age 28. Son of Frank Edgar and Sarah Jane Glanville, of Baythorp, King's Road, Paignton, Devon. Born 17th March, 1888 at Leicester. Resided at 8, Radcliffe Road. Lithographic artist. Enlisted 1915. Commemorated St. Barbara's Memorial. Memorial Ref. Pier and Face 5 C and 12 C. Thiepval Memorial, Somme, France.

GLINDONI, Lance Corporal, Sydney. 201967, 2/5th Bn., Manchester Regiment. Died, 28th September, 1918. Age 21. Son of William and Evangeline Glindoni, of 152, Brynn Street, St. Helens, Lancs. Born Coventry. Enlisted St. Helens, Lancs. Memorial Ref. Le Quesnoy Mem. 5. Valenciennes (St. Roch) Communal Cemetery, France.

GLYNN, Private, William. 7334, 1st Bn., King's Shropshire Light Infantry. Killed in action, 2nd January, 1915. Born Birmingham. Enlisted Coventry. Resided Birmingham. Memorial Ref. Panel 8. Ploegsteert Memorial, Belgium.

GODDARD, Private, Ernest Herbert. 43366, 8th Bn., Royal Berkshire Regiment. Killed in action, ,21st September, 1918. Born 21st October, 1897 at Coventry. Enlisted Coventry. Resided 30, Thomas Street. Miller, Daimler Works. Enlisted May, 1918. Grave Ref. II. A. 3. Unicorn Cemetery, Vend'huile, France.

GODDARD, Private, William. 35636, 1st /4th Bn., Duke of Cornwall's Light Infantry formerly 1115, 92 T. RES. BN. Lost in the torpedoed HMT Transylvania, 4th May, 1917. Age 27. Son of William Goddard. Husband of Edith R. Lynn (formerly Goddard, nee East), of 3, Wheatley Street, Coventry. Born 26th September, 1890 at Coventry. Enlisted Coventry. Greengrocer's Assistant. Enlisted 1916. Memorial Ref. Savona Memorial, Italy.

GODFREY-PAYTON, Captain, Arthur. "C" Coy., 1st /7th Bn., Royal Warwickshire Regiment. Died of wounds, received at the Battle of the Somme, 29th August, 1916. Age 27. Son of Harly George and Janet Park Godfrey-Payton, of The Bridge House, Myton, Warwick. Educated at Oundle School. Professional Associate of the Surveyors' Institution. and Valuer on the staff of the Valuation Dept., Inland Revenue, Coventry. Born 29th March, 1889 at Warwick. Enlisted August, 1914. Grave Ref. I. D. 53. Puchevillers British Cemetery, Somme, France.

GODSELL, Private, Horace. 3909, 2/7th Bn., Royal Warwickshire Regiment. Killed in action 19th July, 1916. Born Foleshill. Enlisted Coventry. Grave Ref. VI. B. 3. Aubers Ridge British Cemetery, Aubers, France.

GOLBY, Gunner, William Thomas. 163771, 33rd Bty. 33rd Bde., Royal Field Artillery. Killed in action, Ypres, 19th July, 1917. Age 30. Son of William Henry and Eliza Golby. Husband of Rachel Golby, of 54, Henley Road, Bell Green, Foleshill, Coventry. Native of Bell Green. Enlisted August, 1916, Coventry. Resided Coventry. Born 3rd October, 1886 at Foleshill. Plate Polisher. Grave Ref. I. G. 23. Vlamertinghe New Military Cemetery, Ieper, West-Vlaanderen, Belgium.

GOLDING, Private, Hubert James. 19375, 10th Bn., Royal Warwickshire Regiment. Died of wounds, 28th July, 1917. Employed Coventry. Enlisted Coventry. Memorial Ref. Panel 8. Ypres (Menin Gate) Memorial, Belgium.

GOLLY, Gunner, W. Royal Garrison Artillery. Commemorated Dunlop Memorial.

GOMM, Private, William. 33024, 1st Bn., Royal Berkshire Regiment. Killed in action, 3rd May, 1917 reports suggest wounded 29th April, 1917. Resided 27, Wood Street, Collycroft, Bedworth. Native of Bedworth. Enlisted Nuneaton. Grave Ref. V. A. 15. Tournai Communal Cemetery Allied Extension, Belgium.

GOODALL, Private, Samuel. 10236, 1st Bn., Grenadier Guards. Died of wounds, 21st November, 1915. Age 32. Husband of Ellen Agnes Maud Goodall, of 104, Red Lane, Coventry. Born 7th February, 1883 at Pudsey, near Leeds. Employed Messrs Courtaulds Ltd. Reservist. Leaves a widow and four children. Grave Ref. IV. N. 1. Merville Communal Cemetery, Nord, France.

GOODE, Corporal, Absalom. 3930, 2/7th Bn., Royal Warwickshire Regiment. Killed in action, 19th July, 1916. Born 19th May, 1891 at Blackheath, Birmingham. Resided at 609, Foleshill Road. Artificial Silk Spinner. Enlisted January, 1915 at Coventry. Memorial Ref. Panel 22 to 25. Loos Memorial, France.

GOODE, Private, Albert. 7th Bn., South Staffordshire Regiment. Died of wounds, home, 1st October, 1916. Born Aldridge, Staffs. Resided Exhall. Employed Coventry. Grave Ref. M. I. 365. Walsall (Bloxwich) Cemetery.

GOODE, Private, Harold. 20916, 1st Bn., Dorsetshire Regiment formerly 36097, Wiltshire Regiment. Killed in action, 30th September, 1918. Born 3rd September, 1900 at Styechale. Resided Styechale. Striker. Enlisted November, 1917. Commemorated Styechale (St. James's) War Memorial Grave Ref. V. I. D11. Grand-Seraucourt British Cemetery, France.

GOODE, Company Sergeant Major, William. 11309, Oxfordshire and Buckinghamshire Light Infantry. Killed in action, 16th August, 1917. Aged 24. Born Exhall. Son of Alfred W. Goode, of 5, Cleavers Yard, Bedworth. Enlisted Nuneaton. Memorial Ref. Panel 96 to 98. Tyne Cot Memorial, Belgium.

GOODE, Private, William John. 266673, 2/7th Bn., Royal Warwickshire Regiment. Died 5th July, 1918. Born 8th August, 1894 at Keresley. Resided at 8, Colledge Road, Holbrook Lane. Labourer. Enlisted 1915 at Coventry. Grave Ref. V. K. 6. Niederzwehren Cemetery, Germany.

GOODFELLOW, Gunner, Ernest Henry. 91431, "C" Bty. 55th Bde., Royal Field Artillery. Died, 21st August, 1916. Age 35. Son of George and Rose Goodfellow, of 97, Foleshill Road, Coventry. Born Burton-on-Trent. Enlisted Burton-on-Trent. Grave Ref. XIV. E. 13. Amara War Cemetery, Iraq

GOODWIN, Rifleman, Harry Thomas. 7921, 1/12th Bn., London Regiment formerly 22969, Northamptonshire Regiment. Killed in action, 9th September, 1916. Age 23. Son of Henry Thomas and Mary Ann Goodwin, of 68, Warwick Street, Daventry, Northants. Employed Swift Motor Works. News requested by Miss. C. Stevens, 86, Smith Street, Red Lane, Coventry. Enlisted Coventry. Memorial Ref. Pier and Face 9 C. Thiepval Memorial, Somme, France.

GOODWIN, Private, Leslie. 15897, 6th Bn., Oxfordshire and Buckinghamshire Light Infantry. Killed in action, 3rd September, 1916. Born Prestwood, Cheshire. Enlisted Coventry. Resided Prestwood, Cheshire. Memorial Ref. Pier and Face 10A and 10D. Thiepval Memorial, Somme, France.

 GOODWIN, Private, Thomas Arthur. 14, 2nd Bn., Royal Warwickshire Regiment. Killed in action, 3rd September, 1916. Born 1881 at Thelsford, Warwicks. Resided 13, Coventry Street. Reservist. Enlisted Coventry. Memorial Ref. Pier and Face 9 A 9 B and 10 B. Thiepval Memorial, Somme, France.

GOODYEAR, Private, Albert Edward. 32141, 7th Bn., Northamptonshire Regiment. Died of wounds, 22nd June, 1917. Age 19. Son of Mr. and Mrs. John Goodyear, of 12, Milton Street, Watford. Born Coventry. Enlisted Watford. Grave Ref. III. D. 39. Dickebusch New Military Cemetery Extension, Belgium.

 GOODYEAR, Lance Corporal, Frederick, Arthur. 10149, 1st Bn., Royal Welsh Fusiliers. Killed in action, 25th September, 1915. Born Foleshill. Resided Foleshill. Commemorated Exhall Memorial. Relative of Mrs. F. Moore, Tailoress, Woodshires Green, Longford. Commemorated Saint Thomas the Apostle, Longford. Memorial Ref. Panel 50 to 52. Loos Memorial, France.

GOODYEAR, Private, Timothy. 3345, 5th Bn., Connaught Rangers. Killed in action, Gallipoli, 22nd August, 1915. Age 35. Husband of Charlotte Goodyer, of 1, Quarry Road, Blacker Hill, Barnsley, Yorks. Born Coventry. Enlisted Birdwell, Yorks. Resided Barnsley. Memorial Ref. Panel 181 to 183. Helles Memorial, Turkey.

GOODYEAR, Private, Timothy. 3345, 5th Bn., Connaught Rangers, formerly York and Lancaster Regiment. Killed in action, Gallipoli, 22nd August, 1915. Age 35. Husband of Charlotte Goodyer, of 1, Quarry Road, Blacker Hill, Barnsley, Yorks. Born Coventry. Resided Barnsley. Memorial Ref. Panel 181 to 183. Helles Memorial, Turkey.

 GORMAN, Lance Sergeant, Arthur William. 9749, 2nd Bn., Royal Welsh Fusiliers. Killed in action, 27th May 1917. Age 26. Son of Thomas and Catherine Gorman, of, 41, Leicester Street, Coventry. Born 1st June, 1890 at Plymouth. Enlisted Warwick. Resided Coventry. Soldier. Memorial Ref. Bay 6. Arras Memorial, Pas de Calais, France.

 GORMAN, Second Lieutenant, Gerald Francis. 14th Bn., Royal Warwickshire Regiment. Killed Battle of the Somme, 30th July, 1916 between Longueval and High Wood. Age 19. Son of John and Annie Gorman, of 105, Pershore Road, Edgbaston, Birmingham. Born 27th December, 1896 at Whitehaven. Resided Coventry. Journalist, employed Midland Daily Telegraph, Coventry. Enlisted March, 1915. Commemorated Iliffe & Sons Ltd Memorial. Memorial Ref. Pier and Face 9 A 9 B and 10 B. Thiepval Memorial, Somme, France.

GOUGH, Gunner, Bernard. 151493, 99th Siege Battery, Royal Garrison Artillery. Died of wounds, 30th June, 1918. Born Longton, Staffs. Enlisted Coventry. Resided Longton. Grave Ref. IV. B. 10A. Les Baraques Military Cemetery, Sangatte, France.

GOUGH, Private, P. J. T/384175, 1034th Mechanical Transport Coy., Royal Army Service Corps. Died 15th March, 1919. Employed Coventry. Grave Ref. I. E. 1. Arquata Scrivia Communal Cemetery Extension, Italy.

GOUGH, 3rd Class Aircraft Mechanic, Wilfred Morris. Royal Flying Corps. Died, home, 16th July, 1917. Born 1st September, 1880 at 73, King William Street. Resided Birmingham. Printer on metal. Enlisted December, 1915. Grave Ref. Coventry (London Road) Cemetery.

GOUGH, Steward 1st Class, William John. L/115, HMS Cowslip, Royal Navy. Drowned at sea, 25th April, 1918. Born 4th January, 1892 at 6c. 4h. Far Gosford Street. Resided Portsmouth. Memorial Ref. 30. Portsmouth Naval Memorial.

GOULD, Private, Walter, 44935, 8th Bn., Royal Berkshire Regiment formerly 42889, Hampshire Regiment. Killed in action, 2nd September, 1918 as a stretcher bearer. Age 19. Son of Edward and Julia Sarah Gould, of 9, Atkin's Square, Gosford Green, Walsgrave Road, Coventry. Born 30th June, 1899 at Loughborough, Leics. Upholsterer, Comley's, The Burges. Enlisted 5th November, 1917 at Coventry. Memorial Ref. Panel 7. Vis-En-Artois Memorial, Pas de Calais, France.

GOULD, Lance Corporal, William. S/26616, 2nd Bn., Rifle Brigade formerly R/27373, King's Rifle Corps. Killed in action, 12th November, 1916. Born at Hognaston, Derby. Resided Coventry. Enlisted Coventry. Memorial Ref. Pier and Face 16 B and 16 C. Thiepval Memorial, Somme, France.

GOULDEN, Private, Frank. 19692, 1st Bn., Wiltshire Regiment formerly 8848, Oxfordshire and Buckinghamshire Light Infantry. Killed Battle of Hooge, 16th June, 1915. Age 17. Son of James and Maria Goulden, of 7, Lansdowne Street, Coventry. Born 21st April, 1899 at Harpurhey, Manchester. Resided at 7, Landsdowne Street. Enlisted August, 1914, Coventry. Cycle liner. Memorial Ref. Panel 53. Ypres (Menin Gate) Memorial, Ieper, West-Vlaanderen, Belgium.

GRAHAM, Flight Lieutenant, Charles Walter, DSO. No.1 Wing (Dunkerque), Royal Naval Air Service. Accidentally killed off the coast of Belgium, 8th September, 1916. Age 23. Son of Charles Knott Graham and Helen Graham, of "Aiuta," 9, Kitson Road, Barnes. Born 1884. Pupil, Triumph Cycle Company Ltd. Commemorated Triumph & Gloria Memorial. Distinguished Service Order awarded for shooting down a German seaplane near the Belgian coast. Grave Ref. 2. V. 9. Barnes Old Cemetery.

GRAHAM, Captain, Francis Noel. 11th Bn., Royal Warwickshire Regiment. Died of wounds, Beaumont Hamel, 16th November, 1916. Age 31. Son of James G. C. and Sophia F. K. Graham, of Whitley. Husband of Alice Graham, of Whitley, nr. Coventry. Born 31st December, 1885 at Whitley. Resided at Whitley. Enlisted October, 1914. Wine Merchant. Commemorated War Memorial Park. Grave Ref. VIII. A. 5. Contay British Cemetery, Contay, Somme, France.

GRAHAM, Captain, George Lionel. D Company, 7th Bn., Royal Warwickshire Regiment. Died German hands, 11th April, 1918. Born 31st October, 1881. Resided at Whitley. Brewer. Commemorated King Henry VIII School and War Memorial Park. Grave Ref. IX. B. 13. Grand-Seraucourt British Cemetery, France.

GRAINGER, Rifleman, John William. R/7068, 17th Bn., King's Royal Rifle Corps. Killed in action, Ypres, 8th August, 1916. Age 19. Son of Thomas and Mary Ann Grainger, of 28, Gun Lane, Stoke Heath, Coventry. Born 1897, Nottingham. Enlisted Nottingham. Resided 20, Spencer Street, Coventry. Grave Ref. III. D. 16. Essex Farm Cemetery, Ieper, West-Vlaanderen, Belgium.

GRAINGER, Lance Corporal, William Henry. 51186, Princess Patricia's Canadian Light Infantry (Eastern Ontario Regiment). Died of wounds, Vimy Ridge, 16th April, 1917. Age 28. Son of Mr. W. H. and Mrs. E. Grainger, of Rose and Crown, High Street, Coventry, England. Born 23rd May, 1889 at Coventry. Resided Canada. Pattern maker. Enlisted 1914. Grave Ref. IV. D. 23. Boulogne Eastern Cemetery, Pas de Calais, France.

GRANT, Private, Frederick. 13684, C Coy., 5th Bn., Oxfordshire and Buckinghamshire Light Infantry. Killed in action, Battle of Loos, 25th September, 1915. Husband of Rose Hannah Benny (formerly Grant), of 7 Court, 5 House, Much Park Street, Coventry. Born at Quorndon, Leics. Employed by Armstrong Siddeley Motors, Ltd. Enlisted Coventry. Commemorated War Memorial Park and Siddeley Roll of Honour. Leaves a widow and one child. Memorial Ref. Panel 37 and 39. Ypres (Menin Gate) Memorial, Ieper, West-Vlaanderen, Belgium.

GRAVES, Private, Arthur. 4325, 1st Bn., Royal Warwickshire Regiment. Died of wounds, 17th October, 1916. Age 22. Son of E. Graves of Clay Lane, Clay Cross, Derbyshire. Born South Muskham, Newark-on-Trent. Enlisted Coventry. Grave Ref. VIII. B. 10A. Etaples Military Cemetery, France.

GRAZHER, Private, James Henry. 1st Bn., Royal Warwickshire Regiment. Died, home, 22nd October, 1914. Born 25th April, 1884 at Longton, Staffordshire. Resided 13c. 20h. St. John Street. Fitter. Enlisted March, 1916. Grave Ref. Coventry (London Road) Cemetery.

GREATREX, Private, Arthur. 47679, 10th Bn., Essex Regiment formerly 10578, South Staffs Regiment. Died of wounds, 10th November, 1918. Age 29. Husband of Alice Greatrex, of 32, Sidney Street, Grantham. Born Coventry. Enlisted Rugby. Resided Grantham. Electrical wireman. Grave Ref. III. E. 3. Etretat Churchyard Extension, France.

GREAVES, Gunner, James Henry. 830240, "A" Bty. 241st Bde., Royal Field Artillery. Killed in action, 24th July, 1917. Age 21. Son of John Richard and Elizabeth Greaves, of 202, St. George's Road, Coventry. Born at Worcester. Grave Ref. V. A. 4. Vlamertinghe New Military Cemetery, Ieper, West-Vlaanderen, Belgium.

GREAVES, Gunner, Walter. 249185, "C" Bty. 291st Bde., Royal Field Artillery. Killed in action, Battle of the Somme, 29th September, 1918. Enlisted Birmingham. Resided Coventry. Born 7th November, 1889 at Edgbaston. Resided 147, Cross Road. Machine tool setter. Enlisted, 1918. Grave Ref. IV. A. 20. Unicorn Cemetery, Vend'huile, France.

GREELEY, James Horace. South Staffordshire Regiment formerly Royal Army Medical Corps. Died, home, 30th September, 1924. Born 3rd June, 1882 at Birmingham. Resided 10c. 2h. Well Street. Bricklayer. Reservist. Grave Ref. Coventry (London Road) Cemetery.

GREELEY, Private, Steven. 310508, Warwickshire Yeomanry formerly Royal Hussars. Killed in action, Egypt, 19th April, 1917. Born 1879 at Birmingham. Resided 10c. 2h. Well Street. Electrician. Commemorated Electricity Department Memorial, Coventry Corporation. Memorial Ref. 16. Jerusalem Memorial, Israel.

GREEN, Private, Albert. 16883, 15th Bn., Royal Warwickshire Regiment. Killed in action, 3rd September, 1916. Born Badley, Northants. Enlisted Coventry. Resided Lilburn, Warwicks. Memorial Ref. Pier and Face 9A 9B and 10B. Thiepval Memorial, Somme, France.

GREEN, Private, Arthur Edward. 50766, 10th Bn., Royal Warwickshire Regiment. Killed in action, 21st October, 1918 by a shell. Age 19. Youngest son of David and Louisa Green of 50, Spring Lane, Kenilworth. Born Kenilworth. Enlisted Coventry. Resided Kenilworth. Grave Ref. VI. E. 4. Romeries Communal Cemetery Extension, France.

GREEN, B. Employed Rover Company Ltd. Killed in action.

GREEN, Private, Bernard Lawdon. 42828, 2/7th Bn., Royal Warwickshire Regiment. Killed in action, 24th October, 1918. Age 19. Son of William Henry and Lizzie Green of 80, Leicester Street, Leamington. Born Leamington. Enlisted Coventry. Resided Leamington. Grave Ref. B. 10. Canonne Farm British Cemetery, Sommaing, France.

GREEN, Private, James. 10165, 1st Bn., Coldstream Guards. Died of wounds, 6th March, 1917. Age 21. Son of James and Ada Green. Born St. Mary's, Warwick. Enlisted Coventry. Resided Leamington Spa. Grave Ref. III. C. 44. Grove Town Cemetery, Meaulte, France.

GREEN, Private, James. 27983, 14th Bn., Royal Warwickshire Regiment. Killed in action, 4th October, 1917. Age 37. Son of William and Emma Green. Born January, 1881 at Coventry. Enlisted Coventry. Resided Coventry. Painter. Memorial Ref. Panel 23 to 28 and 163A. Tyne Cot Memorial, Belgium.

GREEN, Private, Joseph. 10121, 6th Bn., Leicestershire Regiment. Killed in action, 29th September, 1916. Born Stoke, Coventry. Enlisted Leicester. Memorial Ref. Pier and Face 2C and 3A. Thiepval Memorial, Somme, France.

GREEN, Sergeant, Joseph Henry. 45285, Training Depot, Canadian Engineers. Died, home, 11th February, 1917 at Crowborough Camp, Sussex. Age 34. Son of Charles and Mrs. C. L. Scrimshaw (formerly Green), of 54, Gilbert Street, Coventry. Born 14th July, 1882 in White Friars Lane. Sixteen years service, fourteen in Canada. Illness prevented him from going to the front. Grave Ref. 202. 46. Coventry (London Road) Cemetery.

GREEN, Private, Maurice V. P. 61280, Royal Fusiliers. Died, home at Edinburgh, 15th March, 1917. Age 21. Only son of Dr. C. Green. Commemorated Holy Trinity Panels. Grave Ref. Radford (St. Nicholas) Churchyard, Coventry.

GREEN, Corporal, Reginald. 3991, 9th Bn., King's Royal Rifle Corps. Killed in action, 15th September, 1916. Age 27. Son of George and Ruth Agnes Green of Sand Pit, Bulkington. Enlisted 1907. Served in India. Born Nuneaton. Enlisted Coventry. Resided Nuneaton. Memorial Ref. Pier and Face 13A and 13B. Thiepval Memorial, France.

GREEN, Private, Thomas Littler. 38085, 13th Bn., Gloucestershire Regiment attached Royal Warwickshire Regiment. Killed in action, 17th September, 1917. Age 26. Born 19th January, 1891 at Birmingham. Enlisted 3rd March, 1917. Resided 89, Goring Road. Machinist. Enlisted 3rd March, 1917 at Coventry. Husband of Winifred A. Smith (formerly Green) of 8, Jasmine Place, Aberdeen. Grave Ref. I. J. 9. Voormezeele enclosures No.1 and No. 2. Belgium.

GREEN, Private, William, MM. 15551, 10th Bn., Worcestershire Regiment. Killed in action, 7th November, 1918. Born Coventry. Enlisted Rugby. Resided Ryton-on-Dunsmore. Commemorated Ryton Memorial. Gazetted for Military Medal, 12th December, 1917. Grave Ref. IX. F. 6. Niederzwehren Cemetery, Germany.

GREENGRASS, Private, William. 4525, 1/7th Bn., Royal Warwickshire Regiment. Killed in action, 14th July, 1916. Age 41. Born 22nd September, 1874 at Norwich. Resided 133, Leicester Causeway. Bricklayer. Enlisted November, 1915 at Coventry. Memorial Ref. Pier and Face 9 A 9 B and 10 B. Thiepval Memorial, Somme, France.

GREENING, Able Seaman, Frank Kenneth. J/19974, HMS Strongbow, Royal Navy. Killed in action protecting convoy in North Sea, 17th October, 1917. Age 22. Son of Samuel and Emily Greening, of 39/41, Cox Street, Coventry. Husband of Rose Janet Greening, of 60, Weston Street, Coventry. Born 1886. Employed Singer Cycle Co. Ltd. Educated Bablake School. Memorial Ref. 21. Chatham Naval Memorial, Kent.

GREENSTREET, Private, George Weston. 16100, 2nd Bn., Oxfordshire and Buckinghamshire Light Infantry. Killed in action, Ypres, 28th April, 1917. Born 28th September, 1891 at London. Resided 6c. 5h. New Buildings. Polisher, Triumph Works. Enlisted November, 1914. Commemorated Holy Trinity Panels, Triumph & Gloria Memorial and Barras Green Working Mens Club. Memorial Ref. Panel 6 and 7. Arras Memorial, Pas de Calais, France.

GREENWAY, Private, Arthur Henry. 25167, 8th Bn., East Surrey Regiment formerly 5716, Royal. Warwickshire Regiment. Killed in action, Cherisy, 3rd May, 1917. Age 25. Son of Arthur and Florence Greenway, of 28, Brooklyn Road, Coventry. Husband of Olive Greenway, of 279, Foleshill Road, Coventry. Born 21st February, 1892 at 5, Eagle Street, Coventry. Enlisted June 1916 at Warwick. Hairdresser. Memorial Ref. Bay 6. Arras Memorial, Pas de Calais, France.

GREENWAY, Private, James Victor. 14786, 9th Bn., Royal Warwickshire Regiment. Killed in action, Mesopotamia, 25th January, 1917. Born Warwick. Enlisted Warwick. Resided 11, Duke Street, Coventry. Enlisted September, 1915. Grave Ref. XIX. G. 5. Amara War Cemetery, Iraq.

GREENWAY, Private, Leonard Harry. 12830, A Coy., 5th Bn., Oxfordshire and Buckinghamshire Light Infantry. Killed in action, 25th September 1915. Age 21. Son of Charles Harry and Fanny Greenway, of 7, Canterbury Street, Coventry. Born 1894 at Coventry. Enlisted Warwick. Resided Coventry. Memorial Ref. Panel 37 and 39. Ypres (Menin Gate) Memorial, Ieper, West-Vlaanderen, Belgium.

GREENWOOD, Sergeant, Fred. 265254, Depot, Royal Warwickshire Regiment. Died of pneumonia, 17th November, 1918. Age 28. Son of William and Louisa G. Greenwood, of Dark Lane, Batley. Husband of Winifred May Greenwood, of 127, Holyhead Road, Coventry. Born 12th February, 1890 at Batley, Yorks. Clerk. Enlisted August, 1914. Grave Ref. E. 141. Batley Cemetery, Yorkshire.

GREGORY, Private, Arthur. M2/163574, HQ, Mechanical Transport Coy., Royal Army Service Corps. Died, 24th August, 1917. Born Barrow-in-Furness. Enlisted Coventry. Resided Barrow. Grave Ref I. H. 10. Gwalia Cemetery, Belgium.

GREGORY, Captain (Quartermaster) Herbert. Machine Gun Corps (Infantry). Died of pneumonia, 23rd October, 1919. Age 34. Son of Herbert Gregory, of Coventry. Husband of Clara Gregory, of 54, Lugsmore Lane, St. Helens. Grave Ref. O.G.104. Eccleston (Christ Church) Churchyard, Lancashire.

GREHAM, Private, Augustine. 23056, 5th Bn. Royal Berkshire Regiment. Killed in action, 29th April, 1917. Born Chequerhill, Co. Galway. Enlisted Warwick. Resided Coventry. Memorial Ref. Bay 7. Arras Memorial, France.

GREW, Sapper, Harold. 44849, 83rd Field Coy., Royal Engineers. Died of wounds, 31st May, 1917. Age 24. Son of Mrs. Anne Grew of Wilson Road, Smethwick. Born Birmingham. Enlisted Coventry. Grave Ref. V. C. 2. Grevillers British Cemetery, France.

GREW, Second Lieutenant, Walter Ernest. 3rd Bn., Royal Warwickshire Regiment. Killed in action, near Ypres, 7th October, 1917. Born 15th July, 1898 at 7, Wren Street. Resided 135, Holyhead Road. Bank Clerk. Enlisted November, 1916. Educated Bablake School. Commemorated Bablake School Memorial and St. John's Church. Memorial Ref. Panel 23 to 28 and 163A. Tyne Cot Memorial, Belgium.

GRIFFIN, Private, Elijah. 4235, 1st Bn., Royal Warwickshire Regiment. Killed in action, 18th November, 1915. Born Coventry. Enlisted Birmingham. Grave Ref. II. D. 4. Sucrerie Military Cemetery, Colincamps, France.

GRIFFIN, Private, Herbert Henry. 17953, 2nd Bn., Royal Warwickshire Regiment. Died, Italy, 21st October, 1918. Husband of Mrs. A. M. Griffin, of 36, Meadway, Stoke Heath, Coventry. Born 10th September, 1891 at 35, Yardley Street. Resided at 1 North Street. Enlisted Coventry, April, 1916. Tailor. Commemorated War Memorial Park. Grave Ref. 3. D. 6. Giavera British Cemetery, Arcade, Italy.

GRIFFIN, Sergeant, John. 12758, 9th Bn., Royal Warwickshire Regiment. Died, Mesopotamia, 16th June, 1916. Born Hampton Lucy, Warwicks. Enlisted Coventry. Resided Stratford-on-Avon. Grave Ref V. K. 4. Basra War Cemetery, Iraq.

GRIFFIN, Private, Thomas Edmund. 22678, 16th Bn., Royal Warwickshire Regiment. Died of wounds, 14th March, 1917. Age 24. Husband of Mabel Winifred Griffin, of 69, Nicholls Street, Coventry. Born 8th December, 1893 at Coventry. Resided at 15 Stoke Row. Enlisted Coventry, November 1916. Hairdresser. Commemorated War Memorial Park. Grave Ref. H. 24. Cambrin Military Cemetery, Pas de Calais, France.

GRIFFIN, Private, Walter. 12804, 9th Bn., Royal Warwickshire Regiment. Died of wounds, 9th May, 1916 at Victoria Hospital in Bombay. Age 30. Son of Thomas and Maria Griffin, of Bedworth, Coventry. Husband of Lillian Griffin, of 7, Chamberlain Street, Bedworth. Employed Newdigate Colliery. Left a widow and seven children. Memorial Ref. Face B. Kirkee 1914-1918 Memorial, India.

GRIFFITH, Sapper, John Hepworth. 99117, 81st Field Coy., Royal Engineers. Killed in action, 18th November, 1916. Age 31. Son of Thomas and Sarah Ann Griffiths of 24, Young Street, Wolverton, Bucks. Born Wolverton, Bucks. Enlisted Coventry. Memorial Ref. Pier and Face 8A and 8D. Thiepval Memorial, France.

GRIFFITHS, Private, Arthur. 14218, 2nd Bn., Worcestershire Regiment. Killed in action, 24th August, 1916. Born Chrefteins, Salop. Enlisted London. Resided Coventry. Memorial Ref. Pier and Face 5A and 6C. Thiepval Memorial, Somme, France.

GRIFFITHS, Private, William Henry. 2336, 2nd Bn., Royal Warwickshire Regiment. Died of wounds, Sailly, 19th December, 1914. Age 51. Son of Thomas and Mary Ann Griffiths, of Coventry. Born 4th November, 1869 at Spon Street. Resided at 46, Mount Street. Labourer. Enlisted September, 1914 at Coventry. Grave Ref. B. 6. Sailly-Sur-La-Lys Churchyard, Pas de Calais, France.

GRIMLEY, Private, Harry. 201695, 2nd /5th Bn., Royal Warwickshire Regiment. Killed in action, 13th July, 1916. Age 28. Son of John and Millie Grimley, of 1 Court, 2 House, Spriggs Row, Hales Street, Coventry. Born 6th March, 1885 in Chauntry Place, Coventry. Machinist. Memorial Ref. Panel 22 to 25. Loos Memorial, Pas de Calais, France.

GRIMLEY, Private, Sydney. 202193, "B" Coy. 11th Bn., Royal Warwickshire Regiment. Died of wounds, 23rd April, 1917. Age 19. Son of Mr. and Mrs. W. H. Grimley, of 19, Canal Road, Longford, Coventry. Born 1898, Coventry. Enlisted Warwick. Resided Coventry. Commemorated Saint Thomas the Apostle, Longford and Roll of Honour, Salem Baptist Church. Grave Ref. II. D. 7. Aubigny Communal Cemetery Extension, Pas de Calais, France.

GROGAN, Private, Owen. 57646, 20th Bn., 2nd Canadians, Central Ontario Regiment. Killed in action, 28th March, 1916. Born Coventry. Resided Canada. Farmer. Enlisted 1914. Son of John Grogan, Broomfield Place. Grave Ref. I. D. 9. Ridge Wood Military Cemetery, Belgium.

GROOME, Lance Corporal, John Thomas. 5888, 1st Bn., Leicestershire Regiment. Died of wounds, 12th May, 1915. Born Leicester. Resided at 195, Sovereign Road. Employed Coventry Chain Ltd. Commemorated Coventry Chain Memorial. Grave Ref. I. B. 5. Erquinghem-Lys Churchyard Extension, France.

GROOMS, Guardsman, Edward Alexander. 13788, King's Coy. 1st Bn., Grenadier Guards. Killed in action, 10th March, 1915. Age 26. Husband of Clara Grooms, of 252, Knutsford Road, Warrington, Lancs. A member of the Liverpool City Police. Born Coventry. Enlisted Liverpool. Memorial Ref. Panel 2. Le Touret Memorial, France.

GROVER, Sergeant, James John. 2nd Bn., Worcestershire Regiment. Killed in action 21st May, 1917. Born Brighton. Resided Paddlington, London. Formerly employed Coventry. Memorial Ref. Bay 6. Arras Memorial, France.

GROVES, Private, Joseph Harold. 33139, 1st Bn., Wiltshire Regiment formerly 18969, Royal Warwickshire Regiment. Killed in action, Menin Road, 7th July, 1917. Age 19. Son of Harry and Mary Groves, of 24, Union Street, Coventry. Born 27th November, 1897 at Coventry. Enlisted Coventry. Resided Coventry. Compositor. Commemorated Iliffe & Sons Ltd Memorial. Grave Ref. III. D. 8. Ypres Town Cemetery Extension, Ieper, West-Vlaanderen, Belgium.

GUEST, Private, Samuel. 2041, 1/5th Bn., Royal Warwickshire Regiment. Killed in the big push, 18th July, 1916. Husband of Ada Guest of 3/264, Great Lister Street, Birmingham. Brother of A. Guest, Royal Garrison Artillery and G. M. Guest, Motor Cycle Mechanic, 693rd Company, Motor Transport, Army Service Corps. Memorial Ref. Pier and Face 9A 9B and 10B. Thiepval Memorial, Somme, France.

GUISE, Second Lieutenant, James William. 5th Bn., Oxfordshire and Buckinghamshire Light Infantry formerly Royal Warwickshire Regiment. Died of wounds, Ypres, 19th August 1917. Son of James and Norah Guise, of 51, Paynes Lane, Coventry. Born 15th March, 1899 at Cowley Barracks, Oxford. Clerk. Enlisted October, 1914. Commemorated Bablake School Memorial. Grave Ref. I. B. 23. Brandhoek New Military Cemetery, No.3, Ieper, West-Vlaanderen, Belgium.

GULLIVER, Lance Corporal, Arthur Edward. 10060, 2nd Bn., Worcestershire Regiment. Killed in action, 31st October, 1914. Son of Henry and Betsy Gulliver, of Shottery, Stratford-on-Avon. Age 26. Born 27th August, 1888 at Cubbington. Resided 22, Arden Street. Labourer. Reservist. Employed Alfred Herbert Works. Commemorated St. Barbara's Memorial. Memorial Ref. Panel 34. Ypres (Menin Gate) Memorial, Belgium.

GUNN, Private, Henry Edwin. 265749, 1st /7th Bn., Royal Warwickshire Regiment. Died of wounds, 26th June, 1918. Age 22. Son of William F. and Fanny L. Gunn, of Coventry. Born 12th August, 1895 at 56, King William Street. Resided 46, Stockton Road. Clerk. Enlisted September, 1914. Born Coventry. Enlisted Coventry. Educated Bablake School. Commemorated Bablake School Memorial. Grave Ref. 4. A. 2. Montecchio Precalcino Communal Cemetery Extension, Italy.

GUPPY, Private, Edwin John. 701, 1st Bn. Welsh Guards. Killed in action, 27th September, 1915. Age 23. Son of John Guppy of 104, Llangyfelack Road, Brynhyfryd. Husband of Susannah Guppy of 26, New Orchard Street, Swansea. Born Coventry. Enlisted Swansea, Glamorogan. Memorial Ref. Panel 10. Loos Memorial, France.

GUTSELL, Gunner, Leslie Robert. 2518, D Coy., No. 1. Section, Machine Gun Corps (Heavy Branch). Killed in action, 15th September, 1916. Age 20. Born Dorchester. Enlisted Coventry. Resided Shaftesbury. Memorial Ref. Pier and Face 5C and 12C. Thiepval Memorial, Somme, France.

GUTTERIDGE, Private, John Henry. 13941, 2nd Bn., Oxfordshire and Buckinghamshire Light Infantry. Killed in action, Givenchy, 27th August, 1915. Born 25th December, 1892 at Coventry. Enlisted Coventry. Born 25th December, 1892 at Coventry. Resided at 11, Henry Street. Enlisted September 1914. Coremaker, Messrs. Johnson and Mason. Commemorated War Memorial Park. Grave Ref. II. G. 8. Guards Cemetery, Windy Corner, Cuinchy, France.

GUY, Gunner, Percy George Thorne. 352276, Hants Heavy Bty., Royal Garrison Artillery. Died, home, 2nd November 1918. Age 28. Born 8th April, 1890 at Poole. Resided Coventry. Gardener. Enlisted August, 1914. Grave Ref. 211. 141. Coventry (London Road) Cemetery.

GWYNNE, William John Henry. 9236, 1st Bn., Royal Munster Fusiliers. Killed in action, 26th April, 1915. Age 24. Son of William and Alice Gwynne, of 21, Poplar Road, Wichenford, Worcester. Born Rawal Pindi, India. Enlisted Birmingham. Resided Wichenford, Worcester. Billeted Coventry. Memorial Ref. Sp. Mem. A. 55. V Beach Cemetery, Turkey.

HABBERLEY, Private, Thomas Henry. 6334, 1st Bn., Royal Welsh Fusiliers. Killed in action, 16th May, 1915. Age 34. Son of Charles and Margaret Habberley. Husband of Mary Elizabeth Habberley, of 196, St. George's Road, Coventry. Born Barrow, Salop. Enlisted Shrewsbury. Memorial Ref. Panel 13 and 14. Le Touret Memorial, Pas De Calais, France

HACKETT, Private, Edward Finch. 12551, 6th Bn., Oxfordshire and Buckinghamshire Light Infantry. Killed in action, 8th June, 1916. Age 32. Son of William and Eliza Hackett, of 29, Cobden Street, Coventry. Born 1884, Birmingham. Enlisted Nuneaton. Resided Coventry. Memorial Ref. Panel 37 and 39. Ypres (Menin Gate) Memorial, Ieper, West-Vlaanderen, Belgium.

HACKFORD, Private, Frederick. 206139, C Bn., Machine Gun Corps (Heavy Branch) formerly 2813, Machine Gun Corps. Died of wounds, 10th June, 1917. Age 28. Born Belton, Lincs. Enlisted Coventry. Son of William Edward and Emma Hackford of Boston, Lincs. Grave Ref. XXV. H. 4. Etaples Military Cemetery, France.

HADDON, Private, George Henry. 13089, 2nd Bn., Oxfordshire and Buckinghamshire Light Infantry. Killed in action, 16th May, 1915. Born Heyford, Northants. Enlisted Coventry. Resided Lower Heyford, Northants. Memorial Ref. Panel 26. Le Touret Memorial, France.

HADDON, John Herbert. Killed in action, France, 16th May, 1915. Born 18th May, 1889. Resided Coventry. Railway Porter. Enlisted August, 1914.

HADDON, Private, William. 15627, 10th Bn., Royal Warwickshire Regiment. Killed in action, 19th April, 1918. Born Coventry. Enlisted Coventry. Commemorated Coventry Chain Memorial. Grave Ref. III. A. 12. Messines Ridge British Cemetery, Belgium.

HADLAND, Private, William. 2519, "C" Coy. 5th Bn., Leicestershire Regiment. Died of wounds, 13th November, 1915. Age 20. Son of Joseph and Annie Hadland, of Cadeby, Market Bosworth, Nuneaton. Born Coventry. Enlisted Market Bosworth, Leics. Resided Cadeby, Leics. Grave Ref. A. 14. 37. St. Sever Cemetery, Rouen, France.

HADLEY, F. E. Employed by Rover Company Ltd. Killed in action.

HADLEY, Private, Thomas. 29624, 1st Bn., Royal Warwickshire Regiment. Died of wounds, near Poperinghe, 6th October, 1917. Age 19. Son of Thomas and Lucy Hadley, of Roselyn, 37, Holbrooks, Foleshill, Coventry. Born 7th June, 1898 at Birmingham. Needle Swaging. Enlisted March, 1917 at Coventry. Grave Ref. V. H. 12. Dozinghem Military Cemetery, Poperinge, West-Vlaanderen, Belgium.

HAIGH, Private, William, Edward. 12006, 10th Bn., Gloucestershire Regiment. Killed in action, 25th September, 1915. Born St. Michael's Parish. Grave Ref. XII. E. 18. St. Mary's A.D.S. Cemetery, Haisnes, France.

HAINES, Private, Stephen Samuel. 23794, 1st Garrison Bn., Hampshire Regiment formerly 22987, Worcestershire Regiment. Died of wounds, 21st March, 1918. Age 42. Born 16th January, 1876 at Honeybourne. Resided 16c. 9h. Gosford Street. Labourer, Electricity Department. Enlisted June, 1916 at Coventry. Commemorated Electricity Department Memorial, Coventry Corporation. Grave Ref. III. C. 4. Merville Communal Cemetery Extension, France.

HAKES, Sapper, Albert. 88981, II Corps Signals, Royal Engineers. Died of wounds, 29th June, 1917. Age 42. Husband of Lilian Hakes, of 6, Palmerston Road, Earlsdon, Coventry, Warwickshire. Born 1st January, 1874 at Elton, Lancs. Post Office Clerk. Enlisted May, 1915. Grave Ref. XIV. C. 11A. Lijssenthoek Military Cemetery, Poperinge, West-Vlaanderen, Belgium.

HALCOMB, Major, Leslie Broughton. Croix-de-Guerre (Belgium). B Bty., 295th Bde., Royal Field Artillery. Killed in action, 25th October, 1918. Age 21. Son of S. B. and Marion Halcomb, of Beechwood, Broad Lane, Coventry. Native of Sheffield. Grave Ref. A. 4. Hem Communal Cemetery, Nord, Nord, France.

HALEY, Private, William Bernard. 203116, 2nd /5th Bn., Royal Warwickshire Regiment. Killed in action, Ypres, 1st September , 1917. Age 26. Son of Francis and Mary Ann Haley, of Back 12, Jordan Well, Coventry. Born 13th July, 1892 at Coventry. Enlisted June, 1916 at Coventry. Resided Coventry. Universal Grinder. Memorial Ref. Panel 23 to 28 and 163A. Tyne Cot Memorial, Zonnebeke, West-Vlaanderen, Belgium.

HALFORD, Private, Elliot Gostlow. 51000, 9th Bn., Cheshire Regiment formerly Royal Warwickshire Regiment. Killed in action, Messines Ridge, 7th June, 1917. Born 2nd January, 1898 at Wyken. Son of Thomas and Martha Halford, of Binley, Coventry. Educated Brandon School. Resided Binley. Polisher. Enlisted February, 1917 at Coventry. Memorial Ref. Panel 19 –22. Ypres (Menin Gate) Memorial, Belgium.

HALFORD, Private, Sidney Arthur. 16433, 14th Bn., Royal Warwickshire Regiment. Died of wounds, Battle of the Somme, 3rd September, 1916. Age 20. Son of Thomas and Martha Halford, of Binley, Coventry. Born 27th May, 1896 at Wyken. Resided Brandon lane. Brewer's Drayman. Educated Brandon School. Enlisted February, 1916 at Coventry. Memorial Ref. Pier and Face 9 A 9 B and 10 B. Thiepval Memorial, Somme, France.

HALL, Second Lieutenant, Aubrey Frederick. 92nd Field Coy., Royal Engineers. Killed in action, the Somme, 8th August, 1918. Age 22. Son of William Willie and Emma Jane Hall, of 20 Britannia Street, Coventry. Born 12th June, 1896 at Parkside. Architect's Pupil. Enlisted April, 1915. Educated Bablake School. Commemorated Bablake School Memorial. Grave Ref. II. B. 16. Franvillers Communal Cemetery Extension, Somme, France.

HALL, Private, Ernest. 17023, 14th Bn., Royal Warwickshire Regiment. Killed in action, 8th May, 1917. Born 21st February, 1891 at Wirksworth, Derbyshire. Resided 5c. 9h. Spon Street. Carpenter. Enlisted March, 1916 at Coventry. Employed Standard Motor Co., Foleshill Road. Memorial Ref. Bay 3. Arras Memorial, France.

HALL, Ernest James. Private. S/43592, 1st/5th Battalion Seaforth Highlanders formerly 5141094835, Army Service Corps and G/92023 Royal Fusiliers. Killed in action, 13th October, 1918. Born 20th October 1888, at Bretford. Resided at 5c. 3h. Cook Street. Baker. Enlisted May 1915 at Coventry. Commemorated St. John's Church and War Memorial Park. Grave Ref. Row B. Grave 10. Avesnes Le-Sec Communal Cemetery Extension, France.

HALL, Private, F. 4259, King's Own Yorkshire Light Infantry. Died, home, 21st March, 1918. Grave Ref. 222. 19. Coventry (London Road) Cemetery.

HALL, Lance Corporal, Sidney George, MSM. 266586, 2/6th Bn., Royal Warwickshire Regiment. Killed in action, 11th April, 1918. Son of Mr. G. Hall of 31, Alexandria Road, Rugby. Enlisted Coventry. Resided Rugby. Grave Ref. III. C. 11. St. Venant-Robecq Road British Cemetery, Robecq, France.

HAMMERSLEY, Private (Drummer), Ernest. 42338, 2nd Bn., Royal Berkshire Regiment. Killed in action, 28th May, 1918. Son of Mrs. Jessie Hammersley, of 36, White Friar Lane, Coventry. Born Coventry. Enlisted Coventry. Memorial Ref. Soissons Memorial, Aisne, France.

HAMMERTON, Lieutenant, Gilbert. Machine Gun Corps (Infantry). Killed in action, 4th September, 1916. Commemorated King Henry VIII School. Memorial Ref. Pier and Face 5 C and 12 C. Thiepval Memorial, Somme, France.

HAMMOND, R. Commemorated Triumph & Gloria Memorial.

HAMMOND, Private, William. 24998, 2nd Bn., Grenadier Guards. Killed in action, 25th September, 1916. Born 29th January, 1886 at Rugby. Resided at 49, John Street. Employed Mr. G. Bird, Newcombe Road, Painter and Decorator. Enlisted December, 1915 at Coventry. Memorial Ref. Pier and Face 8 D. Thiepval Memorial, Somme, France.

HANCOCK, Private, Frederick Sydney. 17055, 15th Bn., Royal Warwickshire Regiment. Killed in action, 3rd September, 1916. Age 34. Son of Mrs. Sarah Hancock of 8, Castle Lane, Warwick. Born Old Milverton, Warwicks. Enlisted Coventry. Memorial Ref. Pier and Face 9A 9B and 10B. Thiepval Memorial, Somme, France.

HANCOCK, Corporal, Walter H. 7140, 1st Bn., Gloucestershire Regiment. Killed in action, 29th October, 1914. Age 30. Husband of M. A. Hancock, of 12, Humber Rd., Coventry. Employed Swift of Coventry Ltd. Reservist. Memorial Ref. Addenda Panel 57. Ypres (Menin Gate) Memorial, Ieper, West-Vlaanderen, Belgium.

HANCOCK, Rifleman, Wilfred John. R/17405, 11th Bn., King's Royal Rifle Corps. Died of wounds, 3rd September, 1916. Age 21. Son of Sardius and Mary Hancock of 1, Glenfield, Newtown, Malvern, Worcs. Born Harbledown, Kent. Enlisted Coventry. Resided Malvern, Lincs. Commemorated Wesleyan Church. Memorial Ref. Pier and Face 13A and 13B. Thiepval Memorial, Somme, France.

HANCOCK, Private, William Henry. 23042, 4th Bn., Worcestershire Regiment. Killed in action, Gallipoli, 6th August, 1915. Age 24. Son of George Herbert Hancock, of 58, Bond Street, Coventry. Born 1891, Coventry. Enlisted Coventry. Employed Rover Co. Ltd. Memorial Ref. Panel 104 to 113. Helles Memorial, Turkey

HANCOCKS, Private, Ernest John. 42895, "D" Coy. 1st /8th Bn., Royal Warwickshire Regiment. Killed in action, 23rd October, 1918. Age 19. Son of William and Kate Elizabeth Hancocks, of Overtown, Appleby Magna, Burton-on-Trent. Born at Coventry. Born 29Th May, 1899 at Coventry. Resided at 191, Leicester Causeway. Enlisted Coventry. Machinist. Commemorated War Memorial Park. Grave Ref. B. 6. Pommereuil British Cemetery, Nord, France.

HANCOX, Private, Harry. 5219, 1st /6th Bn., Royal Warwickshire Regiment. Killed in action, 18th August, 1916. Age 33. Brother of Mrs. L. Ward, of 8, Ribble Road, Stoke, Coventry. Born 8th April, 1885 at Coventry. Enlisted 1915, Coventry. Resided 26, Ribble Road. Cycle Frame Builder. Memorial Ref. Pier and Face 9 A 9 B and 10 B. Thiepval Memorial, Somme, France (possibly buried near Pozieres).

HANCOX, Private, John Frederick. 25543, 14th Bn., Royal Warwickshire Regiment. Killed in action, 14th April, 1918. Age 24. Son of John and Mary Chatwin Hancox of London Road, Stretton-on-Dunsmore. Born Stretton-on-Dunsmore. Enlisted Coventry. Resided Stretton-on-Dunsmore. Memorial Ref. Panel 2 and 3. Ploegsteert Memorial, Belgium.

HANCOX, Private, Thomas. 9684, 14th Bn., Royal Warwickshire Regiment. Killed in action, Mesopotamia, 10th August, 1915. Age 24. Son of John and Mary Jane Chatwin Hancox of London Road, Stretton-on-Dunsmore, Rugby. Born Longford. Enlisted Coventry. Resided Bishopston, Warwicks. Memorial Ref. Panel 2 and 3. Ploegstreet Memorial, Belgium.

HAND, Private, Albert. 27131, 8th Bn., The Loyal North Lancashire Regiment formerly 35542, Manchester Regiment. Killed in action, 14th October, 1916. Age 26. Husband of Edith May Holiday (formerly Hand), of 37, Mickleton Road, Earlsdon, Coventry. Born Manchester. Enlisted Manchester. Resided Moss Side. Memorial Ref. Pier and Face 11 A. Thiepval Memorial, Somme, France.

HANDLEY, Alfred William. 57322, 8th Bn., Royal Warwickshire Regiment. Died of wounds, 20th October, 1918. Born 1897 at Northampton. Resided 55, Middleborough Road. Fitter. Enlisted May, 1918 at Coventry. Grave Ref. II. C. 20. Roisel Communal Cemetery Extension, France.

HANDLEY, Gunner, G. Killed in action, 1918. Resided 5, Lower Ford Street.

HANDLEY, Sapper, Victor Frederick. 101734, 72nd Field Coy., Royal Engineers. Died of wounds, Mesopotamia, 25th February, 1917. Born Earls Barton, Northants. Enlisted Coventry. Memorial Ref. Panel 5 and 61. Basra Memorial, Iraq.

HANDY, Private, William Edward. G/50114, 11th Bn., Middlesex Regiment formerly 3163, Royal Fusiliers. Died of wounds, 3rd May, 1917 from a piece of shell. Born 12th November, 1893 at 10, Wellington Street, Coventry. Enlisted July, 1916 at Portobello, Midlothian. Resided 8, Sackville Street, Coventry. Stereotyper, Iliffe & Sons. Commemorated Iliffe & Sons Ltd Memorial. Memorial Ref. Bay 7. Arras Memorial, France.

HANKERSON, Private, John. 3038, 2nd Bn., Royal Warwickshire Regiment. Killed in action, 19th December, 1914. Born St. Nicholas, Coventry. Enlisted Warwick. Resided Coventry. Commemorated St. John's Church. Memorial Ref. Panel 2 and 3. Ploegsteert Memorial, Belgium.

HANMER, Second Lieutenant, Alexander, John, MC. 3rd Bn., attached 6th Bn., The Buffs (East Kent) Regiment. Died of wounds, 7th October, 1916 at Rouen. Wounds received in action in the Battle of Pozieres Ridge, 3rd August, 1916. Age 20. Son of John and Constance Catherine Hanmer, of Saynden, Staplehurst, Kent. Native of Newington, Sittingbourne. Name on Roll of Honour in Cathedral Church of St. Michael's. Military Cross displaying exception gallantry in an attack, 3rd August, 1916 in the Battle of Pozieres Ridge, when he led a party to capture and secure flanks, he continued to advance until he fell wounded. Grave Ref. Officer's B. 1. 30. St. Sever Cemetery, Rouen, France.

HANSON, Private, William. 5451, 8th Bn., East Surrey Regiment. Killed in action, 1st July, 1916. Born St. Mark's, Warwickshire. Enlisted Marleybone. Resided Edgeware Road, London. Listed as Coventry, Midland Daily Telegraph. Grave Ref. IV. P. 4. Dantzig Alley British Cemetery, Mametz, France

HARBOURNE, Private, Alfred. CH/1250(S), 1st Royal Marine Bn., Royal Naval Division, Royal Marine Light Infantry. Killed in action, Bapaume, 17th February, 1917. Born 3rd October, 1897 at 44, St. John Street. Resided at 11c. 2h. St. John Street. Moulder, Britannia Foundry. Enlisted November, 1915. Grave Ref. II. K. 13. Queens Cemetery, Bucquoy, France.

HARBOURNE, Acting Bombardier, Arthur Henry. 19158, "D" Bty. 106th Bde., Royal Field Artillery. Killed in action, Battle of the Somme. 25th September, 1916. Born 25th May, 1892 at 44, St. John Street. Resided 11c. 2h. St. John Street. Employed Fitter, Hobart Bird & Co. Coventry. Enlisted 7th September, 1914 at Coventry. Grave Ref. IX. N. 1. Guards' Cemetery, Lesboeufs, France.

HARBOURNE, Private, Walter. 4495, 1/7th Bn., Royal Warwickshire Regiment. Killed in action, 1st July, 1916. Born 1889. Resided 242, Foleshill Road. Employed Daimler Ltd. Enlisted 1916 at Coventry. Memorial Ref. Pier and Face 9 A 9 B and 10 B. Thiepval Memorial, Somme, France.

HARDIMAN, Gunner, Thomas George. 10546, C Bty., 58th Bde., Royal Field Artillery. Died, 21st October, 1916. Born Bedworth. Enlisted Coventry. Grave Ref. VIII. D. 14. Serre Road Cemetery No. 2. France.

HARGREAVES, Private, Frederick. 1016, 2nd Bn., Royal Warwickshire Regiment. Killed in action, 19th December, 1914. Born 1888, St. Michael's, Coventry. Enlisted Warwick. Resided Gulson Road, Coventry. Tool Hardener. Two brothers also lost. Memorial Ref. Panel 2 and 3. Ploegsteert Memorial, Belgium.

HARGREAVES, Private, Herbert. 12910, B Coy., 2nd Bn., Worcestershire Regiment. Killed in action, 25th January, 1915. Born 1891, Coventry. Enlisted Northampton. Resided Gulson Road, Coventry. Labourer. Two brothers also lost. Grave Ref. III. SS. 27. Guards Cemetery, Windy Corner, Cuinchy, France.

HARGREAVES, Private, John Henry. 266506, 11th Bn., Somerset Light Infantry formerly 1966, Royal Warwickshire Regiment. Killed in action, 5th October, 1918. Age 30. Born Holy Trinity, Coventry. Resided with Uncle at 38, Whitefriars Street. Employed Messrs. Wyley Ltd., Chemists. Enlisted Coventry. Two brothers also lost. Grave Ref. I. M. 7. Croix-Du-Bac British Cemetery, Steenwerck, France.

HARLING, Private, Cecil. 16762, 15th Bn., Royal Warwickshire Regiment. Killed in action, 24th April, 1917. Age 24. Son of Edward and Emma Harling, of Wasperton, Warwick. Born 15th March, 1893 at Wasperton, Warwicks. Enlisted February, 1916 at Leamington. Resided Coventry. Labourer. Memorial Ref. Bay 3. Arras Memorial, France. (Buried near Vimy)

HARPER, Private, Harold Hubert. 43250, 8th Bn., Royal Berkshire Regiment. Killed in action, 20th September, 1918. Age 21. Son of Joseph Harper. Husband of Florence Elsie Harper, of 26, Spencer Street, Coventry. Born 11th July 1896, in Thomas Street. Resided at 36 Croft Road. Tool Fitter, Siddeley Deasy Works. Enlisted May, 1918, Coventry. Commemorated War Memorial Park and Siddeley Roll of Honour. Memorial Ref. Panel 7. Vis-En-Artois Memorial, Pas de Calais, France.

HARPER, Private, Harry. 32369, 1st Bn., Sherwood Foresters (Notts and Derby) Regiment. Killed in action, 23rd March, 1918. Age 22. Son of Arthur and Sarah Ann Harper of 79, Regent Street, Beeston, Notts. Born Beeston. Enlisted Coventry. Resided Beeston, Notts. Memorial Ref. Panel 52 to 54. Pozieres Memorial, France.

HARPER, Lance Sergeant, Herbert William. 17912, 15th Bn., Royal Warwickshire Regiment. Killed in action, 21st April, 1917. Age 24. Son of Mr. Harper, of 49, Queen's Road, Coventry. Husband of Lizzie Harper, of 21, Sovereign Road, Coventry. Born 5th July, 1893 at 28, Foleshill Road, Coventry. Enlisted Coventry. Decorator. Commemorated War Memorial Park. Grave Ref. III. D. 19. La Chaudiere Military Cemetery, Vimy, Pas de Calais, France.

HARRINGTON, Private, John Denis. 5423, 9th Bn., Royal Warwickshire Regiment. Killed in action, 10th August, 1915. Age 24. Son of Sarah Harrington, of 49, Weston Street, Coventry. Husband of Alice Harrington, of 47, Weston Street, Coventry. Born 5th November, 1892 at Kidderminster. Stamper. Enlisted September, 1914 at Coventry. Memorial Ref. Panel 35 to 37. Helles Memorial, Turkey.

HARRINGTON, Sergeant, John Joseph. 2694, 21st Bn., Australian Infantry, A.I.F. Killed in action, 21st September, 1917. Age 24. Son of John and Kate Harrington, of 51, West Orchard, Coventry, England. Native of Athlone, Co. Westmeath, Ireland. Memorial Ref. Panel 7 - 17 - 23 - 25 - 27 - 29 - 31. Ypres (Menin Gate) Memorial, Ieper, West-Vlaanderen, Belgium.

HARRINGTON, Ordinary Seaman, Richard. J/30685, HMS Bombala, Royal Navy. Killed in action with submarine, off West Coast of Africa, 2nd May, 1918. Age 20. Son of John and Kate Harrington, of 58, Alma Street, Coventry. Born 1898, Athlone, Ireland. Memorial Ref. 27. Plymouth Naval Memorial, Devon.

HARRIS, Private, Albert George. 37823, 15th Bn., Royal Warwickshire Regiment. Killed in action, 13th April, 1918. Born 4th August, 1885 in Charles Street, Coventry. Enlisted November, 1917 at Coventry. Resided 71, Terry Road. Fitter, Maudslay Motor Co. Ltd. Memorial Ref. Panel 2 and 3. Ploegsteert Memorial, Belgium.

HARRIS, Able Seaman, Arthur John. J/22337, HMS Princess Royal, Royal Navy. Killed in action at Battle of Jutland, 31st May, 1916. Age 19. Son of Henry and Hannah Harris, of 32, Cromwell Street, Coventry. Born 1897 at 32, Cromwell Street. Sailor. Memorial Ref. 13. Portsmouth Naval Memorial, Hampshire.

HARRIS, Private, Edward Joseph. 9358, 1st Bn., Oxfordshire and Buckinghamshire Light Infantry. Died 11th August, 1916. Age 26. Born St Peters in the East, Oxon. Resided Foleshill. Grave Ref. XXI. D. 8. Baghdad (North Gate) War Cemetery, Iraq.

HARRIS, F. Employed by Rover Company Ltd. Killed in action.

HARRIS, Private, Frank. 9158, 1st Bn., Royal Warwickshire Regiment. Killed in action, Meteren, 13th October, 1914. Age 31. Son of James Harris, of Leamington Spa. Husband of Ivy Aminda Southgate (formerly Harris), of 59, Raglan Street, Coventry. Born 1883 at All Saints, Leamington. Reservist. Enlisted Warwick. Resided Coventry. Employed Triumph Cycle Co. Ltd. Commemorated Triumph & Gloria Memorial. Leaves widow and one child. Grave Ref. III. L. 886. (Buried near this spot). Meteren Military Cemetery, Nord, France.

HARRIS, Corporal, Frederick Arthur. 201083, 2nd /4th Bn., Oxfordshire and Buckinghamshire Light Infantry. Killed in action, near St. Quentin, 28th April, 1917. Age 20. Son of Thomas Henry and Emma Harris, of 17, Grove Street, Coventry. A Draughtsman. An old Bablake Schoolboy (Coventry). Enlisted November, 1914 at Oxford. Resided Coventry. Born 4th October, 1896 at 17, Grove Street. Resided 17, Grove Street. Draughtsman. Commemorated Bablake School Memorial and Queens Road Memorial. Memorial Ref. Pier and Face 10 A and 10 D. Thiepval Memorial, Somme, France.

HARRIS, Private, Frederick John. M2/133010, 347th Mechanical Transport Coy., Army Service Corps. Died, 18th October, 1918. Age 32. Son of George and Edith Harris, of Pichford House, Allesley, Coventry. Enlisted Coventry. Resided Coventry. Born Coventry. Grave Ref. Q. 12. Jerusalem War Cemetery, Israel.

HARRIS, Private, Frederick Thomas. 30052, 2nd Bn., Royal Warwickshire Regiment. Killed in action, Battle of the Somme, 3rd September, 1916. Age 28. Husband of Annie Harris, of 567, Stoney Stanton Road, Coventry. Born 28th March, 1888 at 17, St. Agnes Lane, Coventry. Enlisted Coventry. Machinist, Triumph Works. Memorial Ref. Pier and Face 9 A 9 B and 10 B. Thiepval Memorial, Somme, France.

HARRIS, Private, George Benjamin. 41237, 1st Bn., Duke of Cornwalls Light Infantry formerly 19907, Royal Warwickshire Regiment. Died of wounds, 2nd July, 1918. Born 14th June, 1899 at 17, Grove Street. Resided 17, Grove Street. Fettler. Enlisted July, 1917. Coventry. Enlisted Warwick. Resided Coventry. Grave Ref. III. G. 9. Aire Communal Cemetery, France.

HARRIS, Leading Stoker, Herbert Thomas. 302072, HM Submarine, E.18. Submarine reported overdue, believed to have been lost in the Baltic, 11th June, 1916. Age 32. Husband of Mrs. A. Hutchinson (formerly Harris), of 29, Kilmiston Street, Landport, Portsmouth. Born 13th April, 1884 at Coventry. Resided Coventry. Barman. Memorial Ref. 16. Portsmouth Naval Memorial.

HARRIS, Rifleman, Hollis Jordan Bishop. R/15528, 11th Bn., King's Royal Rifle Corps. Killed in action, Ypres, 10th June, 1916. Born 18th June, 1897 at Foleshill. Resided 200, Broad Street. Fettler. Enlisted September, 1915 at Coventry. Brother of Private Oliver Harris. Grave Ref. R. 8. Potijze Burial Ground Cemetery, Belgium.

HARRIS, Private, James. 5893, 2nd Bn., South Staffordshire Regiment. Killed in action, 3rd February 1918. Age 34. Son of Charles and Elizabeth Harris, of Birmingham. Husband of Elizabeth Harris, of 48, Alfred Road, Hillfields, Coventry. Born Birmingham. Enlisted Lichfield. Resided Small Heath, Warwicks. Grave Ref. II. G. 21. Metz-En-Couture Communal Cemetery British Extension, Pas de Calais, France.

HARRIS, Private, John Samuel. 63455, 3rd Bn., Canadian Infantry (Central Ontario Regiment). Killed in action, Givenchy, 16th June, 1915. Age 31. Son of Enoch and Emily Harris, of "Kemscote," Lythall Lane, Coventry. Born 29th May, 1884 at Attleborough. Resided Alberta, Canada. Educated Bablake School. Engineer. Enlisted October, 1914. Commemorated Bablake School Memorial. Memorial Ref. Vimy Memorial, Pas de Calais, France.

HARRIS, Rifleman, Leonard. 315350, 5th Battalion, London Regiment (London Rifle Brigade) formerly 4149 South Staffordshire Regiment. Died of wounds, 28th August, 1918. Born Wolverhampton. Enlisted Wolverhampton. Commemorated War Memorial Park. Grave Ref. III. C. 9. Bac-Du-Sud British Cemetery, Bailleulval, France.

HARRIS, Private, Lionel Arthur. 2700, "A" Coy. 9th Bn., Royal Warwickshire Regiment. Died of wounds, Gallipoli, 14th August, 1915. Age 20. Son of Ernest and Marion Ada Harris, late of Newbury, Berks. Apprenticed to Humber Ltd., Coventry. Born in 1895 at Newbury, Berks. Resided at Newbury. Apprenticed to Humber Ltd. Memorial Ref. Panel 35 to 37. Helles Memorial, Turkey.

HARRIS, Private, Oliver Charles. 9938, 1st Bn., Gloucestershire Regiment. Killed in action, Loos, 8th October, 1915. Age 22. Son of William and Emma Harris, of 200, Broad Street, Coventry. Born 8th July, 1893 at Foleshill. Brickmaker. Enlisted February, 1914 at Coventry. Brother of Rifleman Hollis Harris. Memorial Ref. Panel 60 to 64. Loos Memorial, Pas de Calais, France.

HARRIS, Lieutenant, Reginald William. 4th Bn., West Yorkshire Regiment attached 'Z', 1st Trench Mortar Battery. Killed in action, Longueval, 3rd September, 1916. Age 23. Son of William Henry Harris, of Kyneton, Sidmouth, Devon. Husband of Jessie Harris. Born 6th April, 1893 at Elm Bank, Stoke Park. Farmer and member of Police Force, Rhodesia. Enlisted January, 1915. Memorial Ref. Pier and Face 2 A 2 C and 2 D. Thiepval Memorial, Somme, France.

HARRISON, Private, Allen. 10178, 8th Bn., Royal Fusiliers. Killed in action, 1st May, 1917. Age 21. Son of William and Mary Elizabeth Harrison, of Coventry Side, Southam, Rugby. Born Aston-under-Lyne, Lancs. Enlisted Coventry. Grave Ref. C. 13. Happy Valley British Cemetery, Fampoux, France.

HARRISON, Sapper, Charles Henry. 44961, 2nd Depot Coy., 4th Res. Bn., Royal Engineers. Died, Home, 26th November, 1918. Born Redditch, Worcs. Enlisted Coventry. Memorial Ref. Screen Wall. X5. 3. 7510. Beckenham Crematorium and Cemetery.

HARRISON, Senior Reserve Attendant, Frederick William. M/10080, HMHS Rohilla, Royal Naval Auxiliary Sick Berth Reserve. Drowned in wreck of vessel off Whitby, 30th October, 1914. Age 31. Son of Sarah Harrison, of Coventry. Husband of Ethel Harrison, of 77, Holmsdale Road, Foleshill, Coventry. Born 23rd December, 1881 at Coventry. Chemists Assistant. Enlisted August, 1914. Memorial Ref. 8. Chatham Naval Memorial, Kent.

HARRISON, Gunner, John Edward Albert. 219491, 536th Siege Battery, Royal Garrison Artillery. Died, Home, 8th November, 1918. Born Exhall, Warwick. Enlisted Coventry. Resided Solihull. Grave Ref. South Part. Lydd (All Saints) Churchyard.

HARRISON, Company Quartermaster Sergeant, Leonard Chase. 240002, 1st /5th Bn., King's Own (Royal Lancaster Regiment). Killed in action, 23rd July, 1917. Age 32. Son of George and Elizabeth Harrison. Husband of Sarah Harrison, of Ivy Cottage, Caton, Lancaster. Born at Coventry. Enlisted Lancaster. Grave Ref. VIII. A. 8. Vlamertinghe New Military Cemetery, Ieper, West-Vlaanderen, Belgium.

HARRISON, Lance Corporal, Thomas. 266445, 2/7th Bn., Royal Warwickshire Regiment. Killed in action, 30th March, 1918. Age 21. Son of Alfred and Rosa Harrison of 6, Roadway, Bedworth. Born Bedworth. Enlisted Coventry. Resided Bedworth. Memorial Ref. Panel 18 and 19. Pozieres Memorial, France.

HARRISON, Corporal, William Brough Berrey. 2199, 1st /7th Bn., Royal Warwickshire Regiment. Died of wounds, Messines Ridge, 10th June, 1915. Age 20. Son of Mr. and Mrs. Harrison, of 160, Stoney Stanton Road, Coventry. Born 17th October, 1894 at Solihull. Resided 54, Arden Street, Earlsdon. Coventry Ordnance Works, Clerical Staff. Enlisted August, 1914. Grave Ref. 2. E. 6A. Le Treport Military Cemetery, Seine-Maritime, France.

HARROW, Air Mechanic 2nd Class, Ernest. 405442, 24th Training Sqdn., Royal Air Force formerly Royal Artillery. Accidentally killed by aeroplane near Oxford, 11th June, 1918. Husband of Fanny Harrow. Born in 1881 at 17, Hope Street. Resided 33 White Friars Street. Iron Polisher. Enlisted August, 1915. Commemorated Triumph & Gloria Memorial. Grave Ref. 198. 45. Coventry (London Road) Cemetery.

HARROW, Private, Raymond. 8416, 95th Coy., Machine Gun Corps (Infantry) formerly 19737 Oxfordshire and Buckinghamshire Light Infantry. Killed in action, Battle of the Somme, 27th July, 1916. Age 17. Son of Robert and Mary Harrow, of 4, Berry Street, Coventry. Born 23rd July, 1899 at 4, Berry Street. Resided at 4, Berry Street. Engineers apprentice. Enlisted Nuneaton August 1915. Commemorated War Memorial Park. Memorial Ref. Pier and Face 5 C and 12 C. Thiepval Memorial, Somme, France.

HARTLAND, Private, Frederick Harold. 37435, 14th Bn., Royal Warwickshire Regiment. Killed in action, 8th July, 1918. Born Birmingham. Enlisted Coventry. Grave Ref 3. G. 3. Tannay British Cemetery, Thiennes, France.

HARTLES, Private, Harold. 30176, 8th Bn., Gloucestershire Regiment. Died, 9th September, 1918. Born Redditch. Enlisted Coventry. Memorial Ref. Panel 60 to 64. Loos Memorial, France.

HARTLEY, Private, Nathaniel. 284, 2nd Bn., Lancashire Fusiliers. Killed in action, Cambrai, 26th August, 1914. Age 26. Son of James Hartley, of 53, King Edward Road, Coventry. Commemorated Saint Thomas the Apostle, Longford. Grave Ref. I. Esnes Communal Cemetery, Nord, France.

HARTLEY, Private, William. 11135, 1st Bn., Coldstream Guards. Killed in action, Vermelles, Belgium, 18th October, 1915. Age 22. Son of Mrs. Elizabeth Hartley of 8 Jenner Street, Coventry. Born 7th September, 1892 at 8, Jenner Street. Painter. Enlisted Coventry. Memorial Ref. Panel 7 and 8. Loos Memorial, Pas de Calais, France.

HARTOPP, Private, Ernest. 20476, 6th Bn., Leicestershire Regiment. Killed in action, 29th September, 1916. Born St. Michael's, Coventry. Enlisted Rugby. Resided Coventry. Employed Coventry Corporation. Memorial Ref. Pier and Face 2 C and 3 A. Thiepval Memorial, Somme, France.

HARTOPP, Private, George Joseph. 1285, 2nd Bn., Royal Warwickshire Regiment. Died of wounds, 15th January, 1915. Age 18. Son of William and Sarah Ann Hartopp, of Coventry. Born Redditch. Resided 9, Warwick Lane. Enlisted Coventry. Memorial Ref. Panel 2 and 3. Ploegsteert Memorial, Comines-Warneton, Hainaut, Belgium.

HARTOPP, Rifleman, Walter Herbert. G/44189, 1/21st Battalion, London Regiment (First Surrey Rifles). Killed in action, 1st September, 1918. Born 29th January, 1900 at Coventry. Resided at 11c. 3h. Cox Street. Fitter. Reservist. Commemorated War Memorial Park and Siddeley Roll of Honour. Grave Ref. V. E. 27. Peronne Communal Cemetery Extension, France.

HARTSHORN, Private, William George. 4715, 1st Bn., Royal Warwickshire Regiment. Killed in action, 7th November, 1915. Born in 1881 at Warwick. Resided Warwick. Polisher. Enlisted September, 1914. Grave Ref. II. B. 1. Sucrerie Military Cemetery, Colincamps, France.

HARVEY, E. Comemorated Ryton Memorial.

HARVEY, Private, Frank. 201737, 1/5th Bn., Royal Warwickshire Regiment. Killed in action, Passchendaele, 4th October, 1917. Age 30. Son of Mrs. Sarah Harvey, of Yew Tree Cottage, Whichford, Shipston-on-Stour, Worcs. Born 21st January, 1887 at Whichford. Resided at 127, Aldbourne Road. Baker and confectioner. Enlisted April, 1916 at Coventry. Commemorated War Memorial Park. Memorial Ref. Panel 23 to 28 and 163A.Tyne Cot Memorial, Belgium.

HARVEY, Private, Walter. 587, 2nd Bn., Royal Warwickshire Regiment. Killed in action, 18th December, 1914. Age 23. Son of William and Elizabeth Hannersely Harvey. Husband of L.A. Hannersely Harvey, of 10, Warwick Lane, Coventry. Born St. Michael's Parish. Enlisted Coventry. Memorial Ref. Panel 2 and 3. Ploegsteert Memorial, Comines-Warneton, Hainaut, Belgium.

HARVEY, Driver, Walter. 109788, Royal Field Artillery. Died, home, 2nd April, 1918. Age 29. Husband of Bertha Chamberlain (formerly Harvey), of 16, Butler's Yard, High Street, Bedworth. Enlisted Coventry. Resided Coventry. Grave Ref. I. L44. Bedworth Cemetery.

HASSETT, Private, Michael. 25172, 8th Bn., East Surrey Regiment formerly 5486, Royal Warwickshire Regiment. Died of wounds, 23rd July, 1917. Age 38. Brother of Patrick Hassett, of 12, Castle Street, Dublin. Born Dublin. Enlisted Warwick. Resided Coventry. Grave Ref. XVI. E. 5A. Lijssenthoek Military Cemetery, Belgium.

HASTINGS, Private, John Harold William. Royal Army Service Corps (Motor Transport). Died, home, 19th October, 1919. Born 18th May, 1894 at Oxford. Resided at Coventry. Motor Driver. Enlisted September 1915. Commemorated War Memorial Park. Grave Ref. Coventry (London Road) Cemetery.

HASTINGS, Private, William. 10087, 11th Bn., Royal Warwickshire Regiment. Died of wounds, 22nd November, 1916. Age 24. Son of George and Mary Ann Hastings of 35, Smorrell Lane, Bedworth. Born Coleshill, Warwicks. Enlisted Coventry. Resided Bedworth. Grave Ref. VIII. D. 199. Boulogne Eastern Cemetery, France.

HASWELL, Private, Frank Herbert. 47073, 1st Bn., Royal Inniskilling Fusiliers formerly 40663, Royal Warwickshire Regiment. Killed in action, Gulleghem near Courtrai, Belgium, 14th October 1918 - 15th October 1918. Age 19. Son of George and Clara Haswell, of 61, Oxford Street, Coventry. Born 1st August, 1899 at 1, Oxford Cottage, Little South Street. Dyer. Enlisted September, 1917 at Coventry. Grave Ref. II. A. 11. Dadizeele New British Cemetery, Moorslede, West-Vlaanderen, Belgium.

HATFIELD, Private, Thomas. 43486, 11th Bn., Suffolk Regiment. Killed in action, 28th April, 1917. Born Foleshill. Enlisted Nuneaton. Commemorated Exhall Memorial. Grave Ref. I. F. 5. Bailleul Road East Cemetery, St. Laurent Blangy, France.

HATHAWAY, Private, Albert Frederick. 1937, 1st /7th Bn., Royal Warwickshire Regiment. Killed in action, Somme, 3rd April 1916 by a shell which smashed into his shelter. Age 19. Nephew of Mrs. E. A. Alcock, of 67, North Street, Stoke, Coventry. Adopted son of Mr. and Mrs. F. Alcock, 25, North Street. Born 12th November, 1896 at Coventry. Resided at 25, North Street. Apprentice turner and fitter. Enlisted 1914 at Coventry. Born St. Paul's, Coventry. Grave Ref. I. C. 5. Foncquevillers Military Cemetery, Pas de Calais, France

HATHAWAY, Second Lieutenant, Sidney Cornelious. 11th Squadron, Royal Flying Corps formerly Motor Machine Gun Battery. Killed in action, 12th January, 1916 failed to return from an observation flight. Shot down over Beaumetz. Born 23rd March, 1898 in Stoke Park. Resided Stoneleigh Grove. Engineer's Pupil. Enlisted October, 1914. Son of Mr. C. W. Hathaway, Work's Manager, Triumph Works. Commemorated Triumph & Gloria Memorial. Resided Spencer Avenue. Grave Ref. IV. N. 18. Achiet-Le-Grand Communal Cemetery Extension, France.

HATTERSLEY, Private, Frank Ellis Don. 19041, 8th Bn., South Lancashire Regiment. Killed in action, Battle of the Somme, 15th July, 1916 during an assault on enemy trenches. Age 27. Adopted son of W. H. and Pollie Hattersley, of 253, Swan Lane, Coventry. Born 25th February 1889 at Sheffield. Resided at 253, Swan Lane, Coventry. Mechanic. Enlisted Birmingham May 1915. Commemorated War Memorial Park. Memorial Ref. Pier and Face 7 A and 7 B. Thiepval Memorial, Somme, France.

HATTON, Private, Alfred Thomas. 4512, 1/7th Bn., Royal Warwickshire Regiment. Died of wounds, 3rd September, 1916. Enlisted Coventry. Grave Ref. VIII. C. 122. Boulogne Eastern Cemetery, France.

HAUGHTON, Private, Dan. 18013, 11th Coy., Machine Gun Corps (Infantry) formerly Rifle Brigade. Died of wounds, 1st July, 1916. Born 2nd May, 1897 in St. Michael's Parish. Resided at 32c. 11h. Gosford Street. Employed Coventry Chain Ltd. Memorial Ref. Pier and Face 5 C and 12 C. Thiepval Memorial, Somme, France.

HAUGHTON, Private, Joseph, 7118, 2nd Bn., Royal Warwickshire Regiment. Killed in action, 29th July, 1916. Born 1895 in St. Michael's Parish. Resided Coventry. Enlisted 1914 at Coventry. Memorial Ref. Pier and Face 9 A 9 B and 10 B. Thiepval Memorial, Somme, France.

HAWKINS, Private, George. 20723, 6th Bn., Oxfordshire and Buckinghamshire Light Infantry. Killed in action, 3rd September, 1916. Age 31. Son of George and Annie Hawkins of Croughton, Brackley, Northants. Born Croughton, Northants. Enlisted Coventry. Resided Brackley, Northants. Memorial Ref. Pier and Face 10A and 10D. Thiepval Memorial, Somme, France.

HAWKINS, Corporal, George. 13564, 2nd Bn., Oxfordshire and Buckinghamshire Light Infantry. Killed in action, Arras, 17th April, 1917. Age 27. Son of Caleb and Ellen Hawkins, of 42, Stratford Street, Stoke, Coventry. Born 25th September, 1889 at Stoke. Butcher's Assistant, Mr. David Ward of North Street also night waiter at the Rose and Woodbine. Enlisted September, 1914 at Coventry. Commemorated Barras Green Working Mens Club. Memorial Ref. Bay 6 and 7. Arras Memorial, Pas de Calais, France.

HAWKINS, Private, Walter Edward. 37725, 2nd /7th Bn., Royal Warwickshire Regiment Killed in action, 1st November, 1918. Age 28. Son of Charles Frederick and Eliza Hawkins, of Black Horse Road, Exhall, Coventry. Born 8th October, 1891 at Shilton Fields. Crane Driver. Enlisted Coventry. Resided Exhall. Memorial Ref. Panel 3. Vis-En-Artois Memorial, Pas De Calais, France.

HAWKINS, Private, William. 7285, 2nd Bn., Worcestershire Regiment. Killed in action, 24th October, 1914. Husband of Fanny Hawkins, of 6, Clifford Road, Bearwood, Smethwick, Staffs. Born Coventry. Enlisted Birmingham. Resided Birmingham. Grave Ref. X. B. 25. Perth Cemetery (China Wall), Belgium.

HAWTHORN, Private, George Henry. 28669, 6th Bn., Somerset Light Infantry formerly 35337, Wiltshire Regiment. Died, 4th May, 1918. Age 19. Son of George and Mary Ann Hawthorn, of 121, Allesley Old Road, Coventry. Born 1st July, 1898 at Bradley, Staffs. Clerk. Enlisted February, 1917 at Coventry. Grave Ref. VI. A. Z. Grand-Seraucourt British Cemetery, Aisne, France.

HAWTHORNE, Rifleman, Arthur Edward. 8039, 4th Bn., King's Royal Rifle Corps. Killed in action, 15th May, 1915. Age 28. Son of William Henry and Annie Hawthorn, of Coventry. Born 1887 at Coventry. Enlisted Birmingham. Memorial Ref. Panel 51 and 53. Ypres (Menin Gate) Memorial, Ieper, West-Vlaanderen, Belgium.

HAWTHORNE, Corporal, Herbert William. 235259, 15th Bn., Royal Warwickshire Regiment formerly H/310505, Warwicks Yeomanry. Died of wounds, 4th July, 1918. Age 34. Husband of Lily Hawthorne, of 26, St. Michael's Road, Coventry. Resided 12, Hugh Road. Born in 1885 at Coventry. Enlisted Warwick. Tobacconist. Enlisted October, 1914. Commemorated Bablake School Memorial. Grave Ref. III. H. 5. Aire Communal Cemetery, Pas de Calais, France.

HAWTHORNE, Private, Horace Victor. 8886, 6th Bn., Duke of Cornwall's Light Infantry. Died of wounds, (gun shot wound penetrated the lung), Battle of the Somme, 20th August, 1916 in the 13th Field Ambulance. Age 29. Son of George and Sarah Hawthorne, of Coventry, Warwickshire. Born 6th December, 1888 at 23, Union Street. Resided 23, Union Street. Engineer. Reservist. Enlisted Coventry. Grave Ref. I. B. 18. Dernancourt Communal Cemetery Extension, Somme, France.

HAWTIN, Private, George. 268047, 2/7th Bn., Royal Warwickshire Regiment. Killed in action, 9th April, 1917. Enlisted Coventry. Resided Leamington. Memorial Ref. Pier and Face 9A 9B and 10B. Thiepval Memorial, Somme, France.

HAYCOCK, Private, George Alfred. 17124, 13th Bn., Royal Sussex Regiment. Died whilst prisoner of war, Tincourt, 22nd July, 1918. Born 10th August, 1898 at Withybrook. Resided Withybrook. Artificial silk spinner. Enlisted March, 1917 at Coventry. Grave Ref. IX. C. 13. Tincourt New British Cemetery, France.

HAYCOCK, Private, John. 34635, B Coy., 2/4th Bn., Duke of Wellington's (West Riding Regiment) formerly 183456, Royal Field Artillery. Killed in action, 2nd September, 1918. Age 35. Son of James Haycock of Garmston, Cressage, Salop. Previously served 12 years with Royal Welch Fusiliers. Born Garston, Lancs. Enlisted Coventry. Resided Salop. Grave Ref. III. K. 15. Vaulx Hill Cemetery, France.

HAYDOCK, J. Employed by Humber Ltd. Killed in action. Commemorated Wesleyan Church.

HAYES, Private, Harry. 106644, 51st Bn., Machine Gun Corps (Infantry) formerly 16321, Royal Warwickshire Regiment. Died of influenza, No. 30 Clearing Station, 29th March, 1919. Age 20. Eldest son of Mrs. Emma Hayes, of 7, Court, 1, House, Much Park St., Coventry. Born 22nd July, 1898 at Ansty. Driver, Mr. D. Cooke, Tobacconist. Enlisted January, 1916. Grave Ref. C. 5. La Louviere Town Cemetery, La Louviere, Hainaut, Belgium.

HAYES, James William Henry. Killed in action. Name on Roll of Honour in Cathedral Church of St. Michael.

HAYES, Private, Samuel. M2/050429, G.H.Q. Troop Supply Col., Army Service Corps formerly 11th Hussars. Died, from peritonitis, at St. Omer Hospital, 24th August, 1915. Age 44. Husband of Selina Hayes, of 2, St. Agatha's Road, Stoke, Coventry. Born Brinklow. Enlisted Coventry. Born 16th December, 1870 at Brinklow. Sister, resided at 120, Kensington Road. Van Driver, Messrs, Bushill and sons. Reservist. Grave Ref. II. A. 21. Longuenesse (St. Omer) Souvenir Cemetery, Pas de Calais, France.

HAYES, Private, Thomas. 19729, 2nd Bn., Coldstream Guards. Killed in action, 30th November, 1917. Born Coventry. Enlisted Coventry. Resided at 10c. 1h. St. John Street. Memorial Ref. Panel 2. Cambrai Memorial, Louverval, France.

HAYES, Private, William. 57665, 4th Bn., Royal Warwickshire Regiment. Died, Home, 17th July, 1918. Son of Mr. W. F. Hayes of 24, Smith Street, Chelsea. Born London. Enlisted Coventry. Resided Fulham, London. Grave Ref. M. G. 17. Dover (St. James's) Cemetery.

HAYES, Sergeant, William Thomas. 48726, 2nd Bn., Northumberland Fusiliers formerly 2994, Royal Warwickshire Regiment. Died of typhus, Mesopotamia, 23rd April, 1918. Age 45. Son of W. T. and Harriet Hayes. Husband of H. E. Hayes, of 12 Court, 2 House, Much Park St., Coventry. Born 14th February, 1873 at Fillongley, Warwickshire. Enlisted August, 1914 at Warwick. Carter. Commemorated City Engineer's Department Memorial, Coventry Corporation. Grave Ref. XII. M. 6. Baghdad (North Gate) War Cemetery, Iraq.

HAYFIELD, Private, George Frederick. 41137, 1st Bn., Dorsetshire Regiment. Died of pneumonia, 5th October, 1919. Age 19. Son of Arthur and Ada Maria Hayfield, of 44, Francis Street, Coventry. Born 19th February, 1900 in Narrow Lane. Turner's Apprentice. Enlisted April, 1918. Grave Ref. G. Mil. 5. Londonderry City Cemetery, County Londonderry.

HAYFIELD, Private, Thomas Charles. 45011, 1st Bn., Norfolk Regiment. Died of wounds, 8th November, 1918. Age 20. Son of Charles and Elizabeth Hayfield of Hill Farm, Nether Whitacre, Coleshill. Born Nether Whitacre, Warwick. Enlisted Coventry. Grave Ref. I. A. 9. Caudry British Cemetery, France.

HAYMES, Company Sergeant Major, Arthur. 9098, 17th Bn., Manchester Regiment. Died, home, 30th September, 1915. Age 57. Husband of Ellen Haymes, of 24, Walter Street, Blackburn. Born at Coventry. Enlisted Manchester. Grave Ref. E C.E. 3607. Blackburn Cemetery, Lancashire.

HAYNES, Private, William Thomas. 18532, 10th Bn., Worcestershire Regiment. Killed in action, 18th November, 1915. Born Coventry. Enlisted Birmingham. Resided Birmingham. Grave Ref. III. B. 24. Le Touret Military Cemetery, Richebourg-L'avoue, France.

HAYTER, Private, George Henry. 72999, 182nd Coy., Machine Gun Corps (Infantry) formerly 4793, 7th Bn., Royal Warwickshire Regiment. Killed in action, by a shell, 24th April, 1917. Age 25. Son of Sidney Herbert and Eliza Julia Hayter, of Southsea. Born 29th July, 1892 at Southsea. Resided at 325, Swan lane. Artificial Silk Spinner, Messrs Courtaulds Ltd. Enlisted Coventry. Grave Ref. 3. Savy Communal Cemetery, France.

HAYWOOD, Second Lieutenant, Ernest, DCM., 5th Bn., South Lancashire Regiment attd. 2nd Bn., East Lancashire Regiment. Killed in action, 27th May, 1918. Age 29. Son of Robert and Dinah Haywood, of The Cliff, Cinder Hill, Nottingham. Husband of Annie Maria Haywood, of "Woodside," Arley, Coventry. Memorial Ref. Soissons Memorial, Aisne, France.

HAYWOOD, Private, Herbert. 62, 1st Bn., Royal Warwickshire Regiment. Killed in action, 11th October, 1916. Born Coventry. Enlisted Coventry. Memorial Ref. Pier and Face 9 A 9 B and 10 B. Thiepval Memorial, Somme, France.

HAYWOOD, Private, John. 12795, 2nd Bn., Worcestershire Regiment. Killed in action, Lille, 21st October 1914. Age 20. Son of Mrs. Sarah Ann Haywood, of 8 Court, 8 House, Jordan Well, Coventry. Born 9th September, 1894 in Well Street, Coventry. Enlisted Coventry. Polisher. Reservist. Memorial Ref. Panel 34. Ypres (Menin Gate) Memorial, Ieper, West-Vlaanderen, Belgium.

HAYWOOD, Private, William. 8906, 2nd Bn., Royal Warwickshire Regiment. Killed in action, 24th October, 1914. Born Coventry. Enlisted Coventry. Memorial Ref. Panel 8. Ypres (Menin Gate) Memorial, Belgium.

HAZELWOOD, Private, James Ayres. 265933, 2/7th Bn., Royal Warwickshire Regiment. Killed in action 19th July, 1916. Born 15th December, 1878 at Burnt Post. Resided Coventry. Turner. Enlisted November, 1914 at Coventry. Memorial Ref. Panel 22 to 25. Loos Memorial, France.

HAZLEWOOD, Private, Tom. 9888, 1st Bn., Gloucestershire Regiment. Killed in action, 27th August, 1914. Born St. John Parish. Enlisted Coventry. Grave Ref. Near North Boundary. Prisches Communal Cemetery, France.

HEALD, Lance Corporal, William Gordon. 29612, 2nd Bn., Royal Welsh Fusiliers. Killed in action, 23rd April, 1917. Age 30. Son of Dr. and Mrs. Heald. Born Leeds. Employed Coventry. Memorial Ref. Bay 6. Arras Memorial, France

HEALEY, Private, Patrick. 6930, 1st Bn., Royal Munster Fusiliers. Died of phthisis, 10th April, 1918. Age 34. Born 5th March, 1882. Resided 8, Melbourne Road. Grave Ref. 198. 112. Coventry (London Road) Cemetery.

HEALEY, Lieutenant (Adjutant), Richard Elkanah Hownam. 1st Bn., Royal West Kent Regiment. Killed in action, Battle of the Somme, 22nd July, 1916. Age 31. Son of Randolph E. and Alice M. Healey, of Hownam Lodge, Odiham, Hants. Born in 1885 at Gateacre, Liverpool. Resided St. Thomas's Vicarage. Educated at King Henry VIII School, Uppingham School and Selwyn College, Cambridge. Journalist. Enlisted 1914. Commemorated King Henry VIII School. Memorial Ref. Pier and Face 11 C. Thiepval Memorial, Somme, France.

HEAMES, Private, Sam. 44040, 9th Bn., King's Own Yorkshire Light Infantry formerly 164665, Royal Horse Artillery. Died of wounds, 10th April, 1917. Age 19. Son of John and Clara Heames, of Longford, nr. Coventry. Commemorated Saint Thomas the Apostle, Longford. Born Leicester. Enlisted Leicester. Grave Ref. III. F. 4A. Mont Huon Military Cemetery, Le Treport, Seine-Maritime, France.

HEARN, Aircraftman 2nd Class, James David. 286902, Royal Air Force. Died, home, 24th July, 1919. Age 18. Son of James David and Emma Hearn. Born at Coventry. Grave Ref. 98. 159. Leamington (Whitnash Road) Cemetery, Warwickshire.

HEATH, Private, Arthur. M2/102904, No. 1 Water Tank Coy., Army Service Corps. Killed in action, 23rd August, 1918. Born Northfield. Enlisted Coventry. Resided Birmingham. Grave Ref V. B. 8. Heath Cemetery, Harbonnieres, France.

HEATH, Private, Hubert Frederick. G/17825 6th Bn., Queen's Own (Royal West Kent Regiment) formerly 3164, Royal Fusiliers. Killed in action, 3rd May, 1917. Born Warwick. Enlisted 1916 at Coventry. Resided Coventry. Lithographer. Commemorated Iliffe & Sons Ltd. Memorial Ref. Bay 7. Arras Memorial, France.

HEBBLEWHITE, Private, Edward, MM. 1810, 1/7th Bn., Royal Warwickshire Regiment. Killed in action, whilst firing a machine gun, 14th July, 1916. Born 21st September, 1888 at Thulby, Leics. Resided at 25, Weston Street. Wire Wheel Fitter, Rudge. Enlisted August, 1914. Awarded Military Medal for gallantry on the night of the 8th October, 1915 near Foncquevillers when he showed great courage and devotion to duty by holding an advanced post alone for an hour under intense minenwerfer fire, his comrades being all killed or wounded. Memorial Ref. Pier and Face 9 A 9 B and 10 B. Thiepval Memorial, Somme, France.

HEMMINGS, Private, Charles. G/42821, 4th Bn., Middlesex Regiment formerly DN2/228183, Royal Army Service Corps, Motor Transport. Killed in action, near Ypres, 31st July, 1917. Age 28. Son of Daniel and Mary Ann Hemmings, of Upper Brailes, Banbury, Oxon. Born 12th August, 1888 at Upper Brailes, Warwick. Enlisted October, 1916 at Grove Park, Kent. Resided 104, Oliver Street, Coventry. Storekeeper. Memorial Ref. Addenda Panel 59. Ypres (Menin Gate) Memorial, Belgium.

HEMMINGS, Gunner, Christopher. 1206, D Bty., 93rd Bde., Royal Field Artillery. Killed in action, 13th October, 1916. Born Walsall. Employed Coventry. Grave Ref. XI. N. 3. Guards' Cemetery, Lesboeufs, France.

HEMMINGS, Private, William J. Royal Warwickshire Regiment. Died February, 1917 on a visit to friends house at 9, Upper Well Street, Coventry. Age 21. Resided Wolston. Grave Ref. Coventry.

HENDERSON, Major, Albert Norman. 10th Bn., Royal Warwickshire Regiment. Killed in action, 10th July, 1916. Resided Street Ashton House, Brinklow. Leaves a wife and children. Memorial Ref. Pier and Face 9A 9B and 10B. Thiepval Memorial, Somme, France.

HENDERSON, Private, Samuel. 8641, 2nd Bn., Welsh Regiment. Killed in action, 14th September, 1914. Age 27. Son of James and Sarah Henderson, of 18, Upper Gough Street, Edgbaston, Birmingham. Husband of Anice Ethel Mullane (formerly Henderson), of 194, Munition Cottages, Holbrook Lane, Foleshill, Coventry. Born Ansley, Warwicks. Enlisted Birmingham. Resided Edgbaston. Memorial Ref. La Ferte-Sous-Jouarre Memorial, Seine-et-Marne, France

HENDLEY, Gunner, George. 182377, 59th Siege Bty., Royal Garrison Artillery. Killed in action, 1st September, 1918. Born Coventry. Enlisted 1917 at Coventry. Born 1882 at Coventry. Solicitor's Clerk. Grave Ref. I. D. 16. Tigris Lane Cemetery, Wancourt, France.

HENLEY, Private, Ernest Frederick. 242811, 1/6th Bn., Royal Warwickshire Regiment. Killed in action, 1st April, 1917. Born 22nd October, 1893 at Birmingham. Resided at 41, New Street. Motor Lorry Driver, Brittania Foundry. Enlisted December, 1915. Grave Ref. I. J. 2. Epehy Wood Farm Cemetery, Epehy, France.

HENSON, Sapper, Francis Sidney. 158398, 256th Tunnelling Coy., Royal Engineers. Killed in action, 13th August, 1918. Age 32. Husband of Lavinia Henson, of Exhall, Coventry. Born Foleshill. Grave Ref. A. 19. Montigny Communal Cemetery Extension, Somme, Somme, France

HENSON, Private, George Thomas. 23984, 5th Bn., South Wales Borderers. Killed in action, 22nd November, 1917. Age 21. Son of George James Henson, of 10, Chapil Street, Bedworth. Born Hinckley, Leicestershire. Enlisted Leicester. Resided Coventry. Memorial Ref. Pier and Face 4A. Thiepval Memorial, Somme, France.

HENTON, Gunner, Edgar Charles. 314729, "Q" Anti Aircraft Bty., Royal Garrison Artillery. Died of pneumonia, 8th December, 1918. Age 28. Son of John and Eleanor Henton, of 41, Swanswell Street, Coventry. Born 4th November, 1890 at Coventry. Pattern maker. Grave Ref. XIII. BB. 9. Villers-Bretonneux Military Cemetery, Somme, France.

HENTON, Private, Joseph. 13630, 5th Bn., Oxfordshire and Buckinghamshire Light Infantry. Killed in action, 25th September, 1915. Age 37. Born Bedworth. Son of Joseph and Sarah Henton. Commemorated Saint Thomas the Apostle, Longford. Memorial Ref. Panel 37 and 39. Ypres (Menin Gate) Memorial, Belgium.

HENTON, Private, Wilfred. 266863, 1/7th Bn., Royal Warwickshire Regiment. Killed in action, 3rd November, 1918. Born Mexborough, Yorkshire. Resided Longford. Employed Coventry. Grave Ref. 2. B. 3. Granezza British Cemetery, Italy.

HERBERT, H. Killed in action. Name on Roll of Honour in St. Thomas's Church.

HERBERT, Private, Walter James. 20970, 6th Bn., Oxfordshire and Buckinghamshire Light Infantry. Killed in action, 3rd September, 1916. Age 31. Son of William Henry and Martha Herbert, of Great Bourton, Banbury, Oxon. Born 30th July, 1885 at Hanwell near Banbury. Resided at 248, Harnall Lane East. Fitter, Courtaulds. Enlisted November, 1915. Commemorated Wesleyan Church. Memorial Ref. Pier and Face 10 A and 10 D. Thiepval Memorial, Somme, France.

HERBERT, Private, William. 42463, 3rd Bn., Worcestershire Regiment, formerly 13079, Oxfordshire and Buckinghamshire Light Infantry. Killed in action Steenwerck, 10th April, 1918. Age 28. Brother of George Herbert, of 33/11, Much Park Street, Coventry. Born 11th December 1889 at Coventry. Resided at Coventry. Cycle finisher. Enlisted August, 1914, Coventry. Commemorated War Memorial Park. Grave Ref. Sp. Mem. B. 5. Croix-Du-Bac British Cemetery, Steenwerck, Nord, France.

HETHERINGTON, Gunner, Frederick William. 85396, 2nd /1st Lancashire Heavy Bty., Royal Garrison Artillery. Died of wounds, 29th August, 1917. Age 33. Son of Joseph and Sarah Hetherington. Born at Valetta, Malta. Resided Coventry. Assistant Work's Manager. Commemorated Iliffe & Sons Ltd Memorial. Grave Ref. XXV. O. 16. Etaples Military Cemetery, France.

HEWINS, Private, Frederick. 51005, 9th Bn., Cheshire Regiment formerly Royal Warwickshire Regiment. Killed in action, by a shell, 16th July, 1917. Age 26. Husband of Phyllis Elsie Hewins, of 24, Eagle Street, Leamington Spa. Born 5th June, 1892 at Leamington. Resided 44, Heath Road. Driller, Triumph Works. Enlisted February, 1917. Commemorated Triumph & Gloria Memorial. Memorial Ref. Panel 19 – 20. Ypres (Menin Gate) Memorial, France.

HEWITT, Rifleman, Arthur Edward. R/20351, 3 Platoon, A Coy., 2nd Bn., King's Royal Rifle Corps. Killed in action, 27th September, 1916. Struck by a piece of shell. Born Hawkesbury. Enlisted 30th March 30th, 1916 at Coventry. Employed Coventry Co-Operative Bakery Department. Resided 28, Bulkington Road, Bedworth. Memorial Ref. Pier and Face 13A and 13B. Thiepval Memorial, Somme, France.

HEWITT, Bombardier, Henry. 11895, "D" Bty. 93rd Bde., Royal Field Artillery. Killed in action, 13th October, 1916 by a shell in his dug-out. Age 19. Son of James Mason Hewitt and Caroline Hewitt, of 136, Eden Street, Coventry. Born 14th June, 1897 at Coventry. Enlisted September, 1914 at Coventry. Capstan hand, Rover Works. Grave Ref. XI. N. 2. Guards' Cemetery, Lesboeufs, Somme, France.

HEWITT, Engine Room Artificer 3rd Class, James Moss. M/5451, HMS Queen Mary, Royal Navy. Killed in action, Battle of Jutland, 31st May 1916. Age 24. Son of James Moss and Eliza Mary Hewitt, of 35, Moor Street, Earlsdon, Coventry. Born 22nd November 1891 at 61, Warwick Street. Commemorated St. John's Church Memorial, St. Barbara's Memorial and War Memorial Park. Memorial Ref. 15. Portsmouth Naval Memorial, Hampshire.

HEWITT, Sapper, Percival William. 48746, 73rd Field Coy., Royal Engineers. Died of wounds, Ypres, 24th June, 1917. Age 30. Only son of Mr. and Mrs. J. H. Hewitt, of Spencers Wood, Reading. Born 12th June, 1887 at Basingstoke. Resided Coventry. Motor Body Builder. Enlisted September, 1914. Grave Ref. II. L. 6. Brandhoek Military Cemetery, Belgium.

HEWITT, Private, William Charles. 3013, D Coy., 2nd Bn., Royal Warwickshire Regiment. Killed in action, La Bassee, 18th December, 1914. Age 43. Son of Edward Hewitt, of Wasperton, Warwick. Husband of Louisa E. Hewitt, of 63, St. George's Road, Coventry. Born 9th December, 1872 at Bubbenhall. Enlisted September, 1914 at Warwick. Resided Coventry. Engineer, Rover Co. Ltd. Memorial Ref. Panel 2 and 3. Ploegsteert Memorial, Comines-Warneton, Hainaut, Belgium.

HEWITT, Rifleman, William Charles. 5449, 1st Bn., Rifle Brigade. Killed in action, 19th December, 1914. Age 18. Eldest son of Harry and Sarah Georgina Hewitt of Mill End Kenilworth. Employed Dunlop formerly Messenger, Kenilworth. Memorial Ref. Panel 10. Ploegsteert Memorial, Belgium.

HEWITT, Private, William Henry. 2553, 1/7th Bn., Royal Warwickshire Regiment. Killed in action, Albert, 25th July, 1916. Born 23rd November, 1894 at Coventry. Enlisted September, 1914 at Coventry. Resided 35, Stockton Road. Pattern maker, Singer Co. Ltd. Memorial Ref. Pier and Face 9 A 9 B and 10 B. Thiepval Memorial, Somme, France.

HEWSON, Private, Alfred Walter. 206191, 17th Coy. F Bn., Tank Corps formerly Machine Gun Corps. Died of wounds, Ypres, 2nd August, 1917. Age 19. Son of Mr. and Mrs. A. F. Hewson, of 14, Chandos Street, Stoke, Coventry. Born 9th April, 1898 at Birmingham. Fitter. Enlisted August, 1916. Memorial Ref. Panel 56. Ypres (Menin Gate) Memorial, Ieper, West-Vlaanderen, Belgium

HEWSON, Private, Arthur. 23940, 1st /8th Bn., Royal Warwickshire Regiment. Killed in action, Ypres, 27th August, 1917. Age 31. Husband of Florence Hewson, of 119 Windmill Road, Longford, Coventry. Born 15th February, 1886 at Birmingham. Resided at 22, St. Lawrence Road. Engineer. Enlisted January, 1917 at Coventry. Grave Ref. X. G. 19. Tyne Cot Cemetery, Zonnebeke, West-Vlaanderen, Belgium.

HIATT, Private, John Corbett. 16331, 15th Bn., Royal Warwickshire Regiment. Died of gun shot wounds, 14th September, 1916 at Rouen Hospital, France. Age 22. Son of William Lionel and Charlotte Ann Hiatt, of Upper Swell, Gloucestershire. Employed Keresley Colliery. Grave Ref. I. C. 8. Bois Guillaume Communal Cemetery, France.

HIBBERT, Private, Ernest Leopold. 267503, 16th Bn., Royal Welsh Fusiliers. Killed in action, 19th September, 1917. Age 38. Son of James and Ruth Hibbert, of Manchester. Husband of May Hardaker (formerly Hibbert), of Holmdene, Durbar Avenue, Coventry. Hairdresser. Grave Ref. II. F. 13. Erquinghem-Lys Churchyard Extension, Nord, France.

HICKEN, Private, Joseph. 200591, Brecknock Bn., South Wales Borderers. Died, India, 12th July, 1917 Age 21. Son of William Henry and Alice Louisa Hicken of 53 Emerson Road, Low Hill, Wolverhampton. Born Bridgend, Glam. Enlisted Cefn Coed, Merthyr Tydfil. Commemorated Styechale (St. James) Church. Memorial Ref. Face C. Kirkee 1914 – 1918 War Memorial, India.

HICKIE, Drum Major. Royal Munster Fusiliers. Billeted Coventry. Died Gallipoli, 1915. Helping to bury a bugler when he wa struck by a bullet and killed.

HICKMAN, Bombardier, Thomas. 301, 4th (South Midland) Bde., Royal Field Artillery. Killed in action, 9th April, 1915 by shell fire whilst in an observation post. Age 19. Son of Mrs. Mary A. Hickman, of 8 House, Court 1, Union St., Coventry. Born 23rd June, 1895 in Cow Lane. Engineer. Enlisted Coventry. Grave Ref. X. K. 10. Strand Military Cemetery, Comines-Warneton, Hainaut, Belgium.

HICKS, Private, James. 19635, 5th Bn., Wiltshire Regiment. formerly (13543), Oxfordshire and Buckinghamshire Light Infantry. Killed in action, 9th April, 1916. At that time he was at Basra, on the occasion of the surrender of Kut. Age 31. Son of James and Sarah Hicks, of Rock Farm, Baginton, Coventry. Born Deddington, Oxon. Enlisted Coventry. Resided Coventry. Sister Miss Olive Hicks, New Inn, Gosford Street. Commemorated Baginton Memorial. Memorial Ref. Panel 30 and 64. Basra Memorial, Iraq.

HIGGINS, Private, William. M2/079437, Army Service Corps attached 72nd Field Ambulance, Royal Army Medical Corps. Died, 25th July, 1917. Age 2. Son of Frank Higgins of Rose Farm, Alsager, Cheshire. Born Cheshire. Enlisted Coventry. Resided Stoke-on-Trent. Grave Ref. III. F. 1. Dickebusch New Military Cemetery Extension, Belgium.

HIGGS, Private, Charles. 6367, B Coy., 3rd Bn., Royal Warwickshire Regiment. Died, Home, 9th June, 1917. Age 36. Husband of Florence Getrude Gardner of 104, Washwood Heath Road, Saltley, Birmingham. Served in the South African Campaign. Born Admington, Glos. Enlisted Coventry. Resided Newport. Grave Ref. Screen Wall. 64. 08674. Birmingham (Witton) Cemetery.

HIGH, Troop Cook (Asst.) Frederick William. SS Aragon, (Belfast), Mercantile Marine. Drowned, as a result of an attack by an enemy submarine, 30th December, 1917. Age 18. Son of Walter James and Emily High (nee Tennant), of 19, Lowther Street, Coventry. Born at Cardiff. Memorial Ref. Tower Hill Memorial, London.

HIGH, Private, John. 16500, 2nd Bn., Oxfordshire and Buckinghamshire Light Infantry. Killed in action, 28th April, 1917. Enlisted Coventry. Resided Earsham, Suffolk. Commemorated Coventry Chain Memorial. Memorial Ref. Bay 6 and 7. Arras Memorial, France.

HIGTON, Private, Jacob Ernest. 17300, 2nd Battalion Hampshire Regiment formerly 13107 Oxfordshire and Buckinghamshire Light Infantry. Killed in action, Gallipoli, 6th August, 1915. Born Birmingham. Enlisted Coventry. Employed Armstrong Siddeley Motors Ltd. Commemorated War Memorial Park and Siddeley Roll of Honour. Memorial Ref. Panel 125-134 or 223-226 228-229 & 328. Helles Memorial, Turkey.

HILL, Private, Alfred. 30035, 2nd Bn., Royal Warwickshire Regiment. Killed in action, 3rd September, 1916. Born Coventry. Enlisted Coventry. Grave Ref. XXXII. H. 10. Delville Wood Cemetery, Longueval, France.

HILL, Private, Edgar Manuel. 20911, 1/6th Bn., Royal Warwickshire Regiment. Killed in action, 10th December, 1916. Born 10th August, 1887 at Scarborough. Resided Ford Street. Draper. Enlisted June, 1916 at Coventry. Grave Ref I. J. 5. Warlencourt British Cemetery, France.

HILL, Corporal, Frederick. 16438, 11th Bn., Royal Warwickshire Regiment. Killed in action, 28th April, 1917. Born Menheniot, Cornwall. Enlisted Coventry. Resided Menheniot. Memorial Ref. Bay 3. Arras Memorial, France.

HILL, Gunner, Harry. 840717, "B" Bty. 84th Bde., Royal Field Artillery. Killed in action, 10th October, 1918. Age 29. Son of Mr. and Mrs. Hill, of Tinwell, Stamford, Lincs. Born Coventry. Enlisted Coventry. Born 8th September, 1889 at Hardwick, Rutland. Resided at 106, Lower Ford Street. Tram Driver. Commemorated Transport Department Memorial, Coventry Corporation. Grave Ref. IX. C. 7. Highland Cemetery, Le Cateau, France.

HILL, Private, Harry. 1/7th Bn., Royal Warwickshire Regiment. Died of wounds, received in France, Home, 18th October, 1918. Born 8th April, 1872 at Stourbridge. Resided Coventry. Fitter. Enlisted August, 1914. Grave Ref. Coventry (London Road) Cemetery.

HILL, Gunner, Joseph. 61770, Royal Field Artillery. transf. to (Pte. 595371), Labour Corps. Died, home (gassed), 1st July, 1918. Age 40. Husband of Lizzie Jones (formerly Hill), of 60, Wright Street, Coventry. Born 30th April, 1878 at Kidderminster. Resided 22, Tower Street. Cycle Mechanic. Enlisted Coventry. Grave Ref. 198. 51. Coventry (London Road) Cemetery.

HILL, J. Royal Field Artillery. Died on active service in England, December, 1918. Commemorated Gas Department Memorial, Coventry Corporation.

HILL, S. Employed Humber Ltd. Killed in action.

HILLHOUSE, Sergeant, Robert. 206096, C Bn., Machine Gun Corps (Heavy Branch) formerly 2258, Machine Gun Corps (Infantry). Killed in action, 11th April, 1917. Son of John and Isabella Hillhouse of Stoneywood, Denny. Husband of Janet Hillhouse of 78, Broad Street, Denny, Stirlingshire. Enlisted Coventry. Memorial Ref. Bay 10. Arras Memorial, France.

HILLON, Lance Corporal, John. 242399, 2/5th Bn., 2/5th Bn., East Lancashire Regiment. Killed in action, 21st March, 1918. Born Liverpool. Enlisted Coventry. Resided Liverpool. Grave Ref. III. G. 19. Roisel Communal Cemetery Extension, France.

HILLYER, Lance Corporal, Walter James. R/1308, 12th Bn., King's Royal Rifle Corps. Died of wounds, 11th September, 1917. Age 29. Son of George and Jane Hillyer, of Long Street, Hanslope, Stony Stratford, Bucks. Born 30th October, 1887 at Hanslope, Bucks. Resided at 12, Parkstine Road. Tram Driver. Enlisted September, 1914. Commemorated Transport Department Memorial, Coventry Corporation. Grave Ref. IV. G. 30. Bard Cottage Cemetery, Belgium.

HINCHCLIFFE, Private, Thomas William. 19238, 10th Bn., Royal Warwickshire Regiment. Died of wounds, 1st November, 1916. Born Burton-on-Trent, Staffs. Enlisted Coventry.

HINMAN, Private, Spencer Percy. PO/2425(S), 1st Royal Marine Bn., Royal Marine Light Infantry. Killed in action, 29th September, 1918. Age 26. Only son of F. R. and C. Hinman, of 120, Craven Road, Rugby. Husband of G. M. Hinman, of Rugby. Born 13th March, 1893 at Rugby. Resided Coventry. Clerk. Enlisted August, 1917. Grave Rev. VI. A. 7. Bac-Du-Sud British Cemetery, Bailleulval, France.

HIPPERSON, Private, Albine Gordon. 20249, 1st /6th Bn., Royal Warwickshire Regiment. Killed in action, Somme, 4th February, 1917. Husband of Annie Hipperson, of 153, Terry Road, Coventry. Born 25th October, 1897 at Barford, Norfolk. Employed Co-Operative Society, (Tailoring Department), West Orchard. Enlisted May, 1916 at Coventry. Grave Ref. III. C. 10. Assevillers New British Cemetery, Somme, France.

HIRONS, Private, William. 8947, 9th Bn., Royal Warwickshire Regiment. Killed in action, 10th August, 1915. Son of John and Lydia Hirons of Blackhorse Lane, Longford. Commemorated Saint Thomas the Apostle, Longford. Memorial Ref. Panel 35 to 37. Helles Memorial, Turkey.

HIRONS, Private, William Thomas. 16763, 14th Bn., Royal Warwickshire Regiment. Killed in action, 14th April, 1918. Age 25. Son of William and Hannah Hirons of Lower Hunscote, Wellesbourne. Born Banbury, Oxon. Enlisted Coventry. Memorial Ref. Panel 2 and 3. Ploegsteert Memorial, Belgium.

HITCH, Second Officer, Sydney Charles. SS Polymnia (London), Mercantile Marine. Died 15th May, 1917. Age 38. Son of Edward Hitch. Husband of Sophia Amelia Hitch (nee Lubbock), of 84, Cotton Street, Poplar, London. Born at Eastbourne. Educated Bablake School. Commemorated Bablake School Memorial. Memorial Ref. Tower Hill Memorial.

HOARE, Private, Charles. 131861, 17th Bn., Machine Gun Corps. Killed in action, 4th May, 1918. Age 19. Son of Mr. C. Hoare, of "Boat Caroline," Wyken Colliery, Coventry. Born Banbury. Enlisted Banbury. Grave Ref. II. I. 3. Varennes Military Cemetery, Somme, France

HOARE, Private, James. 43375, 271st Coy., Machine Gun Corps (Infantry) formerly 4478, Royal Warwickshire Regiment. Died at Sea, 27th May, 1918. Enlisted Coventry. Resided Rugby. Memorial Ref. Chatby Memorial.

HOARE, Sergeant, Henry Mark. S/7889, 9th Bn., Seaforth Highlanders. Killed in action, 25th March, 1918. Born 2nd September, 1888 at Hitchin. Resided at 232, Narrow Lane. Leather Dresser. Memorial Ref. Panel 72 and 73. Pozieres Memorial, France.

HOARE, Gunner, Richard Stanley Clent. 334517, 123rd Siege Bty., Royal Garrison Artillery. Killed in action, 12th November, 1917. Age 24. Son of Corporal Alfred S. Hoare, of East Cliff View, West Bay, Bridport. Born 11th August, 1893 at Bridport. Resided Coventry. Hairdresser, F. A. Ghent (Also killed in action). Enlisted November, 1915. Grave Ref. II. C. 49. Level Crossing Cemetery, Fampoux, France.

HOBBIS, Lance Corporal, Henry James. G/42656, 17th Bn., Middlesex Regiment formerly, M/231078, Royal Army Service Corps, Motor Transport. Died of influenza, No. 30, General Hospital, 5th January, 1919 on way home from Germany. Prisoner for 15 months. Age 20. Only son of William and Mary Hobbis, of 7, Meadow Street, Coventry. Born 7th March, 1898 at 24, Henry Street, Coventry. Enlisted October, 1916 at Coventry. Resided 7, Meadow Street, Coventry. Capstan hand, Rover Company. Commemorated St. John's Church. Grave Ref. VII. E. 5A. Les Baraques Military Cemetery, Sangatte, Pas de Calais, France.

HOBBS, Private, Frank Alfred. 2580, C Coy., 2nd Bn., Royal Warwickshire Regiment. Killed in action, 25th September, 1915. Age 20. Son of John and Clara Evline Wingfield(formerly Hobbs) of 276, Marston Lane, Marston Jabbett, Nuneaton. Born Nottingham. Enlisted Coventry. Resided Bulkington. Memorial Ref. Panel 22 to 25. Loos Memorial, France.

HOBBS, Private, Walter Rueben. 2632, 1st /7th Bn., Royal Warwickshire Regiment. Died of wounds, 15th May, 1915 after being shot in the head whilst filling sandbags. Age 16. Son of J. W. and Annie Hobbs, of 'Ferndale', 40, Humber Road, Coventry. Born 1898 in St. John's Parish. Enlisted Coventry. Grave Ref. VIII. D. 4. Boulogne Eastern Cemetery, Pas de Calais, France.

HOBDAY, Private, George. 9076, 11th Bn., Royal Warwickshire Regiment. Killed in action, 16th July, 1916. Born Ryton-on-Dunsmore. Enlisted Coventry. Resided Marton, Warwicks. Commemorated Ryton Memorial. Memorial Ref. Pier and Face 9A 9B and 10B. Thiepval Memorial, Somme, France.

HOBDAY, Rifleman, William Herbert Harrison. 880839, 34th Bn., London Regiment formerly 9/12306, Oxfordshire & Buckinghamshire Light Infantry. Died of wounds, Home, 18th April, 1919. Born Coventry. Enlisted Coventry. Commemorated Ryton Memorial. Grave Ref. Screen Wall. 1 "C." B. 1277. Greenwich Cemetery.

HOBDEN, Second Lieutenant, Ernest. 328th Siege Battery, Royal Garrison Artillery. Killed in action, 20th October, 1918. Employed Town Clerk's Department. Came to Coventry from Middlesbrough in 1912. Leaves a widow and one child. Commemorated Town Clerk's Department Memorial, Coventry Corporation. Grave Ref. C. 50. Quievy Communal Cemetery Extension, France.

HOBSON, Private, Evan. 21627, 14th Bn., Gloucestershire Regiment. Killed in action, 21st August, 1917. Son of Mr. J. Hobson of Ivy Mount, Tyncoed, Gt. Orme's Head, Llandudno. Born Llandudno. Enlisted Coventry. Grave Ref. II. H. 12. Templeux-Le-Guerard British Cemetery, France.

HODGKINS, Private, James. 2nd Bn., Sherwood Foresters. Died 1915 at Boulogne. Resided 27, Cox Street.

HODGKINS, Private, Samuel. 147103, 3rd Bn., Machine Gun Corps (Infantry). Killed in action, 23rd August, 1918. Age 25. Son of William Henry and Hannah Maria Hodgkins, of 27, Grange Avenue, Binley, Coventry. Grave Ref. VI. L. 25. Bucquoy Road Cemetery, Ficheux, Pas de Calais, France.

HODGKINSON, Sergeant, George Henry. 16312, "D" Bty. 91st Bde., Royal Field Artillery. Killed in action, Cambrai, 1st December, 1917. Age 35. Son of George Henry and Millicent Hodgkinson. Born 24th January, 1882 at Middleton. Resided Stoke, Coventry. Smith, Employed Humber Ltd. Enlisted Coventry. Memorial Ref. Panel 1. Cambrai Memorial, Louverval, France.

HODKINSON, Sergeant, James. 5179, 1st Bn., Worcestershire Regiment. Killed in action, 31st July, 1917. Born Coventry. Enlisted Birmingham. Resided Bradley, Staffs. Memorial Ref. Panel 34. Ypres (Menin Gate) Memorial, Belgium.

HOGAN, Private, Francis Joseph. 8623, 3rd Bn., Irish Guards. Died, home, 27th March, 1918. Age 34. Son of James and Jane Hogan, of Coventry. Husband of Ellen Hogan, of 35, New Buildings, Coventry. Born Coventry. Enlisted Coventry. Grave Ref. 193. 207. Coventry (London Road) Cemetery.

HOGAN, Private, Thomas. 4458, 1st /7th Bn., Royal Warwickshire Regiment. Killed in action, Albert , 26th July, 1916. Age 19. Son of William and Lizzie Hogan, of 8, Mill Street, Coventry. Born 2nd October 1896 at Coventry. Resided at 8, Mill Street. Machinist, Triumph Works. Enlisted August 1915 at Coventry. Commemorated Triumph & Gloria Memorial and War Memorial Park. Memorial Ref. Pier and Face 9 A 9 B and 10 B. Thiepval Memorial, Somme, France. (Possibly buried at Tulloch Dump, near Pozieres).

HOGG, Private, John. 2194, 1st Bn., Royal Warwickshire Regiment. Killed in action, 26th August, 1914. Born St. Michael's, Coventry. Enlisted Warwick. Resided Coventry. Memorial Ref. La Ferte-Sous-Jouarre Memorial, France.

HOGG, Private, Thomas Edgar. 242785, 1/6th Bn., Royal Warwickshire Regiment. Killed in action, 27th August, 1917. Born 1st September, 1892 at Coventry. Resided at 54, Cambridge Street. Baker. Enlisted Coventry. Memorial Ref. Panel 23 to 28 and 163A. Tyne Cot Memorial, Belgium.

HOLDER, Acting Bombardier, Thomas. 10544, 47th Bty., 41st Bde., Royal Field Artillery. Killed in action, 19th October, 1917. Born Warwick. Enlisted Coventry. Grave Ref. I. A. 11. St. Julien Dressing Station Cemetery, Belgium.

HOLLAND, Private, Harry. 49811, 1st Battalion, Royal Irish Fusiliers formerly 6506 Oxfordshire and Buckinghamshire Light Infantry. Killed in action, 2nd September, 1918. Born at Birmingham. Employed by Armstrong Siddeley Motors Ltd. Commemorated War Memorial Park and Siddeley Roll of Honour. Memorial Ref. Panel 9. Ploegsteert Memorial, Belgium.

HOLLAND, Private, Sidney William. 41876, 3rd Bn., Worcestershire Regiment. Died whilst prisoner of war in German hands, 4th November 1918. Age 20. Son of Mr. and Mrs. W. Holland, of 219, Alderman's Green, Foleshill, Coventry. Born 24th November, 1899 at Aldermans Green, Coventry. Enlisted March, 1917 at Coventry. Crane driver. Commemorated Saint Thomas the Apostle, Longford. Grave Ref. II. C. 10. Poznan Old Garrison Cemetery, Poland.

HOLLICK, Captain, Percy Hood. 3rd Bn., attd. 15th Bn., Royal Warwickshire Regiment. formerly (Pte. 1267) , Honourable Artillery Company. Killed in action, Fresnoy Wood, near Arras, 9th May 1917. Age 26. Son of Alfred and Fanny Hollick, of "Brooklands", Balsall Common, Coventry. A Solicitor, LL.B. Born 29th January, 1891 at Allesley. Solicitor. Enlisted August, 1914. Mentioned in Despatches. Educated Bablake School. Commemorated Bablake School Memorial. Memorial Ref. Bay 3. Arras Memorial, Pas de Calais, France.

HOLLINS, Sergeant, Horace. 19121, 10th Bn., Royal Welsh Fusiliers formerly Grenadier Guards. Killed in action, 30th April, 1916. Born Rugeley, Staffs. Husband of E. Hollins of 73, Queen Street, Rugeley. Resided 1, Francis Street. South Africa veteran. Enlisted Lichfield. Resided Rugeley. Leaves a widow and two children. Grave Ref. I. J. 5. Lindenhoek Chalet Military Cemetery, Belgium.

HOLLINS, Lance Corporal, William Herbert. 23942, 7th Bn., Duke of Cornwall's Light Infantry. Killed in action, Guillemont, 30th August, 1916. Age 19. Eldest son of William and Amy Hollins, of 11, Francis Street, Coventry. Born 13th May, 1899 at Longford. Coremaker, Matterson, Huxley and Watson Ltd. Enlisted November, 1915 at Coventry. Memorial Ref. Pier and Face 6 B. Thiepval Memorial, Somme, France.

HOLLIS, Private, Arthur James. 12/687, 12th Bn., York and Lancaster Regiment. Killed in action, 1st July, 1916. Age 21. Son of George James and Lilian G. Hollis, of 25, Pinner Road, Sheffield. Born Coventry. Enlisted Sheffield. Grave Ref. 20. Luke Copse British Cemetery, Puisieux, Belgium.

HOLLIS, Private, Frederick. 20300, 2/5th Bn., Royal Warwickshire Regiment. Died home, 13th February, 1917. Age 21. Son of John and Jemima Hollis, of 83, Windmill Road, Longford. Born Coventry. Enlisted Warwick. Resided Foleshill. Grave 37 (In west part). Longford (Salem) Baptist Churchyard.

HOLMES, Lance Corporal, Arthur. 9150, 8th Bn., King's Own (Royal Lancaster Regiment). Died of wounds, 22nd February, 1917. Age 29. Son of Edward and Alice Holmes, of 8, Rugby Road, Milverton, Leamington Spa. Born Coventry. Enlisted Warwick. Grave Ref. IV. B. 16. Avesnes-Le-Comte Communal Cemetery Extension, France.

HOLMES, Lance Corporal, Bert, DCM. 1664, 1st Bn., Royal Warwickshire Regiment. Killed in action, 20th November, 1917. Born 11th May, 1894 at Leicester. Resided Rugby. Moulder and coremaker. Enlisted August, 1914. Awarded Distinguished Conduct Medal, 17th April, 1918 for conspicuous gallantry and devotion to duty. Acting as a company runner for over two years, he has been in the majority of the actions in which the battalion has taken part. He has always proved himself most reliable, and on many occasions has taken messages through very heavy fire, displaying singular devotion to duty. Memorial Ref. Bay 3. Arras Memorial, France.

HOLMES, Private, Charles. 228277, 1st Bn., London Regiment (Royal Fusiliers) formerly 202402, Royal Sussex Regiment. Died, 30th September, 1918. Age 35. Son of Richard and Louise Holmes. Husband of Beatrice Ellen Holmes, of 48, Meadway, Stoke Heath, Coventry. Born and enlisted at Northampton. Grave Ref. Plot IIa. 32. Schoonselhof Cemetery, Antwerpen, Belgium.

HOLMES, Corporal, Harry. 9151, 1st Bn., King's Own (Royal Lancaster Regiment). Killed in action, 14th August, 1917. Age 27. Son of Edward and Alice H. Hunt (formerly Holmes), of 81, Rugby Road, Leamington Spa. Born Coventry. Enlisted Warwick. Grave Ref. II. C. 2. St. Nicolas British Cemetery, France.

HOLMES, Sergeant, Walter. 7962, 2nd Bn., King's Royal Rifle Corps. Killed in action, 9th May, 1916. Age 29. Son of George William and Sarah Ann Holmes, of 1, Railway Cottages, Warwick Road, Coventry. Born 9th July, 1887 at 1, Railway Cottages, Warwick Road. Telegraph clerk. Grave Ref. III. B. 11. St. Patrick's Cemetery, Loos, Pas de Calais, France.

HOLT, Private, Alexander. 50756, 9th Sqdn., Machine Gun Corps (Cavalry) formerly 23827, 19th Hussars. Killed in action, 8th August, 1918. Age 25. Son of John Henry and Sarah Ann Holt, of 3, Primrose Hill Cottages, Leigh Street, Coventry. Born 16th March, 1893 in Hill Street. Resided Vauxhall Street. Turner. Enlisted August, 1914 at Coventry. Memorial Ref. Panel 10. Vis-En-Artois Memorial, Pas de Calais, France.

HOLT, Private, Herbert, MM. 265532, 2/7th Bn., Royal Warwickshire Regiment. Died of wounds, 8th December, 1917. Born 1st May, 1898 in Upper Well Street. Resided at 16, King Fields. Tool maker, Alfred Herbert Ltd. Enlisted August, 1914 at Coventry. Gazetted for Military Medal, 23rd February, 1918. Grave Ref. VII. A. 8. Rocquigny-Equancourt Road British Cemetery, Manancourt, France.

HOLT, Private, Norman. 16397, 15th Bn., Royal Warwickshire Regiment. Died of wounds, 8th September, 1916. Born Coventry. Enlisted Coventry. Born 18th August, 1896 at Coventry. Resided 36, Humber Road. Engine Fitter. Enlisted 1915. Commemorated Dunlop Memorial. Memorial Ref. Pier and Face 9 A 9 B and 10 B. Thiepval Memorial, Somme, France.

HOLT, Private, Oliver. 14713, 10th Bn., Hampshire Regiment. Died of wounds at sea, received at Gallipoli, 10th August, 1915. Age 26. Husband of Minnie Copeland (formerly Holt), of 34, Day's Lane, Coventry. Born 4th December, 1890 at Hillfields, Coventry. Cycle Fitter. Enlisted December, 1914 at Coventry. Memorial Ref. (Soldier, buried at sea) Panel 125-134 or 223-226 228-229 & 328. Helles Memorial, Turkey.

HOLT, Private, Percy Harold. 34021, 1st Bn., Duke of Cornwall's Light Infantry formerly 18828, Royal Warwickshire Regiment. Killed in action, 4th October, 1917. Age 19. Son of Mr. and Mrs. Holt, of 23, Cherry Street, Coventry. Born Coventry. Commemorated St. John's Church. Enlisted Coventry. Memorial Ref. Panel 80 to 82 and 163A. Tyne Cot Memorial, Zonnebeke, West-Vlaanderen, Belgium.

HOLTOM, Private, Edward. 19719, 11th Bn., Royal Warwickshire Regiment. Killed in action, 22nd July, 1917. Age 34. Son of William and Mary Holtom, of Coventry. Husband of Lucy Holton, of 5 Court, 15 House, Chauntry Place, Coventry. Born 1883, Combrook, Warwickshire. Employed Messrs. Garlicks Builders. Enlisted Coventry. Grave Ref. I. A. 16. Derry House Cemetery, No.2, Heuvelland, West-Vlaanderen, Belgium.

HOLTOM, Private, William. 11147, 1st Bn., Royal Dublin Fusiliers. Killed in action, Gallipoli, 30th April, 1915. Born Warwick. Enlisted Warwick. Resided 7c. 1h. Greyfriars Lane, Coventry. Grave Ref. Special Memorial. B. 1. V Beach Cemetery, Turkey.

HOLTON, Private, Enoch. 18581, 6th Bn., Oxfordshire and Buckinghamshire Light Infantry. Killed in action, Cambrai, 20th November, 1917. Born Combrook. Resided 66, New Buildings. Bricklayer. Enlisted Coventry. Commemorated Holy Trinity Panels. Memorial Ref. Panel 7. Cambrai Memorial, Louverval, France.

HOLTON, Private, Thomas. Killed in action, 1915. Resided 7c. Greyfriars Lane.

HOLYOAKE, Private, John Henry. 8696, 2nd Bn., Leicestershire Regiment. Died of wounds, 11th February, 1915. Age 26. Son of William and Mary Holyoake, of Wheelwright Lane, Exhall, Coventry. Native of Sheepy Magna, Leicestershire. Grave Ref. I. H. 3. Merville Communal Cemetery, Nord, France.

HOLYOAKE, Corporal, W, MM. 7403, 6th Bn., Leicestershire Regiment. Died of wounds, 9th October, 1918. Age 31. Son of William and Mary Holyoake, of Wheelwright Lane, Exhall, Coventry. Native of Sheepy Magna, Leicestershire. Gazetted for Military Medal, 21st October, 1918. Grave Ref. IX. A. 10. Rocquigny-Equancourt Road British Cemetery, Manancourt, Somme, France

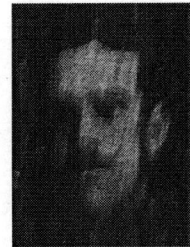

HOOKER, Private, Thomas. 9527, 2nd Bn., South Wales Borderers formerly 6055, Manchester Regiment. Killed in action, 2nd May, 1915. Born London. Resided 28, Canterbury Street. Enlisted Aldershot. Memorial Ref. Panel 80 to 84 or 219 and 220. Helles Memorial, Turkey.

HOOPER, Gunner, Bernard William Cole. 840239, D Bty, 240th Bde., Territorial Force, Royal Field Artillery. Killed in action, 31st August, 1917. Age 22. Son of William Henry and Emily Ada Hooper of Bridestowe, 140, Jerningham Road, New Cross, London. Born London. Enlisted Coventry. Grave Ref. IX. H. 1. Vlamertinghe New Military Cemetery, Belgium.

HOOPER, Gunner, Stanley. 173, 5 Bty., Machine Gun Corps (Motor Branch). Killed in action, shot by sniper, 7th November, 1915. Age 20. Son of James Hooper and of Rhoda Cecilia Hewitt (formerly Hooper), of "Aquata", Parkfield Rd., Wolverhampton. Born 22nd February, 1895 at Bilston, Staffs. Resided in Queen Victoria Road. Brother of Mrs. Jones, 15, Kirby Road. Clerk, British Thompson Houston. Enlisted September, 1914 at Coventry. Commemorated British Thompson Houston Memorial. Grave Ref. II. D. 8. St. Vaast Post Military Cemetery, Richebourg-L'avoue, France.

HOPCROFT, Corporal, George Thomas. 5624, 2nd Bn., Leicestershire Regiment. Died of wounds, Neuve Chapelle, 1st May, 1915. Age 35. Son of George and Elizabeth Hopcroft, of Rowington, Warwick. Husband of Emily Jane Hopcroft, of The Club House, Rowington, Warwick. Born 24th September, 1879 at Redditch. Resided Coventry. Haulier. Enlisted August, 1914. Grave Ref. XVII. C. 34. Cabaret-Rouge British Cemetery, Souchez, France.

HOPE, Private, James. 7696, 2nd Bn., Royal Welsh Fusiliers. Killed in action, 25th September, 1915. Born Cubbington. Enlisted Coventry. Grave Ref. H. 21. Cambrin Churchyard Extension, France.

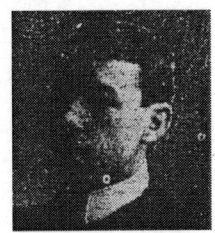
HOPKINS, Bombardier, Charles John. 1383, 1st North Midland Bde., Royal Field Artillery. Killed in action, Loos, 13th October, 1915. Age 36. Son of Mr. and Mrs. J. Hopkins, of The Elms, Coundon, Coventry. Husband of Lizzie May Peace (formerly Hopkins), of The Bungalow, Queen's Road, Boston. Born 28th November, 1878 at Coundon, Coventry. Enlisted September, 1914 at Boston, Lincs. School master at Keresley National School. Commemorated Bablake School Memorial and St. Thomas Memorial. Memorial Ref. Panel 3. Loos Memorial, Pas de Calais, France.

HOPKINS, Private, Ernest. 15693, 3rd Bn., Coldstream Guards. Killed in action, 13th April, 1918. Age 26. Son of Mr. H. and Mrs. S. A. Hopkins of 17, Henry Street, Kenilworth. Born Kenilworth. Enlisted Coventry. Resided Kenilworth. Commemorated St. John's Church. Grave Ref. I. D. 440. Merville Communal Cemetery Extension, France.

HOPKINS, Private, Ernest Mark. 4262, 1/6th Bn., North Staffordshire Regiment. Killed in action, 1st July, 1916. Age 24. Born 1st January, 1892 at Burton-on-Trent. Enlisted Burton-on-Trent. Only son of Mr. and Mrs. Hopkins, 23c. 4h. Spon Street, Coventry. Sand Blower, Daimler Works. Commemorated Queens Road Memorial. Memorial Ref. Pier and Face 14 B and 14 C. Thiepval Memorial, Somme, France.

HOPKINS, Private, Francis. 14405, 7th Bn., Wiltshire Regiment formerly Oxfordshire and Buckinghamshire Light Infantry. Killed in action, 24th April, 1917. Age 21. Son of Mrs. M. A. Hopkins, of 7, Church Lane, Binley Road, Stoke Coventry. Born at Chinnor, Oxon. Enlisted Oxford. Resided Thame. Memorial Ref. Doiran Memorial, Greece.

HOPKINS, George. Private. 266418, 2nd/6th Battalion Royal Warwickshire Regiment. Killed in action, 6th September 1918. Age 24. Born 12th September, 1894 at Coventry. Resided at 70, Mulliner Street. Bottler. Enlisted April 1915 at Coventry. Commemorated War Memorial Park. Grave Ref. III. L. 5. Anzac Cemetery, Sailly-sur-La-Lys, France.

HOPKINS, Private, Harold. 4345, 1/7th Bn., Royal Warwickshire Regiment. Killed in action, 14th July, 1916. Age 17. Son of Mrs. Edith E. Hunt, of 99, Victoria Street, New Bilton, Rugby. Enlisted Coventry. Resided New Bilton, Warwicks. Memorial Ref. Pier and Face 9 A 9 B and 10 B. Thiepval Memorial, Somme, France.

HOPKINS, Private, Henry William. 414732, 7th Coy., Canadian Machine Gun Corps. 7th July, 1917. Age 37. Son of John and Caroline Hopkins, of 1, Gosford St., Coventry, England. Grave Ref. VIII. E. 6. Villers Station Cemetery, Villers-Au-Bois, Pas de Calais, France.

HOPKINS, Private, John Alfred. 152649, 50th Bn., Machine Gun Corps (Infantry) formerly 183454, Royal Field Artillery. Killed in action, 17th October, 1918. Age 22. Son of John Charles and Annie Selina Hopkins, of 35, Duke Street, Nuneaton. Born Bakewell, Derby. Enlisted Coventry. Resided Nuneaton. Grave Ref. A. 2. Quietiste Military Cemetery, Le Cateau, France.

HOPKINS, Private, John Thomas. CH/2209(S), 2nd Royal Marine Bn., Royal Naval Division, Royal Marine Light Infantry. Killed in action, 26th October, 1917. Born 23rd March, 1896 at Rowley Regis, Staffs. Resided at 1, The Hollows, Foleshill Road. Painter, Daimler Works also assisted Mr. W. Jones, Newsagent, Foleshill Road. Enlisted March, 1917. Panel 1 and 162A. Tyne Cot Memorial, Belgium.

HOPKINS, Private, Leonard John. 81288, 4th Bn., Devonshire Regiment. Died, Home, 30th October, 1918. Age 18. Son of Mr. and Mrs. E. Hopkins, of The Green, Dunchurch. Born Dunchurch. Enlisted Coventry. Grave Ref. Dunchurch (St. Peter) Churchyard.

HOPKINS, S. E. Employed by Rover Company Ltd. Killed in action.

HOPKINS, Private, William. 16087, 15th Bn., Royal Warwickshire Regiment. Died of wounds, 7th September, 1916. Age 20. Son of William and Sarah A. Hopkins, of 7, Woodcote Road, Warwick Born Warwick. Resided Warwick. Name on Roll in St. Thomas's Church. Enlisted Coventry. Grave Ref. II. C. 47. Corbie Communal Cemetery Extension, France.

HOPKINS, Private, William Henry. 414732, 7th Coy., Canadian Machine Gun Corps. Killed in action, 7th July, 1917. Age 37. Son of John and Caroline Hopkins, of 1, Gosford St., Coventry, England. Born 21st November, 1879 at Coventry. Resided Canada. Lumberman. Enlisted 1915. Grave Ref. VIII. E. 6. Villers Station Cemetery, Villers-Au-Bois, France.

HOPLEY, Private, Joseph Henry. 19723, 1st Bn., Worcestershire Regiment. Killed in action, 10th October, 1915. Born Birmingham. Enlisted Coventry. Resided 8, Bridge Row, Stoney Stanton Road, Coventry. Grave Ref. I. F. 34. Rue-Petillon Military Cemetery, Fleurbaix, France.

HORDEN, Private, Samuel David. 9435, D Coy., 1st Bn., Cameron Highlanders. Killed in action, Battle of the Aisne, 14th September, 1914. Age 20. Son of Mr. and Mrs. Samuel Horden, of 5, Cobden Terrace, Bradford Street, Hillfields, Coventry. Born 5th September, 1894 at Vauxhall, Birmingham. Enlisted Aldershot, Hants. Soldier. Memorial Ref. La Ferte-Sous-Jouarre Memorial, Seine-et-Marne, France.

HORDERN, Private, Richard. 1310, 2nd Bn., Royal Warwickshire Regiment. Killed in action, 26th January, 1915. Born 22nd February, 1896 at 28, Greyfriars Lane. Resided 28, Greyfriars Lane. Polisher. Enlisted August, 1914 at Coventry. Grave Ref. E. 40. Y Farm Military Cemetery, Bois-Grenier, France.

HORGAN, Private, Daniel. 7214, 2nd Bn., Royal Munster Fusiliers. Killed in action, 21st March, 1918. Born Cork. Enlisted Coventry. Resided Coventry. Memorial Ref. Panel 78 and 79. Pozieres Memorial, France.

HORNBROOK, Sapper, Nelson. 46908, 72nd Field Coy., Royal Engineers. Killed in action, Gallipoli, 22nd September, 1915. Age 30. Son of Mrs. Matilda Arm Hornbrook, of Halgarras, Shortlanesend, Kenwyn, Truro. Born Truro, Cornwall. Enlisted Coventry. Resided Truro, Cornwall. Grave Ref. II. F. 9. Lala Baba Cemetery, Turkey.

HORNE, Private, Fred. 12137, 2nd Bn., Royal Warwickshire Regiment. Died of wounds, 15th April, 1916. Age 24. Son of Jesse and Julia Horne, of "The Cross Keys," Exhall, Coventry. Born Offchurch. Enlisted Nuneaton. Resided Exhall. Commemorated Exhall Memorial. Grave Ref. I. B. 12. Mericourt-L'abbe Communal Cemetery Extension, Somme, France.

HORNER, Private, Charles Frederick. 44163, 24th (Tyneside Irish) Bn., Northumberland Fusiliers formerly 80887, East Yorkshire Regiment. Killed in action, 28th April, 1917. Born Ilkley, Yorks. Enlisted Coventry. Memorial Ref. Bay 2 and 3. Arras Memorial, France.

HORNER, Captain, Frederick Julian, MC. Royal Warwickshire Regiment attd. 2nd Bn., Cheshire Regiment. Died of wounds, 15th April, 1918 when a patrol were outnumbered five to one he managed to escape and was hit by a piece of shell. Age 22. Son of Frederick and Julia Horner, of Burnt Post, Coventry. Born in 1896. Resided at Coventry. Educated King Edward VI School, Birmingham and King Henry VIII, Coventry. Articled pupil, Mr. George Sutton, Town Clerk. Commemorated King Henry VIII School, Town Clerk's Department Memorial, Coventry Corporation and War Memorial Park. Awarded the Military Cross, June 1918, for consistent and conspicuous gallantry in action over an extended period; on one occasion by his prompt grasp of a critical situation, carried through successfully an enterprise which at one period seemed destined to failure. Grave Ref. VII. D. 10. Struma Military Cemetery, Greece.

HORNSBY, Private, Charles Henry. 8188, 1st Bn., Royal Munster Fusiliers. Killed in action, 3rd May, 1915. Born Chelsea. Enlisted London. Memorial Ref. Panel 185 to 190. Helles Memorial, Turkey.

HORNSBY, Private, Richard. 2402, 1st Bn., Royal Warwickshire Regiment. Died of wounds, 29th October, 1916. Born St. Michael's Parish. Grave Ref. O. I. I. 10. St. Sever Cemetery Extension, Rouen, France.

HOROBIN, Private, Arthur. 18135, 1/8th Bn., Royal Warwickshire Regiment. Killed in action, 4th November, 1918. Age 23. Son of Mrs. Ann Horobin, of 24, Anker Street, Nuneaton. Born Nuneaton. Enlisted Coventry. Resided Nuneaton. Grave Ref. B. 25. Landrecies British Cemetery, France.

HORSBURGH, Private, William. 12882, 1st Bn., Coldstream Guards. Killed in action, Ginchy, 15th September, 1916. Born Sparkhill, Warwickshire. Enlisted September, 1914 at Birmingham. Resided Coventry. Born 20th December, 1893 at Birmingham. Bricklayer. Memorial Ref. Pier and Face 7 D and 8 D. Thiepval Memorial, Somme, France.

HORSLEY, Private, Christopher. 2142, D Coy., 7th Bn., Royal Warwickshire Regiment. Died, home, 21st January, 1915 from pneumonia. Age 18. Born in 1896 at Kenilworth. Resided Kenilworth with his Aunt and Uncle at Albion Street. Gardener, with Major Stringer in Coventry. Grave Ref. 44. 8. Coventry (London Road) Cemetery.

HORSWILL, Private, Algernon Sidney. TF/290110, 2/10th Bn., Middlesex Regiment. Killed in action, 26th March, 1917. Age 25. Only son of Charles Henry and Fanny Horswill, of 48, Craven Road, Rugby. Born Holy Trinity Parish. Schoolmaster, Elementary School, Coventry. Commemorated Education Department Memorial, Coventry Corporation and St. Barbara's Memorial. Memorial Ref. Panel 42. Jerusalem Memorial, Israel.

HORTON, Private, Francis Valentine. 36238, 10th Bn., Royal Welsh Fusiliers. Killed in action, 30th April, 1916. Age 27. Son of Mrs. Caroline Horton, of 11, Alfred's Place, Icknield Street, Birmingham. Born Coventry. Enlisted Birmingham. Grave Ref. I. J. 3. Lindenhoek Chalet Military Cemetery, Belgium.

HORTON, Private, George. 254573, 2/3rd Bn., London Regiment (Royal Fusiliers) attached 2/4th London Regiment. Died of wounds, 10th August, 1918. Born Hackney. Enlisted Stratford. Resided Coventry. Grave Ref. IV. C .19. Pernois British Cemetery, Halloy-Les-Pernois, France.

HORTON, Private, Samuel. 240733, 6th Bn., Oxfordshire and Buckinghamshire Light Infantry formerly 7477, Royal Berkshire Regiment. Killed in action, by a shell, 16th August, 1917. Born 1888 at Oldbury, Staffs. Resided 7c. 1h. Brewery Street. Carrier, Messrs Pickfords. Enlisted 1917 at Coventry. Memorial Ref. Panel 96 to 98. Tyne Cot Cemetery, Belgium.

HORTON, Private, William Henry, MM. 2399, A Coy. 1st /7th Bn., Royal Warwickshire Regiment. Killed in action, 14th July, 1916. Age 23. Only son of William and Clara Horton, of 123, Narrow Lane, Coventry. Born 14th June, 1893 at 1c. 3h. Chauntry Place. Gear Cutter and Machinist. Enlisted September, 1914 at Coventry. Awarded Military Medal bravery in the field. Grave Ref. I. J. 6. Pozieres British Cemetery, Ovillers-La Boisselle, Somme, France.

HORTON, Private, William John. 58250, 10th Bn., Royal Warwickshire Regiment. Died of wounds, 8th November, 1918. Born Birmingham. Resided Gulson Road. Enlisted Coventry. Grave Ref. E. 6. Canonne Farm British Cemetery, Sommaing, France.

HOTEN, Private, Frank Cecil. 201472, 4th Bn., Royal Berkshire Regiment. Killed in action, 5th April, 1917. Born Sheffield. Enlisted Reading, Resided Caversham. Commemorated Wesleyan Church. Grave Ref. Sp. Mem. A. 8. Templeux-Le-Guerard British Cemetery, France.

HOTTON, Private, Harold Reginald. 11346, 2nd Bn., Royal Scots. Killed in action, Crux Barbe, Normandy, 15th October, 1914. Age 20. Son of Harold M. and Caroline M. Hotton, 173, Narrow Lane, Coventry. Born 20th May 1894 at Lancaster. Resided at Coventry. Enlisted Coventry. Coach painter. Commemorated War Memorial Park. Grave Ref. VIII. B. 23. Vieille-Chapelle New Military Cemetery, Lacouture, Pas de Calais, France.

HOUGHTON, Private, Dan. 18013, 11th Coy., Machine Gun Corps (Infantry) formerly 4581, Rifle Brigade. Died of wounds, 1st July, 1916. Born St. Michael's, Warwick. Enlisted Coventry. Memorial Ref. Pier and Face 5 C and 12 C. Thiepval Memorial, Somme, France

HOUGHTON, Private, Leonard Wells. 35646, 1st /4th Bn., Duke of Cornwall's Light Infantry formerly 1111, 92 T. RES. Bn. Lost in HMT Transylvania when torpedoed, died at sea, 4th May, 1917. Age 25. Husband of Maud Houghton, of 78, Moor Street, Earlsdon, Coventry. Born 30th December, 1891 at 58, Moor Street, Coventry. Enlisted January, 1917 at Coventry. Accountant's clerk. Memorial Ref. Savona Memorial, Italy.

HOUGHTON, Private, Victor. 3075, 1/7th Bn., Royal Warwickshire Regiment. Killed in action, 14th July, 1916. Son of Mrs. R. E. Houghton, of Station Road, Knowle, Birmingham. Enlisted Coventry. Memorial Ref. Pier and Face 9 A 9 B and 10 B. Thiepval Memorial, Somme, France.

HOUGHTON, Lance Corporal, William. 14738, 8th Bn., Royal Berkshire Regiment. Killed in action, 11th March, 1916. Born Manchester. Enlisted Coventry. Resided Altrincham. Grave Ref. III. E. 6. St. Patrick's Cemetery, Loos, France.

HOUSTON, Lance Corporal, John. 9031, 2nd Bn., Leicestershire Regiment. Killed in action, 14th May, 1915. Born St. Matthew's, Leicester. Enlisted Leicester. Resided Coventry. Grave Ref. I. H. 9. Le Touret Military Cemetery, Richebourg-L'Avoue, France.

HOWARD, Private, Frederick T. 15312, 1st Bn., Worcestershire Regiment. Killed in action, 13th March, 1915. Born Wolston. Enlisted Rugby. Resided Wolston. Commemorated Wolston Memorial. Memorial Ref. Panel 17 and 18. Le Touret Memorial, France.

HOWARD, Lance Corporal, Herbert. 16972, 5th Bn., Oxfordshire and Buckinghamshire Light Infantry. Killed in action, by a shell splinter, Ypres, 9th April, 1917. Born Coventry. Enlisted December, 1914 at Coventry. Born 1st July, 1884 at Coventry. Resided back of 1, Bath Street. Filer, Mr. Rowland Hill, King Street. Grave Ref. III. D. 8. Tilloy British Cemetery, Tilloy-Les-Mofflaines, France.

HOWDLE, Battery Quartermaster Sergeant, James B. 48219, 121st Bty., Royal Field Artillery. Died from acute debility, 12th December, 1916. Age 27. Son of Charles Howdle, of 13, Cambridge Street, Coventry. Commemorated Wesleyan Church. Grave Ref. 112. 2. Coventry (London Road) Cemetery.

HOWE, Gunner, Charles Henry. 840359, D Bty., 242nd Bde., Royal Field Artillery. Killed in action, 5th June, 1917. Age 30. Husband of Ethel Howe, of Kenilworth Road, Berkswell, Coventry. Born 11th December, 1886 at Woolwich. Frame Builder, Fitting Department, Rudge Whitworth Co. Enlisted November, 1914 at Coventry. Grave Ref. II. J. 11. St. Quentin Cabaret Military Cemetery, Heuvelland, West-Vlaanderen, Belgium.

HOWE, Sapper, Edwin Livingstone. 224379, 225th Field Coy., Royal Engineers formerly 58242, West Yorkshire Regiment. Killed in action, 30th March, 1918. Born 7th March, 1889 at Bristol. Enlisted Coventry. Resided Cox Street. Master cooper. Comemorated Triumph & Gloria Memorial. Memorial Ref. Panel 10 – 13. Pozieres Memorial, Ovillers-La-Boiselle, France.

HOWE, Private, John. 37101, 1st /5th Bn., Royal Welsh Fusiliers. Lost in HMT Transylvania when torpedoed. Died, at sea, 4th May, 1917. Age 19. Son of Mr. W. and Mrs. E. E. Howe, of 40, Hope Street, Coventry. Born 21st September, 1897 at 5c. 2h. Moat Street, Coventry. Enlisted November, 1915 at Coventry. Machinist. Grave Ref. E. 15. Savona Town Cemetery, Italy.

HOWE, Sergeant, Joseph, MM. 16003, 14th Bn., Royal Warwickshire Regiment. Killed in action, 29th June, 1918. Age 20. Son of William and Elizabeth Howe, of Coventry. Born 18th January, 1898 in Harnall Lane West, Coventry. Enlisted Warwick. Resided 170, Gulson Road, Coventry. Clerk, Guardians Office, Little Park Street. Commemorated Bablake School Memorial. Awarded Military Medal for bravery in the field, 1917. Grave Ref. 3. F. 3. Tannay British Cemetery, Thiennes, Nord, France.

HOWE, Driver, William. 840374, A Bty,. 317th Bde., Royal Field Artillery formerly South Midland Howitzers. Killed in action, Ypres, 17th October, 1917. Son of William and Elizabeth Howe of 170 Gulson Road, Coventry. Born 25th March, 1887 in Harnall Lane, Coventry. Enlisted November, 1914 at Coventry. Tool Maker, Rudge Whitworth Works. Grave Ref. I. E. 22. Dulhallow ADS Cemetery, Belgium.

HOWELLS, Second Lieutenant, Evan Llewellyn. 23rd Sqdn., Royal Air Force. Killed in action, near Ovillers, 23rd October, 1918. Age 19. Son of Evan O. C. and Florence Howells, of "Haynstone," Stoke Park, Coventry. Born 31st July, 1899 at Coventry. Builder's Pupil. Enlisted January, 1917. Commemorated King Henry VIII School and War Memorial Park. Grave Ref. A. 1. Ovillers New Communal Cemetery, Solesmes, Nord, France.

HOWES, Private, Fred. 242918, 2nd Bn., Royal Warwickshire Regiment. Killed in action, 11th October, 1917. Born 25th February, 1883 at Court House Green, Coventry. Resided 93, Station Street West. Polisher. Enlisted Coventry. Memorial Ref. Panel 23 and 28 and 163A. Tyne Cot Memorial, Belgium.

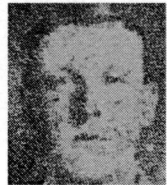

HOWKINS, Private, Charles. 16900, "C" Coy. 10th Bn., Royal Warwickshire Regiment. Killed in action, 18th November, 1916. Age 22. Son of Mrs. S. Howkins, of School Street, Wolston, Coventry. Native of Princethorpe, Rugby. Enlisted Coventry. Commemorated Wolston Memorial. Grave Ref. B. 28. Grandcourt Road Cemetery, Grandcourt, Somme, France.

HOWKINS, Engine Room Artificer 4th Class, Henry Edmund. M/11620, HMS Natal, Royal Navy. Killed by internal explosion of vessel in Cromarty Firth, 30th December, 1915. Age 25. Son of Daniel and Catherine Howkins, of 107, Spon Street, Coventry. Returned from America to enlist. Commemorated St. John's Church. Memorial Ref. 11. Chatham Naval Memorial, Kent.

HOWLETT, Private, George William Billy. 13076, 2nd Bn., Oxfordshire and Buckinghamshire Light Infantry. Killed in action, 25th September, 1915. Age 27. Son of Jonathan and Lucy Howlett, of 26, Elsenham Street, Southfields, London. Born 4th August, 1888 at Knightsbridge. Resided Rugby. Employed Assembly Department, British Thompson Houston Company Ltd. Enlisted September, 1914 at Coventry. Commemorated British Thompson Houston Memorial. Memorial Ref. Panel 83 to 85. Loos Memorial, France.

HOWLETT, Lance Corporal, Seth Edward. G/16875, 10th Bn., Queen's Own (Royal West Kent Regiment). Killed in action, 7th June, 1917. Age 27. Son of Edward and Emily Howlett, of Oakley, Chinnor, Wallingford, Berks. Husband of Kate Edith May Carter (formerly Howlett), of 24, Emscote Road, Coventry. Enlisted High Wycombe. Memorial Ref. Panel 45 and 47. Ypres (Menin Gate) Memorial, Ieper, West-Vlaanderen, Belgium.

HOYLE, Second Lieutenant, Frederick Harold. 2nd Bn., West Yorkshire Regiment (Prince of Wales's Own). Died of wounds, 20th April, 1918. Age 21. Son of William Henry and Elizabeth Hoyle, of Warmleigh, Tile Hill, Coventry. Grave Ref. Officers, B. 6. 18. St. Sever Cemetery, Rouen, Seine-Maritime, France.

HUBBALL, Corporal, James. 1867, 9th Bn., Royal Warwickshire Regiment. Killed in action, 21st April, 1916. Born Birmingham. Resided 149, Villers Street previously Sutton Street, Holloway Head, Birmingham. Memorial Ref. Panel 9. Basra Memorial, Iraq.

HUBBARD, Rifleman, Albert Edward Stanley. C/1581, 17th Bn., King's Royal Rifle Corps. Killed in action, 3rd September, 1916. Born Coventry. Enlisted Rugeley, Staffs. Grave Ref. E. 14. Knightsbridge Cemetery, Mesnil-Martinsart, France.

HUBBARD, Private, Ernest. 7527, 2nd Bn., South Lancashire Regiment. Killed in action, 20th September, 1914. Born Leamington, Warwick. Enlisted Coventry. Resided Leamington. Memorial Ref. La Ferte Sous Jouarre Memorial, France.

HUBBARD, Corporal, Herbert. 2447, 1/7th Bn., Royal Warwickshire Regiment. Killed in action, 28th June, 1916. Age 21. Son of George and Elizabeth Hubbard of Cambridge Cottage, Necton, Swaffham, Norfolk. Born Neeton, Norfolk. Enlisted Coventry. Grave Ref. I. E. 3. Hebuterne Military Cemetery, France.

HUBBARD, Private, Lawrence George. 266018, 2/6th Bn., Royal Warwickshire Regiment. Killed in action, Artres, 2nd November, 1918. Born 28th September, 1897 at Stoke, Coventry. Enlisted November, 1914 at Coventry. Resided 94, King Edward Road. Examiner. Grave Ref. III. D. 25. Valenciennes (St. Roch) Communal Cemetery, France.

HUBY, Private, William Frederick Hacket. 202201, 7th Bn., Royal Warwickshire Regiment. Died home, 7th October, 1918. Age 27. Son of William and Pauline Huby. Born Derby. Resided Bretford. Clerk employed by Coventry Ordnance Works. Enlisted May, 1916 at Coventry. Grave Ref. O. U. 571. Leicester (Welford Road) Cemetery.

HUDSON, C. Employed by Rover Company Ltd.

HUDSON, Private, James Edward. 242093, 1/6th Bn., Royal Warwickshire Regiment. Killed in action, 27th August, 1917. Born Accrington. Enlisted Coventry. Resided at 175, Leicester Causeway. Memorial Ref. Panel 23 to 28 and 163A. Tyne Cot Cemetery, Belgium.

HUDSON, Private, William. 205778, C Bn., Tank Corps formerly 2619, Machine Gun Corps. Killed in action, 22nd August, 1917. Born Birmingham. Enlisted Coventry. Grave Ref XV. C. 17. New Irish Farm Cemetery, Belgium.

HUGGINS, Stanley. Name on Roll of Honour in Cathedral Church of St. Michael's.

HUGHES, Private, Edward. 15656, 11th Bn., Royal Warwickshire Regiment. Killed in action, 16th July, 1916. Age 31. Son of Evan and Elizabeth Hughes, of Wernlas, Llangedwyn, Oswestry, Salop. Resided Coventry. Track labourer. Employed Coventry Corporation Tramways Department. Enlisted Coventry. Commemorated Transport Department Memorial, Coventry Corporation. Memorial Ref. Pier and Face 9 A 9 B and 10 B. Thiepval Memorial, Somme, France.

HUGHES, Lance Sergeant, Geoffrey Leonard. 6465, 24th Bn., Royal Fusiliers. Killed in action, 13th November, 1916. Son of Mr. W. H. Hughes, of Clarendon Hotel, Leamington Spa. Born 9th June, 1894 at Stourbridge. Resided Leamington. Educated Repton School. Solicitors articled clerk. Grave Ref. C. 29. Munich Trench British Cemetery, Beaumont-Hamel, France.

HUGHES, Private, John Thomas. 21391, Gloucestershire Regiment. Died, home, 7th March, 1927. Age 39. Grave Ref. 239. 206. Coventry (London Road) Cemetery.

HUGHES, Private, Josiah. 12907, 6th Bn., Oxfordshire and Buckinghamshire Light Infantry. Died of wounds, 9th October, 1916. Born Foleshill. Resided Longford. Commemorated Saint Thomas the Apostle, Longford. Memorial Ref. Pier and Face 10 A and 10 D. Thiepval Memorial, Somme, France.

HUGHES, Private, Leonard. 17195, 10th Bn., Worcestershire Regiment. Died, France, whilst prisoner of war, 29th August, 1918. Age 25. Son of William and Mary Hughes, of 14, Brunswick Road, Coventry. Born Coventry. Enlisted Nuneaton. Resided Coventry. Grave Ref. II. I. 5. Vendresse British Cemetery, Aisne, France.

HUGHES, Private, Thomas William. 4244, 1/7th Bn., Royal Warwickshire Regiment. Died of wounds, 1st April, 1916. Age 28. Born 1888. Resided Foleshill. Enlisted Coventry. Grave Ref. I. C. 36. Louvencourt Military Cemetery, France.

HUGHES, Stoker 1st Class, William. SS/115891, HMS Southampton, Royal Navy. 20th January, 1919. Age 23. Son of J. T. and L. Hughes, of 4, Swan Street, Coventry. (In the same grave is buried Pte. John Thomas Hughes, 21391, Gloucestershire Regiment. 7th March, 1927. Age 39). Grave Ref. 239. 206. Coventry (London Road) Cemetery.

HUGHES, Sergeant, William Arthur. 3761, 2nd Dragoon Guards (Queen's Bays). Killed in action, Ypres, 13th May, 1915. In Memoriam, sister and brother, Coventry Graphic. Born Stoke on Trent. Enlisted Birmingham. Resided Leamington. Memorial Ref. Panel 3. Ypres (Menin Gate) Memorial, Belgium.

HULL, Sergeant, George. 3066, 1st Bn., Royal Warwickshire Regiment. Killed in action, 12th October, 1916. Age 27. Son of Thomas and Elizabeth Hull of 45, Lowell Street, Worcester. Born Worcester. Enlisted Coventry. Memorial Ref. Pier and Face 9A 9B and 10B. Thiepval Memorial, France.

HUMBER, Private, George James. 17141, 2nd Bn., Hampshire Regiment formerly 13066, Oxfordshire and Buckinghamshire Light Infantry. Killed in action, Gallipoli, 6th August, 1915. Born King's Heath, Warwick. Enlisted Coventry. Resided Shirley, Warwick. Memorial Ref. Panel 125 – 134. Helles Memorial, Turkey.

HUMPAGE, Private, Arthur. 2103, 1/7th Bn., Royal Warwickshire Regiment. Killed in action, 17th February, 1916. Age 26. Son of Edward and Annie Humpage of 26, Prince Albert Street, Dudley. Born Dudley, Staffs. Enlisted Coventry. Grave Ref. I. D. 19. Foncquevillers Military Cemetery, France.

HUMPHREYS, Private, Bert William. 4559, B Coy, 13th Bn., Royal Warwickshire Regiment. Died, home, 13th August, 1915. Age 18. Son of John Thomas and Mary Humphreys, of 151, North Street, Stoke. Enlisted August, 1914. Born 1897, St. Mary's, Wolverhampton. Employed Triumph Cycle Company Ltd. Enlisted Warwick. Grave Ref. 1st Ext. 18. 7. Stoke (St. Michael) Churchyard.

HUMPHREYS, Cyril. Killed in action. Name on Roll of Honour in Holy Trinity Church. Commemorated Holy Trinity Panels.

HUMPHREYS, Private, Harold. 22779, 2/6th Bn., Royal Warwickshire Regiment. Died of wounds, 22nd March, 1918. Born Brighton, Sussex. Enlisted Coventry. Commemorated Triumph & Gloria Memorial. Memorial Ref. Panel 18 and 19. Pozieres Memorial, France.

HUMPHRISS, Gunner, William Thomas. 18334, 6 T. M. Bty., Royal Garrison Artillery. Killed in action, Arras, 4th March, 1916. Age 29. Husband of Norah Turrell (formerly Humphriss), of 65, Pickard Street, Emscote, Warwick. Born 23rd December, 1886 at Leamington. Resided Coventry. Tram Driver. Reservist. Enlisted Coventry. Commemorated Transport Department Memorial, Coventry Corporation. Memorial Ref. Bay 1. Arras Memorial, France.

HUNT, Lance Corporal, Alfred James. 15633, 2nd Bn., Coldstream Guards. Killed in action, 16th September, 1916. Born Herringswell, Suffolk. Enlisted Coventry. Resided Cinderhill, Notts. Grave Ref. VIII. P. 9. Guards Cemetery, Lesboeufs, France.

HUNT, Private, Charles Edward. 268095, 2/7th Bn., Royal Warwickshire Regiment. Killed in action, 24th March, 1918. Age 35. Son of James and Emily Hunt, of 32, Avenue Road, Staines, Middx. Born Staines, Middlesex. Resided Coventry. Stereotyper. Enlisted 1916 at Coventry. Commemorated Iliffe and Sons Ltd Memorial. Memorial Ref. Panel 18 and 19. Pozieres Memorial, France.

HUNT, Pioneer, Charles Wesley. 322064, No. 4. Signal Sect., 19th Div., Signal Coy., Royal Engineers. Killed in action, 25th August, 1918. Age 25. Son of Charles William and Esther Ann Hunt. Husband of Mrs. L. Hunt of the Post Office, Barford. Born Barford, Warwickshire. Enlisted Coventry. Resided Fairford Glos. Grave Ref. E. 14. Le Vertannoy British Cemetery, Hinges, France.

HUNT, Private, Francis William. 266873, 1/7th Bn., Royal Warwickshire Regiment. Killed in action, 28th August, 1917. Enlisted Coventry. Memorial Ref. Panel 23 to 28 and 163A. Tyne Cot Memorial, Belgium.

HUNT, Private, Frederick George. 50699, 2nd Bn., Royal Berkshire Regiment formerly 26908, Royal Warwickshire Regiment. Died of wounds, 11th June, 1918. Age 18. Brother of Miss Dora Hunt, of 14, Hill Cross, Coventry. Born Marden, Kent. Enlisted Coventry. Memorial Ref. Soissons Memorial, Aisne, France.

HUNT, G. Employed by Rover Company Ltd. Killed in action.

HUNT, Private, Stanley, MM. 201464, Tank Corps formerly 38008, Machine Gun Corps. Died, Home, 30th November, 1918. Born Bath, Somerset. Enlisted Coventry. Grave Ref. Church R. 23. 18. Ford Park Cemetery, Plymouth.

HUNT, Sergeant, William George. 1571, 1/7th Bn., Royal Warwickshire Regiment. Killed in action, Battle of the Somme, 14th July, 1916. Born 22nd August, 1893 at Kettering. Resided at 17, The Butts. Engine Fitter. Enlisted Coventry. Memorial Ref. Pier and Face 9 A 9 B and 10 B. Thiepval Memorial, Somme, France.

HUNTER, Sergeant, Herbert Douglas. G/17094, A Coy., 13th Bn., Royal Sussex Regiment. Killed in action, 26th April, 1918. Age 32. Brother of William A. Hunter of 122, Clarendon Street, Leicester. Born Leicester. Enlisted Coventry. Memorial Ref. Panel 86 to 88. Tyne Cot Memorial, Belgium.

HURDLEY, Private, George Harold. 268853, 1/7th Bn., Royal Warwickshire Regiment. Killed in action, 4th October, 1917. Age 23. Son of George and Clara Hurdley of 27, Church Street, Broseley, Salop. Born Broseley, Salop. Enlisted Coventry. Memorial Ref. Panel 23 to 28 and 163A. Tyne Cot Memorial, Belgium.

HURLEY, Gunner, Claude Theodore. 202180, 463rd Bty. 179th Bde., Royal Field Artillery formerly 82218, Royal Garrison Artillery. Killed in action, Ypres, 17th August, 1917. Age 37. Son of Walter and Clara Hurley. Husband of Amie Edith Hurley, of 48, Arden Street, Earlsdon, Coventry. Born 6th January, 1884 at Leytonstone. Enlisted May, 1916 at Coventry. Clerk. Grave Ref. I. M. 4. Aix-Noulette Communal Cemetery Extension, Pas de Calais, France.

HURLOCK, Rifleman, Bertram Thomas. R/34004, 16th Bn., King's Royal Rifle Corps formerly TR/13/839, 16th T.R. Bn. Died, 26th December, 1916. Age 30. Son of Thomas and May Hurlock, of 4, Smith Street, Coventry. Born 1886 at Camberwell, Surrey. Enlisted Stepney. Resided Coventry. Grave Ref. O. III. B. 4. St. Sever Cemetery Extension, Rouen, Seine-Maritime, France.

HURST, Private, James Peter. 9925, 2nd Bn., Oxfordshire and Buckinghamshire Light Infantry. Killed in action, Festubert, 16th May, 1915. Born 1893 at Birmingham. Resided 48 Queen Mary's Road, Coventry. Moulder. Enlisted 1914. Memorial Ref. Panel 26. Le Touret Memorial, France.

HUSSELBY, Cadet, Thomas Law. 184427, Royal Air Force. Died, home, 30th October, 1918. Age 18. Son of T. L. and A. Husselby, of 52, Sir Thomas White's Road, Coventry. Born November, 1900 at Coventry. Clerk. Enlisted September, 1918. Grave Ref. 26. 139. Coventry (London Road) Cemetery.

HUTCHINGS, Private, Leslie. 3175, 1/7th Bn., Royal Warwickshire Regiment. Killed in action, 25th June, 1915. Resided in Paradise Street. Enlisted October, 1914 at Coventry. Grave Ref. II. F. 3. Rifle House Cemetery, Belgium.

HUTCHINSON, W. J. Northumberland Fusiliers. Railway Labourer, Coventry Station. Enlisted August, 1914.

HUTT, Private, Alfred. 25029, 2nd Bn., Dorsetshire Regiment. trans to (436795), Labour Corps. Died, home, 27th November, 1918. Age 27. Son of Samuel and Jane Hutt, of Coventry. Husband of Priscilla Elkington (formerly Hutt), of 20, Howard Street, Coventry. Born 13th January, 1891 in New Buildings. Fitter. Grave Ref. 199. 152. Coventry (London Road) Cemetery.

HUTT, Private, Bertie. 330755, 2/7th Bn., Royal Warwickshire Regiment. Died of wounds, 25th December, 1917. Born 11th November, 1893 at Coventry. Resided 2c. 5h. Gulson Road, Coventry. Polisher, Messrs Calcotts. Enlisted August, 1914 at Coventry. Brother of Corporal Arthur Hutt, VC. Leaves a widow and two children. Grave Ref. P. V. H. 6A. St. Sever Cemetery Extension, Rouen, France.

HUTT, Private, Herbert Henry. 5375, Worcestershire Regiment. Died, home, 28th July, 1916. Born Coventry. Enlisted Birmingham. Resided Birmingham. Grave Ref. B. 20049. Birmingham (Yardley) Cemetery.

HUTTON, Sergeant, William. 34156, 15th Bn., Royal Warwickshire Regiment formerly 16023, Lancers. Killed in action, 27th September, 1918. Born Lynn, Mass., USA. Enlisted Rugby. Resided Coventry. Grave Ref. VII. E. 8. Gouzeaucourt New British Cemetery, France.

HUXHAM, Gunner, Ernest Cyril. 118915, Royal Field Artillery. Died, Belgaum, India, 22nd May, 1919. Age 24. Son of Samuel S. and Emma S. Huxham, of 41, Cambridge Street, Coventry. Born 1st April, 1898 in Victoria Australia. Capstan hand. Enlisted November, 1915. Memorial Ref. Face 1. Kirkee 1914-1918 Memorial, India.

HYDE, Private, Edward. 11619, 9th Bn., Royal Warwickshire Regiment. Killed in action, Mesopotamia, 5th April, 1916. Age 25. Son of John and Mary Hyde of 7, Cottage Row, Daybrook, Nottingham. Born Bulwell, Notts. Enlisted Coventry. Resided Daybrook, Notts. Memorial Ref. Panel 9. Basra Memorial, Iraq.

HYDE, Driver, Ronald Vernon. 845221, 144th Trench Mortar Bty., Royal Field Artillery. attd. 48th Divisional Ammunition Col., Died of wounds, 19th June, 1918. Age 26. Son of Thomas and Elizabeth Hyde, of Coventry. Born 4th October, 1891 at Banbury. Enlisted November, 1914 at Leamington. Resided 49, Waveley Road. Textile manufacturer's assistant. Commemorated Central Methodist Hall. Grave Ref. 4. C. 8. Montecchio Precalcino Communal Cemetery Extension, Italy.

HYDE, Second Lieutenant, Herbert William. Royal Sussex Regiment attached 2nd Bn., Royal Inniskilling Fusiliers. Killed in action, 17th May, 1915. Educated Bablake School. Commemorated Bablake School Memorial. Memorial Ref. Le Touret Memorial, France.

ILIFFE, Private, Cecil Arthur Mountford, BA. 10612, 9th Bn., Royal Fusiliers. Died of wounds, Battle of the Somme, 13th August, 1916. Age 32. Son of Thomas Alfred Soden Iliffe and Emilie Iliffe. Bachelor of Arts, Emmanuel College, Cambridge. Born 31st January, 1888 at Ryton on Dunsmore. Resided at The Elms, Stoke Row. Student at College. Enlisted March, 1916. Commemorated Stoke (St. Michaels) Memorial. Grave Ref. I. F. 79. Puchevillers British Cemetery, France.

IMBER, Second Lieutenant, William Arthur. 7th Bn., Royal Warwickshire Regiment. Killed in action, near St. Julien, Belgium, 27th August, 1917. Shot by a sniper. Age 23. Only son of William and Hannah Imber, of "Astbury," 43, Spencer Avenue, Coventry. Born 6th July 1894 at Coventry. Resided at Coventry. Bankers Clerk, Barclays Bank Ltd. Enlisted 2nd December, 1914. Educated Bablake School. Commemorated Bablake School Memorial and War Memorial Park. Memorial Ref. Panel 23 to 28 and 163A. Tyne Cot Memorial, Zonnebeke, West-Vlaanderen, Belgium.

IMISSON, Lance Corporal, William. 265151, 1/7th Bn., Sherwood Foresters. Killed in action, Battle of the Somme, 1st July, 1916. Born 14th January, 1896 at Cleethorpes. Resided Coventry. Machinist. Enlisted August, 1914. Memorial Ref. Pier and Face 10 C 10 D and 11 A. Thiepval Memorial, Somme, France.

INGERSON, Private, Philip John. 53200, 2nd Bn., Royal Fusiliers formerly S/4/173592, Royal Army Service Corps. Killed in action, 14th April, 1917. Born Barnstaple. Enlisted Coventry. Grave Ref. I. A. 11. Heninel-Croisilles Road Cemetery, France.

INGLEDON, Lance Sergeant, Albert. 9142, 1st Bn., Border Regiment. Killed in action, Gallipoli, 8th May, 1915. Age 30. Son of James and Mary Ingledon. Born Plymouth, Devon. Enlisted Coventry. Resided Chelston, Devon. Memorial Ref. Panel 119 to 125 or 222 and 223. Helles Memorial, Turkey.

INGLES, Private, Richard Ernest. 42898, 1/8th Bn., Royal Warwickshire Regiment. Killed in action, 25th October, 1918. Born Studley, Warwicks. Enlisted Coventry. Resided Studley. Grave Ref. B. 16. Pommereuil British Cemetery, France.

INGLEY, Air Mechanic, Joseph. Royal Air Force. Died, home, 6th December, 1923. Enlisted September, 1914. Fettler. Grave Ref. Coventry (London Road) Cemetery.

INGRAM, Gunner, Ernest Arthur. 362, Royal Field Artillery. Died of sickness, home, 17th November, 1914. Age 19. Son of John Ernest Ingram, of 219, Stoney Stanton Road, Coventry. Born 3rd March, 1895 at Coventry. Resided 123, George Street. Turner. Enlisted August, 1914 at Coventry. Grave Ref. 72. 82. Coventry (London Road) Cemetery.

INGRAM, Private, Leonard. 266513, 15th Bn., Royal Warwickshire Regiment. Died of wounds, 29th May, 1918. Born Rugby. Enlisted Coventry. Resided New Bilton, Warwicks. Grave Ref. II. K. 34. Aire Communal Cemetery, France.

INGRAM, Private, Percy Walter Frederick., 4449, 2nd Bn., Royal Warwickshire Regiment. Killed in action, 21st March, 1916. Age 20. Only son of Walter and Edith Ingram, of Withybrook, Coventry. Grave Ref. D. 16. Point 110 New Military Cemetery, Fricourt, Somme, France.

INSALL, Private, Samuel Henry. 8450, 2nd Bn., Oxfordshire and Buckinghamshire Light Infantry. Killed in action, Festubert, 6th April, 1915. Born Kenilworth. Enlisted Coventry. Resided Kenilworth. Grave Ref. III. F. 4. Brown's Road Military Cemetery, Festubert, France.

IRELAND, Private, C. M. Killed in action, France, 1917. Born 1881. Resided 9, Gas Street.

IRELAND, Private, Edward. 266604, 1/7th Bn., Royal Warwickshire Regiment. Killed in action, 13th August, 1917. Born Coventry. Enlisted Coventry. Memorial Ref. Panel 8. Ypres (Menin Gate) Memorial, Belgium.

IRELAND, Sergeant, Robert. 9967, 1st Bn., Royal Munster Fusiliers formerly 6931, Royal Dublin Fusiliers. Killed in action, Gallipoli, 12th May, 1915 during the night a dug out fell in. Age 35. Husband of Nellie E. Ireland, of 49, Beechwood Road, Litherland, Liverpool. Born Dublin. Enlisted Nass, Co. Kildare. Resided Dublin. Left Coventry, 14th March, 1915. Grave Ref. Sp. Mem. C. 82. Twelve Tree Copse Cemetery, Turkey.

IRESON, Private, Alfred. 20482, 7th Bn., Royal Sussex Regiment. Died, whilst prisoner of war, German Hands, 1st December, 1917. Born Headless Cross, Worcs. Resided 36, Huntingdon Road. Enlisted Coventry. Grave Ref. V. E. 2. Le Cateau Military Cemetery, France.

ISON, Lance Bombardier, Alfred James. 1249, "A" Bty. 79th Bde., Royal Field Artillery. Killed in action, 2nd July, 1918. Age 25. Son of Mr. and Mrs. T. Ison, of 168, Station Street East, Coventry. Born 20th March, 1893 at Coventry. Resided Bristol. Metal Brazier. Enlisted September, 1914 at Bristol. Grave Ref. III. D. 44. Daours Communal Cemetery Extension, Somme, France.

ISON, Corporal, Arthur Ernest. 11230, 2nd Bn., Oxfordshire and Buckinghamshire Light Infantry. Killed in action, Givenchy, France, 27th August, 1915 by a bomb. Age 20. Son of Joseph Albert and Isabella Ison, of 54, Mount St., Allesley Old Road, Coventry. Born 9th August 1895 at Battersea. Resided at 54, Mount Street. Engineer. Enlisted September, 1914. Commemorated British Thompson Houston Memorial and War Memorial Park. Grave Ref. II. C. 10. Guards Cemetery, Windy Corner, Cuinchy, Pas de Calais, France.

ISON, Private, Francis Joseph. 43083, 5th Bn., Royal Berkshire Regiment. Killed in action, Epehy, 27th September, 1918. Age 19. Son of Joseph Albert and Isabella Ison, of 64, Fisher Road, Coventry. Born 17th July 1898 at Wimbledon, Surrey. Resided at 54 Mount Street. Clerk. Enlisted Warwick, April 1918. Grave Ref. VI. E. 14. Villers Hill British Cemetery, Villers-Guislain, Nord, France.

ISON, Private, John William. 267964, 2nd /7th Bn., Royal Warwickshire Regiment attd. to 182nd Light Trench Mortar Bty. Died of wounds, casualty clearing station 17th April, 1917. Age 18. Son of John and Elizabeth Ison, of 26, Albert Street, Hill Fields, Coventry. Born 15th July, 1898 at 22, Bradford Street. Resided 26, Albert Street. Machinist, Sparkbrook Manufacturing Co., Coventry. Enlisted May, 1916 at Coventry. Grave Ref. I. C. 13. Cayeux Military Cemetery, Somme, France.

IZON, Captain, Edgar Godfrey. 14th Bn., Royal Warwickshire Regiment. Killed in action, 27th September, 1918. Age 27. Son of William and Mary Woollaston Izon, of "Hillside," Meriden, Coventry. Enlisted in 2nd Bn. Royal Warwickshire Regiment, 1907. Grave Ref. I. R. 7. Achiet-Le-Grand Communal Cemetery Extension, Pas de Calais, France.

JACKMAN, Lance Corporal, George. 17815, 14th Bn., Royal Warwickshire Regiment. Killed in action, 12th April, 1918. Age 26. Son of Walter Charles and Eliza Jackman, of Coventry. Born 3rd August, 1894 at 97, King William Street, Coventry. Resided 267, Swan Lane. Turret hand. Enlisted. February, 1916 at Coventry. Memorial Ref. Panel 2 and 3. Ploegsteert Memorial, Comines-Warneton, Hainaut, Belgium.

JACKMAN, Private, Sidney. 29206, 8th Bn., East Surrey Regiment. Died of wounds, 20th May, 1918. Age 19. Son of Walter Charles and Eliza Jackman, of 267, Swan Lane, Coventry. Born 14th March, 1899 at 18, Adderley Street, Coventry. Enlisted July, 1917 at Warwick. Miller, in his father's coal business. Grave Ref. I. D. 20. Pernois British Cemetery, Halloy-Les-Pernois, Somme, France.

JACKSON, Private, Albert. 19702, 6th Bn., Oxfordshire and Buckinghamshire Light Infantry. Killed in action, by a shell, Battle of the Somme, 9th October, 1916. Born 19th February, 1881 in Upper Well Street, Coventry. Resided at 1c. 9h. Burges. Polisher, Rudge Whitworth. Enlisted September, 1915 at Coventry. Leaves a widow and five children. Memorial Ref. Pier and Face 10A and 10D. Thiepval Memorial, Somme, France.

JACKSON, Private, Albert Ernest. 17668, 14th Bn., Royal Warwickshire Regiment. Killed in action, 11th November, 1917. Age 20. Son of Albert Edward and C. Jackson, of 69, Whitefriars Street, Coventry. Born 26th January, 1896 in Gosford Street, Coventry. Brazier. Enlisted March, 1916 at Coventry. Memorial Ref. Panel 23 to 28 and 163A. Tyne Cot Memorial, Zonnebeke, West-Vlaanderen, Belgium.

JACKSON, Lance Corporal, Benjamin. 3/8441, 1st Bn., Dorsetshire Regiment formerly 14131, Somerset Light Infantry. Killed in action, (gassed), 3rd May, 1915. Born Walsgrave-on-Sowe. Enlisted Mountain Ash, Glamorgan. Resided Coventry. Brother of Mrs. E. Wright of 68, Smithford Street. Grave Ref. 42. Reninghelst Churchyard Extension, Belgium.

JACKSON, Private, Ernest Alfred. 241619, 1st /6th Bn., Royal Warwickshire Regiment. Killed in action, 27th August, 1917. Age 34. Son of William Jackson, of 96, Spon End, Coventry. Born May, 1890 at 96, Spon End, Coventry. Enlisted Coventry. Resided Bradford Street. Light Porter. Memorial Ref. Panel 23 to 28 and 163A. Tyne Cot Memorial, Zonnebeke, West-Vlaanderen, Belgium.

JACKSON, Private, George. 37226, 1/8th Bn., Royal Warwickshire Regiment. Killed in action, Landrecies, 4th November, 1918. Age 23. Son of William and Emma Jackson. Husband of Ada F. Jackson, of 99, Hurst Road, Longford, Coventry. Born 16th February, 1887 at Longford. Resided Longford. Gear Cutter. Enlisted June, 1918. Commemorated Saint Thomas the Apostle, Longford and Roll of Honour, Salem Baptist Church. Grave Ref. B. 39. Landrecies British Cemetery, France.

JACKSON, Captain, Harold. 41st Sqdn., Royal Flying Corps. and, General List. Killed in action, Messines, 7th June, 1917. Sustained a direct hit from a high explosive with his foot blown off and his left arm practically severed managed to land. Age 21. Brother of Mr. F. H. Jackson, of "Fairhaven," Palmerston Road, Coventry. Born in 1897, at Stoke Green. Resided at Coventry. Apprentice Engineering. Enlisted in 1915. Commemorated Stoke (St. Michaels) Memorial and War Memorial Park. Grave Ref. I. K. 31. Chester Farm Cemetery, Ieper, West-Vlaanderen, Belgium.

JACKSON, Corporal, John. 9405, B Coy. 2nd Bn., Lancashire Fusiliers. Killed in action, shot in the head, Ypres, 29th June, 1915. Age 31. Son of Joshua and Sarah Jackson, of Ratley, Banbury. Husband of Florence Jackson, of 68, Harnall Lane East, Coventry. Born 26th December, 1883 at Ratley, near Banbury. Resided at 68, Harnall Lane East. Accumulator Work. Reservist. Commemorated War Memorial Park. Leaves a widow and one child. Grave Ref. VI. C. 24. Bard Cottage Cemetery, Ieper, West-Vlaanderen, Belgium.

JACKSON, Private, Joseph. 6821, 1st Bn., Northamptonshire Regiment. Killed in action 13th October, 1915. Age 32. Son of Enoch and Lucy Jackson, of Coventry. Husband of Jessie Alice Jackson, of 2, Walker's Buildings, Anstey Road, Alton, Hants. Born Coventry. Enlisted Coventry. Employed Brett's Stamping Works. Reservist. Memorial Ref. Panel 91 to 93. Loos Memorial, Pas de Calais, France.

JACKSON, Private, Lawrence, 515434, 14th Bn., London Regiment (London Scottish) formerly 203559, 5th Bn., Royal Warwickshire Regiment. Killed in action, 25th September, 1917. Age 27. Son of Edward and Ann Jackson, of Coventry. Husband of Phoebe Allen (formerly Jackson), of 67, Butts, Coventry. Born 19th December, 1890 at Coventry. Resided at 28, Broad Street. Clerk. Enlisted Coventry, March, 1917. Commemorated Iliffe & Sons Ltd Memorial and War Memorial Park. Grave Ref. III. F. 85. Anneux British Cemetery, Nord, France.

JACKSON, Private, Thomas Percy, MM. 24869, 16th Bn., Royal Warwickshire Regiment. Died of wounds, 8th September, 1918. Age 32. Son of Henry Ainsworth Jackson and Harriett Jackson, of 112, Earlsdon Avenue North, Coventry. Born 2nd December 1885 at Coventry. Resided at 47 Huntingdon Road. Journalist. Enlisted June 1917. Gazetted for Military Medal, 7th February, 1919. Commemorated War Memorial Park. Grave Ref. VI. F. 25. Bagneux British Cemetery, Gezaincourt, Somme, France.

JACKSON, Private, William. 24279, 10th Bn., Royal Warwickshire Regiment. Killed in action, 19th April, 1918. Born Coventry. Enlisted Coventry. Memorial Ref. Panel 23 to 28 and 163A. Tyne Cot Memorial, Zonnebeke, West-Vlaanderen, Belgium.

JACQUES, Private, Harry. PO/1159(S), 190th Bde. Machine Gun Coy. Royal Naval Division, Royal Marine Light Infantry. Killed in action at Battle of the Ancre, 13th November, 1916. Age 20. Son of Mr. and Mrs. W. H. Jacques, of "Partridge Croft," Bell Green Road, Foleshill, Coventry. Born 1st January, 1896 at Foleshill. Carpenter. Enlisted November, 1915. Carpenter, Mr. Grey. Grave Ref. IV. E. 53. Ancre British Cemetery, Beaumont-Hamel, Somme, France.

JACQUES, Private, William. 240886, 2/1st Bn., Oxfordshire and Buckinghamshire Light Infantry formerly 6776, Norfolk Regiment. Killed in action, 22nd August, 1917. Son of William Jacques. Husband of Betsy Jacques of 10, Spencer Street, St. Albans. Born Bedworth. Resided Bedworth. Enlisted Coventry. Memorial Ref. Panel 96 to 98. Tyne Cot Memorial, Belgium.

JAGGER, Midshipman, Oliver Robin Octavius. HMS Bulwark, Royal Navy. Killed by internal explosion of vessel, off Sheerness, 26th November, 1914. Age 16. Son of A. E. and S. L. Jagger, of Coundon, Coventry. Commemorated St. Thomas Memorial. Memorial Ref. 1. Portsmouth Naval Memorial, Hampshire.

JAMES, Private, Albert. 201738, 15th Bn., Royal Warwickshire Regiment. Killed in action, by a shell, 26th October, 1917. Age 20. Brother of Mr. L. James, of 8, Russell Street, Coventry. Born 6th March, 1897 at Wollaston, Northants. Resided at 215, Swan Lane. Employed Triumph Cycle Company Ltd. Commemorated Triumph & Gloria Memorial and Queens Road Church Memorial. Enlisted April, 1916. Memorial Ref. Panel 23 to 28 and 163A. Tyne Cot Memorial, Zonnebeke, West-Vlaanderen, Belgium. (Possibly buried Polderhoek, near Gheluvelt).

JAMES, Lance Corporal, Alfred. 2329, A Coy., 1/7th Bn., Royal Warwickshire Regiment. Died of wounds, 4th December, 1915. Age 28. Son of Alfred and Adelaide James, of 455, Hedon Road, Hull. Born 23rd August, 1887 at Woodhouse, Yorks. Resided 41, Hill Street. Storekeeper. Enlisted August, 1914. Grave Ref. 315. 92. Hull (Hedon Road) Cemetery.

JAMES, Gunner, Charles Alfred. 110136, 275th Siege Battery, Royal Garrison Artillery. Killed in action, Ypres, 29th September 1917. Age 29. Son of Samuel and Hannah James, of Coventry. Husband of Lily James of 18 Caludon Road, Stoke, Coventry. Born 8th March 1888, at Coventry. Resided at 18, Caludon Road. Insurance agent. Enlisted Coventry, August, 1916. Commemorated War Memorial Park. Grave Ref. Plot VIII. Row C. Grave 10. Huts Cemetery, Dickebusch, Belgium.

JAMES, Lance Corporal, Edgar William. 2135, 2/8th Bn., Worcestershire Regiment. Killed in action, 15th August, 1916. Son of Fanny James, of 39, Stourbridge Road, Bromsgrove, Worcs. Born Bromsgrove. Employed Coventry. Grave Ref. III. C. 34. Laventie Military Cemetery, La Gorgue, France.

JAMES, Bombardier, Harry, DCM. 29568, 32nd Bty. 33rd Bde., Royal Field Artillery. Killed in action, 6th February, 1915. Born 27th May, 1882 at Hackney. Resided at 42, Stanley Street. Employed Daimler Company Ltd. Enlisted August, 1914. Awarded the Russian Medal of St. George, 2nd Class in recognition of his gallant conduct in the field also awarded the Distinguished Conduct Medal for keeping open communication between trenches and his battery for two months, and especially laying wire along the trenches under fire on January 25th, 1915. Grave Ref. II. F. 29. Rue-Des-Berceaux Military Cemetery, Richebourg-L'avoue, France.

JAMES, Sergeant, John. 266468, 2/5th Bn., Royal Warwickshire Regiment. Killed in action, 3rd December, 1917. Born 17th February, 1892 in Northamptonshire. Resided 6, Highland Road. Police Constable. Enlisted May, 1915. Commemorated Police Force Memorial, Coventry Corporation. Memorial Ref. Panel 3. Cambrai Memorial, Louverval, France.

JAMES, Private, John Henry. 40929, 10th Bn., Lincolnshire Regiment formerly 20267, South Staffordshire Regiment. Killed in action, 28th April, 1917. Age 31. Son of Walter and Clara James, of 6, Pearson Street, Wolverhampton. Husband of Mary Jane James, of 21, Lawyer's Field, Charles Street, Wolverhampton. Born Coventry. Enlisted Wolverhampton. Memorial Ref. Bay 3 and 4. Arras Memorial, France.

 **JAMES**, Private, Sidney Francis. 225265, 1st Bn., London Regiment (Royal Fusiliers) formerly 5595, Essex Regt. Killed in action, Ypres, 31st July, 1917. Age 28. Brother of John James, of 24, Aylesford Street, Hillfields, Coventry. Born 16th June, 188 at Gosford Street, Coventry. Enlisted Coventry. Resided 50, Gilbert Street. Coventry. Miller, Auto Co., Hood Street, Coventry. Memorial Ref. Panel 52. Ypres (Menin Gate) Memorial, Ieper, West-Vlaanderen, Belgium. (Possibly buried Zonnebeke Wood, Ypres).

JANE, A. Royal Warwickshire Regiment. Commemorated British Thompson Houston Memorial.

JANE, Sergeant, William Joseph. 38139, 5th Bty., Royal Field Artillery. Died of wounds, 27th August, 1917. Age 30. Husband of Catherine McNamara (formerly Jane) of Kielley Cottage, Thomondgate, Limerick. Born Brighton. Enlisted Brighton. Commemorated Iliffe & Sons Ltd. Grave Ref. Scadden's. 8. 36. Portsmouth (Kingston) Cemetery.

 **JARRETT**, Major, Charles Harry Brownlow. 1st Bn., Royal Munster Fusiliers. Killed in action, 25th April, 1915 at Sed-el-Bahr, Cape Helles. Age 40. Son of Col. H. S. Jarrett, C.I.E., and Mrs. Jarrett. Billeted Coventry. Born 26th November, 1874. Grave Ref. L. 4. Lancashire Landing Cemetery, Turkey.

JARVIS, Gunner. Royal Artillery. Killed in action, January, 1917. Resided Foleshill.

 **JEACOCK**, Gunner, Charles Ernest. 115871, "X"/31st Trench Mortar Bty., Royal Field Artillery. Died, appendicitis, Weymouth Hospital, 11th January, 1919. Age 22. Son of Alexander and Lillie Gertrude Jeacock, of 57, Stanley Road, Earlsdon, Coventry. Born 20th June, 1896 at Coventry. Butcher. Enlisted November, 1915. Commemorated St. Barbara's Memorial. Grave Ref. 178. 200. Coventry (London Road) Cemetery.

 **JEACOCK**, Sergeant, Royal Field Artillery. F. Died after recovering from being a prisoner in Germany.

JEFFCOAT, Gunner, John Arthur. 1191, "D" Bty. 307th Bde., Royal Field Artillery. Died of wounds, 11th July, 1916. Age 25. Son of Walter and Emily Jeffcoat, of 18, St. Mary's Road, Nuneaton. Enlisted Coventry. Resided Coventry. Grave Ref. V. B. 14. Merville Communal Cemetery, France.

JEFFERY, Private, Frank. 28656, 7th Bn., King's Shropshire Light Infantry formerly 8/11934, T. R. Bn. Killed in action, 2nd September, 1918. Born Northampton. Enlisted Coventry. Grave Ref. I. A. 16. Vraucourt Copse Cemetery, Vaulx-Vraucourt, France.

JEFFERY, Private, Frank. 9956, 14th Bn., Royal Warwickshire Regiment. Killed in action, 30th July, 1916. Born Bugbrooke, Northants. Enlisted Coventry. Resided Weedon, Northants. Memorial Ref. Pier and Face 9 A 9 B and 10 B. Thiepval Memorial, Somme, France.

JEFFREY, Private, Eardley Robert Preston. G/205098 7th Battalion, Royal Sussex Regiment formerly Royal Fusiliers. Killed in action, Cambrai, 30th November 1917. Born 18th October, 1889 at Bath. Resided in Spencer Avenue. Gas collector. Enlisted April, 1915. Commemorated War Memorial Park and Gas Department Memorial, Coventry Corporation. Memorial Ref. Panel 7. Cambrai Memorial, Louverval, France.

JEFFS, Private, Albert. 2626, 1st /7th Bn., Royal Warwickshire Regiment. Killed in action, 14th July 1916. Age 22. Son of Harry and Hannah Booton (formerly Jeffs), of 77, Newcombe Road, Coventry. Born 21st February, 1894 in St. Johns Parish. Resided at 6, Broomfield Terrace, Spon End, Coventry. Chain Examiner, Coventry Chain. Commemorated Coventry Chain Memorial and War Memorial Park. Enlisted Coventry, September 1914. Memorial Ref. Pier and Face 9 A 9 B and 10 B. Thiepval Memorial, Somme, France.

JEFFS, Corporal, Harry Edward. 45433, 87th Field Coy., Royal Engineers. Killed in action, 19th July, 1917 by a sniper. Age 26. Husband of Laura Jeffs, of 66, Butts, Coventry. Age 26. Born 14th September, 1890 at Coventry. Enlisted 3rd September, 1914 at Coventry. Parents resided 24, Peel Street. Planer, Ordnance Works. Memorial Ref. Bay 1. Arras Memorial, Pas de Calais, France.

JEFFS, Private, William Arthur. 6378, 1st Bn., Gordon Highlanders. Killed in action, 14th December, 1914. Age 16. Son of James William and Annie Florence Jeffs, of 100, Avon Street, Upper Stoke, Coventry. Born 30th March, 1898 at Birmingham. Resided 136, North Street. Collier. Enlisted September, 1914. Memorial Ref. Panel 38. Ypres (Menin Gate) Memorial, Ieper, West-Vlaanderen, Belgium.

JENKINS, Trooper, Frederick Alfred. 11th Hussars. Died home, 11th June, 1916. Born 22nd October, 1885 at Birmingham. Resided 7, Albert Street. Turner. Reservist. Grave Ref. Coventry (London Road) Cemetery.

JENKINS, Gunner, George Reginald. 353, 4th Bty., 4th Bde., Royal Field Artillery. Died of wounds, caused by accident, Hebuterne, 14th March, 1916. Age 20. Son of Alfred and Sarah Ann Jenkins, of 141, Hearsall Lane, Chapel Fields, Coventry. Born 15th May at Coventry. Resided at 46, Craven Street. Messrs. Hamilton, Sign writer. Enlisted Coventry, August, 1914. Commemorated Queens Road Memorial and War Memorial Park. Grave Ref. D. 17. Beauval Communal Cemetery, Somme, France.

JENKINS, Private, George William. 8558, 1st Bn., South Staffordshire Regiment. Killed in action, Ypres, 7th November, 1914. Age 25. Son of Joseph and Isabella Jenkins. Born Coventry. Enlisted Warwick. Resided Coventry. Born 6th April, 1891 at 405, Stoney Stanton Road. Resided, 21, Cobden Street. Soldier. Grave Ref. IX. A. 21. Perth Cemetery (China Wall), Belgium.

JENKINS, Private, Leonard. 16863, 10th Bn., Royal Warwickshire Regiment. Died of wounds, Battle of the Somme, 6th July, 1916. Age 24. Son of Joseph and Anne Jenkins, of 48, Heath Road, Stoke, Coventry, Warwickshire. Born 24th June, 1892 at Jordan Well, Coventry. Enlisted February, 1916 at Coventry. Cycle Mechanic, Challenge Motor and Cycle Co. Grave Ref. VIII. C. 99. Boulogne Eastern Cemetery, Pas de Calais, France.

JENKINSON, Stoker 1st Class, Ernest Percy. 309255, HMS Indefatigable, Royal Navy. Killed in action, Battle of Jutland, 31st May 1916. Age 28. Son of Mr. T. and Mrs. B. Jenkinson, of 32, Castle Street, Coventry. Husband of Mrs. A. M. Patchot (formerly Jenkinson), of 49, St. George's Avenue, Forest Gate, London. Born 28th December, 1887 in Cox Street. Resided 45, Castle Street. Polisher, Triumph Works prior to the Navy. Reservist. Memorial Ref. 17. Chatham Naval Memorial, Kent.

JENKINSON, Corporal, Thomas. 2795, 16th Bn., Royal Warwickshire Regiment. Killed in action, Ypres, 9th October, 1917. Age 36. Son of Thomas and Agnes Jenkinson, of 32, Castle Street, Coventry. Also served 8 years with Duke of Cornwall's Light Infantry. Born 1882 in Spon Street. Labourer. Enlisted August, 1914 at Coventry. Memorial Ref. Panel 23 to 28 and 163A. Tyne Cot Memorial, Zonnebeke, West-Vlaanderen, Belgium.

JENNINGS, Corporal, Thomas. 6414, 71st Coy., Machine Gun Corps formerly 12761, Royal Warwickshire Regiment. Killed in action, 15th September, 1916. Age 30. Husband of Catherine Jennings, of 8, Trenville Avenue, Fulham Road, Sparkhill, Birmingham. Born 4th April, 1886 at Aston. Resided 12, Ransom Road. Police Constable. Enlisted June, 1915 at Coventry. Commemorated Police Force Memorial, Coventry Corporation. Memorial Ref. Pier and Face 5 C and 12 C. Thiepval Memorial, Somme, France.

JENNINGS, Private, Thomas. 5980, 1/19th Bn., London Regiment formerly 18898, King's Royal Rifle Corps. Killed in action, 2nd October, 1916. Born West Ham. Enlisted Coventry. Resided Coventry. Memorial Ref. Pier and Face 9 D 9 C 13 C and 12 C. Thiepval Memorial, Somme, France.

JENNINGS, Private, Walter. 9427, 1st Bn., Royal Warwickshire Regiment. Killed in action, 1st July, 1916. Age 27. Son of Tom and Emma Jennings, of Station Road, Balsall Common, Coventry. Employed Coventry. Memorial Ref. Pier and Face 9 A 9 B and 10 B. Thiepval Memorial, Somme, France.

JENNINGS, Private, Walter. 4522, 1/7th Bn., Royal Warwickshire Regiment. Killed in action, 1st July, 1916. Age 19. Enlisted Coventry. Born Kidderminster. Memorial Ref. Pier and Face 9 A 9 B and 10 B. Thiepval Memorial, Somme, France.

JENNINGS, Private, William. 20274, No. 1 Works Co., Royal Berkshire Regiment. Died, home, 24th July, 1916. Son of Mr. E. Jennings, of 1, Wargrave Road, Henley-on-Thames. Grave Ref. 177. 170. Coventry (London Road) Cemetery.

JENSON, Private, William Walter. 16030, 9th Bn., Royal Warwickshire Regiment. Died, Mesopotamia 22nd September, 1918. Age 21. Son of Mr. and Mrs. William Ernest Jenson, of Coventry. Born 22nd October, 1896 at 40, Trafalgar Street, Coventry. Resided 5, Mount Street. Trimmer. Enlisted January, 1916 at Coventry. Commemorated St. John's Church and Queens Road Church Memorial. Memorial Ref. Panel 2. Column 2. Tehran Memorial, Iran. (Possibly buried Kazian).

JEPHCOTT, Private, John. 266263, 2/7th Bn., Royal Warwickshire Regiment. Killed in action, 19th July, 1916. Born Hillfields, Coventry. Enlisted Coventry. Memorial Ref. Panel 22 to 25. Loos Memorial, France.

JEPHCOTT, Private, Oliver. 425, 1st Bn., Royal Warwickshire Regiment. Killed in action, by a shell, 13th October, 1914. Born 6th January, 1890 in Grove Street. Resided Coventry. Labourer. Reservist. Enlisted Coventry. Grave Ref. III. L. 88. Buried near this spot. Meteren Military Cemetery, France.

JEROME, J. Commemorated St. Barbara's Memorial.

JERRIMS, F. W. Employed Rover Company Ltd. Killed in action.

JEWSBURY, Private, Joseph Vincent. 48911, 7th Bn., Leicestershire Regiment. Killed in action, 28th September, 1918. Age 19. Son of Arthur and Emily Ann Jewsbury, of 138, Gulson Road, Coventry. Born 15th September, 1899, at Measham, Leics. Resided at 138, Gulson Road. Miller. Enlisted April, 1918 at Coventry. Commemorated War Memorial Park. Grave Ref. VIII. E. 2. Gouzeaucourt New British Cemetery, Nord, France.

JOB, Private, Andrew. 15364, 11th Bn., Sherwood Foresters (Notts and Derby Regiment). Died, home, 29th January, 1915. Age 31. Husband of Clara Job, of 66, Brownlow Road, Mansfield. Born Coventry. Enlisted Mansfield. Resided Coventry. Grave Ref. C17462. Mansfield (Nottingham Road) Cemetery.

JOCELYN, Lance Sergeant, Ernest. 266351, 2/7th Bn., Royal Warwickshire Regiment. Killed in action, 19th July, 1916. Age 20. Son of Charles and C. E. Jocelyn, of 56, Tavistock Crescent, Westbourne Park, London. Born Kensington, London. Enlisted Coventry. Resided London. Memorial Ref. Panel 22 to 25. Loos Memorial, France

JOHNSON, Sergeant, Albert Joseph. 266341, 2/7th Bn., Royal Warwickshire Regiment. Killed in action, 17th September, 1916. Age 24. Son of Joseph and Agnes Johnson, of Bridgnorth, Salop. Born St. Leonards, Bridgnorth, Salop. Enlisted Coventry. Resided Bridgnorth. Grave Ref. VI. C. 4. Aubers Ridge British Cemetery, Aubers, France.

JOHNSON, Private, Arthur. 5379, 6th Dragoon Guards (Carabineers). Killed in action, Battle of Ypres, 1st November, 1914. Age 38. Son of Rosa and Henry Johnson. Husband of Kathleen Johnson, of 21, Maycock Road, Foleshill, Coventry. Born 2nd January 1877 at Coventry. Resided at Coventry. Enlisted Nuneaton. Watchmaker. Reservist. Commemorated War Memorial Park. Memorial Ref. Panel 5. Ypres (Menin Gate) Memorial, Ieper, West-Vlaanderen, Belgium.

JOHNSON, Lance Corporal, Charles. 10514, 2nd Bn., Royal Warwickshire Regiment. Killed in action, 25th September 1915. Age 32. Son of Samuel Edward and Emma Johnson. of Exhall Green, Exhall, Coventry. Born Exhall. Enlisted Coventry. Commemorated Exhall Memorial. Resided Exhall. Memorial Ref. Panel 22 to 25. Loos Memorial, Pas De Calais, France.

JOHNSON, Private, George Alfred. 10005, 10th Bn., Royal Warwickshire Regiment. Killed in action, 25th March, 1916. Age 35. Son of George and Hannah Johnson. Husband of Rose Florence Taylor (formerly Johnson), of 112, Price Street, Smethwick, Birmingham. Employed Rileys Ltd. Leaves widow and three children. Grave Ref. II. F. 16. Rue-Du-Bacquerot No.1 Military Cemetery, Laventie, France.

JOHNSON, Private, George Plant. 266637, 2/7th Bn., Royal Warwickshire Regiment. Killed in action, 5th December, 1917. Born 1879 at Birmingham. Resided 37, Grove Street. Painter's Labourer. Enlisted Coventry. Commemorated Transport Department Memorial, Coventry Corporation. Memorial Ref. Panel 3. Cambrai Memorial, Louverval, France.

JOHNSON, Private, Harry. 702250, 2/23rd Bn., London Regiment formerly 74186, Royal Army Medical Corps. Killed in action, 31st October, 1917. Age 24. Son of Thomas James and Sarah Ann Johnson, of 68, Croft Road, Nuneaton. Born Nuneaton. Enlisted Coventry. Resided Coventry. Grave Ref. J. 18. Beersheba War Cemetery, Israel.

JOHNSON, Private, John. 201959, 1/5th Bn., Royal Warwickshire Regiment. Killed in action, 9th September, 1918. Son of George and Elizabeth Johnson, of Bedworth. Born Bedworth. Enlisted Coventry. Resided Bedworth. Memorial Ref. Giavera Memorial, Italy.

JOHNSON, Private, Montague. 15/1576, 16th Bn., Royal Warwickshire Regiment. Killed in action, Battle of the Somme 3rd September, 1916 by a shell. Age 21. Son of Herbert Arnold and Fanny Sophia Johnson, of 14, Northumberland Road, Coventry. Took his degree (Royal College of Music) as a violinist when he was 14 years of age. Born 17th March 1895 at Coventry. Resided at 14, Northumberland Road. Clerk, Rudge Works and professor of violin. Enlisted Birmingham, November 1915. Commemorated St. John's Church and War Memorial Park. Memorial Ref. Pier and Face 9 A 9 B and 10 B. Thiepval Memorial, Somme, France.

JOHNSON Private, Oliver. 12972, 7th Bn., Oxfordshire and Buckinghamshire Light Infantry. Killed in action, Salonika, 26th April, 1917. Born Longford. Enlisted Warwick. Resided Longford. Commemorated Exhall Memorial and Saint Thomas the Apostle, Longford. Grave Ref. F. 1328. Karasouli Military Cemetery, Greece.

JOHNSON, Corporal, Thomas Frederick. 751, E Coy., Machine Gun Section, 1/7th Bn., Royal Warwickshire Regiment. Killed in action, 9th May, 1915. Age 21. Son of Thomas and Margaret Johnson, of 76, Lawford Road, Rugby. Born Atherstone. Employed Armstrong Siddeley Motors Ltd. Grave Ref. V. C. 5. La Plus Douve Farm Cemetery, Belgium.

JOHNSON, Private, William Alfred. 26218, 10th Bn., Royal Warwickshire Regiment. Killed in action, 20th October, 1918. Born 16th January, 1892 at Ulverston, Lancs. Resided at 165, Narrow Lane. Clerk. Enlisted August, 1917 at Coventry. Memorial Ref. Panel 3. Vis-En-Artois Memorial, France.

JOHNSON, Private, William Harrison. 19102, 7th Bn., Lincolnshire Regiment. Died of wounds, 23rd May, 1917. Age 38. Son of Thomas and Margaret Johnson, of Washingborough, Lincoln. Born Lincoln. Enlisted Coventry. Resided Washingborough, Lincs. Grave Ref. III. N. 35. Duisans British Cemetery, Etrun, France.

JOLLY, Private, Frederick William. 1492, 15th Bn., Royal Warwickshire Regiment. Died of wounds, 11th August, 1916. Age 24. Son of William and Catherine Jolly, of Neatishead, Norwich. Born 9th November, 1891 at Norwich. Resided Coventry. School Teacher, Elementary School, Coventry. Enlisted August, 1915. Commemorated Education Department Memorial, Coventry Corporation. Grave Ref. B. 28.5. St. Sever Cemetery, Rouen, France.

JONES, Sergeant, Alfred William. 9999, 2nd Bn., South Wales Borderers. Killed in action, 28th June, 1915. Billeted Coventry. Born St. Catherines, Glocs. Enlisted Glocs. Memorial Ref. Sp. Mem. C. 201. Twelve Tree Copse Cemetery, Turkey.

JONES, Lance Sergeant, Alec. 4483, 3rd Bn., Rifle Brigade. Killed in action, 2nd July, 1918. Born Wilton, Wilts. Enlisted Northampton. Resided Coventry. Grave Ref. V. E . 14. Bully-Grenay Communal Cemetery, British Extension, France.

JONES, A. S. Commemorated Triumph & Gloria Memorial.

JONES, Private, Archibald Edwin. 16410, 11th Bn., Royal Warwickshire Regiment. Killed in action, 11th November, 1917. Born Warwick. Enlisted Coventry. Memorial Ref. Panel 23 to 28 and 163A. Tyne Cot Memorial, Belgium.

JONES, Gunner, Charles John. HMS Queen Mary, Royal Navy. Killed in action, Battle of Jutland, 31st May, 1916. Born 23rd June 1881, in Spencer Street. Resided at 44c. 1h. Gosford Street. Sailor. Educated Bablake School and St. Michael's School. Commemorated Bablake School Memorial and War Memorial Park. Leaves a widow. Memorial Ref. Portsmouth Naval Memorial.

JONES, Sergeant (Pilot), Dafelyn Tawelog Austin. 205675, Royal Air Force formerly 2196, Machine Gun Corps. Died, Home, 1st October, 1918. Age 21. Due to be gazetted to a Commission in R.A.F. on the day of death. Son of Mr. and Mrs. J. Orton Jones, of 22, Eureka Place, Ebbw Vale. Born Dowlais, Glamorgan. Enlisted Coventry. Grave Ref. K. North. 4. 2. Ebbw Vale Cemetery.

JONES, Private, Ernest. 13096, 2nd Bn., Oxfordshire and Buckinghamshire Light Infantry. Killed in action, Loos, 25th September, 1915. Age 36. Son of Mr. and Mrs. Jones, of 4, Victoria Place, Far Gosford Street, Coventry. Husband of Mrs. E. Jones, of 11, All Saints Lane, Coventry, Warwickshire. Born in 1879 in Far Gosford Street. Resided at 1 All Saints lane. Cycle Mechanic, Messrs. O'Brien Ltd. Enlisted September 1914, Coventry. Leaves a wife and eight children. Memorial Ref. Panel 83 to 85. Loos Memorial, Pas de Calais, France

JONES, Private, Frederick Charles Maurice. 20296, "A" Coy. 7th Bn., Queen's Own (Royal West Kent Regiment) formerly 231256, Mechanical Transport, Royal Army Service Corps. Killed in action, near Albert, 18th June, 1918. Age 19. Son of William Christopher and Georgina French Jones, of 37, Widdrington Road, Coventry. Born 28th November, 1898 at Wet Boldon, Durham. Resided at Coventry. Fitter. Enlisted Warwick, October 1916. Commemorated War Memorial Park. Grave Ref. III. A. 9. Ribemont Communal Cemetery Extension, Somme, France.

JONES, Private, George. 19385, 3rd Bn., South Wales Borderers. Killed in action, 16th August, 1917. Son of Mr. G. Jones, of 40, Station Road, Brimington, Chesterfield. Born Coventry. Enlisted Chesterfield. Grave Ref. VII. 8. A. Artillery Wood Cemetery, Belgium.

JONES, Private, George. 18518, A Coy., 6th Bn., Leicestershire Regiment. Killed in action, 8th October, 1918. Age 32. Brother of Mrs. B. E. Hensworth, of 27, Weymouth Street, Leicester. Born Leicester. Employed Coventry. Grave Ref. I. V. F8. Prospect Hill Cemetery, Gouy, France.

JONES, Private, George. 18588, 13th Bn., Gloucestershire Regiment. Killed in action, 14th March, 1917. Age 40. Son of Frederick and Mary Jones, of 46, St. George's Road, Leamington Spa. Born Leamington. Resided 15c. 2h. Gosford Street. Enlisted Coventry. Grave Ref. VI. B. 11. Vlamertinghe Military Cemetery, Belgium.

JONES, Sapper, George Longworth. 98, 2nd Field Coy., Australian Engineers. Died of sickness, 27th September, 1915. Age 52. Son of George and Selina Jones, of Port Melbourne, Australia. Husband of Ida Mary Jones. Born at Coventry. Grave Ref. C.E. 1729. Netley Military Cemetery, Hampshire.

JONES, H. Commemorated Radford Memorial.

JONES, Private, Harry William. 17675, Royal Warwickshire Regiment. Died of wounds, 16th September, 1916 at Middlesex Hospital. Age 23. Son of Mrs. Charlotte Jones, of 73, Checketts Lane, Worcester. Enlisted April, 1916. Employed Humber Ltd. Enlisted Coventry. Grave Ref. 542. Claines (St. John the Baptist) Churchyard.

JONES, Able Seaman, Harold. J/5219, HMS Bulwark, Royal Navy. Killed off Sheerness, 26th November, 1914 by an internal explosion of vesel. Age 22. Son of John and Eleanor Jones, of Wellingborough. Resided 40, Marlborough Road. Memorial Ref. 2. Portsmouth Naval Memorial.

JONES, Private, Herbert. 11376, 1st Bn., Sherwood Foresters (Notts and Derby) Regiment attached 24th Trench Mortar Battery. Killed in action, 4th March, 1917. Age 30. Son of Thomas and Eliza Jones, of 545, Bridge Street, Wednesbury, Staffs. Born Wednesbury. Enlisted Coventry. Resided Wednesbury, Staffs. Memorial Ref. Pier and Face 10 C 10 D and 11 A. Thiepval Memorial, Somme, France.

JONES, Lance Corporal, Ishmael. 9510, F Coy., 11th Bn., Royal Warwickshire Regiment. Killed in action, 10th August, 1916. Age 41. Son of Ishmael and Charlotte Parkes (formerly Jones), of Stockingford, Nuneaton, Warwickshire. Born Bilston. Resided Stockingford. Employed Coventry. Grave Ref. III. D. 20. Heilly Station Cemetery, Mericourt-L'abbe, France.

JONES, Driver, John Thomas. T/364502, 667th H.T. Coy., Army Service Corps. Died, home (gassed), 10th November, 1918. Husband of Clara Jones, of 619A, Stoney Stanton Road, Coventry. Born 12th March, 1890 at Foleshill, Coventry. Enlisted Coventry. Resided 108, Holmsdale Road. Fruiterer and Greengrocer, Coventry. Grave Ref. 42. 34. Coventry (London Road) Cemetery.

JONES, Lance Corporal, Joseph. 6825, 2nd Bn., South Staffordshire Regiment. Killed in action, Givenchy, 10th March, 1915. Age 28. Born 1887 at Birmingham. Enlisted Birmingham. Resided Coventry. Beltman. Reservist. Employed Messrs Courtaulds. Memorial Ref. Panel 21 and 22. Le Touret Memorial, France. (possibly buried Givenchy Cemetery)

JONES, Private, Leslie Thomas. 42908, 1st /8th Bn., Royal Warwickshire Regiment. Died of wounds, Landrecies, 4th November, 1918. Age 19. Son of Charles Arthur and Frances H. E. Jones, of "Avonmore," 33, Earlsdon Avenue South, Coventry. Born 29th December, 1898 in Queen Victoria Road. Resided at "Avonmore". Electrical Engineer. Enlisted Coventry, June 1918. Commemorated Bablake School Memorial, St. Barbara's Memorial and War Memorial Park. Grave Ref. B. 30. Landrecies British Cemetery, Nord, France.

JONES, Bombardier, Percy. Royal Field Artillery. Born Coventry. Resided Coventry. Photo Engraver. Commemorated Iliffe & Sons Ltd Memorial.

JONES, Able Seaman, Robert. J/34057, HMS Vanguard, Royal Navy. Killed by internal explosion of vessel at Scapa Flow, 9th July, 1917. Age 19. Son of Griffith Jones, of 20, Gun Hill, Arley, Coventry. Native of Bedworth, Warwickshire. Memorial Ref. 21. Plymouth Naval Memorial, Devon.

JONES, Lance Corporal, Thomas. 14734, 8th Bn., Royal Berkshire Regiment. Killed in action, 25th September, 1915. Age 29. Brother of James D. Jones, of 2, Radnor Street, Gorton, Manchester. Born Manchester. Enlisted Coventry. Resided Bradford, Yorks. Memorial Ref. Panel 93 to 95. Loos Memorial, France.

JONES, Drummer, W. South Wales Borderers. Died 1915. Billeted Coventry.

JONES, Private, Walter Henry. 22040, 1st Bn., Gloucestershire Regiment. Died of wounds, 14th October, 1915. Age 24. Son of Alfred and Emma Maria Jones, of 86, Station Street East, Coventry. Born 11th June, 1891 at Little Heath. Resided 86, Station Street East. Turner, Rover Works Ltd. Enlisted September, 1914. Grave Ref. I. E. 17. Noeux-Les-Mines Communal Cemetery, Pas de Calais, France

JONES, Private William Henry. 4367, 1/7th Bn., Royal Warwickshire Regiment. Killed in action, 24th June, 1916 by shell fire when leaving the trenches for rest. Born 1876 in Coventry. Resided 5c. 2h. Whitefriars Street. Mechanic, Humber Works. Enlisted December, 1914 at Coventry. Enlisted Coventry. Leaves a widow and four children. Grave Ref. I. E. 7. Hebuterne Military Cemetery, France.

JONES, Private, William Henry. 3068, 1/7th Bn., Royal Warwickshire Regiment. Killed in action, 14th July, 1916. Age 20. Son of Frederick and Esther Louise Jones of 5, Lime Grove, Hoole, Chester. Born 18th July, 1895 at Chester. Resided 18, Gordon Street. Florist. Enlisted September, 1914. Memorial Ref. Pier and Face 9A 9B and 10B. Thiepval Memorial, Somme, France.

JORDAN, Private, Arthur Stanley. 41224, 1stBn., Worcestershire Regiment formerly 24420, Royal Warwickshire Regt. Died of wounds, 24th November, 1917. Age 20. Son of John and Harriet Jordan, of 3, Broomfield Place, Spon End, Coventry. Born 23rd September, 1897 at Broome, Norfolk. Enlisted March, 1917 at Coventry. Chain Finisher. Resided Coventry. Commemorated Coventry Chain Memorial. Grave Ref. XXVII. B.B. 14A. Lijssenthoek Military Cemetery, Poperinge, West-Vlaanderen, Belgium.

JORDAN, F. Sherwood Foresters. Died (repatriated prisoner of war), Home, 1919.

JOSEPH, Private, Gatcliff Gilbert. 20369, 11th Bn., Royal Warwickshire Regiment. Died of wounds, 12th May, 1917. Age 23. Husband of C. B. Gilbert of Black Bank, Bedworth nr Nuneaton. Born Bedworth. Enlisted Coventry. Resided Bedworth. Commemorated Exhall Memorial. Grave Ref. XVIII. M. 8A. Etaples Military Cemetery, France.

JOYCE, Corporal, Edwin Henry. 48250, "B" Bty. 50th Bde, Royal Field Artillery, formerly 289th A.T. Coy., Royal Engineers. Died of wounds, Boulogne, 6th October, 1918. Enlisted September, 1914 at Nuneaton. Resided Coventry. Born 2nd December, 1892 at Shornicliffe. Resided at 32, New Buildings. Tinsmith. Grave Ref. IV. I. 9. Duhallow ADS Cemetery, Belgium.

JOYNES, Private, Albert Thomas. 2394, 1/1st Bn., Oxfordshire and Buckinghamshire Light Infantry. Killed in action, Allouagne, 12th July, 1915. Age 23. Son of Albert Joseph and Mary Annie Joynes, of Mickleton, Campden, Glos. Born 27th October, 1891 at Chipping Norton. Resided Coventry. Fitter. Enlisted October, 1914. Grave Ref. 4. Allouagne Communal Cemetery, France.

JUDSON, Sapper, John West. 63232, 89th Field Coy., Royal Engineers. Died of wounds, 3rd July, 1915. Age 27. Son of Henry and Ann Elizabeth Judson, of 6, Princess Street, West Hartlepool. Born 6th March, 1887 at West Hartlepool. Resided at 77, Earlsdon Avenue. Builder. Enlisted January, 1915 at Coventry. Commemorated St. Barbara's Memorial and Central Methodist Hall. Grave Ref. Enclosure No.2 V. B. 32. Bedford House Cemetery, Belgium.

JUKES, Private, Arthur. 5089, 1/6th Bn., Royal Warwickshire Regiment. Killed in action, 18th August, 1916. Born 3rd November, 1888 at Coventry. Enlisted Warwick. Resided 4a Bramble Street, Coventry. Carpenter. Grave Ref. IV. F. 39. Pozieres British Cemetery, Ovillers-La Boisselle, France.

JUKES, Corporal, Harry Lancaster. 87115, Royal Garrison Artillery. Killed in action, Ypres, 7th July, 1917. Born 21st May, 1886 at Oldbury. Resided Coventry. Publican. Enlisted May, 1916 at Coventry. Grave Ref. Possibly buried Ypres.

KAYE, Sergeant, Lister Walter. 202712, 2/6th Bn., Royal Warwickshire Regiment. Killed in action, St. Quentin, 21st March, 1918. Age 25. Son of Frederick William and Elizabeth Kaye, of 15, Astley Road, Irlam, Manchester. Born at Workington, Cumberland. Born 28th December, 1892 at Workington, Cumberland. Resided Coventry. Motor Accessories Factor. Enlisted March, 1916 at Coventry. Grave Ref. II. G.14. Chapelle British Cemetery, Holnon, France.

KAYE, Lance Corporal, William. DM2/196093, Mechanical Transport, Army Service Corps. Killed in action, 26th May, 1918. Age 29. Husband of Rosina Kaye, of Victoria Stores, Brays Lane, Coventry. Born 30th August, 1888 at Coventry. Enlisted Coventry. Resided Coventry. Publican. Grave Ref. Plot 1. Row D. Grave 8. Acheux British Cemetery, Somme, France.

KEEFE, Private, Frederick Richard. 3936, 1/7th Bn., Royal Warwickshire Regiment. Died of wounds, base hospital, 22nd August, 1916. Age 20. Born April, 1898 at 6c. 14h. Far Gosford Street, Coventry. Resided at 39, Hood Street. Wheel Builder, Gloria Cycle Works. Commemorated Triumph & Gloria Memorial. Enlisted June, 1915 at Coventry. Grave Ref. I. A. 26. Varennes Military Cemetery, France.

KEEFE, Gunner, Herbert Edward. 87265, 92nd Bty. 17th Bde., Royal Field Artillery. Killed in action, Ypres, 20th September, 1917 by a shell. Age 23. Husband of Violet Alice Keefe (nee Carter), of 4, Sherbourne Street, Coventry. Enlisted April, 1915 at Coventry. Born 22nd February, 1893 at 6c. 4h. Far Gosford Street, Coventry. Polisher, Rotherams factory. Commemorated St. John's Church. Grave Ref. I. B. 24. Artillery Wood Cemetery, Ieper, West-Vlaanderen, Belgium.

KEENE, Private, Joseph. 48877, 2nd Bn., Bedfordshire Regiment. Killed in action, 22nd August, 1918 just south of Albert. Born Coventry. Enlisted Warwick. Resided Coventry. Commemorated Coventry Chain Memorial. Grave Ref. II. A. 9. Albert Communal Cemetery Extension, France.

KEIGHTLEY, Frank. Commemorated Holy Trinity Panels.

KELL, T. Commemorated Coventry Chain Memorial.

KELLEY, Private 2nd Class, Percy. 295264, Royal Air Force. Died, home, 27th November, 1918. Born 19th December, 1900 at Foleshill. Resided Foleshill. Enlisted August, 1918. Commemorated King Henry VIII School. Grave Ref. Foleshill Congregational Burial Ground.

KELLEY, Lance Corporal, Walter. 144515, 213th Army Troops Coy., Royal Engineers. Killed in action, Amiens, 30th March, 1918. Born 6th March, 1888 at Foleshill. Resided Chapel Lane. Builder's Manager. Enlisted November, 1915 at Coventry. Memorial Ref. Panel 10 to 13. Pozieres Memorial, France.

KELLEY, Private, Walter. 24537, 1st /5th Bn., Royal Warwickshire Regiment. Killed in action, 22nd August, 1917. Age 19. Son of Robert and Emma Kelley, of Foleshill, Coventry. Born Foleshill. Enlisted Coventry. Grave Ref. VIII. G. 21. Tyne Cot Cemetery, Zonnebeke, West-Vlaanderen, Belgium.

KELLY, Private, Edward Arthur. 16449, 9th Bn., Royal Warwickshire Regiment. Died of wounds, Mesopotamia, 16th March, 1917. Born 31st July 1895, at Foleshill. Resided at 38, Princess Street. Enlisted Coventry, February, 1916. Clerk. Commemorated War Memorial Park. Grave Ref. Shaikh Saad Old Cemetery. Mem. Amara War Cemetery, Iraq.

KELLY, Private, Richard Frederick. 20324, 16th Bn., Royal Warwickshire Regiment. Died of wounds, 11th May, 1917. Age 23. Son of Mr. and Mrs. Kelly, of Rose Cottage, Ballybrack, Co. Dublin. Husband of Mabel Kelly, of 4, Hooker's Cottages, Ashurst Wood, Sussex. Born Ballybraik, Co. Dublin. Resided Allesley. Enlisted Coventry. Employed Coventry. Grave Ref. III. B. 7. Barlin Communal Cemetery Extension, France.

KELLY, Private, William Reginald Thomas. G/90014, C Coy. 2nd /4th Bn., London Regiment (Royal Fusiliers) formerly 40717, Somerset Light Infantry. Killed in action, the Somme, 30th May, 1918. Age 18. Son of Capt. John Thomas Kelly and Alice Kelly, of 242, Gulson Road, Coventry. Born 31st May, 1899 at Malta. Motor Driver. Enlisted June, 1917 at Coventry. Grave Ref. VIII. G. 18. Warloy-Baillon Communal Cemetery Extension, Somme, France.

KELSEY, Gunner, Edmund, MM. 95978, 211th Siege Bty., Royal Garrison Artillery. Died of wounds, (gas) 31st October, 1918. Age 23. Son of John and Matilda Kelsey, of 96, Foleshill Road, Coventry. Born 16th December, 1894 at Coventry. Enlisted June, 1916 at Coventry. Clerk, Binley Colliery. Commemorated Holy Trinity Panels. Awarded the Military Medal for advancing through the enemy barrage to repair the broken telephone wires on the 21st March, 1918. Grave Ref. IV. F. 9. Tourgeville Military Cemetery, Calvados, France.

KEMP, Rifleman, John Henry. 19789, 212th Coy., Machine Gun Corps (Infantry) formerly King's Royal Rifle Corps. Killed in action, July, 1917. Age 25. Son of Mrs. Alice Elias Kemp, of Row 8, 63, South Howard Street, Great Yarmouth. Resided 66, Spon End. Tram Conductor. Enlisted May, 1915 at Coventry. Grave Ref. H. 2. Noreuil Australian Cemetery, France.

KENDALL, Private, Arthur. 4624, 2nd /7th Bn., Royal Warwickshire Regiment. Died of wounds, received the previous day, 20th July, 1916. Age 21. Son of Robert and Mary Ann Kendall, of 50, St. John Street, Coventry. Born 6th December, 1894. Labourer. Enlisted November, 1915 at Coventry. Grave Ref. XI. A. 38. Merville Communal Cemetery, Nord, France.

KENDALL, Private, Joseph. 10729, 5th Bn., Oxfordshire and Buckinghamshire Light Infantry. Killed in action, 25th September, 1915. Age 20. Son of William and Hannah Kendall, of 136, Gun Hill, Arley, Coventry. Born Chilvers Coton. Enlisted Nuneaton. Memorial Ref. Panel 37 and 39. Ypres (Menin Gate) Memorial, Ieper, West-Vlaanderen, Belgium.

KENDALL, Private, Reginald George. 16504, 1st Bn., Royal Warwickshire Regiment. Died of wounds, 14th July, 1916. Age 23. Son of Charles James and Annie Kendall, of 435, Stoney Stanton Road, Coventry. Native of Coventry. Born 11th January, 1893 at 54, Stoney Stanton Road, Coventry. Bricklayer. Enlisted January, 1916 at Warwick. Resided Coventry. Grave Ref. XIV. A. 10. Etaples Military Cemetery, Pas de Calais, France.

KENDALL, Gunner, William. 16059, "D" Bty. 88th Bde., Royal Field Artillery. Killed in action, Ypres, 10th October, 1917. Born 24th January, 1895 in Spon Street, Coventry. Enlisted September, 1914 at Coventry. Resided at 48, Milton Street. Only son. Driller, Alfred Herbert's Ltd, Edgewick. Grave Ref. I. L. 6. Voormezeele Enclosures No.1 and No.2, Belgium.

KENDRICK, Lance Corporal, Henry. 266406, 2nd /7th Bn., Royal Warwickshire Regiment. Killed in action, Ypres, 4th October, 1917. Age 20. Son of Henry and Charlotte Kendrick, of 37, Cobden Street, Coventry. Born 13th August, 1897 at Coventry. Moulder, Sterling Metal works, George Street. Enlisted March, 1915 at Coventry. Memorial Ref. Bay 3. Arras Memorial, Pas de Calais, France.

KENDRICK, Private, Richard George, 12984, 6th Bn., Dorsetshire Regiment. Died of wounds, 3rd December, 1915. Age 19. Son of Nathaniel and Elizabeth Kendrick, of 23, Trentham Road, Coventry. Native of Newbold-on-Avon, Rugby. Born 5th September, 1896 at Rugby. Enlisted 1915 at London. Resided Coventry. Grave Ref. II. C. 14A. Lijssenthoek Military Cemetery, Poperinge, West-Vlaanderen, Belgium.

KENNEDY, Private, Robert. M2/121664, 282nd Mechanical Transport Coy., Army Service Corps. Died of wounds, 10th November, 1917. Born Inverness. Enlisted Coventry. Resided Inverness. Grave Ref. III. M. 9. Menin Road South Military Cemetery, Belgium.

KENNEY, Private, Herbert Harold. 5224, 1/6th Bn., Royal Warwickshire Regiment. Killed in action, 4th February, 1917. Born at Alcester, Warwickshire. Resided Wolston. Employed Coventry. Commemorated Wolston Memorial. Memorial Ref. Pier and Face 9 A 9 B and 10 B. Thiepval Memorial, Somme, France.

KENNELL, Private, William Samuel. 42516, 10th Bn., Royal Warwickshire Regiment. Killed in action, 8th November, 1918. Age 33. Son of Samuel and Mary Ann Kennell. Husband of Mary Annie Louisa Kennell, of 267, Baker Street, Derby. Born Easenhall, Warwickshire. Employed Coventry. Enlisted Coventry. Grave Ref. West of main path. Malplaquet Communal Cemetery, France.

KENNEY, Sergeant, Richard Isaac. 2096, 1/7th Bn., Royal Warwickshire Regiment. Killed in action, 14th July, 1916. Age 23. Age 23. Son of Thomas and Jane Kenney, of Stretton-under-Fosse, Rugby. Enlisted Coventry in 1914.. Resided Brinklow. Born 5th April, 1893 at Brinklow. Employed Courtaulds Ltd. Grave Ref. I. C. 14. Pozieres British Cemetery, Ovillers-La Boisselle, France.

KENNEY, Lance Corporal, Stanley. 29550, 14th Bn., Worcestershire Regiment. Killed in action, 15th January, 1918. Age 27. Son of Oliver Herbert (Surveyor) and Sussanah Kenney of 105, St. John's Road, Walthamstow, Essex. Born East Ham, London. Enlisted Coventry. Resided Walthamstow, London. Memorial Ref. Pier and Face 5A and 6C. Thiepval Memorial, Somme, France.

KENNING, Lance Corporal, Arthur George. 266074, 7th Bn., Royal Warwickshire Regiment. Died of sickness, Catterick Military Hospital, 9th June 1917. Wounded 19th July, 1916. Age 22. Son of Mrs. Ann House, of 24, Adelaide Street, Coventry. Born 11th May 1895 in Little Church Street. Resided at 24, Adelaide Street. Painter. Enlisted November, 1914. Brother also lost. Grave Ref. 26. 5. Hipswell (St. John) churchyard, Yorkshire.

KENNING, Private, John William. 16542, 10th Bn., Royal Warwickshire Regiment. Killed in action by shrapnel, Battle of the Somme, 1st November, 1916. Age 23. Eldest son of Mrs. Ann House, of 24, Adelaide Street, Coventry. Born 29th April, 1893 at 77, Albert Street, Coventry. Painter, Triumph Works. Enlisted November, 1914 at Warwick. Commemorated Triumph & Gloria Memorial. Resided Coventry. Brother also lost. Memorial Ref. Pier and Face 9 A 9 B and 10 B. Thiepval Memorial, Somme, France.

KENNING, Private, Joseph. 36634, 1st /6th Bn., Gloucestershire Regiment. Killed in action, 22nd August, 1917. Age 29. Son of Joseph and Sarah Kenning, of The Square, Corley Ash, Coventry. Born 1888 at Coventry. Enlisted Coventry. Commemorated St. Thomas Memorial. Memorial Ref. Panel 72 to 75. Tyne Cot Memorial, Zonnebeke, West-Vlaanderen, Belgium.

KENNY, Private, Stephen. 36312, 2nd Bn. , Yorkshire Regiment formerly 14th Reserve Cavalry, 15th Hussars. Killed in action, 2nd April, 1917. Born in 1883 at Birmingham. Resided at 117, Colchester Street. Employed by Humber Ltd. Enlisted August, 1914 at Coventry. Memorial Ref. Hen-sur-Coj Mem. 7. Bucquoy Road Cemetery, Ficheux, France.

KERBY, George. Killed in action. Name on Roll of Honour in St. John the Baptist Church.

KERBY, Private, Phillip Charles. 2140, Warwickshire Yeomanry. Died, At Sea, 11th April, 1915. Age 22. Son of Henry and Mahlda Kerby of Mollington, Banbury. Born Eydon. Enlisted Coventry. Resided Towcester. Memorial Ref. Hollybrook Memorial, Southampton.

KERR, Major, Robert Goodman Kerr, MC. 7th Bn., Royal Inniskilling Fusiliers. Killed in action, 10th July, 1918. Age 28. Named in St. Thomas Parish Magazine, Roll of Honour. Husband of Mrs. C. J. Kerr, of Hillside, Delgany, Co. Wicklow. Grave Ref. II. F. 8. Bertenacre Military Cemetery, Fletre, France.

KETTERIDGE, Private, William. 13106, 1st Bn., Royal Warwickshire Regiment. Killed in action, 5th October, 1917. Age 18. Son of Albert Edward and Bertha Minnie Ketteridge, of 163, Cato Street, Saltey, Birmingham. Born Coventry. Enlisted Birmingham. Memorial Ref. Panel 23 to 28 and 163A. Tyne Cot Memorial, Belgium.

KETTLE, Private, George Henry. 34988, 5th Bn., Royal Berkshire Regiment formerly 7/710, T. R. Bn. Died of wounds, 28th November, 1917. Age 34. Son of C. and L. M. Kettle. Husband of Susan Ellen Kettle, of Rectory Cottage, Allesley, Coventry. Born Birmingham. Enlisted Coventry. Grave Ref. XXX. N. 2A. Etaples Military Cemetery, Pas de Calais, France.

KIGHTLEY, Sidney Frank. 17427, 14th Bn., Royal Warwickshire Regiment. Killed in action, Longueval, 30th July, 1916. Born Coventry. Enlisted Coventry. Born 30th April, 1896 at 21, Chauntry Place. Resided 21, Chauntry Place. Machinist, Daimler Ltd. Enlisted March, 1916. Memorial Ref. Pier and Face 9 A 9 B and 10 B. Thiepval Memorial, Somme, France.

KIGHTLEY, Lance Corporal, Wilfred Henry. 19434, 5th Bn., Oxfordshire and Buckinghamshire Light Infantry. Killed in action, Arras, 24th August, 1916. Age 19. Brother of Miss Hilda G. Kightley, of 417, Foleshill Road, Coventry. Born 10th May, 1897 at Foleshill. Clerk, Coventry Ordnance Works. Enlisted August, 1915 at Coventry. Memorial Ref. Pier and Face 10 A and 10 D. Thiepval Memorial, Somme, France.

KILDING, Rifleman, Alfred Craddock. C/12880, 21st Bn., King's Royal Rifle Corps. Killed in action, 17th September, 1916. Born Yorkshire. Resided Leyburn. Formerly employed Coventry. Grave Ref. V. G. 10. Guards' Cemetery, Lesboeufs, France.

KILLER, Gunner, Alfred. 40648, 217th Siege Bty., Royal Garrison Artillery. Killed in action, 30th August, 1917. Age 23. Son of Alfred Killer, of 39, Herga Road, Wealdstone, Middlesex. Born Coventry. Enlisted Mill Hill, Middlesex. Resided Wealdstone, Middx. Grave Ref. V. E. 30. Vlamertinghe New Military Cemetery, Belgium.

KILPACK, Private, Ernest. 22725, 4th Bn., Worcestershire Regiment. Killed in action, Suvla Bay, 2nd November, 1915. Age 21. Son of Samuel and Mary Ann Kilpack, of Radford, Coventry. Born 18th July, 1894 at Radford. Resided 124, Radford. Fitter, Daimler Coy. Enlisted May, 1915 at Coventry. Commemorated Radford Memorial. Grave Ref. II. B. 10. Azmak Cemetery, Suvla, Turkey.

KIMBERLEY, Private, Harry Edward. 12330, 2nd /4th Bn., Oxfordshire and Buckinghamshire Light Infantry. Killed in action, 22nd August, 1917. Age 24. Husband of Florence Lily Kimberley, of 3, Court, 2, House, Union Street, Coventry. Born 8th April 1893, in Gilbert Street. Resided at 53, Well Street. Fitter. Enlisted September, 1914. Employed Singer and Co. Ltd. Commemorated War Memorial Park. Memorial Ref. Panel 96 to 98. Tyne Cot Memorial, Zonnebeke, West-Vlaanderen, Belgium.

KIMBERLEY, Private, Reuben. 4303, 1/7th Bn., Royal Warwickshire Regiment. Killed in action, 1st July, 1916. Age 29. Husband of Mrs Allen (formerly Kimberley) of 1, Collingham Row, Newark. Enlisted Coventry. Resided Bedworth. Leaves a widow and one child. Memorial Ref. Pier and Face 9A 9B and 10B. Thiepval Memorial, Somme, France.

KIMBERLEY, Driver, Sydney Charles. 793, Warwickshire, Royal Horse Artillery. Died, home, 5th April, 1916 of pneumonia. Age 19. Son of Alfred Kimberly, of 36, Stanley Road, Coventry. Born 18th June, 1897 in Thomas Street, Coventry. Enlisted October, 1915 at Leamington. Printer. Member of Well Street Congregational Church. Grave Ref. 25. 106. Coventry (London Road) Cemetery.

KIMBERLEY, Private, Thomas. 42394, 1st Bn., Royal Warwickshire Regiment. Died of wounds, Verchain, 24th October, 1918. Age 34. Son of Thomas and Rose Kimberley, of Coventry. Husband of Elizabeth Townsend (formerly Kimberley), of 7, Northfield Road, Coventry. Born 17th August, 1881 in Gosford Street. Resided at 7 Northfield Road. Cycle finisher. Enlisted Coventry, May, 1918. Commemorated Triumph & Gloria Memorial. Grave Ref. D. 4. Verchain British Cemetery, Verchain-Maugre, Nord, France.

KIMBERLEY, Lance Corporal, Walter. 1st Bn., Coldstream Guards . Died home, 22nd April 1917. Age 32. Son of Charles and Myra Kimberley. Born 28th September 1884 at Birmingham. Resided in Cromwell Street. Professional Footballer (formerly Coventry City), also employed by Coventry Ordnance Works. Enlisted August 1914. Repatriated August, 1916 on health grounds. Husband of Ada Kimberley. Grave Ref. Witton Cemetery, Birmingham.

KING, Private, Albert. 53651, 2/5th Bn., Manchester Regiment formerly 38151, North Lancashire Regiment. Killed in action, 21st March, 1918. Born Coventry. Enlisted Oldham. Memorial Ref. Panel 64 to 67. Pozieres Memorial, France.

KING, Lieutenant, Charles Kenneth. 1st /1st Glamorgan Bty., Royal Horse Artillery. Died of wounds, Arras, 10th May, 1917. Age 26. Son of Charles Harry and Charlotte King, of The Chantry House, Billericay, Essex. Born 10th January, 1891 in Stoney Stanton Road, at Coventry. Resided Clacton-on-sea. General Manager, Motor Omnibus Company. Enlisted August, 1914. Commemorated King Henry VIII School. Grave Ref. VI. G. 32. Faubourg D'Amiens Cemetery, Arras, Pas de Calais, France.

KING, Private, Frederick. 19552, 1st Bn., Oxfordshire and Buckinghamshire Light Infantry. Died of wounds received at Kut, Persian Gulf, 8th April, 1916. Age 35. Born Thomas Street, Coventry. Enlisted Coventry. Resided No. 2, Paybody's Buildings, Moat Street. Cycle Fitter, Humber Works. Enlisted August, 1915. Memorial Ref. Panel 26 and 63. Basra Memorial, Iraq.

KING, Private, George. 19132, 2nd Bn., Lancashire Fusiliers. Died of wounds, 4th July, 1916. Age 38. Born Coventry. Enlisted April, 1915 at Coventry. Born 28th July, 1879 at 2, Weston Street. Resided 16c. 2h. Spon Street. Brass Furnaceman, Reliance Works. Commemorated St. John's Church. Leaves a widow and two children. Grave Ref. II. A. 6. Gezaincourt Communal Cemetery Extension, France.

KING, John. Commemorated Holy Trinity Panels.

KING, Private, John. 34900, C Coy. 10th Bn., Worcestershire Regiment. Killed in action, 7th July, 1917. Age 32. Son of James and Caroline King, of 7, Chauntry Place, Coventry. Born Birmingham. Enlisted Coventry. Resided Coventry. Born 20th April, 1885 at Birmingham. Resided at 7 Chauntry Place. Fruiterer. Enlisted September 1916. Commemorated War Memorial Park. Memorial Ref. Panel 34. Ypres (Menin Gate) Memorial, Ieper, West-Vlaanderen, Belgium.

KING, Private, John. 45778, 10th Bn., South Wales Borderers formerly M/286518, Royal Army Service Corps. Killed in action, 30th June 1917. Age 37. Son of John and Elizabeth King, of Coventry. Husband of Elizabeth King, of Back 11 Burges, Coventry. Born in 1880, at Coventry. Resided at Coventry. Commemorated War Memorial Park. Grave Ref. II. I. 16. Bard Cottage Cemetery, Ieper, West-Vlaanderen, Belgium.

KING, Private, Thomas George. 16998, 1st Bn., Coldstream Guards. Killed in action 31st July, 1917. Born 1898 at Coleshill. Resided 214, Melbourne Road. Printer's Machinist, Parbury Bros. Enlisted October, 1915. Memorial Ref. Panel 11. Ypres (Menin Gate) Memorial, Belgium.

KINGS, Sergeant, George. 33104, 1st Bn., Wiltshire Regiment formerly 11837, Royal Warwickshire Regiment. Died of wounds, 27th May, 1918. Born 24th July, 1889 at Upton Warren, Worcestershire. Resided Coventry. Police Constable. Enlisted May, 1915 at Coventry. Commemorated Police Force Memorial, Coventry Corporation. Memorial Ref. Soissons Memorial, France.

KINGDON, Private, Edward Pratt. 24594, 11th Bn., Sherwood Foresters (Notts and Derby Regiment). Killed in action, 17th July, 1916. Born Methwold, Norfolk Enlisted Burton-on-Trent, Staffs. Resided Coventry. Memorial Ref. Pier and Face 10C 10D and 11A. Thiepval Memorial, Somme, France.

KINZETT, Private, Arthur Walter. 98398, 3/7th Bn., Royal Warwickshire Regiment attached 188th Bn., Machine Gun Corps formerly 4316, Royal Warwickshire Regiment. Died of wounds, 21st December, 1917 received 2nd December, 1917. Age 24. Son of Edward and Ellen Elizabeth Kinzett, of Wolverton, Warwickshire. Born 23rd April, 1893 at Dunchurch. Resided 23, Marlborough Road. Fitter, Daimler Works. Enlisted June, 1915 at Coventry. Member of the Amalgamated Toolmakers Society and Barras Green Working Mens Club. Commemorated Barras Green Working Mens Club. Grave Ref. VI. B. 8A. Wimereux Communal Cemetery, France.

KIRBY, Private, Charles. 12818, 2nd Bn., Worcestershire Regiment. Killed in action, 29th September, 1915. Age 22. Son of Henry and Ellen Kirby. Born Hill Morton, Warwicks. Enlisted Coventry. Resided Leicester. Memorial Ref. Panel 64 and 65. Loos Memorial, France.

KIRBY, Sergeant, Charles Ernest. 5268, A Coy., 2nd Bn., Manchester Regiment. Killed in action on patrol, Ypres, 11th June, 1915. Age 28. Son of Edward and Mary Ann Kirby, of Manchester. Husband of F. M. Brain (formerly Kirby), of 48, Broad Street, Foleshill, Coventry. Born 28th December, 1884 at Saltley, Birmingham. Enlisted August, 1914 at Manchester. Resided 45, Princess Street, Coventry. Stamper. Grave Ref. I. B. 10. Chester Farm Cemetery, Ieper, West-Vlaanderen, Belgium.

KIRBY, Private, Percy Herbert. 17438, 2nd Bn., Coldstream Guards. Killed in action, Arras, 27th August 1918. Age 22. Son of Mr. and Mrs. G. Kirby, of 10, Park Side, Coventry. Born 28th December, 1895 at Earlsdon, Coventry. Enlisted November, 1915 at Coventry. Warehouseman. Grave Ref. III. C. 8. Croisilles British Cemetery, Pas de Calais, France.

KIRBY, W. Educated and commemorated Bablake School.

KIRKBRIGHT, Private, Harold William. 41763, 8th Bn., Royal Inniskilling Fusiliers. Killed in action, 16th August, 1917. Born 2nd June, 1898 at Saltley. Enlisted December, 1916 at Warwick. Resided 8c. 10h. Jordan Well, Coventry. Employed Singer's Cycle Works. Memorial Ref. Panel 70 to 72. Tyne Cot Memorial, Belgium.

KIRKBRIGHT, Private, John. 11327, 10th Bn., Royal Warwickshire Regiment. Died of wounds, 4th August, 1916. Age 21. Son of John and Eleanor Kirkbright, of 8 Court, 10 House, Jordan Well, Coventry, Warwickshire. Born 16th February, 1896 at Saltley. Moulder. Enlisted September, 1914 at Coventry. Grave Ref. II. C. 54. Puchevillers British Cemetery, Somme, France.

KIRKLAND, Lance Corporal, Samuel Albert. 7259, 1st Bn., South Wales Borderers. Killed in action, Langemarck, 23rd October, 1914. Age 31. Son of John and Ada Kirkland, of Stoke Golding, Nuneaton. Husband of Maud Kirkland, of 20, Manor Street, Hinckley, Leicestershire. Born 17th January, 1883 at Stoke Golding. Resided Coventry. Engineer. Enlisted August, 1914. Memorial Ref. Panel 22. Ypres (Menin Gate) Memorial, Belgium.

KNIBBS, Private, James Henry. 10728, 2/4th Bn., Oxfordshire and Buckinghamshire Light Infantry. Killed, 22nd August, 1917. Born Bedworth. Resided Foleshill. Commemorated Exhall Memorial and Saint Thomas the Apostle, Longford. Enlisted Nuneaton. Memorial Ref. Panel 96 to 98 Tyne Cot Memorial, Belgium.

KNIGHT, Private, Albert. 94080, 1st Bn., Kings Liverpool Regiment formerly 37756, Royal Warwickshire Regiment. Died of wounds, 29th September, 1918. Born Bedworth. Enlisted Coventry. Resided Bedworth. Memorial Ref. XII. D. 1. Grevillers British Cemetery, France.

KNIGHT, Corporal Alfred Leonard. 92nd Canadians. Only son of Mr. John Knight. Draper and outfitter. Resided 143, New Street, Kenilworth. Born 12th January, 1895. Electrician. Commemorated Bablake School Memorial. Attended Bablake prior to emigrating. No record of being a casualty.

KNIGHT, Private, Arthur. 40394, 9th Bn., Leicestershire Regiment. Killed in action, 1st October, 1917. Age 23. Husband of Annie Robbins (formerly Knight), of 9, Sandy Lane, Coventry. Born Northampton. Enlisted Northampton. Memorial Ref. Panel 50 to 51. Tyne Cot Memorial, Zonnebeke, West-Vlaanderen, Belgium.

KNIGHT, Private, George Henry. 10563, 11th Bn., Royal Warwickshire Regiment. Killed in action, 11th April, 1917. Age 23. Son of George and Hannah Knight of Claybroke Magna, Rugby. Born Meriden. Enlisted Coventry. Resided Claybrook, Leics. Grave Ref. IV. D. 4. Tilloy British Cemetery, Tilloy- Les- Mofflaines, France.

KNIGHT, Private, Tom Percy. 79, 1st Bn., Royal Warwickshire Regiment. Killed in action, Meteren, 13th October, 1914. Born 5th November, 1887 at Upper Radford. Resided 261, Radford. Miner, Binley Colliery formerly in the Birmingham Police Force. Enlisted August, 1914 at Coventry. Commemorated Radford Memorial. Left a wife and a child. Reservist. Grave Ref. III. L. 890. Buried near this spot. Meteren Military Cemetery, France.

KNIGHTON, Corporal, Albert Dennis. 12129, 19th Bn., Manchester Regiment. Died of wounds, Battle of the Somme, 4th July, 1916. Age 25. Son of John William and Ellen Knighton, of 250, Harnall Lane East, Coventry. Born 10th January, 1892 at Kentish Town, Middlesex. Enlisted August, 1914 at Manchester. Resided Coventry. Draper. Grave Ref. II. B. 22. Daours Communal Cemetery Extension, Somme, France.

KNIGHTON, Private, Frederick William. 24571, 2/7th Bn., Royal Warwickshire Regiment. Killed in action, 24th March, 1918. Born 13th June, 1898 at Sheffield. Resided Coventry. Clerk. Enlisted 1917 at Coventry. Memorial Ref. Panel 18 and 19. Pozieres Memorial, France.

LAING, Arthur. Killed in action. Name on Roll of Honour in Cathedral Church of St. Michael.

LAKE, Sergeant, Arthur. 888, 10th Bn., Royal Warwickshire Regiment. Killed in action, 21st, October, 1918. Age 30. Son of Mr. Robert and Mrs. Jane Lake of Albion Street, Kenilworth. Brother of Mrs. Colley of 22, Waterloo Street, Hillfields, Coventry. Memorial Ref. Panel 3. Vis-en-Artois Memorial, France.

LALLY, Rifleman, Patrick Thomas. R/2540, 10th Bn., King's Royal Rifle Corps. Killed in action, 3rd September, 1916. Age 25. Son of John and Margaret Lally. Born Birmingham. Enlisted Birmingham. Resided Coventry. Memorial Ref. Pier and Face 13 A and 13 B. Thiepval Memorial, Somme, France.

LAMB, Private, Alfred. 3206, 2nd /7th Bn., Royal Warwickshire Regiment. Died whilst prisoner of war, 19th July, 1916. Age 19. Son of Arthur Henry and Ann Eliza Lamb, of 24, Russell Street, Coventry. Memorial Ref. Panel 22 to 25. Loos Memorial, Pas de Calais, France.

LAMB, Private, John Alfred. 73001, 162nd Coy., Machine Gun Corps (Infantry) formerly 4644, Royal Warwickshire Regiment. Killed in action, by a shell, St. Quentin, 26th April, 1917. Age 21. Son of Mrs. Lucy Lamb, of 2, Arthur Street, Coventry, Warwickshire. Born 5th September, 1895 at Coventry. Enlisted December, 1915 at Coventry. Machinist, Challenge Cycle Co. Memorial Ref. Pier and Face 5 C and 12 C. Thiepval Memorial, Somme, France.

LANCHBURY, Sergeant, Alfred. 5420, 3rd Bn., Coldstream Guards. Killed in action, Loos, 27th September, 1915. Shot whilst leading hand bombers. Age 32. Son of Alfred and Sarah Lanchbury, of 81, Grange Road, Longford, Coventry. Husband of Ida Margaret Lanchbury, of 24, Medina Road, Finsbury Park, London. Born Coventry. Enlisted Coventry. Resided Hove, Sussex. Employed Exhall Colliery. Leaves a wife and three children. Brother also lost. Commemorated Saint Thomas the Apostle, Longford. Memorial Ref. Panel 7 and 8. Loos Memorial, Pas de Calais, France.

LANCHBURY, Lance Sergeant, William. 8711, 3rd Bn. Coldstream Guards. Killed in action, 25th August, 1914. Seen by his brother Alfred injured on an ambulance. Son of Alfred and Sarah Lanchbury, of 81, Grange Road, Longford, Coventry. Brother also lost. Commemorated Saint Thomas the Apostle, Longford.Grave Ref. A. 11. Landrecies Communal Cemetery, France.

LAND, V. C. Employed Humber Ltd. Killed in action, France.

LANE, Private, Ephraim Bunny. 8883, 1st Bn., Royal Warwickshire Regiment. Killed in action, Ypres, 25th April 1915. Age 31. Son of Alfred and Emily Lane, of 2, Croft Terrace, Rudge Road, Coventry. Husband of Emily Lane, of 444, Stoney Stanton Road, Coventry. Born 5th February, 1884 at Coventry. Enlisted Coventry. Cycle Finisher, Challenge Cycle Works. Reservist. Memorial Ref. Panel 8. Ypres (Menin Gate) Memorial, Ieper, West-Vlaanderen, Belgium.

LANE, Private, Herbert. 35097, 2nd /8th Bn., Worcestershire Regiment. Killed in action, St. Quentin, 21st March 1918. Age 19. Son of Arthur Lane, of 146, Bolingbroke Road, Coventry. Born 25th March 1900 at Coventry. Resided at 146 Bolingbroke Road. Miner, Binley Colliery. Enlisted Coventry, 1916. Commemorated War Memorial Park. Memorial Ref. Panel 41. Pozieres Memorial, Somme, France.

LANE, John. Killed in action, November, 1917. Resided Foleshill.

LANGFORD, Private, Clarence Adrian. 42725, 1st /8th Bn., Royal Warwickshire Regiment. Killed in action, Landrecies, 4th November, 1918. Age 21. Son of John and Elizabeth Langford. Husband of Lizzie Adkins (formerly Langford), of 2, Helen Street, Coventry. Born 14th November, 1896 at Sheffield. Fitter. Enlisted May, 1918. Grave Ref. C. 22. Landrecies British Cemetery, Nord, France.

LANGRIDGE, Private, Thomas. 3416, 3rd /7th Bn., Royal Warwickshire Regiment. transf. to (145593), Labour Corps. Died, home, 14th February, 1919. Age 28. Grave Ref. D. 26. Coventry (Windmill Road) Cemetery.

LAPWORTH, Private, Alec. PLY/17151, 1st Royal Marine Bn., Royal Naval Division, Royal Marine Light Infantry. Died of wounds, Arras, 4th October, 1918. Age 21. Son of Mr. J. H. Lapworth, of 111, Gulson Road, Coventry. Born 1897 in Much Park Street. Machinist, Rover Works. Enlisted September, 1914. Grave Ref. III. C. 3. Sunken Road Cemetery, Boisleux-st. Marc, Pas de Calais, France.

LAPWORTH, Private, Arthur. 24517, 1st /5th Bn., Royal Warwickshire Regiment. Killed in action, Poelcapelle, 4th October, 1917. Age 22. Son of Mrs. A. Lapworth, of 102, King Edward Road, Coventry. Born 1st August, 1895 in Freehold Street. Tailor. Grave Ref. II. C. 14. Dochy Farm New British Cemetery, Langemark-Poelkapelle, Belgium.

LAUGHTON, Lieutenant, Henry Phillip Walter. Royal Air Force. 27th May, 1918. Age 28. Son of Walter Edwin and Louisa Laughton, of Mount Villa, Mount Road, Rondebosch, Cape Town, South Africa. Served in German South West Africa with 2nd Natal Light Horse. Proceeded to England and joined Royal Berkshire Regiment, served in Egypt, Mesopotamia, and on the North-West Frontier of India (where he was wounded). Grave Ref. Radford (St. Nicholas) Churchyard.

LAURISTON, Sapper, Hamilton Walker. 98203, 90th Field Coy., Royal Engineers. Killed in action near Montauban, Longueval, 14th July, 1916. Born 28th January, 1893 at Edinburgh. Resided Coventry. Turner. Enlisted January, 1915. Commemorated Holy Trinity Panels. Memorial Ref. Pier and Face 8 A and 8 D. Thiepval Memorial, France.

LAW, Private, Hodgson. 66238, 24th Bn., Canadian Infantry (Quebec Regiment). Died of sickness following wounds (gas), 7th March, 1918. Age 34. Son of Robert Hodgson Law and Helena Law, of Irthington, Cumberland. Husband of Margaret Law, of 89, Glendower Avenue, Coventry. Grave Ref. Binley (St. Bartholomew) Churchyard.

LAWLEY, Lance Corporal, J. A. 43633, 2nd Bn., Royal Berkshire Regiment formerly 011707, Army Ordnance Corps. Killed in action, 27th April, 1918. Brother of Mr. W. Lawley, of 23, Wyley Road, Coventry. Born Woverhampton. Enlisted Hednesford. Resided Hednesford. Grave Ref. II. N. 14. Adelaide Cemetery, Villers-Bretonneux, Somme, France.

LAWRENCE, Private, John. 1295, 2nd Bn., Royal Warwickshire Regiment. Killed in action, Ypres, 25th October, 1914. Born 6th January, 1892 at Aston. Resided at 121, Broad Street. Stamper's Driver. Reservist. Seen service in Malta and Albania. Memorial Ref. Panel 8. Ypres (Menin Gate) Memorial, Belgium.

LAWRENCE, Sergeant, John. 7296, 2nd Bn., Leicestershire Regiment. Killed in action, 8th April, 1917. Born in Holy Trinity Parish. Memorial Ref. Panel 12. Basra Memorial, Iraq.

LAWRENCE, Private, Walter Joseph. 2921, 7th Bn., Royal Warwickshire Regiment. Age 22. Son of Mr. and Mrs. Lawrence, of Warwick. Death recorded Coventry Graphic. Enlisted Leamington. Resided Warwick. Grave Ref. A.11. Villers-Bocage Communal Cemetery Extension, France.

LAWRENSON, Rifleman, Herbert. 2326, 1st Bn., King's Royal Rifle Corps. Killed in action, Festubert, 15th May, 1915. Killed in between the first and second line of captured German trenches. Age 34. Son of John and Emily Lawrenson, of Coventry. Husband of Annie Louise Lawrenson, of 27, Trafalgar Street, Coventry. Born 23rd March, 1882 in St. Thomas Parish. Resided at 27, Trafalgar Street. Motor mechanic, Rex Motor Works formerly Williamson Motor Works. Reservist, originally enlisted 1899. Commemorated St. John's Church and War Memorial Park. Leaves a wife and one child. Memorial Ref. Panel 32 and 33. Le Touret Memorial, Pas de Calais, France.

LAWSON, Sergeant, Charles, MM. 6409, 10th Bn., Sherwood Foresters (Notts and Derby Regiment). Killed in action, 18th September, 1918. Age 38. Son of Charles Lawson, of Lenton's Lane. Husband of Edith Lawson, of Lenton's Lane, Hawkesbury, Coventry. Born Coventry. Enlisted Nuneaton. Resided Hawkesbury. Commemorated Walsgrave-On-Sowe Memorial and Saint Thomas the Apostle, Longford. Gazetted for Military Medal, 25th January, 1918. Memorial Ref. Panel 7. Vis-En-Artois Memorial, Pas de Calais, France.

LAWSON, Private, George William. 25136, 14th Bn., Royal Warwickshire Regiment. Killed in action, 23rd August, 1918. Born Birmingham. Employed Coventry. Grave Ref. IV. C. 27. Adanac Military Cemetery, Miraumont, France.

LAYCOCK, Private, Arthur William. 3083, 9th Bn., Royal Warwickshire Regiment. Died of wounds, 31st December, 1915. Shot whilst returning from a raiding party. Age 20. Son of Mrs. Mary Arm Laycock, of 15, Harnall Row, Coventry. Born 5th September, 1895 at Scarborough. Resided 11, South Street. Driller, Standard Motor Co. Enlisted August, 1914. Memorial Ref. Panel 35 to 37. Helles Memorial, Turkey.

LAYTE, Private, Alfred. 12876, 1st/5th Bn., Leicestershire Regiment. Killed in action, 24th September, 1918. Age 27. Brother of Mrs. E. Gardiner, of 11, Gun Hill, Arley, Coventry. Born Newhall, Derbyshire. Resided Arley. Employed Coventry. Grave Ref. II. J. 13. Roisel Communal Cemetery Extension, Somme, France.

LAYTON, Private, Albert Edward. 10233, "B" Coy. 7th Bn., King's Shropshire Light Infantry. Killed in action, Arras, 1st April 1917. Shot when retuning from a raiding party. Age 20. Son of Thomas Henry and Clara Layton, of 23, Enfield Road, Stoke, Coventry. Born 9th June, 1897 at Shrewsbury. Soldier. Commemorated Stoke (St. Michaels) Memorial. Grave Ref. II. N. 11. Faubourg D'Amiens Cemetery, Arras, Pas de Calais, France.

LAZSTON, J. Employed Rover Company Ltd. Killed in action.

LEATHER, Private, William. 8580, 9th Bn., Royal Warwickshire Regiment. Killed in action, Gallipoli, 10th August, 1915. Born Coventry. Enlisted Coventry. Resided Primrose Hill Street. Memorial Ref. Panel 35 to 37. Helles Memorial, Turkey.

LEATHER, Corporal, William. 10468, 9th Bn., Royal Warwickshire Regiment. Died of wounds, 29th April 1916. Age 22. Son of John and Margaret Jane Leather, of 86, Radford, Coventry. Born 4th March, 1894 at 90, Radford. Resided 344, Radford Road. Moulder, Alfred Herbert Ltd., Edgewick Enlisted September, 1914. Grave Ref. V. H. 4. Basra War Cemetery, Iraq.

LEAVESLEY, Rifleman, Joseph. S/1658, 11th Bn., Rifle Brigade. Killed in action, near Ypres, 17th February, 1916. Age 23. Husband of Minnie Victoria Leavesley, of 32 Court 2 House, Spon Street, Coventry. Born 9th October, 1891 at 30, Gosford Street, Printer. Coventry. Enlisted September, 1914 at Rugby. Resided Coventry. Commemorated St. John's Church. Grave Ref. I. T. 2. Essex Farm Cemetery, Ieper, West-Vlaanderen, Belgium

LEDBROOKE, Private, Henry Charles. 52372, 1st Bn., Worcestershire Regiment. Killed in action, 24th April, 1918. Age 19. Son of William Thomas and Lily Ledbrooke, of "Glendower," Earlsdon Avenue, Coventry. Born 31st March, 1899 at Leamington Spa. Born Leamington. Enlisted March, 1917 at Coventry. Resided 240, Sovereign Road. Apprentice, machine tools. Grave Ref. I. E. 6. Adelaide Cemetery, Villers-Bretonneux, Somme, France.

LEDUC, F. Corporal. Belgian Army. Died of wounds, April, 19th, 1918. Employed by Armstrong Siddeley Motors Ltd. Awarded Croix De Guerre, 15th April, 1918 for pluck and daring. Wounded 17th April, 1918. Commemorated War Memorial Park and Siddeley Roll of Honour.

LEE, Private, Frank. 42392, 4th Bn., Yorkshire Regiment formerly 18331, Royal Field Artillery. Killed in action, 12th April, 1918. Age 40. Father of Ellen Lee, of 24, Orwell Road, Coventry. Born 22nd July, 1878 at Coventry. Enlisted Coventry. Resided 46, Irving Road. Coal Merchant and Haulage Contractor. Enlisted 1916. Memorial Ref. Panel 4. Ploegsteert Memorial, Comines-Warneton, Hainaut, Belgium.

LEE, Private, William. 4243, "A" Coy. 1st /7th Bn., Royal Warwickshire Regiment. Died of wounds, 29th July, 1916. Age 30. Son of Samuel and Frances May Lee, of 5, Park Side, Coventry, Warwickshire. Born 16th October, 1895 at Sheffield. Resided 5, Park Side. Motor Fitter. Enlisted May, 1915. Grave Ref. II. C. 1. Puchevillers British Cemetery, Somme, France.

LEE, Private, William Richard Howard. 266050, 1/7th Bn., Royal Warwickshire Regiment. Died of wounds, St. Julien, 27th August, 1917. Born 19th April, 1895 at Walsgrave-on-Sowe. Resided Stoneleigh. Turner. Enlisted November, 1914. Brother of Miss F. Lee, Eaton Lodge, Eaton Road, Coventry. Memorial Ref. Panel 23 to 28 and 163A. Tyne Cot Memorial, Belgium.

LEESON, Sergeant, Frederick William. 13064, 5th Bn., Oxfordshire and Buckinghamshire Light Infantry. Killed 25th September, 1915. Age 23. Son of Francis William and Eliza Leeson, of 70, Hartington Road, Leicester. Born 7th August, 1892 at Rugby. Resided at Leicester. Assembler. Enlisted September, 1914. Commemorated British Thompson Houston Memorial. Memorial Ref. Panel 37 and 39. Ypres (Menin Gate) Memorial, Belgium.

LEITH, Lieutenant, Sydney Angus. 38th Squadron, Royal Air Force. Killed while flying (crashed), 19th April, 1918. Son of Mrs. Mary Parker, of Forest Avenue, Forest Hall, Northumberland. Grave Ref. 198. 91. Coventry (London Road) Cemetery.

LENTON, Private, John Henry. 24534, 1/5th Bn., Royal Warwickshire Regiment. Killed in action, 13th August, 1917. Born Coventry. Enlisted Coventry. Resided Hawkesbury. Commemorated Saint Thomas the Apostle, Longford. Memorial Ref. Panel 8. Ypres (Menin Gate) Memorial, Belgium.

LESTER, Private, Alec. 10255, "B" Squadron, 11th (Prince Albert's Own) Hussars. Died of wounds, home, 3rd June 1915. Age 20. Son of John and Hannah Marsh (formerly Lester), of II, West Street, Stourbridge, Worcs. Born at Coventry. Born Coventry. Enlisted Wolverhampton. Resided Brierley Hill. Grave Ref. South-West of Church. Brierley Hill (St. Michael) Churchyard, Staffordshire.

LESTER, Private, Fred. 20985, 1st Bn., Coldstream Guards. Killed in action 19th October, 1917. Born 30th March, 1885 at Wolverhampton. Resided 21, Wren Street. Tool Fitter. Enlisted 1916. Memorial Ref. Panel 9 to 10. Tyne Cot Memorial, Belgium.

LESTER, Stoker 1st Class, William Edward. K/7497, HMS Defence, Royal Navy. Killed in action, Battle of Jutland, 31st May, 1916. Age 26. Son of Elizabeth Lester, of 42, Smith Street, Coventry. Born 1890 in Cook Street. Resided Cox Street. Sailor previously employed Messrs Calcott Bros. Memorial Ref. 16. Plymouth Naval Memorial.

LEWIS, Rifleman, Frank. (Known as Frank Hickman). S/1657, 11th Bn., Rifle Brigade. Died of wounds, 19th March, 1916. Born 8th May, 1896 in Spon Street, Coventry. Enlisted Rugby. Resided 28c. 5h. Spon Street. Brewer's Assistant. Enlisted August, 1914. Coventry. Commemorated St. John's Church as F. Hickman. Grave Ref. VD. 7. A. Lijssenthoek Military Cemetery, Belgium.

LEWIS, Private, Frederick, 19819, 2nd Bn., Wiltshire Regiment formerly 980, Royal Warwickshire Regiment. Killed in action, 15th June, 1915. Age 25. Son of Fred Lewis, of Foleshill, Coventry, and Harriett Lewis. Born Fritwell, Oxon. Enlisted Coventry. Resided Coventry. Memorial Ref. Panel 33 and 34. Le Touret Memorial, Pas de Calais, France.

LEWIS, Private, Frederick George. 9774, 2nd Bn., Oxfordshire and Buckinghamshire Light Infantry. Killed in action, Poelcapelle, 24th October, 1914. Age 21. Son of Walter Lewis, of 12, Caludon Road, Stoke, Coventry. Born Coventry. Enlisted Coventry. Born 21st June, 1893 at 20, King William Street. Chain maker, Coventry Chain Co. Memorial Ref. Panel 37 and 39. Ypres (Menin Gate) Memorial, Ieper, West-Vlaanderen, Belgium.

LEWIS, Private, Frederick John. 15070, 2nd /7th Bn., Royal Warwickshire Regiment. Killed in action, 24th October, 1918. Age 19. Son of Mr. H. J. T. and Mrs. R. Lewis, of 79, King Edward Road, Coventry. Born 29th July, 1899 at Bromsgrove. Engineer, Singer Co., Canterbury Street. Enlisted October, 1915. Memorial Ref. Panel 3. Vis-En-Artois Memorial, Pas de Calais, France. (Possibly buried Cambrai).

LEWIS, Corporal, Thomas. 200550, 4th Bn., Oxfordshire and Buckinghamshire Light Infantry. Died, Home, 27th October, 1918. Born Hillfields. Resided Grimsbury, Oxon. Grave Ref. 10478. Banbury Cemetery.

LIGGINS, Gunner, Frederick Thomas. 840559, "D" Bty. 307th Bde., Royal Field Artillery. Killed in action, Ypres, 15th August, 1917. Born Foleshill. Resided 25, George Street. Grave Ref. III. E. 11. White House Cemetery, St. Jean-les-ypres, Belgium.

LIGGINS, Private, Reginald John. PO/1375(S), 1st Royal Marine Bn., Royal Naval Division, Royal Marine Light Infantry. Killed in action, Miraumont, 17th February, 1917. Age 21. Son of Fred and Eliza Liggins, of Waterworks, Keresley, Coventry. Born 7th November, 1895 in Station Street East. Resided Water Pumping Station, Keresley. Tailors Apprentice. Enlisted February, 1916. Commemorated St. Thomas Memorial. Memorial Ref. Pier and Face 1 A. Thiepval Memorial, Somme, France.

LINDER, Private, Edward. 10752, 2nd Bn., Royal Warwickshire Regiment. Killed in action, 23rd April, 1916. Born Rushall, Norfolk. Employed Coventry. Grave Ref. IV. B. 3. Citadel New Military Cemetery, Fricourt, France.

LINDON, Private, Daniel. 26283, Canterbury Regiment, New Zealand Expeditionary Force. Died, 14th June, 1919. Age 42. Born at Coventry. Grave Ref. Soldiers Plot. Row A. Grave 4. Blenheim (Omaka) Public Cemetery, Marlborough District, New Zealand.

LINES, A. Employed Humber Ltd. Killed in action, France.

LINES, Private, John. 9886, 2nd Bn., Royal Warwickshire Regiment. Killed in action, Loos, 25th September, 1915. Husband of Mrs. T. Lines, of 1 Court, 17 House, Leicester Street, Coventry. Born Birmingham. Enlisted 1914. Memorial Ref. Panel 22 to 25. Loos Memorial, Pas de Calais, France.

LINNETT, Private, Frederick. 1155, 2nd Bn., Royal Warwickshire Regiment. Killed in action, 3rd September, 1916. Son of William and Harriett Linnett of Stretton-on-Dunsmore. Born Stretton. Enlisted Coventry. Resided Stretton-on-Dunsmore. Memorial Ref. Pier and Face 9A 9B and 10B. Thiepval Memorial, Somme, France.

LISSAMAN, Private, Edwin. 19466, 2/6th Bn., Royal Warwickshire Regiment. Killed in action, 20th August, 1918. Age 26. Born Coventry. Enlisted Coventry. Grave Ref. 5. E. 3. Tannay British Cemetery, Thiennes, France.

LIXENFIELD, Lance Corporal, John Charles. 41457, Royal Engineers. Died, home, Manchester, 13th May, 1917. Injured due to shrapnel wounds in the head. Resided School Street, Wolston. Age 22. Son of John and Ada Emily Lixenfield, of School Street, Wolston. Enlisted August, 1914. Employed Messrs. Bluemels Ltd. Commemorated Queens Road Church and Wolston Memorial. Grave Ref. Q. 34. Wolston Cemetery.

LLOYD, Private, Harry, DCM. 2965, 1/7th Bn., Royal Warwickshire Regiment. Killed in action, 25th July, 1916. Age 30. Employed Coventry. Son of Thomas and Annie Lloyd. Husband of Eliza Lloyd, of 1, Back, 98, Bridge Street, West Hockley, Birmingham. Also served on North-West Frontier of India, with 1st Bn. (1908). Memorial Ref. Pier and Face 9 A 9 B and 10 B. Thiepval Memorial, Somme, France.

LLOYD, Second Lieutenant, William Merrick Ellis. 40th Bde., Royal Field Artillery. Killed in action, 19th May, 1917. Age 23. Son of William Ellis and Hannah M. U. Allen (formerly Lloyd), of Asleton House, 69, Compton Road, Wolverhampton. Educated Radley College. Employed Daimler Co. Ltd. Enlisted 1915. Grave Ref. V. F. 9. Faubourg D'Amiens Cemetery, Arras, France

LOAKES, Private, George William. 265845, 11th Bn., Royal Warwickshire Regiment. Killed in action, Arras, 23rd April, 1917. Age 22. Son of Mr. and Mrs. G. W. Loakes, of 52, St. John Street, Coventry. Born 26th September, 1895 at 26, St. John Street. Resided 30, St. John Street. Butcher. Enlisted September, 1914. Grave Ref. A. 10. Hervin Farm British Cemetery, St. Laurent-Blangy, Pas de Calais, France.

LOCK, E. Employed Humber Ltd. Killed in action.

LOCKE, Private, Albert Edward. 8314, 1st Bn., Royal Munster Fusiliers. Killed in action, outside his dugout, 27th November, 1915. Age 30. Son of Frederick Locke, of 14, Connors Lane, Boherbee Tralee, Co. Kerry. Memorial Ref. Panel 185 to 190. Helles Memorial, Turkey.

LOGAN, Second Lieutenant, Robert. 4th Battalion, Kings Own Scottish Borderers. Killed in action, Landrecies, 20th October, 1918. Age 25. Only son of James and Mary Dickinson Logan, of Birkhill, Earlston, Berwickshire. Commemorated War Memorial Park. Grave Ref. IV. G. 24. Caudry British Cemetery, France.

LOMAS, Electrical Artificer 4th Class, Harold. M/8858, HMS Invincible. Killed in action, Naval Battle of Jutland, 31st May, 1916. Born 1892 at 119, Humber Avenue. Tester, Humber Ltd. Memorial Ref. 20. Portsmouth Naval Memorial.

LOMAS, Private, Joseph. 3/7859, 1st Bn., Norfolk Regiment. Died of wounds, 25th July 1916. Age 34. Son of Mr. J. Lomas, of Coventry. Born 1882, in St. Michael's Parish. Grave Ref. VI. A. 14. Abbeville Communal Cemetery, Somme, France.

LOMBARD, Private, Ernest. 242732, 1st /6th Bn., Royal Warwickshire Regiment. Killed in action, Bullecourt, near Arras, 19th June, 1917. Age 33. Son of William and Sarah Lombard, of The New Inn, Little Heath, Foleshill. Husband of Emma Lombard, of 124, Little Heath Road, Foleshill, Coventry. Born 4th April, 1884 in Station Street West. Barman. Enlisted June, 1916. Memorial Ref. Bay 3. Arras Memorial, Pas de Calais, France.

LOMBARD, Private, Harry. 44662, 8th Bn., Royal Berkshire Regiment formerly 26552, Royal Warwickshire Regiment. Killed in action, 12th May, 1918. Age 19. Son of William Henry and Ellen Maria Lombard, of 110, Broad Street, Coventry. Born 24th November, 1898 at 11, Holbrook Lane, Coventry. Enlisted Coventry. Machinist. Enlisted March, 1917. Commemorated St. Paul's Foleshill formerly Lockhurst Lane Methodist Church. Grave Ref. VI. I. 1. Dernancourt Communal Cemetery Extension, Somme, France.

LONG, Acting Sergeant, Ernest Harold, DCM, MM. 4765, 10th Bn., Royal Warwickshire Regiment formerly 13994, Northumberland Regiment. Killed in action, Somme, 31st May, 1918. Age 30. Son of Frederick and Sarah Long. Enlisted September, 1914 at Northampton. Resided Coventry. Born 29th May, 1888 at Berkswell Park. Employed Goods Station, Coventry. Awarded the Military Medal for Gallantry, 1916. Distinguished Conduct Medal awarded 1917 for conspicuous gallantry and devotion to duty during a raid on the enemy's trenches. He personally captured two prisoners after a hand to hand struggle and showed great courage and determination. Memorial Ref. Soissons Memorial, France.

LONGDEN, Private, Harry. 1434, 2nd Bn., Royal Warwickshire Regiment. Killed in action, Loos, 25th September, 1915. Age 23. Son of Mrs. E. Richard, of 8 Court, 6 House, Bond Street, Coventry. Born 1891 at Birmingham Soldier. Memorial Ref. Panel 22 to 25. Loos Memorial, Pas de Calais, France.

LONGHURST, Private, Thomas William. 17154, 9th Bn., Essex Regiment. Killed in action, 18th May, 1918. Age 39. Husband of Amy Alice May Longhurst, of 3, Wyatts Lane, Wood Street, Walthamstow, London. Born Coventry. Enlisted Walthamstow, Essex. Resided Walthamstow. Grave Ref. II. L . 12. Mailly Wood Cemetery, Mailly-Maillet, France.

LORD, Sapper, Arthur Rowland. 36831, 1st Field Coy., Royal Engineers. Killed in action, 10th March, 1918. Age 22. Born at Coventry. Enlisted Portsmouth. Son of Mr. A. W. and Mrs. C. Lord of 198, Albert Road, Southsea, Portsmouth. Commemorated War Memorial Park. Grave Ref. I. B. 8. Vadencourt British Cemetery, Maissemy, France.

LORD, Gunner, Ernest Arthur. 19161, B Reserve Bde., Royal Horse Artillery formerly Royal Field Artillery. Died, home, 8th May, 1921. Born 22nd June, 1895 at Coventry. Resided Coventry. Butcher. Enlisted August, 1914. Grave Ref. 148. 42130. Highgate Cemetery.

LORD, Private, Fred. 235066, 1st Battalion, Kings Own (Royal Lancaster Regiment). Killed in action, Arras, 2nd April 1918. Age 39. Son of Fred and Selina Lord. Husband of Clara Lord of 6 Winterton Road, Reddish, Stockport. Born 20th June, 1878 at Radford. Resided at Manchester. Master butcher. Enlisted Manchester, May 1917. Commemorated War Memorial Park. Grave Ref. Sp. Mem. V. C. 10. Buried near this spot. Bailleul Road East Cemetery, St Laurent-Blangy, France.

LOUDON, Private, William Alexander. 40470, 7/8th Bn., King's Own Scottish Borderers formerly 4159, Royal Scots. Killed in action, 28th March, 1918 at Pelves, East of Arras. Born 8th February, 1896 at Holyhead House, Holyhead Road. Coventry. Enlisted February, 1916 at Portobello, Midlothian. Resided Portobello, Edinburgh, Midlothian. Clerk. Educated Bablake School. Commemorated Bablake School Memorial. Memorial Ref. Bay 6. Arras Memorial, France.

LOUNTON, Private, George. 18/317, 18th Bn., Durham Light Infantry. Killed in action, 25th June, 1916. Born Bishop Wearmouth, Sunderland. Resided South Shields. Journalist (previously with The Midland Daily Telegraph). Grave Ref. 1. D. 11. Bertrancourt Military Cemetery, France.

LOVATT, Private, John. 205295, "A" Bn., Tank Corps. Killed in action, Ypres, 31st July, 1917. Son of Mrs. Ada Lovatt, of 16, Kingston Road, Coventry. Memorial Ref. Panel 56. Ypres (Menin Gate) Memorial, Ieper, West-Vlaanderen, Belgium.

LOVEGROVE, Rifleman, Thomas Henry. 301860, 5th Bn., London Regiment (London Rifle Brigade). Killed in action, 20th September, 1917. Age 21. Son of Thomas and Emma Lovegrove, of Coventry. Born 18th September, 1896 at 20, South Street, Coventry. Enlisted London. Resided 125, St. George's Road, Coventry. Clerk Grave Ref. X. A. 24. Tyne Cot Cemetery, Zonnebeke, West-Vlaanderen, Belgium.

LOVEITT, Second Lieutenant, Alan Percy Charles. 7th Bn., Royal Warwickshire Regiment. Killed in action, near Pozieres, 25th July, 1916. Age 20. Son of Mr. and Mrs. Percy G. Loveitt (auctioneer and estate agent), of "Anlaby", Davenport Road, Coventry. Born 26th September 1895, at Kingston-upon-Thames. Resided at Anlaby, Davenport Road. Undergraduate, St. Johns College Oxford University and educated Rugby School. Enlisted August 1915. Commemorated War Memorial Park. Memorial Ref. Pier and Face 9 A 9 B and 10 B. Thiepval Memorial, Somme, France.

LOVELL, Corporal, Walter. 92873, 213th Army Troops Coy. Royal Engineers. Killed in action, 25th July, 1916 when working on the construction of a water track at the rear of the front line trenches. Age 34. Son of William and Annie Lovell, of 177, Team Terrace, Leamington Spa. Born Leamington. Employed Rover Co. Ltd. Grave Ref. II. Z. 17. Essex Farm Cemetery, Belgium.

LOVERIDGE, Private, John William. 20921, 1st /6th Bn., Royal Warwickshire Regiment. Died of wounds, Rouen, 18th February, 1917. Age 33. Son of Frederick and Eliza Loveridge. Husband of Florence Loveridge, of 5 Court, 1, Matthew Square, Bond Street, Coventry. Born 23rd April, 1884 at Fenny Stratford. Gardener. Enlisted June, 1916. Commemorated St. John's Church. Grave Ref. O.V. I. 6. St. Sever Cemetery Extension, Rouen, Seine-Maritime, France.

LOWE, Corporal, Charles. 7129, 1st Bn., Essex Regiment. Died of wounds, 16th October, 1916. Born Coventry. Enlisted Stratford, Essex. Resided King's Norton, Birmingham. Grave Ref. III. G. 74. Heilly Station Cemetery, Mericourt-L'abbe, France.

LOWE, Private, Henry Arthur. 266861, 1st /7th Bn., Royal Warwickshire Regiment. Died of wounds, 12th August, 1917. Age 25. Son of Joseph and Elizabeth Lowe, of Bull's Head Inn Yard, Bishop Street, Coventry. Born 4th May, 1892. Carter. Employed Carter in the Coal Trade. Grave Ref. V. F. 4. Brandhoek New Military Cemetery, Ieper, West-Vlaanderen, Belgium.

LOWE, Private, William Henry. 24550, 2/5th Bn., Royal Warwickshire Regiment. Died of wounds, Belgium, 12th August, 1917. Memorial Ref. Panel 23 to 28 and 163A. Tyne Cot Memorial, Belgium.

LUCAS, Lance Corporal, Abraham. 7084, 1st Bn., Leicestershire Regiment. Died of wounds, 5th February, 1915. Born 1887 at Highbridge, Somerset. Resided Carmelite Road. Police Constable. Reservist. Enlisted August, 1914. Commemorated Police Force Memorial, Coventry Corporation. Memorial Ref. 4. Ploegsteert Memorial, Belgium.

LUCAS, Private, Arthur William. 241621, 1st Bn., Royal Warwickshire Regiment. Died, home, 1st November, 1919. Resided Dolphin Inn, Market Square. Tailor. Enlisted March, 1916. Grave Ref. 111. 164. Coventry (London Road) Cemetery.

LUCAS, Private, Albert. 59348, 1/8th Bn., Worcestershire Regiment. Killed in action, 4th November, 1918. Enlisted Coventry. Resided Coventry. Grave Ref. B. 37. Landrecies British Cemetery, France.

LUCAS, Company Sergeant Major, Bertie, MM. 265476, B Coy., 1st /7th Bn., Royal Warwickshire Regiment. Killed in action, Ypres, 11th August, 1917. Age 25. Son of John Thomas and Emma Elizabeth Lucas, of 404, Radford Road, Coventry. Born 21st December, 1893. Resided at 146, Radford. Cycle Finisher, Rudge Whitworth Works. Enlisted August, 1914. Awarded Military Medal for gallantry in volunteering for and undertaking difficult patrol work on July, 26th, 1916 near Pozieres, he formed and led a successful bombing party, and held up a German counter attack. Memorial Ref. Panel 8. Ypres (Menin Gate) Memorial, Belgium.

LUCAS, Lance Corporal, Ernest. 266383, 2nd /7th Bn., Royal Warwickshire Regiment. Killed in action, 18th April, 1918. Husband of Mrs. E. Lucas, of 2, Court, 4, House, Warwick Lane, Coventry. Born 25th September, 1886 at Gosford Street, Coventry. Enlisted January, 1915. Grave Ref. III. A. 5. St. Venant-Robecq Road British Cemetery, Robecq, Pas de Calais, France.

LUCAS, Lance Corporal, Frederick. 2595, 1/7th Bn., Royal Warwickshire Regiment. Killed in action, 14th July, 1916. Born 12th September, 1893 at Coventry. Resided at 11, Moat Street. Motor Wheel Builder, Rudge works. Enlisted September, 1914. Grave Ref. I. E. 16. Pozieres British Cemetery, Ovillers-La Boisselle, France.

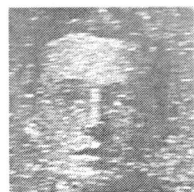
LUCAS, H. Commemorated Radford Memorial. Died of wounds.

LUCAS, Private, Leonard. 1603, 1st Bn., Royal Warwickshire Regiment. Died of wounds, 14th October, 1916. Age 19. Son of George and Harriett Lucas. Native of Coventry. Born 1897 at 13, Waterloo Street. Resided 13, Waterloo Street. Mechanic. Enlisted June, 1914. Grave Ref. I. L. 13. Grove Town Cemetery, Meaulte, Somme, France.

LUCAS, Corporal, Reginald Arthur, DSM. 202927, Royal Air Force. Drowned at sea, subsequent to enemy engagement, 27th April, 1918. Age 21. Son of Thomas Henry and Fanny Francis Lucas, of 6, Gordon Street, Coventry. Born 8th August, 1896 at Coventry. Resided at 6, Gordon Street. Mechanic. Enlisted in 1915. Commemorated War Memorial Park. Awarded Distinguished Service Medal for sinking a submarine. Memorial Ref. Hollybrook Memorial, Southampton, Hampshire.

LUCAS, Able Seaman, Richard Bert. SS/120, (RFR/PO/B/6081). HMS Bayano, Royal Navy. Killed in action in action with a submarine, off the Clyde, 11th March, 1915 when torpedoed and sunk by U-27. Age 31. Son of William and Sarah Lucas, of Eurek Villa, Park Road, Bedworth, Warwickshire. Husband of Beatrice Lucas, of 30, Longford Road, Foleshill, Coventry. Born 1884. Memorial Ref. 7. Portsmouth Naval Memorial, Hampshire.

LUCKETT, Private, George Edward. 23891, 1st Bn., Royal Warwickshire Regiment. Killed in action, 25th April, 1915. Age 22. Son of Mr. and Mrs. Herbert Luckett, of Rose Cottage, 36 Victoria Street, Small Heath, Birmingham. Born 20th August, 1896 at Brentford. Resided Coventry. Printer's Apprentice. Enlisted August, 1914. Grave Ref. A. 23. Landrecies British Cemetery, France.

LUDERS, Private, George Augustus. 1/2nd Bn., West Yorkshire Regiment. Killed in action, Nueve Chapelle, 11th March, 1915. Born 5th July, 1892 at Stepney. Resided at 59, Earlsdon Street. Soldier.

LUDFORD, Private, Henry Edward. 29116, 1st Bn., Hampshire Regiment. Killed in action, 1st November, 1918. Born 10th February, 1900 at 14c. 6h. Much Park Street. Coventry. Enlisted March, 1918 at Leamington. Resided 14c. 6h. Much Park Street, Coventry. Aeroplane Tile Rod Threader. Grave Ref. D. 13. Preseau Communal Cemetery Extension, France.

LUDFORD, Private, Lawrence. 2646, 1st /7th Bn., Royal Warwickshire Regiment. Killed in action, 14th July, 1916. Age 21. Son of Charles John and F. Ludford, of 67, Thomas Street, Coventry. Born Greyfriars Lane. Memorial Ref. Pier and Face 9 A 9 B and 10 B. Thiepval Memorial, Somme, France.

LUDFORD, Private, Percy William. 62628, 16th Bn., Royal Warwickshire Regiment. Killed in action, 10th August, 1918. Born 24th October, 1899 in Lockhurst Lane. Resided 8, Whitefriar's Street. Textile Worker. Enlisted November, 1917. Grave Ref. V. C. 5. Bouchoir New British Cemetery, France.

LUDFORD, R. Commemorated Coventry Chain Memorial.

LUDFORD, Private, S. Royal Warwickshire Regiment. Killed in action. Name on roll of Honour in St. Thomas's Church.

LUDGATE, Lance Corporal, Joseph. 10658, 5th Bn., Oxfordshire and Buckinghamshire Light Infantry. Killed in action, 11th July, 1915. Age 21. Son of Ben Ludgate, of 21, Henry Street, Coton, Nuneaton. Husband of Florence Powell (formerly Ludgate), of 76, Bottrill Street, Nuneaton. Born Coventry. Enlisted Nuneaton. Memorial Ref. Panel 37 and 39. Ypres (Menin Gate) Memorial, Belgium.

LUGGAR, Private, Gerald Percy. 2589, 1st/1st Warwickshire Yeomanry. Killed in action, 21st August, 1915. Age 25. Son of Walter James and Elizabeth Luggar, of 97, Tachbrook Street, Leamington. Husband of Gertrude Hetty Luggar. Related to Mr. C. W. Townsend, of 78, Queen Mary's Road, Coventry. Memorial Ref. Panel 16. Helles Memorial, Turkey.

LUKE, Charles Henry. Resided 35, Vine Street. Print Storeman. Enlisted August, 1914.

LUMBERT, Private, Ernest. 71493, 27th Bn., Canadian Infantry (Manitoba Regiment). St. Eloi, 4th April, 1916. Age 33. Son of Clara Lumbert, of "The Hawthorns", Harefield Road, Stoke, Coventry. Born 15th November 1883, at Birmingham. Resided at Winnipeg, Canada previously at "Claremont", Northumberland Road. Employed Post Office. Commemorated War Memorial Park. Memorial Ref. Panel 24 - 26 - 28 - 30. Ypres (Menin Gate) Memorial, Ieper, West-Vlaanderen, Belgium.

LUMBY, Private, John William. Royal Warwickshire Regiment. Died of wounds, received in France, home, 1st April, 1919. Born 4th May, 1893 at Swalwell, Durham. Resided at 70, Bedlam Cottages, Foleshill. Filer. Enlisted December, 1915. Grave Ref. Salem Chapel Cemetery, Longford.

LUNN, Private, William. 24579, 2/5th Bn., Royal Warwickshire Regiment. Killed in action, 8th November, 1917. Employed Coventry. Grave Ref. I. C. 16. Sunken Road Cemetery, Fampoux, France.

LUTY, Sergeant, Arthur. 8393, "D" Coy., 2nd Bn., Royal Berkshire Regiment. Killed in action, 11th November 1916. Age 39. Son of Ernest and Julia Luty, of Coventry. Husband of Emily Luty, of 15, Theatre Street, Warwick. Born Warwick. Reservist. Memorial Ref. Pier and Face 11 D. Thiepval Memorial, Somme, France.

LYDIATT, Lance Corporal. J. M/098295, 562nd Coy., Royal Army Service Corps. Died Wimereux Hospital, 9th April, 1919. Born 1884. Resided 86, Bolingbroke Road. Grave Ref. XIV. A. 5. Terlincthun British Cemetery, Wimille, France.

LYNCH, Private, John W. PO/10585, HMS Invincible, Royal Marine Light Infantry. Killed in action, Battle of Jutland, 31st May, 1916. Scholar at St. Mary's Roman Catholic School. Raised by Mrs. Branson. Commemorated Exhall Memorial. Memorial Ref. 22. Portsmouth Memorial.

LYNCH, Rifleman, Nicholas D. A/3575, 10th Bn., Kings Royal Rifles. Died of wounds, 28th June, 1916. Resided at Neales Green, Exhall. Cycle Mechanic. Enlisted August, 1914. Born Manchester. Enlisted Nuneaton. Employed Ed. O' Brien's Ltd. First man from Exhall to enlist. Raised by Mrs. Branson. Commemorated Exhall Memorial. Grave Ref. I. C. 26. Ypres Reservoir Cemetery, Belgium.

LYNDON, Private, Thomas. 90022, 2/4th Bn., London Regiment, Royal Fusiliers formerly 40720, Somerset Light Infantry Regiment. Killed in action, 25th April, 1918. Age 18. Son of Thomas and Alice Lyndon, of 25, Windsor Street, Leamington Spa. Born Coventry. Enlisted Leamington. Resided Leamington. Memorial Ref. Panel 19 to 21. Pozieres Memorial, France.

LYNES, Private, Bert Frederick. 6835, 2nd Bn., Coldstream Guards. Died of wounds, Battle of the Aisne, 18th September, 1914. Born 1884 in St. John's Parish. Commemorated St. John's Church. Grave Ref. I. 733. Villeneuve-St. Georges Old Communal Cemetery, France.

LYNES, Private, Thomas. 9590, 11th Bn., Royal Warwickshire Regiment. Died of wounds, 19th July, 1916. Age 32. Husband of Jane Lynes, of 2 Court, 2 House, London Road, Coventry. Born 1884 at 13c. 11h. Gosford Street, Polisher. Enlisted Coventry. Reservist. Commemorated St. John's Church. Grave Ref. II. D. 45. Heilly Station Cemetery, Mericourt-L'abbe, Somme, France.

LYNES, Private, William, 8173, 1st Bn., East Lancashire Regiment. Killed in action, 14th November, 1914. Son of Mr. C. Lynes, of 4 Court, 5 House, Hill Street, Coventry. Born 1880 at Coventry. Enlisted Coventry. Grave Ref. I. A. 5. Lancashire Cottage Cemetery, Comines-Warneton, Hainaut, Belgium.

LYONS, Corporal, Charles. 192631, "G" Special Coy., Royal Engineers formerly 58404, Royal Field Artillery. Killed in action, 7th October, 1918. Age 24. Son of Emily Lyons, of Hall Hill Lane, Keresley, Coventry. Born 1894 at Coventry. Enlisted Coventry. Employed New Colliery, Keresley. Commemorated St. Thomas Memorial. Grave Ref. III. A. 1. Haynecourt British Cemetery, Nord, France.

MacDERMOT, Private, Martin. 69162, 1/5th Bn., Northumberland Fusiliers. Killed in action, 10th April, 1918. Age 19. Brother of John McDermott, of 9, Strickland Street, Hessle, Hull. Born Hull. Employed Coventry. Memorial Ref. 2. Ploegsteert Memorial, Belgium.

MacDONALD, Private, Alexander Ross. 425586, 31st Bn., Canadian Infantry (Alberta Regiment). Killed in action, Courcelette, 15th September, 1916. Age 32. Son of John and Isabella MacDonald, of 19, Butts, Coventry. Born 13th December 1884 at Glasgow. Resided at Lidstone, Canada (previously 19, Butts). Engineer. Enlisted September 1915. Commemorated War Memorial Park. Memorial Ref. Vimy Memorial, Pas de Calais, France.

MacNAMARA, Private, Charles Henry. 27922, 1/7th Bn., Royal Warwickshire Regiment. Killed in action, 27th August, 1917. Born 28th March, 1896 at Edinburgh. Resided Coventry. Stereotyper, Stereotyping Department, Iliffe and sons Ltd. Enlisted September, 1914. Son of Mr. and Mrs. C. MacNamara of 1, St. Agatha's Road, Coventry. Commemorated Iliffe & Sons Ltd Memorial. Grave Ref. XII. B. 6. New Irish Farm Cemetery, Belgium.

MADDOCKS, Lieutenant, John Anslow. 15th Bn., Royal Warwickshire Regiment. Killed in action, Arras, 4th June, 1916 in his dugout by a large shell. Age 19. Son of Sir Henry Maddocks, K.C., and Lady Maddocks, of "Wytheford," Sandy Lodge, Northwood. Middx . Born 20th January, 1897 at Coventry. Resided Hatch End, Middlesex. Schoolboy. Enlisted November, 1914. Commemorated King Henry VIII School and Stoke (St. Michaels) Church. Grave Ref. I. D. 29. Faubourg D'Amiens Cemetery, Arras, France.

MADELIN, Private, Thomas Cyril. 18682, 2nd Bn., Northamptonshire Regiment. Killed in action, 16th August, 1917. Born 19th November, 1891. Resided Coventry. Railway Clerk. Enlisted May, 1915. Memorial Ref. Panel 104 to 105. Tyne Cot Memorial, Belgium.

MAGSON, Private, Samuel. 2199, 1st Bn., Royal Warwickshire Regiment. Killed in action, 13th October, 1914. Age 19. Born 12th April, 1895 at 22, Bridge Row, Foleshill. Enlisted Warwick. Resided 11c. 20h. Gosford Street, Coventry. Soldier. Memorial Ref. III. L. 891. (Buried near this spot). Meteren Military Cemetery, Belgium.

MAHER, Matthew. Killed in action, February, 1917. Resided Foleshill.

MAHERS, Corporal, John. 1224, 11th Bn., Manchester Regiment. Killed in action, 26th September, 1916. Born Manchester. Resided Hillfields. Memorial Ref. Pier and Face 13 A and 14 C. Thiepval Memorial, Somme, France.

MAHERS, Private, William. 8577, 2nd Bn., Manchester Regiment. Killed in action, 20th October, 1914. Age 32. Son of James and Kathleen Mahers, of 54, Castle Street, Coventry. Husband of Mary Griffiths (formerly Mahers), of 30 Court, 3 House, Spon St., Coventry. Born Salford, Lancs. Enlisted Ashton-Under-Lyne, Lancs. Resided Coventry. Commemorated Coventry Chain Memorial. Memorial Ref. Panels 34 and 35. Le Touret Memorial, Pas de Calais, France.

MALL, S. Royal Munster Fusiliers. Killed in action, Gallipoli. Billeted Coventry.

MALLABONE, Lance Corporal, Thomas. 12694, 11th Bn., Royal Warwickshire Regiment. Killed in action, 12th March, 1916. Age 32. Son of J. T. Mallabone, of Rowley's Green, Foleshill, Coventry. Born Chilvers Coton. Enlisted Coventry. Resided Collycroft. Grave Ref. III. A. 4. Bienvillers Military Cemetery, Pas de Calais, France.

MALLON, Edward. Killed in action, Mesopotamia, October, 1918. Resided Foleshill.

MANDER, Captain, Alfred Ernest. "A" Coy, 4th Bn., Duke of Wellington's (West Riding Regiment). Killed in action, Passchendaele Ridge, 9th October, 1917. Reported to have been shot in the head. Age 38. Third son of Alderman and Mrs. H. Mander, of Spon House, Coventry. Born 15th September 1879 at Spon End. Resided at Spon House. Educated at Trinity College, Dublin. Schoolmaster. Enlisted September, 1914. Commemorated Bablake School Memorial and War Memorial Park. Memorial Ref. Panel 82 to 85 and 162A. Tyne Cot Memorial, Zonnebeke, West-Vlaanderen, Belgium.

MANN, Sergeant, Albert Ernest. A/34490, 10th Bn., Canadian Infantry (Alberta Regiment). Killed in action, Vimy Ridge, 9th April, 1917. Age 25. Husband of Irene Frances Annie Mann, of St. Dunstan's School, Stoke Green, Coventry, England. Born in 1892 at Matlock. Resided at Calgary, Canada (formerly Coventry). Engineer. Commemorated Stoke (St. Michael's) Church and War Memorial Park. Memorial Ref. Vimy Memorial, Pas de Calais, France.

MANN, Private, Charles Edward. 1978, 2nd Battalion, Royal Warwickshire Regiment. Died of wounds, 24th May, 1916. Age 23. Son of John and Laura Mann, of 1 Ufton, Southam, Warwickshire. Commemorated War Memorial Park. Grave Ref. Plot 1. Row A. Grave 28. Corbie Communal Cemetery Extension, France.

MANN, H. Commemorated Coventry Chain Memorial.

MANNERS, Lance Corporal, George. 6749, 2nd Bn., York and Lancaster Regiment. Killed in action, 11th May, 1915. Age 31. Son of James Manners, of Coundon. Husband of Elsie M. Manners, of 100, Lockhurst Lane, Coventry. Born 14th January, 1884 at Coundon. Employed in running shed, Standard Motor Co. Ltd. Enlisted August, 1914. Commemorated St. Thomas Memorial. Grave Ref. II. E. 4. Houplines Communal Cemetery Extension, Nord, France.

MANNING, Private, Harold Frank Victor. 645, 16th Service Battalion, Royal Warwickshire Regiment. Died, home from illness, 21st November, 1915 at a Military Hospital, Codford, Wiltshire. Born 1885 at Hunstanton, Norfolk. Enlisted Birmingham. Resided 36, Chester Street, Coventry. Solicitor's Clerk, Messrs Twist & Sons. Commemorated St. John's Church. Grave Ref. Radford (St. Nicholas) Churchyard, Coventry.

MANNION, Private, Patrick. 32542, 1st /5th Bn., Devonshire Regiment. Killed in action, 27th September, 1918. Son of Mrs. Mannion, of 346, Grange Road, Longford, Coventry. Born Bloxwich, Staffs. Enlisted Leamington. Resided Coventry. Commemorated Saint Thomas the Apostle, Longford. Grave Ref. B. 1. Lowrie Cemetery, Havrincourt, Pas de Calais, France.

MANSFIELD, Lance Corporal, Harold. 16500, 14th Bn., Royal Warwickshire Regiment. Killed in action, 3rd September, 1916. Born 6th April, 1893. Resided Coventry. Railway Clerk. Enlisted February, 1916. Memorial Ref. Pier and Face 9 A 9 B and 10 B. Thiepval Memorial, Somme, France.

MANTLE, Private, Harry Bolderson. 82592, 2nd Bn., London Regiment, Royal Fusiliers formerly 3219, 12th Middlesex Regiment. Killed in action, 3rd June, 1918. Age 33. Husband of Ethel Maud Mantle, of 11, Kenneth Road, West Kensington, London. Born Coventry. Enlisted Richmond, Surrey. Grave Ref. VIII. J. 5. Heath Cemetery, Harbonnieres, France.

MANTON, E. H. Employed by Rover Company Ltd. Killed in action.

MANTON, Private, Harry. PLY/2454(S), 1st Royal Marine Bn., Royal Naval Division, Royal Marine Light Infantry. Died whilst prisoner of war, 28th August, 1918. Resided Kenilworth. Millwright's Labourer. Enlisted September, 1917. Grave Ref. V. G. 9. Valenciennes (St. Roch) Communal Cemetery, France.

MAPLEY, Private, Arthur William. 4209, 2nd /7th Bn., Royal Warwickshire Regiment. Died of wounds, Merville, 21st August, 1916. Age 20. Son of George Frederick Mapley, of 192, Sovereign Road, Earlsdon, Coventry. Born 3rd September, 1894 at London. Motor Car Body trimmer. Enlisted March, 1915. Grave Ref. XI. A. 2. Merville Communal Cemetery, Nord, France.

MARGESSON, Major, Edward Cunningham. 2nd Bn., South Wales Borderers. Killed in action 25th April, 1915. Age 43. Son of Lt. Col. W. G. and Mrs. Margesson of Findon Place, Sussex. Husband of Marian Rowsell of 5, Sloane Court, Chelsea. Billeted Coventry. Educated Wellington and Sandhurst. Memorial Ref. Panel 80 to 84 or 219 to 220. Helles Memorial, Turkey.

MARIHAUL, John. Commemorated Walsgrave-On-Sowe Memorial

MARLOW, Lance Corporal, Charles. R/1312, 12th Bn., King's Royal Rifle Corps. Killed in action, 5th July, 1916. Age 25. Tramway pointsman. Son of Thomas and Annie Marlow, of East Gate, Hallaton, nr. Market Harborough, Leicestershire. Grave Ref. II. B. 23. Vlamertinghe Military Cemetery, Belgium.

MARRIOTT, Private, Joseph Leonard. 16218, 10th Bn., Royal Warwickshire Regiment. Killed in action, near Albert, 30th July, 1916. Age 20. Son of Henry and Sarah Ann Marriott, of 127, Bell Green Road, Foleshill, Coventry. Born 15th September, 1895 at Foleshill. Haulier. Enlisted January, 1916. Commemorated Iliffe & Sons Ltd Memorial. Memorial Ref. Pier and Face 9 A 9 B and 10 B. Thiepval Memorial, Somme, France.

MARSH, Arthur. Commemorated Radford Memorial.

MARSH, Corporal, Edward. 1177, "C" Bty. 78th Bde., Royal Field Artillery Died of wounds, 29th July, 1916. Born 5th April, 1893 in Cromwell Street, Coventry. Eldest son of Mr. and Mrs R. Marsh. Resided 6, Red Lane. Turner, Rover Co. Ltd. Enlisted September, 1914 at Nuneaton. Grave Ref. A. 13. 51. St. Sever Cemetery, Rouen, France.

MARSH, Private, Harold Martineau. 46185, C Coy., 1st Bn., Worcestershire Regiment. Killed in action, 27th May, 1918. Age 18. Son of Henry and Elizabeth Marsh. Born 11th March 1898 at Coventry. Enlisted Coventry. Resided at 21, Canterbury Street. Mechanic. Enlisted January, 1917. Commemorated Triumph & Gloria Memorial. Grave Ref. II. I. 20. La Ville-Aux-Bois British Cemetery, France.

MARSHALL, Private, Arthur Sidney. 1634, 1/7th Bn., Royal Warwickshire Regiment. Died of wounds, Boulogne, 19th July, 1916. Age 19. Son of Arthur and Louisa Marshall, of 31, Vauxhall Street, Coventry. Born 24th December, 1896 at Kirkstall, Yorks. Resided Coventry. Driller, Messrs. Calcott Bros. Enlisted August, 1914. Grave Ref. VIII. A. 124. Boulogne Eastern Cemetery, France.

MARSHALL, J. P. Employed Humber Ltd. Killed in action.

MARSHALL, John William. Commemorated Saint Thomas the Apostle, Longford.

MARSHALL, Second Lieutenant, Laurence Herbert. 9th Field Coy., Royal Engineers. Died Rouen, 22nd April, 1918. Age 33. Son of Frank Herbert and Lucy Harriet Marshall (nee Jordison), of "Sunnyside," Prestbury, Cheltenham. Born at Middlesbrough. Born 5th July, 1884 at Middlesbrough. Resided Iquique, Chile (formerly Coventry). Engineer. Enlisted June, 1916. Commemorated King Henry VIII School. Grave Ref. Officers. B. 7. 6. St. Sever Cemetery, Rouen, France.

MARSHALL, Private, Thomas Herbert. 42397, 1st Bn., Royal Warwickshire Regiment. Killed in action, 24th October, 1918. Age 37. Husband of Agnes Emma Marshall, of 101, Clarendon Street, Leamington. Born 12th January, 1881 at Leamington. Resided Leamington. Stores Labourer, Rudge Works. Enlisted May, 1918. Grave Ref. A. 2. Verchain British Cemetery, Verchain-Maugre, France.

MARSTON, Lance Sergeant, Henry. 242469, 2/6th Bn., Royal Warwickshire Regiment. Killed in action, 3rd April, 1918. A native of Lubenham, Leicestershire. Enlisted Nuneaton. Resided Foleshill, Coventry. Memorial Ref. Panel 18 and 19. Pozieres Memorial, France.

MARSTON, Lance Corporal, Thomas. 14336, 10th Bn., Royal Warwickshire Regiment. Killed in action, 1st September, 1916. Age 18. Killed due to the bursting a German grenade and he lived for two minutes after being struck. Son of Mr. and Mrs. Marston of Villa Park Road, Bedworth. Enlisted September, 1915 at the aged of 17 at Nuneaton. Born Bedworth. Employed Courtaulds. Grave Ref. I. H. 2. Dranoutre Military Cemetery, Belgium.

MARSTON, Lance Sergeant, William Henry. 242469, 2/6th Bn., Royal Warwickshire Regiment. Killed in action, St. Quentin, 3rd April, 1918. Born Lubenham, Leics. Resided Foleshill. Miner. Memorial Ref. Panel 18 and 19. Pozieres Memorial, France.

MARTIN, Private, Albert. 265877, 1st /7th Bn., Royal Warwickshire Regiment. Killed in action, Battle of the Somme, 14th July, 1916. Age 18. Son of Mr. and Mrs. F. Waters, of 90, Harnall Lane East, Coventry. Born 2nd April, 1898 in Arthur Street. Resided 25, Cambridge Street. Motor Fitter, Singer Ltd. Enlisted September, 1914. Memorial Ref. Pier and Face 9 A 9 B and 10 B. Thiepval Memorial, Somme, France.

MARTIN, Private, Alfred. 16379, 2nd Bn., Royal Warwickshire Regiment. Killed in action, Battle of the Somme, 6th September, 1916. Age 21. Son of Alfred and Ada Martin, of 60, Mill Street, Bedworth. Born 18th December, 1893 at Bedworth. Resided Bedworth. Spinner. Enlisted January, 1916. Grave Ref. XXXVIII. C. 14. Serre Road Cemetery No.2, France.

MARTIN, Private, Austin. 154, 1st Bn., Royal Warwickshire Regiment. Wounded in action, 6th October, 1914 died from wounds, 15th June, 1920. Age 34. Severely wounded arm became septic. Son of Mr. Edward and Mrs. Elizabeth Martin, 34, Spring Lane, Kenilworth. Husband of Minnie Martin, 51, Albion Street, Kenilworth. Brother of Charles James W. Martin. Grave Ref. C. 1014. Kenilworth Cemetery.

MARTIN, Private, John Thomas. 24287, 11th Bn., Royal Warwickshire Regiment. Killed in action, 9th October, 1917. Age 20. Son of William and Rhoda Martin of Husbands Bosworth, Rugby. Born Husbands Bosworth, Leics. Enlisted Coventry. Resided Husbands Bosworth. Grave Ref. IV. B. 16. Zantvoorde British Cemetery, Belgium.

MARTIN, Private, Robert George. 27786, 2nd Bn., Oxfordshire and Buckinghamshire Light Infantry. Killed in action, 1st May, 1918. Age 33. Son of George Martin. Husband of Rose Hollowell (formerly Martin), of 154, Broad Street, Foleshill, Coventry. Born 21st November, 1885 at Northampton. Bricklayer. Enlisted November, 1916 at Coventry. Grave Ref. VIII. Q. 5. Cabaret-Rouge British Cemetery, Souchez, Pas de Calais, France.

MARTIN, Private, Walter Thomas Stanley. 12351, 5th Bn., Royal Berkshire Regiment. Killed in action, 20th November, 1917. Born Coventry. Enlisted Birmingham. Memorial Ref. Panel 8. Cambrai Memorial, Louverval, France.

MASCORD, Second Lieutenant, Alfred Edgar. 6th Bn., Royal Warwickshire Regiment. Killed in action 6th May, 1918 by a machine gun bullet. Age 26. Son of Alfred and Emma Mascord, of Keresley, Coventry. Resided Coventry. School Teacher, Elementary School, Coventry. Commemorated King Henry VIII School, St. Thomas Memorial and Education Department Memorial, Coventry Corporation. Grave Ref. 3. Isbergues Communal Cemetery, Pas de Calais, France.

MASON, Private, Charles Henry. 7981, 2nd Bn., Royal Welsh Fusiliers. Killed in action, 20th July, 1916. Age 31. Husband of Phoebe Mason, of 26, Sowe Lane, Binley, Coventry. Born Birmingham. Employed Coventry. Memorial Ref. Pier and Face 4 A. Thiepval Memorial, Somme, France.

MASON, Driver, Edward Ernest., 87870, 277th Bde. Ammunition Col., Royal Field Artillery. Died of wounds, 23rd July, 1917. Age 18. (Served as Flinn). Son of Frederick William and Esther Mason, of Earlsdon, Coventry. Born 2nd January 1899 at Budbrook. Resided at 70, Stanley Road. Apprentice Machine Tools. Enlisted July 1915. Commemorated War Memorial Park. Grave Ref. I. N. 19. Brandhoek Military Cemetery, Ieper, West-Vlaanderen, Belgium.

MASON, Second Lieutenant, Edward. 3rd Battalion attached 2nd Battalion, Northamptonshire Regiment. Killed in action near Fromelles, 9th May 1915. Age 36. Son of Jeremiah and Sarah Mason of 1 Ingoldsby Mansions, Avonmore Road, West Kensington, London. Husband of Jessie Mason (professionally known as Jessie Grimson), of Chelsea, London. A.R.C.M, Royal Collge of Music, London. 17 years on the music staff at Eton College. Principal 'Cellist' Royal Albert Hall Orchestra. Founder and conductor of the Edward Mason Choir. Born 24th June, 1878 at Coventry. Resided at London. Enlisted August, 1914. Commemorated Holy Trinity Panels and War Memorial Park. Memorial Ref. Panel 7. Ploegsteert Memorial, Belgium. (Buried near Fromelles).

MASON, F. G. Commemorated St. Barbara's Memorial.

MASON, Private, Frederick Thomas. 16261, 9th Bn., Royal Warwickshire Regiment. Killed in action, Mesopotamia, 7th January, 1917. Age 20. Son of Evan and Ellen Mason, of Halvins, Alfrick, Worcester. Born Skethrury, South Wales. Enlisted Coventry. Resided Broad Marston, Warwicks. Grave Ref. XIV. A. 7. Amara War Cemetery, Iraq.

MASON, Sergeant, G. 65209, 24th Div. Ammunition Column, Royal Field Artillery. Died, home, 1st February, 1919. Employed Coventry. Grave Ref. Binley (St. Bartholomew) Churchyard.

MASON, Corporal, Leonard. 15066, 4th Bn., Worcestershire Regiment. Killed in action, Gallipoli, 6th August, 1915. Born Martley, Worcs. Enlisted Coventry. Resided Brampton Abbotts, Hereford. Commemorated Saint Thomas the Apostle, Longford. Memorial Ref. Panel 104 to 113. Helles Memorial, Turkey.

MASSEY, Private, Herbert John. 5115, 1/6th Bn., Royal Warwickshire Regiment. Killed in action, 18th August, 1916. Born Meriden. Resided Meriden. Employed Coventry. Grave Ref. IV. A. 28. Pozieres British Cemetery, Ovillers-La Boisselle, France.

MASSEY, Private, Sidney Charles. 45738, 13th Bn., Royal Scots. Died of wounds, 21st September, 1918. Born Balsall, Worcs. Enlisted Warwick. Resided Coventry. Grave Ref. III. C. 3. Pernes British Cemetery, France.

MASSINGHAM, Private, Harry. 203399, 5th Bn., Royal Berkshire Regiment. Killed in action, 25th May 1918. Husband of E. M. Massingham, of 56, Arden Street, Earlsdon, Coventry. Born 5th July, 1882 at Foulsham, Norfolk. Baker, Mr. H. Box of Earlsdon. Enlisted May, 1917 at Coventry. Commemorated Earlsdon Working Mens Club. Grave Ref. II. N. 10. Mailly Wood Cemetery, Mailly-Maillet, Somme, France.

MASTERS, Lieutenant, Ernest Harold, Croix de Guerre with Palm (France). 45th Squadron, Royal Air Force. Accidentally killed whilst flying at Duisans, near Arras, 24th December, 1918. Age 19. Son of George and Fanny Masters, of 176, Humber Avenue, Coventry. Born 25th January, 1899 at Langley, Birmingham. Resided at 1, Swan Lane. Engineer. Enlisted May, 1917. Commemorated War Memorial Park. Grave Ref. VIII. B. 60. Duisans British Cemetery, Etrun, Pas de Calais, France.

MASTERS, Private, Herbert. 268139, 2/7th Bn., Royal Warwickshire Regiment. Killed in action, 21st March, 1918. Born November, 1897 at 3, Albert Street. Resided at 62, St. John Street. Turner. Enlisted November, 1916 at Coventry. Grave Ref. I. F. 2. Chapelle British Cemetery, Holnon, France.

MASTERS, Private, Thomas Stevens. 306486, (4622). 1st /8th Bn., Royal Warwickshire Regiment. Killed in action, 1st July 1916. Age 24. Son of Henry S. and Fanny Masters, of 58, Stratford Street, Coventry. Born 12th January, 1892 at Stoke, Coventry. Enlisted February, 1916 at Coventry. Memorial Ref. Pier and Face 9 A 9 B and 10 B. Thiepval Memorial, Somme, France.

MASTERS, Corporal, William. SE/14769, 18th Veterinary Hospital, Army Veterinary Corps. Died of malaria, 21st June, 1918. Age 45. Son of John and Fanny Masters, of Badby, Daventry. Husband of V. G. Masters, of 39, Dean Street, Stoke, Coventry. Born 3rd July, 1873 at Badby, Northants. Labourer. Grave Ref. 1426. Salonika (Lembet Road) Military Cemetery, Greece.

MATHESON, Private, John Smith. Scots Guards. Died, home, 20th March, 1919. Born at Penicuik. Resided Coventry. Linotype Operator. Enlisted January, 1916. Commemorated Central Methodist Hall and Iliffe & Sons Ltd. Grave Ref. Bitton near Bristol.

MATTHEWS, Lance Corporal, Albert. 19356, 10th Platoon, C Coy., 2nd Bn., Royal Warwickshire Regiment. Killed in action, near Polygon Wood, 9th October, 1917. Born 16th May, 1886 at Leamington. Resided 8, Lincoln Street. Silk Spinner, Courtaulds Ltd. Enlisted Coventry. Memorial Ref. Panel 23 to 28 and 163A. Tyne Cot Memorial, Belgium.

MATTHEWS, Private, Albert Herbert. 55338, 9th Bn., Royal Fusiliers formerly S4/173639, Royal Army Service Corps. Killed in action, Monchy near Arras, 9th August, 1917. Born Corley Moor, Warwick. Enlisted March, 1916 at Coventry. Resided 146, Lockhurst Lane. Coventry. Born 27th October, 1895 at Corley Moor. Baker. Grave Ref. I. H. 25. Monchy British Cemetery, Monchy-Le-Preux, France.

MATTHEWS, Private, Alfred Edward. 19229, 1st Bn., Royal Warwickshire Regiment. Killed in action, 18th July, 1918. Born 21st March, 188 at Chalford, Glos. Resided at 186, Harnall Lane East. Insurance Agent. Enlisted May, 1916. Memorial Ref. Panel 22 to 25. Loos Memorial, France. (Possibly buried near Bethune)

MATTHEWS, Private, E. 135683, 44th Motor Amb. Convoy, Royal Army Medical Corps. 13th December, 1918. Age 22. Son of James and Ellen Matthews. of 54, Far Gosford Street, Coventry. Employed Coventry. Grave Ref. B. 28. Fillievres British Cemetery, Pas de Calais, France.

MATTHEWS, Company Sergeant Major, Ethelbert Balfour, DCM. 48215, 101st Field Coy., Royal Engineers. Killed in action, Ypres, 11th June, 1917. Age 23. Son of Mr. and Mrs. J. Matthews, of Arley, nr. Coventry. Born Bentley, Warwickshire. Enlisted Nuneaton. Resided Coventry. Grave Ref. I. B. 41. Hop Store Cemetery, Ieper, West-Vlaanderen, Belgium.

MATTHEWS, F. Commemorated Triumph & Gloria Memorial.

MATTHEWS, Private, Frank William, MM. 11248, 1st Bn., Coldstream Guards. Died of wounds, 21st August, 1918. Age 21. Son of Mrs. M. Matthews, of Lower Keresley, Coventry. Born Chilworth, Oxford. Employed Coventry. Commemorated Exhall Memorial. Enlisted Coventry. Gazetted for Military Medal, 25th June, 1918. Grave Ref. III. A. 23. Bac-Du-Sud British Cemetery, Bailleulval, Pas de Calais, France.

MATTHEWS, Private, Frank William. 201746, 2nd /5th Bn., Royal Warwickshire Regiment. Killed in action, 17th April, 1917. Age 35. Son of Seymour Matthews, of Fillongley, Coventry. Born 1889 at Fillongley. Employed Coventry. Resided Coventry. Enlisted Coventry. Memorial Ref. Pier and Face 9 A 9 B and 10 B. Thiepval Memorial, Somme, France.

MATTHEWS, Bombardier, Frederick. 212493, "D" Bty. 45th Bde., Royal Field Artillery. Killed in action, 2nd December, 1917. Age 28. Native of Bristol. Son of James and Emma Matthews, of Bristol. Husband of Elizabeth Matthews, of 19, Sir Thomas White's Road, Coventry. Enlisted Coventry. Resided Coventry. Grave Ref. V. A. 10. Oxford Road Cemetery, Ieper, West-Vlaanderen, Belgium.

MATTHEWS, Private, Horace Ernest. 42198, 10th Bn., Essex Regiment formerly 47370, Northamptonshire Regiment. Killed in action, 21st March, 1918. Born Wroxhall, Warwickshire. Enlisted Coventry. Resided Coventry. Commemorated Triumph & Gloria Memorial. Memorial Ref. Panel 51 and 52. Pozieres Memorial, France.

MATTHEWS, Private, John. 18602, 1st Bn., Royal Welsh Fusiliers. Died of wounds, 31st May, 1916. Age 25. Son of Elizabeth and Benjamin Matthews, of 7, Pickerd Row, Warwick. Born Coventry. Enlisted Birmingham. Resided Chauntry Place. Employed Dunlop Wheel and Rim Co. Ltd. Commemorated Dunlop Memorial. Grave Ref. 1. A. 22. Corbie Communal Cemetery Extension, France.

MATTHEWS, Corporal, Joseph William. 3609, 2nd /6th Bn., Royal Warwickshire Regiment. Killed in action, 12th April, 1918. Age 40. Son of William and Jane Matthews, of Kilsby, Rugby. Husband of Elizabeth Hannah Matthews, of Coventry Road, Thurlaston, Rugby. Born Barby, Rugby. Enlisted Coventry. Resided Dunchurch. Memorial Ref. Panel 2 and 3. Ploegsteert Memorial, Comines-Warneton, Hainaut, Belgium.

MATTOCKS, Driver, William. Commemorated War Memorial Park.

MATTS, Fitter Staff Sergeant, Charles. Royal Field Artillery. Died Home, 29th March, 1927. Born 29th January, 1880 at Birmingham. Resided 9, Stanton Street. Machine Tool Fitter. Enlisted February, 1915. Grave Ref. St Paul's Cemetery, Coventry.

MATTS, Second Lieutenant, Frank. 1/5th Bn., Royal Warwickshire Regiment. Killed in action, Pozieres, 24th July, 1916 leading a bombing party. Born 16th June, 1891 in Payne's Lane. Resided 7, Grantham Street. Builder's Clerk. Enlisted August, 1914. Commemorated Bablake School Memorial and Stoke (St. Michael's) Church. Son of Arthur Matts, Builder. Grave Ref. I. VK. 51. Pozieres British Cemetery, Ovillers-La Boisselle, France.

MAUND, Private, Charles. 9263, 17th Bn., Manchester Regiment. Killed in action, 30th April, 1918. Born Worcester. Enlisted Coventry. Resided Birmingham. Memorial Ref. Panel 120 to 124 and 162 to 162A and 163A. Tyne Cot Memorial, Belgium.

MAWBY, Rifleman, William Thomas. 11502, 1st Bn., King's Royal Rifle Corps. Died of wounds, home, (received Battle of the Aisne), 16th October, 1914. Age 21. Son of Mr. and Mrs. Thomas Mawby, of 454, Foleshill Road, Coventry. Born 9th February, 1894 at Rushall, Staffs. Soldier. Enlisted Coventry. Grave Ref. D. 1012. Lincoln (Newport) Cemetery, Lincolnshire.

MAXIM, Gunner, Ernest Frederick. 241503, "A" Bty. 180th Bde., Royal Field Artillery. Killed in action, 21st March, 1918. Resided at 11, Silverton Road. Labourer. Born 3rd December, 1890. Enlisted Coventry. Born Burton-on-Trent. Grave Ref. IV. C. 10. Ste. Emilie Valley Cemetery, Villers-Faucon, France.

MAXWELL, Edward Wallace (served as William Leigh). Carpenters crew, 347388, HMS Formidable, Royal Navy . Killed on the 1st January 1915 when sunk by a submarine. Commemorated War Memorial Park. Memorial Ref. Chatham Naval Memorial.

MAYCOCK, Sergeant, A. 2043050, 38th Bn., Canadian Infantry (Eastern Ontario Regiment). Killed in action, 29th September, 1918. Age 29. Son of Frederick William and Eliza Maycock, of Coventry, England. Grave Ref. II. A. 13. Bourlon Wood Cemetery, Pas de Calais, France.

MAYCOCK, Sapper, Joseph. WR/504200, No. 1 Mechanical Unit Inland Water Transport., Royal Engineers. Died, 27th June, 1918. Age 30. Son of Sergeant Major G. Maycock and Charlotte Maycock. Born at Warwick. Resided Pantrick, Lancashire. Formerly employed at Coventry. Enlisted Glasgow. Grave Ref. A. 4. Bleue-Maison Military Cemetery, Eperlecques, France.

MAYCOCK, R. Commemorated Ryton Memorial.

MAYERS, W. Commemorated St. John's Church.

MAYFIELD, Private, William Hector. 2/1st Bn., Mobile Cyclist Corps, Royal Wiltshire Yeomanry formerly O.T.T.C., Royal Flying Corps. Drowned, June, 1919 whilst on leave with his brother when his canoe upturned on the River Leam. Resided 63, Newcombe Road, Earlsdon. Son of Mr. W. H. Mayfield. Educated Bablake School. Previously employed Maudslay Works. Grave Ref. Coventry (London Road) Cemetery.

MAYNARD, Private, Harold. 16602, 9th Bn., Royal Warwickshire Regiment. Killed in action, Mesopotamia, 25th January, 1917. Age 26. Son of William and Phoebe Maynard, of 17, Broomfield Place, Spon End, Coventry. Born Coventry. Enlisted 1915 at Coventry. Born 31st July, 1892 at Coventry. Cycle builder. Commemorated St. John's Church and Triumph & Gloria Memorial. Resided Coventry. Grave Ref. XIX. K. 6. Amara War Cemetery, Iraq .

MAYNARD, Private, Thomas Alfred. 5800, 10th Bn., Royal Warwickshire Regiment. Killed in action, 21st October, 1918. Age 39. Son of William and Phoebe Maynard, of 17, Broomfield Place, Spon End, Coventry. Born 18th March, 1880 in St. Thomas's Parish. Packer, Packing Department, Rudge Works. Enlisted September, 1914 at Coventry. Grave Ref. IV. D. 20. Romeries Communal Cemetery Extension, Nord, France.

McCABE, Ordinary Seaman, Albert. Bristol Z/6066, SS Seagull, Merchant Service, Royal Naval Volunteer Reserve. Drowned, torpedoed 17th March, 1918. Age 26. Son of Owen and Rebecca McCabe, of 37, Bonsall Street, Leicester. Resided Coventry. Process Artist. Commemorated Iliffe & Sons Ltd Memorial. Memorial Ref. 30. Plymouth Naval Memorial.

McARTHUR, Corporal, Alexander. 14739, 4th Bn., Worcestershire Regiment. Killed in action, 20th October, 1918. Born 1891 at Renton, Dumbarton. Enlisted Coventry. Resided 236, Foleshill Road, Coventry. Upholsterer. Grave Ref. A. 17. Stasegem Communal Cemetery, Belgium.

McCARTHY, Private, William. 10537, 2nd Bn., South Wales Borderers. Killed in action, 8th May, 1915. Born Rhymney, Mon. Enlisted Merthyr Tyfdil. Memorial Ref. Panel 80 to 84 or 219 and 220. Helles Memorial, Turkey.

McCARTHY, Sergeant, William. 11095, 82nd Bty., Royal Field Artillery. Died of sickness, whilst a prisoner, 2nd June, 1916. Age 35. Son of James and Sara McCarthy. Husband of Martha McCarthy, of 13, Crossways Cottages, Wood End, Fillongley, Coventry. Born in London. Employed Coventry. Grave Ref. X. K. 11. Baghdad (North Gate) War Cemetery, Iraq.

McCUTCHION, Private, Charles Allan. 99890, 167th Coy., Labour Corps formerly 53484, Devon Regiment. Died of wounds, Bapaume, 9th March, 1918. Born 1st May, 1878 in New Buildings, Coventry. Enlisted Coventry. Resided 77, Much Park Street. Labourer, Co-Operative Stores (Coal Dept). Commemorated St. John's Church. Grave Ref. XI. B. 6. Grevillers British Cemetery, France. (Possibly buried Bapaume).

McDONAGH, Gunner, John. 40198, 262nd Siege Bty., Royal Garrison Artillery. Killed in action, 20th August, 1917. Age 22. Son of James and Winifred McDonagh, of 17, Upper Abbey Street, Nuneaton. Born St. Mary's, Nuneaton. Enlisted Coventry. Resided Nuneaton. Grave Ref. IV. D. 24. Bard Cottage Cemetery, Belgium.

McDONNELL, Private, Thomas Vincent. 19324, 10th Bn., Royal Warwickshire Regiment. Killed in action, 19th April, 1918. Resided 67, Chandos Street. Clerk. Enlisted 1916 at Coventry. Memorial Ref. Panel 23 to 28 and 163A. Tyne Cot Cemetery, Belgium.

McDOUGALL, Gunner, George Strachan. 10525, 58 Bde., Royal Field Artillery. Died of wounds, 11th October, 1917. Born 6th January, 1890 at Peterhead. Enlisted Coventry. Resided Coventry. Acetylene Welder. Enlisted August, 1914. Grave Ref. XI. J. 11. Dozinghem Military Cemetery, Belgium.

McDOUGALL, Sergeant, Thomas McIntosh. 52738, D Bty., 15th Bde., Royal Field Artillery. Died of wounds, 7th November, 1917. Born 12th May, 1888 at Peterhead. Resided Newcastle-on-Tyne (Formerly Coventry). Blacksmith. Grave Ref. XXI. GG. 12A. Lijssenthoek Military Cemetery, Belgium.

McGHIE, Lance Corporal, William Ironside. 40145, "A" Bn., Machine Gun Corps (Heavy Branch). Died, 12th Stationary Hospital, St. Pol, 6th February, 1917 from bronchitis. Age 38. Son of James and Edith McGhie. Husband of Annie E. McGhie, of 36, Northumberland Road, Coventry. Born 26th October, 1877 at Rugby. Resided Coventry. Joint Editor, 'The Midland Telegraph'. Enlisted Coventry. Commemorated Iliffe & Sons Ltd Memorial. Educated Edinburgh. Grave Ref. D. 14. St. Pol Communal Cemetery Extension, Pas de Calais, France.

McGOWRAN, Private, Harry. 276890, 20th Bn., Durham Light Infantry. Killed in action, 31st July, 1917. Born 15th March, 1892 at 1c. 1h. Hill Street, Coventry. Resided 224, Leicester Causeway. Cycle Polisher. Enlisted September, 1916 at Coventry. Commemorated St. John's Church. Memorial Ref. Panel 36 and 38. Ypres (Menin Gate) Memorial, Belgium.

McGRATH, Sergeant, Ernest James. 20721, 1st Bn., Devonshire Regiment. Killed in action, 14th April, 1917. Born Jersey. Resided Instow, Devonshire. Formerly employed Coventry. Memorial Ref. Bay 4. Arras Memorial, France.

McGUIRE, W.I. Commemorated St. John's Church.

McKNIGHT, Private, Horace. S/26968, 1st /6th Bn., Seaforth Highlanders. Died of wounds, 11th November, 1918. Age 20. Son of John James and Annie Elizabeth McKnight, of 36, Day's Lane, Coventry. Born 6th October, 1898 in Day's Lane, Coventry. Turner. Enlisted May, 1918 at Coventry. Commemorated Triumph and Gloria Memorial. Grave Ref. XLIX. F. 3. Etaples Military Cemetery, Pas de Calais, France.

McKNIGHT, Private, Leonard. 9689, 9th Bn., Royal Warwickshire Regiment. Killed in action, 5th April, 1916. Age 21. Son of John James and Anne Elizabeth McKnight, of 36, Days Lane, Coventry. Born 30th March, 1895 at 19, Day's Lane. Turner, Humber Works Ltd. Enlisted September, 1914. Memorial Ref. Panel 9. Basra Memorial, Iraq.

McLACHLAN, Private, Robert. 203553, 2nd Bn., Royal Warwickshire Regiment. Died of sickness, 3rd March 1918. Age 37. Son of Robert and Jessie McLachlan, of Scotland, Husband of Susan McLachlan, of 41. Grove Street, Coventry. Born 16th February, 1882 at Oban, Argylls. Enlisted March, 1917 at Warwick. Machinist, Maudslay Works. Grave Ref. In South quarter. Villafranca Padovana Communal Cemetery, Italy.

McMAHON, Assistant Steward, John. S.S. "Eskmere" (Liverpool), Mercantile Marine. Drowned, as a result of an attack by an enemy submarine, 13th October, 1917. Age 32. Son of Peter Patrick and Mary McMahon. Husband of Catherine McMahon (nee Gangbran), of Hostel 16, Government Housing Colony, Holbrook Lane, Coventry. Born at Belfast. Memorial Ref. Tower Hill Memorial, London.

McQUIGGAN, Private, William. 25124, 8th Bn., East Surrey Regiment formerly Royal Warwickshire Regiment. Killed in action, 12th October, 1917. Age 20. Son of Mrs. Lydia McQuiggan, of 38, Court, 10, House, Gosford Street, Coventry. Born 30th July, 1898 at 1c. 20h. Leicester Street. Machinist. Enlisted March, 1915 at Coventry. Grave Ref. III. B. 4. Poelcapelle British Cemetery, Langemark-Poelkapelle, Belgium.

MEAD, Bombardier, Simeon Leonard. 66618, D Bty, 282 Bde., Royal Field Artillery. Killed in action, 16th November, 1917. Son of Mr. S. and Mrs. M. J. Mead, of 12, Medway Road, Bethnal Green, London. Born Coventry. Enlisted Stratford. Grave Ref. XXX. L. 16A. Etaples Military Cemetery, France.

 **MEADEN**, Lance Corporal, Charley. 1708, "C" Coy. 1st Bn., Royal Warwickshire Regiment. Died of wounds, Canadian Casualty Clearing Station, 12th April, 1917. Age 23. Son of Alfred John and Elizabeth Ann Meaden, of 72, Arden Street, Earlsdon, Coventry. Born 17th January, 1894 at Radford, Notts. Brass Finisher. Enlisted August, 1914 at Coventry. Grave Ref. II. A. 50. Aubigny Communal Cemetery Extension, Pas de Calais, France.

MEEK, Private, Fredrick Charles. 7647, 1/6th Bn., Royal Warwickshire Regiment. Killed in action, 4th February, 1917. Resided at 141, Melbourne Road. Manager, Retail Tobacconist Shop. Enlisted Coventry. Memorial Ref. Pier and Face 9 A 9 B and 10 B. Thiepval Memorial, Somme, France.

MEEKS, Lance Corporal, William Henry. 4798, 1st Bn., Coldstream Guards. Killed in action, 25th October, 1914. Age 34. Son of Edward and Martha Meeks. Husband of Elizabeth Emma Meeks, of 3, Aspley Road, Bedford. Born Tetworth, Hunts. Enlisted Coventry. Resided Islington, Middx. Memorial Ref. Panel 11. Ypres (Menin Gate) Memorial, Belgium.

MEIKLE, Second Lieutenant, Allan John Brian. 4th Training Depot Station, Royal Air Force. Accidentally killed at Charlton Abbots, Andoversford, 6th August, 1918. Age 18. Son of James C. and Elizabeth Meikle, of Cotehay Farm, Andoversford. Born 23rd May, 1900 at Barham, Staffs. Resided at Willenhall. Apprentice, Machine tools. Enlisted December, 1916. Grave Ref. On East boundary. Charlton Abbots (St. Martin) Churchyard, Hooton Park, Cheshire.

MELARANGI, Private, Michael Albert. 9209, 6th Dragoon Guards. Killed in action, 25th February, 1915. Age 21. Son of Mary Melarangi, of 27, Bidder Street, Islington, Liverpool. Born Chorlton-on-Medlock, Manchester. Enlisted Coventry. Resided Liverpool. Memorial Ref. Panel 5. Ypres (Menin Gate) Memorial, Belgium.

 **MELLON**, Sapper, Edward John. 503859, 4th Cav. Division, Signal Sqn., Royal Engineers. Died, Damascus, 8th October, 1918. Born 16th April, 1894 at Bolton. Resided at 20, Goring Road. Engineer. Enlisted August, 1914. Grave Ref. B. 20. Damascus Commonwealth War Cemetery, Syria.

MELLON, Gunner, Henry Carrados. 684, "D" Bty. 306th Bde., Royal Field Artillery. Killed in action, Battle of the Somme, 18th July, 1916. Signalling at an observation post, when he was buried in a dugout by a shell, a further shell struck the same place killing him and his comrades. Age 20. Born 11th March, 1896 at Bolton. Enlisted Coventry. Son of Henry C. and Annie Mellon, of 38, Trefusis Road, Redruth, Cornwall. Resided 20, Goring Road. Sign writer. Enlisted August, 1914. Grave Ref. II. E. 12. Laventie Military Cemetery, La Gorgue, France.

MELLON, Rifleman, Percival James. S/36651, 1/7th Bn., London Regiment formerly M/319327, Army Service Corps. Killed in action, near Cambrai, 6th October, 1918. Age 20. Son of Henry and Annie Mellon, of 38, Trefusis Road, Redruth, Cornwall. One of three sons killed in the war. Native of Bolton, Lancs. Born 6th September, 1898 at Bolton. Resided at 20, Goring Road. Painter's apprentice. Enlisted May, 1917 at Coventry. Grave Ref. VI. D. 40. Ration Farm Military Cemetery, La Chapelle-Darmentieres, France.

MELTON, Private, Richard , 8946, 1st Bn., Royal Warwickshire Regiment. Died of wounds, 25th May, 1915. Age 29. Husband of A. E. Bowns (formerly Melton), of 15, Wyken Terrace, Walsgrave Road, Coventry. Born Durham. Enlisted Warwick. Grave Ref. II. B. 25. Hazebrouck Communal Cemetery, Nord, France.

MELLY, Lieutenant, Reginald Ernest. No. 1 Coy., 17th Bn., King's Liverpool Regiment. Killed in action, Battle of the Somme, 30th July, 1916. Age 28. Son of Ernest Louis and Florence Melly, of Highbury Bank, Meriden. Born 5th June, 188 at Fornby, Lancs. Resided at Wakefield, Yorks. Educated at King Henry VIII School and Malvern College. Solicitor. Enlisted August, 1914. Commemorated King Henry VIII School. Memorial Ref. Pier and Face 1 D 8 B and 8 C. Thiepval Memorial, Somme, France.

MENCE, Private, Frederick Henry. 1802, 1st /7th Bn., Royal Warwickshire Regiment. Killed in action, Foncquevillers, 8th October, 1915. Age 22. Son of Frederick Henry and Mary M. Elizabeth Mence, of 35, Priory Street, Coventry. Born 27th June 1893 at Coventry. Resided at 35, Priory Street. Engineer. Enlisted August, 1914, Coventry. Commemorated Holy Trinity Panels and War Memorial Park. Grave Ref. I. D. 24. Foncquevillers Military Cemetery, Pas de Calais, France.

MENCE, Sapper, Horace. 144545, 105th Field Coy., Royal Engineers. Died Le Cateau, 30th November, 1918. Age 23. Son of William Henry and Mary Louisa Mence, of Chapel House, Outwood Lane, Horsforth, Leeds. Resided in Avondale Road, Earlsdon. Grave Ref. VIII. B. 42. Busigny Communal Cemetery Extension, France.

MERRETT, Sapper, Royston Stephen. 101850, S.S.T.C (Worcester), Royal Engineers. Drowned at sea, 5th May 1917. Born 19th October, 1897 at 64, Oxford Street. Resided at 34, Sparkbrook Street. Fitter, Humber Works Ltd. Enlisted July 1915. Commemorated War Memorial Park. Memorial Ref. Doiran Memorial, Greece.

MERRIMAN, Lance Corporal, Ernest Mark. 241992, 1/6th Bn., Gloucestershire Regiment. Killed in action, 16th June, 1918. Born 30th September, 1888 at Campden, Glos. Resided at Campden. Employed Coventry Ordnance Works Ltd. Enlisted August, 1914. Grave Ref. I. C. 4. Boscon British Cemetery, Italy.

MERRY, Private, Arthur Stewart. Royal Warwickshire Regiment. Killed in action, 11th August, 1916. Born in 1899. Employed Coventry Chain Co. Ltd. Enlisted March, 1915.

MERRY, Private, James Frederick. 6356, 1st Bn., Royal Warwickshire Regiment. Died of wounds, 29th March, 1916. Age 19. Son of James and Harriet Merry, of St. Ives, Holbrook Lane, Foleshill, Coventry. Born in 1897 at Barwell, Hinckley, Leicester. Enlisted Birmingham. Resided Coventry. Grave Ref. A. 19. 5. St. Sever Cemetery, Rouen, Seine-Maritime, France.

MERRY, Private, James Samuel. 1381, 10th Bn., Australian Infantry, A.I.F., Killed in action, 7th October, 1915. Age 34. Son of James Samuel and Ann Maria Merry, of 30, Farman Road, Coventry, England. Born 17th February, 1882 in Gas Street. Resided Broken Hill, New South Wales formerly resided Trafalgar Street. Silver Miner. Enlisted 1st December, 1914. Grave Ref. II. I. 1. Shell Green Cemetery, Turkey.

METCALF, Lance Corporal, Harry John. 2543, 1st /7th Bn., Royal Warwickshire Regiment. Killed in action, Foncquevillers, 12th September, 1915. Age 21. Son of Ernest Harry John and Martha Metcalf, of 38, Bolingbroke Road, Coventry. Born 24th September, 1893 in St. Peter's Parish. Wages Clerk, Humber Co. Ltd. Enlisted September, 1914 at Coventry. Commemorated St. Thomas's Church. Grave Ref. I. D. 27. Foncquevillers Military Cemetery, Pas De Calais, France.

METCALFE, Private, Thomas. 10447, 1st Bn., Cheshire Regiment. Killed in action, 8th May, 1915 whilst in trenches at Freezenburg. Memorial Ref. Panel 19 - 22. Ypres (Menin Gate) Memorial, Belgium.

MEWIS, Arthur. Killed in action. Born 6th April, 1891. Railway Porter. Enlisted June, 1915.

MEYRICK, Private, James Ivor. 57351, 10th Bn., Royal Warwickshire Regiment. Died of wounds, 8th November, 1918. Age 21. Son of Walter Henry and Katherine Meyrick of Bedworth. Born Foleshill, Warwicks. Enlisted Coventry. Resided Bedworth. Grave Ref. III. B. 7. Awoingt British Cemetery, France.

MIDDLETON, Gunner, Alfred George. 546, "D" Bty. 240th (South Midland) Bde., Royal Field Artillery. Killed in action, Aveluy, France, 27th August 1916. Age 23. Third son of Edward and Rebecca Middleton, of 78, Richmond Street, Stoke, Coventry. Born in 1893 at Collycroft, Bedworth. Resided at 572 Foleshill Road. Engineer, Triumph Works Ltd. Enlisted October, 1914. Commemorated Bablake School Memorial, Triumph and Gloria Works Memorial and War Memorial Park. Grave Ref. G. 45. Aveluy Communal Cemetery Extension, Somme, France.

MILES, Private, Alfred Robert. 17176, 2nd Bn., Hampshire Regiment formerly Oxfordshire and Buckinghamshire Light Infantry. Killed in action, 6th August, 1915. Age 19. Son of Mr. and Mrs. Miles, of 14, Broomfield Place, Spon End, Coventry. Born 21st February, 1894 in Chapel Yard, Spon Street. Chain Finisher. Enlisted September, 1914. Memorial Ref. Panel 125-134 or 223-226 228-229 & 328. Helles Memorial, Turkey.

MILES, Private, Frank., 205, 1st Bn., Royal Warwickshire Regiment. Killed in action, 5th February 1915. Age 35. Son of James and Ann Miles, of 12c. 4h Spon Street, Coventry. Husband of Ellen Miles, of 104, Broad Street, Coventry. Born 1880, St. Michael's, Coventry. Enlisted Warwick. Reservist. Attended Trinity School. Employed Daimler formerly Siddeley-Deasy works, Post Office and Railway Station. Leaves a wife and one child. Grave Ref. I. D. 5. Prowse Point Military Cemetery, Comines-Warneton, Hainaut, Belgium.

MILES, Corporal, 265525, Percy Henry. 1/7th Bn., Royal Warwickshire Regiment. Killed in action, St. Julien, Ypres, 22nd August, 1917. Born 9th December, 1891 at Coventry. Resided at 4c. 14h. Sherbourne Street. Motor Mechanic, Triumph Works. Enlisted September, 1914 at Coventry. Commemorated Triumph and Gloria Works Memorial and St. John's Church. Memorial Ref. Panel 23 to 28 and 163A. Tyne Cot Memorial, Belgium.

MILES, Private, Robert. 17176, 2nd Bn., Hampshire Regiment formerly 12299, Oxfordshire and Buckinghamshire Light Infantry. Killed in action, 6th August, 1915. Age 19. Born in 1896 at St. John, Coventry. Resided at 14, Broomfield Place, Spon End. Employed Coventry Chain Co. Ltd. Enlisted Coventry. Memorial Ref. Panel 125-134 or 223-226 228-229 & 328. Helles Memorial, Turkey.

MILES, Driver, Samuel. 93959, 6th Depot, Royal Field Artillery. Died of pneumonia, 18th February, 1915. Age 37. Son of Richard and Jane Miles. Husband of Maria Benson (formerly Miles, nee Kimberly), of 6, Laburnum Terrace, Hawkes Street, Small Heath, Birmingham. Born at Coventry. Grave Ref. H. 1444A. Glasgow Western Necropolis, Glasgow.

MILES, Private, William Albert. 30440, 61st Bn., Machine Gun Corps (Infantry) formerly 2680, Middlesex Regiment. Killed in action, St. Quentin, 22nd March 1918. Born 17th August, 1897 at Gosford Street, Coventry. Enlisted October, 1915 at Woldingham. Resided 2c. 4h. Gulson Road, Coventry. Motor Body Trimmer. Memorial Ref. Panel 90 to 93. Pozieres Memorial, France.

MILES, Gunner, William Joseph. 40066, A Coy., Machine Gun Corps (Tanks). Killed in action, 13th November, 1916. Born Birmingham. Resided at 190, Clay Lane. Enlisted Coventry. Commemorated Barras Green Working Mens Club. Grave Ref. II. B. 9. Mill Road Cemetery, Thiepval, France.

MILES, Private, William Nathaniel. 485, 1st Bn., Royal Warwickshire Regiment. Killed in action, Hill 60, 25th April, 1915. Age 26. Son of Mr. T. H. Miles, of 5, Queen Street, Coventry. Born 20th August, 1890 at Burton-on-Trent. Soldier. Memorial Ref. Panel 8. Ypres (Menin Gate) Memorial, Ieper, West-Vlaanderen, Belgium.

MILLER, Private, Alfred Fred William. 24154, 11th Bn., Royal Warwickshire Regiment. Killed in action, 9th October, 1917. Age 28. Son of Alfred James and Matilda Miller of 4, Paradise Square, Bath Road, Banbury. Born Sussex. Enlisted Coventry. Memorial Ref. Panel 23 to 28 and 163A. Tyne Cot Memorial, Belgium.

MILLER, Rifleman, Frederick. 44994, 1st Bn., King's Royal Rifle Corps formerly 31498, Dorset Regiment. Killed in action, Mesnil, 1st April, 1918. Born 2nd January, 1899 at Whitfield, Northants. Resided 120, Station Street West. Turner. Enlisted 1916 at Coventry. Grave Ref. II. C. 14. Mesnil Communal Cemetery Extension, France.

MILLER, Private, Robert Charles. 18492, 10th (Prince of Wale's Own) Hussars. Killed in action, 23rd March, 1918. Born Wisbech. Enlisted Coventry. Resided Coventry. Commemorated Coventry Chain Memorial. Memorial Ref. Panel 4. Pozieres Memorial, France.

MILLERCHIP, Pioneer, Charles Henry. 44851, 203rd Coy., Royal Engineers. Died of wounds, Meaulte, 6th October, 1916. Shot by a sniper on return from mending the wires. Age 24. Son of Arthur and Lucy Millerchip, of 30, Sherbourne Street, Coventry. Born 26th July, 1892 at 19, Sherbourne Street, Coventry. Resided 100, Spon Street. Motor Fitter, Singer's Cycle Co. Ltd. Enlisted September, 1914 at Coventry. Commemorated St. John's Church. Grave Ref. I. J. 2. Grove Town Cemetery, Meaulte, Somme, France.

MILLERCHIP, Private, Edward James. 5174, 1st /6th Bn., Royal Warwickshire Regiment. Killed in action, Battle of the Somme, 18th August 1916. Age 22. Only son of Charles and M. Millerchip, of 20, Sherbourne Street, Coventry. Born 21st November, 1894 at Coventry. Enlisted March, 1916 at Warwick. Resided Coventry. Haulier. Commemorated St. John's Church. Memorial Ref. Pier and Face 9 A 9 B and 10 B. Thiepval Memorial, Somme, France.

MILLERCHIP, Private, Joseph. 10425, 9th Bn., Royal Warwickshire Regiment. Killed in action, 10th August, 1915. Age 37. Son of Charles and Elizabeth Millerchip, of Foleshill, Coventry. Husband of Eliza Ellen Millerchip, of 6, Clifton Road, Stockingford, Nuneaton. Born Foleshill. Memorial Ref. Panel 35 to 37. Helles Memorial, Turkey.

MILLERCHIP, Driver, William Ernest. 840679, 61st Div. Ammunition Col., Royal Field Artillery. Killed in action, 23rd May, 1918. Age 28. Husband of Annie Marion Pavey (formerly Millerchip), of 160, Broad Street, Foleshill, Coventry. Born 17th March, 1891 at 6, Sherbourne Square, Coventry. Resided 3c. 5h. Sherbourne Enlisted 1915 at Coventry. Machinist. Commemorated St. John's Church. Grave Ref. C. 6. Berguette Churchyard, Pas de Calais, France.

MILLS, Private, Alfred. 12315, 2nd Bn., Oxfordshire and Buckinghamshire Light Infantry. Killed in action, Loos, 25th September 1915. Age 18. Son of William and Hannah Mills, of 13, Rudge Road, Coventry. Born 13th October, 1896 at 5, Springfield Cottage, Trafalgar Street, Coventry. Enlisted October, 1914 at Coventry. Machine Fitter. Memorial Ref. Panel 83 to 85. Loos Memorial, Pas de Calais, France.

MILLS, Corporal, Arthur James. 52442, 8th Bn., West Yorkshire Regiment formerly 34862, 5th Reserve Cavalry Regiment. Killed in action, 27th September, 1918. Son of Mrs. Mary Ann Mills of Bubbenhall, Kenilworth. Enlisted Coventry. Resided Bubbenhall, Kenilworth. Grave Ref. II. A. 8. Noyelles-Sur-L'Escaut Communal Cemetery Extension, France.

MILLS, Private, Clement Edwin. 103079, 7th Bn., Canadian Expeditionary Force. Killed in action, Lens, 15th August, 1917. Eldest son of Mrs. Mills, 5, Rudge Road, Coventry. Born 16th July, 1882 at Coventry. Resided Canada. Estate Agent. Reservist. Enlisted October, 1916. Memorial Ref. Vimy Memorial, France.

MILLS, Able Seaman, Frank Herbert. J/7266, HMS Queen Mary, Royal Navy. Killed in action, Battle of Jutland, 31st May 1916. Age 22. Son of Thomas Richard and Amanda Root Mills, of IA, Redcar Road, Coventry. Native of Brightlingsea, Essex. Born 13th December, 1893 at Brightlingsea, Essex. Resided Coventry. Memorial Ref. 13. Portsmouth Naval Memorial, Hampshire.

MILLS, Private, Francis Herbert. 2980, 1st Bn., Welsh Guards. Killed in action, 27th September, 1918. Age 27. Son of Mr. and Mrs. F. H. Mills, of Birmingham. Husband of Mattie Mills, of "Ivydene," Rhoose, Glam. Born Coventry. Enlisted Cardiff, Glamorgan. Grave Ref. I. D. 2. Sanders Keep Military Cemetery, Graincourt-Les-Havrincourt, France.

MILLS, Gunner, Thomas. 130180, 68th Bty. 14th Bde., Royal Field Artillery. Killed in action, Flers, 27th October, 1916. Age 34. Son of John and Sarah Ann Mills, of Coombe Street Nurseries, Stoke, Coventry. Enlisted Coventry. Resided Harefield Road, Coventry. Born 4th November, 1883 at Ardens Grafton, Warwickshire. Driver. Enlisted 1916. Commemorated Stoke (St. Michaels) Church. Grave Ref. XIII. E. 7. Guards' Cemetery, Lesboeufs, Somme, France.

MILLS, Bombardier, Walter Robert. 81644, 190th Heavy Bty., Royal Garrison Artillery. Died, home, 20th February, 1919. Age 25. Son of Mrs. Mary Ann Mills, of Bubbenhall, Kenilworth. Bricklayer's Labourer, Electricity Department, Coventry Corporation. Commemorated Electricity Department Memorial, Coventry Corporation. Grave Ref. North of Church. Bubbenhall (St. Giles) Churchyard.

MILLS, Private, William Henry. 182380, Machine Gun Corps (Infantry). Died, home, 15th December, 1918. Age 38. Son of Joseph and Hannah Mills, of Baginton. Husband of Ethel Mills, of Baginton. Employed by Coventry Corporation, City Engineer's Department. Commemorated Baginton Memorial and Sewage Disposal Memorial, Coventry Corporation. Grave Ref. East of Church. Baginton (St. John the Baptist) Churchyard.

MILLWARD, Gunner, George. 19160, 51st Ammunition Sub. Park, Royal Field Artillery. Died of wounds, received at Arras, 9th April, 1917. Age 24. Son of Mr. and Mrs. G. Millward, of 99, Spon Street, Coventry. Born 4th November, 1894 at Coventry. Motor Wheel Builder. Enlisted September, 1914. Grave Ref. I. B. 10. Anzin-St. Aubin British Cemetery, Pas de Calais, France.

MILNER, Private, Samuel. 35095, 2nd Bn., Wiltshire Regiment formerly 18945, Warwickshire Regiment. Killed in action, 8th August, 1918. Age 19. Son of Samuel and Nellie Milner, of Back, 444, Stony Stanton Road, Coventry. Born 19th December, 1898 at Aston, Warwick. Enlisted Coventry. Employed Bretts Stamping Co. Ltd. Memorial Ref. Panel 102. Loos Memorial, Pas De Calais, France.

MILNER MOORE, Captain, Douglas Owen. Royal Engineers attached East African Railways, Died of sickness, 23rd April, 1918. Age 33. Son of Milner M. Moore and Caroline Marie M. Moore, of 81, Hartfield Terrace, Eastbourne. District Superintendent on Bombay and Baroda Railway. Born at Coventry. Grave Ref. I. O. 7. Mombasa (Mbaraki) Cemetery, Kenya.

MILSOM, Private, William Henry. 148702, Machine Gun Corps (Infantry) formerly 4702, Royal Warwickshire Regiment. Died, 19th June, 1918. Age 22. Son of Mr. and Mrs. W. H. Milsom of 1, Crompton Street, Warwick. Enlisted Coventry. Resided Warwick. Grave Ref 84. U. 24. Warwick Cemetery.

MINSTRELL, Private, Herbert. 42135, 2nd /6th Bn., Royal Warwickshire Regiment. Killed in action, Laventie, 3rd September, 1918. Age 20. Son of Henry and Mary Charlotte Minstrell, of 2, Aylesford Street, Hillfields, Coventry. Born 6th January, 1898 in Albert Street, Hillfields, Coventry. Enlisted Coventry. Clerk. Commemorated Holy Trinity Panels. Grave Ref. II. K. 10. Royal Irish Rifles Graveyard, Laventie, Pas de Calais, France.

MITCHELL, Chief Boatswain, James. HMS Tiger, Royal Navy. Killed in action, Battle of Jutland, 31st May, 1916. In charge of ammunition supply when a shell burst near close to the magazine, rushed to get the magazine flooded and overcome by fumes, his last order was 'Flood the magazines'. Age 42. Son of Charles and Mary Anne Mitchell, of Cornwall. Husband of Lydia Mason Mitchell, of Brownshill Green, Coundon, Coventry. Buried at sea. Commemorated St. Thomas Memorial. Memorial Ref. 10. Plymouth Naval Memorial, Devon.

MITCHELL, Private, James Albert. 24738, 7th Bn., North Staffordshire Regiment. Killed in action, Mesopotamia, 29th March, 1917. Born Long Eaton, Derbys. Enlisted Coventry. Memorial Ref. Panel 34. Basra Memorial, Iraq.

MITCHELL, Lieutenant, James Campbell. Indian Army Reserve of Officers attd. 56th Punjabi Rifles (Frontier Force). Shot in the head, Battle of the Wadi, 13th January, 1916. Age 32. Son of John and Mary Mitchell, of Arden House, Allesley, Coventry. Late of Mercantile Bank of India, Ltd., Calcutta. Born Boreland, Dumfries, 22nd September, 1883. Memorial Ref. Panel 43 and 65. Basra Memorial, Iraq. (Buried on the left bank of the Tigris a mile from where he fell).

MITCHELL, Pioneer, John. 130389, 5th Bn. Special Bde., Royal Engineers formerly Royal Field Artillery. Killed in action, 3rd July, 1916. Born 1894 at Offchurch. Resided Cubbington. Machinist. Enlisted January, 1916. Memorial Ref. Pier and Face 8 A and 8 D. Thiepval Memorial, Somme, France.

MITCHELL, Private, William. 125675, 2nd Bn., Machine Gun Corps. Died, Germany, 9th February, 1919. Born 9th December, 1898 at West Buildings, Stoney Stanton Road. Resided at 125, George Street. Turner. Enlisted May, 1917. Commemorated Wesleyan Church. Grave Ref II. B. 13. Cologne Southern Cemetery, France. (Originally buried Sudgried Bey Cemetery, Germany).

MITCHINSON, Corporal, Thomas. 6842, "A" Coy. 2nd Bn., South Staffordshire Regiment. Killed in action, 1st November, 1914. Age 35. Son of William John and Olivia Ann Mitchinson. Husband of Sarah Ann Mitchinson, of 17, St. Lawrence Road, Foleshill, Coventry. Served in the South African Campaign. Born 28th April, 1879 at Small Heath, Birmingham. Stoker. Reservist. Enlisted Coventry. Memorial Ref. Panel 35 and 37. Ypres (Menin Gate) Memorial, Ieper, West-Vlaanderen, Belgium.

MITCHNER, Rifleman, George. A/3702, 10th Bn., King's Royal Rifle Corps. Died of wounds, 12th December, 1915 on a hospital train going from Hazebrouck to Etaples. Age 19. Son of Thomas and Elizabeth Mitchner, of 162 Warwick Road, Kenilworth, Warwick. Born 1894 at Kenilworth. Employed Dunlop Rim and Wheel Co. Ltd. Grave Ref. VI. A. 17A. Etaples Military Cemetery, France.

MOLE, Private, Arthur Henry. 5303, 1st Bn., Royal West Surrey Regiment. Died of wounds, 28th August, 1916. Age 23. Youngest son of Henry and Isabel Mole. Born 15th January, 1894 at Charlecote. Resided Coventry. Butcher. Enlisted 1915. Grave Ref. III. G. 30. Heilly Station Cemetery, Mericourt-L'abbe, France.

MOLE, Corporal, Benjamin. 9773, 1st Bn., Royal Warwickshire Regiment, Killed in action, 10th December, 1914. Age 29. Son of Henry and Isabell Mole, of Charlecote, Warwick. Born 12th January, 1881 at Stoneleigh. Enlisted Warwick. Resided 37, Britannia Street, Coventry. Fitter, Daimler works. Served seven years in India. Reservist. Grave Ref. I. B. 6. Prowse Point Military Cemetery, Belgium.

MOLE, Sergeant, Herbert. 6067, 1st Bn., Royal West Surrey Regiment. Died of wounds, Poperinghe, 27th October, 1914. Born 22nd May, 1876 at Coleshill. Resided 37, Britannia Street. Postman. Reservist. Commemorated Post Office Memorial. Served five years in Africa. Leaves a wife and two children. Grave Ref. I. L. 1. Poperinghe Old Military Cemetery, Belgium.

MOLESWORTH, Private, Alfred. TR/8/9402, 35th Bn., Training Reserve. Died of sickness, 18th April, 1917. Age 17. Son of Arthur and Julia Molesworth, of 6, Princess Street, Coventry. Born 23rd October, 1898 in Gulson Road. Warehouse Assistant. Enlisted Coventry. Grave Ref. 41. 51. Coventry (London Road) Cemetery.

MOLESWORTH, Private, Ernest George. 19486, 15th Bn., Royal Warwickshire Regiment. Killed in action, near Lens, 24th April 1917. Age 32. Son of John and Mary E. Molesworth, of 77, Cox Street, Coventry. Husband of Eliza Molesworth, of 13, Terry Road, Coventry. Born 12th December, 1883 at Coventry. Enlisted June, 1916 at Coventry. Traveller. Memorial Ref. Bay 3. Arras Memorial, Pas de Calais, France.

MOLESWORTH, Lance Corporal, Harry. 29733, 4th Bn., Worcestershire Regiment. Killed in action, Ypres, 29th September, 1918. Age 21. Son of Arthur and Julia Molesworth, of 6, Princess Street, Coventry. Born 20th October, 1896 in Gulson Road, Coventry. Enlisted Coventry. Carpenter's Apprentice. Grave Ref. IX. F. 1. Hooge Crater Cemetery, Ieper, West-Vlaanderen, Belgium.

 **MOLLOY**, Private, Thomas William. 20902, 10th Bn., Royal Warwickshire Regiment. Killed in action, Hazebrouck, 24th July 1917. Died of wounds to the head and eye. Born 6th December, 1888 in New Buildings, Coventry. Resided at 3, Spon End. Enameller, Messrs Calcott's. Enlisted Coventry, July, 1916. Commemorated War Memorial Park. Grave Ref. Plot III. Row D. Grave 38. Hazebrouck Communal Cemetery.

MONCK, Pioneer, Ayler John Ashley. 40015, 14th Signal Coy., Royal Engineers. Died 17th August, 1920. Born 18th December, 1893. Resided Warwick. Apprentice Machine Tools. Enlisted August, 1914. Grave Ref. 189. "C." 17. Warwick Cemetery.

MONKS, Private, Henry. 200759, D Bn., Tank Corps formerly 1699, Machine Gun Corps. Killed in action, 20th November, 1917. Born Pemberton, Lancs. Enlisted Coventry. Grave Ref. VIII. E. 9. Flesquieres Hill British Cemetery, France.

MONTGOMERY, Private, Albert. 21139, 14th Bn., Royal Warwickshire Regiment. Died of wounds, 26th October, 1917. Born Ashby St. Ledgers, Northants. Enlisted Coventry. Memorial Ref. Panel 23 to 28 and 163A. Tyne Cot Memorial, Belgium.

MONTGOMERY, Private, Charles Paul. 9396, 2nd Bn., Royal Warwickshire Regiment. Killed in action, 24th October, 1916. Born Coventry. Enlisted Doncaster, Yorks. Born 11th November, 1883 in Far Gosford Street. Resided Coventry. Miner. Grave Ref. I. I. 1. Berks Cemetery Extension, Belgium.

 **MONTGOMERY**, Able Seaman, Joseph Robert. J/12871, HM Submarine K17, Royal Navy. Drowned through collision in North Sea, 31st January, 1918. Age 23. Son of Arthur and Sarah Montgomery, of 4, Hertford Square, Butts, Coventry. Resided Coventry. Born 29th August, 1894 at 4, Hertford Square. Sailor. Memorial Ref. 27. Plymouth Naval Memorial, Devon.

MONTGOMERY, Sergeant, William James. 658, C Squadron, South Nottinghamshire Hussars. Killed in action, Suvla Bay, Gallipoli, 12th September, 1915. Age 23. Son of Mr. and Mrs. H. Montgomery, of 1, Sophie Road, Nottingham. Born 6th January, 1892 at 14, Queen Victoria Road, Coventry. Soldier. Enlisted Nottingham. Resided Nottingham. Grave Ref. I. B. 1. Green Hill Cemetery, Turkey.

MOODY, Private, Harry. Worcestershire Regiment. Died home, 21st December, 1928. Born 10th December, 1898 at Coventry. Resided 16, Hales Street. Machinist. Enlisted 1916. Grave Ref. Buried Coventry.

MOONEY, Rifleman, Christopher. 12036, 4th Bn., King's Royal Rifle Corps. Died of wounds, 9th May, 1915. Born Bradford. Enlisted Coventry. Resided Bradford. Memorial Ref. Panel 51 and 53. Ypres (Menin Gate) Memorial, Belgium.

MOORE, Lance Corporal, Frank. 8137, 5th Bn., Northamptonshire Regiment. Died of wounds, 8th August, 1916. Age 27. Son of Robert and Ellen Moore. Native of Northampton. Born Northampton. Employed Coventry. Grave Ref. B. 28. 25. St. Sever Cemetery, Rouen, France.

MOORE, Private, John. 1st Bn., Leicestershire Regiment. Died, home, 21st August, 1924. Born 19th November, 1882 at Coventry. Resided Coventry. Labourer. Employed Coventry Corporation. Reservist. Grave Ref. Coventry (London Road) Cemetery.

MOORE, Private, Thomas. 6462, 1/5th Bn., Royal Warwickshire Regiment. Killed in action, 8th December, 1916. Enlisted Bedworth. Resided Longford, Coventry. Commemorated Saint Thomas the Apostle, Longford. Memorial Ref. Pier and Face 9 A 9 B and 10 B. Thiepval Memorial, Somme, France.

MOORE, Private, Thomas. 266167, 2/7th Bn., Royal Warwickshire Regiment. Killed in action, Battle of the Fromelles, 19th July, 1916. Born 29th March, 1890 at back of 35, Well Street, Coventry. Enlisted Coventry. Served apprenticeship at the Midland Daily Telegraph, Linotype Operator. Freeman of the City. Commemorated Iliffe & Sons Ltd Memorial. Enlisted November, 1914. Memorial Ref. Panel 22 to 25. Loos Memorial, France.

MOORE, Sergeant, Thomas Ernest. 496, "B" Coy. 10th Bn., Lincolnshire Regiment. Killed in action, 1st July, 1916. Age 25. Son of Mr. and Mrs. P. T. Moore, of "The Rest", Old Clee Rd., Cleethorpes, Lincs. Husband of Letty Mary Goodman (formerly Moore), of 6, Abercorn Road, Earlsdon, Coventry. Born Grimsby. Enlisted Grimsby. Memorial Ref. Pier and Face 1 C. Thiepval Memorial, Somme, France.

MOORE, Private, Walter. 203200, 2/5th Bn., Royal Warwickshire Regiment. Killed in action, 6th September, 1917. Age 39. Son of William and Maria Moore, late of Chilvers Coton, Nuneaton. Husband of Matilda Ellen Moore, of "Wilana," Long Shoot, Nuneaton, Warwickshire. Resided 508, Foleshill Road. Memorial Ref. Panel 23 to 28 and 163A. Tyne Cot Memorial, Belgium.

MOORE, Private, Walter. 37971, 2nd /6th Bn., Royal Warwickshire Regiment. Died, whilst prisoner of war, Germany, 15th August, 1918. Age 19. Son of Mrs. Elizabeth Ann Moore, of 13A, The Jetty, Broad Street, Coventry. Born 6th November, 1898 at Foleshill. Resided at 132, Broad Street. Carter. Enlisted 1917 at Coventry. Grave Ref. XIII. E. 33. Cologne Southern Cemetery, Koln(Cologne), Nordrhein-Westfal, Germany

MOORE, Private, William. 478, 30th Bn., Australian Infantry, A.I.F., Killed in action, 23rd June, 1918. Age 34. Son of John and Lucy Moore. Husband of F. Waterston (formerly Moore), of 225, Rankin Street, Bathurst, New South Wales. Native of Coventry, England. Born 1884 at Coventry. Grave Ref. III. D. 1. Mericourt-L'abbe Communal Cemetery Extension, Somme, France.

MOORE, Lance Corporal, William Charles. 11867, 6th Bn., Dorsetshire Regiment formerly 5680, Royal Warwickshire Regiment. Killed in action, 1st September, 1918. Age 21. Son of Fredrick and Jenny Moore, of 2A, Bracebridge Street, Birmingham. Born Coventry. Enlisted Birmingham. Memorial Ref. Panel 7. Vis-En-Artois Memorial, France.

MORAN, Private, Alfred. 201809, B Coy., 6 Platoon, 1/5th Bn., Royal Warwickshire Regiment. Killed in action, Battle of the Somme, 19th August, 1916. Born 10th October, 1899 at Coventry. Enlisted Coventry. Resided Gosford Street. Motor Mechanic. Enlisted May, 1916. Mother resided Tadmore, Tedworth, Surrey. Memorial Ref. Pier and Face 9 A 9 B and 10 B. Thiepval Memorial, Somme, France.

MORAN, Corporal, Charles Frederick. S/43605, 2nd Bn., Gordon Highlanders formerly S/4184, Argyll and Sutherland Highlanders. Died of wounds, 11th April, 1917. Age 29. Son of Charles and Catherine Moran, of Mansfield. Nephew of Jessie Ann Moran, of 106, Churchill Avenue, Foleshill, Coventry Born at Mansfield. Enlisted Glasgow. Resided Coventry. Grave Ref. XXII. F. 17. Etaples Military Cemetery, Pas de Calais, France.

MORAN, Sergeant, Thomas. R/5618, 4th Bn., King's Royal Rifle Corps. Died of wounds, received at Hill 60, 3rd September, 1915. Age 51. Born 23rd December, 1865 at Bilston. Served in the South African Campaign. Resided at 8 Day's Lane. Millwright. Reservist. Grave Ref. D. I. 5. Calais Southern Cemetery, France.

MORAN, Gunner, William. 113729, D Bty., 78th Bde., Royal Field Artillery. Killed in action, Ypres, 6th November, 1917. Born 13th March, 1896 at 35, Harnall Lane, Coventry. Enlisted October, 1915 at Coventry. Resided at 108, Red Lane. Puller Stamper. Grave Ref. II. A. 18. Solferino Farm Cemetery, Belgium.

MORETON, Private, Allan Edmund. M2/105079, Mechanical Transport Reinforcements, Army Service Corps. Died, East Africa, 26th January, 1917. Born Wandsworth. Enlisted Coventry. Resided Leicester. Grave Ref. VII. E. 12. Morogoro Cemetery, Tanzania.

MORFETT, Private, Henry. 1885, 1/7th Bn., Royal Warwickshire Regiment. Died of wounds, (shock and loss of blood) 4th June, 1916. Born 1893 at Peckham, London. Resided at 84, Highfield Street. Employed Courtaulds Ltd. Enlisted Coventry. Leaves a widow. Grave Ref. I. A. 2. Couin British Cemetery, France.

MORGAN, Private, John Charles. 22464, 10th Bn., Royal Warwickshire Regiment. Died of wounds, 10th June, 1917. Age 34. Husband of Annie Morgan, of 104, Albion Street, Kenilworth. Born 10th June, 1884 at Coventry. Enlisted June, 1916 at Coventry. Chain Finisher. Grave Ref. III. H. 5A. Mont Huon Military Cemetery, Le Treport, France.

MORGAN, Private, William David. M2/102632, 1st Siege Coy., Mechanical Transport, Army Service Corps. Died, 14th August, 1918. Age 22. Son of D. J. and Mary Morgan of Pontypridd, Glam. Born Newport, Mon. Enlisted Coventry. Resided Cardiff. Grave Ref. IV. B. 7. Aire Communal Cemetery, France.

MORLEY, Cadet, Hubert Arthur. 180148, No. 7 Sqdn. No. 7 Observers School of Aeronautics, Royal Air Force. Died of pneumonia, home, 27th October 1918. Age 18. Son of Arthur O. and Annie S. Morley, 67, Far Gosford Street, Coventry. Born 28th July, 1900 at Coventry. Resided at 67, Far Gosford Street. Engineers apprentice. Enlisted June 1918. Commemorated Bablake School Memorial and War Memorial Park. Grave Ref. C. D. 97. Bath (Locksbrook) Cemetery, Somerset.

MORRIS, Gunner, A. 830738, No. 4 Depot, Royal Field Artillery. 13th December, 1918. Age 38. Son of Mrs. Annie Morris, of 35, Leopold Road, Hillfields, Coventry. Born at Worcester. Grave Ref. I. 265. Bedford Cemetery, Bedfordshire.

MORRIS, Private, Alfred James. 10207, 3rd Bn., Coldstream Guards. Killed in action, Vermelles, 23rd October, 1915. Age 20. Son of Frederick and Emma Morris, of 55, Cambridge Street, Hillfields, Coventry. Born 14th April, 1895 at Smethwick. Soldier. Enlisted Coventry. Grave Ref. VII. J. 18. Brown's Road Military Cemetery, Festubert, Pas de Calais, France.

MORRIS, Private, Charles. 2nd Bn., South Lancashire Regiment. Killed in action, 24th October, 1914. Born 7th July, 1876 at West Bromwich. Resided at 21, Weston Street. Employed Coventry Ordnance Works Ltd. Enlisted August, 1914.

MORRIS, Private, Charles Edwin. G/90028, "C" Coy. 2nd /4th Bn., London Regiment (Royal Fusiliers). formerly 40724, 4th RES., Somerset Light Infantry Regiment. Killed in action, near Albert, 30th May, 1918. Age 18. Son of E. H. and U. J. Morris, of 58, Coronation Road, Coventry. Born 4th June, 1899 at Bromsgrove. Enlisted July, 1917 at Coventry. Resided Coventry. Clerk. Grave Ref. VIII. G. 20. Warloy-Baillon Communal Cemetery Extension, Somme, France.

MORRIS, E. Commemorated Iliffe & Sons Ltd.

MORRIS, Private, Frederick. DM2/189620, 1st Reserve M.T. Depot (Grove Park), Army Service Corps. Died, home 6th September, 1916. Born Birmingham, Enlisted Coventry. Resided Coventry. Grave Ref. 194. 81. Coventry (London Road) Cemetery.

MORRIS, Lance Corporal Frederick Henry. 2842, 2nd Bn., Royal Warwickshire Regiment previously Rifle Brigade. Died, 20th February, 1915 accidentally fell into a dug-out. Born 18th January, 1880 in Cow Lane. Resided at 2c. 3h. Cox Street. Sand Blaster, Mills and Fullard. Enlisted August, 1914 at Coventry Attended St. Osburg's School. Grave Ref. F. 5. Bois-Grenier Communal Cemetery, France.

MORRIS, Rifleman, George Thomas. R/38001, 13th Bn., King's Royal Rifle Corps formerly M2/269569, Army Service Corps. Killed in action, Arras, 27th April, 1917. Age 29. Husband of A. A. Rogers (formerly Morris), of 58, Crabmill Lane, Coventry. Born 18th October, 1887 in Chapel Lane. Painter and Decorator. Born Edgehill, Warwick. Enlisted Coventry. Grave Ref. VIII. E. 37. Orchard Dump Cemetery, Arleux-En-Gohelle, Pas De Calais, France.

MORRIS, Lance Corporal, Leonard. 1754, 1/7th Bn., Royal Warwickshire Regiment. Killed in action, 14th July, 1916. Believed to have died when a trench caved in. Born 3rd April, 1892 at 1c. 4h. Hill Cross. Resided at 2c. 4h. Cox Street. Frame Filer. Reservist. Commemorated St. Thomas Memorial. Memorial Ref. Pier and Face 9 A 9 B and 10 B. Thiepval Memorial, Somme, France.

MORRIS, Private, Thomas. 266046, 1/7th Bn., Royal Warwickshire Regiment. Killed in action, 27th March, 1917. Born 6th January, 1891 at Bristol. Resided Coventry. Machine Hand. Enlisted September, 1914 at Coventry. Grave Ref. V. F. 19. Peronne Communal Cemetery Extension, France.

MORRIS, Private, Tom Stanley. 12080, 4th Bn., Grenadier Guards. Killed in action by a shell, 25th November, 1916. Born 22nd February, 1886 at Islington, London. Resided 10, Tile Hill Lane. Presser, Rudge Works. Reservist. Memorial Ref. Pier and Face 8D. Thiepval Memorial, Somme, France.

MORRIS, Private, Walter. 13590, 7th Bn., Oxfordshire and Buckinghamshire Light Infantry. Killed in action, Salonica, 18th Match, 1918. Age 25. Son of Joseph and Elizabeth Morris, of Stoneleigh, Kenilworth, Warwickshire. Born 22nd June, 1892 at Stoneleigh. Resided Stoneleigh. Driller. Enlisted September, 1914. Grave Ref. F. 1387. Karasouli Military Cemetery, Greece.

MORRIS, Private, William Hubert. 11096, 2nd Bn., Oxfordshire and Buckinghamshire Light Infantry. Killed in action, 25th September, 1915. Age 18. Son of John Charles and Miriam Morris, of Wolston, Coventry. Commemorated Bablake School and Wolston Memorial. Born Wolston. Enlisted Rugby. Resided Shenton. Grave Ref. II. B. 6. Guards Cemetery, Windy Corner, Cuinchy, Pas de Calais, France.

MORTON, Bombardier, Tom. 27384, 17th Siege Bty., Royal Garrison Artillery. Died, at Sea, 19th October, 1915. Age 26. Son of William and Sarah Morton of Pailton, Rugby. Born Pailton. Enlisted Coventry. Resided Pailton. Memorial Ref. Panel 23 to 325. Helles Memorial, Turkey.

MOSELEY, Private, Charles Francis. 9390, 1st Bn., Royal Warwickshire Regiment. Killed in action, 13th October, 1914. Born Birmingham. Enlisted Coventry. Resided Selly Oak, Birmingham. Grave Ref. V. E. 696. (Buried near this spot). Meteren Military Cemetery, France.

MOSELEY, Lance Corporal, Harry. 16434, 1st Bn., Royal Warwickshire Regiment. Died of wounds, 16th April, 1918. Age 22. Son of Eliza Moseley, of The Cottage, File Hill, Coventry. Born Berkswell. Resided Tile Hill. Employed Coventry. Grave Ref. VIII. D. 4. Lapugnoy Military Cemetery, Pas de Calais, France.

MOSELEY, Private, Harold. 204224, 2nd Bn., Worcestershire Regiment. Killed in action, 11th April 1918. Age 21. Son of Charles and Ada Matilda Moseley, of 8, Welford Place, Lockhurst Lane, Coventry. Born 10th September, 1896 at Astley. Enlisted May, 1917 at Coventry. Resided Coventry. Fitter. Memorial Ref. Panel 5. Ploegsteert Memorial, Comines-Warneton, Hainaut, Belgium.

MOSS, Second Lieutenant, Percy William. 59th Bn., Machine Gun Corps (Infantry). Killed in action, Arras, 22nd August, 1918. Age 36. Son of Frank and Mary Moss, of 25, Southampton Road, Fareham, Hants. Born 1882 at Fareham, Hants. Resided Elastic Inn, Lower Ford Street. Body Builder. Enlisted June, 1915. Grave Ref. VIII. N. 19. Cabaret-Rouge British Cemetery, Souchez, France.

MOTTASHAW, Warrant Officer Class 2, William Henry, MM. 8620, 7th Bn., Duke of Cornwall's Light Infantry. Killed in action, 5th October, 1918. Born Stafford, Staffs. Enlisted Coventry. Resided Crieff, Scotland. Gazetted for Military Medal, 13th June, 1919. Grave Ref. VI. A. 1. Sucrerie Cemetery, Ablain-St. Nazaire, France.

MOULT, Private, Alwyn Percy. 512467, 2/14th Bn., London Regiment. Killed in action, Palestine, 1st May, 1918. Age 32. Son of Charles and Annie Moult. Born 25th November, 1885. Resided Coventry. Railway Clerk. Enlisted December, 1915. Grave Ref. 34. Jerusalem War Cemetery, Israel.

MOUNTFORD, Lance Corporal, Arthur James. R/8981, 12th Bn., King's Royal Rifle Corps. Killed in action, Battle of the Somme, 5th September, 1916. Age 33. Husband of Henrietta Mountford, of Walcott, Lincoln. Born 14th January, 1883 at Emscote. Resided Leamington. Railway Accounts Clerk. Enlisted January, 1915. Memorial Ref. Pier and Face 13 A and 13 B. Thiepval Memorial, Somme, France.

MOWE, Gunner, Jesse. 840482, D Bty., 307th Bde., Royal Field Artillery. Died of wounds, 3rd January, 1917. Born Kenilworth. Enlisted Coventry. Grave Ref. O. IV. G. 10. St. Sever Cemetery Extension, Rouen, France.

MOXHAM, Private, Bertie, 33033, 1st Bn., Wiltshire Regiment formerly 2198, Wiltshire Yeomanry. Died, home, 29th April, 1917. Age 27. Born Ebbesbourne Wake, Wilts. Enlisted Salisbury. Resided Salisbury. Grave Ref. 226. 124. Coventry (London Road) Cemetery.

MOY, Private, Arthur Robert Rotherham. M/288141, 37th M.T. Motor Amb. Convoy, Army Service Corps. Died, 25th October, 1918. Age 33. Son of James Thomas and Elizabeth Moy. Husband of Lilian Kate Moy, of "Roisel," 19, Spencer Avenue, Coventry. Born 25th October 1885 at "The Crescent" Holyhead Road. Resided at 51, Broadway. Grocer. Enlisted February 1917. Commemorated King Henry VIII School and War Memorial Park. Member of Well Street Congregational Church. Grave Ref. II. D. 3. Roisel Communal Cemetery Extension, Somme, France.

MOY, Gunner, William Henry. 840201, 56th Bty. 34th Bde., Royal Field Artillery. Died of wounds, Beaumetz, 27th September, 1918. Age 22. Son of William Henry and Amy Elizabeth Moy, of 25, Broomfield Place, Coventry. Born 28th August 1896 at Coventry. Resided at Coventry. Tool Maker. Enlisted August 1914. Commemorated War Memorial Park. Grave Ref. N. 8. Ruyaulcourt Military Cemetery, Pas de Calais, France.

MOYCE, Second Lieutenant, George Herbert Stanley. 2/8th Bn., Manchester Regiment. Died of wounds, Rouen, 19th April, 1918. Age 42. Husband of Beatrice Moyce, of The Rectory Cottage, Ashby Magna, Lutterworth, Leicestershire. Born 1878. Resided Spon Street. Journalist. Grave Ref. Officers, B. 10. 12. St. Sever Cemetery, Rouen, France.

MUGGERIDGE, Private, Stephen. PO/11648, HMS Bulwark, Royal Marine Light Infantry. Killed in action at sea, 26th November, 1914. Age 30. Name on Roll of Honour in Cathedral Church of St. Michael. Son of Robert and Elizabeth Muggeridge of 65, High Street, Cosham, Hants. Native of Banstead, Surrey. Memorial Ref. Panel 6. Portsmouth Naval Memorial.

MULLINER, Private, Neville. 18962, 5th Bn., Oxfordshire and Buckinghamshire Light Infantry. Killed in action, 23rd March, 1918. Born Nantwich, Cheshire. Resided Stoke. Enlisted Coventry. Memorial Ref. Panel 50 and 51. Pozieres Memorial, France.

MURFIN, Corporal, George, MM. 44974, . 93rd Field Coy., Royal Engineers. Killed in action, 23rd March, 1918. Age 24. Son of Mr. and Mrs. E. Murfin, of Court House Green, Foleshill, Coventry formerly Rising Sun Hotel, Spon Street. Born 31st November, 1893 Hucknall, Notts. Enlisted Nuneaton. Resided 181, Spon Street, Coventry. Turner. Enlisted September, 1914. Commemorated St. John's Church. Awarded Military Medal for gallantry in the field, 1917. Gazetted 27th July, 1917. Memorial Ref. Panel 10 to 13. Pozieres Memorial, Somme, France.

MURPHY, Corporal, Sidney James. 50, 1st Bn., Royal Warwickshire Regiment. Killed in action, near St. Julien, 25th April, 1915. Born 1887 at Leamington. Resided Leamington. Employed Coventry. Enlisted August, 1914 at Coventry. Memorial Ref. Panel 8. Ypres (Menin Gate) Memorial, Belgium.

MURR, Private, John. G/58828, 4th Bn., Royal Fusiliers. Killed in action, 14th December, 1917. Age 24. Son of George Henry and Mary Murr, of 32, Commercial Road, Grantham, Lincs. Born Grantham. Enlisted Coventry. Resided Coventry. Grave Ref. II. F. 3. Mory Abbey Military Cemetery, Mory, France.

MURRAY, Second Lieutenant, John Claude. 2nd Bn., South Wales Borderers. Killed in action, 9th July, 1916. Teacher, Bablake School. Commemorated Bablake School Memorial. Memorial Ref. Pier and Face 4A. Thiepval Memorial, Somme, France.

MUSGROVE, Private, Sydney Charles. 11028, 6th Bn., Oxfordshire and Buckinghamshire Light Infantry. Killed in action, 23rd September, 1917. Born Coventry. Enlisted Birmingham. Resided Sparkbrook, Warwicks. Memorial Ref. Panel 96 to 98. Tyne Cot Memorial, Belgium.

MUSSON, Private, Ernest. 307648, 1/6th Bn., Royal Warwickshire Regiment. Killed in action, 27th August, 1916. Enlisted Nuneaton. Resided Stockingford. Name on Roll of Honour in Cathedral Church of St. Michael. Memorial Ref. Pier and Face 9 A 9 B and 10 B. Thievpal Memorial, Somme, France.

MUSSON, Lance Corporal, John. 8618, 2nd Bn., King's Own (Royal Lancaster Regiment). Killed in action, 5th May, 1915. Born Ulverston. Enlisted Barrow-In-Furness. Commemorated War Memorial Park. Grave Ref. II. D. 25. Hazebrouck Communal Cemetery, France.

MUSTON, Lance Corporal, Charles Norman. Royal West Kent Regiment. Died, home, 22nd October, 1920. Born 17th May, 1895 at Coventry. Resided Coventry. Lithographic printer. Commemorated Iliffe & Sons Ltd. Grave Ref. Coventry (London Road) Cemetery.

MYLREA, Private, Henry Walter. 204985, 1/5th Bn., Devonshire Regiment formerly Royal Warwickshire Regiment. Killed in action, 30th September, 1918. Born 14th July 1896 at Highgate, London. Resided at 108, Broomfield Road. Capstan Turner. Enlisted November, 1914. Grave Ref. VI. C. 9. Flesquieres Hill British Cemetery, France. (Originally buried Crevecoeur Sur-L'escaut Cemetery).

MYNETT, Lance Corporal, Leonard Samuel. 45082, 2nd /6th Bn., South Staffordshire Regiment. Killed in action, Bullecourt, 21st March, 1918. Age 19. Son of Mrs. Mary Elizabeth Mynett, of 21, George Street, Coventry. Born 29th October, 1898 at London. Miller, British Thompson Houston, Ford Street, Coventry. Enlisted November, 1914. Memorial Ref. Bay 6. Arras Memorial, Pas de Calais, France.

NASH, Private, Alfred George. 44966, 8th Bn., Royal Berkshire Regiment formerly 43017, Hampshire Regiment. Killed in action, 19th September, 1918. Age 19. Son of Alfred and M. S. Nash of 55, Longford Street, Derby. Born Limpsfield, Surrey. Enlisted Coventry. Commemorated Triumph & Gloria Memorial. Resided Derby. Memorial Ref. Panel 7. Vis-en-Artois Memorial, France.

NASH, Sergeant, Frederick. 203098, 1/4th Bn., Royal Berkshire Regiment. Died of wounds, 19th May, 1918. Born Keresley. Enlisted Reading. Resided Faringdon, Berks. Grave Ref. III. A. 18. Aire Communal Cemetery, France.

NAUNTON, Private, Ernest William. 16730, 1/7th Bn., Royal Warwickshire Regiment. Killed in action, 12th October, 1916. Born 10th January, 1898 at London. Resided 51, Freeman Street. Engineer's Apprentice. Enlisted Coventry. Born Bethnal Green, Middlesex. Memorial Ref. Pier and Face 9 A 9 B and 10 B. Thiepval Memorial, Somme, France.

NAYLOR, Gunner, William. 1740, Machine Gun Corps (Motors). Died, East Africa, 25th April, 1916. Age 20. Son of Henry Naylor of 51, Rochdale Road, Bacup, Leics. Born Bacup. Enlisted Coventry. Resided Bacup. Grave Ref. VI. B. 7. Taveta Military Cemetery, Kenya.

NEAL, Private, David. 16843, 11th Bn., Royal Warwickshire Regiment. Died of wounds, 19th July, 1916. Age 24. Son of David and Rebecca Neal, of 169, Grange Road, Longford, Coventry. Born Banbury. Employed Coventry. Enlisted Coventry. Resided Longford. Commemorated Saint Thomas the Apostle, Longford. Grave Ref. A. 33. 15. St. Sever Cemetery, Rouen, Seine-Maritime, France.

NEAL, Private, Ernest Joseph. 204082, 2/5th Bn., Gloucestershire Regiment. Killed in action, 12th September, 1917. Born Stockton, Warwickshire. Enlisted Coventry. Grave Ref. Enclosure No. 4. IV. D. 11. Bedford House Cemetery, Belgium.

NEAL, R.T. Commemorated Coventry Chain Memorial.

NEAL, Private, Walter Ernest. 17456, 11th Bn., Royal Warwickshire Regiment. Killed in action, 26th November, 1916. Age 39. Son of John Neal, of Allesley, Coventry. Enlisted Coventry. Born Fillongley. Memorial Ref. Pier and Face 9 A 9 B and 10 B. Thiepval Memorial, Somme, France.

NEALE, Private, Alexander Grant. 266506, 2/7th Bn., Royal Warwickshire Regiment. Killed in action, 19th July, 1916. Enlisted Coventry. Resided Bedworth. Memorial Ref. Panel 22 to 25. Loos Memorial, France.

NEALE, Private, Arthur. 307594, 1/8th Bn., Royal Warwickshire Regiment. Killed in action, 24th October, 1918. Born Balsall Heath, Birmingham. Enlisted Coventry. Grave Ref. B. 49. Pommereuil British Cemetery, France.

NEALE, Private, Frederick Ernest. 1509, 1st /7th Bn., Royal Warwickshire Regiment. Died, home, 12th February, 1917. Age 39. Son of William Neale. Husband of Maude Marion Neale, of 5, Odells Buildings, Stoney Stanton Rd., Coventry. Born at Leicester. Grave Ref. 8. 50. Coventry (St. Paul's) Cemetery.

NEALE, Private, George. 14479, "B" Coy. 8th Bn., Royal Berkshire Regiment. Killed in action, Battle of the Somme, 14th July, 1916. Age 23. Youngest son of Mrs. A. M. Neale, of 10, Albert Street, Coventry. Husband of Katherine Amy Neale, of 97, Chandos Street, Stoke, Coventry and married nine weeks at the time of his death. Born 9th April, 1898 at 7c. 3h. Brewery Street, Coventry. Enlisted September, 1914 at Rugby. Moulder, Britannia Foundry. Grave Ref. IV. H. I. Flatiron Copse Cemetery, Mametz, Somme, France.

NEALE, Private, Sydney Joseph. 68082, 2nd Bn., Highland Light Infantry. Killed in action, 1st October, 1918. Born 23rd March, 1899 at 38, Moat Street, Coventry. Resided 11, Percy Street. Watch Maker. Enlisted April, 1917 at Coventry. Commemorated St. John's Church. Memorial Ref. Panel 9 and 10. Vis-En-Artois Memorial, France.

NEALE, Private, Walter Henry. 3388, 1st Bn., Royal Warwickshire Regiment formerly 251466, Royal Engineers. Killed in action, 31st March, 1918. Born 7th November, 1882 in Spon Street, St. Michael's, Coventry. Enlisted September, 1914 at Warwick. Resided 37, Howard Street, Coventry. Iron Polisher. Commemorated Triumph & Gloria Memorial. Memorial Ref. Bay 3. Arras Memorial, France.

NEEDLE, Private, Reginald. 24366, 4th Bn., Grenadier Guards. Killed in action, 25th September, 1916. Age 20. Son of John and Jane Needle, of 182, Gulson Road, Coventry. Born 1895 at Coventry. Enlisted February, 1915 at Coventry. Fitter, Standard Motor Co. Ltd. Memorial Ref. Pier and Face 8 D. Thiepval Memorial, Somme, France.

NELSON, Private, Charles. 8138, 2nd Bn., Royal Welsh Fusiliers. Killed in action, 27th October, 1914. Born 15th September, 1882 at 1, Junction Street, Coventry. Resided 48c. 1h. Spon Street. Armourer, Coventry Drill Hall. Reservist. Enlisted Coventry. Commemorated St. John's Church. Leaves a widow and three children. Grave Ref. XI. C. 3. Pont-Du-Hem Military Cemetery, La Gorgue, France.

NELSON, Company Quartermaster Sergeant, Edward Russell. 1975, Machine Gun Corps (Motors) attached Gold Coast Regiment, RWAFF. Killed in action, East Africa, 3rd February, 1917. Age 28. Born Warham, Norfolk. Enlisted Coventry. Resided Warham. Grave Ref. 4. B. 2. Dar Es Salaam War Cemetery, Tanzania.

NELSON, H. Commemorated Coventry Chain Memorial.

NELSON, Second Lieutenant, Herbert. Royal Flying Corps. Killed in flying accident, Hemel Hempstead, 19th March, 1918. Machine nose-dived and he suffrered injuries to the head and face. Born 28th January, 1895 at 2, Brook Street. Resided at 136, Earlsdon Avenue. Draughtsman, Rudge Whitworth Drawing Office. Educated Bablake School. Commemorated Bablake School Memorial. Grave Ref. 159. 166. Coventry (London Road) Cemetery.

NELSON, Private, Herbert. 27914, 1st Bn., Royal Warwickshire Regiment. Died of wounds, 3rd May, 1917. Born 1888 at Coventry. Enlisted Coventry. Son of Mrs. Nelson, 48c. 1h. Spon Street, Coventry. Employed as a Polisher, Middlemore and Lamplugh. Memorial Ref. Bay 3. Arras Memorial, France.

NELSON, Private, Horace William. 47625, 1st Bn., Sherwood Foresters (Notts and Derby Regiment). 29th May, 1918. Age 28. Son of Charles and Martha Nelson, of 122, Harnell Lane East, Coventry. Husband of Gladys Nelson, of 48, Highfield Road, Coventry. Born 22nd January, 1891 at Burton-upon-Trent. Tailor. Enlisted Sunderland, August, 1914. Commemorated St. John's Church, Holy Trinity Panels and War Memorial Park. Memorial Ref. Soissons Memorial, Aisne, France.

NELSON, Corporal, James Frederick. M2/135613, G.H.Q Troops, Motor Transport Company, Royal Army Service Corps. Accidentally killed, 26th July, 1919. Born 3rd October, 1894 at Birmingham. Resided at 165, Leicester Causeway. Turner. Eldest son of Mr. and Mrs. Nelson, 165 Leicester Causeway, Coventry. Husband of Beatrice Sophia Nelson (nee Lowe). Commemorated War Memorial Park. Grave Ref. Plot XIV. Row B. Grave 19. Terlincthun British Cemetery, Wimille, France.

NELSON, Private, Percy Harold. 52879, 1st /8th Bn., Worcestershire Regiment. Killed in action, 24th October, 1918. Age 19. Son of Alfred and Miriam Nelson, of 50, Mickleton Road, Earlsdon, Coventry. Born 23rd May, 1899 at Burton-on-Trent, Staffs. Enlisted April, 1918 at Coventry. Machinist. Grave Ref. IV. A. 25. Cross Roads Cemetery, Fontaine-Au-Bois, Nord, France.

NESBIT, Private, Henry Robert. 57327, 1/8th Bn., Royal Warwickshire Regiment. Killed in action, 9th October, 1918. Age 23. Son of Henry and Ellen Jane Nesbit, of 102, Hyde Park Street, Gatehsead. Born Newcastle-on-Tyne, Northumberland. Enlisted Coventry. Resided Gateshead-on-Tyne, Durham. Grave Ref. 35. Maurois Communal Cemetery, France.

NEVEY, Second Lieutenant, Frank, MA. 6th Bn., Duke of Wellington's (West Riding Regiment). Killed in action, 12th October, 1918. Age 36. Son of George Richard and Annie Nevey of London. Husband of Gertrude Nevey of 29, Therapia Road, Honor Oak, London. Obtained MA degree London and was a Master in LCC Central School. Educated Bablake School and King's College, London. Commemorated Bablake School Memorial. Grave Ref. I. C. 17. Selridge British Cemetery, Montay, France.

NEVILLE, Captain, Frank Septimus. 6th Bn., Northamptonshire Regiment. Killed in action, 24th November, 1917. Age 26. Educated Bablake School. Born Dunchurch. Son of Mrs. L. Neville and T. J. Neville of 1 Bilton Road, Rugby. Commemorated Bablake School Memorial. Grave Ref. XIII. E. 9. Dozinghem Military Cemetery, Belgium.

NEVILLE, Senior Reserve Attendant, Maurice Alfred. M/10087, HMS Rohilla, Royal Naval Auxiliary Sick Berth Reserve. Drowned in wreck of vessel off Whitby, 30th October, 1914. Age 27. Son of Arthur and Ellen Neville, of 18, Castle Street, Coventry. Born 28th June, 1887 at Coventry. Resided 18, Castle Street. Printer's Machinist. Enlisted August, 1914. Commemorated Iliffe & Sons Ltd Memorial. Memorial Ref 8. Chatham Naval Memorial, Kent.

NEWBOLD, Private, Edward Walter. 10979, 10th Bn., Royal Fusiliers. Killed in action, 28th April, 1917. Age 26. Son of Francis and Eliza Newbold, of Coventry. Husband of Elsie Newbold, of 72, Humber Avenue, Coventry. Born Coventry. Enlisted March, 1916 at Coventry. Born 10th July, 1890 at Coventry. Resided at 7, Palace Buildings, Little Park Street. Auctioneers Clerk, Eaves and Bird, Bishop Street. Enlisted Coventry May 1916. Commemorated Holy Trinity Panels and War Memorial Park. Grave Ref. Sp. Mem. A. 7. Chili Trench Cemetery, Gavrelle, Pas de Calais, France.

NEWCOMBE, Private, Christopher. 2091, 1/7th Bn., Royal Warwickshire Regiment. Killed in action, 14th July, 1916. Born Foleshill. Enlisted Coventry. Memorial Ref. Pier and Face 9 A 9 B and 10 B. Thiepval Memorial, Somme, France.

NEWDIGATE, Captain, Richard Francis. 1st Bn., Border Regiment. Killed in action, 4th September, 1916. Age 22. Son of Lt. Gen. Sir Henry Newdigate, K.C.B., Rifle Brigade, and Lady Newdigate. Proceeded to France December, 1914 and wounded at Neuve-Chappelle 1915. Returned to the Front November, 1915. Born 1893. Resided Allesley. Enlisted August, 1914. Memorial Ref. Panel 35. Ypres (Menin Gate) Memorial, France.

NEWEY, Private, Arthur Thomas. 310605, "D" Sqdn., Warwickshire Yeomanry formerly Warwickshire Yeomanry. Died of pneumonia, 17th October, 1918. Age 23. Son of James and Francis Ada Newey, of 104, Harnall Lane East, Coventry. Born 10th January, 1895 at Coventry. Enlisted October, 1914 at Warwick. Resided Coventry. Clerk. Grave Ref. A. 202. Alexandria (Hadra) War Memorial Cemetery, Egypt.

NEWMAN, Private, Alfred, 42137, 14th Bn., Royal Warwickshire Regiment. Killed in action, 27th September, 1918. Age 24. Son of John and Mary Jane Newman, of 77, Westwood Road, Earlsdon, Coventry. Born 30th April, 1894 at 1c. 8h. Upper Well Street, Coventry. Capstan hand Enlisted April, 1918 at Coventry. Grave Ref. II. C. 11. Fifteen Ravine British Cemetery, Villers-Plouich, Nord, France.

NEWMAN, Private, Arthur. 7570, "A" Coy. 4th Bn., Middlesex Regiment. Died of wounds, 14th December, 1914. Gunshot wound to the back and treated at No. 13 General Hospital. Age 32. Husband of Kate Newman, of 41 Court, 3 House, Gosford Street, Coventry. Served in the South African Campaign. Born 1st June, 1881 at Loughborough. Labourer. Reservist. Enlisted Coventry. Grave Ref. III. B. 63. Boulogne Eastern Cemetery, Pas de Calais, France.

NEWMAN, Rifleman, Charles. 7176, 1st Bn., Rifle Brigade. Killed in action, 20th June, 1915. Age 33. Husband of Elsie Miranda Newman, of 1, Third Avenue, Camel's Head, Devonport. Born Coventry. Enlisted Hounslow, Middx. Resided North Hyde, Middx. Memorial Ref. Panel 46 to 48 and 50. Ypres (Menin Gate) Memorial.

NEWMAN, Sergeant, Herbert James. 205642, Depot, Tank Corps formerly 2104, Machine Gun Corps. Died, Home, 18th May, 1918. Born Mere, Wilts. Enlisted Coventry. Grave Ref. 1201. Mere Cemetery.

NEWMAN, Private, John Charles. 265785, 1st /7th Bn., Royal Warwickshire Regiment. Killed in action, 27th August, 1917. Age 23. Son of John and Martha Newman, of 111, Chandos Street, Coventry. Born 3rd July, 1896 at Nuneaton. Painter. Enlisted August, 1914 at Coventry. Memorial Ref. Panel 23 to 28 and 163A. Tyne Cot Memorial, Zonnebeke, West-Vlaanderen, Belgium.

NEWSOME, Second Lieutenant, Theo Edward. 2nd Bn., Royal Warwickshire Regiment. Killed in action, 25th September, 1915. Age 21. Eldest son of Samuel Theo and Kate Newsome, of "Fairhill", Warwick Road, Coventry formerly Oaklands, Belvedere Road. Born 24th February, 1894 at Coventry. Resided at Coventry. Motor Engineer, Daimler Works. Educated Coventry Grammar School and Birmingham University. Enlisted August 1914. Commemorated King Henry VIII School and War Memorial Park. Memorial Ref. Panel 22 to 25. Loos Memorial, Pas de Calais, France.

NEWTON, Gunner, Frederick. 128602, B Bty., 331st Bde., Royal Field Artillery. Killed in action, 28th March, 1918. Enlisted Coventry. Resided Warwick. Memorial Ref. Panel 7 to 10. Pozieres Memorial, France.

NEWTON, Lance Corporal, Frederick. 9311, 2nd Bn., Coldstream Guards. Died of wounds, 9th September, 1914. Born Small Heath, Warwicks. Enlisted Coventry. Resided Ashow, Warwick. Grave Ref. A. 3. Coulommiers Communal Cemetery, France.

NICHOLAS, James. 7923, 6th Dragoons (Inniskilling). Died, 11th March, 1917. Born Coventry. Resided Swainshill. Born Coventry. Grave Ref. C. 13. St. Riquier British Cemetery, France.

NICHOLL, Company Quarter Master Sergeant, Duncan. 2851, 2/7th Bn., Royal Warwickshire Regiment. Died of wounds, 16th December, 1916. Age 35. Son of John William and Eleanor Nicholl, of Berkswell. Born Berkswell. Resided Berkswell. Educated King Henry VIII School, 1891 to 1895. Commemorated King Henry VIII School. Enlisted Coventry. Grave Ref. VIII. D. 26. Warloy-Baillon Communal Cemetery Extension, France.

NICHOLLS, Private, Frederick George. 27282, 6th Bn., Wiltshire Regiment formerly 19th Hussars. Killed in action, 10th January, 1918. Age 36. Son of Frederick and Adeline Nicholls, of Leamington Spa. Husband of Agnes Mary Nicholls, of 4, Holly Street, Leamington Spa. Served 12 years with 15th The King's Hussars. Born 29th January, 1881 at Merton. Resided at 61, Broomfield Road. Postman. Reservist. Commemorated Post Office Memorial. Grave Ref. II. C. 7. Ribecourt British Cemetery, France.

NICHOLLS, Private, John Henry. A Coy., 2nd Bn., Oxfordshire and Buckinghamshire Light Infantry. Killed in action, by a bomb, 26th August. Resided 11, Henry Street. Mother Mrs. E. Nicholls.

NICHOLLS, Second Lieutenant, Horace William, MC. Northumberland Fusiliers attached 1st Bn., East Yorkshire Regiment. Killed in action 24th August, 1918. Born 29th February, 1893 in Eagle Street. Resided on Newcastle on Tyne. Employed Daimler Ltd. Awarded the Military Cross for conspicuous gallantry and devotion to duty on 22nd August, 1918. He went forward with his platoon to reconnoiter and on gaining touch with the enemy, routed a machine gun post. Later he sent valuable information which enabled his company to move forward. Throughout the operation he showed cool courage and fine leadership. He lost his life during this operation. Grave Ref. VIII. G. 13. Regina Trench Cemetery, Grandcourt, France.

NICHOLLS, Private, Percy Douglas. 28859, 6th Bn., Somerset Light Infantry formerly 35072, Wiltshire Regiment. Died of wounds, 23rd October, 1917. Age 19. Son of G. and M. A. Nicholls of 57, West Street, Stratford-on-Avon. Born Stratford-on-Avon. Enlisted Coventry. Resided Stratford-on-Avon. Grave Ref. XXII. D. 12. Lijssenthoek Military Cemetery, Belgium.

NICHOLLS, Private, William. 7156, 2nd Bn., Norfolk Regiment. Killed in action, Monchy, 28th August, 1917. Age 31. Son of John Benjamin and Harriet Nicholls, of Station Road, Pulham Market, Harleston, Norfolk. Born 25th April, 1886 at Diss, Norfolk. Resided at 92, Princess Street. Drayman. Reservist. Grave Ref. I. K. 29. Monchy British Cemetery, Monchy-Le-Preux, France.

NICHOLS, Sergeant, George Henry. 144838, 78th Bn., Canadian Infantry (Manitoba Regiment). 30th October, 1917. Age 33. Son of R. H. and Elizabeth Nichols, of 35, Huntingdon Road, Earlsdon, Coventry. Native of Tenby, Pembrokeshire. Wales. Grave Ref. XVIII. A. 11. Tyne Cot Cemetery, Zonnebeke, West-Vlaanderen, Belgium.

NICHOLS, Private, Harry William. 20552, 1st Bn., Royal Warwickshire Regiment formerly 10114, A.C.C. Killed in action, 20th October, 1916. Born Norwich. Enlisted Coventry. Memorial Ref. Pier and Face 9A 9B and 10B. Thiepval Memorial, France.

NICHOLS, Private, Henry. 242557, 1/6th Bn., Royal Warwickshire Regiment. Killed in action, 11th March, 1917. Born Coventry. Enlisted Coventry. Resided 98 Westwood Road. Grave Ref. II. C. 4. Assevillers New British Cemetery, France.

NICHOLAS, Private, James. 7923, 6th Dragoons (Innsikilling). Died, 11th March, 1917. Born Coventry. Enlisted Newport, Mon. Resided Swainshill. Grave Ref. C. 13. St. Riquier British Cemetery, France.

NICHOLSON, Private, Charles Alister. 267371, 2/7th Bn., Royal Warwickshire Regiment. Killed in action, 1st November, 1918. Born Coventry. Enlisted September, 1916 at Coventry. Resided 47, Gordon Street. Aeroplane Tie Rod Threader. Grave Ref. South end east. Maresches Communal Cemetery, France.

NIDDLE, A. Employed by Rover Company. Killed in action.

NIXON, Lieutenant, Gerald William. 1st Bn., Hampshire Regiment attached Trench Mortar Battery. Killed in action, Beaumont Hamel, 1st July, 1916. Born 8th June, 1896 at Bengal, India. Resided Coventry. Educated at Bedford Grammar School. Pupil at Daimler Ltd. Enlisted August, 1914. Brother of Mrs. Edward Manville. Memorial Ref. Pier and Face 7 C and 7 B. Thiepval Memorial, Somme, France.

NIXON, Private, Joseph. 12526, 6th Bn., Oxfordshire and Buckinghamshire Light Infantry. Killed in action by a shell, 26th September, 1916. Enlisted September, 1914. Resided at Ryton/Bulkington. Memorial Ref. Pier and Face 10 A and 10 D. Thiepval Memorial, Somme, France.

NIXON, Private, Walter Harry. 25057, 2nd Bn., South Staffordshire Regiment. Killed in action, 1st August, 1918. Age 28. Son of Reuben and Laura Nixon, of Hinckley. Husband of E. M. Nixon, of 100, Munition Cottage, Foleshill, Coventry. Born Hinckley. Enlisted Hinckley. Grave Ref. XVIII. D. 13. Bienvillers Military Cemetery, Pas de Calais, France.

NORBURY, Private, Albert. 1816, 1st Bn., Royal Warwickshire Regiment. Killed in action 7th July, 1915. Born St. Peter's parish. Memorial Ref. Panel 8. Ypres (Menin Gate) Memorial, Belgium.

NORBURY, Private, Charles Jesse. 17659, "A" Coy. 1st Bn., Royal Warwickshire Regiment. Killed in action, near Arras, 11th April, 1917. Age 20. Son of Charles Jesse and Louisa Norbury, of 81, Guild Road, Foleshill, Coventry. Born 17th February, 1897 at Coventry. Enlisted March, 1916 at Coventry. Commemorated St. Pauls Church, Foleshill. Grave Ref. B. 24. Fampoux British Cemetery, Pas de Calais, France.

NORMAN, Private, Roland Stephen. 6402, 2nd Bn., Royal Warwickshire Regiment. Killed in action, near Lille, 19th December, 1914. Age 33. Son of Henry and Hannah Norman. Husband of Emma Louisa Norman, of 16, Queensland Avenue, Coventry. Born 23rd April, 1881 at Dunchurch. Enlisted Warwick. Resided 101, Kensington Road, Coventry. Postman, eight years. Reservist. Commemorated Post Office Memorial and St. Barbara's Memorial. Leaves a widow and two children. Memorial Ref. Panel 2 and 3. Ploegsteert Memorial, Comines-Warneton, Hainaut, Belgium.

NORRIS, Private, Frank. 6059, 3rd Bn., Coldstream Guards. Died of wounds, 26th August, 1914. Age 26. Husband of Sarah Louisa Norris of 92, St. Yoris Vest, Antwerp, Belgium. Born Long Buckley, Northamptonshire. Enlisted Coventry. Resided Rugby. Grave Ref. A. 3. Landrecies Communal Cemetery, France.

NORRIS, Second Lieutenant, Sydney Frank. Royal Field Artillery. Died, 28th April. 1919. Age 22. Son of Frank H. and Bertha Annie Norris, of 791, Foleshill Road, Coventry. Grave Ref. In small plot against N. West side. Turin Town Cemetery, Italy.

NORRIS, Lance Sergeant, William Charles, MM. 265566, 1/7th Bn., Royal Warwickshire Regiment. Died of wounds, 16th June, 1918. Age 28. Son of Tom and Kate Norris, late of Neate Street, Camberwell, London. Born 5th August, 1890 at London. Resided 9, Percy Street. Dial writing. Enlisted September, 1914 at Coventry. Awarded the Military Medal on 15th August, 1916 for carrying messages under heavy fire. Commemorated St. John's Church. Grave Ref. III. A. 2. Montecchio Precalcino Communal Cemetery Extension, Italy.

NORTH, Private, Arthur Allen. 43082, 5th Bn., Royal Berkshire Regiment. Killed in action, 18th September 1918. Age 32. Husband of Annie Morgan (formerly North), of 9, Lansdowne Street, Coventry. Born Maidenhead, Berks. Enlisted April, 1918 at Leamington. Resided 31, Whitefriar's, Coventry. Born 28th July, 1886 at Maidenhead, Berks. Frame Filer, Humber works. Left a widow and one child. Grave Ref. II. G. 17. Epehy Wood Farm Cemetery, Epehy, Somme, France.

NORTH, Private, Charles William. 15430, 15th Bn., Royal Warwickshire Regiment. Killed in action, 3rd September, 1916. Age 19. Son of William Henry and Mary Winifred North, of 30, Gilbert Street, Coventry. Born 5th April, 1897 in George Street, Coventry. Enlisted October, 1915 at Coventry. Machinist. Commemorated Triumph and Gloria Memorial. Grave Ref. XXVI. H. 2. Delville Wood Cemetery, Longueval, Somme, France.

 NORTH, Gunner, James. 94553, 35th Bde., Royal Field Artillery. Killed in action, 28th June, 1916. Enlisted Coventry. Resided Fillongley. Grave Ref. I. D. 19. Bronfay Farm Military Cemetery, Bray-sur-Somme, France.

NORTHALL, Gunner, William Richard. 681623, "B" Bty. 286th Bde., Royal Field Artillery. Died of wounds, 7th July, 1917. Age 21. Son of William and Fanny Northall, of Manchester. Husband of Violet Northall, of 30, St. George's Road, Coventry. Born at Newton Heath, Lancs. Enlisted Wolverhampton. Name on Roll in St. Thomas's church and commemorated War Memorial Park. Grave Ref. IV. A. 7. Estaires Communal Cemetery and Extension, Nord, France.

NORTHWOOD, Private, Alfred. 2747, 1/3rd Bn., London Regiment (Royal Fusiliers). Killed in action, 8th October, 1916. Born Whitstable. Enlisted Harrow. Resided Coventry. Memorial Ref. Pier and Face 9 D and 16 B. Thiepval Memorial, Somme, France.

NORTON, Private, Albert James. 14898, 9th Bn., East Lancashire Regiment. Killed in action, 13th December, 1916. Age 33. Son of James Norton, of Coventry. Husband of Harriet Alice Norton, of 9, Carrfield, Fortsmouth, Todmorden. Born Whitstable. Resided Fortsmouth. Enlisted Burnley. Memorial Ref. Doiran Memorial, Greece.

NORTON, Private, Richard. 612370, 19th Bn., London Regiment. Died home, of illness contracted whilst a prisoner of war in Germany, 18th February, 1919. Age 19. Son of John and E. J. Norton, of 62, Much Park Street, Coventry. Born 21st January, 1900 at Coventry. Miller and Driller. Enlisted November, 1915. Commemorated Queen's Road Church Memorial. Grave Ref. 88. 41. Coventry (London Road) Cemetery.

OAKES, Private, George Thomas. S/383755, Horse Transport and Supply, Army Service Corps. Died, 12th October, 1918. Age 29. Husband of Laura Oakes, of 50, Leicester Causeway, Coventry, Warwickshire. Born 20th March, 1889 at Solihull. Butcher. Enlisted September, 1916 at Coventry. Resided Coventry. Grave Ref. Div. 62. V. I. 12. Ste. Marie Cemetery, Le Havre, Seine-Maritime, France.

OAKLEY, Percy Perkins. Northamptonshire Regiment. Killed in action, 27th August, 1916. Conductor, employed by Coventry Corporation, Tramways Department. Commemorated Transport Department Memorial, Coventry Corporation.

O'CALLAGHAN, Private, Francis. J. 45283, 11th Bn., Sherwood Foresters (Notts and Derby) Regiment. Age 28. Killed in action, 8th October, 1916. Born Nottingham. Enlisted Derby. Resided Coventry. Son of Charles Michael and Mary Ann O'Callaghan, of 68, Talbot Street, Nottingham. Memorial Ref. Pier and Face 10 C 10 D and 11 A. Thiepval Memorial, Somme, France.

O'CONNELL, Private, James. 3088, 7th Bn., Royal Warwickshire Regiment. Died, Home, 17th April, 1915. Born Athy, Co. Kildare. Enlisted Coventry. Grave Ref. In North East Corner. Witham (Holy Family) Roman Catholic Churchyard.

 O'CONNELL, Private, Terence James. 10725, 2nd Bn., South Wales Borderers. Killed in action, 25th April, 1915. Age 23. Son of Sarah Ann Mottram (formerly Connell), of 21, New Street, Bently, Doncaster. Memorial Ref. Panel 80 to 84 or 219 and 220. Helles Memorial, Turkey.

ODEY, Rifleman, George. R/16566, 13th Battalion, Kings Royal Rifle Corps. Died of wounds, 28th April 1917. Son of Mrs. Maria Odey of 15, Edward Street, Milverton, Leamington Spa. Born at Burton-upon-Trent. Employed by Armstrong Siddeley Motors Ltd. Commemorated War Memorial Park and Siddeley Roll of Honour. Grave Ref. IV. H. 25. Duisans British Cemetery, Etrun, France.

O'DONNELL, Sergeant, John Patrick. 11393, 5th Bn., Connaught Rangers formerly 10043, Leinster Regiment. Died, Rouen, 24th October, 1918. Born 21st March, 1894 at Leicester. Enlisted 1914 at Drogheda. Resided Coventry. Clerk. Grave Ref. S2. AA. 12. St. Sever Cemetery Extension, Rouen, France

O'GARA, Sergeant, Peter. 7413, 2nd Bn., Hampshire Regiment. Killed in action, 30th November, 1917. Born Coventry. Enlisted Portsmouth. Memorial Ref. 7. Cambrai Memorial, Louverval, France.

O'GRADY, Private, Thomas. 36639, 1st/5th Bn., Gloucestershire Regiment. Died of wounds, 19th October, 1917. Enlisted Coventry. Grave Ref. IV. E. 56. Longuenesse (St.Omer) Souvenir Cemetery, France.

O'HANLAN, Sergeant, William. 7282, 1st Bn., Royal Munster Fusiliers. Killed in action, 25th April, 1915. Age 27. Billeted Earlsdon, Coventry. Acted as referee for Earlsdon hockey matches. Memorial Ref. Special Memorial. B. 19. V Beach Cemetery, Turkey.

OLDFIELD, Gunner, Walter. 840621, "D" Bty. 242nd Bde., Royal Field Artillery. Died of wounds, 20th September, 1917. Age 20. Son of Walter J. and Margaret Alice Oldfield, of 51, Gordon Street, Coventry. Born 18th December, 1897 at Birmingham. Enlisted September, 1914 at Coventry. Mechanic. Commemorated Coventry Chain Memorial. Grave Ref. Enclosure No.2 I. F. 37. Bedford House Cemetery, Ieper, West-Vlaanderen, Belgium.

OLIVER, Gunner, Frank Albert. 184254, 343rd Siege Battery, Royal Garrison Artillery. Died of wounds, 30th November, 1917. Age 26. Son of Frank and Mary Jane Oliver, of Warwick. Born 1st June, 1891. Resided at Leamington. Railway Loader. Enlisted April, 1917. Grave Ref. XXVI. B. 2. Lijssenthoek Military Cemetery, Belgium.

O'MARA, Private, Joseph. 10779, 1st Bn., Leicestershire Regiment. Killed in action, the Ancre, 15th September, 1916. Age 23. Son of Ted and Violet O'Mara, of 81, Little Heath, Coventry. Husband of Jane Satchwell (formerly O'Mara), of 91, Much Park Street, Coventry. Born 8th October, 1893 at Heathtown, Staffs. Enlisted August, 1914 at Leicester. Resided 17c. 13h. Gosford Street, Coventry. Turner, Daimler Works. Memorial Ref. Pier and Face 2 C and 3 A. Thiepval Memorial, Somme, France.

O'NEIL, Private, Albert. 17674, "C" Coy. 11th Bn., Royal Warwickshire Regiment. Killed in action, 13th August 1916. Age 29. Son of James and Elizabeth O'Neil, of 2, Croft Cottages, Albion Street, Coventry. Born 9th August, 1887 in Spon Street, Coventry. Enlisted March, 1916 at Coventry. Polisher. Memorial Ref. Pier and Face 9 A 9 B and 10 B. Thiepval Memorial, Somme, France.

O'NEIL, Private, James. 15106, "A" Coy. 15th Bn., Durham Light Infantry. Died of wounds, 13th November, 1915. Age 23. Youngest son of James and Elizabeth O'Neil, of 2, Croft Cottages, Albion Street, Coventry. Born 13th August, 1892 in Spon Street. Enlisted September, 1914 at Winlaton, Durham. Iron Apprenticed Polisher, Edward O'Brien Ltd. Resided Coventry. Grave Ref. I. C. 29. Bailleul Communal Cemetery Extension (Nord), Nord, France.

OPENSHAW, Lieutenant, Harold. 1st Bn., Norfolk Regiment. Died, 28th August, 1914 at Thulin off wounds received at Mons on the 24th. Second son of Lt. Col. and Mrs B. D. Openshaw of "Fairlawn", 11 Christchurch Rd., Winchester. Born 9th November, 1889. Name on Roll of Honour in Cathedral Church of St. Michael. Originally buried at Thulin New Communal Cemetery, but whose grave is now lost. Memorial Ref. Kipling Memorial, Cement House Cemetery, Belgium.

ORANGE, Private, Cecil Bernard. 18276, 15th Bn., Royal Warwickshire Regiment. Killed in action, 9th April, 1917. Age 19. Son of Arnold and Edith Orange of 34, Warwick Place, Leamington. Born Leamington. Enlisted Coventry. Resided Leamington. Grave Ref. II. B. 1. Thelus Military Cemetery, France.

ORMSBY, Second Lieutenant, Francis John. 14th Bn., attached 13th Bn., Royal Sussex Regiment formerly Natal Light Horse. Killed in action, 3rd September, 1916. Age 32. Son of Col. John Becher Ormsby, R. A. South African Constabulary. Educated King Henry VIII School, 1896 to 1904. Commemorated King Henry VIII School. Brother of Horatio Nelson Ormsby. Grave Ref. II. A. 44. Hamel Military Cemetery, Beaumont –Hamel, France.

ORMSBY, Lieutenant, Horatio Nelson. 12th Cameroonians attached 1st Bn., King's Own Scottish Borderers. Killed in action, Gallipoli, 4th June, 1915. Resided Dener, South Africa. South African Constabulary. Educated King Henry VIII School, 1896 – 1900. Commemorated King Henry VIII School. Brother of Francis John Ormsby. Memorial Ref. Panel 92 to 97. Helles Memorial, Turkey.

OSBORN, Private, Bernard John. 6144, 1st/5th Bn., Royal Warwickshire Regiment. Killed in action, 10th November, 1916. Enlisted Coventry. Memorial Ref. Pier and Face 9A 9B and 10B. Thiepval Memorial, Somme, France.

OSBORN, Sapper, Howard John. 44497, 78th Field Coy., Royal Engineers. Killed in action, 4th March, 1916. Age 23. Son of John and Jane Louisa Osborn, of 72, Eagle Street, Coventry. Born 11th April, 1892 at Kenilworth. Turner, Dunlop Rim and Wheel Co. Enlisted September, 1914 at Coventry. Commemorated Dunlop Memorial. Grave Ref. XI. A. 9. Voormezeele Enclosure No.3, Ieper, West-Vlaanderen, Belgium.

OSBORNE, Gunner, David. 87169, "B" Bty. 84th Bde., Royal Field Artillery. Killed in action by a shell, 3rd April 1918 when a working party moving ammunition were shelled. Age 23. Son of Mrs. E. Osborne, of Keresley, Coventry. Enlisted Coventry. Resided Coventry. Apprentice, Mr. Wetton, Sign Writer, Jordan Well, Coventry. Commemorated St. Thomas Memorial. Grave Ref. III. A. 2. Beuvry Communal Cemetery Extension, Pas de Calais, France.

OSBORNE, Private, Harold Colin Jesse. 4540, 1/7th Bn., Royal Warwickshire Regiment. Killed in action, 4th June, 1916. Age 18. Son of Jesse and Sarah Ann Osborne of Honeysuckle Villa, Himbleton, Droitwich. Born Worcester. Enlisted Coventry. Grave Ref. I. E. 9. Hebuterne Military Cemetery, France.

OSBORNE, Private, William Matthew. 2229, "C" Coy., 1st Bn., Royal Warwickshire Regiment. Died of wounds, received the previous day, 10th November, 1914. Age 21. Son of Mr. and Mrs. W. Osborne, of 44, Stockton Road, Coventry. Native of Leamington Spa. Grave Ref. IX. B. 82. Cite Bonjean Military Cemetery, Armentieres, Nord, France.

OSMOND, D. Killed in action. Employed Humber Ltd.

OSWIN, Private, Herbert Henry. M1/07764, 93rd Mechanical Transport Coy., Army Service Corps. Died of disease, 22nd November, 1918. Age 30. Son of Herbert Henry and Annie Elizabeth Oswin, of Coventry. Born 22nd September, 1888 at Coventry. Resided at 46, Stanley Road. Motor body builder. Enlisted October, 1914. Commemorated St. Barbara's Memorial and War Memorial Park. Grave Ref. Plot 9. Row A. Grave 30. Montecchio Precalcino Communal Cemetery Extension, Italy.

OUGHTON, Lance Corporal, Ernest Henry. 266298, 2/7th Bn., Royal Warwickshire Regiment. Killed in action, near St. Quentin, 23rd March, 1918. Born Keresley. Resided Allesley. Printer's Assistant. Enlisted Coventry. Commemorated Iliffe & Sons Ltd Memorial and St. Thomas Memorial. Memorial Ref. Panel 18 and 19. Pozieres Memorial, France.

OVER, Private, Albert Edward. 2827, 2nd /7th Bn., Royal Warwickshire Regiment. Died of wounds, 18th May, 1918. Age 28. Son of Albert Edward and Fanny Elizabeth Over, of 40, Henrietta Street, Coventry. Born 13th December, 1889 at 2c. 4h. Well Street. Cycle Wheel Maker. Enlisted August, 1914 at Coventry. Grave Ref. III. C. 2. Les Baraques Military Cemetery, Sangatte, Pas de Calais, France.

OVER, Private, Charles. 1368, 2nd Bn., Royal Warwickshire Regiment. Died of wounds, 20th October, 1914. Born Brinklow. Enlisted Coventry. Grave Ref. II. B. 2. Ypres Reservoir Cemetery, Belgium.

OVER, Corporal, Walter. 266203, "C" Coy. 2nd /7th Bn., Royal Warwickshire Regiment. Killed in action at Fampoux, 29th September, 1917. Age 22. Son of John and Minnie Over, of 49, Chapel Lane, Foleshill, Coventry. Born 19th July, 1895 at 49, Chapel Lane. Apprentice at Coventry Tramway depot. Enlisted December, 1914 at Coventry. Commemorated Transport Department Memorial, Coventry Corporation and Roll of Honour, Salem Baptist Church. Grave Ref. IV. B. 39. Brown's Copse Cemetery, Roeux, Pas de Calais, France.

OVERTON, Sergeant, Albert Ernest. 1193, 2nd Bn., Royal Warwickshire Regiment. Killed in action, 25th September, 1915. Son of John Overton, of 72, Henry Street, Kenilworth, Warwickshire. Born Coventry. Enlisted Birmingham. Resided Coventry. Memorial Ref. Panel 22 to 25. Loos Memorial, France.

OVERTON, Private, Arthur William. 11044, 25th Coy., Machine Gun Corps (Infantry) formerly 18843, Oxfordshire and Buckinghamshire Light Infantry. Killed in action, 21st March, 1918. Age 20. Son of Arthur and Zelpha Sophia Overton, of 60, Mount Street, Coventry. Born 19th January, 1898 at South Wigston, Leics. Enlisted 1915 at Coventry. Commemorated Queens Road Church Memorial. Engineer. Memorial Ref. Bay 10. Arras Memorial, Pas de Calais, France.

OVERTON, Private, Ernest Henry. 265902, 2/7th Bn., Royal Warwickshire Regiment. Killed in action, Cambrai, 3rd December, 1917 by a shell. Age 21. Husband of Annie Poulton (formerly Overton), of 6, Hearne Road, Chiswick, London. Born 28th August, 1897 in Russell Street, Coventry. Enlisted October, 1914 at Coventry. Resided 41, Albert Street. Printer. Commemorated Iliffe & Sons Ltd Memorial. Memorial Ref. 3. Cambrai Memorial, Louverval, France.

OVERTON, Sapper, Fred Thomas. 126098, Inland Water Transport, Royal Engineers. Died, home, 13th October, 1916. Accidentally drowned after falling from a barge on the River Stour, Thanet, Sandwich. Age 23. Son of Fred and Emma Overton, of 707, Stoney Stanton Road, Coventry. Born 9th July, 1893 at Foleshill, Coventry. Enlisted September, 1916 at Birmingham. Resided Coventry. Carpenter. Grave Ref. 21. 33. Coventry (St. Paul's) Cemetery.

OWEN, Gunner, Frank. 203614, 108th Siege Bty., Royal Garrison Artillery. Died of wounds, 2nd October, 1918. Husband of Mrs. H. Owen, of Berkswell Village, Coventry. Born Berkswell. Employed Coventry. Enlisted Coventry. Grave Ref. VIII. A. 65. Duisans British Cemetery, Etrun, Pas de Calais, France.

OWEN, Lance Corporal, Frank Leslie. PS/10096, 8th Bn., Royal Fusiliers. Killed in action, Arras, 3rd May, 1917. Born 6th May, 1893 at Birmingham. Resided Birmingham. Solicitors Clerk, Messrs Browetts. Freeman of the City. Enlisted January, 1916 at Coventry. Memorial Ref. Bay 3. Arras Memorial, France.

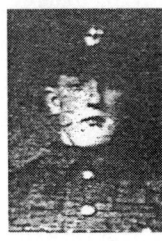
OWEN, Private, George Ernest. 2824, 1st Bn., Royal Warwickshire Regiment. Killed in action, 25th April, 1915. Age 19. Son of Arthur and Annie Owen, of Brook Street, Wolston, Coventry. Born Wolston. Enlisted Coventry. Resided Wolston. Commemorated Wolston Memorial. Memorial Ref. Panel 8. Ypres (Menin Gate) Memorial, Ieper, West-Vlaanderen, Belgium.

OWEN, Leslie. Royal Warwickshire Regiment. Killed in action. Name on Roll of Honour in West Orchard Chapel.

OWEN, Private, William Alfred. 2490, 9th Bn., Royal Warwickshire Regiment. Killed in action, Mesopotamia, 25th January, 1917. Killed manning a Lewis gun in a captured Turkish trench. Age 23. Son of Mr. and Mrs. J. Owen, of 107, Nicholls Street, Coventry. Born 20th May, 1894, at 9c. 5h. Chauntry Place. Resided at 67, Northfield Road. Labourer, Bretts Stamping Works Ltd. Enlisted in 1914 at Coventry. Commemorated War Memorial Park. Grave Ref. XIX. K. 10. Amara War Cemetery, Iraq.

OWEN, Wynn H Meredith. Commemorated Wolston Memorial.

PACKWOOD, Private, Sydney. 20181, 10th Bn., Worcestershire Regiment. Killed in action, 10th February, 1917. Age 24. Son of Edward and Frances Packwood, of 9, Williams Street, Brierley Hill, Staffs. Born Coventry. Enlisted Worcester. Resided Brierley Hill, Staffs. Grave Ref. E. 12. Courcelles-Au-Bois Communal Cemetery Extension, France.

PACKWOOD, Private, Thomas Joseph, 9030, 2nd Bn., Royal Warwickshire Regiment. Died of wounds at Sailly, 20th November, 1914. Age 35. Husband of Alice Rose Packwood, of 78, Thomas Street, Butts, Coventry. Born 1882 at Coventry. Enlisted Coventry. Reservist. Grave Ref. A. 4. Sailly-Sur-La-Lys Churchyard, Pas De Calais, France.

PADBURY, Lance Corporal, John Hercules. 10167, 6th Bn., Somerset Light Infantry. Killed in action, 18th August, 1916. Born Coventry. Enlisted Bristol. Resided Coventry. Memorial Ref. Pier and Face 2 A. Thiepval Memorial, Somme, France.

PADMORE, Private, Charles. 26714, 1st Bn., Royal Warwickshire Regiment. Killed in action, 29th August, 1918. Age 21. Son of William Padmore, of 19, Graiseley Street, Wolverhampton. Born 1897 at Wolverhampton. Resided 33, Coniston Road. Enlisted Coventry. Grave Ref. III. A. 1. Feuchy Chapel British Cemetery, Wancourt, France.

PAGE, Gunner, Frederick George. 944531, 49th Bty. 40th Bde., Royal Field Artillery. Killed in action, 16th September, 1918. Age 22. Son of Frederick and Selina Page, of 13, Bond Street, Coventry. Born 18th May, 1896 at Coventry. Resided at 13, Bond Street. Iron Turner employed Siddeley. Enlisted January 1915. Commemorated St. John's Church, Holy Trinity Panels, Siddeley Roll of Honour and War Memorial Park. Grave Ref. C. 5. Morchies Australian Cemetery, Pas de Calais, France.

PAGE, Private, George Samuel. 34677, 1st Garrison Bn., Somerset Light Infantry formerly 5177, Royal Warwickshire Regiment. Died, India, 1st August, 1918. Born West Down, Bristol. Enlisted Coventry. Memorial Ref. Karachi 1914-1918 War Memorial, Pakistan.

PAGE, Corporal, Louis Henry. 310258, Warwickshire Yeomanry. Died, 19th October, 1918. Age 32. Son of William and Mabel Page, of Wolston, Coventry. Husband of Annie Page, of 6, Smithford Street, Coventry. Enlisted August, 1914 at Warwick. Resided Coventry. Born 28th July, 1886 at Hatton. Hay and Corn Merchant. Commemorated Wolston Memorial. Grave Ref. E. 18. Alexandria (Hadra) War Memorial Cemetery, Egypt.

PAGE, Private, Samuel. 2761, 1st Bn., Royal Warwickshire Regiment. Killed in action, 18th February, 1915. Age 35. Son of Samuel Page of Birmingham. Husband of Louisa Ellen Page of 109, Sherlock Street, Birmingham. Born Birmingham. Enlisted Coventry. Served 15 years (11 in India). Grave Ref. I. D. 12. Prowse Point Military Cemetery, Belgium.

PAGETT, Private, Henry. 2529, 1st /7th Bn., Royal Warwickshire Regiment. Killed in action, 2nd July, 1916. Age 23. Son of Mr. T. Pagett, of 47, Primrose Hill Street, Coventry. Born St. Peter's Parish. Resided 50, St. John Street. Employed Humber Works. Enlisted Coventry. Grave Ref. I. F. 10. Hebuterne Military Cemetery, Pas de Calais, France.

PAILS, Rifleman, Hugh Conrad. 7118, 1st/12th Bn., London Regiment (The Rangers) formerly 6377, 16th London Regiment. Killed in action, Battle of the Somme, 7th October, 1916. Age 19. Son of Hugh William and Clara Emma Pails, of 7, Starley Road, Coventry. Born 16th April 1897, at 7, Starley Road. Resided at 7, Starley Road. Textile warehouse men. Enlisted April, 1916, Coventry. Educated Bablake School. Commemorated Bablake School Memorial and War Memorial Park. Memorial Ref. Pier and Face 9 C. Thiepval Memorial, Somme, France.

PAINTING, Private George Henry. 8383, 1st Bn., Oxfordshire and Buckinghamshire Light Infantry. Died, 21st March, 1917. Born Hook Norton. Enlisted Banbury. Commemorated Exhall Memorial. Grave Ref. XXI. Y. 31. Baghdad (North Gate) War Cemetery, Iraq.

PAINTING, Private, William Arthur. 42744, 8th Bn., North Staffordshire Regiment. Killed in action, Messiness, 10th April, 1918. Age 23. Son of Henry and Elizabeth Lucy Painting, of 26, Warwick Road, Coventry. Born 16th December, 1895 at Lichfield. Railway Parcel Porter. Enlisted November, 1916 at Coventry. Commemorated Central Methodist Hall. Memorial Ref. Panel 124 to 125 and 162 to 162A. Tyne Cot Memorial, Zonnebeke, West-Vlaanderen, Belgium.

PALFREYMAN, Private, Bert. 9868, 1st Bn., Royal Warwickshire Regiment. Killed in action, 13th October, 1914. Born Atherstone. Enlisted Coventry. Resided Chilvers Coton. Grave Ref. IV. C. 606. (Buried near this spot). Meteren Military Cemetery, France.

PALFREYMAN, Lance Corporal, Charles. 9705, 2nd Royal Berkshire Regiment formerly 327, Royal Warwickshire Regiment. Killed in action, 25th September, 1915. Age 29. Son of Mr. and Mrs. Charles Palfreyman of 9, Gotts Terrace, Utley, Yorks. Born Atherstone. Enlisted Coventry. Resided Chilvers Coton. Memorial Ref. Panel 7 and 8. Ploegsteert Memorial, Belgium.

PALMER, Private, Alfred. Royal Berkshire Regiment. Died, home, 3rd October, 1917. Born 6th August, 1893 at 8, Sovereign Terrace. Resided 8, Sovereign Terrace. Cycle Finisher. Enlisted December, 1915. Grave Ref. Coventry (London Road) Cemetery.

PALMER, Private, Alfred Albert. 7942, Duke of Wellington (West Riding Regiment). Died, home, 4th August, 1917. Age 35. Born Coventry. Enlisted Warwick. Resided Birmingham. Husband of Mary Parnell (formerly Palmer), of 51, Larches Street, Sparkbrook, Birmingham. Born in Birmingham. Grave Ref. Screen Wall. E. 24494. Birmingham (Yardley) Cemetery.

PALMER, Lance Corporal, Herbert John. R/2542, 13th Bn., King's Royal Rifle Corps. Killed in action, 1st July, 1917. Born Coventry. Enlisted West Bromwich. Grave Ref. II. D. 32. Messines Ridge British Cemetery, Belgium.

PALMER, Private, Isaac George. 34997, 5th Bn., Royal Berkshire Regiment. Killed in action, Monchy, 28th April, 1917. Son of Mrs. Palmer of 52, Coventry Street, Stoke, Coventry. Born Coventry. Resided 15, Coventry Street. Employed Mills and Fulford. Enlisted December, 1916. Commemorated Barras Green Working Mens Club. Memorial Ref. Bay 7. Arras Memorial, France.

PALMER, Rifleman, Sydney Charles. 844, 2nd Bn., Rifle Brigade. Killed in action, 9th May, 1915. Age 32. Brother of John Palmer, of 70, Springfield Road, Coventry. Memorial Ref. Born Guildford, Surrey. Enlisted New Cross, Surrey. Resided Coventry. Memorial Ref. Panel 10. Ploegsteert Memorial, Comines-Warneton, Hainaut, Belgium.

PALMER, Private, Tom Felix. 25855, 9th Bn., Cameroonians. Killed in action, 23rd March, 1918. Born 6th March, 1895 at Walford, Herts. Resided at 124, Lower Ford Street. Assembler speedometer. Enlisted September, 1914 at Coventry. Commemorated British Thompson Houston Memorial. Memorial Ref. Panel 37 and 38. Pozieres Memorial, France.

PALMER, Private, William James. 1862, "B" Coy. 1st /7th Bn., Royal Warwickshire Regiment. Died of wounds, 29th September, 1916. Had his leg amputated and died afterwards, wounded whilst on observation duty. Age 24. Brother of Clara Caroline Palmer, of 59, Coronation Road, Coventry. Born 27th August, 1892 at St. Phillips, Bristol. Artificial silk spinner. Enlisted Coventry. Grave Ref. I. D. 13. Abbeville Communal Cemetery Extension, Somme, France.

PANCOUST, Lance Corporal, Horace Smith. 16099, 2nd Bn., Coldstream Guards. Killed in action, 16th September, 1916. Born All Saints, Northants. Enlisted Coventry. Resided Gayton, Northants. Memorial Ref. Pier and Face 7D and 8D. Thiepval Memorial, Somme, France.

PARGETER, Corporal, William. 9860, 1st Bn., South Wales Borderers. Killed in action, 10th November, 1917. Age 30. Son of Edward and Elizabeth Pargeter. Husband of Beatrice Pargeter, of 25, Godiva Street, Coventry. Commemorated War Memorial Park. Memorial Ref. Panel 65 to 66. Tyne Cot Memorial, Zonnebeke, West-Vlaanderen, Belgium.

PARISH, Private, Herbert. 24644, 2/7th Bn., Royal Warwickshire Regiment. Killed in action, 14th April, 1918. Son of Mr. J. T. Parish of Osborne Heath, Stainforth, Doncaster. Born Doncaster. Enlisted Coventry. Resided Stainforth, Yorks. Grave Ref. II. B. 2. St. Venant-Robecq Road British Cemetery, Robecq, France.

PARKER, Battery Sergeant Major, Charles Edward Hayden, VC. 90029, Royal Field Artillery. Died, home, 9th August, 1918. Age 49. Son of William Parker (Crimean Veteran). Husband of Louisa Parker, of 2 Court, 4 House, The Butts, Coventry. Born 11th March, 1869 at Woolwich, London. Examiner Coventry Ordnance Works. Enlisted December, 1914. .Decoration, for their conspicuous bravery during the action at Korn Spruit on the 31st March 1900. Grave Ref. 198. 1. Coventry (London Road) Cemetery.

PARKER, Private, Ernest Arthur Edward. 266551, B Coy., 1/7th Bn., Royal Warwickshire Regiment. Killed in action, 27th August, 1917. Age 19. Son of Edward and Edith Parker of Waverley, Osmaston Park Road, Derby. Enlisted Coventry. Memorial Ref. Panel 23 to 28 and 163A. Tyne Cot Memorial, Belgium.

PARKER, Lance Corporal, Harold Thomas. 265491, 1st /7th Bn., Royal Warwickshire Regiment. Killed in action, whilst asleep by a shell, 23rd September, 1918. Age 22. Son of Richard C. and Elizabeth Parker, of Coventry. Born 30th March, 1896 at Coventry. Enlisted 3rd September, 1914 at Coventry. Resided 2, Trentham Road. Fitter, Humber Co. Ltd. Grave Ref. Plot 1. Row E. Grave 3. Granezza British Cemetery, Italy.

PARKER, Captain, Roland Gaskell. 2nd Bn., South Wales Borderers. Killed in action, 25th April, 1915. Age 38. Son of Herbert and Emily Palmer of 16, Ovington Gardens, Chelsea, London. Husband of Olive Palmer of 38, Park Mansions, Knightsbridge. Billeted Coventry. Memorial Ref. Panel 80 to 84. Helles Memorial, Turkey.

PARKER, Private, William. 69153, 6th Labour Coy., The King's (Liverpool Regiment). transf. to 76th Coy., Labour Corps formerly Loyal North Lancashire Regiment. Died, 6th August, 1917. Husband of Mrs. M. A. Parker, of 849, Station Street, Coventry. Born Kirkham, Lancs. Employed Coventry. Grave Ref. G. 18. St. Pol Communal Cemetery Extension, Pas de Calais, France.

PARKER, Private, William Arthur. 19722, 1st Bn., Wiltshire Regiment formerly 3/8644, Oxfordshire and Buckinghamshire Light Infantry. Killed in action, 1st September, 1915. Born St. Thomas, Warwick. Enlisted Coventry. Resided Coventry. Grave Ref. I. I. 5. La Brique Military Cemetery No.2, Belgium.

PARKER, Corporal, W. H. 195281, Signal Service, Royal Engineers. Died, home, 26th February, 1919. Age 33. Son of Mrs. F. Gibbs, of 531, Stoney Stanton Road, Coventry. Grave Ref. M. "U." 664. Leicester (Welford Road) Cemetery, Leicestershire.

PARKES, Private, Charles William. 44908, 2nd Bn., Royal Berkshire Regiment formerly 42714, Hampshire Regiment. Killed in action, 11th June, 1918. Age 19. Son of George and Madeline Parkes, of 20, Crossways Cottages, Wood End, Fillongley, Coventry. Born Coventry. Enlisted Coventry. Memorial Ref. Soissons Memorial, Aisne, France.

PARKIN, Private, Ernest. 13677, 7th Bn., King's Own (Royal Lancaster Regiment). Killed in action, 31st July, 1917. Age 22. Son of Albert and Harriett Parkin, of 208, Gulson Road, Coventry. Born Cape Town, South Africa. Enlisted Ulverston. Memorial Ref. Panel 12. Ypres (Menin Gate) Memorial, Ieper, West-Vlaanderen, Belgium.

PARKINSON, Corporal, Arthur. 206135, F Bn., Tank Corps formerly 2691, Machine Gun Corps. Killed in action, 31st July, 1917. Age 28. Son of Thomas and Sarah Parkinson of 47, Berry Lane, Longbridge, Preston. Born Longbridge, Lancs. Enlisted Coventry. Memorial Ref. Panel 56. Ypres (Menin Gate) Memorial, Belgium.

PARMITER, Private, George Geoffrey. DM2/180236, 648th Mechanical Transport Coy., Army Service Corps. Died, East Africa, 11th January, 1918. Age 19. Son of the Rev. George Parmiter of Doseley Vicarage, Dawley, Salop. Born Leicester. Enlisted Coventry. Resided Dawley, Salop. Grave Ref. 6. H. 11. Dar Es Sallam War Cemetery, Tanzania.

PARNELL, Private, Henry. 48483, 3rd Bn., Worcestershire Regiment. Killed in action, 18th October 1918. Born 27th October, 1882 at Withybrook. Resided 14, Station Street West. Artificial Silk Spinner. Enlisted June, 1917 at Coventry. Grave Ref. IV. E. 3. Romeries Communal Cemetery Extension, France.

PARNELL, Acting/Bombardier, Henry Walter. 221513 "A" Battery 103rd Brigade, Royal Field Artillery. Killed in action, Ypres 20th August 1917. Born 23rd December 1892 at Coventry. Resided at York Minster, Musician at York Minster. Commemorated St. John's Church and War Memorial Park. Memorial Ref. Panel 4 to 6 and 162. Tyne Cot Memorial, Belgium.

PARNELL, Corporal, James William George. 4448, 1st Bn., Royal Warwickshire Regiment. Killed in action, 23rd July 1917. Age 22. Son of James and Ellen Parnell, of Withybrook, Coventry. Born Withybrook. Employed Coventry. Grave Ref. I. B. 8. Crump Trench British Cemetery, Fampoux, Pas de Calais, France.

PARRATT, Lance Corporal, Samuel William. 15038, 11th Bn., Royal Warwickshire Regiment. Killed in action, Arras, 10th April, 1917. Born 1st May, 1887 at Bradford. Resided 94, Broad Street. Artificial silk spinner. Enlisted October, 1915 at Coventry. Grave Ref. I. A. 21. Feuchy Chapel British Cemetery, Wancourt, France.

PARSONAGE, Private, Fred Waldensian. 15667, 3rd Bn., Worcestershire Regiment. Died of wounds, 8th July, 1916. Age 25. Son of Thomas Henry and Mary Ann Parsonage. Born Crewe. Enlisted Coventry. Resided Crewe. Grave Ref. L. D. M18. Hastings Cemetery, Sussex.

PARSONS, Gunner, Charles. 614291, 2nd /1st (Warwick) Bty., Royal Horse Artillery. Killed in action, 20th July, 1917. Born Stratford on Avon. Employed Coventry. Grave Ref. III. G. 15. Vlamertinghe New Military Cemetery, Belgium.

PARSONS, Lance Corporal, Charles Warden. 1st /28th Bn., London Regiment (Artists' Rifles). Killed in action, 31st December, 1917. Born 1st June, 1898. Resided Coventry. Railway Clerk. Enlisted May, 1917. Grave Ref. A. 43. Sunken Road Cemetery, Villers-Plouich, France.

PARSONS, Gunner, Herbert William. 36924, 114th Heavy Bty., Royal Garrison Artillery formerly 8600, 5th Bn., Worcester Regiment. Killed in action, 27th March, 1918. Age 24. Born Coventry. Enlisted Birmingham. Son of Elizabeth J. Parsons, of 4, Defford Place, Clifford Street, Aston, Birmingham. Grave Ref. II. G. 7. Ribemont Communal Cemetery Extension, Somme, France.

PARSONS, Sergeant, Joseph. 387, 2nd Bn., Royal Warwickshire Regiment. Died of wounds, 7th July, 1917. Born Birmingham. Enlisted Coventry. Resided Birmingham. Grave Ref. I. N. 18. Acchiet-Le-Grand Communal Cemetery Extension, France.

PARSONS, Private, Joseph. 20660, 8th Bn., Gloucestershire Regiment. Died of wounds, 16th July, 1916. Age 38. Born 4th December, 1877 in Steam Yard, East Street, Coventry. Resided 7, The Hollows, Foleshill. Employed Standard Motor Co. Ltd. Enlisted March, 1915 at Coventry. Leaves a widow and three children. Grave Ref. VIII. D. 123. Boulogne Eastern Cemetery, France.

PARSONS, Joseph. Killed in action. Resided at 4c. 1h. Leicester Street. Welder.

PARSONS, Private, Victor Reginald. TR/7/1085, 92nd Bn., Training Reserve and 1/7th Bn., Royal Warwickshire Regiment. Died, Home of sickness, 30th May, 1917. Born Leamington. Enlisted Coventry. Grave Ref. I. AA. 24. Bedworth Cemetery.

PARSONS, Private, William Henry. 6847, 1st Bn., The Loyal North Lancashire Regiment. Died of wounds at Hotel Astoria, Paris, 1st October, 1914. Age 31. Son of James and Emma Parsons, of 37, Vernon Street, Hill Fields, Coventry. Born 1884 at Coventry. Enlisted Coventry. Reservist. Grave Ref. 6. 20. 32. City Of Paris Cemetery, Pantin, Seine-St-Denis, France.

PARTRIDGE, Private, Arthur John. 8485, 2nd Bn., Norfolk Regiment. Died, 20th September, 1916. Son of Thomas and Mary Partridge, of 48, Leicester Street, Coventry. Born St. Mary, Ely, Cambs. Enlisted King's Lynn. Grave Ref. XXI. M. 35. Baghdad (North Gate) War Cemetery, Iraq.

PASTON, Private, George Edward. 8885, 1st Bn., King's Liverpool Regiment. Died of wounds, 21st September, 1914. Born Berkswell. Enlisted Coventry. Resided Bulkington. Age 32. Husband of Gertrude Elizabeth Paston, of 6, Gorwell Street, Leicester. Grave Ref. II. E. 4. Valley British Cemetery, France.

PASTON, Private, William. 9702, 2nd Bn., Oxfordshire and Buckinghamshire Light Infantry. Killed in action, 14th April, 1917. Age 38. Son of George and Ann Paston. Husband of Emma Paston of 50, Long Street, Ryton. Born Coundon. Enlisted Coventry. Resided Bulkington. Memorial Ref. Bay 6 and 7. Arras Memorial, France.

PATCHETT, Private, William Ivens. 310976, 1st/1st Warwickshire Yeomanry. 14th November, 1917. Age 38. Husband of Ellen Patchett, of 6, Rowland Street, Rugby Born Clifton, Warwick. Enlisted Warwick. Commemorated War Memorial Park. Grave Ref. P. 29. Beersheba War Cemetery, Israel.

PATIENCE, Private, Frank Herbert. EMT/61896, 35th Motor Amb. Convoy, Royal Army Service Corps. Died, 15th August, 1920. Age 18. Son of John and Sarah Patience, of 9, Spencer Street, Coventry. Grave Ref. P. 106. Cairo War Memorial Cemetery, Egypt.

PATRICK, Private, James. 203274, 2/5th Bn., Royal Warwickshire Regiment. Killed in action, 3rd December, 1917 reported as wounded. Born 1889 at Foleshill. Resided 4, Market Street, Longford. Employed White and Poppe. Commemorated Saint Thomas the Apostle, Longford and Roll of Honour, Salem Baptist Church. Memorial Ref. Panel 3. Cambrai Memorial, Louverval, France.

PATRICK, Private, William. 7th Bn., Royal Warwickshire Regiment. Died, home, 8th September, 1916. Born 3rd February, 1896 at 6, Leicester Row. Resided 230, Stoney Stanton Road. Machinist. Enlisted 1914. Grave Ref. Coventry (London Road) Cemetery.

PATTERSON, Private, John Edward. 85366, Royal Defence Corps. 30th November, 1920. Age 43. Son of J. E. Patterson, of Coventry. Husband of Maud Patterson (nee Joll), of 25, Wesley Avenue, Peverell, Plymouth. Served in the South African Campaign. Grave Ref. General M. 30. 32. Ford Park Cemetery (Formerly Plymouth Old Cemetery) (Pennycomequick), Devon.

PATTINSON, Corporal, Gerald Edmond. 206126, C Coy., Machine Gun Corps (Heavy Branch) formerly 2212, Machine Gun Corps. Killed in action, 15th September, 1916. Age 31. Son of Charles Reginald and Helen Pattinson of Bridge Park, Gosforth, Newcastle-on-Tyne. Born Sunderland. Enlisted Coventry. Grave Ref. VII. A. 21. Combles Communal Cemetery Extension, France.

PAUL, Private, Harry. 13636, Oxfordshire and Buckinghamshire Light Infantry. Died, home, 11th October, 1919. Born 19th December, 1894 at Sunderland. Resided at 4, Sunny Bank, Abbots Lane. Driller. Enlisted September, 1914. Grave Ref. 197. 119. Coventry (London Road) Cemetery.

PAUL, Private, William. 6865, 11th Bn., Royal Warwickshire Regiment. Killed in action, 10th April, 1917. Born Coventry. Enlisted Ross, Herts. Resided Winston Green, Birmingham. Grave Ref. I. B. 18. Feuchy Chapel British Cemetery, Wancourt, France.

PAXTON, Sergeant, Leslie Hamilton. 10674, 5th Bn., Oxfordshire and Buckinghamshire Light Infantry. Killed in action, 12th July, 1915. Born Brackley, Northants. Enlisted Coventry. Resided Brackley, Northants. Grave Ref. LVIII. D. 12. Poelcapelle British Cemetery, Belgium.

PAXTON, Private, R. 7517, 1st Bn., Northamptonshire Regiment. Died, Germany, whilst a prisoner of war, 4th November, 1918. Age 30. Husband of Sarah Paxton, of 5 Court, 3 House, Chauntry Place, Coventry. Born 10th July, 1888. Miller. Reservist. Grave Ref. XIII. C. 8. Berlin South-Western Cemetery, Berlin, Brandenburg, Germany.

PAXTON, Sapper, William Henry. 9533, 11th Field Coy., Australian Engineers. Died of wounds, 16th February, 1917. Age 34. Son of William and Clare Paxton. Husband of F. Paxton, of 1st Avenue Bulimba, Brisbane, Queensland. Native Coventry, England. Born 7th June, 1880 in Bond Street. Bricklayer. Enlisted 31st December, 1915. Grave Ref. I. F. 2. Trois Arbres Cemetery, Steenwerck, Nord, France.

PAYNE, A. C. Commemorated Wesleyan Church.

PAYNE, Bombardier, Albert Edward. 1548, 123rd Bde., Royal Field Artillery. Killed in action, 11th October, 1915. Age 25. Son of William and Minnie Payne of 201, Munster Road, Fulham, London. Born Birmingham. Enlisted Coventry. Grave Ref. R. 4. Berles-Au-Bois Churchyard Extension, France.

PAYNE, Sapper, Arthur. 43397, 78th Field Coy., Royal Engineers. Killed in action, 29th April, 1918. Age 24. Son of John and Susannah Payne, of 31, Court, 5 House, Spon St., Coventry. Born 13th May, 1894 at Coventry. Turner. Enlisted September, 1914 at Coventry. Employed Rex Works. Commemorated St. John's Church. Grave Ref. B. 10. Englebelmer Communal Cemetery Extension, Somme, France.

PAYNE, Gunner, Ewart. 128328, 130th Bty., 40th Bde., Royal Field Artillery. Killed in action, Passchendaele, 10th October, 1917. Age 25. Son of Susanna Payne, of 266, Harnall Lane East, Coventry. Enlisted Coventry. Resided Coventry. Born 16th December, 1891 at 52, Vine Street. Painter and decorator. Grave Ref. II. G. 20. Potijze Chateau Grounds Cemetery, Ieper, West-Vlaanderen, Belgium.

PAYNE, Pioneer, Herbert Joseph. 43212, 72nd Field Coy., Royal Engineers. Killed in action, Gallipoli, 8th August, 1915. Age 34. Son of Alfred and Ellen Elizabeth Payne, of 4 Court, 2 House, Cox St., Coventry. Served in the South African War as Trooper in The Imperial Yeomanry. Born 3rd August, 1882, at 72 West Orchard. Resided at 16, Gas Street. Examiner, Daimler Co. Ltd. Enlisted August,1914, Coventry. Educated Bablake School. Commemorated Bablake School Memorial and War Memorial Park. Memorial Ref. Panel 23 to 25 or 325 to 328. Helles Memorial, Turkey.

PAYNE, Private, John. 9710, 1st Bn., Coldstream Guards. Died of wounds, 28th March, 1918. Age 23. Son of Edward and Anne Payne of 9, Church Terrace, Leamington. Born All Saints, Warwick. Enlisted Coventry. Resided Leamington. Grave Ref. VIII. R. 52. Cabaret-Rouge British Cemetery, Souchez, France.

PAYNE, Private, Victor James. 7th Bn., Royal Warwickshire Regiment. Died, home, 15th January, 1921. Born 23rd June, 1897 in Whitefriars Street. Resided at 28, Hood Street. Turner. Enlisted November, 1914. Grave Ref. Coventry (London Road) Cemetery.

PAYNE, Private, William John Henry. 19336, 2nd Bn., Royal Warwickshire Regiment. Killed in action, 4th May, 1916. Enlisted May, 1915 went to France in December, 1915. Farm worker. Husband of Mrs. Payne of 34, Middlemarch Road, Coventry. Memorial Ref. Bay 3. Arras Memorial, France.

PEACE, Lance Corporal, Arnold Ross. 200567, 3rd Bn., Tank Corps formerly 2682, Machine Gun Corps. Died of wounds, 8th October, 1918. Age 25. Husband of Gertrude M. Green (formerly Peace), of 51, High St., Grantham. Born Heanor, Derby. Enlisted Coventry. Grave Ref. S. II. L. 3. St. Sever Cemetery Extension, Rouen, France.

PEACEY, Corporal, Arthur. 200707, 5th Bn., Yorkshire Light Infantry. Killed in action, 30th July, 1918. Employed Coventry. Enlisted Wakefield. Grave Ref. I. H. 9. Courmas British Cemetery, France.

PEACOCK, Private, Harry. 978, D Coy., 2nd Bn., Royal Warwickshire Regiment. Killed in action, Loos, 25th September, 1915. Age 24. Son of Mrs. Ellen Randle, of 96, Crabmill Lane, Coventry. Born 21st August, 1891 at Nuneaton. Resided 11, Stoney Stanton Road. Labourer. Reservist. Enlisted Coventry. Memorial Ref. Panel 22 to 25. Loos Memorial, Pas de Calais, France.

PEAKE, Gunner, William Henry, 194389, 194th Siege Bty., Royal Garrison Artillery. Killed in action, 17th May 1918. Age 31. Husband of H. Peake, of Allesley, Coventry. Born 26th December, 1887 in Stephen Street, Coventry. Filer. Enlisted July, 1917 at Coventry. Grave Ref. XV. C. 14. Bienvillers Military Cemetery, Pas de Calais, France.

PEARCE, Private, Frederick. 13292, 8th (King's Royal Irish) Hussars. Killed in action, 31st March, 1918. Born Derby. Enlisted Dublin. Resided Coventry. Memorial Ref. Panel 3 and 4. Pozieres Memorial, France.

PEARCE, Private, George William Henry. 24552, 2/5th Bn., Royal Warwickshire Regiment. Killed in action, 6th September, 1917. Born 19th December, 1886 at Coventry. Resided at 109, Caludon Road. Brazier. Enlisted March, 1917 at Coventry. Commemorated Barras Green Working Mens Club. Memorial Ref. Panel 23 to 28 and 163A. Tyne Cot Memorial, Belgium.

PEARCEY, Private, Harold Thomas. 9884, 2nd Bn., Oxfordshire and Buckinghamshire Light Infantry. Died of wounds, 2nd November, 1914. Wounded 22nd October, 1914. Age 18. Son of Arthur and Anne Pearcey, of 106, Westwood Road, Earlsdon, Coventry. Born 12th May, 1896 at Northampton. Soldier. Grave Ref. I. A. 9A. Bois Guillaume Communal Cemetery, Seine-Maritime, France.

PEARMAN, Cadet, Herbert Carl. 768847, 28th Bn., County of London Regiment. Died, home, 4th November, 1918. Born in 1895 at Ryton on Dunsmore. Resided Ryton on Dunsmore. Educated King Henry VIII School. Farmer. Enlisted June, 1918. Commemorated King Henry VIII School and Ryton Memorial. Grave Ref. In East part. Ryton on Dunsmore (St. Leonard) Churchyard.

PEARS, Seaman, Arthur Reynolds. SS/4958, HMS Bulwark, Royal Navy. Killed off Sheerness, 26th November, 1914. Age 22. Son of Thomas Reynolds and Susannah Pears, of Leamington Spa., Warwickshire. Born 21st October, 1892 at Leamington. Resided at 49, Coronation Road. Miller, Triumph Works. Enlisted 1914. Memorial Ref. 3. Portsmouth Naval Memorial.

PEARS, Private, Frederick. 18713, 3rd Bn., Canadian Infantry (Central Ontario Regiment). Killed in action, 2nd May, 1915. Age 48. Son of George and Jane Pears. Husband of Rose Pears, of IOO/2, 107th Avenue, Edmonton, Alberta. Enlisted in 9th Bn. at Edmonton. Memorial Ref. Panel 18 - 24 - 26 – 30. Ypres (Menin Gate) Memorial, Belgium.

PEARSALL, Private, William. 38580, 2nd Bn., Royal Berkshire Regiment. Killed in action, 27th April, 1918. Age 19. Son of Mr. and Mrs. John Pearsall, of 141, Windmill Road, Longford, Coventry. Born Branstone, Northants. Enlisted Coventry. Memorial Ref. Panel 56 and 57. Pozieres Memorial, Somme, France.

PEARSON, Gunner, Arthur George. 98673, 116th Siege Battery, Royal Garrison Artillery. Died of wounds. 31st October, 1917. Age 25. Son of Fred and Emma Pearson, of Wheelwrights Lane, Exhall, nr. Coventry. Born at Exhall. Resided at Keresley. Employed Coventry. Commemorated Exhall Memorial. Enlisted Coventry. Grave Ref. VIII. A. 17. Nine Elms British Cemetery, Poperinge, West-Vlaanderen, Belgium.

PEARSON, Corporal, George Henry. 840660, 48th Div. Ammunition Col., Royal Field Artillery. Died of wounds, Home, 6th March, 1917. Born Coventry. Enlisted Coventry. Grave Ref. II. B. 25. Bray Military Cemetery, France.

PEARSON, Lance Corporal, John Carr. 24047, 3rd Bn., Grenadier Guards. Killed in action, 31st July, 1917. Born 31st June, 1894 at 12, Henry Street. Resided Station Street West. Coremaker and Moulder. Enlisted June, 1915 at Coventry. Memorial Ref. Panel 9 and 11. Ypres (Menin Gate) Memorial, Belgium.

PEARSON, Private, Thomas Speight. 5273, 1st/10th Battalion, The Kings (Liverpool Regiment). Killed in action, 9th August, 1916. Age 24. Son of Arthur and Alice Pearson, of 68, Fishergate, Preston. Born in 1892 at Preston. Resided at 55, Park Road. Enlisted Liverpool. Traveller. Commemorated War Memorial Park. Memorial Ref. Pier and Face 1D 8B and 8C. Thiepval Memorial, Somme, France.

PEART, Ordinary Seaman, Oswald Alfred. Bristol Z/9401, SS Ravensworth, Royal Naval Volunteer Reserve. Drowned through collision, 15th September, 1917. Age 25. Son of William John and Elizabeth Peart, of 6, Melville Road, Coventry. Born 19th April, 1892 at 7, Hertford Terrace. Analytical Chemist. Enlisted July, 1916. Educated Bablake School. Commemorated Bablake School Memorial. Memorial Ref. 25. Plymouth Naval Memorial, Devon.

PEBODY, Sergeant, Richard. 206118, D Coy. Machine Gun Corps (Heavy Branch) formerly 1672, Machine Gun Corps. Killed in action, 16th September, 1916. Age 21. Nephew of Mr. J. T. Pebody, of 24, Stephen St., Rugby. Born Rugby. Enlisted Coventry. Grave Ref. III. G. 12. A.I.F. Burial Ground, Flers, France.

PECKHAM, Sergeant, Walter. 5788, 1st Bn., Dorsetshire Regiment. Died of wounds, 1st June, 1915. Age 35. Son of Joseph William and Mary Ellen Peckham, of The Furlong, Ringwood, Hants. Grave Ref. 226. 124. Coventry (London Road) Cemetery.

PEDDIE, Private, Joseph. 18980, 1st Battalion, North Staffordshire Regiment. Killed in action, 30th April, 1916. Age 42. Husband of Mary Peddie, of 67, High Street, Bucknall, Stoke on Trent. Born Stoke-on-Trent. Enlisted Nuneaton. Resided Coventry. Commemorated War Memorial Park and Siddeley Roll of Honour. Grave Ref. I. D. 8. Dranoutre Military Cemetery, Belgium.

PEEL, Private, Edward. 19255, 15th Bn., Royal Warwickshire Regiment. Killed in action, Ypres, 5th October, 1917. Born 1889 in Gildersone near Leeds. Resided at 219, Sovereign Road. Grocer's Assistant. Enlisted April, 1916 at Coventry. Commemorated War Memorial Park. Memorial Ref. Panel 23 to 28 and 163A. Tyne Cot Memorial, Belgium.

PEERS, Private, John. 1414, 1st Bn., Royal Warwickshire Regiment. Killed in action, 12th October, 1916. Born 15th November, 1896 at 1c. 2h. Butts. Resided at 96, East Street. Enameller. Enlisted August, 1914 at Coventry. Memorial Ref. Pier and Face 9 A 9 B and 10 B. Thiepval Memorial, Somme, France.

PEET, Private, Charles William. 22170, 1st Bn., Royal Warwickshire Regiment. Killed in action, 3rd May, 1917. Born Greenfield, Beds. Enlisted Coventry. Resided Luton, Beds. Memorial Ref. Bay 3. Arras Memorial, France.

PEGG, Private, Richard Foster. 49791, 2nd Bn., Middlesex Regiment. Killed in action, 24th April, 1918. Born 24th April 1899 at Stockingford. Resided Exhall. Moulder. Enlisted May, 1917 at Coventry. Born 24th April, 1899 at Stockingford. Moulder. Commemorated Exhall Memorial and Roll of Honour, Salem Baptist Church. Memorial Ref. Panel 60 and 61. Pozieres Memorial, France.

PEIRSON, Assistant Paymaster, Edward Leslie. HMS Vanguard, Royal Naval Reserve. Killed by internal explosion of vessel at Scapa Flow, 9th July, 1917. Age 26. Son of Sidney T. and Edith E. Peirson, of 12, Park Road, Coventry. Born 7th February, 1891 at Coventry. Resided at 12, Park Road. Educated at King Henry VIII School and Heidelberg College, Germany. Chartered Accountant., Messrs E. T. Peirson & Son. Enlisted November, 1914. Commemorated King Henry VIII School, Queens Road Church Memorial and War Memorial Park. Memorial Ref. 25. Chatham Naval Memorial, Kent.

PENN, Arthur. Killed in action. Name on Roll of Honour in St. John Baptist Church. Commemorated St. John's Church.

PENN, Private, Ernest. 16221, 15th Bn., Royal Warwickshire Regiment. Died of wounds, whilst prisoner of war, 26th June, 1917. Born 1896 at Birmingham. Resided at 20, Smith Street. Employed Premier Cycle Company. Enlisted Coventry. Grave Ref. I. C. 17. Niederzwehren Cemetery, Germany.

PEPPER, Company Sergeant Major, Charles Arthur. 7613, 7th Bn., King's Royal Rifle Corps. Killed in action, Battle of the Somme, 18th August, 1916. Age 27. Son of John and Mary Pepper, of 25, Albert Street, Coventry. 9 years service. Twice previously wounded. Gold wire drawer. Reservist. Commemorated St. Johns Church. Memorial Ref. Pier and Face 13 A and 13 B. Thiepval Memorial, Somme, France.

PEPPER, Private, Edward Frederick. 26094, 2nd Bn., Worcestershire Regiment. Killed in action, 21st May, 1917. Age 31. Son of Frederick David and Sarah A. Pepper, of Edgbaston, Birmingham. Born Coventry. Enlisted Birmingham. Resided Birmingham. Memorial Ref. Bay 6. Arras Memorial, France.

PEPPER, Private, William. 203310, 2nd /6th Bn., Royal Warwickshire Regiment. Believed killed, 31st March, 1918. Age 21. Son of Mr. George Pepper and Mrs. E. Graham (formerly Pepper), of 198, Stoney Stanton Rd., Coventry, Warwickshire. Born 6th July, 1897 at 55, New Buildings, Coventry. Vanman, Bakery Department, Co-Operative Society. Enlisted November, 1915 at Coventry. Memorial Ref. Panel 18 and 19. Pozieres Memorial, Somme, France.

PERKINS, Corporal, Percy. 18919, 8th Bn., South Lancashire Regiment. Killed in action, 27th August, 1916. Born Kettering, Northants. Enlisted Coventry. Resided Kettering. Grave Ref. VI. P. 10. Lonsdale Cemetery, Authuile, France.

PERKINS, Private, William John. 202864, 5th Bn., Royal Berkshire Regiment. Killed in action, 30th November, 1917. Born Claybrook Magna, Leics. Enlisted Coventry. Resided Lutterworth. Memorial Ref. Panel 8. Cambrai Memorial, France.

PERKS, J.C. Commemorated Central Methodist Hall.

PERKS, Private, William Herbert. 201681, 1/5th Bn., Royal Warwickshire Regiment. Killed in action, 13th July, 1916. Born 11th June, 1887 at Lockhurst Lane, Coventry. Enlisted March, 1916 at Coventry. Resided 200, Lockhurst Lane. Hosiery Worker. Commemorated St. Pauls Foleshill formerly Lockhurst Lane Methodist Church. Memorial Ref. Pier and Face 9 A 9 B and 10 B. Thiepval Memorial, Somme, France.

PERRINS, Private, George Harry. 10760, 1st Bn., Royal Fusiliers. Killed in action, 25th March, 1918. Age 21. Son of George H. and Ellen Perrins, of 239, Longford Road, Longford, Coventry. Born 7th July, 1896 at Manchester. Enlisted Coventry. Resided Coventry. Clerk. Enlisted April, 1916. Commemorated Saint Thomas the Apostle, Longford and Roll of Honour, Salem Baptist Church. Memorial Ref. Panel 19 to 21. Pozieres Memorial, France.

PETERS, Private, G. Commemorated War Memorial Park.

PETERS, Private, George William. 33586, 1st /1st Bucks Bn., Oxfordshire and Buckinghamshire Light Infantry formerly 5451 Rifle Brigade. Died of wounds, received in Marseilles, Italy, 8th October, 1918. Age 23. Son of Arthur and Ada Peters, of 30, Primrose Hill Street, Coventry. Born 15th December, 1895, at Sowe Coventry. Resided at Coventry. Ribbon dresser, Hammerton's, Much Park Street. Enlisted August, 1914 at Coventry. Commemorated War Memorial Park. Grave Ref. III. A. 26. Mazargues War Cemetery, Marseilles, Bouches-du-Rhone, France.

PETERS, Gunner, Herbert Charles. 170080, 249th Siege Bty., Royal Garrison Artillery. Killed in action, Ypres, 8th July, 1918. Born 12th May, 1880 at Dulwich. Resided at 23a, Burges. Boot Shop Manager. Enlisted June, 1917 at Coventry. Grave Ref. I. J. 1. Hagle Dump Cemetery, Belgium.

PETFORD, Private, John. 10949, 2nd Bn., Worcestershire Regiment. Killed in action, 12th November, 1917. Born Wolverhampton. Enlisted Dudley, Worcs. Resided Coventry. Grave Ref. I. D. 13. Messines Ridge British Cemetery, Belgium.

PETTIFOR, Private, Wilfred Thomas. 260297, 2/8th Bn., Worcestershire Regiment. Killed in action, 3rd December, 1917. Enlisted Coventry. Resided Corley. Memorial Ref. Panel 6. Cambrai Memorial, France.

PHELPS, Private, Edward. 266356, 2nd Bn., Royal Warwickshire Regiment. Killed in action, 9th October, 1917. Born Foleshill. Resided Foleshill. Son of Mrs. Mary Ann Phelps, of 30, Homer Street, Hanley, Stoke-on-Trent. Memorial Ref. Panel 23 to 28 and 163A. Tyne Cot Memorial, Belgium.

PHILLIPS, Lieutenant, Charles Ernest, MC. 4th Bn., attached 7th Bn., South Irish Horses, Royal Irish Regiment. Killed in action, 22nd October, 1918. Age 31. Son of Evan Charles Phillips and Martha Phillips, of Newtown, Montgomeryshire. An Official in Lloyd's Bank, Limited. Born 25th July, 1887. Resided Cheltenham, previously Coventry. Bank clerk. Enlisted August, 1914. Grave Ref. V. D. 4. Vichte Military Cemetery, Belgium.

PHILLIPS, Corporal, George. (Alias see Biddle true family name). 27369, Machine Gun Corps formerly 21277, Oxfordshire and Buckinghamshire Light Infantry. Killed in action, 7th July, 1916. Age 24. Born Coventry. Enlisted Leamington. Resided Wyken. Memorial Ref. Thiepval Memorial.

PHILLIPS, Private, George Noel. 12986, 10th Bn., Royal Warwickshire Regiment formerly 3529, Life Guards. Died of wounds, 14th March, 1918. Aged 28. Husband of Ann Sarah Phillips, of 66, Marston Lane, Collycroft, Bedworth. Son of Leonard and Hannah Phillips of Bedworth. Born in Stockingford. Enlisted Coventry. Grave Ref. VIII. F. 3. St. Pierre Cemetery, Amiens, France.

PHILLIPS, Joseph. Killed in action. Resided Foleshill.

PHILLIPS, Private, William. 6424, 2nd Bn., York and Lancaster Regiment. Killed in action, Hooge, 9th August, 1915. Age 34. Son of George and Ellen Phillips, of 30, Greyfriars Lane, Coventry. Husband of Matilda Phillips, of 63, Godiva Street, Coventry. Born 29th May, 1882 at Birmingham. Turner., Triumph Works. Reservist. Commemorated Triumph and Gloria Works Memorial. Leaves a widow and one child. Memorial Ref. Panel 36 and 55. Ypres (Menin Gate) Memorial, Ieper, West-Vlaanderen, Belgium.

PHILLIPS, Rifleman, William Henry. 6493, 2nd Bn., Royal Irish Rifles. Killed in action, 21st September, 1914. Age 31. Born Coventry. Enlisted Coventry. Employed Standard Motor Works. Commemorated Saint Thomas the Apostle, Longford. Memorial Ref. La Ferte-Sous-Jouarre Memorial, France.

PHILPOTT, Private, R. 9495, 4th Bn., Middlesex Regiment. Killed in action, 12th October, 1915. Age 25. Brother of Charles William Philpott, of Brook Cottages, Allesley, Coventry. Grave Ref. I. B. 10. Lijssenthoek Military Cemetery, Poperinge, West-Vlaanderen, Belgium.

PHILPOTT, Private, Reginald Albert. 59321, 1st /8th Bn., Worcestershire Regiment. Killed in action, 4th November, 1918. Age 19. Son of Harry and Elizabeth Philpott, of 27, Holmsdale Road, Coventry. Husband of Kate Philpott. Born 16th July, 1899 at Foleshill, Coventry. Toolmaker. Enlisted June, 1918 at Coventry. Grave Ref. B. 51. Landrecies British Cemetery, Nord, France.

PICKARD, Private, George Alfred. DM2/179130, Mechanical Transport, Army Service Corps. attd. 298th Siege Bty. Royal Garrison Artillery, Died of disease, 9th September, 1918. Age 41. Son of William and Maria Pickard, of Coventry. Born 7th April, 1878 at Coventry. Enlisted May, 1916 at Coventry. Resided Coventry Cross Hotel. Publican. Commemorated Wesleyan Church. Grave Ref. Plot 4. Row D. Grave 3. Montecchio Precalcino Communal Cemetery Extension, Italy.

PICKARD, Private, James. 15252, 11th Bn., Royal Warwickshire Regiment. Killed in action, Ypres, 9th October, 1917. Born 31st July, 1898 at 7, Harnall Row, Coventry. Enlisted October, 1915 at Coventry. Resided 25, Payne's Lane. Capstan Hand, Messrs Clarke and Cluley. Memorial Ref. Panel 23 to 28 and 163A. Tyne Cot Cemetery, Belgium.

PICKARD, Private, Thomas William. 9134, C Coy., 2nd Bn., Royal Warwickshire Regiment. Killed in action, 31st October, 1914. Born 1888 at Coventry. Enlisted 1914 at Coventry. Resided 65, Lockhurst Lane, Coventry. Polisher. Memorial Ref. Panel 8. Ypres (Menin Gate) Memorial, Belgium.

PICKERILL, Private, Sydney Mornington. 265917, 2nd /7th Bn., Royal Warwickshire Regiment. Killed in action, St. Quentin, 23rd March, 1918. Age 22. Son of Isaac and Rose Pickerill, of "Oak Mount", Windmill Lane, Berkswell, Coventry. Born 8th April, 1895, at Sutton Coldfield. Resided at 69, Shakespeare Street. Butcher's assistant, London and Central Meat Co. Ltd. Enlisted Coventry, October, 1914. Commemorated Bablake School Memorial and War Memorial Park. Memorial Ref. Panel 18 and 19. Pozieres Memorial, Somme, France

PICKERING, Private, William Harold. 268075, 2/7th Bn., Royal Warwickshire Regiment attached Trench Mortar Battery. Killed in action, 21st March, 1918. Born 1, Bristle Hill, Buckingham. Enlisted Coventry. Employed Mr. Curzons Bakery. Resided 26, Albert Street, Coventry. Memorial Ref. Panel 18 and 19. Pozieres Memorial, France.

PICKUP, Surgeon Lieutenant, William Howard. HMS Prince Rupert, Royal Navy. Died of pneumonia, 27th November, 1918. Age 35. Son of William J. and Emily Pickup, of Swanswell, Coventry. Born 1884 at Coventry. Resided Coventry. Enlisted August, 1914. Commemorated King Henry VIII School. Grave Ref. Radford (St. Nicholas) Churchyard.

PIERCE, Stanley. Killed in action. Name on Roll of Honour in Cathedral Church of St. Michael.

PIGGOTT, Private, Albert. 3269, 1st /7th Bn., Royal Warwickshire Regiment. Killed in action, by a bomb, 25th June, 1915. Age 24. Son of Joseph Piggott, of 29 Court, 4 House, Spon St., Coventry. Born 15th September, 1890 at 5c. 4h. Chauntry Place. Polisher, Triumph Works. Enlisted November, 1914 at Coventry. Commemorated Holy Trinity Panels, St. John's Church and Triumph and Gloria Works Memorial. Grave Ref. II. E. 3. Rifle House Cemetery, Comines-Warneton, Hainaut, Belgium.

PIGGOTT, Private, Phillip John. 352937, "C" Coy. 7th Bn., London Regiment formerly 24152, 9th Duke Cornwall's Light Infantry. Died of wounds, 3rd December, 1917. Age 19. Son of Mr. and Mrs. Piggott, of 44, Bond Street, Coventry. Born 28th April, 1898 at Coventry. Enlisted December, 1915 at Nuneaton. Resided 44, Bond Street, Coventry. Apprentice, Coach and Body Building, Pass and Co. Ltd. Commemorated St. John's Church. Grave Ref. VI. E. 30. Rocquigny-Equancourt Road British Cemetery, Manancourt, Somme, France.

PILBROW, Gunner, William. 872, 4th Bty. 2nd/4th South Midland Howitzer Bde., Royal Field Artillery. Died, Home, 10th June, 1915. Age 19. Son of Phillip and Mary Elizabeth Pilbrow, of 1, Bath Terrace, Northampton. Born Northampton. Enlisted Coventry. Grave Ref. C. 104. Chelmsford (Writtle Road) Cemetery.

PILGRIM, Private, Neville Arthur. S4/039226, 13th Field Bakery, Army Service Corps. Died, Home, 9th June, 1918. Born Southsea, Hants. Enlisted Coventry. Resided Cambridge. Grave Ref. Newport (St. Woolos) Cemetery.

PIMM, Private, George. 1858, 1st Bn., Royal Warwickshire Regiment. Killed in action, 26th August, 1914. Born Coventry. Enlisted Birmingham. Grave Ref. I. B. 27. Fontaine-Au-Pire Communal Cemetery, France

PINFOLD, Private, William Robert. 42301, 1/5th Bn., North Staffordshire Regiment formerly 35259, Worcestershire Regiment. Died of wounds, 16th April, 1918. Age 19. Son of Mr. R. Pinfold, of The Forge, Witney. Native of Middleton Cheney, Banbury. Born Middleton Cheney, Oxford. Enlisted Warwick. Resided Coventry. Grave Ref. II. E. 6. Haringhe (Bandaghem) Military Cemetery, Belgium.

PIPER, Private, Albert Charles. 14323, 2nd Bn., Coldstream Guards. Died of wounds, 20th March, 1916. Age 22. Son of Charles and Edith Piper, late of Wellington Rd., Hounslow, Middx. Born Sunbury, Middx. Enlisted Coventry. Resided Hanworth, Middx. Grave Ref. V. D. 8A. Lijssenthoek Military Cemetery, Belgium.

PIPER, Private, Francis. 268807, 10th Bn., Royal Warwickshire Regiment. Killed in action, 22nd September, 1917. Born 17th June, 1886 at Birmingham. Resided 105, Spon Street. Licensed Victualler. Enlisted January, 1917 at Coventry. Memorial Ref. Panel 23 to 28 and 163A. Tyne Cot Memorial, Belgium.

PITCHFORD, Private, Frederick Ernest. 31975, 1st Bn., Devonshire Regiment. Killed in action, 24th September, 1918. Age 18. Son of Noah and Florence Elizabeth Pitchford, of 138, Elmsdale Avenue, Foleshill, Coventry. Native of Nuneaton, born 1900. Grave Ref. II. H. 27. Lebucquiere Communal Cemetery Extension, Pas de Calais, France

PITT, Private, Leslie Richard. 220021, 2nd Bn., Wiltshire Regiment. Died of wounds, 9th June, 1917. Age 19. Son of Mrs. E. M. Pitt, of Hawkesbury Junction, Longford, Coventry. Native of Oxford. Grave Ref. IV. B. 52. Boulogne Eastern Cemetery, Pas de Calais, France.

PLACKETT, Private, Horace. 10223, 2nd Bn., Royal Irish Regiment. Killed in action, 22nd November, 1917. Age 21. Son of Mary Jane Plackett, of Hayes Lane, Exhall, Coventry. Born Colin, Warwickshire. Enlisted Nuneaton. Resided Exhall. Commemorated Exhall Memorial. Grave Ref. II. D. 32. Heninel-Croisilles Road Cemetery, Pas De Calais, France.

PLANT, Second Lieutenant, Herbert. 14th Bn., Royal Warwickshire Regiment formerly Oxfordshire and Buckinghamshire Light Infantry. Died of wounds, 20th December, 1916 at No. 33, Casualty Clearing Station. Severely wounded, 13th December, 1916 by a shell. Age 25. Son of Alfred and Barbara Plant, of Eastern Green, Coventry. Born Styechale, 6th January, 1892. Educated Earlsdon School. Grave Ref. III. K. 45. Bethune Town Cemetery, Pas De Calais, France.

PLESTER, Sergeant, John William Bloxham. 6123, 1st Bn., Duke of Cornwall's Light Infantry. Killed in action, 3rd October, 1917. Born Fenny Compton. Employed Coventry. Memorial Ref. Panel 80 to 82 and 163A. Tyne Cot Memorial, Belgium.

PLIMMER, Flight Sergeant, Frederick. Royal Air Force. Died, home, 27th October, 1919. Born 30th January, 1897 at 32, Winchester Street. Resided 155, Shakespeare Street. Pattern Maker. Enlisted May, 1915. Grave Ref. Coventry (London Road) Cemetery.

PODMORE, Private, Francis George. 10749, 2nd Bn., Royal Warwickshire Regiment. Killed in action, 14th July, 1916. Age 19. Son of Alfred and Sarah Maria Podmore, of 133, Colony Cottages, Holbrooks Lane, Coventry. Memorial Ref. Pier and Face 9 A 9 B and 10 B. Thiepval Memorial, Somme, France.

POINTER, W. Killed in action. Employed by Rover Company, Ltd.

POLLARD, Captain, Gerald Evelyn Gustavus. 1st Bn., Royal Munster Fusiliers. Killed in action, 25th April, 1915. Aged 26. Billeted Coventry. Memorial Ref. Panel 185 to 190. Helles Memorial, Turkey.

PONDER, Private, Charles, DCM. 8959, 2nd Bn., Duke of Cornwall's Light Infantry. Killed in action, Hill 60, 15th February, 1915. Age 26. Son of Thomas Martin Ponder and Mary Ann Ponder, of 171, Walsgrave Road, Coventry. Born 21st December, 1888, at Stoke, Coventry. Resided at Coventry. Metal Worker, Triumph and Smith and Molesworth. Reservist. Awarded the Distinguished Conduct Medal for conspicuous gallantry near St. Eloi on the 14th and 15th February, 1915 when he rushed forward at great risk under heavy fire and dragged back a seriously wounded officer. Enlisted Warwick. Commemorated Stoke (St. Michaels) Church and War Memorial Park. Memorial Ref. Panel 20. Ypres (Menin Gate) Memorial, Ieper, Belgium.

PONTING, Private, Edwin Stanley. 200226, 1st /4th Bn., Wiltshire Regiment. Died, 30th June, 1916. Age 22. Son of William and Elizabeth Ponting, of 42, Gorton Road, Coventry. Born at Swindon. Enlisted Swindon. Resided Swindon. Grave Ref. Nisibin Mem. 245. Baghdad (North Gate) War Cemetery, Iraq.

POOLE, Leonard Ralph, MM. Royal Horse Artillery. Employed Gas Collector. Awarded Military Medal. Commemorated Gas Department Memorial, Coventry Corporation.

POOLE, Second Lieutenant, Roland Barrett. 62nd Wing 221st Sqdn., Royal Air Force. Accidentally killed whilst flying, 20th December, 1918. Age 19. Son of James and Mary Elizabeth Poole, of 17, Strathearn Road, Leamington Spa. Warwickshire. Born 6th June, 1899 at Leamington. Resided Leamington. Engineers Apprentice. Enlisted April, 1918. Grave Ref. V. B. 23. East Mudros Military Cemetery, Greece.

POOLE, Private, Samuel. 18862, 16th Bn., Royal Warwickshire Regiment. Killed in action, 9th October, 1917. Age 19. Son of Samuel and Amelia Copeland (formerly Poole), of 29, Coventry Street, Upper Stoke, Coventry. Born 1898 at Coventry. Enlisted Coventry. Memorial Ref. Panel 23 to 28 and 163A. Tyne Cot Memorial, Zonnebeke, West-Vlaanderen, Belgium.

POOLE, Private, William. 13055, 5th Bn., Oxfordshire and Buckinghamshire Light Infantry. Killed in action, Loos, 17th October, 1915. Born in 1888 at London. Resided Ryton-on-Dunsmore. Employed Courtaulds Ltd. Enlisted August, 1914 at Coventry. Commemorated Ryton Memorial. Memorial Ref. Panel 37 and 39. Ypres (Menin Gate) Memorial, Belgium.

PORTELLI, Corporal, Joseph Paul. 14649, 3rd Bn., Worcestershire Regiment. Killed in action, 26th September, 1915. Age 19. Son of Paul and Elizabeth Portelli, of 215, Mount Pleasant Rd., Hastings. Born Sheerness, Kent. Enlisted Coventry. Resided Sheerness. Memorial Ref. Panel 34. Ypres (Menin Gate) Memorial, Belgium.

PORTER, Private, Ernest. 12889, 9th Bn., Royal Warwickshire Regiment. Killed in action, 5th April, 1916. Age 28. Son of Mr. F. and Mrs. P. Porter, of 95, Colchester Street, Coventry. Husband of Lizzie Porter, of 84, Station Street East, Coventry. Born 21st January, 1888 at Coventry. Moulder, Mattersons Huxley and Watson. Resided little Heath. Enlisted 1915 at Coventry. Commemorated Holy Trinity Panels. Memorial Ref. Panel 9. Basra Memorial, Iraq.

PORTER, Private, Henry. 20168, 6th Bn., King's Own (Royal Lancaster Regiment). Died, Mesopotamia, 11th June, 1916. Born Coventry. Enlisted Coventry. Memorial Ref. Panel 7. Basra Memorial, Iraq.

PORTER, Private, James. 19115, 15th Bn., Royal Warwickshire Regiment. Killed in action, 24th April, 1917 by a shell. Born 24th December, 1890 in Stoney Stanton Road. Resided 2, Edgwick Road. Bleacher, Courtaulds Ltd. Enlisted April, 1916 at Coventry. Leaves a wife and three children Memorial Ref. Bay 3. Arras Memorial, France.

PORTER, Bugler, John William. 9137, "G" Coy. 2nd Bn., Oxfordshire and Buckinghamshire Light Infantry. Died of wounds, 14th September, 1915. Age 23. Son of Mr. and Mrs. F. Porter, of Reading, Berks. Husband of Emily Walker (formerly Porter), of 449, Brooklyn Street, St. James', Winnipeg, Canada. Born Reading. Enlisted Oxford. Resided Coventry. Grave Ref. I. D. 99. Chocques Military Cemetery, France.

PORTMAN, Private, Albert. 266488, 2nd /7th Bn., Royal Warwickshire Regiment. Killed in action, 19th July, 1916. Age 19. Son of George William and Jane Portman, of 56, Little Park Street, Coventry. Born 11th May, 1897 at Whitley. Clerk. Enlisted May, 1915 at Coventry. Memorial Ref. Panel 22 to 25. Loos Memorial, Pas de Calais, France.

POTTER, Sergeant, Charles Henry. 8822, 4th Bn., Coldstream Guards. Died of wounds, 2nd October, 1918. Age 29. Son of Joseph and Annie Potter, of Coventry. Husband of Gertrude Lily Potter, of 38, Rye Street, Bishops Stortford, Herts. Born 1889 at Birmingham. Grave Ref. V. C. 13. Terlincthun British Cemetery, Wimille, Pas de Calais, France.

POTTS, Private, John Charles Stanley. 2814, 9th Bn., Royal Warwickshire Regiment. Died of wounds, Gallipoli, 12th August, 1915. Age 21. Son of George Potts, of 440, Coventry Rd., Small Heath, Birmingham. Husband of F. N. A. Allton (formerly Potts), of The Hollies, Station Rd., Hinckley, Leicestershire. Born Southam, Warwicks. Enlisted Coventry. Resided Small Heath, Birmingham. Memorial Ref. panel 35 to 37. Helles Memorial, Turkey.

POULTNEY, Lance Corporal, William. 19864, 2nd Bn., Wiltshire Regiment formerly 2838, Royal Warwickshire Regiment. Killed in action, 25th November, 1915. Born Atherstone, Warwick. Enlisted Coventry. Resided Atherstone. Grave Ref. II. G. 5. Guards Cemetery, Windy Corner, Cuinchy, France.

POULTON, Lieutenant, Frederick James. 9th Bn., Royal West Surrey Regiment attached 1/8th Bn., Hampshire Regiment. Killed in action, 2nd November, 1917. Born 28th October, 1894 at Birmingham. Resided Coventry. Articled Clerk to Chartered Accountant. Educated Bablake School. Commemorated Bablake School Memorial, Iliffe & Sons Ltd and Queens Road Memorial. Enlisted 1915. Grave Ref. XIII. A. 4. Gaza War Cemetery, Israel.

POWELL, Private, Bertram Brown. 24325, 12th Bn., Devonshire Regiment. Killed in action, 22nd September, 1916. Age 21. Brother of Mr. J. H. Powell, of 22, Kimpton Rd., Luton. Born St. Olives, York. Enlisted Coventry. Grave Ref. A. 4. Fricourt New Military Cemetery, France.

POWELL, Sapper, C. L. Royal Engineers. Killed in action, 8th August, 1918. Born 22nd April, 1898. Resided 106, Lower Ford Street. Tester. Enlisted November, 1916. Commemorated British Thompson Houston Memorial.

POWELL, E. Commemorated Post Office Memorial.

POWELL, Private, Egbert William. 8940, 16th Bn., Royal Warwickshire Regiment. Killed in action, Battle of the Somme, 3rd September, 1916. Went over the top with a fatigue party of 15 men, none returned. Age 35. Son of Joseph and Elizabeth Powell. Husband of Jane Elizabeth Powell, of 13, Peel Street, Coventry. Born 30th September, 1882 at Leek, Staffs. Enlisted Warwick. Watchman, Rudge Whitworth. Reservist. Resided Coventry. Recommended for Distinguished Conduct Medal for shooting a sniper, April 1916. Memorial Ref. Pier and Face 9 A 9 B and 10 B. Thiepval Memorial, Somme, France.

POWELL, Sergeant, Frank Thomas. 18708, 10th Bn., Worcestershire Regiment. Killed in action, 11th February, 1917. Age 22. Son of Luther Powell, of 22, Taff St., Ferndale (Rhondda), Glam. Husband of E. Powell, of 9, Wells Place, Holloway, Bath. Born Ystradfodwg, Glam. Enlisted Ferndale, Glam. Resided Coventry. Grave Ref. D. 17. Queens Cemetery, Puisieux, France.

POWELL, Bombardier, Frederick James. 16241, 91st Bde., Royal Field Artillery. Killed in action, 3rd November, 1916 by a shell. Born 1893 at Rugby. Resided 106, Eagle Street. Employed Triumph Cycle Company Ltd. Enlisted Coventry. Commemorated Saint Thomas the Apostle, Longford. Grave Ref. X. 3. Carnoy Military Cemetery, France.

POWELL, Able Seaman, John. SS/1861, HMS Good Hope, Royal Navy. Killed in action, Battle of Coronel, 1st November, 1914. Age 25. Husband of Ada Jeffries (formerly Powell), of 34, Colony Cottage, Holbrooks Lane, Coventry. Memorial Ref. 2. Portsmouth Naval Memorial, Hampshire.

POWELL, Driver, Kenneth Merrick, 840547, "B" Bty. 306th Bde., Royal Field Artillery. Killed in action near Cambrai, 19th October, 1918. Age 20. Son of Arthur S. and Annie Mary Powell, of 33, Catherine Street, Coventry. Native of Hay, Breconshire. Born 9th June 1899 at Hay, Breconshire. Resided at 33, Catherine Street. Apprentice Engine Fitter, Maudslay Works. Enlisted February 1915 at Coventry. Commemorated War Memorial Park. Grave Ref. II. C. 3. St. Aubert British Cemetery, Nord, France.

POWELL, Thomas. Commemorated Wolston Memorial.

POWELL, Major, Vernon Harcourt De Butts, MC. 53rd Bty. 13th Bde., Canadian Field Artillery. Killed in action, 2nd January, 1918. Age 31. Son of Rev. Harcourt Powell, of Wollaston Vicarage, Wellingborough, Northants, and of Cecile H. Powell, of 5, Regent Street, Coventry. Name on Roll of Honour in St. Thomas's Church. Grave Ref. North of Church. Little Shelford (All Saints) Churchyard, Cambridgeshire.

POWELL, Rifleman, William. 8226, 3rd Bn., King's Royal Rifles. Died, India, 8th October, 1914. Born Coventry. Enlisted Coventry. Commemorated Triumph and Gloria Memorial. Memorial Ref. Delhi 1914-1918 War Memorial, India.

POWER, Private, Reginald Colin. 5486, 10th Bn., Royal Fusiliers. Killed in action, 10th July, 1916. Born Atherstone. Enlisted Coventry. Resided Atherstone. Memorial Ref. Pier and Face 8 C 9 A and 16 A. Thiepval Memorial, Somme, France.

POWERS, Private, George Frederick. 16652, 9th Bn., Royal Warwickshire Regiment. Killed in action, by a shell, 5th January, 1917. Age 26. Son of Frederick and Annie Powers, of Pickford Green, Allesley, Coventry. Dairyman. Born Allesley. Enlisted Warwick. Resided Allesley. Grave Ref. XIX. K. 13. Amara War Cemetery, Iraq.

POWERS, Private, Sutcliffe. M2/046681, M.T. 1st Heavy Repair Shop, Royal Army Service Corps. Died, 6th September, 1918. Age 28. Son of the Rev. Henry and Mary Powers. Husband of Queenie Powers, of Queenscliffe Cafe, Margate. Born at Leeds. Born Hull. Enlisted London. Resided Coventry. Grave Ref. 6. 19. 24. City Of Paris Cemetery, Pantin, France.

POXTON, Ralph. Commemorated Holy Trinity Panels.

PRATT, Gunner, Albert Edwin. Royal Garrison Artillery. Died, home, 30th March, 1921. Born 15th October, 1881 at Brailes. Resided 28, Irving Road. Postman. Enlisted November, 1916. Grave Ref. Coventry (London Road) Cemetery.

PRATT, Regimental Sergeant Major, Edward Joseph. 2469, 10th Bn., Royal Warwickshire Regiment. Died of wounds, 20th September, 1917. Born 5th August, 1875 at Westwood Heath. Resided Foleshill. School Attendance Officer. Enlisted September, 1914. Grave Ref. I. 7. Bus House Cemetery, Belgium.

PRATT, Private, William Andrew. 148703, 48th Bn., Machine Gun Corps formerly 3280, Royal Warwickshire Regiment. Died of accidental injuries, 4th July, 1918 during musketry practice with the discharge of a comrades rifle. Age 22. Son of William and Alice Pratt, of Coventry. Born 28th September, 1895 at 17, George Street. Resided 41, George Street. Motor Cycle Finisher, Triumph and formerly Deasy Works. Enlisted November, 1914 at Coventry. Grave Ref. 9. A. 13. Montecchio Precalcino Communal Cemetery Extension, Italy.

PREEDY, Gunner, Horace. 845172, 48th Div. Ammunition Col., Royal Field Artillery. attd. 48th Trench Mortar Bty., Died of wounds, 25th August, 1917. Wounded in the head by a shrapnel bullet. Age 23. Son of Thomas and Elizabeth Preedy, of 17, Jenner Street, Coventry. Born 16th November, 1893 at 17, Jenner Street. Resided at 17, Jenner Street. Employed at concrete works, Foleshill Road. Enlisted August, 1914. Commemorated War Memorial Park. Grave Ref. I. B. 36. Duhallow A.D.S. Cemetery, Ieper, West-Vlaanderen, Belgium.

PRESCOTT, Private, Albert. 10518, 2nd Bn., Royal Warwickshire Regiment. Killed in action, 4th May, 1917. Age 30. Son of Thomas Prescott, of Bromsgrove. Hsband of Beatrice Prescott, of 77, Blakefield Rd., St. John's, Worcester. Born Upton, Worcs. Enlisted Coventry. Memorial Ref. Bay 3. Arras Memorial, France.

PRESCOTT, Private, Job. 28678, 6th Bn., Somerset Light Infantry. Killed in action, 3rd November, 1917. Age 18. Son of Charles and Polly Prescott, of 3, Grange Terrace, Walsgrave Road, Coventry. Native of Blackheath, Staffs. Grave Ref. II. I. 15. Hooge Crater Cemetery, Ieper, West-Vlaanderen, Belgium.

PRESTON, William Albert. 131, 14th Bn., Royal Warwickshire Regiment. Killed in action, 23rd July, 1916. Age 23. Son of Albert and Jane Anne Preston, of 17, Coventry Road, Coleshill, Birmingham. Born Coventry. Enlisted Birmingham. Resided Coventry. Memorial Ref. Pier and Face 9 A 9 B and 10 B. Thiepval Memorial, Somme, France.

PRETTY, Private, William Henry. 35329, 14th Bn., Royal Warwickshire Regiment. Died of wounds, 14th April, 1918. Born 24th November, 1898 at 13, Little South Street, Coventry. Enlisted September, 1917 at Coventry. Resided 16, East Street. Apprentice Carpenter. Grave Ref. I. VF. 19. Aire Communal Cemetery, France.

PRICE, Private, A. W. (Billie). 269894, 124th Bn., Canadian expeditionary Force transferred to Princess Patricia's Canadian Light Infantry. Killed in action, 17th May, 1917. Born Coventry. Resided Toronto, Canada in January, 1916. Previously employed Daimler Company Ltd. Grave Ref. III. F. 12. La Chaudiere Military Cemetery, Vimy, France.

PRICE, Corporal, Arthur Richard. 24854, 13th Bn., Gloucestershire Regiment. Died, 30th March, 1918. Born Aldershot. Enlisted Coventry. Memorial Ref. Panel 40 and 41. Pozieres Memorial, France.

PRICE, Private, Ernest. 266540, 1/7th Bn., Royal Warwickshire Regiment. Killed in action, Ypres, 13th August, 1917. Born 19th February, 1890 at Coventry. Resided 11, Church Street. Polisher. Enlisted June, 1915 at Coventry. Memorial Ref. Panel 8. Ypres (Menin Gate) Memorial, Belgium.

PRICE, Private, George Enos. 9966, 2nd Bn., Royal Warwickshire Regiment. Killed in action, Loos, 25th September, 1915. Born 1884 at Huddersfield. Resided 35, Radford. Moulder, Daimler Ltd, Radford Foundry. Enlisted August, 1914 at Coventry. Memorial Ref. Panel 22 to 25. Loos Memorial, France.

PRICE, Private, Herbert George. 1st Bn., Royal Warwickshire Regiment. Killed in action, Ypres, 26th April, 1915. Born September, 1889 at Leamington. Resided Chandos Street. Machinist. Reservist.

PRICE, Private, Herbert William. 1240, 1st Bn., Royal Warwickshire Regiment. Killed in action, 26th April, 1915. Age 22. Son of James and Elizabeth Price. Husband of Ada Summerlin (formerly Price) of 118, Princess Street, Luton. Born Milverton, Warwick. Enlisted Coventry. Resided Milverton. Born September, 1889 at Leamington. Resided Chandos Street. Machinist. Reservist. Memorial Ref. Panel 8. Ypres (Menin Gate) Memorial, Belgium.

PRICE, Lance Corporal, Isaac Norman. 2503, 1st /6th Bn., South Staffordshire Regiment. Killed in action, 13th October, 1915. Age 19. Son of Isaac and Mary Price, of 43, Churchill Avenue, Coventry. Born 22nd March, 1896 at Worksop. Engineer. Enlisted August, 1914. Memorial Ref. Panel 73 to 76. Loos Memorial, Pas de Calais, France.

PRICE, Driver, John. Royal Field Artillery. Died, home, repatriated prisoner of war, 8th April, 1918. Born 1892 at Coventry. Resided Coventry. Agricultural Labourer. Enlisted 1914. Grave Ref. Coventry (London Road) Cemetery.

PRICE, Acting Sergeant, Joseph. 962, 14th Bn., Royal Warwickshire Regiment. Died of wounds, 1st September, 1916. Age 25. Son of William Isaac and Caroline Price, of Walsall Wood. Born Walsall, Staffs. Enlisted Birmingham. Resided Coventry. Grave Ref. II. B. 26. La Neuville British Cemetery, Corbie, France.

PRICE, Lance Corporal, Leonard Joseph Walter. 10090, 9th Bn., Royal Fusiliers. Killed in action, 7th October, 1916 at Bapaume. Age 21. Son of Joseph and Alice Price. Born 16th August, 1895 at 9, Stanley Terrace, Allesley Old Road, Coventry. Enlisted Coventry. Resided 58, Craven Street, Coventry. Clerk. Enlisted January, 1916. Educated Bablake School. Commemorated Bablake School Memorial and St. John's Church. Memorial Ref. Pier and Face 8 C 9 A and 16 A. Thiepval Memorial, Somme, France.

PRICE, Lance Corporal, Thomas Martin. 7811, 2nd Bn., Leicestershire Regiment. Killed in action, 25th September, 1915. Born St. Margaret's, Leicester. Enlisted Leicester. Resided Coventry. Memorial Ref. Panel 42 to 44. Loos Memorial, France.

PRICE, Walter. Royal Marine Light Infantry. Killed in action. Born 1897. Resided 15, Little Field, Stoke Heath. Enlisted 1915.

PRICE, Sapper, William Allan. 43841, 86th Field Coy., Royal Engineers. Killed in action, 16th August, 1917. Born 11th December, 1893 at 17, Spring Street, Coventry. Enlisted August, 1914 at Coventry. Resided 23, Hood Street. Son of Mr. F. Price. Machinist, Humber Ltd. Grave Ref. L. F. 7. Poelcapelle British Cemetery, Belgium.

PRIDMORE, Harry. Royal Warwickshire Regiment. Killed in action, July 1918. Commemorated Gas Department Memorial, Coventry Corporation.

PRIDMORE, Private, Henry Alfred. 22532, 14th Bn., Royal Warwickshire Regiment. Killed in action, 27th September, 1918. Born Desborough, Northants. Enlisted Coventry. Memorial Ref. 3. Vis-En-Artois Memorial, France.

PRIDMORE, Captain, Percy Malin, MC. 2nd /6th Bn., Royal Warwickshire Regiment. Killed in action, 2nd September, 1917. Age 31. Son of Alexander Percy and Florence Louise Pridmore, of Coventry. Husband of Constance Margaret Mitchell (formerly Pridmore), of Coventry. Born 7th January, 1886 at Coventry. Resided at Burnt post. Manufacturer of small wares. Enlisted August, 1914. Awarded the Military Cross for gallant conduct whilst in charge of a Trench Mortar battery. Commemorated War Memorial Park. Grave Ref. VII. G. 2. Vlamertinghe New Military Cemetery, Ieper, West-Vlaanderen, Belgium.

PRIDMORE, Major, Reginald George, MC. "C" Bty. 240th Brigade, Royal Field Artillery. Killed in action near the Piave River, Arcade, 13th March, 1918. Age 31. Only son of George William and Sarah Louisa Pridmore, of Coventry. The inscription on his original wooden cross erected by his comrades read. "A most Gallant Sportsman and Comrade". Born 29th April, 1886 at Birmingham. Stockbroker. Enlisted September, 1914. Awarded the Military cross for conspicuous gallantry during operations as Forward Observing officer. He displayed great coolness under fire, notably on one occasion when his observation post was very heavily shelled, both he and his look out man were partially buried but he carried on and send in valuable reports. Grave Ref. Plot 1. Row D. Grave 5. Giavera British Cemetery, Arcade, Italy.

PRIEST, Lance Corporal William Joseph, MM. 11038, 11th Bn., Royal Warwickshire Regiment. Died 29th January, 1917 at Beaumont Hamel at the time of his death, being seized with illness in the trenches and died within half an hour. Aged 45. Son of Thomas and Harriet Priest, of Bedworth. Born Bedworth. Employed at a Nottinghamshire Colliery formerly Newdigate Colliery and Courtaulds. Enlisted Hucknall, Nottinghamshire. Decorated in the field for bravery with the Military Medal. Grave Ref. I. D. 4. Vielle-Chapelle New Military Cemetery, Lacouture, France.

PRIOR, Private, Ernest Peter. 9901, 2nd Bn., Border Regiment. Killed in action, 28th October, 1914. Age 26. Son of Peter and Rachel Prior, of 7, Craven Street, Chapel Fields, Coventry. Born 25th January 1889 at Banbury. Resided at 25, Allesley Old Road. Soldier. Enlisted Coventry. Commemorated War Memorial Park. Clerk, Ordnance Works formerly Wood Machinist, Hancox's Memorial Ref. Panel 35. Ypres (Menin Gate) Memorial, Ieper, West-Vlaanderen, Belgium.

PRITCHARD, Lance Corporal, Frank Hubert. 21959, 14th Bn., Royal Warwickshire Regiment. Killed in action, near Arras, 18th May, 1917. Born 22nd August, 1880 at Warwick. Enlisted Warwick. Resided 95, Poplar Road, Coventry. Dental Mechanic. Enlisted July, 1916. Grave Ref. IX. A. 32. Orchard Dump Cemetery, Arleux-En-Gohelle, France.

PROBERT, Private, Herbert. 266626, 1st /6th Bn., Royal Warwickshire Regiment. Killed in action, Ypres, 27th August, 1917. Age 31. Son of William and Mary Ann Probert, of Coventry. Born 16th April, 1886 in New Court, Gosford Street. Resided at 5c. 5h. Birds Yard, Smithford Street. Window Cleaner. Enlisted November, 1915 at Coventry. Grave Ref. XIII. B. 5. Tyne Cot Cemetery, Zonnebeke, West-Vlaanderen, Belgium.

PROCTOR, Private, Frank. 10275, 143rd Machine Gun Corps (Infantry) formerly Royal Berkshire Regiment. Died, 24th December, 1916. Age 35. Son of Mr. and Mrs. Thomas Proctor, of 2, Marston's Buildings, Holbrooks Lane, Foleshill, Coventry. Born 29th August, 1881 at Little Heath. Resided at 2, Martson's Building, Holbrook Lane. Brick Maker. Enlisted Coventry. Grave Ref. I. R. 41. Albert Communal Cemetery Extension, France.

PROCTOR, Corporal, Harry. 45790, 94th Bty. 18th Bde., Royal Field Artillery. Died of wounds, 30th September, 1917. Born Coventry. Enlisted Coventry. Grave Ref. III. E. 141. Bailleul Communal Cemetery Extension (Nord), France.

PROCTOR, Private, Henry. 16810, 8th Bn., Royal Berkshire Regiment. Killed in action, 25th September, 1915. Born 11th August, 1874 at Little Heath. Resided at 2, Martson's Building, Holbrook Lane. Labourer. Enlisted Coventry. Memorial Ref. Panel 93 to 95. Loos Memorial, France

PROCTOR, Driver, Herbert Edward. 109688, "B" Bty. 177th Bde., Royal Field Artillery. Died of wounds, caused by the bursting of a 5.9 shell, 12th July, 1917. Age 19. Son of Leonard Proctor, of 3, Red Lane, Coventry, Warwickshire. Husband of Emily Kate Proctor. Born 26th March, 1898 at Foleshill, Turner, Herberts Ltd. Enlisted October, 1915 at Coventry. Grave Ref. I. F. 31. Vlamertinghe New Military Cemetery, Ieper, West-Vlaanderen, Belgium.

PROCTOR, Leonard, St. Pauls Foleshill formerly Lockhurst lane Methodist church.

PROFFITT, Private, Thomas Henry. 36934, A Coy., 1st Bn., Wiltshire Regiment. Died whilst prisoner of war, 1st April, 1918. Born 27th November, 1899 at 18, Harnall Lane East, Coventry. Enlisted Coventry. Resided 18, Harnall Lane East, Coventry. Employed Mr. T. H. Spencer & Co. Ltd, Slay and Harness maker, Priory Street. Grave Ref IX. A. 6. Strand Military Cemetery, Belgium.

PRUE, Gunner, Richard Matthew Price. 212219, "D" Bty. 106th Bde., Royal Field Artillery. Died of wounds, 6th August, 1917. Enlisted Coventry. Resided Coventry. Grave Ref. IV. A. 36. Mendinghem Military Cemetery, Belgium.

PRYCE, Rifleman, Stanley Theodore. S/13349, 12th Bn., Rifle Brigade. Killed in action, 14th August, 1916. Born Coventry. Enlisted Coventry. Resided Birmingham. Butcher's Assistant. Memorial Ref. Pier and Face 16 B and 16 C. Thiepval Memorial, Somme, France.

PUGH, Lieutenant, John Edwin. 210th Sqdn., Royal Air Force. Died of injuries received whilst flying 10th November, 1918. Shot down near Grand Reng. Age 19. Son of John Vernon Pugh, of Meriden House, Meriden, Warwickshire, and of Edith Georgina French (formerly Pugh), of Hertford House, Coventry. Born 21st February, 1899 at Primrose Hill House. Resided Allesley. Student. Enlisted April, 1917. Grave Ref. In the S. East part, near the South wall. Gosselies Communal Cemetery, Charleroi, Hainaut, Belgium.

PULLEN, Private, George. 511656, Labour Corps formerly 122275, Royal Army Service Corps. Died, 21st May, 1918. Born Nuneaton. Enlisted Coventry. Resided Harbighan, Nuneaton.

PULLFORD, Private, Cyril Charles. 62925, 7th Bn., Royal Fusiliers formerly 39320, Queen's Royal West Surrey Regiment. Killed in action, 20th April, 1917. Age 19. Son of George Ernest and Elizabeth Pulford, of 81, Pellatt Grove, Wood Green, London. Born Coventry. Enlisted Mill Hill. Resided Wood Green. Memorial Ref. Bay 3. Arras Memorial, France.

PUNSHON, Gunner, George Nixon. 92805, "D" Battery, 47th Brigade, Royal Field Artillery. Died of wounds, 22nd July 1917. Born 6th October, 1892 at London. Resided at Coventry. Cycle Liner. Enlisted Coventry, September, 1914. Commemorated War Memorial Park. Grave Ref. XVI. E. 5. Lijssenthoek Military Cemetery, Belgium.

PURKISS, Private, Henry. 17200, 2nd Bn., Hampshire Regiment formerly 17987, Oxfordshire and Buckinghamshire Light Infantry. Killed in action, Gallipoli, 6th August, 1915. Age 48. Husband of Clara Elizabeth Purkiss, of 184, Gadsby St., Attleborough Nuneaton. Born St. Mary's, Reading, Berks. Enlisted Coventry. Resided Nuneaton. Grave Ref. Panel 125 -134. Helles Memorial, Turkey.

PURNELL, Private, Eric Keppell. 241541, 1st /6th Bn., Royal Warwickshire Regiment. Killed, Battle of the Somme, 1st July, 1916. Son of E. J. and A. Purnell, of Coventry. Born 6th January, 1887 at Kenilworth. Resided at 20, Sir Thomas Whites Road. Tailors manager. Enlisted October, 1915. Commemorated King Henry VIII School and War Memorial Park. Memorial Ref. Pier and Face 9 A 9 B and 10 B. Thiepval Memorial, Somme, France

PURNELL, Private, George. 14447, 8th Bn., Royal Berkshire Regiment. Killed in action, Loos, 25th September, 1915. Born 7th February, 1892 at Birmingham. Enlisted September, 1914 at Nuneaton. Resided Upper Stoke, Coventry. Machinist. Memorial Ref. Panel 93 to 95. Loos Memorial, France.

QUINNEY, Gunner, Percy Reginald. 944536, D Bty., 31st Bde, Royal Field Artillery. Died of wounds, 28th November, 1917. Enlisted Coventry. Resided Nottingham. Memorial Ref. Garter Point Cem. Mem. 31.Perth (China Wall) Cemetery, Belgium.

QUINNEY, Private, Sidney Thomas. 1629, 1st Bn., Royal Warwickshire Regiment. Died of wounds, caused by the bursting of a shell as he was entering the trenches, 24th April, 1916. Age 20. Son of George Henry and Ellen Quinney, of 1, Court, 8, House, Swanswell Terrace, Coventry. Born 7th August, 1895 at 1c. 4h. Burges. Machinist, Edward O' Briens Ltd. Enlisted August, 1914 at Coventry. Grave Ref. III. B. 4. Bienvillers Military Cemetery, Pas de Calais, France.

RABY, Lance Corporal, Ernest William. 3314, 9th Bn., Royal Warwickshire Regiment. Killed in action, 10th August, 1915. Born 3rd May, 1895 in Albion Street. Resided at 61, Poplar Road. Turner. Enlisted August, 1914. Commemorated Central Methodist Hall. . Born St. John's, Coventry. Enlisted Coventry. Memorial Ref. Panel 35 to 37. Helles Memorial, Turkey.

RADBURN, Private, Charles Walter. 16420, 1st Bn., Hampshire Regiment. Killed in action, 1st July, 1916. formerly 13950, Oxfordshire and Buckinghamshire Light Infantry. Born Ryton-on-Dunsmore. Enlisted Coventry. Resided Ryton-on-Dunsmore. Commemorated Ryton Memorial. Grave Ref. I. D. 91. Sucrerie Military Cemetery, Colincamps, France.

RADBURN, Private, Joseph. 28544, 11th Bn., Royal Warwickshire Regiment. Believed killed at Monchy, 29th April, 1917. Age 32. Son of William and Mary Radburn. Husband of Mary Jane Ball (formerly Radburn), of 412, Stoney Stanton Road, Coventry. Born 6th June, 1884 at Holy Trinity, Coventry. Resided at 10, Henry Street. Labourer. Enlisted February, 1914 at Coventry. Commemorated Coventry Chain Memorial. Memorial Ref. Bay 3. Arras Memorial, Pas de Calais, France.

RADFORD, Private, Harold James. 10090, "B" Coy. 2nd Bn., Royal Warwickshire Regiment. Killed in action, Battle of the Somme, 3rd September, 1916. Age 19. Son of William and Emma Radford, of 1 House, 1 Court, Heney Street, Coventry. Born Devonshire. Resided Warwick. Employed Coventry. Memorial Ref. Pier and Face 9 A 9 B and 10 B. Thiepval Memorial, Somme, France.

RADFORD, Sergeant, George Thomas. SR/508, 16th Bn., Royal Fusiliers. Died, Home, 19th November, 1918. Age 46. Son of Oliver and Jane Radford, of London. Husband of Phoebe Elizabeth Radford, of 59, Smith Street, Coventry. Born 1874 at London. Resided Raglan Street. Miller. Reservist. Grave Ref. 197. 78. Coventry (London Road) Cemetery.

RADLEY, Lance Corporal, Ernest. 8085, 2nd Bn., Oxfordshire and Buckinghamshire Light Infantry formerly 25883, Royal Field Artillery. Died of wounds (received in Ypres), in hospital at Exeter, 25th November, 1914. Age 31. Husband of S. Radley, of 103, Richmond Street, Coventry. Born 3rd May, 1884 at Romford, Essex. Enlisted Hounslow, Middx. Resided Coventry. Driller. Served eight years in India. Reservist. Left a wife and one child. Grave Ref. 183. 88. Coventry (London Road) Cemetery.

RAFFERTY, Private, Louis Frank (Known as W. Hancox). 5451, 8th Bn., East Surrey Regiment. Killed in action, Battle of the Somme, 1st July, 1916. Born 17th July, 1894 at 35, Cobden Street. Resided 35, Cobden Street. Labourer. Enlisted September, 1914. Grave Ref. IV. P. 4. Dantzig Alley British Cemetery, Mametz, France.

RAINBOW, Sapper, Henry Charles. 44853, 416th Field Coy., Royal Engineers. Killed in action, 4th September, 1918. Age 28. Son of William Moses and Ann Rainbow, of 75, King Edward Road, Coventry. Resided Nottingham. Born 26th April, 1890 at Coventry. Coach Body maker. Enlisted September, 1914. Grave Ref. IV. H. 35. Queant Road Cemetery, Buissy, Pas de Calais, France.

RAINSDEN, Lance Corporal, John. 18526, 1st Bn., Bedfordshire Regiment. Killed in action, Longueval, 27th July, 1916. Age 33. Son of Mrs. Dinah Rainsden, of 17, Charterhouse Road, Coventry. Husband of Annie Rainsden, of 61, Beech Road, Luton, Beds. Memorial Ref. Pier and Face 2 C. Thiepval Memorial, Somme, France.

RANDALL, Private, Charles. 16333, 10th Bn., Royal Warwickshire Regiment. Died of wounds, 6th April, 1918. Born St John Street, Coventry. Enlisted Coventry. Resided at 5c. 12h. Chauntry Place. Employed Triumph Motor Co. Ltd. Memorial Ref. Panel 23 to 28 and 163A. Tyne Cot Memorial, Belgium.

RANDALL, Sergeant, George Frederick, MM and Bar. 52903, 56th Bty. 34th Bde., Royal Field Artillery. Killed in action, Arras, by a shell, 5th May, 1917. Age 28. Son of John William and Mary Ann Randall, of 23, Stratford Street, Coventry. Born 16th January, 1899, at Woodford, Northants. Resided at 23, Stratford Street. Mechanic. Commemorated Triumph and Gloria Memorial and War Memorial Park. Awarded the Military Medal for bravery in the field. Served for nine years in the army. Memorial Ref. Bay 1. Arras Memorial, Pas de Calais, France.

RANDALL, Private, George Sidney. 20400, 9th Bn., Essex Regiment formerly 58256, Royal Field Artillery. Killed in action, 9th April, 1917. Born Gaydon. Enlisted Coventry. Resided Earlsdon. Grave Ref. C. 1. Houdain Lane Cemetery, Tilloy-Les-Mofflaines, France.

RANDALL, Leading Stoker, James William. K/8899, HMS Arabis, Royal Navy. Killed in action with destroyer in North Sea, 11th February, 1916. Age 26. Son of John William and Mary Ann Randall, of 23, Stratford Street, Stoke, Coventry. Native of Finedon, Northants. Born 6th December 1891, at Finedon, Northants. Resided at 23, Stratford Street. Commemorated War Memorial Park. Memorial Ref. 15. Plymouth Naval Memorial, Devon.

RANDLE, Sergeant, George William. 201047, 1/4th Bn., Welsh Regiment. Killed in action, Gaza, 26th March, 1917. Age 33. Son of Richard and Jane Randle, of 2, Lodge Road, Stourport, Worcs. Born 25th July, 1883 at Stourport. Resided Coventry. Artificial Silk Spinner. Enlisted August, 1914. Memorial Ref. Panel 30 to 32. Jerusalem Memorial, Israel.

RANDLE, Private, Joseph George. 7124, 1st Bn., Cameroonians (Scottish Rifles). Killed in action, 22nd October, 1914. Age 31. Son of George Randle, of Kenilworth Rd., Berkswell, Coventry. Husband of Fanny Maria Randle, of 463, Park Road, Soho, Birmingham. 9 years' service. Also served in Africa and India. Born Handsworth. Enlisted Birmingham. Memorial Ref. Panel 5. Ploegsteert Memorial, Comines-Warneton, Hainaut, Belgium.

RANDLE, Lance Corporal, Oliver. 16635, 10th Bn., Royal Warwickshire Regiment. Killed in action, 18th November, 1916. Age 26. Son of Fred and Mary Ann Randle, of 13, Coventry Road, Coleshill, Birmingham. Born 23rd January, 1890 at Shipston-on-Stour. Resided Foleshill Police Station. Police Constable. Enlisted February, 1916 at Coventry. Commemorated Police Force Memorial, Coventry Corporation. Memorial Ref. Pier and Face 9 A 9 B and 10 B. Thiepval Memorial, Somme, France.

RANDLE, Corporal, Percy Knight. Royal Engineers. Died, home, 15th March, 1921. Born 18th August, 1891 at Foleshill. Resided in Heath Road, Stoke, Coventry. Engine Fitter. Enlisted August, 1914. Grave Ref. Foleshill Cemetery.

RANN, Private, Louis Frederick. 35, 2nd Bn., Royal Warwickshire Regiment. Died of wounds, Festubert, 18th May, 1915 wounded 17th May. Age 29. Son of Daniel and Sanders Elizabeth Rann, of Birmingham Born 29th June, 1884 at Birmingham. Resided at 13, Ranby Road. Mechanic. Commemorated Barras Green Working Mens Club. Grave Ref. III. D. 14. Bethune Town Cemetery, France.

RAPER, Private, Charles. 26066, 2nd Bn., Duke of Wellington's (West Riding Regiment) formerly 076237, Army Service Corps. Died of wounds, 10th October, 1917. Age 23. Son of John and Susan Raper, of 151, Bolingbroke Road, Stoke, Coventry. Born in 1894, at Wheatley, Yorks. Resided at Coventry. Commemorated War Memorial Park. Grave Ref. X. J. 8. Dozinghem Military Cemetery, Poperinge, West-Vlaanderen, Belgium.

RATHBONE, Private, Arthur. 27991, 1st Bn., Royal Warwickshire Regiment. Killed in action, 15th April, 1918. Age 20. Son of William and Georgina Elizabeth Rathbone, of Abbey Green, Southam, Rugby. Born Southam, Warwicks. Enlisted Coventry. Resided Southam. Memorial Ref. Panel 2 and 3. Ploegsteert Memorial, Belgium.

RATLIFFE, Private, George Alexander. 28173, Northamptonshire Regiment formerly 2206, Northamptonshire Yeomanry. Died of wounds, 18th October, 1918. Born Coventry. Enlisted West Haddon, Warwick. Commemorated King Henry VIII School. Grave Ref. S. II. J. 12. St. Sever Cemetery Extension, Rouen, France.

RATTEY, Battery Acting Quarter Master Sergeant Arthur George. 131, Royal Horse Artillery (Warwickshire). Died, home, 17th May, 1915. Age 43. Son of George Alfred and Susanah Jane Rattey of 157, Pershore Road, Birmingham. Born Edgbaston. Resided Coventry. Grave Ref. Screen Wall. B 10. 3. 277A. Birmingham (Lodge Hill) Cemetery.

RAVEN, Private, Albert. G/15522, The Buffs (East Kent Regiment) formerly G/12394, 3rd Battalion, Royal West Kent Regiment. Killed in action, 25th September, 1916. Born Coventry. Enlisted Deptford, Kent. Resided Birmingham. Memorial Ref. Pier and Face 5 D. Thiepval Memorial, Somme, France.

RAVENHALL, Private, William Sidney. 1819, 9th Bn., Royal Warwickshire Regiment. Died Mesopotamia, 2nd July, 1916. Age 22. Son of William and Jane Ravenall, of 1/54, Wheeler Street, Birmingham. Born Birmingham. Resided Birmingham. Employed Coventry. Enlisted Coventry. Memorial Ref. Panel 9. Basra Memorial, Iraq.

RAVENSCROFT, Rifleman, Frederick. R/7772, 9th Bn., King's Royal Rifle Corps. Killed in action, 24th August, 1916. Born Audley, Staffs. Enlisted Newcastle. Resided Coventry. Grave Ref. IX. K. 1. Delville Wood Cemetery, Longueval, France.

RAWLINGS, Lance Corporal, Henry. 9011, 1st Bn., Worcestershire Regiment. Killed in action, 26th September, 1915. .Born Hornsey, London. Enlisted Coventry. Resided Palmers Green, London. Grave Ref. M. 25. Y Farm Military Cemetery, Bois-Grenier, France.

RAWLINS, Private, Bert. 7262, 1st Bn., Royal Warwickshire Regiment. Killed in action, Ypres, 25th April 1915. Age 34. Son of William Rawlins. Husband of Mrs. M. A. Rawlins, of 13, Lower Ford Street, Coventry. Born 18th November 1881 in Far Gosford Street. Resided at 51, Much Park Street. Commemorated War Memorial Park. Memorial Ref. Panel 8. Ypres (Menin Gate) Memorial, Belgium.

RAYBOULD, Private, Albert Alfred. 16849, "C" Coy. 11th Bn., Royal Warwickshire Regiment. Killed in action, 8th July, 1916. Age 24. Son of William and Fanny Raybould, of 35, Alma Street, Coventry. Born All 4th April, 1892 at Saints, Coventry. Enlisted December, 1915 at Warwick. Resided 35, Alma Street, Coventry. Fitter, Frame Building Department, Rudge Works. Grave Ref. XXXVI. M. 10. Serre Road Cemetery No.2, Somme, France.

RAYNER, Private, Percy Richard (real family name, Ravenor). 13564, 2nd Bn., Grenadier Guards. Killed in action, 1st September, 1914. Age 24. Son of Richard and Matilda Ravenor, of 30, Dartford Road, Dartford, Kent. Born Chislehurst, Kent. Resided Coventry. Memorial Ref. La Ferte-Sous-Jouarre Memorial, France.

REA, Private, Ernest Frederick. 10058, 1st Bn., Coldstream Guards. Killed in action, Neuve Chappelle, 17th March, 1915. Age 21. Son of Edwin and Elizabeth Rea, of 68, Dibble Road, Smethwick, Staffs. Born at Winson Green. Employed Coventry Chain Company Ltd. Enlisted Coventry. Grave Ref. I. C. 7. Le Touret Military Cemetery, Richebourg-L'avoue, France.

READ, Trooper, Edward John. 841, Household Battalion. Died of wounds, Germany, 3rd June, 1917. Age 24. Son of Charles and Hannah Read, of 29 Friars Wharf, Oxford. Born Oxford. Enlisted Coventry. Resided Oxford. Grave Ref. I. D. 4. Hamburg Cemetery, Germany.

READE, Private, Charles. 11376, 1st Bn., Sherwood Foresters (Notts and Derby) Regiment. Killed in action, 4th March, 1917. Born Wednesbury. Enlisted Coventry. Resided Wednesbury.

READER, Private, Percy Hutchinson. 4688, 9th Bn., Royal Warwickshire Regiment. Killed in action, 10th August, 1915. Age 19. Son of William Arthur and Mary Elizabeth Reader. Resided 7, Lockhurst Lane. Enlisted August, 1914. Born 30th August, 1895 at Warwick. Labourer. Employed Daimler Co. Ltd. Cousin of Mr. G. Reader of Wolston. Memorial Ref. Panel 35 to 37. Helles Memorial, Turkey.

READING, Charles. Royal Field Artillery. Born 1894. Resided Leamington. Labourer employed by Rowland Hill and Sons Ltd.

REASON, Lance Corporal, Charles Joseph. 5451, 10th Bn., Royal Warwickshire Regiment. Died of wounds, 30th July, 1916. Age 23. Enlisted September, 1914. Employed Gardener, Ven. Archdeacon Bree of Allesley. Son of Charles and Frances Louisa Reason, of Tysoe, Kineton. Enlisted Coventry. Grave Ref. XVI. C. 29. Caterpillar Valley Cemetery, Longueval, France.

REAVES, Gunner, William John. 121105, "C" Bty. 157th Bde., Royal Field Artillery. Killed in action, 5th November, 1917. Age 24. Son of Henry and Zara Anne Reaves, of 187, Leicester Causeway, Coventry. Born 27th September, 1893 in Howard Street, Coventry. Enlisted November, 1915 at Coventry. Clerk. Memorial Ref. Panel 4 to 6 and 162. Tyne Cot Memorial, Zonnebeke, West-Vlaanderen, Belgium. (possibly buried at Langemarck).

REDDINGTON, Sergeant, John. 1828, 1st/7th Battalion, Royal Warwickshire Regiment. Died of wounds, 18th July, 1916 caused by machine gun fire. Born 15th February, 1893 in Vauxhall Terrace, East Street. Resided at 12 Hartlepool Road. Enameller, Rudge Works. Enlisted August, 1914, Coventry. Husband of Mrs. H. Reddington (nee Parkes). Commemorated War Memorial Park. Grave Ref. II. D. 36. Heilly Station Cemetery, Mericourt-L'Abbe, France.

REDGRAVE, Private, Charles. 9798, 1st Bn., Coldstream Guards. Killed in action, Ginchy, 15th September, 1916. Born 10th June, 1894 at Willenhall. Resided at Swift Corner Cottages, Whitley. Soldier. Enlisted Coventry. Memorial Ref. Pier and Face 7 D and 8 D. Thiepval Memorial, Somme, France.

REDGRAVE, Lance Corporal, Frederick Alfred. 116, 2nd Bn., Royal Warwickshire Regiment. Died of wounds, 24th May, 1916. Born 10th November, 1885 at Coventry. Resided at 25, Caludon Road. Stamper. Enlisted August, 1914 at Coventry. Grave Ref. I. A. 27. Corbie Communal Cemetery Extension, France.

REDGRAVE, Private, Herbert. 15374, 9th Bn., Royal Warwickshire Regiment. Killed in action, Mesopotamia, 25th January, 1917. Born 14th October, 1880 in Much Park Street, Coventry. Enlisted October, 1914 at Coventry. Resided at 35, Gosford Street. Stamper. Employed Red Lane. Leaves a widow and four children. Grave Ref. XIX. K. 14. Amara War Cemetery, Iraq.

REED, Corporal, Joseph William. 09325, Royal Army Ordnance Corps. Died home, 14th October, 1918. Age 29. Born 23rd February, 1889 at Twyford. Resided at 33, Ludlow Road. Railway Clerk. Enlisted August, 1915. Commemorated Central Methodist Hall. Grave Ref. 119. 69. Coventry (London Road) Cemetery.

REENE, Private, Walter Charles. S/33969, G.H.Q. 2nd Echelon (Intelligence Dept.), Army Service Corps. Died, 5th November, 1917. Age 30. Husband of Drusilla Reene, of 68, Nicholls Street, Coventry. Born Epsom, Surrey. Enlisted Colchester. Resided Coventry. Grave Ref. F. 327. Cairo War Memorial Cemetery, Egypt.

REES, Private, Harold Axalandra. 9763, 1st Bn., Gloucestershire Regiment. Died of wounds, 25th December, 1914. Born 10th October, 1895 at Coventry. Resided at 92, Station Street East. Moulder. Grave Ref. III. B. 7. Bethune Town Cemetery, France.

REEVE, Corporal, Leonard Henry, DCM. 11935, 2nd Bn., King's Royal Rifle Corps. Died of wounds, 18th July, 1916. Born Kenilworth. Enlisted Coventry. Resided Kenilworth. Grave Ref. II. D. 13. Heilly Station Cemetery, Mericourt-L'Abbe, France.

REEVES, A. Commemorated Wesleyan Church.

REEVES, Private, Alfred. 4733, 1/7th Bn., Royal Warwickshire Regiment. Killed in action, 25th July, 1916 by a mortar trench shell. Resided at Kenilworth. Labourer, Rudge Works. Enlisted January, 1916. Memorial Ref. Pier and Face 9 A 9 B and 10 B. Thiepval Memorial, France.

REEVES, Private, Arthur. 1/7th Bn., Royal Warwickshire Regiment. Died (gassed), Home 30th October, 1917. Born 16th December, 1879 in Smithford Street. Resided at 47, Springfield Road. Polisher. Commemorated Triumph and Gloria Memorial. Enlisted August, 1914. Grave Ref. Coventry (London Road) Cemetery.

REEVES, F. Commemorated Radford Memorial.

REEVES, Private, John. 17455, 1st Bn., Royal Warwickshire Regiment. Killed in action, 29th April 1918. Age 39. Husband of Clara Reeves, of 10, Sherbourne Street, Coventry. Born 28th December, 1878 at 57, Leicester Street, Coventry. Enlisted March, 1916 at Coventry. Resided at 10, Leicester Street. Polisher. Grave Ref. VII. F. 1. Vieille-Chapelle New Military Cemetery, Lacouture, Pas de Calais, France.

REGAN, Private, M. 93935, 1st Bn., Royal Munster Fusiliers. Killed in action, 9th May, 1915. Age 25. Son of Michael and Mary Regan (nee Riordan), of Mount Bridget, Churchtown, Buttevant, Co. Cork. Grave Ref. E. 54. Lancashire Landing Cemetery, Turkey.

REID, Private, James Livingstone. 18713, 2nd Bn., Oxfordshire and Buckinghamshire Light Infantry. Died of wounds, 29th April, 1917. Born Springburn, Glasgow. Enlisted Oxford. Resided Coventry. Grave Ref. II. J. 10. Aubigny Communal Cemetery Extension, France.

REID, Sergeant, Walter James. 3302, 9th Bn., Royal Warwickshire Regiment. Killed in action, 10th August, 1915. Born 5th August, 1872 at St. Thomas, Coventry. Resided Vincent Street. Machinist, Humber Works. Enlisted 1914 at Coventry. Seen 21 years in the Army. Sister, Mrs. Ashby resided at 33, King William Street. Memorial Ref. Panel 35 to 37. Helles Memorial, Turkey.

REVELL, Private, George. 14697, 4th Bn., Coldstream Guards. Killed in action, 7th July, 1918. Born Bungay, Suffolk. Enlisted Coventry. Resided Buhgay, Suffolk. Grave Ref. VIII. K. 19. Cabaret-Rouge British Cemetery, Souchez, France.

REVERE, Corporal, Alfred Joseph. 207, 1st /4th (Warwick) Heavy Bty., Royal Field Artillery. Died of wounds, 25th September, 1916. Age 25. Born 16th January, 1891 at St. Pancras, London. Soldier. Son of George and Harriet Revere, of 120, Villiers Street, Coventry. Enlisted Coventry. Employed Triumph Co. and Carpenter by trade. Commemorated Wesleyan Church. Grave Ref. IV. E. 5. Puchevillers British Cemetery, Somme, France.

REYNOLDS, Private, Charles. 35023, 5th Bn., Royal Berkshire Regiment. Died of wounds, 9th May, 1917. Born Coventry. Enlisted Warwick. Resided Bedworth. Grave Ref. I. C. 23. Feuchy British Cemetery, France.

REYNOLDS, Private, George Henry. 5667, 2nd Bn., Coldstream Guards. Killed in action, 25th September, 1916. Born Worcester. Enlisted Coventry. Resided Minworth, Warwick. Memorial Ref. Pier and Face 7D and 8D. Thiepval Memorial, Somme, France.

REYNOLDS, Private, James. 22782, 11th Bn., Royal Warwickshire Regiment. Killed in action, 28th April, 1917. Born Kinton, Staffs. Enlisted Coventry. Resided Kenilworth. Memorial Ref. Bay 3. Arras Memorial, France.

REYNOLDS, Private, James. 22991, 9th Bn., Royal Warwickshire Regiment. Died, 11th November, 1918. Born Ryton. Enlisted Bedworth. Memorial Ref. 2. 2. Tehran Memorial, Iran.

REYNOLDS, Private, John. 102244, 2/5th Bn., Sherwood Foresters formerly 3707, East Kent Regiment. Killed in action 16th April, 1918. Resided Coventry. Enlisted Coventry. Memorial Ref. Panel 7. Ploegsteert Memorial, Belgium.

REYNOLDS, Private, Lewis Mawson. 6483, 22nd (Tyneside Scottish) Bn., Northumberland Fusiliers. formerly, 9454, Durham Light Infantry. Died, 11th April, 1918. Age 33. Son of George and Mary Ann Reynolds. Husband of Isabel Maud Reynolds, of 9, Coventry Street, Bradford, Yorks. Born Halifax. Memorial Ref. Panel 2. Ploegsteert Memorial, Comines-Warneton, Hainaut, Belgium.

REYNOLDS, Sapper, L. N. 91824, 214th Army Troops Coy., Royal Engineers. Died, home, 27th February, 1919. Age 24. Son of Mrs. Adelaide Reynolds, of 18, Lynton Road, Foleshill, Coventry. Grave Ref. 239. 196. Coventry (London Road) Cemetery.

RHODES, Private, Fred. 59392, 1st /8th Bn., Worcestershire Regiment. Killed in action, 4th November, 1918. Age 19. Son of William H. and Jane Rhodes, of "Woodville," Lythalls Lane, Coventry. Born Coventry. Enlisted Coventry. Employed Rover Co. Ltd. Grave Ref. I. B. 35. Landrecies British Cemetery, Nord, France.

RICE, Lieutenant, Edmund Gabriel. No. 2 School of Instruction (Redcar), Royal Air Force. Killed while flying (crashed), 3rd May, 1918 in Yorkshire. Age 19. Only son of Dr. Charles E. and Elsie Garrett Rice, of Mansfield, Stoke Green, Coventry. Grave Ref. 34/35. 42. Coventry (London Road) Cemetery.

RICE, Private, George. 7944, 2nd Bn., Royal Welsh Fusiliers. Killed in action, 23rd February, 1915. Age 26. Husband of Annie Clarke (formerly Rice), of 38, Court, 4, House, Gosford Street, Coventry. Born 22nd July, 1886 at 11c. 1h. Gosford Street, Coventry. Enlisted Coventry. Polisher, British Thompson Houston. Reservist. Commemorated British Thompson Houston Memorial. Leaves a widow and three children. Memorial Ref. Panel 5. Ploegsteert Memorial, Comines-Warneton, Hainaut, Belgium.

RICE, Lance Corporal, James. Killed in action, October, 1918. Resided Foleshill.

RICE, Lance Corporal, John. Killed in action, May, 1918. Resided at Foleshill.

RICE, Private, Josiah Henry. 3/1419, New Zealand Medical Corps. Killed in action, Passchendaele Ridge, 16th October, 1917. Age 33. Son of Henry and Lydia Rice, of Epsom, Auckland, New Zealand. Born 17th March, 1883 at Foleshill. Resided at Auckland, New Zealand. Painter. Enlisted November, 1915. Grave Ref. IV. E. 47. Longuenesse (St. Omer) Souvenir Cemetery, France.

RICE, Sergeant, Samuel. 8952, 2nd Bn., Worcestershire Regiment. Killed in action, 26th September, 1915. Born Wolverhampton. Enlisted August, 1914 at Lichfield, Staffs. Resided 6, Vauxhall Terrace, Coventry. Memorial Ref. Panel 64 and 65. Loos Memorial, France.

RICHARDS, Private, George. 6261, 1st Bn., Lincolnshire Regiment. Died, 10th May, 1915. Age 26. Husband of Elizabeth Davidson (formerly Richards), of 31, First Avenue, Copeswood, Stoke, Coventry. Born St. Helens, Lancs. Enlisted Manchester. Resided Rotheram. Grave Ref. VII. A. 6. Niederzwehren Cemetery, Kassel, Hessen, Germany.

RICHARDS, Joseph. Commemorated Holy Trinity Panels.

RICHARDS, Fitter Corporal, Joseph. 840249, 35th Bty. 22nd Bde., Royal Field Artillery. Killed in action by shell fire, 26th January, 1918. Age 21. Son of Joseph and Hannah Richards, of Coventry. Born 26th November 1897 at Coventry. Resided at 7, Stockton Road. Fitter. Employed Ordnance Works. Commemorated War Memorial Park. Grave Ref. Plot 2. Row D. Grave 3. Giavera British Cemetery, Arcade, Italy.

RICHARDS, Private, Joseph. 8514, 2nd Bn., Worcestershire Regiment. Killed in action, 13th April, 1915. Age 30. Son of Charles Edwin and Annie Maria Richards, of Birmingham. Husband of Laura Lucy Richards, of 8, Newland Street, Coleford, Glos. Born Birmingham. Enlisted Worcester. Resided Coventry. Grave Ref. I. C. 6. Gorre British And Indian Cemetery, France.

RICHARDS, Captain, Joseph Arthur. 1st/8th Battalion, Royal Warwickshire Regiment. Killed in action, Landrecies, 4th November, 1918. Age 26. Son of James and Anne Richards of 45, Cartland Road, Stirchley, Birmingham. Native of Shustoke, Birmingham. Born 20th May 1892 at Tenterden, Kent. Resided at Coventry. Police Constable. Enlisted in 1915. Commemorated War Memorial Park and Police Force Memorial, Coventry Corporation. Grave Ref. A. 31. Landrecies British Cemetery, France.

RICHARDS, Thomas. Commemorated Stoke (St. Michaels) Memorial.

RICHARDSON, Lieutenant, Richard Francis. 2nd Bn., Royal Warwickshire Regiment. Killed in action, 30th September, 1915. Age 21. Son of Edward Taswell Richardson (Clerk in Holy Orders) and Muriel Richardson of 23, Clifton Wood Road, Bristol. Born Moreton Morrell, Warwickshire. Only son of the Vicar of Binley. Grave Ref. Officers. A. 1. 2. St. Sever Cemetery, Rouen.

RICHARDSON, Lance Corporal, Frederick. 25400, 37th Coy., Machine Gun Corps formerly 17759, Royal Warwickshire Regiment. Killed in action, 5th April, 1918. Born 21st September, 1896 at Darlaston. Resided at 149, Terry Road. Capstan hand, British Thompson Houston. Enlisted April, 1916 at Coventry. Memorial Ref. Bay 10. Arras Memorial, France.

RICHARDSON, Private, Joseph Wilfred Reeley. 136419, 25th Bn., Machine Gun Corps (Infantry) formerly 3382, Royal Warwickshire Regiment. Believed killed, 27th May, 1918. Age 23. Son of Charles James and Sarah Anne Richardson, of 5, Priory Street, Coventry. Born 21st February, 1897 at Holyhead Road, Coventry. Enlisted August, 1914 at Leamington. Resided 9, Jesson Street, Coventry. Pawnbroker's Assistant. Memorial Ref. Soissons Memorial, Aisne, France.

RICHARDSON, Private, Thomas. 26883, 12th Bn., Duke of Cornwall's Light Infantry formerly 20644, Royal Berkshire Regiment. Died, 26th September, 1916. Age 34. Son of Thomas and Sarah A. Richardson, of Hill Top, West Bromwich, Staffs. Born Tipton, Staffs. Enlisted Coventry. Grave Ref. I. C. 7. Guillemont Road Cemetery, Guillemont, France.

RICHARDSON, Private, William. 29693, 124th Coy., Machine Gun Corps formerly 14437, Royal Warwickshire Regiment. Killed in action, 8th October, 1916. Born Coventry. Enlisted Birmingham. Memorial Ref. Pier and Face 5 C and 12 C. Thiepval Memorial, Somme, France.

RICKMAN, Sergeant, Robert Melville. 37701, 73rd Bty., Royal Field Artillery. Died of disease, 10th August, 1916. Age 29. Son of George and Annie Rickman, of Acton, London. Husband of Nellie Rickman, of 39, Colchester St., Coventry. Grave Ref. VII. B. 22. Warloy-Baillon Communal Cemetery Extension, Somme, France.

RIDER, Private, Joseph. 28555, 11th Bn., Royal Warwickshire Regiment. Killed in action, 10th April, 1917. Age 19. Son of Joseph and Lucy Charlotte Rider, of 246, Marston Lane, Bedworth, Nuneaton. Born Coventry. Enlisted Warwick. Resided Bedworth. Memorial Ref. Bay 3. Arras Memorial, France.

RIDGWAY, Private, Alexander. 59526, 3rd Reserve Bn., Machine Gun Corps (Infantry) formerly 5339, Cheshire Regiment. Died, 15th September, 1918. Born Rossett, Denbigh. Enlisted Coventry. Grave Ref. 4244. Chester (Overleigh) Cemetery.

RIDLEY, Rifleman, Eustace Bernard. R/7649, 1st Bn., Kings Royal Rifle Corps. Died of wounds, 31st July, 1916. Age 23. Son of Henry and Mary Louisa Ridley, of Bury St. Edmunds, Suffolk. Born Bury St. Edmunds. Enlisted Letchworth. Resided Coventry. Grave Ref. VI. F. 4. Abbeville Communal Cemetery, France.

RIDLINTON, Private, Lawrence Piersey (Pete). 202857, 10th Bn., Royal Warwickshire Regiment. Killed in action, Vierstraat, 10th June, 1917. Age 19. Son of Mr. H. J. and Mrs. S. A. Ridlinton, of 110, Stoney Stanton Rd., Coventry. Enlisted 9th November, 1916. Resided Coventry. Born 30th March, 1898 at Warwick. Fitter, Triumph Co. Grave Ref. II. C. 13. Klein-Vierstraat British Cemetery, Heuvelland, West-Vlaanderen, Belgium.

RIGBY, Gunner, Edward Thomas. 238611, "C" Bty. 108th Bde., Royal Field Artillery. Killed in action, 9th June, 1918. Age 23. Brother of Mrs. L. Hughes, of 15, St. Michael's Road, Stoke, Coventry. Born 1895 at Worcester. Enlisted June, 1916 at Coventry. Resided Coventry. Miller and turner. Grave Ref. VII. C. 23. Contay British Cemetery, Contay, Somme, France.

RILEY, Private, Arthur. 241366, 1/6th Bn., Royal Warwickshire Regiment. Killed in action, 1st April, 1917. Born 17th July, 1897 at Foleshill, Coventry. Resided at 56, King George's Avenue. Painter and decorator. Enlisted December, 1915 at Birmingham. Grave Ref. III. H. 16. Unicorn Cemetery, Vend'huile, France.

RILEY, Private, Henry Herbert. 16848, 1st Bn., Royal Warwickshire Regiment. Killed in action, 11th April, 1917. Age 24. Son of John and Elizabeth Riley, of 71, Huntingdon Road, Coventry. Born 31st October, 1893, at London. Resided at 71 Huntingdon Road. Coach painter (tramways), Coventry Corporation Tramways Department. Enlisted Leamington, February, 1916. Commemorated St. Barbara's Church, War Memorial Park and Transport Department Memorial, Coventry Corporation. Memorial Ref. Bay 3. Arras Memorial, Pas de Calais, France.

RILEY, Private, Joseph. 1293, 2nd Bn., Royal Warwickshire Regiment. Died, Malta, 19th August, 1914. Born St. Michael's Parish. Enlisted Coventry. Grave Ref. IV. IB. 1. Imtarfa Military Cemetery, Malta.

RILEY, Lance Corporal, Sydney James. G/18219, 7th Bn., Queen's Own (Royal West Kent Regiment), formerly PS/10961, Royal Fusiliers. Killed in action, 12th October, 1917. Age 20. Son of Harry and Elizabeth Riley, of 22, Kensington Road, Coventry. Born 6th April, 1897 at 88 Foleshill Road. Resided at 22 Kensington Road. Assistant works manager (textiles). Enlisted April, 1916. Previously employed Franks Weaving Factory, West Orchard. Commemorated War Memorial Park. Memorial Ref. Panel 106 to 108. Tyne Cot Memorial, Zonnebeke, West-Vlaanderen, Belgium. (Possibly buried Poelcapelle).

RILEY, Thomas. Priest. Killed in action. Name on Roll of Honour in St. John Baptist Church.

RIX, Rifleman, Albert Percy. 6647, 3rd Bn., Rifle Brigade. Died (Home) of wounds received at Mons, 11th December, 1914. Age 32. Son of Anna Broughton, of Norwich. Husband of Emily Rix, of 134, Nicholas Street, Norwich. Born North Heigham, Norfolk. Resided 74, Queen Victoria Road. Grave Ref. 1291. Fort Pitt Military Cemetery.

ROBBINS, Private, Arthur John. 31446, 34th Bn., Royal Fusiliers attached 60459, 101st Coy., Labour Corps formerly 25311, Duke of Cornwall's Light Infantry. Died of wounds, 22nd May, 1918. Born 27th February, 1886 in Weston Street, Coventry. Resided Broad Street. Cycle fitter. Enlisted March, 1916 at Coventry. Grave Ref. Q. III. N. 22. St. Sever Cemetery Extension, Rouen, France.

ROBBINS, Lance Corporal, Frederick. 2833, 2nd Bn., Royal Warwickshire Regiment. Killed in action, 30th April, 1916. Born Stretton-on-Dunsmore, Warwicks. Enlisted Coventry. Resided Stretton-on-Dunsmore.

ROBBINS, Sapper, Fredrick William. 102385, 185th Tunnel Field Coy., Royal Engineers. Died of accidental injuries, 12th November, 1917. Age 48. Son of William and Harriett Robbins, of Tiddington, Stratford-on-Avon. Husband of Alice Robbins, of 11, St. Wilfred's, Arley, Coventry. Born Stratford-on-Avon. Enlisted London. Grave Ref. VI. D. 23. Duisans British Cemetery, Etrun, Pas de Calais, France.

ROBBINS, Gunner, Herbert. 840512, Base Details, Royal Field Artillery. Died of malaria, 13th November, 1917. Age 22. Son of Mrs. Maria Robbins, of 197, Broad Street, Foleshill, Coventry. Born 25th June, 1895 in Weston Street, Coventry. Enlisted February, 1915 at Coventry. Resided at 39, Wright Street. Cycle Fitter. Commemorated Triumph and Gloria Memorial. Grave Ref. 2. Bralo British Cemetery, Greece.

ROBBINS, Private, Thomas Arthur. PO/2426(S), 2nd Royal Marine Bn. Royal Naval Division, Royal Marine Light Infantry. Died, whilst prisoner of war, 13th October, 1918. Age 31. Son of Mrs. Elizabeth Jeffries. Husband of Emily Scanlan (formerly Robbins), of 109, Broad Street, Coventry. Born 5th December, 1886 at Stretton-on-Dunsmore. Artificial silk worker. Enlisted September, 1917. Grave Ref. At the North end, to the right of the path. Hennuyeres Communal Cemetery, Braine-le-Comte, Hainaut, Belgium.

ROBERTS, Private, Albert. 9373, 1st Bn., Royal Warwickshire Regiment. Killed in action, 27th August, 1914. Age 30. Born Birmingham. Enlisted Birmingham. Resided 28, Highfield Road, Coventry. Commemorated Coventry Chain Memorial. Grave Ref. I. C. 56. (Sp. Mem.). Honnechy British Cemetery, France.

ROBERTS, Private, Alfred Valletort. 32079, B Coy., 10th Bn., Hampshire Regiment formerly 15980, Royal Warwickshire Regiment. Killed in action, Balkans, 1st September, 1918. Age 32. Son of Alfred and Annie Roberts, of 28, Second Avenue, Camel's Head, Devonport. Born Devonport. Enlisted Coventry. Resided Keyham, Devon. Grave Ref. C. 663. Karasouli Military Cemetery, Greece.

ROBERTS, Private, Christopher. 3492, Royal Army Medical Corps attd. 115th Siege Bty., Royal Garrison Artillery. Killed in action 22nd August, 1916. Born 28th December, 1882 at Hope under Dinmore, Herefordshire. Grave Ref. VII. S. 5. Dantzig Alley British Cemetery, Mametz, France.

ROBERTS, Sergeant, Fred. MM. 67680, 32nd Bn., Machine Gun Corps formerly York and Lancaster Regiment. Died of wounds, 2nd April, 1918. Born Galasbrough, Rotheram. Employed Coventry. Gazetted for Military Medal, 19th November, 1917. Grave Ref. VI. E. 15. Doullens Communal Cemetery Extension No.1, France.

ROBERTS, Private, Frederick. 983, 2nd Bn., Royal Warwickshire Regiment. Killed in action, 25th September, 1915. Born 26th August, 1893 at 16, Arthur Street. Resided 121, Broad Street. Moulder. Enlisted August, 1914 at Coventry. Memorial Ref. 22 to 25. Loos Memorial, France.

ROBERTS, Private, George Harold. 17421, 11th Bn., Royal Warwickshire Regiment. Died of wounds, 12th August, 1917. Age 23. Son of Charles and Elizabeth Roberts, of 177, Birkin Avenue, Hyson Green, Nottingham. Born Nottingham. Enlisted Coventry. Memorial Ref. Panel 8. Ypres (Menin Gate) Memorial, Belgium.

ROBERTS, Private, Herbert. 14619, 10th Bn., Royal Warwickshire Regiment. Killed in action, 20th September, 1917. Born 19th November, 1892 in 2c. Jordan Well, Coventry. Enlisted Coventry. Resided at back of 29, Hill Street. Silk dyer. Enlisted August, 1915. Commemorated St. John's Church. Grave Ref. II. H. 18. Perth Cemetery (China Wall), Belgium.

ROBERTS, Lance Corporal, James. 10422, 2nd Bn., South Wales Borderers. Died of wounds, 29th April, 1915. Age 21. Son of Reuben Roberts of 63, Poplar Street, Everton, Liverpool and Ellen Roberts of Newtown, Montgomery. Served in Tsingtao. Billeted 37, Monk's Road, Coventry. Killed in action, Dardanelles. Born Llanwchairn, Newtown, Montgomeryshire. Enlisted Brecon. Grave Ref. Panel 80 to 84 or 219 and 220. Helles Memorial, Turkey.

ROBERTS, Able Seaman, John. HMS Ivy, Royal Navy. Died, home, 19th July, 1915. Born 1878 in Worcestershire. Resided at 66, Much Park Street. Employed Humber Ltd. Enlisted September, 1914. Grave Ref. Coventry (London Road) Cemetery.

ROBERTS, Gunner, John. 33260, 73rd Bty. 5th Bde., Royal Field Artillery. Died of wounds, 29th October, 1918. Born Coventry. Enlisted Wakefield, Yorks. Grave Ref. II. A. 13. Premont British Cemetery, France.

ROBERTS, Gunner, John Tydwal. 2693, 15th Squadron, Machine Gun Corps (Motors). Killed in action, India, 1st June, 1919. Born New Tredegar, Mon. Enlisted Coventry. Resided Liyerorwerth. Grave Ref. Buried Peshawar (Left) B.C. VIII. 444.). Face 23, Delhi Memorial, India.

ROBERTS, Private, Laurence. 3285, 1st Middlesex Hussars. Killed in action, Gallipoli, 23rd October, 1915. Age 19. Son of Robert James and Martha Louisa Roberts, of 35, Knighton Road, Forest Gate, London. Born Coventry. Enlisted Chelsea. Resided Forest Gate. Memorial Ref. Panel 19. Helles Memorial, Turkey.

ROBERTS, Private, Leonard Arthur. 41846, 1st Bn., Royal Irish Fusiliers formerly T/37296, Royal Army Service Corps. Died, 7th May, 1918. Born Willenhall, Staffs. Enlisted Willenhall. Resided Coventry. Grave Ref. B. 18. Nesle Communal Cemetery, France.

ROBERTS, Private, Percy Thomas. 22585, 1st Bn., Coldstream Guards formerly 2954, Household Battalion. Died of wounds, 8th November, 1918. Age 23. Brother of George William Roberts, of 29, Hartopp Road, Saltley, Birmingham. Born Manchester. Resided Birmingham. Cost clerk. Enlisted May, 1917 at Coventry. Commemorated British Thompson Houston Memorial. Grave Ref. In East Part. Bavay Communal Cemetery, France.

ROBERTS, Private, Sidney Herbert Harold. 9695, 9th Bn., Royal Warwickshire Regiment. Died of wounds, received at Gallipoli, 22nd August, 1915. Age 24. Son of John Thomas Roberts, of 27, Howard Street, Coventry. Born 28th January, 1892 at 30, Jenner Street. Resided at 121, Broad Street. Miller, White and Poppe Ltd. Enlisted September, 1914 at Coventry. Commemorated Central Methodist Hall. Grave Ref. A. VIII. 3. Pieta Military Cemetery, Malta.

ROBERTS, W. Commemorated St. John's Church

ROBERTS, W. A. Educated at Bablake School. Killed in action. Commemorated Bablake School Memorial.

ROBERTS, Private, William. 8961, 1st Bn., Royal Warwickshire Regiment. Died, home, of wounds received in France, 19th October, 1914 at Leeds. Age 30. Seventh son of William Roberts of 29, Hill Street, Coventry. Born 16th August, 1884 at Nottingham. Cycle finisher, Gloria Cycle Works. Reservist. Enlisted Coventry, August, 1914. Commemorated Triumph & Gloria Memorial. Grave Ref. 86. 6. Coventry (London Road) Cemetery.

ROBERTS, Private, William Edward. 10895, 9th Bn., Royal Warwickshire Regiment. Killed in action, Gallipoli, 7th August, 1915. Age 27. Son of John and Polly Roberts. Husband of Alice Maud Wheeler (formerly Roberts), of 11, Palmer Lane, Coventry. Born 1887 at 30, Jenner Street. Resided 11, Palmer Lane. Iron Rim Polisher. Enlisted August, 1914. Enlisted Warwick. Resided Coventry. Memorial Ref. Panel 35 to 37. Helles Memorial, Turkey.

ROBERTSON, Private, William. 64261, 216th Coy., Machine Gun Corps (Infantry) formerly 17125, Argyll and Sutherland Highlanders. Killed in action, 10th July, 1917. Born Ayr. Enlisted Coventry. Grave Ref. VII. D. 6. Ramscappelle Road Military Cemetery, Belgium.

ROBINSON, Corporal, Alexander George. 22209, 2/8th Bn., Royal Warwickshire Regiment. Died, 14th January, 1918 in hospital. Born 2nd January, 1885 at Coventry. Enlisted October, 1916 at Coventry. Resided 3, Mansell Street, Foleshill formerly 156, St. Georges Road. Iron Polisher. Grave Ref. II. A. 5. Cerisy-Gailly Military Cemetery, France.

ROBINSON, Private, Alfred. 42449, 13th Bn., Yorkshire Regiment formerly 183662, Royal Field Artillery. Killed in action, 26th July, 1917. Born Bradford. Enlisted Coventry. Grave Ref. I. E. 11. Fins New British Cemetery, Sorel-Le-Grand, France.

ROBINSON, Gunner, Arthur Raymond. 11006, Royal Field Artillery attached 'Z' 41st Trench Mortar battery. Died of wounds, 30th July, 1917 to the head and upper body. Age 23. Son of George and Annie Stimpson, of Burton Lazars, Melton Mowbray, Leicestershire. Born 7th October, 1893 at Melton Mowbray. Resided Coventry. Printer's Rotary Machine Assistant, Iliffe and Sons Ltd. Commemorated Iliffe & Sons Ltd Memorial. Enlisted September, 1914 at Coventry. Grave Ref. I. A. 29. Godewaersvelde British Cemetery, France.

ROBINSON, Lieutenant, Ernest Charles. 10th Sqdn., Royal Air Force. Died, pleurisy, 20th January, 1919. Age 30. Son of Thomas and Ann Robinson. Husband of Ethel Gertrude Robinson, of 28, Starley Road, Coventry. Born 2nd April 1888,at Stafford. Resided at 114, Nicholls Street. Engineer. Enlisted September 1914. Commemorated War Memorial Park and Siddeley Deasy, Roll of Honour. Grave Ref. I. D. 11. Lille Southern Cemetery, Nord, France.

ROBINSON, Private, Ernest Edward. 3873, 9th Bn., Royal Warwickshire Regiment. Killed in action, Gallipoli, 10th August, 1915. Age 28. Son of Edwin James and Mary Robinson. Born Burton-on-Trent, Staffs. Enlisted Coventry. Resided Burton-on-Trent. Memorial Ref. Panel 35 to 37. Helles Memorial, Turkey.

ROBINSON, Private, H. 16930, 4th Coy., 7th Bn.,, British Columbia Regiment. Killed in action, 24th April, 1915. Age 34. Mother resided 4, Sandy Lane, Coventry. Memorial Ref. Panel 18 – 28 –30. Ypres (Menin Gate) Memorial, Belgium.

ROBINSON, Private, Harold. 7799, D Coy., 2nd Bn., South Lancashire Regiment. Killed in action, 20th September, 1914. Age 28. Son of Mrs. Annie Elizabeth Robinson, of 1, Chesham Terrace, Chesham St., Leamington Spa. Born Leamington. Enlisted Coventry. Resided Leamington. Memorial Ref. La Ferte-Sous-Jouarre Memorial, France.

ROBINSON, Private, John Walter. 32958, 10th Bn., Oxfordshire and Buckinghamshire Light Infantry formerly Royal Warwickshire Regiment. Killed in action, 7th October, 1916. Born at Huntingdon. Resided Whitley, Coventry. Gravedigger. Enlisted Coventry. Commemorated Parks and Cemeteries Memorial, Coventry Corporation. Memorial Ref. Pier and Face 10 A and 10 D. Thiepval Memorial, Somme, France.

ROBINSON, Private, Sidney Herbert. 265613, 1st /7th Bn., Royal Warwickshire Regiment. Died, 30th July, 1918. Age 22. Son of George and Jane Elizabeth Robinson, of Coventry. Born 8th October, 1895 at Coventry. Resided St. Georges Road, Coventry. Painter. Enlisted August, 1914 at Coventry. Grave Ref. Plot 5. Row C. Grave 1. Montecchio Precalcino Communal Cemetery Extension, Italy.

ROBINSON, Private, Sydney. 41065, 7th Bn., Somerset Light Infantry. Killed in action, 10th June, 1918. Born 30th October, 1899 at Leamington. Resided at 19, Lower Ford Street. Motor Body Builder, Humber Ltd. Enlisted March, 1917 at Coventry. Grave Ref. IV. C. 11. Sucrerie Cemetery, Ablain-St. Nazaire, France.

ROBINSON, William. Commemorated Holy Trinity Panels.

ROBINSON, Corporal, William, MSM. 10825, Royal Warwickshire Regiment transf. to (Company Sergeant Major, 95401, Labour Corps. Badly gassed which set up cancer, died 25th May, 1919. Age 44. Born 13th August, 1874 at Bedworth. Resided Coventry. Iron Polisher, Polishing Shop, Rudge Works. Enlisted January, 1915. Awarded Meritorious Service Medal. Discharged 19th May, 1919. Grave Ref. 197. 143. Coventry (London Road) Cemetery.

ROBINSON, Private, William. 16034, 1st Bn., Royal Warwickshire Regiment. Killed in action, 3rd May, 1917. Born 6th February, 1898 at New Jersey, USA. Resided at 101, Brook Street. Machinist. Enlisted September, 1915 at Coventry. Employed Sparkbrook Cycle Works. Memorial Ref. Bay 3. Arras Memorial, France.

ROCHELL, Rifleman, Thomas Albert. 4172/ 371836, 8th Bn., City of London Regiment (Post Office Rifles). Killed in action, 7th October, 1916. Age 28. Son of William and Mary Jane Rochelle, of Stafford. Fifteen years in Post Office service. Enlisted London. Resided Coventry. Commemorated Post Office Memorial. Grave Ref. I. B. 8. Warlencourt British Cemetery, France.

ROCK, Private, Alfred. 203335, 1/4th Bn., Norfolk Regiment. Killed in action, 19th April, 1917. Born 28th December, 1897 at King's Bramley, Staffs. Resided Coventry. Railway Van Setter. Enlisted November, 1916 at Coventry. Memorial Ref. Panel 12 to 15. Jerusalem Memorial, Israel.

ROCK, Private, Sydney James. 62845, 3rd Bn., Royal Warwickshire Regiment attached Labour Centre, British Military Mission. Died, South Russia, 1st February, 1920. Age 19. Son of James and Sarah Rock, of 529, Kingsbury Road, Erdington, Birmingham.(buried Novorossisk New Cemetery). Born Coventry. Enlisted Coventry. Memorial Ref. Haidar Pasha Memorial, Turkey.

RODDY, Private, Alfred Henry (Harry). 3770, "B" Coy. 1st /7th Bn., Royal Warwickshire Regiment. Killed in action, 14th July, 1916. Age 19. Son of Mrs. Resided Pantlin, of 2, Tower Street, Coventry. Born 14th February, 1897 at 23, Leicester Street, Coventry. Resided at 2, Tower Street. Coremaker. Enlisted December, 1914. Memorial Ref. Pier and Face 9 A 9 B and 10 Thiepval Memorial, Somme, France.

RODDY, Private, Edward Charles. 50712, 2nd Bn., Royal Berkshire Regiment. Died of wounds while a Prisoner of War, 28th May, 1918. Age 18. Son of Mrs. Resided Pantlin, of 2, Tower Street, Coventry. Born Coventry. Enlisted Warwick. Grave Ref. 1827. Rethel French National Cemetery, Ardennes, France.

RODEN, Private, Arthur Edward. 21713, 14th Bn., Gloucestershire Regiment. Died of wounds, 12th June, 1916. Born 17th October, 1884 at West Bromwich. Resided at 15, Princess Street. Moulder. Enlisted July, 1915 at Coventry. Grave Ref. II. C. 6. Longuenesse (St. Omer) Souvenir Cemetery, France.

RODEN, Private, John. 202806, 1/8th Bn., Royal Warwickshire Regiment. Killed in action, 4th November, 1918. Born 4th February, 1896 in Broad Street. Resided at 55, Princess Street. Moulder. Enlisted Coventry. Grave Ref. B. 29. Landrecies British Cemetery, France.

RODEN, Sergeant, Thomas. 4722, 3rd Bn., Rifle Brigade. Killed in action, 20th December, 1916. Age 22. Son of Arthur Edward and Alice Roden, of 55, Princess Street, Coventry. Born 4th February, 1894 at Smethwick. Enlisted Coventry. Resided Coventry. Moulder. Reservist. Grave Ref. II. A. 2. Philosophe British Cemetery, Mazingarbe, Pas de Calais, France.

ROE, Private, Charles Wilfred., 81204, 4th Bn., Devonshire Regiment. Died, home, 7th March, 1919. Age 19. Born 25th February, 1900 in Arden Street. Resided at 12, Meadow Street. Turner. Enlisted August, 1918. Commemorated War Memorial Park. Grave Ref. 98. 144. Coventry (London Road) Cemetery.

ROE, Private, Leonard Michael. 356654, 15th Bn., Hampshire Regiment. Killed in action, 20th September, 1917. Born 21st August, 1887 at Coventry. Enlisted August, 1916 at Coventry. Hairdresser. Resided at 64, Bramble Street. Memorial Ref. Panel 88 to 90 and 162. Tyne Cot Memorial, Belgium.

ROGERS, Sergeant. South Wales Borderers. Killed in action, 1915. Billeted Coventry.

ROGERS, Lance Corporal, Ernest. 10993, 2nd Bn., King's Royal Rifle Corps. Killed in action, 25th September, 1915. Age 21. Son of Mrs. A. E. Rogers, of 12, Park Avenue, Holbrook's Lane, Foleshill, Coventry. Memorial Ref. Panel 101 and 102. Loos Memorial, Pas de Calais, France.

ROGERS, Sapper, Henry James. 213812, Inland Water Transport, Royal Engineers. Died, Home, 2nd December, 1916. Enlisted Coventry. Grave Ref. T. 87. Herne Bay Cemetery, Kent.

ROGERS, Acting Bombardier, Herbert James. 110940, 249th Siege Bty., Royal Garrison Artillery. Died of wounds, 27th October, 1916. Born in 1874 at London. Resided in Earlsdon Street. Postman. Enlisted 1916 at Coventry. Commemorated Post Office Memorial. Grave Ref. II. A. 20. Outtersteene Communal Cemetery Extension, Bailleul, France.

ROLLASON, Bombardier, Harold Eugene. 614105, 1st Warwick Bty. 15th Brigade, Royal Horse Artillery. Killed in action, 11th April, 1917. Age 24. Only son of James Eugene Herbert and Nellie Annie Rollason, of 24, Park Rd., Coventry. Born 27th November, 1892 at Nicholls Street, Coventry. Enlisted August, 1914 at Coventry. Educated Bablake School. Resided 1, Grantham Street. Tailor's Cutter. Commemorated Bablake School Memorial. Grave Ref. IV. B. 5. Tilloy British Cemetery, Tilloy-Les-Mofflaines, Pas de Calais, France.

ROLLASON, Private, Mark Welch. 11673, 1st Battalion, Royal Warwickshire Regiment. Killed, Battle of the Somme, 23rd October, 1916. Born 29th February, 1876, at West Bromwich. Resided at 25, Swan Street. Labourer, Daimler Foundry. Enlisted Coventry, January, 1915. Leaves a widow and five children. Commemorated War Memorial Park. Memorial Ref. Pier and Face 9 A 9 B and 10 B. Thiepval Memorial, Somme, France.

ROLLASON, Private, William Thomas. 4908, 1/7th Bn., Royal Warwickshire Regiment. Killed in action, 20th August, 1916. Age 24. Son of Jacob and Keziah Rollason. Born 20th November, 1891 in Broad Street. Resided at 308, Foleshill Road. Iron Worker. Enlisted March, 1916 at Coventry. Coventry Chain Co. Nephew of J. Gilbert, Foleshill Road. Commemorated Coventry Chain. Memorial Ref. Pier and Face 9 A 9 B and 10 B. Thiepval Memorial, Somme, France.

ROOTS, Private, Joseph Edward. 164883, 100th Bn., Machine Gun Corps (Infantry) formerly 2044, C Coy., Warwick Yeomanry. Killed in action, 6th October, 1918. Born 18th July, 1896 at Coventry. Enlisted August, 1914 at Warwick. Resided 18, Croft Road, Coventry. Educated Bablake School. Electrician, Rover Company Ltd. Eldest son of Mr. and Mrs. George Roots. Commemorated Bablake School Memorial. Memorial Ref. Panel 10. Vis-en-Artois Memorial, France.

ROPER, Private, William. 2594, "A" Coy. 9th Bn., Royal Warwickshire Regiment. Killed in action, 10th August, 1915. Age 21. Son of John Thomas and Jane Ann Roper, of 13, Argyll St., Stoke, Coventry. Born 13th February, 1895 at Wolverhampton. Miner, Binley Pit previously Daimler Works. Enlisted August, 1914 at Coventry. Father, Driver in the Royal Field Artillery. Memorial Ref. Panel 35 to 37. Helles Memorial, Turkey.

ROSE, Private, Arthur. 187150, 78th Bn., Winnipeg Rifles, Canadian Expeditionary Force. Killed in action, 9th April, 1917. Age 33. Born 1st January, 1885 at Foleshill. Resided Canada. Farmer. Enlisted 1916. Memorial Ref. Vimy Memorial, France.

ROSE, Private, Arthur Henry. 72155, A Coy., 21st Bn., Machine Gun Corps (Infantry) formerly 2884, Royal Warwickshire Regiment. Killed in action, 21st March 1918. Age 33. Son of George Rose, of 45, Harnall Lane West, Coventry. Enlisted in 1914 at Coventry. Born 4th February, 1874 at 51, East Street. Compositor, Iliffe and Sons Ltd. Commemorated Iliffe and Sons Ltd Memorial. Memorial Ref. Panel 90 to 93. Pozieres Memorial, Somme, France.

ROSE, Private, John. 3087, 2nd Bn., Royal Warwickshire Regiment. Killed in action, Neuve Chappelle, 13th March, 1915. Struck by shrapnel. Age 30. Husband of Florence Allen (formerly Rose), of 12, Bell Stiles, Bell Green, Coventry. Born 28th January, 1885 at 3, Upper Well Street. Resided Princess Street. Labourer, Swift Motor Co. Ltd. Enlisted August, 1914 at Coventry. One of three sons of Mr. and Mrs. Rose of 78, Station Street East. Memorial Ref. Panel 6. Le Touret Memorial, Pas de Calais, France.

ROSEBY, Gunner, Iddlesleigh. 224497, 52nd Anti-Aircraft Coy., Royal Garrison Artillery. 12th October, 1918. Age 26. Son of Thomas William and Mary Roseby, of 85, Colchester Street, Coventry. Born at Stockingford. Enlisted Coventry. Grave Ref. In North East part. Stockingford (St. Paul) Churchyard, Warwickshire.

ROSS, Private, George Wilson. 153310, 6th Bn., Black Watch (Royal Highlanders), Scottish Horse. Killed in action, 29th July, 1918. Age 19. Son of John and Margaret Ross, of Knowes of Elrick, Aberchirder, Banffshire. Native of Aberdeen. Born Coventry. Enlisted Aberdeen. Grave Ref. VII. C. 4. Chambrecy British Cemetery, France.

ROSSITER, Private, John William. 530, "I" Coy. 2nd Bn., Royal Warwickshire Regiment. Killed in action, Hazebrouck, 27th October, 1914. Age 27. Son of Charles James Rossiter, of 19, Stockton Road, Coventry. Educated Wheatley Street School and Bablake School. Born 28th August, 1887 at Coventry. Turner. Reservist. Commemorated Bablake School Memorial. Enlisted Coventry. Memorial Ref. Panel 2 and 3. Ploegsteert Memorial, Comines-Warneton, Hainaut, Belgium. (Possibly buried Hazebrouck).

ROTHERAM, Lieutenant, Donald Kenneth. HMS Cadmus, China Station. Died of syncope, following bronchitis contracted during duty, 24th March, 1916. Son of Kenneth and Frances Elizabeth Rotherham, of 46, Heath Terrace, Leamington Spa. Born 1891. Resided Coventry. Commemorated St. Thomas Memorial. Grave Ref. 18A. 8146. Hong Kong Cemetery, China.

ROTTENBURY, Lance Corporal, Henry John. 5004, 9th Bn., Royal Warwickshire Regiment. Died, Gallipoli, 26th July, 1915. Age 21. Son of Mrs. Fanny Rottenbury, of Parracombe. North Devon. Born 26th April, 1894 at Paracombe, Devonshire. Resided Coventry. Tram Driver. Enlisted August, 1914 at Coventry. Commemorated Transport Department Memorial, Coventry Corporation. Memorial Ref. Panel 35 to 37. Helles Memorial, Turkey.

ROUE, Private, William George. 12309, 2nd Bn., Oxfordshire and Buckinghamshire Light Infantry. Killed, in action, Loos, 25th September, 1915. Age 19. Son of Frank and Alice Roue, of 15, Highfield Road, Stoke, Coventry. Born 17th August, 1896 at Liverpool. Coach Painter. Enlisted September, 1914 at Coventry. Employed Singer. Memorial Ref. Panel 83 to 85. Loos Memorial, Pas de Calais, France.

ROULSON, Private, George Harry. 20065, 5th Bn., Royal Wiltshire Regiment formerly 21089, Royal Field Artillery. Died on way to Mesopotamia,19th July, 1916. Born 24th December, 1876 at Attercliffe, Yorks. Enlisted Sheffield. Resided Charterhouse Mill, London Road, Coventry. Blacksmith's striker. Reservist. Memorial Ref. Panel 30 and 64. Basra Memorial, Iraq. (Buried at sea).

ROUND, Private, Howard. 2404, 1/7th Bn., Royal Warwickshire Regiment. Killed in action, Pozieres, 25th July, 1916 bringing in a wounded man. Born 4th April, 1896 at Dudley. Resided at Whoberley. Draughtsman, Messrs. Harper, Son and Bean, Dudley. Enlisted 3rd September, 1914 at Coventry. Educated Bablake School. Commemorated Bablake School Memorial. Memorial Ref. Pier and Face 9 A 9 B and 10 B. Thiepval Memorial, France.

ROUND, Private, Hubert E. TR/8/17193, 35th Bn., Training Reserve. Died, home, 11th June, 1917. Resided 11, Coniston Road. Employed by Coventry Brace, Manufacturing Company. Enlisted Coventry Grave Ref. 13. 28. Coventry (London Road) Cemetery.

ROUSE, Private, Walter Jack. 45147, 2nd Bn., Royal Inniskilling Fusiliers. Killed in action, 28th April, 1918. Born St. John's Parish. Grave Ref. I. A. 41. New Irish Farm Cemetery, Belgium.

ROW, Private, Albert. 33189, 6th Bn., Oxfordshire and Buckinghamshire formerly 19757, Royal Warwickshire Regiment. Died, 11th January, 1917. Enlisted Coventry. Resided Kidderminster.

ROWE, Private, Bertram Thomas. 266599, 1st /7th Bn., Royal Warwickshire Regiment. Killed in action. 8th October, 1917. Age 21. Son of Charles and Ada Rowe, of 1, Pridmore Road, Coventry. Born 27th August, 1896 at 24, New Buildings, Coventry. Enlisted Coventry. Lithographer. Enlisted October, 1915. Memorial Ref. Panel 23 to 28 and 163A. Tyne Cot Memorial, Zonnebeke, West-Vlaanderen, Belgium.

ROWE, Pioneer, Charles Herbert. 130645, 1st Special Coy., Royal Engineers formerly Royal Warwickshire Regiment. Killed in action, 24th March, 1918. Age 21. Son of Thomas Arthur and Edith Rowe, of 124, Coventry Road, Bedworth, Nuneaton. Born 14th July, 1896 at Leicester. Resided Bedworth. Labourer. Enlisted November, 1915. Memorial Ref. Panel 10 to 13. Pozieres Memorial, Somme, France.

ROWE, Corporal, William Henry. 7438, H.Q. Coy. 6th Bn., Dorsetshire Regiment. Killed in action, 23rd March, 1918. Age 33. Son of Mrs. Mary Rowe, of 8/3, Grey Friars Lane, Coventry. Husband of Caroline Rowe, of 8 Court, 3 House, Grey Friars Lane, Coventry. Born 24th April, 1885, at Dublin. Grinder, Dunlop Works. Reservist. Resided 5c. 4h. East Street. Enlisted August, 1914 at Southampton. Commemorated War Memorial Park. Memorial Ref. Bay 6. Arras Memorial, Pas de Calais, France.

ROWE, Private, W. G. Oxfordshire and Buckinghamshire Light Infantry. Employed Singer. Resided 15, Highfield Road. Employed Singer. Commemorated Wesleyan Church.

ROWNTREE, Driver, Alma Wyndham. 154752, "B" Bty. 251st Bde., Royal Field Artillery. Died of wounds, 23rd April, 1917. Enlisted 1916 at Coventry. Resided Coventry. Leather merchant's assistant. Grave Ref. Wancourt Road Cem. No. 2 Mem., Panel 1. London Cemetery, Neuville-Vitasse, France.

RUBLEY, Corporal, Arthur Albert. 61339, 39th Battalion, Machine Gun Corps (Infantry) formerly 3596 Royal Warwickshire Regiment. Killed in action, Mesopotamia, 13th February 1917 by a high explosive shell. Born 18th February, 1894, in 30c. Spon Street. Resided at 91, Butts. Fitter, Siddeley Deasy works. Enlisted August, 1914 at Coventry. Commemorated St. Barbara's Church, St. John's Church, War Memorial Park and Siddeley Roll of Honour. Grave Ref. XXIX. B. 41. 51. Amara War Cemetery, Iraq.

RUDDICK, Gunner, Louis Allan. 845250, "D" Bty. 241st Bde., Royal Field Artillery. Killed in action, Italy, 15th June, 1918. Age 23. Son of Robert and Josephine Ruddick, of Greenhead, Northumberland. Born 20th August, 1894 at Coventry. Enlisted Coventry. Resided at 643, Stoney Stanton Road. Labourer. Grave Ref. 2. B. 6. Magnaboschi British Cemetery, Italy.

RUDGE, Private, Sam. 110461, Royal Army Medical Corps. Died, home, 28th July, 1918. Age 37. Husband of Sarah Ellen Rudge, of 35, Tile Hill Lane, Coventry. Born West Bromwich. Enlisted Birmingham. Grave Ref. C. 24. Penn Fields (St. Philip) Churchyard, Staffordshire.

RUFF, Private, Alfred. M/353074, Mechanical Transport, Army Service Corps. Died of wounds, 26th May, 1918. Age 28. Husband of May Ruff, of 75, Cox Street, Coventry. Born Brentford, Middlesex. Resided Coventry. Born 1890 at Brentford. Grave Ref. Div. 62. III. I. 2. St. Marie Cemetery, Le Havre, Seine-Maritime, France.

RUSCOE, Private, J. 6607, 1st Bn., North Staffordshire Regiment. Died of sickness, 15th October, 1917. Age 35. Son of George and Mary Ruscoe. Husband of Caroline M. Brayford (formerly Ruscoe), of 34, Stockton Road, Coventry. Born at Silverdale. Grave Ref. N.C. 380. Newcastle-Under-Lyme (Silverdale) Cemetery, Staffordshire.

RUSSELL, Private, Alfred Charles. 16337, 10th Bn., Royal Warwickshire Regiment. Killed in action, 3rd July, 1916. Age 20. Son of Mrs. Annie E. Griffiths, of 8, Ash Grove, Stoney Stanton Road, Coventry. Born 5th June, 1897 at Wednesbury. Resided at 132, Humber Avenue. Turner. Enlisted January, 1915. Commemorated Triumph and Gloria Ltd and Wesleyan Church. Memorial. Memorial Ref. Pier and Face 9 A 9 B and 10 B. Thiepval Memorial, Somme, France.

RUSSELL, Private, Leonard. 9114, 14th Bn., Royal Warwickshire Regiment. Killed in action, 13th April, 1918. Age 31. Son of Edward Russell. Born Meriden. Resided Meriden. Employed Coventry. Memorial Ref. Panel 2 and 3. Ploegsteert Memorial, Belgium.

RUSSELL, Private, Thomas Henry. 3055, 1st /5th Bn., Sherwood Foresters (Notts and Derby Regiment). Died of pneumonia, 9th January, 1916. Age 36. Son of George Henry and Emma Russell, of Tusses Bridge, Sowe. Resided Coventry. Grave Ref. I. L. 14A. Wimereux Communal Cemetery, Pas de Calais, France.

RUSSELL, Sergeant, William George. 993, 14th Bn., Royal Warwickshire Regiment. Killed in action, 26th October, 1917 struck by a bomb. Born Chippenham. Resided at 85, Lower Ford Street. Employed Messrs. Aitkens & Turton. Memorial Ref. Panel 23 to 28 and 163A. Tyne Cot Memorial, Belgium.

RUSSELL, Lance Sergeant, William Thomas, DCM. 181, 1st Bn., Royal Warwickshire Regiment. Killed in action, 15th March, 1915 at St. Yves. Born 1889 at Leamington. Resided Coventry. Postman. Enlisted August, 1914. Recommended for Distinguished Conduct Medal for returning with a wounded man, treating him and returning to the firing line. Leaves a widow and five children. Commemorated Post Office Memorial. Resided 7, Spon End. Memorial Ref. Panel 2 and 3. Ploegsteert Memorial, Belgium.

RYAN, Private, John Edmund Alexander. 23075, 4th Bn., Worcestershire Regiment. Killed in action, Gallipoli, 6th August, 1915. Son of James and Mary Ryan, of The Heath, Keresley, Coventry. Born 17th February, 1897 at Keresley. Enlisted Coventry. Employed Materson, Huxley and Watson Limited. Enlisted April, 1915. Commemorated St. Thomas Memorial. Memorial Ref. Panel 104 to 113. Helles Memorial, Turkey.

RYAN, Second Lieutenant, Patrick Joseph. Royal Warwickshire Regiment attd. 6th Bn., North Staffordshire Regiment. Killed in action, Bullecourt, 21st March, 1918. Age 32. Husband of Rose Hopcraft (formerly Ryan), of 12, Welland Road, Coventry. Born 1885 at Coventry. Turner, Triumph Works. Reservist. Commemorated Triumph and Gloria Memorial. Memorial Ref. Bay 3. Arras Memorial, Pas de Calais, France.

RYCROFT, Second Lieutenant, Nelson Wynne. 6th Bn., Bedfordshire Regiment. Killed in action, during heavy shelling, 25th September, 1917. Born 21st September, 1896 at Sleaford, Lancashire. Resided Coventry. Apprentice Engineer. Enlisted November, 1914. Memorial Ref. Panel 48 to 50 and 162A. Tyne Cot Memorial, Belgium.

RYE, Private, Walter Harold. 16748, 9th Bn., Royal Warwickshire Regiment. Killed in action, 25th January, 1917. Age 28. Son of George Rye, of Albion House, Lower Bridge Street, Chester formerly Police Court Missioner for Mid-Warwickshire. Born 25th January, 1889. Husband of Marion Rye, of 1, Umberslade Road, Selly Park, Birmingham. Born at Hoo, Kent. Resided Chemsleigh, Copsewood Estate. Grave Ref. XIX. K. 15. Amara War Cemetery, Iraq.

SABIN, Sergeant, Stanley George. 10903, 5th Bn., Oxfordshire and Buckinghamshire Light Infantry. Killed in action, 24th August, 1916. Born in 1890 at Chalcombe, Oxon. Resided at 21, Wright Street. Employed Coventry Co-Operative Society. Enlisted Coventry. Grave Ref. XI. D. I. Delville Wood Cemetery, Longueval, France.

SADLER, Private, Frank. G19126, A Coy., 7th Bn., East Kent Regiment formerly Royal Fusiliers. Killed in action, 3rd May, 1917. Age 29. Son of Frank W. and Emma Sadler, of The Retreat, The Elms, Ramsgate. Born 2nd June, 1887 at Droitwich. Resided at Brecon (previously Coventry). Banker's Clerk. Enlisted May, 1916. Memorial Ref. Bay 2. Arras Memorial, France

SADLER, Private, Joseph Charles. 76806, 11th Bn., Durham Light Infantry formerly 138828, Royal Engineers. Missing, believed killed, 22nd March, 1918. Age 23. Son of Joseph and Emily Sadler, of 28, Gas Street, Coventry. Husband of Gertrude May Sadler, of 27, Providence Street, Earlsdon, Coventry. Born 24th May, 1896 at 42, Spon Street, Coventry. Motor Body Maker, Messrs Hollick and Pratt. Enlisted Coventry, April, 1916. Commemorated St. John's Church and St. Barbara's Church. Memorial Ref. Panel 68 to 72. Pozieres Memorial, Somme, France.

SALMON, Private, Tom. 35647, 1st/4th Bn., Duke of Cornwall's Light Infantry formerly 1128, 92nd T. Res. Bn. Died, at sea, 4th May, 1917. Born Leamington. Enlisted Coventry. Resided Leamington. Memorial Ref. Savona Memorial, Italy.

SALMONS, Second Lieutenant, William John, MM. 65th Sqdn., Royal Air Force. Accidentally killed whilst flying, 23rd April, 1918. Age 21. Son of William and Annie Maria Salmons, of 26, Norfolk Street, Coventry. Educated Bablake School. Born 27th April, 1896 at 13, Gulson Road. Auctioneers Clerk. Enlisted September, 1914. Awarded Military Medal for excellent work in sniping, observing and collecting trench intelligence. Commemorated Bablake School Memorial, Central Methodist Hall and St. John's Church. Grave Ref. 26. 153. Coventry (London Road) Cemetery.

SALT, Private, Edward. 214543, 9th Bn., Royal Warwickshire Regiment. Died Mesopotamia, 6th October, 1918. Born Wolverhampton. Resided Foleshill. Grave Ref. IV. C. 3. Tehran War Cemetery, Iran.

SALT, Private, John William. 30770, 14th Bn., Worcestershire Regiment. Killed in action, 13th November, 1916. Born Fenton, Staffs. Enlisted Coventry. Resided Fenton. Memorial Ref. Pier and Face 5 A and 6 C. Thiepval Memorial, Somme, France.

SANDERS, Private, Albert Hayes. Northern C. L. C. Corps formerly Norfolk Regiment. Died, home, 23rd March, 1919. Born 5th February, 1883 at 62, Gosford Street. Resided at 34, Cook Street. Mechanic. Enlisted November, 1915. Grave Ref. Coventry (London Road) Cemetery.

SANDERS, Private, Edmund. G/38690, 23rd Bn., Royal Fusiliers. Killed in action, Albert, 17th February, 1917. Born 18th April, 1897 at Birmingham. Enlisted Coventry. Resided Earlsdon, Coventry. Warehouseman. Enlisted July, 1916. Commemorated St. John's Church. Grave Ref. IV. G. 22. Regina Trench Cemetery, Grandcourt, France.

SANDERS, Rifleman, Montague William. 6145, 1/17th Bn., London Regiment formerly 3rd Dorsets. Killed in action, 15th September, 1916. Born Keresley. Enlisted Warwick. Resided Coventry. Commemorated St. Thomas Memorial. Memorial Ref. Pier and Face 9 D 9 C 13 C and 12 C. Thiepval Memorial, Somme, France.

SANGSTER, Lieutenant, Frederick Charles. 16th Bn., Royal Warwickshire Regiment. Died of wounds, received on the Somme, 6th September, 1916. Age 22. Son of Charles and Louisa Sangster, of Overdale, Russell Road, Moseley, Birmingham. Born in 1894 at Coventry. Educated at Hurstpierpoint College, Sussex. Commercial School, Leipzig and Technical School, Rouen. Enlisted September, 1914. Employed Dunlop Tyre Mill. Grave Ref. II. C. II. Corbie Communal Cemetery Extension, France.

SANT, Private, Albert George. 97669, 73rd Coy., Machine Gun Corps (Infantry) formerly 268846, Royal Army Service Corps. Killed in action, 24th July, 1917. Age 20. Son of Mrs. Louisa Treen, of 27, Newcombe Road, Coventry. Born Coventry. Enlisted Coventry. Memorial Ref. Panel 56. Ypres (Menin Gate) Memorial, Ieper, West-Vlaanderen, Belgium.

SATCHWELL, Bombardier, George William. 10919, "B" Bty. 330th Brigade, Royal Field Artillery. Killed in action, 28th October, 1918. Age 23. Son of George William Satchwell, of 72, Bramble Street, formerly 51, East Street, Coventry. Born 16th June, 1895 at Coventry. Enlisted August, 1914 in Nuneaton. Grocer's Assistant. Grave Ref. B. 42. Pommereuil British Cemetery, Nord, France.

SATCHWELL, Lance Bombardier, Sidney Charles. 840770, 264th Brigade, Royal Field Artillery. Killed in action, 26th November, 1918. Age 21. Son of Mr. Satchwell, of 51, East Street, Coventry. Enlisted May, 1915 at Coventry. Resided Coventry. Born Coventry. Grocer's Assistant. Grave Ref. 325. Beirut War Cemetery, Lebanese Republic.

SATCHWELL, Private, William Charles. 1473, 7th Bn., Royal Warwickshire Regiment. Died, home, 7th January, 1916. Age 18. Son of Thomas and Martha Satchwell. Born 15th June, 1897 at 7, Duke Street. Resided at 19, Mount Street. Turner. Enlisted August, 1914 at Coventry. Commemorated Queens Road Church. Grave Ref. 183. 20. Coventry (London Road) Cemetery.

SAUL, Lance Corporal, Frederick Arthur. 14490, 7th Bn., Wiltshire Regiment formerly 14779, Oxfordshire and Buckinghamshire Light Infantry. Died of wounds, Rouen, 28th October, 1918 received the 8th October. Age 22. Youngest son of Mr. F. G and Mrs Caroline Saul, of 74, Mayfield Road, Coventry. Born 13th February, 1896 at Wood Green, Middlesex. Enlisted September, 1914 at Coventry. Resided 18, St. George's Road, Coventry. Aeroplane Engine Fitter, Standard Motor Co. Ltd. Grave Ref. S. II. G. 1B. St. Sever Cemetery Extension, Rouen, Seine-Maritime, France.

SAUL, Private, William Jackson. 2919, 1st /1st , Warwickshire Yeomanry. Killed in action, 6th August, 1916. Age 35. Son of Joseph and Georgina Saul, of 87, Highfield Street, Foleshill, Coventry. Husband of Lottie Saul. Born 1881. Grave Ref. F. 235. Kantara War Memorial Cemetery, Egypt.

SAUNDERS, Private, John Kirby. 18580, 5th Bn., Oxfordshire and Buckinghamshire Light Infantry. Killed in action, 9th April, 1917. Age 24. Son of Mr. and Mrs. J. K. Sanders, of 14, Matthew's Square, Bond Street, Coventry. Born 30th December, 1893 at Coventry. Cylinder Moulder, Britannia Foundry. Enlisted May, 1916 at Coventry. Commemorated St. John's Church. Grave Ref. III. C. 5. Tilloy British Cemetery, Tilloy-Les-Mofflaines, Pas de Calais, France.

SAUNDERS, Private, John Ernest Albert, MM. 1446, 14th Bn., Royal Warwickshire Regiment. Killed in action, 29th May, 1918. Age 22. Son of Albert and Ada Saunders, of 447, Foleshill Road, Foleshill, Coventry. Born 6th October, 1895 at Brill, Buckinghamshire. Engine Cleaner. Awarded the Military Medal for conspicuous bravery in repairing telephone wires upon several occasions, whilst under heavy shell fire. Enlisted Coventry. Grave Ref. Row A. Grave 12. Thiennes British Cemetery, Nord, France.

SAVAGE, Rifleman, George. R/15990, 10th Bn., King's Royal Rifle Corps. Killed in action, 28th July, 1916. Born Hook Norton. Enlisted Coventry. Grave Ref. I. B. 11. Hebuterne Communal Cemetery, France.

SAVAGE, Private, Harry. 13953, 6th Bn., Oxfordshire and Buckinghamshire Light Infantry. Killed in action, 19th September, 1916. Age 30. Son of William and Fanny Savage, of Bradley Green, Redditch, Worcs. Husband of Ada Savage, of Walsgrave-on-Sowe, Coventry. Enlisted Coventry. Commemorated Stoke (St. Michaels) Church. Carter. Memorial Ref. Pier and Face 10 A and 10 D. Thiepval Memorial, Somme, France.

SAVAGE, Private, Joseph. 18075. 1st Bn., Coldstream Guards. Died of wounds, 31st July, 1917. Age 23. Son of Joseph and Eliza Savage, of Station Cottages Hampton-in-Arden, Birmingham. Born 26th July, 1894 at Hampton in Arden. Resided Coventry. Apprentice, Railway Clerk. Enlisted January, 1916 at Coventry. Memorial Ref. 11. Ypres (Menin Gate) Memorial, Belgium.

SAWARD, Private, George Vivian. 202171, 9th Bn., Essex Regiment. Died of wounds, 5th October, 1918. Age 19. Son of Samuel John and Edwina Saward, of "Glendale," Castle Road, Hartshill, Atherstone, Warwickshire. Native of Essex. Born Coventry. Resided Chelmsford. Grave Ref. Div. 62. V. H. 9. Ste. Marie Cemetery, Le Havre, France.

SCANDLON, Private, Basil. 17304, 4th Bn., Worcestershire Regiment. Died of wounds (received at Gallipoli), at sea, 14th August, 1915. Born 18th September, 1891 at 4c. 7h. Greyfriars Lane, Coventry. Resided 6c. 1h. Greyfriars Lane. Iron Polisher. Enlisted August, 1914 at Coventry. Memorial Ref. Panel 104 to 113. Helles Memorial, Turkey.

SCATTERGOOD, Private, Charles William. 60057, 5th Bn., Royal Warwickshire Regiment. Died, Home, 11th November, 1918. Enlisted Coventry. Resided Leamington. Grave Ref. Q. U. 41 Newcastle Upon Tyne (St. Andrew's and Jesmond) Cemetery.

SCOTT, Lance Corporal, Walter. R/15920, 17th Bn., King's Royal Rifle Corps. Killed in action, 28th May, 1917. Age 28. Husband of Lilian A. Scott, of 22, Gloucester St., Swindon. Born Nuneaton. Enlisted Coventry. Resided Swindon. Grave Ref. II. D. 10. New Irish Farm Cemetery, Belgium.

SCOTT, Sergeant, William. K. 7237, 2nd Bn., Kings Royal Rifle Corps. Killed in action, Richebourg, 9th May, 1915. Born 1888 at Moseley, Yorkshire. Resided at 112, Walsgrave Road. Drapers Assistant., Co-Operative Society. Reservist. Grave Ref. II. J. 16. Arras Road Cemetery, Roclincourt, France.

SCRUTON, Rifleman, Sam. R/18201, 18th Bn., King's Royal Rifle Corps. Killed in action, 10th October, 1916. Born Leeds. Enlisted Coventry. Resided Middlesbrough. Memorial Ref. Pier and Face 13A and 13B. Thiepval Memorial, Somme, France.

SEAL, Lance Corporal, William. 20752, 9th Bn., York and Lancaster Regiment formerly 16427, Hussars. Killed in action, 1st July, 1916. Born Shenton, Wigan. Enlisted Nuneaton. Resided Coventry. Memorial Ref. Pier and Face 14 A and 14 B. Thiepval Memorial, Somme, France.

SEAMARK, Private, Walter Ernest. 3/9128, 1st Bn., Northamptonshire Regiment. Killed in action, 24th October, 1914. Age 20. Son of Mrs. Georgiana Durose, of II, Oliver Street, Coventry. Born 1894. Memorial Ref. Panel 43 and 45. Ypres (Menin Gate) Memorial, Ieper, West-Vlaanderen, Belgium.

SEATON, Lance Corporal, William Richard. 1st Bn., Welsh Guards. Killed in action, Langemarck, 11th October, 1917. Born 3rd April, 1886 at Bilton. Resided at 79, Aldbourne Road. Driller. Enlisted June, 1915.

SEDGLEY, Private, Frank. 125327, 25th Bn., Machine Gun Corps (Infantry) formerly 6719, Royal Warwickshire Regiment. Died of wounds, 25th September, 1918. Enlisted Coventry. Grave Ref. I. F. 8. Pont-Du-Hem Military Cemetery, La Gorgue, France.

SEDGLEY, Private, Jonathan William. 55809, 14th Bn., Welsh Regiment. Killed in action, 20th October, 1918. Age 20. Son of Charles and Mary E. Sedgley, of 34A, Drapers Fields, Coventry. Born 24th June, 1898 at 1c. 1h. Freeth Street, Coventry. Enlisted March, 1917 at Warwick. Resided Coventry. Boatman. Grave Ref. II. B. 8. Montay-Neuvilly Road Cemetery, Montay, Nord, France.

SEDGLEY, Private, Thomas. 7077, 1st Bn., Leicestershire Regiment. Killed in action, 21st December, 1915 when carrying stores to trenches, killed by a shell. Born 27th December, 1878 in Well Street, St. Michael's, Coventry. Enlisted Leicester. Resided 21, St. Agnes Lane, Coventry. Frame filer, Messrs Smith and Molesworth, Coventry. Reservist. Grave Ref. I. F. 12. White House Cemetery, St. Jean-Les-Ypres, Belgium.

SEELEY, Rifleman, Robert Sutherland. 5/3370, 1st Bn., Kings Royal Rifle Corps. Killed in action, 17th May, 1915. Employed by Rover Company Ltd. Memorial Ref. Panel 32 and 33. Le Touret Memorial, France.

SELBY, Private, Alfred William. 242506, 2/6th Bn., Royal Warwickshire Regiment formerly Worcestershire Regiment. Died of wounds, Ypres, 9th September, 1917. Born 1878. Resided at 38, Princess Street. Labourer, employed at Foleshill Gas works. Enlisted Coventry. Commemorated Gas Department Memorial, Coventry Corporation. Grave Ref. XVIII. E. 4. Lijssenthoek Military Cemetery, Belgium.

SELFE, Shoeing Smith, Frank. 52875, "Z" Bty. 5th Brigade, Royal Horse Artillery. Died of disease, 23rd October, 1918. Age 27. Son of Henry John Selfe, of Plaistow, London. Husband of Eva Selfe, of Meadow Cottage, Berkswell, Coventry. Born London. Employed Coventry. Grave Ref. IV. H. 24. Abbeville Communal Cemetery Extension, Somme, France.

SELMAN, Private, Joseph Newton. 327639, 9th Bn., Suffolk Regiment formerly Royal Fusiliers. Died of wounds, 29th November, 1917. Age 28. Husband of May A. Selman, of 8, Stanley Road, Earlsdon, Coventry. Born Freemantle, Hants. Grave Ref. IV. A. 13. Rocquigny-Equancourt Road British Cemetery, Manancourt, Somme, France.

SETCHELL, Rifleman, John William. A/200215, 10th Bn., King's Royal Rifle Corps formerly Leicestershire Regiment. Killed in action, 28th February, 1917. Age 24. Husband of Mrs. M. Setchell, of 41, Sherbourne Street, Coventry. Born 1893 at Coalville. Commemorated St. John's Church. Enlisted Ashby De La Zouch. Grave Ref. IX. W. 6. Guards' Cemetery, Lesboeufs, Somme, France.

SETTLE, Private, John. 29186, 6th Bn., Somerset Light Infantry. Killed in action, 21st March, 1918. Age 19. Son of Mrs. Alice H. Settle, of 5 Court, 1 House, Sherbourne Street, Coventry. Born 24th December, 1898 at Coventry. Enlisted 1918, Coventry. Machinist. Grave Ref. Urvillers German Cem. Mem. 45 St. Souplet British Cemetery, France.

SEVERN, Bombardier, John Wilfred. 466, A Bty., 241st Bde., Royal Field Artillery. Died of wounds, 29th October, 1916. Age 22. Son of Charlie and Annie Sarah Severn, of Cossall, Nottingham. Enlisted Aug. 1914. Born Kimberley, Notts. Enlisted Coventry. Grave Ref. IV. C. 16. Couin British Cemetery, France.

SEXTON, Private, Arthur Edward. G/18221, 7th Bn., Queen's Own (Royal West Kent) Regiment formerly PS/10959, Royal Fusiliers. Killed in action, 31st October, 1916. Age 25. Son of Jane Lydia and William Sexton, of 26, Victoria Avenue, Hunstanton, Norfolk. Born Hunstanton-on-Sea, Norfolk. Enlisted Coventry. Resided Coventry. Memorial Ref. Pier and Face 11 C. Thiepval Memorial, Somme, France.

SHADBOLT, Private, William. 19335, 4th Bn., Grenadier Guards. Died of wounds, received in France, home, 30th October, 1915. Age 22. Son of William George Shadbolt of Silver Street School, Upper Edmonton. Born 1895 at Winchmore Hill, Middlesex. Resided Coventry. Employed Humber Limited. Grave Ref. Sq. 182, Grave 45. Coventry (London Road) Cemetery.

SHAFFIR, Sergeant, Herbert Meredith. 266007, 2nd /7th Bn., Royal Warwickshire Regiment. Died of wounds, 21st March, 1918. Age 21. Only son of Mr. and Mrs. Mary Adele Shaffir, of 67, Radford Road, Coventry. Born in 1897, at Coventry. Resided at 5, Trinity Terrace, Radford Road. Assistant Analytical Chemist, Rudge Whitworth Chemical Laboratory. Enlisted Coventry November, 1914. Educated Radford Council School and King Henry VIII School. Mentioned in Despatches. Commemorated King Henry VIII School, Holy Trinity Panels and War Memorial Park. Grave Ref. I. E. 26. Ham British Cemetery, Muille-Villette, Somme, France.

SHAKESPEARE, Private, Harry. 18253, B Coy., 5th Bn., Oxfordshire and Buckinghamshire Light Infantry. Missing, believed, Killed Battle of Loos, 25th September, 1915. Age 24. Son of Mrs. E. Shakespeare, of 91, Kensington Road, Coventry. Born 6th August, 1892 in Meadow, Street, Coventry. Enlisted Coventry. Upholsterer. Enlisted April, 1915. Memorial Ref. Panel 37 and 39. Ypres (Menin Gate) Memorial, Ieper, West-Vlaanderen, Belgium.

SHANAHAN, Private, Patrick. 9275, 1st Bn., Royal Munster Fusiliers. Killed in action, 28th June, 1915. Age 28. Son of Mr. and Mrs. Shanahan, of Portmagee, Co. Kerry. Billeted Coventry. Memorial Ref. Panel 185 to 190. Helles Memorial, Turkey.

SHARLAND, Corporal, Robert Montague. 614136, "Warwick" Bty. 15th Brigade, Royal Horse Artillery. Killed in action, Monchy-le-Preux, 20th May, 1917. Age 28. Son of William Claridge Sharland and Hannah Sharland, of Bournemouth. Husband of Elizabeth Ellen Sharland, of 29, King Street, Coventry. Born 17th April, 1889 at Bournemouth. Engineer. Enlisted September, 1914. Commemorated Holy Trinity Panels. Grave Ref. I. E. 30. Monchy British Cemetery, Monchy-Le-Preux, Pas de Calais, France.

SHARMAN, Private, Alfred. 20346, 7th Bn., Royal Warwickshire Regiment. Died of tuberculosis, 26th April, 1917. Son of Letitia Sharman of 24 Queen Street, Coventry. Born 1st May, 1894 at Coventry. Process Engraver and photographer. Enlisted July, 1916. Commemorated Iliffe & Sons ltd Memorial. Grave Ref. Square 159. Grave 194. Coventry (London Road) Cemetery.

SHARMAN, Private, Charles Wilfred. 30365, 2nd Bn., Seaforth Highlanders. Died of accidental injuries, 19th November, 1919 at the Stationary Hospital, Meerut, India. Age 19. Second son of Mr. and Mrs. John Thomas Sharman, of 20, Hertford Square, Coventry. Enlisted August 13th 1918. Employed Rudge Whitworth Ltd. Memorial Ref. Delhi 1914-1918 War Memorial, India.

SHARMAN, Sapper, Frederick John. 48172, 100th Field Coy., Royal Engineers. Died, Malta, 9th May, 1918. Age 26. Husband of Emily Florence Sharman, of 71, Cambridge Street, Coventry. Born 18th May, 1893 at Coventry. Enlisted October, 1914 at Coventry. Resided 24, Queen Street. Coach Body Builder. Grave Ref. C. XVIII. 1. Pieta Military Cemetery, Malta.

SHARMAN, S. Employed by Rover Company. Killed in action.

SHARMAN, Private, Thomas Henry. 21673, 10th Bn., Royal Warwickshire Regiment. Killed in action, 5th April, 1918. Born Old Humberstone, Leics. Enlisted Coventry. Resided Old Humberstone. Grave Ref. IV. H. 6. Euston Road Cemetery, Colincamps, France.

SHARPE, Private, Clement. 23601, 7th Bn., Duke of Cornwall's Light Infantry. Died of wounds, 25th September, 1916. Age 25. Son of Mary Sharpe, of Lincoln. Born Lincoln. Enlisted Coventry. Grave Ref. I. C. 7. Abbeville Communal Cemetery Extension, France.

SHARPLES, Private, William Arnold. 18155, 14th Bn., Royal Warwickshire Regiment. Killed in action, 3rd September, 1916. Age 31. Son of William and Alice Sharples, of 53A, Clarendon Street, Chesham, Bury. Born Bury, Lancashire. Employed Coventry. Enlisted Coventry. Memorial Ref. Pier and Face 9 A 9 B and 10 B. Thiepval Memorial, France.

SHARRATT, Private, George Albert. 23885, 2nd Bn., Devonshire Regiment. Killed in action, Ypres, 31st July, 1917. Age 22. Son of Mrs. Annie Agnes Sharratt, of 8 Court, 2 House, New Buildings, Coventry. Born 28th January, 1896 at London. Driver, Messrs. Phillips and Marriott. Enlisted February, 1915 at Coventry. Grave Ref. XXVI. H. 23. Tyne Cot Cemetery, Zonnebeke, West-Vlaanderen, Belgium.

SHARRATT, Lance Corporal, Joseph. 1716, 2nd Bn., Royal Warwickshire Regiment. Killed in action, Bullecourt, 4th May, 1917. Age 30. Brother of William Sharratt of 81, East Street, Coventry. Born in 1886 at St. Michaels, Coventry. Resided at Coventry. Fitter. Enlisted August, 1914 at Coventry. Commemorated War Memorial Park. Memorial Ref. Bay 3. Arras Memorial, Pas de Calais, France.

SHARROD, Private, Harold Jason. 103144, Machine Gun Corps formerly M/298690, Army Service Corps. Died of wounds, 17th April, 1918. Age 25. Son of Michael and Mary Sharrod, of 28, William Street, Nuneaton. Husband of Ellen Mary Sharrod, of 4, Granville Road, Tunbridge Wells, Kent. Born 24th May, 1893 at Attleborough. Resided at 52, Booth Fields, Foleshill. Turner. Enlisted 1917 at Coventry. Grave Ref. VIII. D. 2. Laougnoy Military Cemetery, France.

SHAW, Lance Corporal. Resided at 181, St. George's Road. Killed in action, 1917.

SHAW, Lance Corporal, Archibald. 307745, 1/8th Bn., Royal Warwickshire Regiment. Killed in action, 15th June, 1918. Age 21. Son of Samuel and Jane Bertie Shaw, of Nottingham. Born 12th May, 1897 at Nottingham. Resided 18, Clara Street. Mechanic, Coventry Ordnance Works. Enlisted November, 1914 at Coventry. Grave Ref. II. D. 11. Magnaboschi British Cemetery, Italy.

SHAW, Private, Arnold. 26715, 16th Bn., Royal Warwickshire Regiment. Killed in action, 15th March, 1918. Age 28. Son of William Baily Shaw. Husband of Mrs. M. E. Shaw, of 5, Laurel Street, Kingswood, Bristol. Born at Long Eaton, Derby. Employed Coventry. Commemorated Coventry Chain Memorial. Enlisted Coventry. Grave Ref. 2. E. 10. Giavera British Cemetery, Arcade, Italy.

SHAW, Rifleman, Frank Ernest. S/13111, 11th Bn., Rifle Brigade. Killed in action, 13th March, 1916. Age 36. Son of Aron Shaw, of Smethwick. Husband of C. E. Washbrook (formerly Shaw), of 36, Gun Hill Cottages, Arley, Coventry. Enlisted Smethwick. Grave Ref. II. D. 8. Essex Farm Cemetery, Ieper, West-Vlaanderen, Belgium.

SHAW, Private, George Henry. 28584, 2nd /5th Bn., Royal Warwickshire Regiment. Killed in action, Cambrai, 3rd December, 1917. Age 22. Second son of Mr. and Mrs. G. Shaw, of 68, Villiers Street, Stoke, Coventry. Born 11th March, 1896 at London. Resided 29, Freeth Street. Enameller, Rudge Whitworth Co. Ltd. Enlisted August, 1914 at Coventry. Grave Ref. VII. A. 19. Fifteen Ravine British Cemetery, Villers-Plouich, Nord, France.

SHAW, Lance Corporal, John Phillip. 1751, 11th Bn., Royal Warwickshire Regiment. Killed in action, 15th November, 1916. Age 19. Son of Phillip and Lucy Charlotte Shaw, of 13/11, Far Gosford Street, Coventry. Born 11th September, 1896 at 29, George Street. Enlisted Coventry. Grave Ref. B. 7. Redan Ridge Cemetery No.3, Beaumont-Hamel, Somme, France.

SHAW, Apprentice, Leonard Bruce. S.S. "Treverbyn" (St. Ives), Mercantile Marine. Drowned as a result of an attack by an enemy submarine, or killed by mine 3rd September, 1917. Age 19. Son of John and Sarah Shaw (nee Arrowsmith), of 65, Knighton Road, Plymouth. Born at Coventry. Memorial Ref. Tower Hill Memorial, London.

SHEAR, Regimental Sergeant Major, Arthur. 3562, 11th Bn., Royal Warwickshire Regiment. Killed in action, 14th November, 1916. Age 45. Husband of L. Shear, of 15, Guy St., Warwick. Born Birmingham. Enlisted Coventry. Resided Warwick. Grave Ref. II. R. 5. Euston Road Cemetery, Colincamps, France.

SHEARGOLD, Private, Sidney George Allen. 40863, 2/7th Bn., Royal Warwickshire Regiment. Killed in action, 14th April, 1918. Born 22nd October, 1899 at Cheltenham, Glos., Enlisted October, 1917 at Warwick. Resided Upper Stoke, Coventry. Stamper, Smith's Stamping Works. Educated Stoke Council School. Memorial Ref. Panel 2 and 3. Ploegsteert Memorial, Belgium.

SHEASBY, Gunner, Edwin. 662, 109th Heavy Bty., Royal Garrison Artillery. Died, 19th March, 1915. Age 29. Son of Arthur E. Sheasby, of Icknield Street, Bidford-on-Avon, Warwickshire. Born Stoke, Coventry. Resided Bidford-on-Avon. Enlisted Gosport. Grave Ref. A. 6. 20. St. Sever Cemetery, Rouen, France.

SHEER, Private, Frank. 11392, 3rd Bn., Coldstream Guards. Killed in action, Battle of the Somme, 15th September, 1916. Age 21. Son of John and Helen Louisa Sheer, of 14, Ivor Road, Little Heath, Foleshill, Coventry. Born 17th August, 1895 at Bristol, Glos. Enlisted September, 1914. Nuneaton. Resided Coventry. Driller. Grave Ref. XVI. B8. Delville Wood Cemetery, Longueval, Somme, France.

SHEFFIELD, Lance Corporal, Sidney. 4618, "B" Coy. 2nd /7th Bn., Royal Warwickshire Regiment. Missing believed killed, 19th July, 1916. Age 24. Son of Walter John and Mary Ann Sheffield, of 13, Stoke Row, Coventry. Born 18th March, 1892 in Foleshill Road. Assistant Storekeeper. Enlisted November, 1915 at Coventry. Memorial Ref. Panel 22 to 25. Loos Memorial, Pas de Calais, France.

SHENSTONE, Private, Amos. 18026, Depot, Royal Warwickshire Regiment. Died, home, 10th April, 1916. Born Coventry. Enlisted Coventry. Grave Ref. 177. 106. Coventry (London Road) Cemetery.

SHENSTONE, Signalman, George. J/24441, HMS Invincible, Royal Navy. Killed in action, Battle of Jutland, 31st May, 1916. Age 19. Son of Mr. and Mrs. R. Shenstone, of 24, Lamb Street, Coventry formerly Harnall Lane. Born 23rd August, 1897 in Queen Victoria Road. Resided at 5, Bond Street. Commemorated St. John's Church. Memorial Ref. 14. Portsmouth Naval Memorial, Hampshire.

SHEPHERD, Private, Arthur. 242213, 2nd /8th Bn., Worcestershire Regiment. Died of wounds, 17th August, 1917. Age 30. Brother of Mrs. Selina Small, of 12th Grove, Mount Pleasant, Coventry. Born Birmingham. Grave Ref. I. A. 1. Brandhoek New Military Cemetery No.3, Ieper, West-Vlaanderen, Belgium.

SHEPHERD, Private, Ernest John. 206102, D Bn., Machine Gun Corps (Heavy Branch) formerly 32100, Machine Gun Corps. Killed in action, 3rd May, 1917. Born Birmingham. Enlisted Coventry. Commemorated Wolston Memorial. Memorial Ref. Bay 10. Arras Memorial, France.

SHEPPARD, Private, Herbert Benjamin. 265192, 2nd /7th Bn., Royal Warwickshire Regiment. Missing, believed killed 19th July, 1916. Age 18. Son of Herbert Benjamin Sheppard, of 18, Stockton Road, Coventry. Enlisted 1914, Coventry Born 7th June, 1898 in Spon End. Machinist, Rudge Whitworth Ltd. Memorial Ref. Panel 22 to 25. Loos Memorial, Pas de Calais, France.

SHEPPARD, Rifleman, Hubert Edwin. C/9880, 20th Bn., King's Royal Rifle Corps. Killed in action, 21st June, 1918. Born Westwood, Wiltshire. Employed Coventry. Grave Ref. II. J. 10. Sandpits British Cemetery, Fouquereuil, France.

SHEPPARD, Private, James William. 17730, 11th Bn., Worcestershire Regiment. Died, home, 2nd October, 1914. Age 25. Son of Joseph and Annie Sheppard, of Coventry. Husband of Amy, of 30, Court, 3, House, Much Paul Street., Coventry. Born 8th July, 1889 at Coventry, Enlisted September, 1914 at Coventry Machinist. Grave Ref. 187. 68. Coventry (London Road) Cemetery.

SHEPPERD, Gunner, Fredrick Stanley. 262, 4th South Midland Howitzer Brigade, Royal Field Artillery. Killed in action, Battle of the Somme, 2nd July, 1916. Age 21. Son of Mrs. E. M. Shepperd, of 67, Broomfield Rd., Coventry. Born 31st December, 1894 at 52, Winchester Street. Engineer. Enlisted 1914 at Coventry. Commemorated War Memorial Park. Memorial Ref. Pier and Face 1 A and 8 A. Thiepval Memorial, Somme, France. (Possibly buried Carnoy Military Cemetery).

SHERGOLD, Private, James Ernest. 203568, 1/7th Bn., Royal Warwickshire Regiment. Killed in action, 4th October, 1917. Born Aston, Birmingham. Resided at 78 Uplands, Stoke Heath. Enlisted Coventry. Memorial Ref. Panel 23 to 28 and 163A. Tyne Cot Memorial, Belgium.

SHERWOOD, Private, Alfred. 7776, 1st Bn., Royal Welsh Fusiliers. Killed in action, 16th May, 1915. Age 33. Born Swindon, Wilts. Enlisted Coventry. Resided Wolverhampton. Memorial Ref. Panel 13 and 14. Le Touret Memorial, France.

SHEWARD, Sergeant, Henry J. 6465, 2nd Bn., Leinster Regiment. Killed in action, 20th October, 1914. Born Coventry. Enlisted Coventry. Resided 10, Eagle Street. Reservist. Commemorated Holy Trinity Panels. Memorial Ref. Panel 10. Ploegsteert Memorial, Belgium.

SHEWARD, Private, William Charles. 4424, 1st /7th Bn., Royal Warwickshire Regiment. Killed in action, 14th July, 1916. (Roll of Honour states 14th October, 1916). Age 44. Son of Mrs. Sheward, of Alma Street, Coventry. Husband of Gwendoline F. Pearson (formerly Sheward), of 5, Tower Street, Coventry. Born in 1883. Window Cleaner. Enlisted January, 1915 at Coventry. Memorial Ref. Pier and Face 9 A 9 B and 10 B. Thiepval Memorial, Somme, France.

SHIERS, Private, Albert. 17759, 5th Bn., Oxfordshire and Buckinghamshire Light Infantry. Died of wounds, after having a leg amputated at the 3rd General Hospital, 16th August, 1915. wounds received by a rifle grenade. Age 35. Born 19th August, 1879 in Freeth Street, Coventry. Enlisted February, 1915 at Coventry. Resided 35, Howard Street. Iron Polisher, Daimler Works. Left a widow and four children. Grave Ref. I. G. 4. Le Treport Military Cemetery, France.

SHILLCOCK, Driver, Aubrey Harry. 113330, B Bty., 177th Bde., Royal Field Artillery. Killed in action, 19th July, 1917. Son of Arthur and Emma Elizabeth Shillcock of Black Bank, Bedworth. Commemorated Exhall Memorial. Commemorated Exhall Memorial. Enlisted Coventry. Grave Ref. I. M. 35. Brandhoek Military Cemetery, Belgium.

SHILTON, Private, George James Joseph. 17955, 16th Bn., Royal Warwickshire Regiment. Killed in action, Ypres, 7th October, 1917. Age 21. Only son of James and Mary H. Shilton, of 8, Station Road, West Longford, Coventry. Born 1896 at Birmingham. Apprenticed Mr. J. Bicknell, Foleshill Road. Enlisted Coventry. Commemorated Saint Thomas the Apostle, Longford. Memorial Ref. Panel 23 to 28 and 163A. Tyne Cot Memorial, Zonnebeke, West-Vlaanderen, Belgium.

SHILTON, Private, William Henry. 27896, 1st Bn., Royal Warwickshire Regiment. Killed in action, 11th April, 1917. Age 39. Son of W. H. Shilton, of Smethwick, Birmingham. Husband of A. A. Shilton, of 38, Mount Street, Coventry. Born 10th May, 1878 at Birmingham. Licenced Victualler. Enlisted 1916 at Coventry. Memorial Ref. Bay 3. Arras Memorial, Pas de Calais, France.

SHIPP, Private, George Thomas. 58573, 6th Bn., Northamptonshire Regiment. Killed in action, 18th September, 1918. Age 38. Son of George and Rebecca Shipp. Husband of Alice Maud Shipp, of 5, Gordon Street, Coventry. Born 20th January, 1880 at Northampton. Machinist. Enlisted May, 1918 at Coventry. Grave Ref. I. F. 12. Unicorn Cemetery, Vend'huile, Aisne, France.

SHIRES, Private, Harry. 21188, "C" Coy. 8th Bn., East Surrey Regiment formerly 5645, Royal Warwickshire Regiment. Killed in action, 3rd May, 1917. Age 40. Son of Mr. and Mrs. Mason Shires, of "Home Croft," Dunkirk Road, Birkdale, Southport. Husband of Louisa Elizabeth Shires, of "Ingledene," Hilldale, Parbold, Lancs, late of 123, Holyhead Road, Coventry. Enlisted Coventry. Memorial Ref. Bay 6. Arras Memorial, Pas de Calais, France.

SHIRLEY, Corporal, Percy John. 10481, 10th Bn., Royal Warwickshire Regiment. Killed in action, 20th September, 1917. Born 1892 at Meriden. Son of Mr. John Shirley. Resided Malt Shovel, Stonebridge. Employed Roulette, Cycle Company, Gosford Street. Enlisted Coventry. Memorial Ref. Panel 23 to 28 and 163A. Tyne Cot Memorial, Belgium.

SHORE, Private, James Harold. 35343, 14th Bn., Royal Warwickshire Regiment. Killed in action, 14th April, 1918. Age 19. Son of James and Amelia Shore, of 43, Pole Street, Stepney, London. Clerk to Surveyor of Taxes. Coventry. Educated at St. Olaves Grammar School, Southwark, London. Born London. Enlisted Coventry. Memorial Ref. Panel 2 and 3. Ploegsteert Memorial, Comines-Warneton, Hainaut, Belgium.

SHORT, Acting Corporal, Oliver Calloway. 14400, 8th Bn., Duke of Wellington's Regiment. Killed in action, 21st August, 1915. Age 28. Husband of Edith Short, of 6, Somerset Place, Mulberry St., Moldgreen, Huddersfield. Born 25th November, 1887 at 59, Well Street, Coventry. Enlisted August, 1914 at Huddersfield. Resided Moldgreen, Yorks. Painter and Decorator. Memorial Ref. Panel 117 to 119. Helles Memorial, Turkey.

SHORT, Gunner, Thomas Richard. 150273, 303rd Brigade Ammunition Col., Royal Field Artillery. Died, home, (gassed), 23rd December, 1917. Age 40. Son of Thomas and Agnes Calloway Short. Born 6th March, 1879 at 59, Well Street, Coventry. Resided Coventry. Reservist. Enlisted Coventry. Grave Ref. 191. 72. Coventry (London Road) Cemetery.

SHORTLEY, Private 1st Class, Herbert John. 9111, 45th Kite Balloon Section, Royal Air Force. Died of disease, 3rd December, 1918. Age 23. Only son of William and Alice Shortley, of Coventry. Born 9th December, 1894 in Queen Victoria Road. Resided at 20, Albany Road. Bookbinder and Machine Ruler. Enlisted August, 1915. Grave Ref. V. E. 34. Abbeville Communal Cemetery Extension, Somme, France.

SHUFFLEBOTHAM, Acting Corporal, Alfred Edwin. 20364, 9th Bn., Leicestershire Regiment. Killed in action, 25th September, 1916. Age 34. Born Holy Trinity Parish. Resided 2c. 2h. Leicester Street. Employed Messrs S. Peters and Son. Enlisted Coventry. Memorial Ref. Pier and Face 2 C and 3 A. Thiepval Memorial, Somme, France.

SHUFFLEBOTHAM, Lance Corporal, Edward. 1645, 2nd Bn., Royal Warwickshire Regiment. Killed in action, 4th May, 1917. Age 21. Second son of Edwin A. Shufflebotham, of 5/11 House, Far Gosford Street, Coventry. Born 9th May, 1896 at 2c. 2h. Spon Street. Grinder, Dunlop. Enlisted August, 1914 at Coventry. Memorial Ref. Bay 3. Arras Memorial, Pas de Calais, France.

SHUFFLEBOTHAM, Private, Frank Albert. 9353, 1st Bn., Northamptonshire Regiment. Killed in action, Mons, 3rd November, 1914. Son of Mr. Edwin. A. Shufflebotham, of Court 5, House II, Far Gosford Street, Coventry. Born 22nd April, 1891 at back of 2, Spon Street, Coventry. Enlisted Northampton. Soldier. Memorial Ref. Panel 43 and 45. Ypres (Menin Gate) Memorial, Ieper, West-Vlaanderen, Belgium.

SHUFFLEBOTTOM, Frederick. Resided in Thomas Street. Labourer. Killed in action.

SHUFFLEBOTTOM, Sergeant, George Henry. 33965, 6th Bn., Duke of Cornwall's Light Infantry formerly 21358, Hussars. Killed in action, 23rd September, 1917. Born Hanley, Staffs. Enlisted Nuneaton. Resided Exhall. Employed Coventry. Commemorated Exhall Memorial. Grave Ref. V. A. 16 Messines Ridge Cemetery, Belgium.

SHUTTLEWORTH, E.H. Iliffe & Sons Ltd

SIDEBOTTOM, Gunner, Arthur. 2694, 7th Light Armoured Car Bty., Machine Gun Corps (Motors). Killed in action, East Africa, 21st October, 1917. Born Reddish, Stockport. Enlisted Coventry. Resided Stockport. Grave Ref. 6. L. 4. Dar Es Salem War Cemetery, Tanzania.

SIDWELL, Lance Corporal, Cecil. 310549, 1st /1st , Warwickshire Yeomanry. Died of sickness (on H.S. Kalyan), 30th January, 1918. Age 27. Husband of Marion Grace Sidwell of 7 Wren Street, Coventry. Enlisted Warwick. Resided Coventry. Educated Bablake School. Born 22nd December, 1889 at Hook Norton, Oxon. Resided at Branksome, King Richard Street. Assistant Clerk to Guardians. Enlisted October, 1914. Son of Mr. S. Sidwell of 2, King Richard Street. Commemorated Bablake School Memorial. Grave Ref. Square 53. Grave 97. Coventry (London Road) Cemetery.

SIDWELL, Private, Ernest. 9043, 1st Bn., The King's (Liverpool Regiment). Died of wounds, Mons, 15th September, 1914. Son of William Sidwell, of 132, Lower Ford Street, Coventry. Born 26th September, 1886 at Stoke, Coventry. Enlisted Warwick. Engineer. Reservist. Grave Ref. IV. D. 9. Vendresse British Cemetery, Aisne, France.

SIDWELL, Private, Percy Arthur. 103239, 53rd Coy., Machine Gun Corps (Infantry) formerly 24317, Royal Warwickshire Regiment. Killed in action, 22nd October, 1917. Born 1898 at Coventry. Enlisted 1917 at Coventry. Resided Stoke. Driller. Memorial Ref. Panel 154 to 159 and 163A. Tyne Cot Memorial, Belgium.

SIDWELL, R. Commemorated Coventry Chain Memorial.

SIDWELL, Private, Wilfred Herbert. PS/9984, 17th Bn., Royal Fusiliers. Died, 25th March, 1917. Born 28th March, 1896 at Coventry. Enlisted December, 1915, Coventry. Resided at Branksome, King Richard Street, Coventry. Educated Bablake School. Son of Mr. S. Sidwell of 2, King Richard Street. Clerk, Public Health Department, Coventry Corporation. Commemorated Bablake School Memorial and Public Health Department Memorial, Coventry Corporation. Grave Ref. XXII. C. 10A. Etaples Military Cemetery, France.

SILCOCKS, Private, Francis Herbert. 11110, 1st Bn., Coldstream Guards. Missing, believed, killed 22nd December, 1914. Age 19. Son of Frank and Lydia Silcocks, of 12, Ransom Road, Foleshill, Coventry. Born 23rd April, 1896 at 12, Charterhouse Road. Barber's Apprentice. Enlisted August, 1914 at Coventry. Memorial Ref. Panels 2 and 3. Le Touret Memorial, Pas de Calais, France.

SILLITOE, Driver, Henry. 132015, 7th T. F. Training School, Royal Field Artillery. Died, Home, 16th May, 1916. Son of Richard and Priscilla Sillitoe of Hartshill, Stoke-on-Trent. Born Stoke-on-Trent. Enlisted Coventry. Grave Ref. 16272. Winchester (West Hill) Old Cemetery, Hampshire.

SILSWORTH, Private, F. . 5th Bn., Oxfordshire and Buckinghamshire Light Infantry. Killed in trenches, 16th October, 1915. Enlisted Coventry.

SIMMONDS, Private, Aubrey Henry. 39463, 10th Bn., Royal Warwickshire Regiment Killed in action, near Haussy, Cambrai, 24th October, 1918. Age 19. Son of Rev. Charles Simmonds, M.A., and Helen Simmonds, of Exhall Vicarage, Coventry. Born Exhall. Enlisted Leamington. Resided Exhall. Commemorated Exhall Memorial. Grave Ref. B. 14. Crucifix Cemetery, Vendegies-Sur-Ecaillon, Nord, France.

SIMMONDS, Private Charles. 35500, 7th Bn., Wiltshire Regiment. Killed in action, 7th October, 1918. Born 6th December, 1898 at 22, Sherbourne Street, Coventry. Enlisted March, 1916 at Coventry. Resided 22, Sherbourne Street, Coventry. Commemorated St. John's Church. Grave Ref. II. E. 11. Prospect Hill Cemetery, Gouy, France.

SIMMONDS, Private, Thomas Henry. 3324, 9th Bn., Royal Warwickshire Regiment. Died of wounds, 22nd August, 1915. Age 21. Son of Mr. and Mrs. Thomas Simmonds, of 10, Little South Street, Coventry. Born 2nd January, 1894 in Gosford Street. Employed Humber Limited. Enlisted August, 1914 at Coventry. Grave Ref. A. X. 1. Pieta Military Cemetery, Malta.

SIMMONDS, Private, William. 16973, 7th Bn., Oxfordshire and Buckinghamshire Light Infantry formerly Royal Munster Fusiliers. Killed in action, Kidney Hill, 2nd January, 1917 by a shell dropping close-by. Born Studley, Warwicks. Enlisted Coventry. Employed Filing Department, Rudge Works. Grave Ref. F. 1251. Karasouli Military Cemetery, Greece.

SIMMONS, Stoker 1st Class, Charles. SS/114748, HMS Tipperary, Royal Navy. Killed in action, Battle of Jutland, 31st May, 1916. Age 21. Son of George and Mary Simmons, of Byfield Place, Berkswell, Coventry. Memorial Ref. 19. Portsmouth Naval Memorial, Hampshire.

SIMMONS, Private, Henry. 9058, 1st Bn., Royal Warwickshire Regiment. Killed in action, at Mons, 13th October, 1914. Born Berkswell, Coventry. Enlisted Coventry. Resided Mere End, Kenilworth. Grave Ref. IV. C. 610. (Buried near this spot). Meteren Military Cemetery, France.

SIMMONS, Lance Corporal, Thomas James. 532412, 490th Field Coy., Royal Engineers. Died of wounds, 27th March, 1918. Enlisted Slough. Resided Coventry. Grave Ref. I. C. 2. Namps-Au-Val British Cemetery, France.

SIMMONS, Private, William. 2567, 1st /7th Bn., Royal Warwickshire Regiment. Shot by a sniper, whilst on sentry duty, 23rd June, 1915. Age 26. Son of Walter and Emily Simmons, of 29, Rudge Road, Coventry. Born 23rd March 1889 in Spon Street. Resided at 29 Rudge Road. Machinist. Enlisted September, 1914, Coventry. Commemorated Queens Road Church and War Memorial Park Grave Ref. II. G. 3. Rifle House Cemetery, Comines-Warneton, Hainaut, Belgium.

SIMMS, Gunner, Thomas Henry. 930, "D" Bty. 306th Brigade, Royal Field Artillery. Killed in action, Battle of the Somme, 18th July, 1916. Age 18. Son of H. Ralph and Ellen E. Simms, of 68, Spon Street, Coventry. Born 21st August, 1897 at Barnt Green, Worcestershire. Resided at 6c. 2h. Freeth Street, Coventry. Mechanic. Enlisted March, 1915 at Coventry. Grave Ref. II. E. 13. Laventie Military Cemetery, La Gorgue, Nord, France.

SIMMS, Private, William. 2192, Depot, Royal Warwickshire Regiment. Died of wounds, received in Gallipoli, 23rd June, 1918. Age 36. Son of George Simms. Husband of Lucy Ann Simms, of 54, Aldbourne Road, Radford, Coventry. Born 29th April, 1882 at Handsworth. Resided 157, Cambridge Street. Grave Ref. 198. 61. Coventry (London Road) Cemetery.

SIMONS, Private, William. 10119, 1st Bn., Royal Welsh Fusiliers. Died, home, 2nd February, 1917. Born Coventry. Enlisted Wrexham. Resided Leicester. Grave Ref. 213. 7. 23. (Screen Wall.). Kensal Green (All Souls') Cemetery, London.

SIMPSON, Brian. Killed in action. Name on Roll of Honour in Cathedral Church of St. Michael.

SIMPSON, Private, Frederick. 266371, 1/7th Bn., Royal Warwickshire Regiment. Killed in action, 8th October, 1917. Born Coventry. Resided Foleshill. Enlisted Coventry. Memorial Ref. Panel 23 to 28 and 163A. Tyne Cot Memorial, Belgium.

SIMPSON, Company Sergeant Major, Harold, DCM. 66186, 2nd /10th Bn., Royal Scots formerly 12904, Shropshire Light Infantry. Died of wounds, Russia, 13th October 1918. Age 24. Son of Thomas and Elizabeth Simpson. Husband of Emily Gertrude Simpson, of 29, Paynes Lane, Coventry. Born Madeley, Shrops. Enlisted Shrewsbury. Resided Coventry. Memorial Ref. Archangel Memorial, Russian Federation.

SIMPSON, Captain, John Edmund. 2nd Bn., Kings Own Yorkshire Light Infantry. Killed in action, 31st October, 1914. Age 41. Son of Rev. John Curwen Simpson and Mrs. Frances Maria Simpson. Mentioned in Despatches. Name on Roll of Honour in Cathedral Church of St. Michael. Memorial Ref. Addenda Panel 57. Ypres Menin Gate Memorial, Belgium.

SIMPSON, Lance Corporal, Joseph Richard. 11228, 1st Bn., North Staffordshire Regiment. Died of wounds, 2nd July, 1916. Age 23. Born at Emscote, Warwick. Son of Joseph Francis and Mary Simpson, of 85, Grafton Street, Coventry. Grave Ref. VIII. B. 119. Boulogne Eastern Cemetery, Pas de Calais, France.

SIMS, Rifleman, Frederick Arthur. B/203121, 9th Bn., Rifle Brigade formerly King's Royal Rifle Corps. Killed in action, 3rd May, 1917. Age 23. Son of Josiah and Ellen Sims, of 9, Newdigate Road, Coventry. Husband of Alice Mary Sims, of 93, Raglan Street, Coventry. Born 3rd April, 1894 at Handsworth. Enlisted November, 1915 at Coventry. Resided 9, Nelson Street, Coventry. Wood Machinist, Dunlop Works, Wellington Street. Commemorated Dunlop Memorial. Memorial Ref. Bay 9. Arras Memorial, Pas de Calais, France.

SINCLAIR, Private, Norman Edward. 58424, 70th Field Ambulance, Royal Army Medical Corps. Killed in action, 15th October, 1917. Born 1st September, 1895 at Southwark. Resided 74, Eagle Street. Clerk. Memorial Ref. Panel 160. Tyne Cot Memorial, Belgium.

SKINNER, Private, G. 8872, 1st Bn., Royal Munster Fusiliers. Killed in action, 1st May, 1915. Billeted Coventry. Age 22. Son of George and Mary Skinner. Memorial Ref. Panel 185 to 190. Helles Memorial, Turkey.

SKINNER, Private, William Matthew. 20296, 2nd Bn., Duke of Cornwall's Light Infantry formerly 4462, Royal Warwickshire Regiment. Killed in action, Balkans, 17th November, 1916. Age 25. Son of Mrs. Teresa Ford of Bedworth Hill, Nuneaton. Commemorated Exhall Memorial. Born Exhall. Enlisted Nuneaton. Resided Exhall. Memorial Ref. Doiran Memorial, Greece.

SLATER, Lance Sergeant, Harold. 3617, 1st Bn., Royal Warwickshire Regiment. Died of wounds, 26th August, 1916. Age 27. Son of Hedley and Hannah Slater, of 10, Lincoln Street, Coventry. Native of Stanningley, Leeds. Born 10th March, 1889. Resided 71, Station Street West. Coremaker. Enlisted August, 1914. Grave Ref. VI. L. 5. Railway Dugouts Burial Ground, Ieper, West-Vlaanderen, Belgium.

SLATER, Corporal, John Rowland Jennings. 10303, 2nd Bn., South Wales Borderers. Died 19th May, 1915. Age 25. Son of John and Selina Slater. Born St. Matthews, Walsall. Enlisted Swansea. Son of Mrs. Jennings Slater of No. 6. Town Hall Villas, Swansea. Billeted Mrs. Eadon, 59, Hamilton Road. Grave Ref. IV. A. 11. Pink Farm Cemetery, Helles, Turkey.

SLATER, T. H. Killed in action. Name on Roll of Honour in St. Thomas's Church.

SLATER, Private Walter. 302039, 10th Bn., Essex Regiment formerly 9830, Oxfordshire & Buckinghamshire Light Infantry. Killed in action, 23rd August, 1917. Age 28. Born 1889 at Macclesfield. Enlisted Coventry. Resided Coventry. Employed Rover Company Ltd. Enlisted November, 1914. Memorial Ref. Panel 88 to 89. Tyne Cot Memorial, Belgium.

SLATER, Gunner, William Samuel. 1164, Royal Field Artillery. Died (repatriated prisoner of war) of pneumonia, 16th April, 1919. Age 21. Son of William and Alice Elizabeth Slater, of 24, Welford Place, Coventry. Born 24th July, 1899 at Wordesley, Staffordshire. Moulder. Enlisted September, 1914. Grave Ref. 55. 29. Coventry (London Road) Cemetery.

SLATTERY, William. Resided Foleshill. Killed in action, March, 1918.

SLAUGHTER, H, MSM. The Hussars. School Teacher, Elementary School, Coventry. Commemorated Education Department Memorial, Coventry Corporation. Awarded the Meritorious Service Medal, 1920.

SMALLEY, Private, Albert. 27185, 6th Bn., Leicestershire Regiment attached 110th Trench Mortar Battery. Killed in action, 18th September, 1918. Age 27. Husband of Mrs. A. R. Ison (formerly Smalley), of 60, Gladstone Street, Leicester. Born Coventry. Enlisted Leicester. Memorial Ref. panel 5. Vis-En-Artois Memorial, France.

SMART, Private, Albert Edward. 201483, 4th Bn., Canadian Infantry (Central Ontario Regiment). Killed in action, 8th October, 1916. Age 18. Son of Ellen Rose and Frederick Smart of 94, Cox Street, Coventry. Memorial Ref. Vimy Memorial, Pas de Calais, France.

SMART, Private, Ernest Frank. 11534, 3rd Bn., Coldstream Guards. Killed in action, 13th April, 1918. Age 27. Husband of Sarah Whiting (formerly Smart), of 337, New Houses, Stafford Road, Cannock, Staffs. Born at Chestnuts, Gloucestershire. Resided Arley. Employed Coventry. Memorial Ref. Panel 1. Ploegsteert Memorial, Belgium.

SMITH, Rifleman, Albert. S/16541, 12th Bn., Rifle Brigade. Killed in action, 5th September, 1916. Born Earlsdon. Enlisted 11th April, 1916 at Coventry. Resided Coventry. Only son of Mrs. Mary Smith, Tollgate Cottage, Stivichall. Under gardener, Stivichall Hall. Commemorated St. James Church. Memorial Ref. Pier and Face 16 B and 16 C. Thiepval Memorial, Somme, France.

SMITH, Private, Albert. 22516, 10th Bn., Royal Warwickshire Regiment. Died of wounds, 26th April, 1918. Brother of Mr. E. F. Smith, of 38, Court House, Gosford Street, Coventry. Born February, 1879 in Canterbury Street, Coventry. Enlisted February, 1917 at Coventry. Iron Polisher. Grave Ref. XXVIII. A. 7A. Lijssenthoek Military Cemetery, Poperinge, West-Vlaanderen, Belgium.

SMITH, Sergeant, Albert Edward. 12763, 15th Bn., Royal Warwickshire Regiment. Killed in action, 26th October, 1917. Born Stourbridge, Worcestershire. Resided 31, Edgewick Road. Police Constable. Commemorated Police Force Memorial, Coventry Corporation. Memorial Ref. Panel 23 to 28 and 163A. Tyne Cot Memorial, Belgium.

SMITH, Private, Arthur. 15692, 9th Bn., Royal Warwickshire Regiment. Died, 4th July, 1916. Age 35. Son of Mrs. Ann Smith, of 8, St. John Street, Coventry. Born 29th May, 1881 at Coventry. Lithographic printer. Enlisted 20th November, 1915. Employed Messrs. Thomas Bushill and Sons printers, Cow Lane. Grave Ref. VIII. A. 6. Amara War Cemetery, Iraq.

SMITH, Private, Arthur. 17832, 15th Bn., Royal Warwickshire Regiment. Killed in action, 20th August 1916. Age 32. Son of Mrs. Eliza Smith, of 7, Coventry Road, Bulkington, Nuneaton. Born in Witherley, Leicestershire. Enlisted Nuneaton. Resided Bedworth formerly Navigation Inn, Foleshill. Employed milk round in Bedworth. Memorial Ref. Pier and Face 9 A 9 B and 10 B. Memorial Ref. Thiepval Memorial, Somme, France.

SMITH, Aircraftman 2nd Class, Aubrey Lawrence. 263755, 141st Sqdn., Royal Air Force. Killed while flying (crashed), 30th April 1920. Age 19. Son of George H. and Harriett Smith, of Coventry. Grave Ref. 84. 73. Coventry (London Road) Cemetery.

SMITH, Private, Charles. 20943, 14th Bn., Worcestershire Regiment. Killed in action, 6th November, 1917. Born Warwick. Enlisted Nuneaton. Resided Whitefriars Lane, Coventry. Employed Humber Ltd. Grave Ref. XLII. C. 14. Poelcapelle British Cemetery, Belgium.

SMITH, Rifleman, Dennis. R/6340, 7th Bn., King's Royal Rifle Corps. Killed in action, 12th October, 1917. Husband of Frances S. Smith, of 31, Tidy Street, Brighton. Born Ledbury, Hereford. Enlisted Marylebone, Middx. Resided Coventry. Memorial Ref. Panel 115 to 119 and 162A and 163A. Tyne Cot Memorial, Belgium.

SMITH, Private, Eli. 14563, 2nd Bn., Royal Warwickshire Regiment. Killed in action, 5th November, 1915. Age 21. Only son of William and Prudence Smith, of Walsgrave-on-Sowe, Coventry, Warwick. Enlisted August, 1914. Commemorated Walsgrave Memorial. Grave Ref. III. B. 7. Guards Cemetery, Windy Corner, Cuinchy, Pas de Calais, France.

SMITH, Private, Frank. 307778, 15 Platoon, D Coy., Machine Gun Section, 1/8th Bn., Royal Warwickshire Regiment. Killed in action, 27th August, 1917. Born 18th November, 1888 at Coventry. Resided 81, Guild Road with his sister, Mrs. Norbury. Silk Spinner, Courtaulds Ltd. Enlisted February, 1916. Memorial Ref. Panel 23 to 28 and 163A. Tyne Cot Memorial, Belgium.

SMITH, Private, Frank Edmund. PLY/2407(S), 1st Royal Marine Bn., Royal Marine Light Infantry. Killed in action, 19th May, 1918. Age 36. Son of Mr. and Mrs. Fred Smith, of Alma Street, Wellingborough. Husband of Frances S. Smith. Motorman. Employed by Coventry Corporation, Tramways Department. Commemorated Transport Department Memorial, Coventry Corporation. Grave Ref. II. F. 31. Hamel Military Cemetery, Beaumont-Hamel, France.

SMITH, Private, Frank Leonard. 18246, 9th Bn., Royal Warwickshire Regiment. Killed in action, 25th January, 1917. Born 15th December, 1891 at Broughton Green near Droitwich. Resided at 64, Much Park Street. Storekeeper. Grave Ref. XIX. K. 16. Amara War Cemetery, Iraq.

SMITH, Second Lieutenant, Frederick George, Royal Flying Corps. Killed while flying at Basingstoke, 8th February, 1918. Age 20. Son of Henry and Alice Smith, of 14, Gloucester Street, Coventry. Born 15th November 1897, at Kingston-upon-Hull. Resided at 14, Gloucester Street. Engineer, British Thompson Houston. Enlisted July 1917. Educated Rugby School. Commemorated St. John's Church and War Memorial Park. Grave Ref. 141. 173. Coventry (London Road) Cemetery.

SMITH, Private, Fredrick James. 9699, "C" Coy. 2nd /7th Bn., Royal Warwickshire Regiment. Died of wounds, 31st December, 1917. Age 19. Son of Jane Burdett, of 144, Cross Road, Foleshill, Coventry. Born 18th April, 1899 in Malta. Enlisted 7th September, 1914. Mechanic, Daimler Works. Grave Ref. VI. C. 12A. Mont Huon Military Cemetery, Le Treport, Seine-Maritime, France.

SMITH, Sergeant. G. S. Royal Field Artillery. Killed in action by a shell, 2nd August, 1917. Son of Mr. and Mrs. Arthur Smith of Clarendon Street, Earlsdon. Employed Coventry Chain. Commemorated Coventry Chain Memorial.

SMITH, Private, Geoffrey George. 81248, 4th Bn., Devonshire Regiment. Died, Home, 1st November, 1918. Age 18. Son of Mr. and Mrs. C. E. Smith, of 29, Eagle Street, Leamington Spa. Born Coventry. Enlisted Coventry. Resided Leamington. Employed Rover Co. Ltd. Grave Ref. 89. 26. Leamington (Whitnash Road) Cemetery.

SMITH, Private, George, MM. 9505, 1st Bn., Royal Warwickshire Regiment. Killed in action, 30th August, 1918. Born Coventry. Commemorated Saint Thomas the Apostle, Longford. Grave Ref. C. 9. Eterpigny British Cemetery, France.

SMITH, Private, George Edward. 17368, 15th Bn., Royal Warwickshire Regiment. Killed in action, 30th July, 1916. Age 30. Son of Mrs. Ann Smith, of 128, Eden Street, Coventry. Born 12th June, 1888 at Coventry, Enlisted 1914 in Coventry. Haulier, Mr. Cotton. Memorial Ref. Pier and Face 9 A 9 B and 10. Thiepval Memorial, Somme, France.

SMITH, Private, George William, 43093, 5th Bn., Royal Berkshire Regiment. Died of wounds, 31st October, 1918. Age 19. Son of George J. and Maggie G. Smith, of 37, Drapers Fields, Coventry. Born 30th August 1899, at Coventry. Resided at Coventry. Engineers Apprentice. Enlisted Coventry, April 1918. Commemorated War Memorial Park. Grave Ref. VI. F. 4. Terlincthun British Cemetery, Wimille, Pas De Calais, France.

SMITH, Private, H. W. Killed in action.

SMITH, Private, Harold Herbert. 28685, 11th Bn., Royal Warwickshire Regiment. Killed in action, 17th July, 1917. Born Coventry. Enlisted Coventry. Resided Foleshill. Grave Ref. H. 30. Kemmel Chateau Military Cemetery, Belgium.

SMITH, Sapper, Harry. 41455, 54th Field Coy., Royal Engineers. Died of pneumonia, 7th November 1918. Age 25. Son of George and Elizabeth Smith, of Wolston, Coventry. Commemorated Woslton Memorial. Grave Ref. II. B. 10. Staglieno Cemetery, Genoa, Italy.

SMITH, Private, Henry Arthur. 17710, 2nd Bn., Worcestershire Regiment. Killed in action, 26th September, 1917. Born 3rd August, 1894 at Meadow Street, Coventry. Enlisted September, 1914 at Coventry. Resided 27 Yardley Street. Capstan Hand, Rover Company. Memorial Ref. Panel 75 to 77. Tyne Cot Memorial, Belgium.

SMITH, Pioneer, Henry George, MM. 48446, 31st Div. Signal Coy., Royal Engineers. Died of disease, 10th November, 1918. Age 32. Son of Mr. and Mrs. C. Smith, of Down, Hatherley, Gloucester. Husband of Margaret Smith, of 25, Shackleton Road, Earlsdon, Coventry. Born 16th September, 1887 at Gloucester. Mechanic. Enlisted September, 1914. Awarded Military Medal for bravery on 10th November, 1917. Grave Ref. X. D. 9. Terlincthun British Cemetery, Wimille, Pas de Calais, France.

SMITH, Sapper, Herbert James. 43894, 18th Signal Coy., Royal Engineers. Killed in action, Trones Wood, 14th July, 1916 when leading a party to repair a telephone wire. Second son of Mrs. Edwin Smith of Mile End, Kenilworth. Born 10th August, 1896 at Wasperton, Warwick. Resided Kenilworth. Apprentice Fitter, Mr. Bloomfield of Coventry later Alfred Herbert. Enlisted August, 1914. Memorial Ref. Pier and Face 8 A and 8 D. Thiepval Memorial, Somme, France.

SMITH, J. L. Employed by Rover Company. Killed in action.

SMITH, J. R. Commemorated Post Office Memorial.

SMITH, Private, James. 1888, 2nd Bn., Royal Warwickshire Regiment. Killed in action, 19th December, 1914. Age 40. Husband of Martha Smith, of 36, Spon End, Coventry. Born in November, 1875 at Coventry. Driller. Enlisted August, 1914. Memorial Ref. Panel 2 and 3. Ploegsteert Memorial, Comines-Warneton, Hainaut, Belgium.

SMITH, Private, James Thomas. 58432, 10th Bn., Royal Warwickshire Regiment. Killed in action, 7th November, 1918. Born 1898 at Coventry. Enlisted May, 1918 at Coventry. Resided at 129, Harnall Lane. Employed by Armstrong Siddeley Motors Limited. Son of Mr. and Mrs. W. H. Smith of Coventry Street, Coventry. Commemorated War Memorial Park and Siddeley Roll of Honour. Grave Ref. I. D. 7. Cross Roads Cemetery, Fontaine-Au-Bois, France.

SMITH, Private, Jesse Herbert. 242821, 1/6th Bn., Royal Warwickshire Regiment. Killed in action, 1st April, 1917. Born Luton. Resided Foleshill. Grave Ref. I. J. 4. Epehy Wood Farm Cemetery, Epehy, France.

SMITH, Gunner, John. 53446, 124th Siege Battery, Royal Garrison Artillery. Died of wounds, 22nd October, 1917. Son of Samuel and Mary Agnes Smith, of Wirksworth, Derbyshire. Born 6th September, 1889 at Wicksworth, Derbyshire. Resided Coventry. Compositor. Enlisted November, 1914. Memorial Ref. VI. E. 16A. Wimereux Communal Cemetery, France.

SMITH, Private, John. 266752, 2/6th Bn., West Riding Regiment. Killed in action, 3rd May, 1917. Resided Foleshill. Memorial Ref. Bay 6. Arras Memorial, France.

SMITH, Private, John Charles. 11098, 1st Bn., Coldstream Guards. Killed in action, 22nd December, 1914. Age 21. Son of Joseph and Ann Smith, of Park Lane, Berkswell, Coventry. Memorial Ref. Panels 2 and 3. Le Touret Memorial, Pas de Calais, France.

SMITH, Private, John Norman. 68072, 7th Bn., Royal Fusiliers formerly 7835, 2/5th Queen's Royal West Surrey Regiment. Killed in action, 30th December, 1917. Born Bedworth. Enlisted Coventry. Resided Coventry. Memorial Ref. Pier and Face 8 C 9 A and 16 A. Thiepval Memorial, Somme, France.

SMITH, J. T. Royal Warwickshire Regiment. Commemorated Siddeley Roll of Honour.

SMITH, Private, John Thomas. 201458, 1/4th Bn., Northamptonshire Regiment. Killed in action, 19th April, 1917. Born Northampton. Tram Conductor. Commemorated Transport Department Memorial, Coventry Corporation. Memorial Ref. Panel 40. Jerusalem Memorial, Israel.

SMITH, Private, John William. 36004, 14th Bn., Worcestershire Regiment. Killed in action, 5th February, 1917. Born Exhall. Enlisted Stratford-on-Avon. Commemorated Exhall Memorial. Resided Alcester. Memorial Ref. Pier and Face 5A and 6C Thiepval Memorial, France.

SMITH, Gunner, Leonard. 44384, 46th Bty. 39th Bde., Royal Field Artillery. Killed in action, La Bassee, 1st November, 1914. Age 27. Son of David John and Eliza Frances Smith, of 14, Belfry Avenue, Bell Hill, St. George, Bristol. Born in 1888 at Bristol. Resided Coventry. Machine Moulder. Reservist. Memorial Ref. Panel 5 and 9. Ypres (Menin Gate) Memorial, Belgium.

SMITH, Second Lieutenant, Leslie George. 20th Sqdn., Royal Air Force. Killed in action, brought down near Le Cateau, 26th September, 1918. Age 21. Son of Sidney and Kate Smith, of "Malmsmead," Rochester Road, Earlsdon, Coventry. Born 19th March, 1897 at Coventry. Engineer's Apprentice, Alfred Herbert Ltd. Enlisted June, 1917. Commemorated King Henry VIII School and St. Barbara's Church. Grave Ref. VIII. G. 9. Gouzeaucourt New British Cemetery, Nord, France

SMITH, Private, Mark Henry. 6211, 2nd Bn., Royal Warwickshire Regiment. Died of wounds, Festubert, 16th May 1915. Age 35. Son of Thomas Smith, of Coventry. Husband of Mary A. Smith, of 10, Stanway Road, Earlsdon, Coventry. Born 29th July, 1879 at Coventry. Resided at Coventry. Mechanic, Rover Works. Reservist. Held South African war medal with four clasps. Commemorated War Memorial Park. Grave Ref. III. D. 32. Bethune Town Cemetery, Pas de Calais, France.

SMITH, Private, Oliver Thomas. 16441, 15th Entrenching Bn., late 11th Bn., Royal Warwickshire Regiment. Died of wounds, 22nd March, 1918. Son of John Oliver Smith and Agnes Smith, of The Post Office, Bulkington, Nuneaton. Born 30th July, 1894 at Bulkington. Resided Bulkington. Carpenter. Enlisted February, 1916. Memorial Ref. Panel 18 and 19. Pozieres Memorial, France. (Possibly buried near St. Quentin).

SMITH, Private, Percival James. 265402, 1/7th Bn., Royal Warwickshire Regiment. Died, 7th March, 1917. Born 16th January, 1896 at Newton Abbot, Devonshire. Resided 30. Howard Street. Driller. Enlisted August, 1914. Grave Ref. XXII. 16. A. Etaples Military Cemetery, France.

SMITH, Sergeant, Percy. 840591, "D" Bty. 306th Brigade, Royal Field Artillery. Killed in action, 22nd August, 1917. Age 21. Son of Joseph and Emma Smith, of II Court, 22 House, Gosford Street, Coventry. Born 16th May, 1896 at Coventry. Enlisted 1914 at Coventry. Trimmer, Montgomery's Lower Ford Street. Grave Ref. III. K. 7. White House Cemetery, St. Jean-les-Ypres, Ieper, West-Vlaanderen, Belgium.

SMITH, Private, Percy Arthur. 4060, 10th Bn., Royal Warwickshire Regiment. Died of wounds, La Bassee, 26th February, 1916. Wounds received through running into an enemy shell whilst taking a message to a first aid station. Age 19. Son of Arthur and Emily M. Smith, of 4, Aylesford Street, Coventry. Born 17th March, 1898 at 6, South Street. Machinist. Enlisted September, 1914. Commemorated Triumph and Gloria Memorial. Grave Ref. VI. M. 4. Merville Communal Cemetery, Nord, France.

 **SMITH**, Corporal, Percy Francis. 16323, 9th Bn., Royal Warwickshire Regiment. Killed in action, Mesopotamia, 29th March, 1917. Age 21. Born 6th March, 1896 at 18, South Street, Coventry. Enlisted January, 1916. Enlisted Coventry. Resided at 84, East Street. Miller, Triumph works. Only son of Mrs. Munton, 84 East Street, Coventry. Commemorated Triumph and Gloria Memorial. Memorial Ref. Panel 9. Basra Memorial, Iraq.(Possibly buried Baghdad Cemetery).

SMITH, Second Lieutenant, Reginald Iredale. 10th Bn., Argyll and Sutherland Highlanders. Killed in action, Deville Wood, 18th July, 1916. Age 20. Son of Mr. and Mrs. James Laurence Smith, of Rayrigg Hall, Windermere. Born 20th September, 1895 at Workington. Resided Workington. Pupil at Daimler Limited. Enlisted September, 1914. Memorial Ref. Pier and Face 15 A and 16 C. Thiepval Memorial, Somme, France.

SMITH, Private, Richard Lewis. 985, 1st Bn., Royal Warwickshire Regiment. Died of wounds (received in Ypres), home, 24th May, 1915. Age 21. Son of Company Sergeant Major R. Smith and Mrs. Smith, of Guernsey. Born 7th February, 1894 at Gosport. Resided at 144, Cross Road. Polisher. Enlisted August, 1914. Grave Ref. 1319. Fort Pitt Cemetery, Chatham.

SMITH, Private, Roy Basil Ireland. PLY/247(S), 2nd Royal Marine Bn., Royal Naval Division, Royal Marine Light Infantry. Killed in action, 27th March, 1918. Born 8th December, 1897. Resided at 63, Earlsdon Street. Planer. Enlisted September, 1917. Memorial Ref. Bay 1. Arras Memorial, France.

SMITH, S. E. Employed by Humber Limited. Killed in action.

SMITH, Sergeant, Samuel Arthur., 91889, "D" Bty, 62nd Brigade, Royal Field Artillery. Killed in action, 2nd August, 1917. Age 25. Only son of Arthur and Rosa Smith, of 22, Clarendon Street, Earlsdon, Coventry. Native of Gainsborough. Born 10th September 1892, at Gainsborough, Lincolnshire. Resided at 22 Clarendon Street. Machine Tool Maker. Enlisted Coventry, August, 1914. Commemorated War Memorial Park. Grave Ref. I. J. 8. Tilloy British Cemetery, Tilloy-Les-Mofflaines, Pas de Calais, France.

SMITH, Samuel Charles. Killed in action. Name on Roll of Honour in Cathedral Church of St. Michael.

SMITH, Private, Stewart. 15/1103, 15th Bn., Royal Warwickshire Regiment. Killed in action, 4th June, 1916. Age 22. Son of Mr. and Mrs. A. Harrison Smith, of "Bodowen," Orphanage Rd., Erdington, Birmingham. Born Manchester. Resided Birmingham. Draughtsman employed by Coventry Corporation, Gas Dept. Grave Ref. I. C. 57. Faubourg D'Amiens Cemetery, Arras, France.

SMITH, Sergeant, Sydney Harry. G/53674, 1st/19th Bn., London Regiment. Died of wounds, 24th August, 1918. Age 24. Son of Harry Daulby Smith and Sarah Ann Smith, of 28, Berkeley Road, Earlsdon, Coventry. Born in 1894, in Northampton. Resided at Coventry. Enlisted Northampton. Commemorated St. Barbara's Church and War Memorial Park. Grave Ref. VI. B. 29. Daours Communal Cemetery Extension, Somme, France.

SMITH, Corporal, Thomas, MM. 265979, 2/7th Bn., Royal Warwickshire Regiment. Died of wounds, 28th October, 1918. Resided Stoke, Coventry. Gazetted for Military Medal, 29th August, 1918. Grave Ref. II. F. 28. Awoingt British Cemetery, France.

SMITH, Lance Corporal, Thomas. 6379, 9th Bn., Royal Welsh Fusiliers. Killed in action, 11th August, 1916. Born Coventry. Enlisted Liverpool. Resided Coventry. Grave Ref. VII. D. 8. La Laiterie Military Cemetery, Belgium.

SMITH, Private, Thomas. 20912, 1/8th Bn., Royal Warwickshire Regiment. Died of wounds, 7th October, 1916. Age 26. Son of Annie Clayton, of 1/129, Sandpits, Birmingham. Born Birmingham. Resided Birmingham. Employed Coventry. Grave Ref. I. H. 2. Warlincourt Halte British Cemetery, Saulty, France.

SMITH, Second Lieutenant, Thomas Eli. Royal Air Force formerly Private, Worcestershire Regiment. Killed accidentally whilst flying at Thetford, 11th June, 1918. Age 24. Eldest son of George and Edith M. Smith, of Mount Pleasant, Walsgrave-on-Sowe, Coventry. Born 4th June, 1894 at Walsgrave-on-Sowe. Clerk. Enlisted August, 1914. Clerk, Laying Department, Humber Works. Commemorated Walsgrave Memorial and British Thompson Houston Memorial. Grave Ref. In South-West part. Wyken (St. Mary Magdalene) Churchyard.

SMITH, Private, Thomas Henry. 11221, Royal Fusiliers. transf. to (275716), Labour Corps. Died of wounds, 17th March 1918. Age 32. Son of Mr. and Mrs. Lewin, of High Street, Braunston. Husband of Maria Clarke (formerly Smith), of Low Common, Walsgrave, Coventry. Grave Ref. Braunston (All Saints) Churchyard Extension, Daventry, Northamptonshire.

SMITH, Corporal, Thomas Joseph, MM. 618345, "A" Bty. 298th Bde., Royal Field Artillery. Died of wounds, 22nd March, 1918. Born 24th October, 1888 at Stoke, Coventry. Resided at 2, Kingsway. Draughtsman. Enlisted 5th August, 1914. Awarded the Military Medal for conspicuous conduct and attending the wounded under heavy fire. Employed British Thompson Houston Ltd. Grave Ref. I. E. 21. Ham British Cemetery, Muille Villette, France.

SMITH, Private, Thomas William Edward. 10456, 9th Bn., Royal Fusiliers formerly Army Ordnance Corps. Killed in action, 22nd July, 1916. Age 23. Son of John and Harriet Smith. Born 24th March, 1895 at Swynford, Leicestershire. Resided Coventry. Railway Clerk. Enlisted February, 1916. Memorial Ref. Pier and Face 8 C 9 A and 16 A. Thiepval Memorial, Somme, France.

SMITH, Private, Tom. 36359, 12th Coy., Machine Gun Corps (Infantry) formerly Royal Warwickshire Regiment. Killed in action, by a shell, 3rd May, 1917. Age 27. Son of Mr. and Mrs. John Smith, of Waste Lane, Balsall Common, Coventry. Born 22nd February, 1890 at Beausale near Warwick. Resided 58, Cromwell Street. Van salesman. Enlisted December, 1915. Memorial Ref. Bay 10. Arras Memorial, Pas De Calais, France.

SMITH, Private, W. H. 19966, 11th Bn., Sherwood Foresters. Killed in action, 1st July, 1916. Born at Worksop, Nottinghamshire. Employed Coventry. Memorial Ref. Pier and Face 10 C 10 D and 11 A. Thiepval Memorial, Somme, France.

SMITH, Private, Walter. 7270, C Coy., 1st Bn., Royal Warwickshire Regiment. Killed in action, 25th April, 1915. Age 41. Husband of Mary A. Bibb (formerly Smith), of 31, Beale Street, Aston, Birmingham. Relative of Mr. Dagley, 230 Lockhurst Lane, Coventry. Memorial Ref. Panel 8. Ypres (Menin Gate) Memorial, Belgium.

SMITH, Lance Corporal, Walter. 4480, 1st Bn., Royal Warwickshire Regiment. Killed in action, 10th May, 1917. Born Bedworth. Enlisted Nuneaton. Resided Coventry. Commemorated Saint Thomas the Apostle, Longford. Grave Ref. II. B. 25. Crump Trench British Cemetery, Fampoux, France.

SMITH, Private, Walter Thomas. 306768, 1st /8th Bn., Royal Warwickshire Regiment. Died of wounds, 1st September, 1917. Age 23. Son of Annie and Alfred Smith, of 83, Godiva Street, Coventry. Born 8th April, 1894 at Stoke, Coventry. Dairyman. Enlisted March, 1915. Commemorated Stoke (St. Michael's) Church. Grave Ref. IV. D. 13. Dozinghem Military Cemetery, Poperinge, West-Vlaanderen, Belgium.

SMITH, Private, William. 15432, 10th Bn., Royal Warwickshire Regiment. Killed in action, 3rd July, 1916. Born Meriden. Resided Meriden. Employed Coventry. Memorial Ref. Pier and Face 9 A 9 B and 10 B. Thiepval Memorial, Somme, France.

SMITH, Private, William. 48109, 13th Bn., Royal Inniskilling Fusiliers formerly 23134, Royal Warwickshire Regiment. Killed in action, 19th July, 1918. Born Exhall. Enlisted Warwick. Resided Coventry. Grave Ref. II. D. 13. Borre British Cemetery, France.

SMITH, Private, William Harvey. 10417, 2nd Bn., South Wales Borderers. Killed in action, 25th April, 1915. Billeted Coventry. Memorial Ref. Panel 80 to 84 or 219 and 220. Helles Memorial, Turkey.

SMITH, William Henry. 10115, 11th Bn., Royal Warwickshire Regiment. Killed in action, 24th September, 1917. Age 25. Son of William Henry and Jane Smith. Born 9th January, 1892 at Coventry. Resided at 20, Bradford Street. Carpet Weaver. Enlisted January, 1915 at Coventry. Memorial Ref. Panel 23 to 28 and 163A. Tyne Cot Memorial, Belgium.

SMITH, Sergeant, William John. 28048, 14th Bn., Royal Warwickshire Regiment. Killed in action, 7th May, 1917. Born Birmingham. Resided 45, Well Street. Memorial Ref. Bay 3. Arras Memorial, France.

SMITHSON, Private, George. 10088, 11th Bn., Royal Warwickshire Regiment. Killed in action, 15th July, 1916. Born 12th December, 1893 at Copsewood Grange, Stoke. Resided 51, Hamilton Road. Gardener. Enlisted December, 1914. Commemorated Stoke (St. Michaels) Church. Memorial Ref. Pier and Face 9 A 9 B and 10 B. Thiepval Memorial, Somme, France.

SMYTHE, Private, George Thomas. 15777, 7th Bn., Leicestershire Regiment. Killed in action, 22nd March, 1918. Age 32. Husband of Mrs. Dorothy Elsie Isabel Manderfield (formerly Smythe), of 10, Chapel Street, Shepshed, Leicestershire. Born Coventry. Enlisted Coalville, Leics. Memorial Ref. Panel 29 and 30. Pozieres Memorial, France.

SMYTHE, Captain, Rudolph Meade. 5th Bn., Bedfordshire Regiment. Killed in action, 14th September, 1915. Shot in the head by a sniper and did not regain consciousness, died at 16th Casualty Clearing Station. Born 15th June, 1885 at Caxton. Eldest son of the Reverend Henry Meade and Fanny Smythe (nee Pritchard). Educated at King Henry VIII School, 1894 to 1902. Employed Barclays Bank. Commemorated King Henry VIII School. Memorial Ref. Panel 54 and 218 Helles Memorial, Turkey.

SNAITH, Gunner, Thomas Henry. 2546, 4th Bty., Machine Gun Corps (Motors). Killed in action, 29th April, 1918. Born Elsdon, Northumberland. Enlisted Coventry. Resided Elsdon, Northumberland. Grave Ref. IIA. E. 1. Wytschaete Military Cemetery, Belgium.

SNOW, Private, Charles Richard. 266577, 1/7th Bn., Royal Warwickshire Regiment. Died of wounds, 14th August, 1917. Age 21. Son of Albert and Mary E. Snow, of Moat Road, Taynton, nr. Gloucester. Born in 1896 at Gloucester. Resided the Butts. Dairyman. Enlisted May, 1915 at Coventry. Grave Ref. VI. E. 14. Brandhoek New Military Cemetery, Belgium.

SOUSTER, Private, Albert George. 109743, 12th Bn., Machine Gun Corps (Tanks) formerly Royal Field Artillery. Killed in action, 29th August, 1918. Born 24th May, 1898 at Rugby. Resided Rugby. Railway Clerk. Enlisted February, 1917. Memorial Ref. Panel 11. Vis-En-Artois Memorial, France.

SOUTH, Private, Amos Joseph. 20742, 1/6th Bn., Royal Warwickshire Regiment. Died of wounds, 6th February, 1917. Age 28. Son of Joseph T. and H. South, of 795, Foleshill Road, Coventry. Born 1889. Resided at 795, Foleshill Road. Employed Messrs. Courtaulds Ltd. Enlisted 13th March, 1916 at Coventry. Grave Ref. I. D. 2. Bray Military Cemetery, Bray-sur-Somme, France.

SOUTHAM, Private, William. 6734, 1st Bn., Royal Warwickshire Regiment. Killed in action, 25th April, 1915. Age 34. Son of Mrs. J. E. Davis, of 130, Red Lane, Coventry. Born 1881 at Coventry. Enlisted Coventry. Memorial Ref. Panel 8. Ypres (Menin Gate) Memorial, Ieper, West-Vlaanderen, Belgium.

SOWTER, Private, Albert Harold. 41023, 6th Bn., Dorsetshire Regiment. Killed in action, 16th October, 1918. Age 19. Son of Mrs. M. Sowter, of Back 44, Spon Street, Coventry. Born 16th March 1899 at Coventry. Resided at 44, Meadow Street. Turner, Siddeley works. Enlisted April 1918, Coventry. Commemorated St. John's Church, War Memorial Park and Siddeley Roll of Honour. Memorial Ref. Panel 7. Vis-En-Artois Memorial, Pas De Calais, France.

SPARKES, Gunner, Arthur Ernest. 840200, . Killed in action, Ypres, 18th August, 1917. Born 17th September 1896, at 19c. 6h., Much Park Street. Resided at 82, Much Park Street. Turner. Enlisted Coventry, August 1914. Commemorated War Memorial Park. Grave Ref. Plot VII. Row C. Grave 12. Vlamertinghe New Military Cemetery, Belgium.

SPARKES, Lance Corporal, Edward. 8987, 1st Bn., Royal Warwickshire Regiment. Died of wounds, 10th May, 1915. Age 34. Son of Sarah Sparkes, of Payne Lane, Coventry. Born 1st August, 1880 at Sheffield. Resided Coventry. Cycle Hand. Reservist. Enlisted Coventry. Commemorated Dunlop Memorial. Grave Ref. I. G. 11. Wimereux Communal Cemetery, Pas de Calais, France.

SPARKES, Corporal, William Henry. 24280, 10th Bn., Royal Warwickshire Regiment. Killed in action, Cambrai, 23rd March, 1918. Born 13th June, 1877 at Sheffield. Resided at 87, Chandos Street. Cycle Liner. Enlisted February, 1917 at Coventry. Memorial Ref. Bay 3. Arras Memorial, France.

SPARROW, Private, Walter. 16030, 5th Coy., Machine Gun Corps (Infantry) formerly 12316, Oxfordshire & Buckinghamshire Light Infantry. Died of wounds, 21st November, 1916. Wounded 14th November. Born 14th December, 1897 at 7, Tower Street, Coventry. Enlisted Coventry. Resided at 79, St. Georges Road. Fitter, Singer and Co. Ltd. Enlisted August, 1914. Grave Ref. III. F. 5. Warlincourt Halte British Cemetery, Saulty, France.

SPENCER, Private, Albert Edward. 59362, 1/8th Bn., Worcestershire Regiment. Killed in action, 4th November, 1918. Age 19. Son of William P. and E. Spencer, of 3, Cooperation Street, Enderby, Leicester. Born 9th March, 1899 in Station Street, Coventry. Resided at 104, Lockhurst Lane. Miller. Enlisted June, 1918. Enlisted Coventry. Grave Ref. I. I. 1. Cross Roads Cemetery, Fontaine-Au-Bois, France.

SPENCER, Second Lieutenant, Charles Herbert Slingsby. "C" Bty. 330th Bde., Royal Field Artillery. Killed in action, 5th October, 1918. Age 25. Husband of Gertrude Mary Spencer, of 94, Ashbourne Road, Aigburth, Liverpool. Born 7th May, 1893 at London. Resided Leamington. Apprentice Britannia Foundry Company Ltd. Enlisted August, 1914. Grave Ref. III. E. 2. Pont d'Achellles Military Cemetery, Nieppe, France.

SPENCER, Lance Corporal, James Thomas. 2610, 1st /7th Bn., Royal Warwickshire Regiment. Killed in action, Hebuterne, 1st July, 1916. Age 29. Son of Thomas and Hannah Elizabeth Spencer, of 12, Drapers Field, Coventry. Born 7th January, 1888 in Leicester Street. Resided at 12, Drapers Field. Machinist. Enlisted September, 1914. Memorial Ref. Pier and Face 9 A 9 B and 10 B. Thiepval Memorial, Somme, France.

SPENCER, Private, John. 155729, 30th Bn., Machine Gun Corps formerly Royal Warwickshire Regiment. Killed in action, 2nd August, 1918. Age 38. Son of Mary Spencer of Stockingford and Henry Spencer. Husband of Isabella Spencer of 44 Church Road, Stockingford. Educated Bablake School. Born 16th October, 1880 at Stocklingford. Brewer's Agent. Commemorated Bablake School Memorial. Grave Ref. VI. E. 9. La Clytte Military Cemetery, Reninghelst, Belgium.

SPENCER, Private, John Thomas. 35911, 14th Bn., Worcestershire Regiment. Killed in action, Grandcourt, 5th February, 1917. Son of John Henry and Elizabeth Spencer, of 67, Park Road, Bedworth, Warwickshire. Born 6th November, 1897 at Bedworth. Resided at 67, Park Road, Bedworth. Employed by Coventry Ordnance Works Ltd and formerly Courtaulds. Enlisted August, 1916 at Coventry. Memorial Ref. Pier and Face 5 A and 6 C. Thiepval Memorial, Somme, France.

SPENCER, Private, Joseph. 266505, 1/6th Bn., Royal Warwickshire Regiment. Killed in action, 19th June, 1917. Brother of Mr. W. Spencer, 28, Hertford Place. Born Burton-on-Trent, Staffs. Enlisted Coventry. Memorial Ref. Bay 3. Arras Memorial, France.

SPENCER, Private, Samuel. 2052, B Coy., 2nd Bn., Royal Warwickshire Regiment. Killed in action, 24th October, 1914. Age 25. Son of John and Jemima Spencer, of 250, Marston Lane, Marston Jabbett, Nuneaton. Brother of Mrs. Gibbs, Rowley's Green, Foleshill. A native of Hangingheaton, Dewsbury, Yorkshire. Enlisted in Nuneaton. Resided Bedworth. Memorial Ref. Panel 8. Ypres (Menin Gate) Memorial, Belgium.

SPENCER, Private, William Edward. 2191, 1/7th Bn., Royal Warwickshire Regiment. Killed in action, 26th June, 1916. Aged 18. Born 23rd December, 1898 at Winchester. Resided 23, Marlborough Road, Coventry. Liner, Employed Humber Works. Enlisted August, 1914 at Coventry. Commemorated Stoke (St. Michaels) Church. Grave Ref. I. E. 5. Hebuterne Military Cemetery, France.

SPICER, Gunner, Thomas. 259, 4th Warwick Bty., 4th South Midland Bde., Royal Field Artillery. Killed in action, by a shell, 31st January, 1916. Born 12th October, 1894 in Wellington Street. Resided at 42, Parkside. Engineer, Rover Works. Enlisted August, 1914 at Coventry. Employed Grave Ref. I. N. 18. Hebuterne Military Cemetery, France.

SPRAGG, Private, William Henry. 38076, 2/4th Bn., Somerset Light Infantry formerly 11864, Royal Warwickshire Regiment. Died of wounds, Egypt, 12th December, 1917. Age 29. Son of Henry and Emma Spragg, of 102 Boscombe Road, Greet, Birmingham. Born 2nd December, 1885 at Birmingham. Resided at 28, Hugh Road. Millwright. Enlisted May, 1915 at Coventry. Grave Ref. H. 52. Ramleh War Cemetery, Israel (Previously recorded as Junction Station Military Cemetery, Egypt).

SPRAGGITT, Private, George Leonard. 330794, 15th Bn., Royal Warwickshire Regiment. Died of wounds, 7th October 1917. Age 22. Only son of Benjamin and Harriett Spraggitt, of Rose Cottage, Keresley Heath, Coventry. Enlisted Coventry. Commemorated St. Thomas Memorial. Grave Ref. I. F. 5. Godewaersvelde British Cemetery, Nord, France.

SPRIGGS, Private, Alfred. 9278, 5th Bn., Worcestershire Regiment. Died, Home, 11th February, 1917. Born Walsall, Staffs. Enlisted Coventry. Resided Wolverhampton. Grave Ref. Mil. Con. C. 3497. Plymouth (Weston Mill) Cemetery.

SPRIGGS, Private, Alfred William. 55345, 9th Bn., Royal Fusiliers formerly 157697, Army Service Corps. Killed in action, 3rd May, 1917. Born Bruntingthorpe. Enlisted Coventry. Resided Coventry. Memorial Ref. Bay 3. Arras Memorial, France.

SPRIGGS, Gunner, Arthur Thomas. 64736, 42nd Bty., Royal Field Artillery. Died of wounds, 29th September, 1917. Enlisted Coventry. Resided Coventry. Grave Ref. I. M. 17. Choques Military Cemetery, France.

SPROUL, Leading Seaman, Benjamin. Royal Navy. Died, home, 14th June, 1920. Born 30th March, 1884 in Whitefriars Street. Resided Ryton-on-Dunsmore. Sailor. Grave Ref. Coventry (London Road) Cemetery.

SPROUL, Quartermaster Sergeant, Rochester Illingworth. S/20996, 1st Indian Div. Supply Col., Army Service Corps formerly Kings Royal Rifle Corps. Died of accidental injuries, 28th March, 1915. Age 36. Husband of M. E. Sproul, of 25, Dudley Road, Folkestone. Native of Coventry. Served in the South African Campaign. Born April, 1878 at Paisley. Resided Coventry. Butcher. Completed Apprenticeship with Mr. Weston. Reservist. Grave Ref. I. H. 3. Aire Communal Cemetery, Pas De Calais, France.

SQUIRE, Corporal, Arthur John. 200063, A Bn., Tank Corps. Killed in action, 20th November, 1917. Age 21. Son of Mrs. Bessie A. Squire of Castle Hill, Lynton, Devon. Born Lynton, Devon. Enlisted Coventry. Memorial Ref. Panel 13. Cambrai Memorial, Louveral, France.

SQUIRES, Sergeant, Edgar Cumberland. 9611, 1st Bn., Royal Warwickshire Regiment. Killed in action, 4th October, 1917. Born 14th May, 1897 at Ruddington, Nottinghamshire. Resided 28c. 2h. Gosford Street. Fitter, Humber Works. Enlisted December, 1914 at Coventry. Leaves a widow and four children. Grave Ref. XLV. A. 12. Poelcapelle British Cemetery, Belgium.

SQUIRES, Gunner, William Henry. 701, 4th South Midland Bde., Royal Field Artillery. Killed in action, 18th July, 1916. Born 22nd March, 1894 at Warwick. Enlisted January, 1915 at Coventry. Resided 13, Warwick Lane. Son of Mr. and Mrs. Squires Grey Friar's Lane. Machinist, Swift Works. Grave Ref. II. C. 15. Laventie Military Cemetery, La Gorgue, France.

STAFFORD, Private, Alfred Joseph. 9843, 10th Bn., Royal Warwickshire Regiment. Killed in action, 30th July, 1916. Born 14th June, 1894 at Whitley. Resided at 35, Castle Street. Cycle Liner. Enlisted December, 1914 at Coventry. Son of Mr. and Mrs. Stafford of 35, Castle Street. Employed O' Briens Ltd. Memorial Ref. Pier and Face 9 A 9 B and 10 B. Thiepval Memorial, Somme, France. (Possibly buried Bazentin-le-Petit Communal Cemetery)

STAGG, Sergeant, Arthur. 10224, 1st Bn., Royal Welsh Fusiliers. Died of wounds, 17th May, 1915. Age 23. Son of Mr. and Mrs. A. Stagg, of 10, Castle Street, Coventry. Husband of M. Box (formerly Stagg), of 11, Villiers Street, Wrexham. Born 12th March 1891 in Spon Street. Resided at 3c. 10h. Castle Street. Soldier. Enlisted Coventry. Commemorated War Memorial Park. Grave Ref. III. D. 71. Bethune Town Cemetery, Pas De Calais, France.

STAGG, Private, William. 8936, 9th Bn., Royal Warwickshire Regiment. Killed in action, Gallipoli, 8th August, 1915. Age 22. Son of Mr. and Mrs. A. Stagg, of 3 Court, 10 House, Castle Street, Coventry. Born 6th December in Well Street. Resided at 3C. 10h., Castle Street. Hardener. Enlisted August 1914. Commemorated War Memorial Park. Memorial Ref. Panel 35 to 37. Helles Memorial, Turkey.

STANLEY, Rifleman, Frederick Richard. R/721, 7th Bn., King's Royal Rifle Corps. Killed in action, 30th July, 1915. Age 26. Son of Mr. and Mrs. Thomas Stanley, of Hawkeswell, Coleshill, Birmingham. Born Coventry. Enlisted Nuneaton. Resided Birmingham. Memorial Ref. Panel 51 and 53. Ypres (Menin Gate) Memorial, Belgium.

STANLEY, Private, Harry. 1702, 10th Bn., Royal Warwickshire Regiment. Killed in action, 23rd March, 1918. Born Anstey, Warwicks. Enlisted Coventry. Grave Ref. II. D. 9. Harlebebke New British Cemetery, Belgium.

STANLEY, Private, John. 177028, 287th Coy., Machine Gun Corps formerly 204547, Oxfordshire and Buckinghamshire Light Infantry. Died India, 17th October, 1918. Age 20. Born Foleshill. Commemorated Saint Thomas the Apostle, Longford. Memorial Ref. Face E. Kirkee 191 – 1918 Memorial, India.

STANLEY, Sergeant, John T. 2321, A Coy., 11th Bn., Royal Warwickshire Regiment. Killed in action, 1st October, 1916 by a shell burst in the trench. Husband of Ellen Elizabeth Stanley, of 15, Weston Street, Coventry. Born 7th March, 1817 at St. Nicholas, Coventry. Enlisted September, 1914 at Warwick. Resided 15, Weston Street, Coventry. Wheel Truer, Rudge Whitworth Works. Served 16 years with the Volunteers. Left a widow and four children. Grave Ref. J. 17. Tranchee De Mecknes Cemetery, Aix-Noulette, Pas De Calais, France.

STANLEY, Private, William Joseph. 41541, Devonshire Regiment. transf. to (141531), Labour Corps, formerly 41541, Devon Regiment. Died of pneumonia, home, 14th October, 1917. Age 28. Son of Thomas and Maria Stanley, of Coventry. Born 16th January, 1889 at 6, Mill Terrace, Coventry. Enlisted September, 1916 at Coventry. Resided at 12, Godiva Street. Mechanic. Grave Ref. 126. 207. Coventry (London Road) Cemetery.

STANNARD, Able Seaman, Harry Bridges. J/12822, HMS Vanguard, Royal Navy. Killed by internal explosion of vessel at Scapa Flow, 9th July, 1917. Age 24. Son of Charles Albert and Hannah Elizabeth Stannard, of 28, Kingsland Avenue, Earlsdon, Coventry. Memorial Ref. 22. Chatham Naval Memorial, Kent.

STANTON, Private, Frank Montague. 8815, 2nd Bn., Royal Warwickshire Regiment. Killed in action, 31st October, 1914. Employed Coventry Chain Ltd. Resided Spon Street, Coventry. Sister resided 39, Lower Ford Street, Coventry. Memorial Ref. Panel 8. Ypres (Menin Gate) Memorial, France.

STANWAY, Corporal, Herbert William. 265295, 7th Bn., Royal Warwickshire Regiment. Killed in action, 19th July, 1916. Born 3rd May, 1897 at Frazerburgh, Scotland. Resided 36, Sherbourne Street. Machine Tool Maker, Coventry Chain. Appeal by Miss. A. Dagley of 26, Meadow Street, Coventry. Enlisted August, 1914 at Coventry. Commemorated Coventry Chain Memorial. Memorial Ref. Panel 22 to 25. Loos Memorial, France

STAPLES, Sergeant, Charles Victor. 11661, 47th Coy., Machine Gun Corps (Infantry) formerly Royal Field Artillery. Killed in action, 16th August, 1917. Son of Walter Staples, of 36, Hill Road, Keresley, Coventry. Born Leicester. Enlisted Lichfield. Resided Kingsbury. Memorial Ref. Panel 154 to 159 and 163A. Tyne Cot Memorial, Zonnebeke, West-Vlaanderen, Belgium.

STAPLETON, Boatswain (Bosun) Frank Thomas (Served as Webb). SS Cape Finisterre (Glasgow), Mercantile Marine. Drowned, as a result of an attack by an enemy submarine, 2nd November, 1917. Age 53. Born at Coventry. Memorial Ref. Tower Hill Memorial, London.

STATHAM, Private, Arthur. 17141, 8th Bn., East Yorkshire Regiment. Killed in action, 26th September, 1915. Born Coventry. Enlisted Newcastle-on-Tyne. Resided Coventry. Born 29th November, 1884 in Coventry Street. Turner. Enlisted 1914. Memorial Ref. Panel 40 and 41. Loos Memorial, France.

STATHAM, Private, Ephraim. A/21767, 10th Bn., Cheshire Regiment. Died of wounds, 15th September, 1916. Born in 1889 in St. Peter's Parish. Employed by the Daimler Company Ltd. Enlisted December, 1914 at Coventry. Resided 9, Sovereign Row, Coventry. Grave Ref. IV. C. 33. Puchevillers British Cemetery, France.

STEAD, Private, Thomas. M2/118633, 605th Mechanical Transport Coy., Army Service Corps. Died, At Sea, 8th January, 1916. Age 31. Son of Thomas and Lucy Stead. Husband of Ethel Stead of 155, Oxford Street, Grimsby. Born Lincoln. Enlisted Coventry. Resided Grimsby. Grave Ref. 14. G. 14. Bari War Cemetery, Italy.

STEBBING, Gunner, Sydney Reginald. 181, 3rd Battery, Machine Gun Corps (Motors). Died of wounds received at Zonnebeke by maxim fire, the previous day, died 4th May, 1915. Age 21. Son of Edwin Robert and Annabella Rebecca Stebbing, of 100, Craven Road, Rugby. Born at 3rd October, 1893 in Springfield Terrace, Coventry. Resided at Coventry. Machine Tool Maker, Rudge Works. Enlisted 28th November 1915 at Coventry. Commemorated War Memorial Park. Grave Ref. II. D. 9. Hazebrouck Communal Cemetery, Nord, France.

STEELE, J. Employed Humber Limited. Killed in action.

STEELEY, Sergeant, Alfred Walter. C/291, 16th Bn., King's Royal Rifle Corps. Killed in action, 23rd April, 1917. Born Coventry. Enlisted Nuneaton. Memorial Ref. Bay 7. Arras Memorial, France.

STEELEY, Gunner, Herbert Walter. 58396, 9th Div. Ammunition Col., Royal Field Artillery. Drowned in La Bassee Canal, 3rd July, 1915. Age 27. Son of Mr. and Mrs. C. Steeley, of Old House Lane, Corley, Coventry. Husband of Elizabeth Steeley, of Stone House, Red Hill, Fillongley. Born 22nd November, 1887 at Corley, Coventry. Enlisted December, 1914 at Coventry. Grave Ref. 11. Robecq Communal Cemetery, France.

STEVENS, Private, Henry George. 28659, 6th Bn., Somerset Light Infantry formerly 35213, Wiltshire Regiment. Killed in action, 21st March, 1918. Born Leighton Buzzard, Bedfordshire. Enlisted Coventry. Grave Ref. I. H. 35. St. Souplet British Cemetery, France.

STEVENS, Private, J. 205731, 4th Bn., Devonshire Regiment. Died, home, 17th June, 1917. Grave Ref. 194. 146. Coventry (London Road) Cemetery.

STEVENS, Private, John Alfred. 7680, B Coy., 2nd Bn., Royal Warwickshire Regiment. Died of wounds, 6th October, 1917 in the 37th Clearing Station. Aged 22. Son of John and Emma Stevens. Resided Woodlands Lane, Bedworth. Born Newtown, Leicester. Enlisted September, 1914 at Rugby. Previously employed at Binley Colliery. Grave Ref. I. N. 34. Godewaersvelde British Cemetery, France.

STEVENS, Private, Percy. 328, Australian Naval and Military Expeditionary Force. Died, due to Dysentery at Rabaul, 7th May, 1915. Australian Naval and Military Expeditionary Force. Born Coventry. Brother of Alice Stevens of Hollybank, Earlsdon, Coventry. Enlisted 8th January, 1915. Grave Ref. AA. B. 6. Rabaul (Bita Paka) War Cemetery, Papua New Guinea.

STEVENSON, A. Commemorated Coventry Chain Memorial.

STEVENSON, Private, Harry. 1722, A Coy., 2nd Bn., Royal Warwickshire Regiment. Believed killed, 16th May, 1915. Age 24. Son of Michael and Ellen Stevenson, of 41, Eagle Street, Coventry. Born 30th May, 1892 at Foleshill, Coventry. Resided Coventry. Fitter. Enlisted August, 1914 at Coventry. Memorial Ref. Panel 6. Le Touret Memorial, Pas De Calais, France.

STEW, Private, Joseph. 43258, 8th Bn., Royal Berkshire Regiment. Killed in action, 23rd October, 1918. Age 29. Son of Mr. and Mrs. Thomas Stew, of 266, Hall Green, Foleshill, Coventry. Born in 1883 at Coleshill. Resided at Coventry. Enlisted Warwick. Commemorated War Memorial Park. Grave Ref. XI. A. 11. Highland Cemetery, Le Cateau, Nord, France.

STEW, Private, Thomas. 306495, 1st /8th Bn., Royal Warwickshire Regiment. Killed in action, 1st July, 1916. Age 22. Son of William and Jane Stew, Rowley's Green, Foleshill, Coventry. Enlisted 10th February, 1916 at Coventry. Employed Messrs. Courtaulds Ltd. Appeal by Miss S. Lawrence, 121, Broad Street, Coventry. Memorial Ref. Pier and Face 9 A 9 B and 10 B. Thiepval Memorial, Somme, France.

STEWART, Thomas. F. Killed in action. Name on Roll of Honour in Cathedral Church of St. Michael.

STILES, Company Sergeant Major, William. 1323, 2nd Bn., Royal Warwickshire Regiment. Died of wounds, 26th July, 1917. Age 26. Brother of Mrs. E. L. Thornley, of Mill House, Gulsa Road, Coventry. Born 27th December, 1891 at Sherbourne, near Warwick. Resided at 5, Passes Row, Station Street West. Soldier. Enlisted Coventry. Grave Ref. I. O. 26. Achiet-Le-Grand Communal Cemetery Extension, Pas de Calais, France

STOCKLEY, Private, George. 23058, 3rd Bn., King's Own Hussars. Died of wounds, 29th March, 1918. Born 1895 at Coventry. Enlisted Coventry. Resided Woollaston. Employed Daimler Company Ltd. Commemorated St. Johns Church. Grave Ref. C. 36. Evreux Communal Cemetery, France.

STOCKTON, Lance Corporal, Richard Henry. 14818, 14th Bn., Royal Warwickshire Regiment. Killed in action, 22nd June, 1917. Born Birmingham. Resided Stoke, Coventry. Enlisted Warwick. Grave Ref. IX. A. 24. Orchard Dump Cemetery, Arleux-En-Gohelle, France.

STOKES, Able Seaman, Arthur Edward. SS/1320, HMS Good Hope. Killed in action, Naval Battle of Coronel, 1st November, 1914. Age 25. Son of George Thomas and Elizabeth Stokes, of Drayton, Uppingham, Rutland. Born in 1889 at Drayton road. Resided at 15, Croft Road. Chain Finisher. Commemorated Coventry Chain Memorial. Memorial Ref. 2. Portsmouth Naval Memorial.

STOKES, Charles. Commemorated Holy Trinity Panels.

STOKES, Lance Corporal, Charles Henry. R/1825, 11th Bn., King's Royal Rifle Corps. Killed in action, 10th August, 1917. Born St. Michaels, Coventry. Enlisted Nuneaton. Resided 2c. 4h. Castle Street, Coventry. Grave Ref. IV. B. 2. Artillery Wood Cemetery, Belgium.

STOKES, Private, Charles John. 42576, 3rd Bn., Worcestershire Regiment. Killed in action, 7th June, 1917. Age 32. Son of William and Mary Stokes, of 6c. 1h. Chauntry Place. Husband of Alice Elizabeth Stokes, of 611, Chauntry Place, Coventry. Born 29th March, 1895 in Spon Street. Driller. Enlisted December, 1915. Memorial Ref. Panel 34. Ypres (Menin Gate) Memorial, Ieper, West-Vlaanderen, Belgium. (Possibly buried at St. Quentin).

STOKES, Private, George John. 11811, 1st Bn., Worcestershire Regiment. Killed in action, Neuve Chapelle, 11th December, 1914. Age 25. Son of William Thomas and Sarah Ann Stokes, of 45, Swanswell Street, Coventry. Born 19th January, 1888 at Coventry. Enlisted Coventry. Soldier. Commemorated War Memorial Park. Memorial Ref. Panel 17 and 18. Le Touret Memorial, Pas de Calais, France.

STOKES, Private, Herbert. 25347, 2/5th Bn., Gloucestershire Regiment. Killed in action, 1st November, 1918. Born Coventry. Enlisted Coventry. Born 6th March, 1896 at 2c. 7h. Chauntry Place. Resided at 22, Yardley Street. Painter. Enlisted November, 1916. Grave Ref. I. H. 18. Cross Roads Cemetery, Fontaine-Au-Bois, France.

STOKES, Private, John Thomas. 6505, 1st Bn., Northamptonshire Regiment. Killed in action, 30th November, 1914. Aged 33. Son of Henry Stokes and Elizabeth Ann Gilkes of 2, Hatter's Arms Yard, Leicester St., Bedworth. A native of Rushden, Northamptonshire. Enlisted Higham Ferrers, Northamptonshire. Soldier, formerly employed Mr. Herbert Goode, Builders of Foleshill. Memorial Ref. Panel 43 and 45. Ypres (Menin Gate) Memorial, Belgium.

STOKES, Private, William John. 12th Battalion Gloucestershire Regiment formerly 44875, Warwickshire Regiment. Killed in action, 23rd August, 1918. Born 12th January 1900, at 27, Peel Street, Foleshill. Resided at 24, Smith Street. Driller. Enlisted Warwick January 1918. Grave Ref. Plot III. Row F. Grave 3. Adanac Military Cemetery, Miraumont-Pys, France.

STONE, Private, Harold. 42745, 1/8th Bn., Royal Warwickshire Regiment. Died, 13th November, 1918. Age 23. Son of Percy Gregory and Margaret Stone. Born Derby. Enlisted Coventry. Grave Ref. 2454. Derby (Uttoxeter Road) Cemetery.

STONE, Private, John. 17700, 14th Bn., Royal Warwickshire Regiment. Killed in action, 3rd September, 1916. Born Leighton Buzzard, Beds. Enlisted Coventry. Grave Ref. XXVII. D. 4. Delville Wood Cemetery, Longueval, France.

STONE, Able Seaman, Thomas. M/9804, 2nd Royal Marine Bn., Royal Naval Division. Died of wounds, 5th April, 1918. Age 39. Employed Coventry. Grave Ref. I. J. 24. Gezaincourt Communal Cemetery Extension, France.

STONEHOUSE, Able Seaman, George. SS/4242, HMS Queen Elizabeth, Royal Navy. Died, 29th October, 1916. Age 21. Son of George James and Lizzie Stonehouse, of 73, Colony Cottages, Holbrook Lane, Foleshill, Coventry. Grave Ref. 648. Dalmeny And Queensferry Cemetery, West Lothian.

STONIER, Private, William. 55130, 23rd Bn., Machine Gun Corps formerly 20256, Royal Warwickshire Regiment. Killed in action, 23rd June, 1918. Age 34. Husband of Alice Stonier, of 152, Widdrington Road, Coventry. Born Macclesfield. Enlisted Warwick. Resided Coventry. Commemorated War Memorial Park. Grave Ref. Plot II. Row C. Grave 1. Granezza British Cemetery, Italy.

STOOK, Private, Albert Edgar. 307646, 1/8th Bn., Royal Warwickshire Regiment. Killed in action, 27th August, 1917. Age 27. Son of Thomas John and Rose Ann Stook of 74, Archers Road, Eastleigh, Hants. Born South Lambeth, Surrey. Enlisted Coventry. Memorial Ref. Panel 23 to 28 and 163A. Tyne Cot Memorial, Belgium.

STORR, Private, Albert Edward. 9208, 1st Bn., Royal Munster Fusiliers. Killed in action, 1st May, 1915. Native of Lower Sydenham, Kent. Friend of Miss Swalwell of Hope Street, Coventry. Billeted Coventry. Enlisted New Cross, Kent. Resided Lower Sydenham. Grave Ref. Special Memorial B. 107. V Beach Cemetery, Turkey.

STORR, Private, Harry. 10/890, 10th Bn., East Yorkshire Regiment. Killed in action, 4th June, 1916. Age 19. Son of Mr. S. Storr, of 30, Elmsdale Avenue, Foleshill Road, Little Heath, Coventry. Born Goole. Enlisted Hull. Resided Goole. Grave Ref. I. F. 40. Sucrerie Military Cemetery, Colincamps, Somme, France.

STRATTON, Lance Corporal, Herbert. G/14868, 13th Bn., Royal Sussex Regiment. Killed in action, British Expeditionary Force, 26th September, 1917. Age 20. Son of Henry and Mary Stratton. Born Coventry. Enlisted Luton. Memorial Ref. Panel 86 to 88. Tyne Cot Memorial, Belgium.

STRATTON, Gunner, John. 89426, 122nd Bty. 52nd Bde., Royal Field Artillery. Killed in action, 28th May, 1917. Born Coventry. Enlisted Birmingham. Grave Ref. II. A. 7. Elzenwalle Brasserie Cemetery, Belgium.

STRETTON, Lieutenant, Sidney. 66th Squadron, Royal Flying Corps. Killed whilst flying, 27th March, 1917. Age 28. Son of Benjamin and Frances Amelia Stretton, of Hammerwich House, nr. Lichfield, Staffs. Born at Derby. Born 1889. Resided in Ellys Road. Representative for Daimler Company Ltd in India. Grave Ref. II. A. 14. Doullens Communal Cemetery Extension No.1, France.

STRINGER, Lance Corporal, Leonard Frank. 307496, 10th Bn., Royal Warwickshire Regiment. Killed in action, 21st March, 1918. Son of Mr. H. Stringer, of 59, Mayfield Road, Earlsdon, Coventry. Born 5th October, 1891 in Hillfields. Hairdresser. Enlisted February, 1916 at Coventry. Grave Ref. III. A. 8. Bancourt British Cemetery, Pas de Calais, France.

STUART, Private, Arthur Charles. 4206, 2/7th Bn., Royal Warwickshire Regiment. Killed in action, near Ypres, 22nd August, 1916. Born 2nd March, 1899 at Coventry. Resided at 264, Narrow Lane. Grinder. Enlisted April, 1915 at Coventry. Commemorated Coventry Chain. Grave Ref. I. K. 13. Rue-Du-Bacquerot No.1 Military Cemetery, Laventie, France.

STUART, William Alexander B. Educated at King Henry VIII School, 1893 – 1901. Killed in action. Commemorated King Henry VIII School.

STUBBS, Private, James. 52494, 43rd Field Ambulance, Royal Army Medical Corps. Died of wounds, 8th September, 1917. Born Hurworth, Durham. Enlisted Newcastle. Resided Coventry. Grave Ref. IV. M. 7. A. Mont Huon Military Cemetery, Le Treport, France.

STUBBS, Private, Percy. 129169, 72nd Bn., Canadian Infantry (British Columbia Regiment). Killed in action, 9th April, 1917. Age 33. Son of Percy and Florence Stubbs, of Sheffield, England. Husband of Elizabeth Pleydell (formerly Stubbs), of 40, Humber Road, Coventry. Grave Ref. F. 25. Givenchy-En-Gohelle Canadian Cemetery, Souchez, Pas de Calais, France.

STURGESS, Lance Corporal, John Henry. 13975, 4th Bn., Coldstream Guards. Killed in action, 29th December, 1916. Age 24. Son of Mr. and Mrs. W. H. Sturgess of 14, Gentry Avenue, Lawrence Hil, Bristol. Born South Wigston, Leics. Enlisted Coventry. Resided S. Wigston, Leicester. Grave Ref. I. C. 16. Guards Cemetery, Combles, France.

STURMAN, Private, Sidney. 242502, 2/6th Bn., Royal Warwickshire Regiment. Killed in action, 6th September, 1917. Age 19. Son of James M. and Annie Sophia Sturman of Ferndale, Exeter Street, Kettering. Enlisted Coventry. Resided Whitley. Memorial Ref. Panel 23 to 28 and 163A. Tyne Cot Memorial, Belgium.

STYLES, Private, Arthur Edward. 10155, 14th Bn., Royal Warwickshire Regiment. Killed in action, 30th July, 1916 near Longueval. Born 1st December, 1877 at Coventry. Enlisted December, 1914 at Birmingham. Resided Birmingham. Enameller and Liner. Memorial Ref. Pier and Face 9 A 9 B and 10 B. Thiepval Memorial, Somme, France.

SUDDENS, Company Sergeant Major, Alfred J. 200849, 2/4th Bn., Oxfordshire and Buckinghamshire Light Infantry. Died whilst prisoner of war in German hands, 21st March, 1918. Enlisted Oxford. Resided Coventry. Born 1890. Educated Bablake School. School Teacher, Elementary School, Coventry. Commemorated Bablake School Memorial and Education Department Memorial, Coventry Corporation. Grave Ref. IV. B. 59. Premont British Cemetery, France.

SULLIVAN, Private, John. 3613, 1st Bn., Royal Warwickshire Regiment. Killed in action, 11th May, 1915. Born Huntingdon. Enlisted Coventry. Resided Birmingham. Memorial Ref. Panel 8. Ypres (Menin Gate) Memorial, Belgium.

SULLIVAN, Second Lieutenant, Timothy. 1st Bn., Royal Munster Fusiliers. Killed in action, 4th May, 1915. Age 31. Son of Michael Sullivan, of Bantry, Co. Cork. Husband of Maud Sullivan (nee Bates) of the Albany Hotel, Coventry. Served in the South African War. Billeted Coventry, January, 1915 to March, 1915. Memorial Ref. Panel 185 to 190. Helles Memorial, Turkey.

SUNNER, Company QuarterMaster Sergeant, Harry. 4932, 1st Bn., Royal Munster Fusiliers. Killed in action, 2nd May, 1915. Age 37. Billeted Coventry with Miss Yardley, Cox Street. Son of James and Frances Sunner, of James St, Mount Morgan, Queensland, Australia. Served in the South African War and on the North West Frontier of India. Memorial Ref. Panel 185 to 190. Helles Memorial, Turkey.

SUTHERLAND, Private, Thomas. 267960, 2/7th Bn., Royal Warwickshire Regiment. Killed in action, 14th April, 1918. Age 37. Born Leamington Spa. Enlisted Coventry. Resided Leamington Spa. Memorial Ref. Panel 2 and 3. Ploegsteert Memorial, Belgium.

SUTTON, Sapper, Aleck. 155608, 459th Field Coy., Royal Engineers. Died of appendicitis, 21st May, 1918. Age 30. Son of Harry Sutton, of Bocking, Essex. Husband of Annie Maud Sutton, of 427, Foleshill Road, Coventry, Warwick. Born 27th August 1887 Bocking, Essex. Enlisted Warwick. Commemorated War Memorial Park. Grave Ref. II. D. 13. Esquelbecq Military Cemetery, Nord, France.

SUTTON, Company Sergeant Major, Hugh Hinds. 205082, Tank Corps formerly 182, Mounted Machine Gun Corps, Royal Field Artillery. Died of pneumonia, 12th October, 1918. Age 35. Son of William Sutton, of Coventry. Born St. Michael's Parish. Resided at 15, Albany Road. Enlisted Coventry. Commemorated Holy Trinity Panels. Grave Ref. 54. 6. Coventry (London Road) Cemetery.

SWADLING, Private, Robert. 16452, 15th Bn., Royal Warwickshire Regiment. Died of wounds, 8th October, 1917. Age 22. son of Mr. and Mrs. Robert John Swadling of Stoke Row Farm, Stoke Row, Henley-on-Thames. Enlisted Coventry. Resided Bampton, Oxon. Born Laleham. Grave Ref. I. N. 42. Godewaersvelde British Cemetery, France.

SWAIN, Private, Frank, 242105, 2nd Bn., Suffolk Regiment formerly 6135, Suffolk Regiment. Killed in action, near Arras, 28th February, 1918. Age 19. Son of Albert Swain, of 17, Mulliner Street, Coventry. Born 23rd January 1899 at 234, Stoney Stanton Road, Coventry. Enlisted October, 1916 at Coventry. Moulder. Grave Ref. Wancourt Road Cem. No. 2 Mem., Panel 2. London Cemetery, Neuville-Vitasse, Pas de Calais, France.

SWAIN, Private, Oliver. 9814, 4th Bn., Worcestershire Regiment. Killed in action, Gallipoli, 6th August, 1915. Age 16. Born Coventry. Enlisted August, 1914 at Coventry. Resided 8, Clarence Street. Assistant in Plating shop, Coventry Swaging Co. Memorial Ref. Panel 104 to 113. Helles Memorial, Turkey.

SWAINSTON, Private, William Ernest. 9486, 1st Bn., Royal Warwickshire Regiment. Killed in action, 26th July, 1915. Born 28th June, 1883 at Darlington, Yorks. Enlisted September, 1914 at Coventry. Resided Coventry. Engineer. Grave Ref. III. A. 9. Sucrerie Military Cemetery, Colincamps, France.

SWAN, Lance Corporal, Albert. S/420, 12th Bn., Rifle Brigade. Killed in action, 6th June, 1916. Born Ladywood, Birmingham. Resided Foleshill. Memorial Ref. Panel 46 - 48 and 50. Ypres (Menin Gate) Memorial, Belgium.

SWAN, Private, George Henry. 21045, 10th Bn., Worcestershire Regiment. Killed in action, 3rd July, 1916. Age 31. Son of William and Mary Ann Swan of 1, Cross Row, Warwick Road, Kenilworth. Born Birmingham. Enlisted Coventry. Resided Kenilworth. Memorial Ref. Pier and Face 5A and 6C. Thiepval Memorial, France.

SWEATMAN, Lance Corporal, William. R/725, 7th Bn., King's Royal Rifle Corps. Killed in action, Delville Wood, 18th August, 1916. Age 22. Son of William and Jane Sweatman, of Eastern Green, Allesley, Coventry. Born 29th August, 1893 at Eastern Green, Coventry. Enlisted September, 1914 at Nuneaton. Resided 54, Windsor Street, Coventry. Moulder, Rover Works Memorial Ref. Pier and Face 13 A and 13 B. Thiepval Memorial, Somme, France.

SWEET, Sidney. Killed in action. Name on Roll of Honour in cathedral Church of St. Michael.

SWIFT, Private, Ernest William.1785, Warwickshire Yeomanry. Killed in action, 21st August, 1915. Age 21. Son of Arthur Sydney and Matilda Swift, of 27, Highfield Street, Great Heath, Foleshill, Coventry. Born 13th January, 1893 at Bodicote, Oxon. Enlisted August, 1914 at Warwick. Resided Coventry. Engineer. Grave Ref. Special Memorial H. 8. Green Hill Cemetery, Turkey.

SWINGLER, Private, Frank. 11128, 5th Bn., Dorsetshire Regiment. Died of wounds, Gallipoli, 9th August 1915. Age 20. Son of John and Ellen, of 35, Bramble Street, Coventry. Born 8th January, 1894 at Coventry. Clerk. Enlisted September, 1914 at Nuneaton. Resided Coventry. Commemorated War Memorial Park and Transport Department Memorial, Coventry Corporation. Grave Ref. II. G. 11. Green Hill Cemetery, Turkey.

SWINGLER, Private, Percy. 268854, 1/7th Bn., Royal Warwickshire Regiment. Killed in action, 8th October, 1917. Born Stanton, Northants. Enlisted Coventry. Memorial Ref. Panel 23 to 28 and 163A. Tyne Cot Memorial, Belgium.

TABOR, Private, Alec John. 77460, 19th Bn., Durham Light Infantry formerly Army Service Corps. Killed in action, 29th March, 1918. Age 19. Son of George Sims Tabor and Mary Ann Tabor, of Lower Green. Woolscott, Rugby. Born Leamington. Resided 11, Station Cottages, Warwick Road. Auto machine setter. Enlisted February, 1917 at Coventry. Memorial Ref. Panel 68 to 72. Pozieres Memorial, France.

TALLIS, Private, Thomas. 4233, 2nd /7th Bn., Royal Warwickshire Regiment. Killed in action, 19th July, 1916. Age 19. Son of Harry and Zilla Tallis, of 118, Coventry Road, Bedworth, Nuneaton. Enlisted Coventry. Memorial Ref. Panel 22 to 25. Loos Memorial, Pas de Calais, France.

TAMS, Private, Henry Francis. 3343, 2nd /7th Bn., Royal Warwickshire Regiment. Died of wounds, 20th July, 1916. Age 19. Son of Charles J. and Elizabeth Tams, of 19, Broad Street, Coventry. Born 5th December, 1897 at Rugeley. Moulder. Enlisted November, 1914 at Coventry. Grave Ref. XI. B. 30. Merville Communal Cemetery, Nord, France.

TANDY, Corporal, Henry. 10598, 1st Bn. Worcestershire Regiment. Killed in action, 31st July, 1917. Age 27. Husband of Edith Tandy, of 7/147, Angelina Street, Highgate, Birmingham. Born Coventry. Enlisted Birmingham. Resided Birmingham. Memorial Ref. Panel 34. Ypres (Menin Gate) Memorial, Belgium.

TANSLEY, Private, Ernest. 49585, 21st Bn., Manchester Regiment. Killed in action, 24th October, 1917. Born 21st November, 1880 at 92, East Street, Coventry. Enlisted December, 1916 at Preston, Lancs. Resided Earlsdon, Coventry. Insurance Agent. Grave Ref. IV. 6. G. Perth Cemetery (China Wall), Belgium.

TANSLEY, Private, Percy William. 16758, 11th Bn., Royal Warwickshire Regiment. Killed in action, 15th July, 1916. Age 27. Eldest son of Mr. and Mrs. T. Tansley, of 34, Bedford Street, Coventry. Born 8th April, 1889 at Coventry. Enlisted February, 1916 at Coventry. Painter and decorator, Sidney Douglas. Enlisted February, 1916. Memorial Ref. Pier and Face 9 A 9 B and 10 B. Thiepval Memorial, Somme, France.

TANSLEY, Private, Walter. 19566, B Coy., 10th Bn., Cameroonians (Scottish Rifles) formerly 94135, Royal Field Artillery. Killed in action, Loos, 25th September, 1915. Born 18th February, 1884 in All Saints Parish. Resided at 13, Henry Street. Railway porter, Coventry Goods Station. Enlisted February, 1915 at Coventry. Memorial Ref. Panel 56 to 59. Loos Memorial, France.

TAPLEY, Corporal, William Harry. 10657, 5th Bn., Oxfordshire and Buckinghamshire Light Infantry. Killed in action, Battle of Messines, 3rd May, 1917. Son of William and Sophia Tapley, of Stowe Hill, Weedon, Northants. Born 31st August, 1892 at Stowe Hill, Weedon. Resided at 49, King William Street. Railway porter. Enlisted August, 1914 at Coventry. Memorial Ref. Bay 6 and 7. Arras Memorial, France.

TATE, Sergeant, William Frederick. 3075, 2nd Bn., Rifle Brigade. Killed in action, 9th May, 1915. Age 24. Enlisted Coventry. Resided Toronto, Canada. Memorial Ref. Panel 10. Ploegsteert Memorial, Belgium.

TAYLOR, A. Commemorated Wesleyan Church.

TAYLOR, Alfred William. Resided Foleshill. Killed in action, February, 1918.

TAYLOR, Private, Arthur. 267856, 1/8th Bn., Royal Warwickshire Regiment. Died of wounds, received at Bray, France, 27th March, 1917. Born 23rd January, 1896 at 1, Leigh Street. Resided 1, Leigh Street. Carter, Mr. Dorrington, Aylesford Street. Enlisted February, 1916 at Coventry. Grave Ref. II. D. 7. Bray Military Cemetery, France.

TAYLOR, Private, Arthur. 25777, "D" Coy. 7th Bn., Leicestershire Regiment. Died of wounds, 22nd June, 1918. Age 26. Son of Charles Taylor, of 8, Highfield, Stoney Stanton, Leicester. Husband of Elizabeth May Taylor, of Fair View Terrace, Keresley, Coventry. Grave Ref. 7. 33. Hook Norton Cemetery, Oxfordshire.

TAYLOR, Private, Arthur. 235022, 12th Bn., Gloucestershire Regiment formerly 5669, Royal Warwickshire Regiment. Killed in action, 25th August, 1918. Born 30th August, 1882 at Radford. Resided at 22, Ena Road. Traveller. Enlisted June, 1916 at Coventry. Commemorated Radford Memorial. Grave Ref. Queens Cemetery

TAYLOR, Lance Corporal, Charles Gordon. 9827, 1st Bn., Coldstream Guards. Killed in action, Battle of the Aisne, 14th September, 1914. Born 10th September, 1893 at Knighton Fields, Leicester. Resided at 19, London Road. Soldier. Sister, Mrs. Haynes resided at 2, Augustus Road. Formerly employed Centaur works and then assistant book-keeper and traveler at Messrs. Blairs, wine and spirit merchant. Enlisted Coventry. Memorial Ref. La Ferte-Sous-Jouarre Memorial, France.

TAYLOR, Private, Daniel. 18808, 11th Bn., Royal Warwickshire Regiment. Killed in action, 29th April, 1917. Born 11th December, 1897 at Coventry. Enlisted May, 1916 at Coventry. Resided at 31, Lower Nelson Street. Fitter, Gloria Cycle Works. Commemorated Triumph and Gloria Works Memorial. Memorial Ref. Bay 3. Arras Memorial, France.

TAYLOR, Private, Frank. 4705, 1/8th Bn., Royal Warwickshire Regiment. Killed in action, 18th July, 1916. Born Coventry. Enlisted Coventry. Memorial Ref. Pier and Face 9 A 9 B and 10 B. Thiepval Memorial, Somme, France.

TAYLOR, Private, Frederick. 203507, 9th Bn., Royal Warwickshire Regiment. Killed in action, 31st August, 1918. Born Ibstock, Leicestershire. Resided Longford. Enlisted Coventry. Commemorated Saint Thomas the Apostle, Longford. Memorial Ref. Panel 9. Basra Memorial, Iraq.

TAYLOR, Driver, George. 840370, 9th Div. Ammunition Col. Royal Field Artillery. Died at Cologne, Germany, 15th January, 1919. Born October, 1891 at Coventry. Resided in Spon End. Turner. Enlisted November, 1914. Grave Ref. I. B. 17. Cologne Southern Cemetery, Germany.

TAYLOR, Private, George Albert. 4369, 2nd /7th Bn., Royal Warwickshire Regiment. Died whilst prisoner of war, Germany, 19th July, 1916. Age 20. Son of William and Margaret E. Taylor, of 19, Huntingdon Road, Earlsdon, Coventry. Born 21st May, 1896 at 25, Sherbourne Street. Driller. Enlisted May, 1915 at Coventry. Commemorated St. John's Church. Memorial Ref. Panel 22 to 25. Loos Memorial, Pas De Calais, France.

TAYLOR, Private, George Everitt. 45705, 3rd Bn., Yorkshire Regiment. Died, home, 29th April, 1917. Born Coventry. Enlisted Middlesborough. Grave Ref. North of church. Marton-In-Cleveland (St. Cuthbert) Churchyard.

TAYLOR, Private, George Harry. Commemorated Saint Thomas the Apostle, Longford.

TAYLOR, Company Sergeant Major, George William Marchant. 6368, 8th Bn., Royal Scots Fusiliers. Killed in action, Balkans, 10th June, 1917. Age 36. Son of George and Mary Emma Taylor of Loughborough. Husband of W. Taylor of 41, Cumberland Road, Loughborough. Born Loughborough, Leicestershire. Enlisted Coventry. Resided Loughborough. Grave Ref. B. 314. Karasouli Military Cemetery, Greece.

TAYLOR, Private, Harry. 20280, B Coy., 6th Bn., King's Own (Royal Lancaster Regiment). Killed in action, 23rd March, 1918. Age 22. Son of Harry and Elizabeth Taylor of Ormes Lane, Tettenhall Wood, Wolverhampton. Born Wolverhampton. Enlisted Coventry. Memorial Ref. Bay 2. Arras Memorial, France.

TAYLOR, Gunner, Harry. 29657, 92nd Bty., Royal Garrison Artillery. Died, India, 13th May, 1915. Born in St. John's Parish. Enlisted Coventry. Memorial Ref. Face 2. Kirkee 1914 – 1918 Memorial, India.

TAYLOR, Gunner, Hector. 183563, 40th Bty., 122nd Bde., Royal Field Artillery. Died, 30th October, 1918. Age 20. Son of Annie Taylor of Nuneaton. Enlisted Coventry. Resided Nuneaton. Grave Ref. S. III. G. 3. St. Sever Cemetery Extension, Rouen, France.

TAYLOR, Private, Henry Joseph. 10536, 10th Bn., Royal Warwickshire Regiment. Died, 5th November, 1918. Born Birmingham. Resided Sheffield. Formerly employed at Coventry. Grave Ref. S. II. Y. 30. St. Sever Cemetery Extension, Rouen, France.

TAYLOR, Private, Herbert, MM. 1222, 2nd Bn., Royal Warwickshire Regiment. Died of pneumonia, 8th November, 1918. Age 33. Son of Walter G. and Ellen A. Taylor, of 32, Grafton Street, Coventry. Born 17th November, 1884 in Holy Trinity Parish. Enlisted Coventry. Awarded Military Medal for bravery in the field. Gazetted 25th January, 1918. Grave Ref. E. 10. Cremona Town Cemetery, Italy.

TAYLOR, Private, Kenneth John. 13419, 4th Bn., Coldstream Guards. Killed in action, Boulincourt, 29th March, 1918. Age 25. Son of John Harrison Taylor and Clara Elizabeth Taylor, of 50, Alfred Road, Coventry. Born 13th April, 1892, at 5, Hales Street. Resided at 50, Alfred Road. Fitter. Enlisted in 1914 at Coventry. Commemorated Triumph and Gloria Memorial and War Memorial Park. Grave Ref. VIII. Q. 15. Cabaret-Rouge British Cemetery, Souchez, Pas de Calais, France.

TAYLOR, Private, Maurice James. 57689, 29th Bn., Machine Gun Corps. Died of wounds, Ypres, 13th April, 1918. Age 20. Son of Mr. and Mrs. James Taylor, of Finham Park Farm, Stoneleigh, Kenilworth, Warwickshire. Born 14th July, 1897 at Epwell near Banbury. Resided at Finham Park Farm, Stoneleigh. Employed A. Williamson & Co. Ltd. Enlisted July, 1917 at Coventry. Grave Ref. I. A. 9. Ebblinghem Military Cemetery, France.

TAYLOR, Lance Sergeant, Robert Gervase. 8864, 2nd Bn., Royal Scots Fusiliers. Killed in action, 23rd October, 1914. Born 14th November, 1891 at South Wigstone, Leicester. Resided in Foleshill Road. Sister, Mrs. Haynes resided at 2, Augustus Road. Butcher in Market Street. Enlisted Coventry. Memorial Ref. Panel 19 and 33. Ypres (Menin Gate) Memorial, Belgium.

TAYLOR, S. Commemorated Post Office Memorial.

TAYLOR, Lance Corporal, Sam. 23076, 10th Bn., Royal Berkshire Regiment attached 122090, 17th Labour Group, Labour Corps formerly 24383, Wiltshire Regiment. Died, 5th September, 1918. Born Attleborough. Employed Coventry. Enlisted Coventry. Grave Ref. Q. IV. G. 6. St. Sever Cemetery Extension, Rouen, France.

TAYLOR, Gunner, Samuel. 11959, Royal Field Artillery. Died at home, (gassed), 21st April, 1916. Gassed at Neuve Chappelle and in hospital unconscious for a few weeks, with no improvement send home. Age 33. Husband of Mary Ann Taylor, of 109 Station Street West, Coventry. Born Abingdon. Labourer. Enlisted September, 1914 at Coventry. Employed Finishing Department, Rudge Works. Grave Ref. 20. 32. Coventry (St. Paul's) Cemetery.

TAYLOR, Private, Sydney John Smith. 32678, 8th Bn., York and Lancaster Regiment formerly 183299, Royal Field Artillery. Killed in action, 7th June, 1917. Age 24. Son of Mr. W. S. Taylor of Ceylon, Saskatchewan, Canada. Born Barton on-the-Heath, Warwicks. Enlisted Coventry. Memorial Ref. Panel 36 and 55. Ypres (Menin Gate) Memorial, Belgium.

TAYLOR, Thomas. Commemorated Saint Thomas the Apostle, Longford.

TAYLOR, Corporal, Thomas. 2598, 7th Bn., Royal Warwickshire Regiment. Killed in action, Battle of the Somme, 14th July, 1916. Age 21. Son of Arthur Taylor, of 51, Brooklyn Road, Coventry. Born 25th February, 1895 at 98, Radford. Motor Body Builder. Enlisted 1914 at Coventry. Grave Ref. III. B 39. Pozieres British Cemetery, Ovillers-La Boisselle, Somme, France.

TAYLOR, Private, Thomas. 2890, 1st/1st Warwickshire Yeomanry. Killed in action, 9th January, 1917. Enlisted Warwick. Resided Longford, Coventry. Grave Ref. E. 12. Kantara War Memorial Cemetery, Egypt.

TAYLOR, Sergeant, Walter. M2/098021, 605th Mechanical Transport Coy., Army Service Corps. Died, At Sea, 8th January, 1916. Born Wakefield. Enlisted Coventry. Resided Wakefield. Memorial Ref. Hollybrook Memorial, Southampton.

TAYLOR, Private, Walter. 26621, 2nd Bn., Wiltshire Regiment formerly 18307, Dorsetshire Regiment. Killed in action, 17th October, 1916. Born Denston, Suffolk. Enlisted Coventry. Resided Denston. Memorial Ref. Pier and Face 13A. Thiepval Memorial, France.

TAYLOR, Private, Walter Charles. 18927, C Coy, 7th Bn., South Lancashire Regiment. Killed in action, 5th July, 1916. Age 18. Son of Walter and Georgina Taylor of Priory Cottage, Rising Lane, Lapworth, Birmingham. Born Olton, Warwick. Enlisted Coventry. Resided Lapworth, Warwick. Memorial Ref. Pier and Face 7A and 7B. Thiepval Memorial, France.

TAYLOR, Private, Walter Edward. 3073, 1/6th Bn., North Staffordshire Regiment. Killed in action, 1st July, 1916. Resided at Winshill. Formerly employed at Coventry. Commemorated St. John's Church. Enlisted Coventry. Memorial Ref. Pier and Face 14B and 14C. Thiepval Memorial, Somme, France.

TAYLOR, William. Commemorated Holy Trinity Panels.

TAYLOR, Private, William. 5918, 2nd Bn., South Lancashire Regiment. Killed in action, 24th October, 1914. Age 37. Son of John and Elizabeth Taylor. Husband of Annie Taylor, of 21, Weston Street, Coventry. Born 7th July, 1876 at Smethwick. Gun Slinger. Enlisted August, 1914. Memorial Ref. Panel 23. Le Touret Memorial, Pas de Calais, France.

TAYLOR, Sapper, William. 71085, 42nd Airline Section, Royal Engineers. Died, Home, 20th August, 1918. Age 37. Husband of annie Loveridge (Formerly Taylor) of 9, Sergeant's Yard, Towcester. Born Towcester, Northants. Enlisted Coventry. Resided Towcester, Northants. Grave Ref. O. 57. Towcester Cemetery.

TAYLOR, Company Sergeant Major, William. 11146, 5th Bn., King's Shropshire Light Infantry. Died of wounds, home, 15th March, 1916. Age 32. Son of Thomas Proctor Taylor, of 25, Tasman Road, Stockwell, London. Born Coventry. Enlisted Shrewsbury. Resided Clapham, Junction. Grave Ref. F. 12. Baschurch (All Saints) Churchyard.

TAYLOR, Private William. 16665, 9th Bn., Royal Warwickshire Regiment. Died of wounds, received at Basra, Mesopotamia, 9th May, 1917. Born 1889 at Coventry. Enlisted February, 1916 at Warwick. Resided 30, Well Street, Coventry. Tinsmith. Grave Ref. XIII. G. 2. Amara War Cemetery, Iraq.

TAYLOR, Sergeant, William Albert. 2386, 1/7th Bn., Royal Warwickshire Regiment. Killed in action, Pozieres, 14th July, 1916. Born 13th February, 1887 at 1, Lilian Terrace, Paynes Lane. Resided at The Firs, Avon Street. House decorator. Enlisted August, 1914 at Coventry. Memorial Ref. Pier and Face 9 A 9 B and 10 B. Thiepval Memorial, Somme, France. (Possibly buried at Pozieres).

TAYLOR, Lance Corporal, William Arthur. 27698, 14th Bn., Royal Warwickshire Regiment. Killed in action, 31st March, 1917. Age 34. Husband of Elizabeth Taylor, of 15, Bond Street, Coventry. Born 22nd December, 1883 in St. Nicholas Parish. Iron Polisher, Polishing Department, Rudge Whitworth works. Enlisted August, 1914 at Coventry. Leaves a wife and four children. Grave Ref. V. B 23. Ecoivres Military Cemetery, Mont-st. Eloi, Pas de Calais, France.

TAYLOR, Private, William Thomas. 43328, 15th Bn., Royal Warwickshire Regiment formerly 357282, Hampshire Regt. Died of wounds, 31st October, 1918. Age 20. Eldest son of Mr. and Mrs. G. Taylor. Born 5th April, 1897 at back, 94, Red Lane, Coventry. Resided back, 94, Red Lane. Employed Hillman Motor Co. Ltd. Enlisted Coventry. Grave Ref. S. III. T. 3. St. Sever Cemetery Extension, Rouen, France.

TAYTON, Quartermaster Sergeant, John Henry. 267116, 1st Bn., Royal Warwickshire Regiment. Killed in action, 29th March, 1918. Age 34. Son of Mr. and Mrs. H. Tayton, of U.S.A. Husband of May Tayton, of Coventry. Born 7th December, 1883 at Macclesfield. Resided at 41, Queen Mary's Road. Assistant Sales Manager. Enlisted August, 1914 at Coventry. Grave Ref. V. F. 68. Duisans British Cemetery, Etrun, Pas de Calais, France.

TAYTON, Second Lieutenant, Wilfred Edward. 6th Bn., Northamptonshire Regiment. Killed in action, 10th August, 1917. Born 25th October, 1880 in Norfolk Street. Resided Chilvers Coton, Nuneaton. School Teacher. Enlisted October, 1916. Memorial Ref. Panel 43 and 45. Ypres (Menin Gate) Memorial, Belgium.

TEAGUE, Private, Arthur William Tyler. 10039, 1st Bn. Shropshire Light Infantry. Killed in action, Ypres, 22nd April, 1916. Age 22. Son of George and Alice Maud Teague, of Glencoe Villas, 31, Green Street, Hereford. Born 1894 at Ross, Herefordshire. Resided 16, Stanley Street. Memorial Ref. Panel 47 and 49. Ypres (Menin Gate) Memorial, Belgium.

TEALE, Private, Charles John. M/333404, Royal Army Service Corps. Died Trinnelgherry, India, 2nd June, 1919. Age 40. Husband of Edith Mary Teale, of 24, Newcombe Road, Earlsdon, Coventry. Born 22nd September, 1879. Chauffer. Enlisted May, 1917. Memorial Ref. Face 26. Madras 1914-1918 War Memorial, Chennai, India. (Originally buried in Trinnelgherry Cantonment Cemetery).

TEDD, Lance Corporal, Herbert. 202021, 1/5th Bn., Royal Warwickshire Regiment. Killed in action, 24th August, 1917. Born 1894 at Coventry. Enlisted Coventry. Resided back of 101, Gosford Street. Employed Courtaulds Ltd. Memorial Ref. Panel 23 to 28 and 163A. Tyne Cot Cemetery, Belgium.

TEDDS, Private, James. 42233, 1st Bn., Royal Warwickshire Regiment. Killed in action, 18th October, 1918. Age 35. Son of William and Hannah Selina Tedds, of 35, Stephen Street, Coventry. Born 7th September, 1885 at Coventry. Butcher. Enlisted April, 1918 at Coventry. Grave Ref. III. B. 23. St. Aubert British Cemetery, Nord, France.

TEDDS, Private, Samuel King (Known as Herbert Cooper). 5736, 1st Bn., Border Regiment. Killed in action, Gallipoli, 28th April, 1915. Nephew of Sarah Oswin, of 5 Court, 3 House, Gosford Street, Coventry. Born Gosford Street. Resided Coventry. Turner. Buried at sea. Memorial Ref. Panel 119 to 125 or 222 and 223. Helles Memorial, Turkey.

TENNANT, Gunner, Harry. 16313, "B" Bty. 92nd Brigade, Royal Field Artillery. Killed in action, 23rd August ,1917. Age 21. Son of Arthur and Annie Tennant, of Ash Green, Exhall, Coventry. Born at Chippington, Oxon. Employed Coventry. Enlisted Coventry. Commemorated Exhall Memorial. Grave Ref. A. 13. Dragoon Camp Cemetery, Ieper, West-Vlaanderen, Belgium.

TERHEEGE, Gunner, Albert. 685, 11th Bty., Machine Gun Corps (Motors). Killed in action, 16th April, 1918. Age 26. Husband of Elsie Terheege, of 30, Aylesford Street, Coventry. Born August, 1892 in St. Michael's Parish. Resided Coventry. Traveller. Enlisted 1915 at Coventry. Grave Ref. I. H. 43. Voormezeele Enclosures No.1 and No.2, Ieper, West-Vlaanderen, Belgium.

TERHEEGE, D. Commemorated St. Thomas Memorial.

TERHEEGE, Private, George. 138425, Devonshire Regiment. transf. to 28266, Labour Corps, Died of pneumonia, 7th November, 1918. Age 34. Son of William Terheege, of Meriden, Coventry. Husband of Emily Terheege, of Stratford Road, Hockley Heath, Birmingham. Grave Ref. S. 3. 4. Umberslade Baptist. Burial Ground, Warwickshire.

TERHEEGE, Private, Percy. 13769, 9th Bn., King's Own Yorkshire Light Infantry. Killed in action, 27th May, 1918. Age 32. Son of Mrs. Mary Ingram, of 30, Holyhead Road, Coventry. Born Pockington, Coleshill. Enlisted Nuneaton. Memorial Ref. Soissons Memorial, Aisne, France.

 **TERRY**, Rifleman, Alfred. 10856, 1st Bn., Kings Royal Rifle Corps. Died of wounds, 14th September, 1914. Born Walsgrave, Warwick. Enlisted Coventry. Resided Walsgrave. Memorial Ref. La Ferte Sous-Jouarre Memorial, France.

TERRY, Private, Frederick. 265956, 2/7th Bn., Royal Warwickshire Regiment. Killed in action, 29th September, 1917. Born 27th January, 1889 at Stoke, Coventry. Resided at 94, Red Lane. Heater (steam hammers). Enlisted November, 1914 at Coventry. Grave Ref. IV. B. 35. Brown's Copse Cemetery, Roeux, France.

TERRY, Private, Henry Arthur. 28459, 14th Bn., Royal Warwickshire Regiment. Killed in action, 7th May, 1917. Age 21. Son of Frederick and Rebecca Terry, of 57, Leicester Street, Coventry. Born 3rd December, 1894 in Cobden Street. Tinplate worker. Enlisted September, 1914 at Coventry. Memorial Ref. Bay 3. Arras Memorial, Pas de Calais, France.

TERRY, Private, Richard. 38454, 1st Bn., King's Shropshire Light Infantry formerly Royal Warwickshire Regiment. Killed in action, 26th May 1918. Age 19. Son of Thomas and Elizabeth Terry, of 4, Wyken Terrace, Walsgrave Road, near Coventry. Born Pailton. Employed Coventry. Grave Ref. XI. A. 14. Nine Elms British Cemetery, Poperinge, West-Vlaanderen, Belgium.

TESTER, Sergeant, Leonard Charles. 19790, 17th Bn., Lancashire Fusiliers. Killed in action, 8th June, 1918. Age 23. Son of Oliver Charles and Rose Tester, of Coventry. Born 1893 at Birmingham. Resided Manchester. Grave Ref. III. F. 17. Varennes Military Cemetery, Somme, France.

TESTOT, Corporal, Edward Charles. 14307, 6th Bn., Royal Dublin Fusiliers formerly Wiltshire Regiment. Killed in action, 10th August, 1915 .Born Coventry. Enlisted Wandsworth, Middx. Resided Earlsfield. Memorial Ref. Panel 190 to 196. Helles Memorial, Turkey.

THAIN, Chief Shipwright 2nd Class, Alfred. 344427, HMS Vivid, Royal Navy. Died of phthisis, 8th November, 1920. Age 34. Son of James and Jane Thain of 11, Craven Avenue, Plymouth. Husband of Ellen R. M. Thain, of 595, Foleshill Road, Coventry. His brother Charles also fell. Grave Ref. General A. 31. Plymouth (Efford) Cemetery, Devon.

THOMAS, Second Lieutenant, Arthur Coke, MC. D Coy., 6th Bn., Oxfordshire and Buckinghamshire Light Infantry. Killed in action, 2nd June, 1916. Age 30. Son of the Rev. David Thomas, of Garsington Rectory, Oxford. Born 18th July, 1886. Resided at London (previously Coventry). Bankers clerk. Enlisted September, 1914. Awarded Military Cross for gallantry in rescuing a wounded fellow officer under heavy fire. Grave Ref. Enclosure No.2 IV. C. 12. Bedford House Cemetery, Belgium.

THOMAS, Private, George Rymill. 2689, The King's (Liverpool Regiment). Killed in action, 11th December, 1914. Age 19. Son of William Rymill Thomas and Maude Jeannette Thomas, of 5, Blacklion St., Brighton. Born at Coventry. Grave Ref. D. C. E.9. Church and Clayton-Le-Moors Joint Cemetery, Lancashire.

THOMAS, Corporal, Lionel Edward. 1752, 2nd Bn., Royal Warwickshire Regiment. Killed in action, 25th September, 1915. Age 22. Son of William Edward Thomas, of 2, King Georges Avenue, Foleshill, Coventry. Born 25th October, 1892 at Foleshill. Resided at 3, Chapel Lane. Commemorated King Henry VIII School. Memorial Ref. Panel 22 to 25. Loos Memorial, Pas de Calais, France.

THOMPSON, Private, Albert Charles. 28586, 15th Battalion, Royal Warwickshire Regiment. Killed in action, 26th October 1917. Age 23. Son of Albert and Lucy Thompson, of 61, Gordon Street, Butts, Coventry. Born 23rd October 1893, at Coventry. Resided at 61, Gordon Street. Lithographic Printer. Commemorated Iliffe & Sons Ltd Memorial and War Memorial Park. Enlisted October, 1915. Memorial Ref. Panel 23 to 28 and 163a. Tyne Cot Cemetery, Belgium.

THOMPSON, Private, Alfred. 1073, D Coy., 2nd Bn., Royal Warwickshire Regiment. Killed in action, 21st November, 1914. Age 25. Son of Charles and Sarah Ann Thompson, of 22, Smith Street, Coventry. Born 10th November, 1889 in Holy Trinity Parish, Soldier. Brother of Mrs. Pullin of 5, Silvester Road, Coventry. Memorial Ref. Panel 2 and 3. Ploegsteert Memorial, Comines-Warneton, Hainaut, Belgium.

THOMPSON, Private, Berry. 22871, 2nd Bn., Northamptonshire Regiment. Killed in action, 3rd July, 1916. Born Coventry. Enlisted Braunston, Northants. Memorial Ref. Pier and Face 11 A and 11 D. Thiepval Memorial, Somme, France.

THOMPSON, Rifleman, Edgar. C/6391, 18th Bn., King's Royal Rifle Corps. Killed in action, 15th September, 1916. Born Coventry. Enlisted London. Resided Coventry. Memorial Ref. Pier and Face 13 A and 13 B. Thiepval Memorial, Somme, France.

THOMPSON, Private, Edwin. 265784, 1/7th Bn., Royal Warwickshire Regiment. Killed in action, 6th April, 1917. Employed Coventry. Enlisted Coventry. Grave Ref. III. J. 12. Epehy Wood Farm Cemetery, Epehy, France.

THOMPSON, Private, George Samuel. G/18223, 7th Bn., Queen's Royal West Kent Regiment formerly PS/11549, Royal Fusiliers. Killed in action, 4th October, 1916. Age 29. Son of G. and C. Thompson, of Knowle, Warwickshire. Husband of Hilda W. Thompson, of 41, College Road, Moseley, Birmingham. Born 13th October, 1885. Enlisted Coventry. Resided Coventry. Banker's clerk. Enlisted May, 1916. Commemorated St. Barbara's Church. Memorial Ref. Sp. Mem. 1. Mill Road Cemetery, Thiepval, France.

THOMPSON, J. H. Employed Rover Company Ltd. Killed in action.

THOMPSON, Private, James Thomas. 202006, 8th Bn., Tank Corps. Killed in action, 29th September, 1918. Age 27. Son of James Thompson, of 1, Percy Street, Coventry. Born 1st January, 1889 at 38, Spon Street, Coventry. Resided at 38, Sherbourne Street. Cabinet maker. Enlisted May, 1916 at Coventry. Memorial Ref. Panel 11. Vis-En-Artois Memorial, Pas de Calais, France.

THOMPSON, Lance Sergeant, Leonard. 265511, 1st /7th Bn., Royal Warwickshire Regiment. Fell in a raid on Ave, south of Asiago, 9th August, 1918. Age 24. Son of George and Eliza Ann Thompson, of Coventry. Born 23rd February, 1894 in Spon Street. Resided at 7c. 23h. Spon Street. Mechanic. Enlisted September, 1914. Commemorated St. John's Church and Triumph and Gloria Memorial. Memorial Ref. Giavera Memorial, Italy.

THOMPSON, Private, Percy. 27162, 11th Bn., Lancashire Fusiliers. Killed in action, 22nd January, 1917. Born Coventry. Enlisted Coventry. Grave Ref. I. M. 8. Berks Cemetery Extension, Belgium.

THOMPSON, Private, Percy John. 33016, 6th Bn., Oxfordshire and Buckinghamshire Light Infantry formerly Royal Warwickshire Regiment. Killed in action, 16th August, 1917. Age 24. Youngest son of Reuben and Maria Thompson, of 40, Day's Lane, Coventry. Born 1st August, 1893 in Mount Street. File cutter and formerly teacher at the Ragged Schools. Enlisted April, 1916. Memorial Ref. Panel 96 to 98. Tyne Cot Memorial, Zonnebeke, West-Vlaanderen, Belgium.

THOMPSON, Lance Sergeant, Reuben. 11274, 1st Bn. Royal Dublin Fusiliers formerly Royal Warwickshire Regiment. Killed in action, Gallipoli, 26th April, 1915. Born 7th November, 188 at Coventry. Enlisted Wedgnock Park. Resided 8c. 9h. Jordan Well, Coventry. Miller. Memorial Ref. Panel 190 to 196. Helles Memorial, Turkey.

THOMPSON, T. Commemorated Triumph & Gloria Memorial.

THOMPSON, Private, Thomas. 50738, 10th Bn., Royal Warwickshire Regiment. Killed in action, 3rd June, 1918. Age 18. Son of Mr. and Mrs. C. Thompson, of 48A, St. John Street, Coventry. . Enlisted Leamington. Resided Coventry. Born Coventry. Grave Ref. A. 40. La Neuville-Aux-Larris Military Cemetery, Marne, France

THOMPSON, Lance Corporal, Thomas Charles. 30760, 2/8th Bn., Worcestershire Regiment. Killed in action, 1st November, 1918. Age 28. Son of William and Helen Jane Thompson, of Solihull, Birmingham. Born Solihull. Resided Knowle. Employed Coventry. Grave Ref. III. A. 11. Cross Roads Cemetery, Fontaine-Au-Bois, France.

THOMPSON, Private Walter. 28446, 14th Bn., Royal Warwickshire Regiment. Died of wounds, received at Arras, 7th May, 1917. Born 18th February, 1893 in Holy Trinity Parish. Resided at 60, New Buildings. Polisher. Enlisted September, 1915. Commemorated Holy Trinity Panels. Grave Ref. I. B. 40. Nine Elms Military Cemetery, Thelus, France.

THOMPSON, Private, Walter Henry. 16105, 6th Bn., Oxfordshire and Buckinghamshire Light Infantry. Killed in action, 3rd September , 1916. Age 34. Son of John and Sarah Ann Thompson, of Castle Street, Coventry. Husband of Sarah Ann Thompson, of 1 Court, 6 House, Grove Street, Coventry. Born 13th April, 1882 at Coventry. Enlisted November, 1914 at Coventry. Labourer, Daimler works. Left a widow and four children. Memorial Ref. Pier and Face 10 A and 10 D. Thiepval Memorial, Somme, France.

THOMPSON, Private, William George. 16641, 9th Bn., Royal Warwickshire Regiment. Mesopotamia, Killed in action, 25th January, 1917. Age 27. Son of James Thompson, of 1, Percy Street, Coventry. Born 24th January, 1890 at 38, Spon Street, Coventry. Enlisted February, 1916 at Warwick. Resided 38, Sherbourne Street, Coventry. Commemorated St. John's Church. Barman. Grave Ref. XIX. K. 18. Amara War Cemetery, Iraq.

THOMSON, J. I. St. John's Church

THORLEY, Lance Corporal, Samuel Ernest. 3593, 9th Bn., Royal Warwickshire Regiment. Died of wounds, received at Gallipoli, 25th August, 1915. Age 20. Son of John and Maria Thorley, of London Lodge, Stoneleigh. Born 3rd October, 1894 at Nuneaton. Resided at Stoneleigh. Mechanic. Enlisted August, 1914. Grave Ref. D. 62. Cairo Cemetery, Egypt.

THORNETT, Private, Albert. 16581, 10th Bn., Royal Warwickshire Regiment. Killed in action at Wytschaete Ridge, Belgium, 10th April, 1918. Age 24. Son of Albert and Elizabeth Thornett, of 10, Drapers Fields, Coventry. Born 27th March, 1894. Resided at 10, Drapers Fields. Warehouseman. Enlisted Birmingham, February, 1916. Commemorated Holy Trinity Panels and War Memorial Park. Memorial Ref. Panel 23 to 28 and 163A. Tyne Cot Memorial, Zonnebeke, West-Vlaanderen, Belgium.

THORNEYCRAFT, D. Commemorated Exhall Memorial.

THORNTON, Private, Fred. 28006, 10th Bn., Royal Warwickshire Regiment. Died 30th October, 1918. Resided at 61, King Richard Street. Grave Ref. I. A. 18. Delsaux Farm Cemetery, Beugny, France.

THORNTON, Second Lieutenant, George Rowland Hart. 16th Heavy Bty., Royal Garrison Artillery. Killed in action, 9th April, 1918. Age 35. Son of Mr. and Mrs. George Marmaduke Hart Thornton of Exeter Villa, Cranham Road, Cheltenham. Commemorated Iliffe & Sons Ltd. Memorial Ref. Panel 3 and 4. Loos Memorial, France.

THORPE, Private, Denis. 43621, 2/7th Bn., Royal Warwickshire Regiment. Died of wounds, 7th September, 1918. Age 18. Son of William and Sarah Thorpe, of Kidlington, Oxon. Born 21st September, 1899 at Kidlington, Oxon. Resided at 102, Bolingbroke Road. Fitter. Enlisted January, 1918. Commemorated War Memorial Park and Siddeley Roll of Honour. Grave Ref. I. V. D15. Aire Communal Cemetery, France.

THORPE, Fred. Commemorated Baginton Memorial.

THORPE, Corporal, Frederick George. 9596, 1st Reserve Bn., Oxfordshire and Buckinghamshire Light Infantry. Died, 14th August, 1919. Age 27. Son of Mr. A. and Mrs. K. Thorpe, of 20, Humber Avenue, Stoke, Coventry. Memorial Ref. Face 23. Delhi Memorial (India Gate), India. (Buried Peshawar (Right) B.C. XLIV. 34.).

THORPE, Private, Walter. 5080, C Company, 2nd Bn., Royal Warwickshire Regiment. Died of wounds, Beuvry, near Bethune, 20th June, 1915. Suffered a head wound caused by a shell and died during the night. Age 22. Husband of Alice Thorpe, of 8 Court, 4 House, Bond Street, Coventry. Born 1st March, 1893 at Worcester. Weaving mechanic. Enlisted September, 1914. Grave Ref. I. F. 6. Gorre British and Indian Cemetery, Pas de Calais, France.

THREADGOLD, Private, Frank. 63290, 52nd Bn., Machine Gun Corps (Infantry) formerly Royal Warwickshire Regiment. Killed in action, 5th May, 1917. Born 6th February, 1897 in Cobden Street, Coventry. Enlisted July, 1916 at Coventry. Resided at 69, Broad Street. Polisher. Commemorated Coventry Chain Memorial. Grave Ref. I. B. 3. Point-Du-Jour Military Cemetery, Athies, France.

THURMAN, Private, Albert. 17161, 2nd Bn., Hampshire Regiment formerly Oxfordshire and Buckinghamshire Light Infantry. Killed in action, 6th August, 1915. Age 20. Son of Alice Thurman, of 42, Trentham Road, Coventry. Born 20th September, 1896 at 26, Highfield Road. Resided 26, Highfield Road. Vanman. Enlisted August, 1914. Commemorated Wesleyan Church. Memorial Ref. Panel 125-134 or 223-226 228-229 & 328. Helles Memorial, Turkey.

TIBBETTS, Private, Jack Abraham. 11632, 6th Bn., Oxfordshire and Buckinghamshire Light Infantry. 25th September, 1915. Age 19. Resided Bedworth. Employed Courtaulds. Enlisted August, 1914. Grave Ref. III. K. 17. Royal Irish Rifles Graveyard, Laventie, France.

TIDMAN, Private, Isaac. 32961, 2/4th Bn., Oxfordshire and Buckinghamshire Light Infantry formerly Royal Warwickshire Regiment. Died prisoner of war in German hands, 14th October, 1918. Born 17th March, 1889 at Shilton, Warwickshire. Resided at Shilton. Artificial Silk Weaver. Enlisted Coventry. Grave Ref. IV. B. 21. Hautmont Communal Cemetery, France.

TIDMAN, Private Thomas. 11390, 5th Bn., Oxfordshire and Buckinghamshire Light Infantry. Killed in action, 24th August, 1916. Age 22. Son of Thomas and Mary Ann Tidman who resided at 13A, Roadway, Bedworth. Born in Bedworth. Employed Exhall Colliery. Enlisted Nuneaton. Memorial Ref. Pier and Face 10A and 10D. Thiepval Memorial, Somme, France.

TIDMAN, Private, Walter. 12785, 9th Bn., Royal Warwickshire Regiment. Doed, 26th September, 1918. Age 45. Husband of Emma Priscilla Tidman, of Walsgrave-on-Sowe, Coventry. Enlisted Coventry. Born Shilton. Commemorated Walsgrave Memorial. Grave Ref. III. A. 16. Tehran War Cemetery, Iran.

TIFFIN, Private, Henry James. 200565, C Bn., Tank Corps formerly 2678, Machine Gun Corps. Killed in action, 20th November, 1917. Age 25. Son of John and Annas E. Tiffin of Ravenbank, Kirkswald, Cumberland. Born Kirkswald, Cumberland. Enlisted Coventry. Memorial Ref. Panel 13. Cambrai Memorial, Louveral, France.

TILLEY, Private, Ernest John. 57672, 36th Coy., Machine Gun Corps formerly 20303, Royal Warwickshire Regiment. Died, 27th February, 1917. Age 31. Son of A. T. Tilley of Northfleet, Kent. Born Northfleet, Kent. Enlisted Coventry. Grave Ref. IV. B. 21. Avesnes-Le-Comte Communal Cemetery Extension, France.

TILLEY, Private, John William. 41405, 3rd Bn., Worcestershire Regiment. Killed in action, 11th April, 1918. Age 19. Son of Charles and Mary Elizabeth Tilley, of 29, Trafalgar Road, Cape Hill, Smethwick, Staffs. Born Coventry. Enlisted Birmingham. Resided Smethwick, Staffs. Memorial Ref, Panel 5. Ploegsteert Memorial, Belgium.

TILLEY, Rifleman, William Henry. 5224, 1st Bn., Rifle Brigade. Killed in action, 18th March, 1915. Born Birmingham. Enlisted Coventry. Resided Birmingham. Grave Ref. IV. J. 6. Rifle House Cemetery, Belgium.

TILSLEY, Rifleman, William. 5480, 2nd Bn., Rifle Brigade. Killed in action, shot by a rifle bullet, 15th June, 1915. Age 23. Son of Mrs. Jane Tilsley, of 11, St. Laurence Avenue, Warwick previously 10, Wheatley Street, Coventry. Born Warwick. Resided Coventry. Grave Ref. VIII. A. 3. Aubers Ridge British Cemetery, Aubers, France.

TILSTON, Private, Leonard. 1326, 9th Bn., Royal Warwickshire Regiment. Died, Mesopotamia, 20th July, 1916. Age 23. Son of Henry and Harriet Tilstone of May Cottage, Milford, Stafford. Born Milford, Stafford. Enlisted Coventry. Resided Milford. Memorial Ref. Face B. Kirkee 1014 – 1918 Memorial, India.

TIMERICK, Private, Norbert. 16780, 11th Bn., Royal Warwickshire Regiment. Killed in action, 9th July, 1916. Age 26. Son of Arthur and Sarah Timerick. Born 1889 at Coventry. Enlisted February, 1916 at Coventry. Employed W. W. Curtis Ltd. Memorial Ref. Pier and Face 9 A 9 B and 10 B. Thiepval Memorial, Somme, France.

TIMMINS, Lance Corporal, Austin. M2/202316, 778th Mortar Trench Company. (Salonika), Royal Army Service Corps. Invalided from Salonica, died at home 16th August, 1919. Age 38. Son of Richard Timmins, of Bridgnorth, Salop. Husband of Agnes Jane Timmins, of 118, Stoney Stanton Road, Coventry. Born 18th March, 1881 at Bridgnorth, Shropshire. Warehouseman. Enlisted August, 1916. Commemorated War Memorial Park. Grave Ref. 59. 90. Coventry (London Road) Cemetery.

TIMMINS, Rifleman, John Henry. 50155, King's Royal Rifle Corps attached London Regiment. Killed in action, 21st September, 1918. Born Wootton, Warwick. Enlisted Coventry. Resided Wootton. Memorial Ref. Panel 9. Vis-en-Artois Memorial, France.

TIMMS, Rifleman, John. R/16740, 7th Bn., King's Royal Rifle Corps. Died of wounds, 25th August, 1916. Age 19. Son of William Edward and Elizabeth Ann Timms, of Four Oaks, Meriden, Coventry. Native of Berkswell, Coventry. Enlisted Coventry. Grave Ref. I. A. 10. Dernancourt Communal Cemetery Extension, Somme, France.

TIMMS, Private, Walter Joseph. 7222, B Coy., 1st Bn., Northamptonshire Regiment. Killed in action, 23rd October, 1914. Age 26. Brother of Jane Elizabeth Frances Timms, of 89, Queen Street, Leamington Spa. Born 20th May, 1883. Resided Coventry. Railway porter. Enlisted August, 1914. Memorial Ref. Panel 43 and 45. Ypres (Menin Gate) Memorial, Belgium.

TIMMS, Corporal, Walter William. 9953, 1st Bn., The Loyal North Lancashire Regiment. Killed in action, 29th September, 1914. Born Coventry. Enlisted Coventry. Memorial Ref. La Ferte-Sous-Jouarre Memorial, France.

TIMS, Private, William. 1868, 1st/7th Bn., Royal Warwickshire Regiment. Killed in action, 7th June, 1915. Shot whilst returning from a working party which pierced his lung. Husband of F. Tims of 4, Francis Street, Foleshill, Coventry,. Born 6th August, 1885 at Leamington. Silk spinner. Enlisted August, 1914 at Coventry. Grave Ref. V. C. 1. La Plus Douve Farm Cemetery, Comines-Warneton, Hainaut, Belgium.

TINSLEY, Private, George Henry. 36th Bn., Oxfordshire and Buckinghamshire Light Infantry. Died, home, 29th August, 1917. Born 5th May, 1894 at Winson Green, Birmingham. Resided 16, Queens Road. Core maker. Enlisted September, 1914. Grave Ref. Coventry (London Road) Cemetery.

TINSLEY, Private, Thomas Edward. 44165, 2nd /4th Bn., Royal Berkshire Regiment. Died of wounds, 28th August, 1918. Age 18. Son of George Henry and Sarah Ellen Tinsley, of Coventry. Born 15th September, 1899 at Rugby. Resided at 49, Bramble Street. Miller. Enlisted October, 1917 at Coventry. Grave Ref. IV. C. 15. Aire Communal Cemetery, Pas de Calais, France.

TOD, Corporal, Alexander Shepherd. 265788, 1st /7th Bn., Royal Warwickshire Regiment. Killed in action, St. Julien, 4th October, 1917. Age 19. Son of Alexander and Marjorie R. Tod, of 41A, Widdrington Road, Coventry. Born 1st March, 1898 at Edinburgh. Resided 141, Narrow Lane. Coach Trimmer, Daimler Works. Enlisted October, 1914 at Coventry. Memorial Ref. Panel 23 to 28 and 163A. Tyne Cot Memorial, Zonnebeke, West-Vlaanderen, Belgium. (Possibly buried Tweedhouse, St. Julien).

TODD, Acting Lance Corporal, Allen. P/13164, Military Foot Police, Military Police Corps formerly 17425, Royal Warwickshire Regiment. Died, home, 6th August, 1918. Born Stretton-on-Fosse. Enlisted Coventry. Resided Coventry. Commemorated Triumph and Gloria Memorial. Grave Ref. In North part. Burmington (St. Barnabas) Churchyard.

TOLLEY, Sapper, William. 175559, 3rd Special Bn., Royal Engineers. Killed in action, 5th March, 1917. Born Brierley Hill, Staffs. Enlisted Coventry. Grave Ref. IV. E. 25. Ecoivres Military Cemetery, Mont-St. Eloi, France.

TOMBS, Private, William. 39654, 1st Bn., Wiltshire Regiment. Killed in action, 27th May, 1918. Age 18. Son of Arthur and Clara Tombs, of 7, Holly Bush Villa, Longford, Coventry. Enlisted Coventry. Resided Coventry. Born Bucknall, Staffs. Commemorated Saint Thomas the Apostle, Longford. Memorial Ref. Soissons Memorial, Aisne, France.

TOMKIES, Second Lieutenant, Henry Lea. 48th Squadron, Royal Flying Corps formerly Sherwood Foresters. Killed, Cambria, 25th April, 1917. Born 6th December, 1893 at Foleshill Lodge. Resided at 6, White Street. Motor Body Builder. Enlisted October, 1914. Memorial Ref. Arras Flying Services Memorial, France.

TOMLINSON, Private, Albert Leonard. M2/114103, Army Service Corps. Killed in action, 4th June, 1917. Born Foleshill. Enlisted Birmingham. Resided Coventry. Grave Ref. I. C. 3. Loker Churchyard, Belgium.

TOMLINSON, Private, Frederick John. 20277, 1st Bn., Dorsetshire Regiment. Died of wounds, 16th August, 1918. Age 19. Son of Mr. and Mrs. A. J. Tomlinson, of 14, David Street, Coventry. Born at King's Norton, Birmingham. Employed Coventry. Grave Ref. VIA. C. 22. Villers-Bretonneux Military Cemetery, Somme, France.

TOMLINSON, Second Lieutenant, Herbert Cecil. 39th Siege Battery, Royal Garrison Artillery. Died of wounds, 21st March, 1918. Resided Warwick. Solicitor's Clerk Enlisted August, 1914. Grave Ref. III. A. 12. Nine Elms British Cemetery, Belgium.

TOMPKINS, Private, Fred. 96796, 162nd Coy., Labour Corps formerly 28191, Royal Berkshire Regiment. Killed in action, 25th February, 1918. Born Ryton-on-Dunsmore, Warwicks. Enlisted Warwick. Resided Coventry. Grave Ref. I. 0. 1. Roisel Communal Cemetery Extension, France.

TOMPKINS, Corporal, George Herbert. 12326, 5th Bn., Oxfordshire and Buckinghamshire Light Infantry. Died of wounds, 23rd October, 1917. Age 35. Son of George William and Jane Tompkins, of Northampton. Husband of Sarah Ann Tompkins, of 70, Hood Street, Northampton. Born Northampton. Resided at 203, Gulson Road. Gateman. Enlisted September, 1914 at Coventry. Grave Ref. I. K. 30. Godewaersvelde British Cemetery, France.

TOMPKINS, Airman 1st Class, George Philip. 6061, 7th Sqdn., Royal Flying Corps. Died of wounds, 17th July, 1916. Age 24. Son of Albert and Susan Tompkins, of Coventry. Husband of Edith Alice Tompkins, of 63, Lawson Villas, Priory Road, Dartford, Kent. Born 28th November, 1891 at 17, Waterloo Street. Resided Dartford. Enlisted June, 1915. Grave Ref. II. E. 28. Bailleul Communal Cemetery Extension (Nord), Nord, France.

TOMPKINS, Driver, George William. RMA/266(S), Howitzer Brigade, Royal Marine Artillery. 25th May, 1917. Age 21. Son of George and Ruth Tompkins, of 42, Hamilton Road, Coventry. Born 1st July, 1894 at Coventry. Clerk. Commemorated British Thompson Houston Memorial. Grave Ref. C. 1. Beaumetz-Les-Loges Communal Cemetery, Pas de Calais, France.

TOMPKINS, Private, Stanley George. G/21161, 2nd Bn., Royal Fusiliers. Killed in action, 1st July, 1916. Husband of Ethel Matilda Tompkins, of 71, London Road, Wembley, Middx. Born 13th September, 1886 at Dunstable. Resided Coventry. Railway (booking and Parcels) Clerk. Enlisted November, 1915. Memorial Ref. Pier and Face 8 C 9 A and 16 A. Theipval Memorial, Somme, France.

TOMS, Sergeant, William. 3023, 2nd/4th Bn., Oxfordshire and Buckinghamshire Light Infantry. Killed in action, Laventie, 3rd July, 1916. Age 24. Husband of M. A. Toms, of 190, Spon Street, Coventry. Born Coventry. Enlisted Oxford. Resided Coventry. Born 14th February, 1892 at Coventry. Resided at Coventry. School Teacher, Elementary School, Coventry. Enlisted Oxford, September, 1914. Educated Bablake School. Commemorated Bablake School Memorial, Education Department Memorial, Coventry Corporation and War Memorial Park. Grave Ref. II. A. 12. Laventie Military Cemetery, La Gorgue, Nord, France.

TONKINSON, Private, Reginald. 10486, 11th Bn., Royal Fusiliers. Died of wounds, 27th February, 1917. Son of Edward and Sarah Tonkinson, of Croft Cottage, Farnworth, Widnes, Lancs. Born Kidderminster. Enlisted Coventry. Resided Coventry. Grave Ref. VIII. B171. Boulogne Eastern Cemetery, France.

TONKS, Private, Harry. 235288, 1st Bn., Worcestershire Regiment. Died of wounds, 24th November, 1917. Age 19. Son of Benjamin and Mary Tonks, of Coventry. Born Coventry. Enlisted Coventry. Born 19th December, 1899 in Vauxhall Yard, East Street. Resided 10, Craner's Road. Tool grinder. Enlisted March, 1917. Grave Ref. XXVII. B. B. 21A. Lijssenthoek Military Cemetery, Poperinge, West-Vlaanderen, Belgium.

TOOKEY, Private, James Pressley. 266230, 1/7th Bn., Royal Warwickshire Regiment. Killed in action, Passchendaele, 4th October, 1917 attempting to save his officer, Captain Croall. Born Rawtenstall, Lancs. Enlisted Coventry. Resided Kenilworth. Age 36, Husband of Jessie Mansell Mary Tookey of 26, Spring Lane, Kenilworth. Leaves a widow and three children. Memorial Ref. Panel 23 to 28 and 163A. Tyne Cot Memorial, Belgium.

TOOMEY, Gunner, David Daniel. 840505, D Bty., 240th Bde., Royal Field Artillery Killed in action, 18th July, 1917. Born Coventry. Enlisted Coventry. Grave Ref. VII. F. 7. Duhallow A.D.S. Cemetery, France.

TOON, Corporal, Charlie. 265215, 1/7th Bn., Royal Warwickshire Regiment. Killed in action, 26th March, 1917. Husband of Mrs. L. Toon of 141, Stockbrook Street, Derby. Born Derby. Enlisted Coventry. Grave Ref. XXII. C. 6A. Etaples Military Cemetery, France.

TOOTH, Driver, John James. 234, 4th Bty., Royal Field Artillery. Accidental death, 12th April, 1915. Born in 1894 at Handsworth. Resided at 29, Redcar Road. Engineer. Enlisted August, 1914 at Coventry. Son of Mr. Humphrey Tooth of 23, Redcar Road. Completed Apprenticeship, Brett's Engineering works. Attended Frederick Bird Elementary School. Grave Ref. Merris Chyd. Mem. 53. Cabaret-Rouge British Cemetery, Souchez, France.

TOPP, Private, Aubrey. 4386, 2/7th Bn., Royal Warwickshire Regiment. Died whilst prisoner of war, 19th July, 1916. Born in 1891. Resided Coventry. Builder. Enlisted Coventry. Memorial Ref. Panel 22 to 25. Loos Memorial, France.

TOSSWILL, Corporal, John Speare. 72726, Northern Signal Service Training Centre, Royal Engineers. Died home, 28th September, 1915. Born at Eastbourne, Sussex. Professional Footballer (formerly with Coventry City Football Club). Grave Ref. UA. 250. Eastbourne (Ocklynge) Cemetery.

TOVEY, Private, Frederick John. 10724, 1st Bn., Coldstream Guards. Died, 25th January, 1915. Born Milton-Under-Wychwood, Oxford. Enlisted Coventry. Resided Heythrop, Oxen. Memorial Ref. Panel 2 and 3. Le Touret Memorial, France.

TOWE, Private, Wallace. 22429, 7th Bn., Gloucestershire Regiment. Died of wounds, received at Suvla Bay, Gallipoli, 20th December, 1915. Age 21. Son of Wallace and Emma Towe, of 30, Mickleton Road, Earlsdon, Coventry. Born 5th February, 1894, at Daltons Cottages, Allesley Old Road. Resided at Yardley, Birmingham. Tailors Cutter. Enlisted September, 1914. Commemorated War Memorial Park. Grave Ref. C. III. 2. Pieta Military Cemetery, Malta.

TOWNEND, Private, Andrew. 147, 2nd Bn., Royal Warwickshire Regiment. Killed in action, 19th December, 1914. Age 27. Husband of Elizabeth Townend, of 1, Court, 5 House, Payne's Lane, Coventry. Born in 1886, in Ford Street. Resided at 1c. 5h. Paynes Lane. Employed by Humber Limited. Reservist. Known as 'Happy'. Enlisted Coventry. Attended All Saints School. Commemorated War Memorial Park. Memorial Ref. Panel 2 and 3. Ploegsteert Memorial, Comines-Warneton, Hainaut, Belgium.

TOWNEND, Private, Edgar George. DM2/178702, 406th Mechanical Transport Coy, Army Service Corps. attd. II Corps Heavy Artillery. Died of wounds, 22nd April, 1918. Son of Mrs. E. Townend, of 42, Binley Road, Coventry. Born Coventry. Enlisted Coventry. Resided Coventry. Commemorated King Henry VIII School and Triumph and Gloria Memorial. Grave Ref. X. B. 38. Mendinghem Military Cemetery, Poperinge, West-Vlaanderen, Belgium.

TOWNLEY, Private, Frederick. 4638, 2/7th Bn., Royal Warwickshire Regiment. Killed in action, 19th July, 1916. Age 28. Employed Courtaulds. Born at Hook Norton, Oxon. Resided Foleshill. Enlisted Coventry. Commemorated Saint Thomas the Apostle, Longford. Memorial Ref. Panel 22 to 25. Loos Memorial, France.

TOWNSEND, Mark. Killed in action, 12th August, 1916. Born 4th April, 1894. Resided Coventry. Railway Porter. Enlisted May, 1915.

TOWNSEND, Rifleman, Mark. R/12853, 2nd Bn., King's Royal Rifle Corps. Died of wounds, 15th July, 1916. Son of Mr. and Mrs. T. Townsend, of Wilmcote, Stratford-on-Avon. Born Smethwick. Resided Stratford-on-Avon. Employed Coventry. Enlisted Coventry. Grave Ref. II. B. 31. Heilly Station Cemetery, Mericourt-L'Abbe, France.

TOWNSEND, Private, William Arthur. 926, 2nd Bn., Royal Warwickshire Regiment. Died of wounds, received at the Battle of Loos, 26th September, 1915. Born 4th June, 1892 at 19, Howard Street. Resided 19, Howard Street. Soldier. Employed as a Fitter, Rudge Whitworth Works Ltd. Left a widow and one child. Enlisted Coventry. Memorial Ref. Panel 22 to 25. Loos Memorial, France.

TOWNSEND, Private, William. 2731, C Coy., 1/7th Bn., Royal Warwickshire Regiment. Killed in action, 9th October, 1915. Age 22. Son of Mr. E. George and Mrs. Ann. Townsend of 14, Gordon Street, Leamington. Born Leamington. Enlisted Coventry. Resided Leamington. Grave Ref. I. D. 21. Foncquevilliers Military Cemetery, France.

TREADGOLD, Lance Corporal, William Henry. 266273, 1/7th Bn., Royal Warwickshire Regiment. Killed in action, 8th October, 1917. Born 27th November, 1895 in Bond Street. Resided at 34, Gresham Street formerly 6, Meadow Street. Clerk. Enlisted 1914 at Coventry. Commemorated St. John's Church. Memorial Ref. Panel 23 to 28 and 163A. Tyne Cot Memorial, Belgium.

TREDELL, Private, Arthur. 48170, 8th Bn., Devonshire Regiment. Killed in action, Passchendaele Ridge, 26th October, 1917. Born Coventry. Resided Coventry. Labourer. Commemorated Stoke (St. Michael's) Church. Enlisted 1916 at Coventry. Memorial Ref. Panel 38 to 40. Tyne Cot Memorial, Belgium.

TREEBY, Air Mechanic 2nd Class, F. J. 297784, Royal Air Force. Died, home, 14th February. 1919. Age 42. Son of John Treeby, of Kingsbridge, Devonshire. Husband of Lillian Bertha Moore (formerly Treeby), of 4 Back, 40 Bromsgrove Street, Birmingham. Grave Ref. Y. 45. Coventry (Windmill Road) Cemetery.

TREEN, Private, Albert George. Machine Gun Corps. Killed in action, Ypres, 24th July, 1917. Born 26th June, 1896 in Allesley Old Road. Resided at 27, Newcombe Road, Earlsdon, Coventry. Turner and Fitter, Rover Works. Enlisted November, 1916.

TREW, Private, Ernest Herbert. 126408, 31st Bn., Machine Gun Corps (Infantry) formerly 18574, Bedfordshire Regiment. Killed in action, 12th April, 1918. Born Coventry. Enlisted Canning Town. Resided Custom House. Memorial Ref. Panel 11. Ploegsteert Memorial, Belgium.

TRICKETT, Private, Arthur. 26204, 14th Bn., Royal Warwickshire Regiment. Killed in action, Vaulx, near Cambrai, 28th August, 1918. Age 19. Son of Edward and Emily Trickett, of 39, Poplar Road, Earlsdon, Coventry. Born 2nd July 1899, at, 10 Raglan Street. Resided at 10, Raglan Street. Green grocers. Enlisted August, 1917. Commemorated War Memorial Park. Grave Ref. V. A. 1. Mory Abbey Military Cemetery, Mory, Pas de Calais, France.

TRICKETT, Corporal, Herbert. 3434663, 2nd Bn., Lancashire Fusiliers. Died, Lahore, 13th June, 1921. Born 27th November, 1899 at Coventry. Resided at 46, South Street. Labourer. Enlisted December, 1916. Memorial Ref. Panel 4. Kirkee 1914 –1918 Memorial, India (Buried Amrisar Cemetery).

TRINDER, Private, Joshua. 12084, 2nd Bn., Leicestershire Regiment. Died of sickness, 4th July, 1916. Age 35. Son of John and Emma Trinder. Husband of Edith Sarah Day (formerly Trinder), of 18, West Street, Coventry. Born 20th September, 1881 at Leamington. Enlisted Warwick. Resided 18, West Street, Coventry. Warehouseman. Enlisted September, 1914. Memorial Ref. Panel 12. Basra Memorial, Iraq.

TROLLEY, Sick Bay Steward, G. M/296, Mentioned in Despatches. HMS Arethusa, Royal Navy. Died, home, 9th October, 1919. Age 30. Husband of Sarah Ann Trolley, of 19, Colony Cottages, Foleshill, Coventry. Grave Ref. 23. 6. Coventry (St. Paul's) Cemetery.

 **TROUGHTON**, Private, Albert. 10853, 1st Bn., Royal Welsh Fusiliers. Shot at dawn, 22nd April, 1915. Reported as met his death in extremely sad circumstances. Age 22. Son of Nathaniel Troughton, of 14, Ash Grove, Stoney Station Road, Coventry. Born 22nd July, 1892 in Eden Street. Resided 14, Ash Grove. Soldier. Grave Ref. Joint grave, III. D. 6. Estaires Communal Cemetery and Extension, Nord, France.

TROUSDELL, Hugh. Killed in action. Name on Roll of Honour in Cathedral Church of St. Michael.

TROUT, Lieutenant, Roy Cumestree. 69th Sqdn., Australian Flying Corps. Killed while flying (crashed), 27th July, 1917. Age 22. Son of Walter John and Alice Trout, of Victoria Street, Red Hill, Brisbane, Queensland. Born at Red Hill, Brisbane, Queensland. Grave Ref. 141. 174. Coventry (London Road) Cemetery.

TROY, Private, Richard. 12670, 9th Bn., Machine Gun Corps (Infantry). Killed in action, 25th April, 1918. Born Enfield Wash, Middx. Enlisted Coventry. Memorial Ref. Panel 154 to 159 and 163A. Tyne Cot Memorial, Belgium.

TRUSLOVE, Driver, Harry. 840762, "C" Bty. 307th Brigade, Royal Field Artillery. Killed in action at Boutillerie, near Cagny, 23rd April, 1918. Age 21. Son of Harry and Mary Ann Truslove, of 116, Nicholls St., Coventry. Enlisted May, 1915. Enlisted May 1915. Born 14th November, 1896 at 6, Vine Street. Resided at 116, Nicholls Street. Machinist. Commemorated War Memorial Park. Grave Ref. III. D. 1. Dive Copse British Cemetery, Sailly-Le-Sec, Somme, France.

TUCK, Private, William. 7606, 1st Bn., Wiltshire Regiment. Killed in action, 21st October, 1914. Age 28. Son of Edward and Mary Ann Tuck, of 1, Bishop Gate Green, Foleshill Road, Coventry. Husband of Bessie Lavinia Maud Hatcher (formerly Tuck), of 84, Park Street, Yeovil, Somerset. Memorial Ref. Panel 33 and 34. Le Touret Memorial, Pas de Calais, France.

TUCKEY, Private, Charles Ernest. 242325, 1st Bn., Royal Warwickshire Regiment. Killed in action, 4th October, 1917. Age 23. Son of Thomas and Sarah Ann Tuckey, of Princethorpe, Rugby. Born Princethorpe. Resided Princethorpe. Employed Coventry. Memorial Ref. Panel 23 to 28 and 163A. Tyne Cot Memorial, Belgium.

TUCKWELL, Sergeant King's Own Scottish Borderers. Killed in action, 26th February, 1917. Tester (employed Humber Limited). Enlisted 1914.

TULLY, Acting Corporal, John Alfred. 11630, 6th Bn., Oxfordshire and Buckinghamshire Light Infantry. Killed in action, 3rd September, 1916. Born Wolverhampton. Enlisted Nuneaton. Resided Coventry. Memorial Ref. Pier and Face 10 A and 10 D. Thiepval Memorial, Somme, France.

TUNNICLIFFE, Private, Ernest. 19610, "A" Coy. 11th Bn., Royal Warwickshire Regiment. Killed in action, 7th October, 1917. Age 40. Husband of Florence Tunnicliffe, of 20, Freeman Street, Coventry. Born 11th May, 1877 at 17, Sherbourne Street. Coventry. Enlisted June, 1916. Coventry. Resided at back of 72, Thomas Street. Packer and Casemaker. Memorial Ref. Panel 23 to 28 and 163A. Tyne Cot Memorial, Zonnebeke, West-Vlaanderen, Belgium.

TURBITT, Driver, Ernest George. 845188, 48th Divisional Ammunition Col., Royal Field Artillery. Died of wounds, Italy, 26th October, 1918. Born 30th June, 1893 at 12, Swanswell Street, Coventry. Enlisted Coventry. Resided 7, Atkins Square, Walsgrave Road. Signwriter. Commemorated Holy Trinity Panels. Grave Ref. 6. G. 10. Montecchio Precalcino Communal Cemetery Extension, Italy.

TURNER, A. Commemorated Coventry Chain Memorial.

TURNER, Private, Albury Charles. SD/2804, 13th Bn., Royal Sussex Regiment. Died of wounds, 30th June, 1916. Age 32. Son of Charles Thomas and Mrs. Maria Georgina Turner, of Coventry. Born 24th August, 1884 at Coventry. Enlisted Brighton. Resided Coventry. Surveyor. Grave Ref. XV. N. 25. Cabaret-Rouge British Cemetery, Souchez, Pas de Calais, France.

TURNER, Private, Alfred. 203718, 14th Bn., Royal Warwickshire Regiment. Killed in action, Merville, 14th April, 1918. Age 32. Son of Henry Turner, of 5, Duke St., Coventry. Husband of Harriett Gertrude Green (formerly Turner), of 164, Stoney Stanton Road, Coventry. Born 8th August, 1885 in Hill Street, Coventry. Enlisted July, 1917, Coventry. Resided at 164, Stoney Stanton Road. Bootmaker and repairer. Memorial Ref. Panel 2 and 3. Ploegsteert Memorial, Comines-Warneton, Hainaut, Belgium.(Possibly buried Merville).

TURNER, Rifleman, Bernard Louis. S/29050, 16th Bn., Rifle Brigade formerly R/16445, King's Royal Rifle Corps. Died of wounds, 8th February, 1917. Age 25. Husband of Clara Maud Turner, of Lentons Lane, Hawkesbury, Coventry. Born 16th May, 1891 at Harbury. Enlisted Coventry. Resided Hillfields, Coventry. Labourer. Enlisted November, 1915. Commemorated Saint Thomas the Apostle, Longford. Grave Ref. I. D. 2. Hazebrouck Communal Cemetery, Nord, France.

TURNER, Private, Edwin. 17687, 8th Bn., Royal Berkshire Regiment. Died of wounds, 1st April, 1916. Born 28th December, 1873 in Well Street, Coventry. Resided at 94, Much Park Street. Cycle finisher, Globe and Premier Works and owner of tobacconist's shop, Much Park Street. Enlisted Coventry. Grave Ref. 2K. 4. C. Le Treport Military Cemetery, France.

TURNER, Private, George. 57334, 16th Bn., Manchester Regiment formerly M/286440, Royal Army Service Corps. Killed in action, 24th March, 1918. Age 21. Son of George and Etty Turner, of 47, Jordan Well, Coventry. Born 23rd November, 1896 at 48, Lower Wellington Street, Coventry, Enlisted February, 1917 at Coventry. Mechanic. Memorial Ref. Panel 64 to 67. Pozieres Memorial, Somme, France.

TURNER, Private, Harry, MM. 1537, 1/8th Bn., Worcestershire Regiment. Killed in action, 8th June, 1915. Resided at 17, St. Michaels Road. Born Worcester. Enlisted Worcester. Grave Ref. IV. C. 3. Calvaire (Essex) Military Cemetery, Belgium.

TURRALL, Petty Officer, Charles William. 204563, HM Submarine E18, Royal Navy. Killed in loss of vessel in the Baltic, 11th June, 1916. Age 32. Son of Joseph and Lucy Turrall, of 25, Guild Road, Coventry. Husband of Selina Olive Turrall, of Huntingdon Cottage, 72, Victoria Road, Netley Abbey, Southampton. Born 1884. Resided Coventry. Served for 17 years in the Navy and was a pensioner, rejoined at the outbreak of war. Memorial Ref. 12. Portsmouth Naval Memorial, Hampshire.

TURRELL, Private, Bertie. PO691/S, Portsmouth Bn., Royal Marine Light Infantry. Killed in action, Gallipoli, 14th October, 1915. Born 2nd December, 1894 in Bull's Head Lane. Resided at 21, Coombe Street. Grinder. Enlisted October, 1914. Commemorated Stoke (St. Michaels) Church. Grave Ref. Sp. Mem. B. 72. Redoubt Cemetery, Helles, Turkey.

TURRELL, Private, Frank. 1176, 2nd Bn., Royal Warwickshire Regiment. Killed in action, 23rd April, 1916. Age 24. Son of William and Esther Turrell. Born Leamington. Resided Leamington. Employed Coventry. Grave Ref. IV. B. 1. Citadel New Military Cemetery, Fricourt, France.

TURRELL, Private, Joe, MM. 9578, 2nd /4th Bn., York and Lancaster Regiment. Killed in action, 21st July, 1918. Age 26. Son of Mr. and Mrs. Joseph Turrell, of 25, Guild Road, Foleshill, Coventry. Born 1892 in Oundle, Northants. Resided Coventry. Enlisted Coventry. Gazetted for Military Medal, 10th December, 1918. Memorial Ref. Soissons Memorial, Aisne, France.

TURRELL, Corporal, Reginald George. 840399, 306th Brigade, Royal Field Artillery. Died of wounds, received Gonnehem, 7th May, 1918. Born 9th March, 1897 at 13, Leicester Causeway. Resided at 72, Bradford Street. Clerk. Enlisted January, 1915. Commemorated War Memorial Park. Grave Ref. Row C. Grave 14. Gonnehem British Cemetery, France.

TWAITES, Private, Horace. 10711, 2nd Bn., Royal Scots Fusiliers. Killed in action, Neuve Chappelle, 13th March, 1915. Born 1891 at Coventry. Enlisted Coventry. Resided at 40, Stockton Road. Soldier. Memorial Ref. Panel 12 and 13. Le Touret Memorial, France.

TWAITES, Private, Leonard. 9773, 1st Bn., Northamptonshire Regiment. Died of wounds, Loos, 2nd October, 1915. Age 19. Son of William and Elizabeth Twaites, of 40, Stockton Road, Harnall Lane, Coventry. Born 1896 in Coventry. Resided 40, Stockton Road. Soldier. Grave Ref. Div. 19. J. 1. St. Marie Cemetery, Le Havre, Seine-Maritime, France.

TWAMLEY, Private, George. 41118, 1st Bn., Worcestershire Regiment formerly Royal Warwickshire Regiment. Killed in action, 31st July, 1917. Age 19. Son of Mrs. Drucilla Twamley, of 52, Godiva Street, Coventry. Born 19th July, 1898 at Stoke Aldermoor, Coventry. Enlisted June, 1916 at Coventry. Turner, Messrs. Guest, Charterhouse. Brother of Private Leonard Twamley. Grave Ref. II. J. 18. Divisional Collecting Post Cemetery And Extension, Belgium.

TWAMLEY, Private, Joseph. 779, H" Coy. 2nd /8th Bn., Royal Warwickshire Regiment. Died, 11th July, 1916. Age 52. Husband of Esther Twamley, of 64, Porchester Street, Birmingham. Born Coventry. Enlisted Aston, Birmingham. Grave Ref. Screen Wall. 31. 037134. Birmingham (Witton) Cemetery.

TWAMLEY, Private, Leonard. 266675, 2nd /7th Bn., Royal Warwickshire Regiment. Killed in action, 19th July, 1916. Age 21. Son of Mrs. Twamley, of 52, Godiva Street, Coventry. Born 9th March, 1896 at Stoke Aldermoor, Coventry. Enlisted Leamington. Turner, Singer Works. Enlisted November, 1915. Brother of Private George Twamley. Memorial Ref. Panel 22 to 25. Loos Memorial, Pas de Calais, France.

TWIGGER, Private, John. 159, 1st Bn., Royal Warwickshire Regiment. Died of wounds, received at Mons, 9th August 1916. Age 30. Husband of Ethel Storer (formerly Twigger), of 13, Hayes Lane, Exhall. Commemorated Exhall Memorial. Leaves a widow and four children. Grave Ref. North of church. Exhall (St. Giles) Churchyard.

TWINING, Private, James John. 483, D Coy., 7th Bn., Australian Infantry. Killed in action, 25th April, 1915. Enlisted 17th August, 1914. Born Coventry. Grave Ref. Sp. Mem. 47. No.2 Outpost Cemetery, Turkey.

TYAS, Driver, George. 720589, A Bty, 330th Bde., Royal Field Artillery. Killed in action, 21st March, 1918. Born Weaste, Lancashire. Employed Coventry. Memorial Ref. Panel 7 to 10. Pozieres Memorial, France.

TYLER, Private, Arthur Charles. 9976, 1st Bn., Royal Welsh Fusiliers. Killed in action, 21st October, 1914. Age 27. Son of Harry and Annie Tyler, of 3 Court, 2 House, Leicester Street, Coventry. Born 1887. Memorial Ref. Panel 22. Ypres (Menin Gate) Memorial, Ieper, West-Vlaanderen, Belgium.

TYLER, Private, Peter. 3280432/8th Bn., Royal Warwickshire Regiment. Killed in action, 15th December, 1917. Age 29. Son of William and Sarah Tyler of Bedworth Hill, Nuneaton. Commemorated Exhall Memorial. Enlisted Coventry. Resided Bedworth. Memorial Ref. Pier and Face 9A 9B and 10B Thiepval Memorial, France.

UDALL, William Sydney. 99080, 214th Tunnelling Coy., Royal Engineers. Killed in action, 3rd June, 1917. Age 33. Son of William and Sarah Udall, of 56, South St., Atherstone, Warwickshire. Born Dunston Heath, Staffs. Enlisted Coventry. Resided Atherstone. Grave Ref. I. C. 17. Poperinghe New Military Cemetery, Belgium.

UMNEY, Lance Corporal, Jack. 13100, 5th Oxfordshire and Buckinghamshire Light Infantry. Killed in action, 2nd April, 1917. Age 25. Son of Mrs. Eliza Umney, of 2, Church Passage, Newport Pagnell, Bucks. Born Buckingham. Enlisted Coventry. Resided Newport Pagnell. Grave Ref. D. 14. Beaurains Road Cemetery, Beaurains, France.

UNDERHILL, Rifleman, Arthur. 52385, 15th Bn., Royal Irish Rifles formerly 3881, Royal Warwickshire Regiment. Died, 15th June, 1918. Born Leamington. Enlisted Coventry. Resided Leamington. Grave Ref. I. B. 22. Gwalia Cemetery, Belgium.

UNDERHILL, Private, Frank. 3517, 1st Bn., Royal Warwickshire Regiment. Killed in action, 1st July, 1916. Age 21. Youngest son of Andrew and Jane Ann Underhill, of 47, Coronation Road, Coventry. Born Hillfields, Coventry. Enlisted Coventry. Employed Messrs. Poole, Lorrimer & Co. Lockhurst Lane. Commemorated Wesleyan Church. Memorial Ref. Pier and Face 9 A 9 B and 10 B. Thiepval Memorial, Somme, France.

UNDERWOOD, A. Educated at Bablake School. Killed in action. Commemorated Bablake School Memorial.

UNDERWOOD, Sapper, Harry Hassall. 49387, 89th Field Coy., Royal Engineers. Killed in action, 26th September, 1915. Age 18. Son of Emily Barnes (formerly Underwood), of 100, Newcombe Road, Earlsdon, Coventry. Enlisted September, 1914 at Coventry. Educated Bablake School. Born 13th October, 1896 at Coventry. Apprentice Machine Tools, Alfred Herbert Ltd. Grave Ref. Menin Road North Mem. 7. Menin Road South Military Cemetery, Ieper, West-Vlaanderen, Belgium.

UPEX, Private, Harry. 20163, 6th Bn., Northamptonshire Regiment. Died, 26th November, 1918. Age 28. Born Warmington, Northants. Enlisted Coventry. Grave Ref. Near North West Corner. Spy Communal Cemetery, Belgium.

UPEX, Private, John William. 20162, 6th Bn., Northamptonshire Regiment. Killed in action, 20th October, 1917. Age 25. Son of John and Louisa Jane Upex, of Warmington, Peterborough. Born Warmington, Northants. Enlisted Coventry. Panel 104 to 105. Tyne Cot Memorial, Belgium.

UPTON, Private, John Christopher. 114829, 35th Bn., Machine Gun Corps formerly 202967, Wiltshire Regiment. Died of wounds, 5th April, 1918. Age 22. Son of Charles Foster Upton and Louisa Upton, of Woodmill, Yoxall, Burton-on-Trent. Enlisted Coventry. Employed Coventry. Commemorated Exhall Memorial. Grave Ref. VI. A. 61. Doullens Communal Cemetery Extension No.1, France.

USHER, Robert. Killed in action. Name on Roll of Honour in Cathedral Church of St. Michael.

VALE, Lance Corporal, Joseph, DCM, MSM. 11103, 2nd Bn., Oxfordshire and Buckinghamshire Light Infantry. Killed in action, 12th September, 1918. Brother of Mrs. F. Anderton of London Road, Stretton-on-Dunsmore, Rugby. Born Allesley. Enlisted Rugby. Resided Clifton, Warwicks. Awarded Distinguished Conduct Medal near Hermies, on 11th and 12th September, 1918. He showed great courage and devotion to duty. Although tired out with relaying lines during two days under shell fire, he went out again on four separate occasions under very heavy barrage to mend lines whose preservation was of the utmost importance. On the third occasion he bought in a wounded man. Memorial Ref. panel 7. Vis-En-Artois Memorial, France.

VALENTINE, Private, Edward. T.F. 200184, 13th Bn., Middlesex Regiment. Killed in action, 24th August, 1917. Born Coventry. Enlisted Tottenham, Middlesex. Memorial Ref. Panel 113 to 115. Tyne Cot Memorial, Belgium.

VALLANCE, Private, Richard. 1785, 1st Bn., Royal Warwickshire Regiment. Killed in action, 25th April, 1915. Age 23. Son of Charles and Frances Vallance of 22, Bedford Street, Leamington. Born Leamington, Spa. Enlisted Coventry. Resided Leamington Spa. Memorial Ref. Panel 8. Ypres (Menin Gate), Belgium.

VALOUR, Private, Edward. 58993, 7th Bn., Royal Fusiliers formerly DN/2/209265, Royal Army Service Corps. Killed in action, 30th October, 1917. Age 19. Son of Edward and Jean Thompson (formerly Valour), of 24, Hamilton Road, Stoke. Born 29th May, 1898 at Dover. Enlisted June, 1916, Coventry. Resided Coventry. Turner. Memorial Ref. Panel 28 to 30 and 162 to 162A and 163A. Tyne Cot Memorial, Zonnebeke, West-Vlaanderen, Belgium.

VARNEY, Bugler, Frederick Willoughby. 9970, 2nd Bn., Oxfordshire and Buckinghamshire Light Infantry. Killed in action, 1st October, 1918. Born Neithrop, Oxon. Resided Earlsdon. Commemorated St. Barbara's Church. Grave Ref. III. D. 1. Anneux British Cemetery, France.

VARNEY, Private, James. 203698, 1st Bn., Royal Warwickshire Regiment. Killed in action, 17th October, 1918. Eldest son of Mr. G. Varney, of 7, Court, 4, House, Chauntry Place, Coventry. Born 8th December, 1897 at 7c. 4h. Chauntry Place. Turner, Gloria Cycle Works. Enlisted 1916 at Coventry. Commemorated Triumph and Gloria Memorial. Grave Ref. III. B. 22. St. Aubert British Cemetery, Nord, France.

VAUGHAN, Sapper, Harry Adrian. Cadet, Officers' Cadet Battalion formerly 74035, Fenny Stratford Signal Depot, Royal Engineers. Accidentally, drowned, home, 20th May 1917. Draughtsman. Enlisted in 1914. Grave Ref. Cambridge City Cemetery.

VAUGHAN, Private, William. G/5723, 8th Bn., The Queen's Royal West Kent Regiment. Killed in action, 15th November, 1915. Born Lambeth, Surrey. Enlisted 1915 at Coventry. Resided Coventry. Stereotyper. Commemorated Iliffe & Sons Ltd Memorial. Grave Ref. I. J. 23. Spoilbank Cemetery, Belgium.

VERNON, Lance Corporal, Edward. 40350, 8th Bn., Royal Inniskilling Fusiliers formerly 14093, Middlesex Regiment Died of wounds, 29th May, 1917. Born Middleton, Lancs. Enlisted Millhill. Resided Coventry. Grave Ref. I. B. 184. Bailleul Communal Cemetery Extension (Nord), France.

VERNON, Private, John. 268102, 2/7th Bn., Royal Warwickshire Regiment. Killed in action, 9th April, 1917. Born Coventry. Enlisted Coventry. Memorial Ref. Pier and Face 9 A 9 B and 10 B. Thiepval Memorial, Somme, France.

VERNON, Private, John. 16666, 16th Coy., Machine Gun Corps (Infantry) formerly 21196, Royal Dublin Fusiliers. Killed in action, 28th June, 1917. Born Aston, Birmingham. Employed Coventry. Enlisted Coventry. Grave Ref. II. C. 5. Mazingarbe Communal Cemetery Extension, France.

VERPILLOT, Private, Aime Constant. 4885, 53rd Bn., Australian Infantry. Killed in action, 19th July, 1916. Age 25. Son of Charles Eugene and Berthe Verpillot, of 15, Barracluff Avenue, Bondi, New South Wales. Native of Neuchatel, Switzerland. Employed Alfred Herbert prior to emigrating. Memorial Ref. 9. V.C. Corner Australian Cemetery Memorial, Fromelles, France.

VIALS, Corporal, Charles David. 7859, 1st Bn., Bedfordshire Regiment. Killed in action, 13th November, 1914. Age 28. Husband of Emma Tansley (formerly Vials), of 268, Longford Road, Longford, Coventry. Born Irlingborough. Enlisted Bedford. Resided Longford. Commemorated Saint Thomas the Apostle, Longford. Memorial Ref. Panel 10 and 11. Le Touret Memorial, Pas De Calais, France.

VICK, Lance Corporal, Bernard C. 2465, 1st/8th Bn., Sherwood Foresters (Notts and Derby Regiment). Killed in action, 14th October, 1915. Son of Victor and Kate Vick of Kintore, Ettrick Road, Chichester. Name on Roll of Honour in Cathedral Church of St. Michael. Memorial Ref. Panel 87 to 89. Loos Memorial, France.

VICKERS, Private, Isaac. 59178, 1st (Garr.) Bn., Devonshire Regiment. Died, 17th November, 1918. Age 20. Son of John and Elizabeth Vickers, of 21, Canal Road, Longford, Coventry. Born 25th February, 1898 at Waterloo, Pilsley near Chesterfield. Artificial silk spinner. Enlisted October, 1916. Commemorated Saint Thomas the Apostle, Longford. Grave Ref. W. 21. Jerusalem War Cemetery, Israel.

VICKERS, T. Killed in action. Employed by Rover Company Ltd.

VIDLER, Private, Charlie. M2/11868, VIII Corps, Army Service Corps. Died of wounds, 12th May, 1918. Age 25. Only son of Walter and Fanny Vidler of Mill House, Hamptons, Tonbridge, Kent. Born Horsmonden, Kent. Enlisted Coventry. Resided Tonbridge. Grave Ref. IX. B. 71. Boulogne Eastern Cemetery, France.

VILLIERS, Private, William Alfred. 12627, 11th Bn., Royal Warwickshire Regiment. Killed in action, 16th July, 1916. Born 17th March, 1886 at 26c. 4h. Gosford Street. Resided 1, Weston Street. Gear case enameller, Speedwell Gear Co. Enlisted June, 1915 at Coventry. Left a widow and two children. Memorial Ref. Pier and Face 9 A 9 B and 10 B. Thiepval Memorial, Somme, France.

VINCENT, Private, Charles. 7400, 2nd Bn., South Lancashire Regiment. Killed in action, 25th September, 1914. Born Hereford. Enlisted Coventry. Resided Leamington. Memorial Ref. La Ferte Sous-Jouarre Memorial, France.

VINCENT, Private, Edgar Arthur. 23724, 16th Bn., Royal Warwickshire Regiment. Killed in action, 10th May, 1917 severely wounded in the head. Age 20. Son of Mr. Edward and Mrs. Charlotte Vincent of 10, White's Row, Warwick Road, Kenilworth. Employed Triumph Works, Coventry. Memorial Ref. Bay 3. Arras Memorial, Pas-de-Calais, France.

VINCENT, Second Lieutenant, Frederick Charles, DCM. 7th Bn., King's Royal Rifle Corps. Killed in action, 21st March, 1918. Age 25. Eldest son of William Charles and Emily Lauria Vincent, of Walsgrave-on-Sowe, Coventry. Awarded Distinguished Conduct Medal for fighting on the Somme. Employed Daimler Co. Ltd. Commemorated Walsgrave Memorial and Bablake School Memorial. Memorial Ref. Panel 61 to 64. Pozieres Memorial, Somme, France.

VINCENT, Private, James. 6040, 1/19th Bn., London Regiment formerly 18024, King's Royal Rifle Corps. Killed in action, 29th September, 1916. Age 18. Son of James and Eliza Vincent of 49, Clarence Street, Nuneaton. Born Leamington. Enlisted Coventry. Resided Hinckley. Memorial Ref. Pier and Face 9D 9C 13 C and 12 C. Thiepval Memorial, France.

VINCENT, Private 2nd Class, Sydney. 276103, Royal Air Force. Died home, 4th November, 1918. Age 28. Husband of Harriet Amelia Vincent, of 1 Sun Street, Brockmoor, Staffs. Born 27th November, 1889 at Quarry Bank, Staffs. Resided Coventry. Crane Driver. Enlisted July, 1918. Memorial Ref. Brookwood (United Kingdom 1914-1918) Memorial. (possibly buried Quarry Bank).

VINCENT, T. Commemorated Triumph & Gloria Memorial.

VINER, Private, Albert Victor. 2602, 1st /7th Bn., Royal Warwickshire Regiment. Killed in action, Foncquevillers, 23rd March, 1916. Age 22. Son of Alfred and Ellen Elizabeth Viner, of Allesley, Coventry. Born August, 1888 at Allesley. Gardener. Enlisted August, 1914 at Coventry. Grave Ref. I. C. 7. Foncquevillers Military Cemetery, Pas de Calais, France.

VINER, Private, Alfred Lawrence Norman. 43089, 1st /10th Bn., Manchester Regiment formerly Oxfordshire and Buckinghamshire Light Infantry. Killed in action, by a shell, 29th March 1918. Age 35. Son of Alfred and Ellen Elizabeth Viner, of Ragland Cottage, Allesley, Coventry. Born 7th March. 1883 at Allesley. Printers machine minder, Iliffe and Sons Ltd. Commemorated Iliffe & Sons Ltd Memorial. Enlisted January, 1915 at Coventry. Memorial Ref. Bay 7. Arras Memorial, Pas De Calais, France.

VOICE, Battery Quartermaster Sergeant, Arthur Richard. 11385, "D" Bty. 66th Brigade, Royal Field Artillery. Died of wounds received, Kut, 13th March, 1916. Age 33. Son of Walter and Emma J. Voice, of Coventry. Born 26th October 1883, at Cardiff. Resided at Coventry. Rate collector. Enlisted Rugby, October, 1914. Commemorated Finance Department Memorial, Coventry Corporation and War Memorial Park. Grave Ref. VI. F. 20. Basra War Cemetery, Iraq.

WADLEY, Corporal, Ralph. 14732, 8th Bn., Oxfordshire and Buckinghamshire Light Infantry. Died, Salonika, 4th January, 1918. Age 27. Husband of Nellie B. Wadley of 83, Middle Street, Trallwn, Pontypridd. Born Drybrook, Glos. Enlisted Coventry. Resided Pontypridd, South Wales. Grave Ref. 204. Mikra British Cemetery, Kalamaria, Greece.

WAGSTAFFE, Private, George. 8059, 1st Bn., Royal Welsh Fusiliers. Killed in action, near Festubert, 16th May, 1915. Age 28. Son of Amos and Anna Wagstaffe, of 150, Nicholls St., Coventry. Husband of Jane Elizabeth Gill (formerly Wagstaffe), of 50, Well Street, Coventry. Born in 1887, at Foleshill. Resided at 183, Cross Road. Engineer, Deasy and Daimler Works. Enlisted Coventry. Commemorated War Memorial Park and Siddeley Roll of Honour. Memorial Ref. Panel 13 and 14. Le Touret Memorial, Pas de Calais, France.

WAINMAN, Private, Harry. 70583, 9th Battalion, Royal Welsh Fusiliers. Died of wounds, 13th May 1918. Age 26. Son of George Wainman of 115, Baughton Street, Birmingham. Husband of Martha Wainman of 59, High Street, Fenton, Stoke-on-Trent. Born at Birmingham. Resided at Birmingham. Enlisted Llanelly. Employed by Armstrong Siddeley Motors, Limited. Commemorated War Memorial Park and Siddeley Roll of Honour.. Grave Ref. I. D. 12. Esquelbecq Military Cemetery, France.

WALDEN, A. J. Royal Fusiliers. Killed in action, Dardanelles. Resided Stoneleigh and District.

WALDEN, Lance Corporal, William Francis. 20779, 3rd Bn., Coldstream Guards. 13th April, 1918. Age 21. Son of William and Agnes Walden, of The Green Man Inn, Hall Green, Foleshill, Coventry. Enlisted Coventry. Memorial Ref. Panel 1. Ploegsteert Memorial, Comines-Warneton, Hainaut, Belgium.

WALDRON, Lance Corporal, Frank. 66222, 24th Bn., Canadian Infantry. Killed in action, near Marcelcave, 8th August, 1918. Born 7th February, 1896 at Coventry. Resided Canada. Trimmer. Enlisted October, 1914. Grave Ref. XVI. E. 7. Villers-Bretonneux Military Cemetery, France.

WALE, Private, William. 66674, 2/7th Bn., Royal Warwickshire Regiment. Killed in action, 19th July, 1916. Born Coventry. Enlisted Coventry. Employed by Rover Co. Ltd. Grave Ref. Sp. Mem. M7. Cabaret-Rouge British Cemetery, Souchez, France.

WALFORD, Corporal, George Herbert. 19898, Royal Air Force formerly Royal Warwickshire Regiment. Died, home, John Coupland Hospital 26th June, 1917. Born 5th August, 1894 at Kenilworth. Resided 68, Harnall Lane East with his Uncle. Fitter, Rover Works. Enlisted September, 1914. Eldest son of Mrs. Morgan, Offchurch. Grave Ref. Offchurch (St. Gregory) Churchyard.

WALKER, Private, Arthur. 265279, 2/7th Bn., Royal Warwickshire Regiment. Died, 21st November, 1918. Born Foleshill. Enlisted Coventry. Grave Ref. XV. A. 64. Cologne Southern Cemetery, Germany.

WALKER, Private, Cuthbert William. 21204, 2nd/7th Battalion, Royal Warwickshire Regiment. Killed in action, near St. Julien, 30th August 1917. Born 5th February, 1898, in Lincolnshire. Resided at Wisteria Cottage, Stivichall Common. Miller. Enlisted February, 1917 at Coventry. Commemorated St. James Church and War Memorial Park. Memorial Ref. Panel 23 to 28 and 163A. Tyne Cot Memorial, Belgium.

WALKER, Private, Ernest Sydney. 9507, 14th Bn., Royal Warwickshire Regiment. Killed in action, 8th November, 1917. Age 35. Husband of Amy Rebecca Walker, of 16, King William Street, Coventry. Born 25th January, 1882 at Coventry. Enlisted August, 1914 at Coventry. Postman. Commemorated Post Office Memorial. Memorial Ref. Panel 23 to 28 and 163A. Tyne Cot Memorial, Zonnebeke, West-Vlaanderen, Belgium.

WALKER, H. Commemorated Triumph & Gloria Memorial.

WALKER, Sapper, H. 236581, Royal Engineers. Died, home, 9th October, 1919. Grave Ref. 188. 48. Coventry (London Road) Cemetery.

WALKER, Private, Harry Henry. 15486, 11th Bn., Royal Warwickshire Regiment. Died of wounds, 18th July, 1916. Age 30. Brother of Miss F. Walker, of 3 Court, 2 House, Union St., Coventry. Born 25th December, 1883 at Foleshill, Coventry. Enlisted December, 1915 at Coventry. Resided Foleshill Road. Machinist. Grave Ref. II. D. 14. Heilly Station Cemetery, Mericourt-L'abbe, Somme, France.

WALKER, Corporal, Henry. 12620, 2nd Bn., Worcestershire Regiment. Killed in action, La Bassee, 7th December, 1915. Age 22. Son of William Henry Walker, of Smethwick, Staffs. Husband of Mabel Hannah Walker, of 258, Cross Road, Foleshill, Coventry. Born Smethwick. Grave Ref. I. B. 13. Woburn Abbey Cemetery, Cuinchy, Pas De Calais, France.

WALKER, Private, John Thomas. 41213, 1st Bn., Worcestershire Regiment. Died of wounds, 19th August, 1917. Born Coventry. Enlisted Bedworth. Resided Bedworth. Grave Ref. VIII. I. 6. Boulogne Eastern Cemetery, France.

WALKER, Private, Oliver John. 25120, 14th Bn., Royal Warwickshire Regiment. Killed 14th April, 1918. Born 3rd July, 1883 at Longford. Resided at 43, King Fields. Labourer, Courtaulds Ltd. Enlisted Coventry. Commemorated Roll of Honour, Salem Baptist Church. Memorial Ref. Panel 2 and 3. Ploegsteert Memorial, Belgium.

WALKER, Private, Thomas William. 14728, 2nd Bn., Worcestershire Regiment. Killed in action, 2nd July, 1916. Age 22. Husband of Maggie Walker of 113 Nuneaton Road, Collycroft, Nuneaton. Born 1891 in Station Street West. Resided at 28, Station Street East. Driller. Enlisted August, 1914 at Coventry. Memorial Ref. Addenda Panel. Loos Memorial, France.

WALL, Private, Charles. 13807, 4th Bn., Coldstream Guards. Died of wounds, 9th July, 1916. Age 19. Son of George and Elizabeth Wall, of Allesley Hall Cottage, Allesley, Coventry. Born Great Packington, near Coventry. Enlisted Coventry. Grave Ref. VIII. C. 8A. Lijssenthoek Military Cemetery, Poperinge, West-Vlaanderen, Belgium.

WALL, Sergeant, George Henry. 265568, 1/7th Bn., Royal Warwickshire Regiment. Killed in action, 18th April, 1917 by a shell in the trenches and buried where he fell. Born 24th September, 1892 at 11, Junction Street. Resided Coventry. Fitter, Rex Co. Ltd. Enlisted September, 1914 at Coventry. Resided 20 Grantham Street. Memorial Ref. Pier and Face 9 A 9 B and 10 B. Thiepval Memorial, Somme, France.

WALL, Lance Corporal, John Thomas. 5743, 1st Bn., Coldstream Guards. Died of wounds, Poperinghe, 29th October, 1914. Born 8th January, 1883 at 2, Thomas Street. Resided Coventry. Cycle Hand. Reservist. Enlisted Coventry. Grave Ref. I. L. 13. Poperinghe Old Military Cemetery, Belgium.

WALLACE, Private, Herbert. 206183, A Bn., Machine Gun Corps (Heavy Branch) formerly 38424, Machine Gun Corps. Killed in action, 8th June, 1917. Age 27. Son of William and Elizabeth Wallace of 21, St. John Street, Rugby. Born Blakesby, Northants. Enlisted Coventry. Grave Ref. III. C. IS. Dickebusch New Military Cemetery Extension, Belgium.

WALLEN, Private, Alfred. 9701, 1st Bn., Royal Warwickshire Regiment. Died of wounds, 24th November, 1914. Age 28. Husband of Margaret Wallen, of 3 Court, 8 House, Sherbourne St., Coventry. Born 9th September, 1886 at Coventry. Enlisted Coventry. Resided 26c. 6h. Gosford Street. Polisher, Rotherams. Reservist. Leaves a widow and three children. Grave Ref. II. I. 33. Trois Arbres Cemetery, Steenwerck, Nord, France. (Originally buried Fortrie Fernie, Romarin).

 **WALLIS**, Private, Albert Edward. 103209, 153rd Coy., Machine Gun Corps (Infantry) formerly Royal Warwickshire Regiment. Killed in action 17th September, 1917. Age 19. Son of Matthew H. and Fanny Wallis, of 72, George Street, Coventry. Born 25th April, 1892 at Brinkworth, Wilts. Turner. Enlisted March, 1917 at Coventry. Grave Ref. L. F. 16. Poelcapelle British Cemetery, Langemark-Poelkapelle, West-V., Belgium.

WALLIS, Private, George. 12590, 2nd Bn., Oxfordshire and Buckinghamshire Light Infantry. Killed in action, Vermelles, 15th October, 1915. Born 9th June, 1892 at Burton-on-Trent. Resided 1, Somerset Road. Labourer. Enlisted September, 1914 at Coventry. Grave Ref. B. 18. Quarry Cemetery, Vermelles, France.

WALLIS, Private, George Claridge. 12074, 17th Entrenching Bn., late 14th Bn., Hampshire Regiment. Killed in action between 21st March, 1918 and 27th March, 1918. Age 39. Brother of Miss F. G. Wallis, of 79, Park Road, West Dulwich, London. Born Norwood, Surrey. Enlisted Lambeth, London. Resided Coventry. Memorial Ref. Bay 6. Arras Memorial, France.

WALLSGROVE, Company Sergeant Major, Louis. 92127, F Bn., Tank Corps formerly 079326, Machine Gun Corps. Killed in action, 20th November, 1917. Age 28. Son of Mr. R. and Mrs. S. Wallsgrove of 41, Clarendon Street, Leamington. Enlisted Coventry. Memorial Ref. Panel 13. Cambrai Memorial, Louveral, France.

WALTER, Rifleman Herbert. G/44189, 1/21st Bn., London Regiment (First Surrey Rifles). Killed in action, 1st September, 1918. Born 29th January, 1900 at Coventry. Resided at 11c. 3h. Cox Street. Fitter. Reservist. Employed Rudge Works. Grave Ref. Peronne Communal Cemetery Extension.

WALTERS, Private, James Henry. 44553, 2nd Bn., Suffolk Regiment formerly SS/49733, South Staffordshire Regiment. Killed in action, 8th October, 1918. Age 34. Son of Albert James and Alice Walters of 119, Bank Street, Brierly Hill, Staffs. Enlisted Coventry. Grave Ref. H. 7. Forenville Military Cemetery, France.

WALTERS, Private, Sidney. 20897, 6th Bn., Oxfordshire and Buckinghamshire Light Infantry. Died of wounds, 7th October, 1916. Born Middleton Cheeney, Northants. Enlisted Coventry. Resided Middleton Cheeney, Northants. Memorial Ref. Pier and Face 10A and 10D. Thiepval Memorial, France.

WALTON, Frank. Killed in action, September, 1915. Resided Foleshill.

WALTON, Private, George Alfred. 64108, 10th Bn., Royal Fusiliers formerly 4905, 4th East Kent Regiment. Died of wounds, 16th September, 1918. Born Homport. Enlisted Coventry. Resided Birmingham. Grave Ref. XIII. C. 15. Grevilliers British Cemetery, France.

WALTON, Private, Joseph John. 266241, 1/7th Bn., Royal Warwickshire Regiment. Died of wounds, 6th April, 1917. Age 18. Son of Joseph Harry and Sarah Ellen Walton of 45, Gadsby Street, Attleborough, Nuneaton. Born Nuneaton. Enlisted Coventry. Resided Attleborough, Warwicks. Grave Ref. E. 81. Villiers-Faucon Communal Cemetery, France.

WALTON, Private, Spencer. 42466, 11th Bn., Suffolk Regiment formerly TR/9/34829, T.R. Bn. Died of wounds, 23rd August, 1918. Age 19. Son of John and Amy L. Walton of 80, Henry Street, Kenilworth. Born Tysoe, Warwick. Enlisted Coventry. Grave Ref. IV. C. 3. Aire Communal Cemetery, France.

 **WARD**, Private, Albert Edward. 17758, A Coy., 3 Platoon, 11th Bn., Royal Warwickshire Regiment. Killed in action, 13th August, 1916. Age 19. Son of Albert Edward and Martha Ward, of 66, Milton Street, Stoke, Coventry. Born 18th March, 1897 at Plumstead, London. Turner, Dunlop Rim and Wheel Co. Ltd., Alma Street, Coventry. Enlisted Aspril, 1916. Resided 66, Milton Street. Commemorated Dunlop Memorial. Memorial Ref. Pier and Face 9 A 9 B and 10 B. Thiepval Memorial, Somme, France.

WARD, Rifleman, Alfred John. R/1824, 11th Bn., King's Royal Rifle Corps. Died of wounds, 30th August, 1916. Age 22. Born 1st September, 1894 at All Saints, Coventry. Enlisted September, 1914 at Nuneaton. Resided 67, Yardley Street, Coventry. Son of Mr. G. Ward. Labourer. Grave Ref. IV. A. 2. St. Pierre Cemetery, Amiens, France.

WARD, Private, Amos. 8363, 10th Bn., Royal Warwickshire Regiment. Died of wounds, 31st August, 1915. Age 29. Son of William and Elizabeth Ward, of Radford Semele, Leamington Spa. Born Radford Semele, Leamington. Resided at 5, Railway Cottages. Railwayman. Enlisted Coventry. Grave Ref. III. V. 7. Merville Communal Cemetery, France.

WARD, Private, Anthony. 24469, 1st Coy., 1st Platoon, 1st Bn., Devonshire Regiment. Killed in action, Ypres, 4th October, 1917. Age 21. Son of William Ward, of 29, London Road, Coventry. Born 27th May, 1896 in Gosford Street, Coventry. Enlisted Coventry. Resided 29, London Road. Machinist, Swift Motor Co. Ltd. Enlisted December, 1915. Grave Ref. XLVII. G. 6. Tyne Cot Cemetery, Zonnebeke, West-Vlaanderen, Belgium.

WARD, Second Lieutenant, Bernard Michael. 11th Battalion, Royal Dublin Fusiliers. Killed in action, Cambrai, 20th November, 1917. Age 19 Son of John P and Mary Ward, of Ballinrobe, Co. Mayo. Born in 1898, at Coventry. Resided at Coventry. Registrar's clerk. Enlisted August, 1916. Educated Bablake School. Commemorated Bablake School Memorial and War Memorial Park. Grave Ref. II. D. 4. Croisilles British Cemetery, France.

WARD, Gunner, Charles. Royal Field Artillery. Killed in action, 6th April, 1917. Aged 22. Resided Keresley. Commemorated St. Thomas Memorial.

WARD, Private, Charles. 41908, 3rd Bn., Worcestershire Regiment formerly 26702, Royal Warwickshire Regiment. Killed in action, 10th April, 1918. Son of Mr. G. and Mrs. E. Ward of 56, West Street, Warwick. Born Wasperton, Warwicks. Enlisted Coventry. Resided Warwick. Memorial Ref. Panel 5. Ploegsteert Memorial, Belgium.

WARD, Rifleman, Charles. S/2758, 10th Bn., Rifle Brigade. Killed in action, 3rd September, 1916. Born and resided Brandon. Enlisted Rugby. Memorial Ref. Pier and Face 16 B and 16 C. Thiepval Memorial, Somme, France.

WARD, Rifleman, Charles. 52222, 15th Bn., Royal Irish Rifles formerly 1600, Royal Warwicks Regiment. Killed in action, 22nd August, 1918. Born 29th March, 1893 at 48, Yardley Street, Coventry. Enlisted August, 1914, Coventry. Resided Bristol. Clerk, Coventry Chain. Commemorated Coventry Chain Memorial. Grave Ref. III. F. 103. Bailleul Communal Cemetery Extension (Nord), France.

WARD, Private, Charles Henry. 148, B Coy., 1st Bn., Royal Warwickshire Regiment. Killed in action, Hill 60, 25th April, 1915. Born 2nd June, 1883 at 3, Paynes Lane, Coventry. Resided at 40c. 3h. Gosford Street. Driller. Reservist. Enlisted Coventry. Memorial Ref. Panel 8. Ypres (Menin Gate) Memorial, Belgium.

WARD, Private, Charles William. 718409, 23rd Bn., London Regiment formerly Notts and Derby Regiment. Killed in action, 14th October, 1918. Age 29. Husband of Alma Ward, of 16, Berridge Road, West Nottingham. Born 28th July, 1889 at Radford, Nottingham. Resided at 5, Uplands, Stoke Heath. Toolsetter. Enlisted April, 1918. Grave Ref. XVII. H. 5. Hooge Crater Cemetery, Belgium.

WARD, Sergeant, Cyril Arthur Morris. 8142, 1st Bn., Northamptonshire Regiment. Killed in action, Festubert, 9th May, 1915. Age 26. Son of Arthur James and Sarah Ann Ward. Husband of Lily Jones (formerly Ward), of 12, Peel Street, Crewe. Born 29th October, 1889 at Gosford Green, Coventry. Enlisted Coventry. Resided Crewe. Machinist. Grave Ref. II. B. 6. Rue-Petillon Military Cemetery, Fleurbaix, France.

WARD, Private, David. 9757, 1st Bn., Royal Warwickshire Regiment. Killed in action, Armentieres, 27th October, 1914. Born 1887 in Foleshill. Resided at 150, Cross Road. Miner formerly employed Stirling Metal Works. Reservist. Left a widow and one child. Enlisted Coventry. Grave Ref. Sp. Mem 4. Houplines Communal Cemetery, France.

WARD, Private, Ernest Thomas. 23034, 3rd Bn., Durham Light Infantry. Died, Home, 22nd January, 1919. Born 24th January, 1894 at Coventry. Resided at 3c. 6h. Sherbourne Street. Cycle Filer. Enlisted September, 1914. Grave Ref. 191. 45. Coventry (London Road) Cemetery.

WARD, Private, F. H. 321364, Royal Wiltshire Yeomanry. Died, home, 15th May, 1919. Age 29. Son of Francis William Ward, of 24, St. Margaret's Road, Stoke, Coventry. Grave Ref. 1583. Newport (Christchurch) Cemetery, Monmouthshire.

WARD, Private, Felix. 75424, 21st Bn., Manchester Regiment. Died of wounds, 8th November, 1918. Born Manchester. Resided at 328, Harnall Lane East. Machine tool repairer. Grave Ref. I.B. 29. Busigny Communal Cemetery Extension, France.

WARD, G. Commemorated Coventry Chain Memorial.

WARD, Private, George Allan. 42875, 10th Bn., Royal Warwickshire Regiment. Killed in action, St. Martin, 21st October, 1918. Age 19. Son of George A. and Maria Ward, of 104, Station Street West, Foleshill, Coventry. Born 22nd September, 1899 at Foleshill, Coventry. Enlisted Coventry. Resided 50, Lockhurst Lane. Turner. Enlisted May, 1918. Commemorated St. Paul's Church. Grave Ref. VI. E. 7. Romeries Communal Cemetery Extension, Nord, France.

WARD, Private, George Frederick. 7512, 7th Bn., King's Shropshire Light Infantry. Died of wounds, 1st April, 1918. Born 4th September, 1887 at Coventry. Enlisted Coventry. Resided 67, Yardley Street. Hardener. Reservist. Grave Ref. XIV. F. 8. Cabaret-Rouge British Cemetery, Souchez, France.

 **WARD**, Lance Sergeant, Herbert. 3354, 2nd /7th Bn., Royal Warwickshire Regiment. Killed in action, Laventie, 19th July, 1916. Age 35. Son of Walter and Mary Ward, of Coventry. Husband of Alice Ward, of 31, Bloomsbury Street, Gloucester Road, Cheltenham. Born 6th February, 1881 at Coventry. Resided Whitley. Mechanic, Sewage Pumping Station. Enlisted November, 1916. Commemorated Bablake School Memorial and Sewage Disposal Memorial, Coventry Corporation. Leaves a widow and four children. Grave Ref. II. E. 16. Laventie Military Cemetery, La Gorgue, Nord, France.

WARD, Private, John. 57354, 1/8th Bn., Royal Warwickshire Regiment. Killed in action, 4th November, 1918. Born Horton-on-the-Hill, Warwick. Enlisted Coventry. Resided Dordon, Warwicks. Grave Ref. A. 30. Landrecies British Cemetery, France.

 **WARD**, Gunner, John Percy. 845308, "D" Bty. 162nd Brigade, Royal Field Artillery. Died of wounds, 26th April, 1918. Husband of L. Ward, of 7, Marsworth Street, Coventry. Born 31st December, 1887, at 8, Waterloo Street. Resided at 7, Marsworth Street. Capstan Hand. Enlisted February, 1915. Commemorated War Memorial Park. Grave Ref. I. D. 14. Arneke British Cemetery, Nord, France.

WARD, Private, Joseph. 266345, 2/7th Bn., Royal Warwickshire Regiment. Killed in action, Pozieres, 14th July, 1916. Born 23rd September, 1899 in Holy Trinity Parish. Resided 28 Day's Lane. Engineer. Enlisted January, 1915 at Coventry. Memorial Ref. Panel 22 to 25. Loos Memorial, France.

WARD, Gunner, Joseph Charles. 62066, 45th Bty. 42nd Bde., Royal Field Artillery. Killed in action, 6th April, 1917. Born Coventry. Enlisted Coventry. Grave Ref. III. O. 15. Faubourg D'Amiens Cemetery, Arras, France.

WARD, Corporal, Leonard. 242493, 2/6th Bn., Royal Warwickshire Regiment. Killed in action, 8th December, 1917. Husband of Edith Ward, of 7, Rue Armand Carrel, Paris. Born 1888 at 6c. 4h. New Buildings, Coventry. Enlisted Coventry. Resided 38, New Buildings. Coal yardman. Enlisted June, 1915. Commemorated Holy Trinity Panels. Grave Ref. II. F. 15. Metz-En-Couture Communal Cemetery British Extension, France.

WARD, Second Lieutenant, Norman John. 11th Bn., Royal Warwickshire Regiment. Killed in action, 11th August, 1916. Age 21. Son of John James and Amelia Ann Ward, of "Glencoe," Barrow Road, Kenilworth, Warwickshire. Born 1895. Resided Kenilworth. Educated King Henry VIII School. Auctioneer. Commemorated King Henry VIII School. Memorial Ref. Pier and Face 9 A 9 B and 10 B. Thiepval Memorial, Somme, France.

WARD, S. Commemorated Ryton Memorial.

WARD, Private, Sidney Frank. 94119, 1st Bn., The King's (Liverpool Regiment) formerly 38092, Royal Warwickshire Regiment. Killed in action, 25th August, 1918. Age 32. Son of George Ward, of 74, St. Patrick's Road, Coventry. Husband of Gertrude Ward, of 11, White Street, Coventry. Born 5th December, 1885 at Stoneleigh Cottage, Butts, Coventry. Enlisted 1915 at Coventry. Educated Bablake School. Resided Stoneleigh Cottage. Bookseller and Stationer. Commemorated Bablake School Memorial. Memorial Ref. Panel 3 and 4. Vis-En-Artois Memorial, Pas de Calais, France.

WARD, Private, Sydney. 13103, "C" Coy. 2nd Bn., Oxfordshire and Buckinghamshire Light Infantry. Killed in action, 15th May, 1915. Age 37. Son of Joseph and Hannah Ward, of 1, Sunnyside, Nuneaton, Warwickshire. Husband of Sarah Ward, of Ryton-on-Dunsmore, Coventry. Enlisted Coventry. Memorial Ref. Panel 26. Le Touret Memorial, Pas De Calais, France.

WARD, William. B Coy., 3rd Bn., Devonshire and Cornwall Light Infantry.

WARD, Sergeant, William. 6030, 3rd Bn., Duke of Cornwalls Light Infantry. Died, Home, 6th January, 1915. Born Leicester. Enlisted Coventry. Grave Ref. K. H. 69. Falmouth Cemetery, Cornwall.

WARD, Private, William George. 31048, 2nd Bn., Hampshire Regiment. Died of wounds, Home, 26th February, 1919. Age 19. Son of George E. and Emma Ward of 22, John Street, Kenilworth. Born Kenilworth. Enlisted Coventry. Resided Kenilworth. Grave Ref. C. 854. Kenilworth Cemetery.

WARDEN, Gunner, Leonard. 118983, "D" Battery, 108th Brigade, Royal Field Artillery. Killed in action, Passchendaele, 18th October, 1917. Born 1st July 1896, at Coventry. Resided at 39, Holyhead Road. Coach Painter. Enlisted November, 1915. Commemorated War Memorial Park. Memorial Ref. Panel 4 to 6 and 162. Tyne Cot Memorial, Belgium.

WARDER, Private, William. 10465, 2nd Bn., Royal Warwickshire Regiment. Killed in action, Loos, 25th September, 1915. Age 34. Son of John Warder, of 15, Beechfield Road, Beechfield Grove, Ladypool, Birmingham. Husband of Rose Lilian Warder, of 172, Whitmore Park Cottages, Holbrooks Lane, Foleshill, Coventry. Born 25th March, 1881 at Birmingham. Resided Gosford Street. Labourer. Enlisted January, 1915 at Coventry. Memorial Ref. Panel 22 to 25. Loos Memorial, Pas De Calais, France.

WARE, Private, Thomas. 20984, 1/8th Bn., Royal Warwickshire Regiment. Died, 16th December, 1916. Son of James and Elizabeth Ware of Torrington, North Devon. Husband of Mrs. L. M. Ware of Toll Marsh, Plymouth Road, Buckfastleigh, Devon.. Born Torrington, Devon. Enlisted Coventry. Resided Buckfastleigh, Devon. Grave Ref. II. B. 7A. Wimereux Cemetery, France.

WARING, Private, Ernest Edward. 1773, 1st /7th Bn., Royal Warwickshire Regiment. Killed in action, 14th July, 1916. Age 28. Son of Joseph Waring, of 22, Lamb Street, Coventry. Husband of Ada Waring, of 24, Moat Street, The Butts, Coventry. Born 11th May, 1888 at 3, West Street. Resided at 22, Lamb Street. Driller. Enlisted August, 1914 at Coventry. Commemorated War Memorial Park and Siddeley Roll of Honour. Memorial Ref. Pier and Face 9 A 9 B and 10 B. Thiepval Memorial, Somme, France.

WARING, Driver, Frank Alfred. 72329, 41st Bty. 42nd Brigade, Royal Field Artillery. Died of wounds, Ypres, 12th October , 1917. Age 25. Son of Joseph and Agnes Waring, of 77, Little Heath, Coventry. Born 25th January, 1893 at Foleshill, Coventry. Enlisted Coventry. Resided Foleshill. Miner, Exhall Colliery. Grave Ref. II. L. 11. Brandhoek New Military Cemetery No.3, Ieper, West-Vlaanderen, Belgium.

WARING, J. I. Commemorated St. John's Church.

WARING, Private, James William. 2204, 1st Bn., Royal Warwickshire Regiment. Killed in action, Mons, 26th August, 1914. Born Longford. Resided at 77, Little Heath Road. Grave Ref. I. B. 26. Fontaine-au-Pire Communal Cemetery, France.

WARING, Private, John. 9456, 1st Bn., Royal Warwickshire Regiment. Killed in action, 27th July, 1916. Age 28. Son of Mr. and Mrs. J. Waring of Bubbenhall. Employed Warwickshire County Council, Road marking. Memorial Ref. Panel 8. Ypres (Menin Gate) Memorial, Belgium.

WARING, Private, John James. 266460, 1st /7th Bn., Royal Warwickshire Regiment. Died of wounds received on the Somme, in clearing station, 7th March, 1917. Age 29. Husband of Emma Waring, of 23 Court, 10 House, Lyon Street, Coventry. Born 18th August, 1887 at Warwick. Resided at 23c. 6h. Spon Street. Painter, Swifts Motor Works. Enlisted 1915 at Coventry. Grave Ref. II. D. 49. Bray Military Cemetery, Somme, France.

WARMINGTON, Private, George Henry. 10188, 11th Bn., Royal Warwickshire Regiment. Killed in action, 15th July, 1916. Born 1st May, 1878 at West Bromwich. Resided at 28a, Lower Nelson Street. Cycle Frame Builder. Commemorated Triumph and Gloria Memorial. Enlisted Coventry. Memorial Ref. Pier and Face 9 A 9 B and 10 B. Thiepval Memorial, Somme, France.

WARNER, Private, Eric Charles Durrant. 68100, "A" Company, 7th Battalion, Royal Fusiliers formerly 7957, 2/5th Royal West Surrey Regiment. Killed in action, Passchendaele, 30th October 1917. Age 20. Youngest son of William Horne Warner and Elizabeth Warner, of 145 Station Street, East, Coventry. Born 17th January, 1897, at Tidings Hill, Halstead, Essex. Resided at 145, Station Street, East. Clerk, Gloria Cycle Works. Enlisted February, 1917 at Coventry. Commemorated Triumph and Gloria Memorial and War Memorial Park. Memorial Ref. Panel 28 to 30 and 162 to 162A and 163A. Tyne Cot Memorial, Zonnebeke, West-Vlaanderen, Belgium.

WARNER, Lance Corporal, George. 10097, 2nd Bn., Welsh Regiment. Killed in action, 23rd September, 1916. Age 31. Son of Mrs. Alice Parnell, of 18, Craven Street, Chapel Fields, Coventry. Born 9th May, 1885 at Coventry. Enlisted Coventry. Resided at 58, Thomas Street. Boot repairer. Reservist. Memorial Ref. Pier and Face 7 A and 10 A. Thiepval Memorial, Somme, France.

WARNER, Lance Corporal, George Percy. 3274, "B" Company, 1st/7th Battalion, Royal Warwickshire Regiment. Killed in action, by a shell, Foncquevillers, 8th October, 1915. Age 21. Third son of William Horne Warner and Elizabeth Warner, of 145, Station Street, East, Coventry. Born 11th November, 1893 at Halstead, Essex. Resided at 145, Station Street, East. Printer, Messrs. W. W. Curtis Ltd. Enlisted November, 1914 at Coventry. Commemorated War Memorial Park. Grave Ref. Plot I. Row D. Grave 26. Foncquevillers Military Cemetery, Pas de Calais, France.

WARNER, Private, Stanley Thomas. G/15027, "B" Coy. 11th Bn., Royal Sussex Regiment. Killed in action, Somme, 21st October, 1916. Age 28. Son of William Horne Warner and Elizabeth Warner, of 145, Station Street East, Coventry. Born 6th March, 1888, of Halstead, Essex. Resided at 145, Station Street East. Decorator. Enlisted Bedford, January 1916. Commemorated War Memorial Park. Grave Ref. VII. M. 26. Regina Trench Cemetery, Grandcourt, Somme, France.

WARNER, Private, Walter. 989, 2nd Bn., Royal Warwickshire Regiment. Killed in action, 18th May, 1918. Age 27. Son of Mr. and Mrs. C. Warner of 22, George Street, Rugby. Born Stockton, Warwicks. Enlisted Coventry. Resided Leamington. Memorial Ref. Panel 6. Le Touret Memorial, France.

WARR, Lance Corporal, Alfred. 2616, 16th Bn., Rifle Brigade. Killed in action, 26th April, 1918. Born Coventry. Enlisted Coventry. Resided Coventry. Commemorated Holy Trinity Panels. Memorial Ref. Panel 145 to 147. Tyne Cot Memorial, Belgium.

WARRREN, Private, George. 32434, 2nd Bn., York and Lancaster Regiment. Killed in action, 17th May, 1917. Age 37. Son of Fredrick and Louisa Warren, of Burton-on-Trent. Husband of Lily Warren, of 4 1/2, Well Lane, Hinckley. Born 6th March, 1881 at Burton-on-Trent. Resided Hinckley. Professional Footballer (formerly with Coventry City Football Club). Enlisted February, 1917. Grave Ref. I. P. 20. Philosophe British Cemetery, Mazingarbe, France.

WARREN, L. Commemorated St. John's Church.

WARWICK, Private, David Samuel. 203998, 4th Bn., Devonshire Regiment. Died, home, 29th April, 1917. Age 21. Son of Mrs. Jane Warwick, of Finedon, Northants. Born Coventry. Enlisted Northampton. Grave Ref. 214. Wellingborough (Finedon) Cemetery.

WATERFALL, Private, Arthur. 17098, Depot, West Yorkshire Regiment (Prince of Wales's Own). Died of sickness, following wounds, 26th July, 1916. Age 26. Son of Walter John and Mrs. Sarah Waterfall, of Butt's Croft, Corley, Coventry. Grave Ref. 4518. Chester (Overleigh) Cemetery, Cheshire.

WATERFALL, Private, Walter John. 10189, 2nd Bn., Worcestershire Regiment. Died of wounds, 2nd November, 1917. Born Coventry. Enlisted Birmingham. Resided Birmingham. Grave Ref. VI. L. 4. Niederzwehren Cemetery, Germany.

WATERS, Private, C. 10080, 2nd Bn., South Wales Borderers. Killed in action, 25th April, 1915. Memorial Ref. Panel 80 to 84 or 219 and 220. Helles Memorial, Turkey.

WATERS, Lance Corporal, Ernest Charles. L/11232, 2nd Bn., Royal Fusiliers. 25th April, 1915. Age 23. Son of Ernest Charles Waters, of 1, Ordnance Road, Coventry. Husband of Christina Mary Waters, of 9, Church Place, Rathmines, Co. Dublin. Memorial Ref. Panel 37 to 41 or 328. Helles Memorial, Turkey.

WATERS, Captain, Reginald Rigden. 4th Bn. attd. 1st Bn., Royal Warwickshire Regiment. Died of wounds, 24th October, 1916 injured between Les Boeufs and Le Transloy on the 23rd October. Age 22. Son of Hubert David and Lucy Fownes Waters, of Oakhurst, Coundon, Coventry. Born 6th March, 1894 at Coventry. Undergraduate Corpus Christi College, Oxford. Enlisted December, 1914. Commemorated St. Thomas Memorial. Memorial Ref. Pier and Face 9 A 9 B and 10 B. Thiepval Memorial, Somme, France. (Possibly buried near Combles).

WATERS, Private, Thomas W. 5868, 13th Bn., Northumberland Fusiliers. Killed in action, 28th June, 1916. Age 28. Husband of Margaret J. Waters, of 21, Woodhorn Road, Hirst, Ashington, Northumberland. Employed Coventry. Grave Ref. I. D. 6. Mericourt-L'abbe Communal Cemetery Extension, France.

WATKINS, Private, Benjamin. 8213, 3rd Bn., Coldstream Guards. Died, 25th August, 1914. Born Brinklow. Enlisted Coventry. Resided Brinklow. Grave Ref. B. 12. Landrecies Communal Cemetery, France.

WATKINS, Private, James. 458, 1st Bn., Royal Warwickshire Regiment. Killed in action, La Bassee, 8th July, 1915. Born 9th September, 1891 at Brinklow. Resided at 5, Gilbert Street. Fettler. Reservist. Left a widow and child. Enlisted Coventry. Memorial Ref. Panel 8. Ypres (Menin Gate) Memorial, Belgium. (Possibly buried La Bassee).

WATKINS, Private, James. 1367, 2nd Bn., Royal Warwickshire Regiment. Killed in action, 25th October, 1914. Age 25. Son of Mrs. Mary Ann Watkins. Born Brinklow, Warwicks. Enlisted Coventry. Memorial Ref. Panel 8. Ypres (Menin Gate) Memorial, Belgium.

WATSON, Private, Arthur James. 2270, 1/7th Bn., Royal Warwickshire Regiment. Killed in action, 2nd July, 1916. Born Long Lawford. Resided New Bilton. Employed Coventry. Grave Ref. I. F. 13. Hebuterne Military Cemetery, France.

WATSON, Private, William Henry. 16122, 1st Bn., Royal Warwickshire Regiment formerly 1871, Royal Army Service Corps. Killed in action, 23rd October, 1916. Born 4th November, 1895 at Kenilworth. Enlisted April, 1916 at Leamington. Resided Coventry. Employed Courtaulds Ltd. Grave Ref. II. F. 7. Thiepval Anglo-French Cemetery, Authuile, France.

WATTS, Private, Albert. 2210, 1st Bn., Royal Warwickshire Regiment. Killed in action, Mons, 26th August, 1914. Born 26th October, 1895 at 14c. 4h. Cow Lane. Resided at 14c. 4h. Gosford Street with his wife. Soldier. Enlisted Coventry. Grave Ref. I. A. 3. Fontaine-Au-Pire Communal Cemetery, France.

WATTS, Private, Albert Mark. 43488, 2nd Bn., Worcestershire Regiment. Killed in action, 6th November, 1918. Age 22. Son of Mark and Sarah Ann Watts, of 735, Stoney Stanton Road, Coventry. Enlisted June, 1918 at Coventry. Resided Coventry. Born 6th April, 1896 at Hucknall, Notts. Moulder. Grave Ref. E. 6. Leval Communal Cemetery, Nord, France.

WATTS, Private, Harry. 295156, 708th Coy., Labour Corps formerly 124036, Royal Engineers. Died, 21st October, 1918. Born Barby, Northants. Enlisted Whitehall, Middx. Resided Coventry. Grave Ref. S. II. W. 3. St. Sever Cemetery Extension, Rouen, France.

WATTS, Private, John Henry. Royal Warwickshire Regiment. Died home. 8th March, 1925. Born 2nd October, 1883 at 22c. 2h. Gosford Street. Resided at 26c. 8h. Gosford Street. Plater. Reservist. Grave Ref. Coventry (London Road) Cemetery.

WATTS, Private, Joseph Thomas. 241608, 1/6th Bn., Royal Warwickshire Regiment. Killed 18th August, 1916. Born 28th February, 1896 at Beeston, Notts. Resided at 20, Hugh Road. Steel storekeeper. Enlisted March, 1916 at Coventry. Memorial Ref. Pier and Face 9 A 9 B and 10 B. Thiepval Memorial, Somme, France.

WATTS, Private, Leonard. 16475, 1st Bn., Hampshire Regiment formerly 13562, Oxfordshire and Buckinghamshire Light Infantry. Killed in action, 1st July, 1916. Born 1893 at 22c. 2h. Gosford Street, Resided at 16c. 4h. Gosford Street. Plater. Coventry. Enlisted September, 1914 at Coventry. Grave Ref. C. 40. Redan Ridge Cemetery No.2, Beaumont-Hamel, France.

WATTS, Private, Walter John. 266520, 1/7th Bn., Royal Warwickshire Regiment. Killed in action, 13th August, 1917. Born 29th December, 1887 at Coventry. Resided Coventry. Labourer. Enlisted 1915 at Coventry. Grave Ref. LI. C. 8. Poelcapelle British Cemetery, Belgium.

WATTS, Private, William. 15048, 1st Bn., Royal Warwickshire Regiment. Killed in action, 11th April, 1917. Age 31. Son of Mr. and Mrs. Richard Watts, of Great Bourton, Banbury, Oxon. Born at Great Bourton, Oxon. Resided at 4, Moreton Place, Castle Street. Carter, Mr. J. Shelton, Little Park Street. Enlisted Coventry. Memorial Ref. Bay 3. Arras Memorial, France.

WATTS, Private, William. 17298, 17th Bn., Royal Warwickshire Regiment Died, home, 26th March, 1916. Age 37. Son of Austin and Annie Watts. Born Coventry. Enlisted Coventry. Born 1881 at Coventry. Resided at 27, Well Street. Licenced Victualler. Grave Ref. 29. 12. Coventry (London Road) Cemetery.

WAYNE, Private, Albert Charles. 32988, 6th Bn., Oxfordshire and Buckinghamshire Light Infantry. Killed in action, 17th October, 1916. Age 31. Son of Charles and S. Wayne, of 4, Oswald Road, Leamington Spa. Husband of Mary F. A. Wayne, of 16, Upper Mounts, Northampton. This name appears on the memorial to the members of the Independent Order of Oddfellows in the Cathedral Church of St. Michael. Memorial Ref. Pier and Face 10 A and 10 D. Thiepval Memorial, Somme, France.

WEATHERBY, Private, David. 307840, 1st /8th Bn., Royal Warwickshire Regiment. Killed in action, 4th October, 1917. Age 23. Son of David and Ellen Weatherby, of Woodshires Green, Exhall, Coventry. Born 18th April, 1893 at Exhall. Resided Exhall. Employed by Albion Drop Forgings Co. Ltd. Enlisted May, 1916 at Coventry. Commemorated Exhall Memorial. Memorial Ref. Panel 23 to 28 and 163A. Tyne Cot Memorial, Zonnebeke, West-Vlaanderen, Belgium.

WEATHERBY, Private, Samuel. 4182, 1st /7th Bn., Royal Warwickshire Regiment. Died, home, 30th August, 1921. Age 30. Son of David and Ellen Weatherby, of 3, Station Road, Longford, Coventry. Born at Exhall. Grave Ref. In South-East part. Exhall (St. Giles) churchyard, Warwickshire.

WEAVING, Private, Walter Reginald. 18603, 6th Bn., Oxfordshire and Buckinghamshire Light Infantry attached Royal Munster Fusiliers. Died, Mesopotamia, 28th September, 1916. Age 28. Son of William and Sarah Weavings. Born Gloucester. Enlisted Coventry. Resided Kidderminster. Grave Ref. 485. Salonika (Lembet Road) Military Cemetery, Greece.

WEAVER, Private, William Alfred. 8581, 1st Bn., Worcestershire Regiment. Killed in action, 6th February, 1915. Born in 1884 at Birmingham. Resided at 14c. 18h. Little Park Street. Polisher, Messrs Rotherams. Reservist. Leaves a widow and two children. Memorial Ref. Panel 17 and 18. Le Touret Memorial, France.

WEBB, Private, Alfred Thomas. 268097, 2/7th Bn., Royal Warwickshire Regiment. Killed in action, 15th November, 1917. Born 6th May, 1895 at Coventry. Resided Poplar Road. Fruiterer. Enlisted June, 1916 at Coventry Grave Ref. I. D. 19. Sunken Road Cemetery, Fampoux, France.

WEBB, Private, Arthur. 35913, 14th Bn., Worcestershire Regiment. Killed in action, 29th October, 1917. Age 26. Son of Thomas and Martha Webb of 326, Blackpool Street, Burton-on-Trent. Born Burton-on-Trent, Staffs. Enlisted Coventry. Resided Burton-on-Trent. Grave Ref. I. M. 12. La Brique Military Cemetery No. 2. Belgium.

WEBB, Private, Ernest. 3681, 1st Bn., Royal Warwickshire Regiment. Accidentally killed, 7th November, 1915. Born 2nd February, 1895 in Whitefriars Street. Resided at 14, Ranby Road. Polisher, Premier Cycle Works. Enlisted September, 1914 at Coventry. Grave Ref. II. B. 2. Sucrerie Military Cemetery, Colincamps, France.

WEBB, Private, Francis Edward. 25640, Royal Warwickshire Regiment. Killed in action, 24th October, 1918. Born Pangbourne, Oxon. Enlisted Coventry. Resided Honington, Shipston-on-Stour. Grave Ref. A. 15. Canonne Farm British Cemetery, Sommaing, France.

WEBB, Sergeant, Frank. 12757, 11th Bn., Royal Warwickshire Regiment. Died of wounds, 26th April, 1917. Age 29. Son of Thomas and Jane Webb, of Hearsall Common, Canley Gates, Coventry. Born 28th December, 1888 at Eastcote, Solihull. Resided Hearsall Common. Police constable. Enlisted June, 1915 at Coventry. Commemorated Police Force Memorial, Coventry Corporation. Grave Ref. IV. H. 5. Duisans British Cemetery, Etrun, Pas de Calais, France.

WEBB, Lance Corporal, Horace Bernard. PO/1384, Portsmouth Bn., Royal Marine Light Infantry. Died, Alexandria, Egypt, 27th June, 1915 due to pneumonia. Born 5th June, 1886 at Burton-on-Trent. Resided at 129, Northfield Road. Carriage Repairer. Reservist. Grave Ref. L. 64. Alexandria (Chatby) Military And War Memorial Cemetery, Egypt.

WEBB, Sergeant, James. 266321, 2/7th Bn., Royal Warwickshire Regiment. Died of wounds, 22nd April, 1918. Son of Mrs. Emily Webb of 19, Bull Street, Stratford-on-Avon. Born Stratford-on-Avon. Enlisted Coventry. Grave Ref. IX. D. 7. Niederzwehren Cemetery, Germany.

WEBB, Private, John Thomas. 267332, 10th Bn., Royal Warwickshire Regiment. Died whilst prisoner of war in German hands, 16th October, 1918. Born 22nd September, 188 at Coventry. Resided at 68 Edgewick Road. House Decorator. Enlisted September, 1916 at Coventry. Grave Ref. VII. C. 23. Cologne Southern Cemetery, Germany.

WEBB, Driver, Joseph. 118838, 20th Bty., Royal Field Artillery. Buried at sea, 14th July, 1916. Age 19. Son of Mrs. Rose Webb, of 136, Much Park Street, Coventry. Born Coventry. Enlisted Coventry. Memorial Ref. Panel 3 and 60. Basra Memorial, Iraq.

WEBB, Sergeant, Reginald William. 80309, Machine Gun Corps (Locker Lampson's Armoured Cars). Died at Hospital in Baghdad, 29th November, 1918. Age 18. Born 22nd January, 1900 at Coventry. Resided at 88, Cox Street. Turner, Grinding Department, Rudge Works. Enlisted May, 1918. Grave Ref. XI. G. 1. Baghdad (North Gate) War Cemetery, Iraq.

WEBB, Private, William. 42325, 3rd Bn., Prince Albert's, Somerset Light Infantry. Died, home, 19th July, 1918. Born at Fulham, Middlesex. Employed by Armstrong Siddeley Motors, Ltd. Enlisted Kenilworth. Commemorated War Memorial Park and Siddeley Roll of Honour. Grave Ref. Belfast City Cemetery.

WEBB, Private, William Henry. 18112, 2nd Bn., Royal Warwickshire Regiment. Killed, Arras, 4th May, 1917. Age 20. Son of Albert and Annie Webb, of 131, Earlsdon Avenue North, Coventry. Born 4th September, 1896 at Cindeford, Gloucestershire. Resided Coventry. Moulder. Enlisted April, 1916 at Coventry. Memorial Ref. Bay 3. Arras Memorial, Pas de Calais, France.

WEBBER, Private, Frederic William. 80069, 31st Bn., Canadian Infantry (Alberta Regiment). Killed in action, St. Eloi, 16th April, 1916. Age 23. Son of George Henry and Fanny Webber, of 5, Dean Street, Kingsway, Coventry, England. Born 3rd August, 1892 at the Rectory, Port Glasgow, Scotland. Resided Alberta, Canada. Farmer (Clerk in Coventry, 1908 to 1911). Enlisted October, 1914. Memorial Ref. Panel 24 - 28 - 30. Ypres (Menin Gate) Memorial, Ieper, West-Vlaanderen, Belgium.

WEBSTER, Private, Alfred Charles. 13690, 6th Bn., Oxfordshire and Buckinghamshire Light Infantry. Killed in action, Guillemont, 3rd September, 1916. Born 20th May, 1890 at Leicester. Resided at 409, Stoney Stanton Road. Labourer. Enlisted September, 1914 at Coventry. Memorial Ref. Pier and Face 10 A and 10 D. Thiepval Memorial, Somme, France.

WEBSTER, Private, Charles Clifford. 25542, 14th Bn., Gloucestershire Regiment. Died of wounds, Battle of the Somme, 24th August, 1916. Age 20. Son of Mr. and Mrs. Frederick Webster, of Coventry. Born 8th September, 1895 at Halifax. Resided at 6, Rayleigh Road. Clerk. Enlisted November, 1915 at Coventry. Commemorated Stoke (St. Michaels) Church and War Memorial Park. Grave Ref. VII. D. 51. Warloy-Baillon Communal Cemetery Extension, Somme, France.

WEBSTER, Private, Edward John. 45719, 2nd/4th Bn., Hampshire Regiment. Killed in action, Avrincourt, 13th September, 1918. Aged 19. Eldest son of Mr. Edward Wheeler and Mrs. Ellen J. Webster of 2, White's Row, Kenilworth. Born Kenilworth. Enlisted Coventry. Resided Kenilworth. Grave Ref. II. E. 4. Hermies Hill British Cemetery, Pas-de-Calais, France.

WEBSTER, Frederick W. Commemorated Holy Trinity Panels.

WEBSTER, Private, Robert William. 2243, 1/7th Bn., Royal Warwickshire Regiment. Killed in action, 3rd April, 1916 when a shell burst in the dug-out. Age 27. Son of Mrs. J. Bradford, of 20, Radnor Gardens, Twickenham, Middx. Husband of Mrs. E. V. Terry (formerly Webster), of 49, Breakspeare Road, Abbots Langley, Herts. Resided at 21, York Street. Blacksmith's striker, Rudge Works. Enlisted August, 1914 at Coventry. Grave Ref. I. C. 6. Foncquevillers Military Cemetery, France.

WEDGE, Sergeant, James. 7967, 9th Bn., Duke of Wellington's West Riding Regiment. Killed in action, 27th April, 1916. Age 32. Husband of Alice Wedge, of Long Handborough, Woodstock, Oxon. Employed by Humber Ltd. Resided 110, Harnall Lane East. Grave Ref. IX. G. 22. Cite Bonjean Military Cemetery, Armentieres, France.

WELCH, Private, Arthur. 17028, 1st Bn., Royal Warwickshire Regiment. Killed in action, 31st August, 1918. Age 30. Son of Arthur and Hannah Welch, of 21, Primrose Hill Street, Coventry. Born 11th September, 1887 at Coventry. Resided at 21, Primrose Hill Street. Enlisted Coventry, March, 1916. Grinder, Triumph Works. Commemorated War Memorial Park. Memorial Ref. Panel 3. Vis-En-Artois Memorial, Pas de Calais, France.

WELCH, Sergeant, Vincent Joseph. 250, 7th Bn., East Surry Regiment attached Royal West Surrey Regiment. Died of wounds, 17th June, 1916. Born 1884 at Chislehurst. Resided at 4, Rudge Road. Labourer. Enlisted August, 1914. Grave Ref. II. D. 1. Dranoutre Military Cemetery, France.

WELDING, Lance Corporal, Edward Victor. 13237, No. 1 Coy., 3rd Bn., Coldstream Guards. Died of wounds, 20th April, 1918. Age 25. Son of Joseph and Annie Welding of 98, Church Road, Stockingfrod, Nuneaton. Born Merthyr Tydvil, Glamorganshire. Enlisted Coventry. Resided Nuneaton. Grave Ref. I. D. 59. Merville Communal Cemetery Extension, France.

WELLS, Private, Alfred William. M2/033710, 283rd Coy. Mechanical Transport, Army Service Corps. Killed in action, 23rd March, 1918. Age 24. Son of Mrs. E. Bates, of 166, Melbourne Road, Coventry. Born 27th April, 1893 at Coventry. Enlisted Coventry. Resided 166, Melbourne Road, Coventry. Motor tester. Enlisted January, 1915. Grave Ref. C. 17. La Neuville Communal Cemetery, Corbie, Somme, France.

WELLS, Private, Arthur James. 32902, (376720) 184th Coy., Labour Corps formerly 3rd Bn., Northumberland Fusiliers. Died of wounds, 29th September, 1918. Age 34. Son of James and Amelia Wells, of 302, Queen's Road, Sheffield. Born Coventry. Resided at Heeley, Sheffield. Grave Ref. III. C. 52. Haringhe (Bandaghem) Military Cemetery, Belgium.

WELLS, Private, Frank. 20413, 2/6th Bn., Royal Warwickshire Regiment. Died of wounds, 27th October, 1916. Age 21. Born 16th October, 1895 at Coventry. Enlisted Coventry. Resided Allesley. Leaves widow and one child. Second son of Mrs. Cooper of Berkswell. Grave Ref. I. A. 34. Merville Communal Cemetery Extension, France.

WELLS, Private, Frank William. 17145, 13th Battalion, Royal Sussex Regiment. Died of wounds, whilst prisoner of war, 3rd October, 1918. Last heard of working behind the German Lines in Northern France. Age 21 Son of Frank W and Alice Wells, of 64 Arden Street, Earlsdon, Coventry. Born 7th September 1898 at Coventry. Resided at 64 Arden Street. Clerk, London and North Western and Midland Railways. Enlisted September 1916. Educated Bablake School. Commemorated Bablake School Memorial, St. Barbara's Memorial and War Memorial Park. Grave Ref. II. F. 17. Glageon Communal Cemetery Extension, Nord, France.

WELLS, Private, Harry. 10444, 1st Bn., Coldstream Guards. Killed in action, 11th May, 1916. Age 22. Son of Mr. and Mrs. Wells of Pakenham, Bury St. Edmonds. Born Ashfield Magna, Suffolk. Enlisted Coventry. Resided Bury St. Edmonds. Grave Ref. I. A. 36. Poperinghe New Military Cemetery, Belgium.

WELLS, Private, John Thomas. 40015, 4th Bn., Tank Corps. Killed in action, 22nd March, 1918. Age 25. Son of John and Hannah Wells and 12, St. James Street, Bradford. Born Harpurhey, Lancs. Enlisted Coventry. Memorial Ref. Panel 94. Pozieres Memorial, France.

WELLS, Lance Corporal, Robert. 15317, 1st Bn., Worcestershire Regiment. Killed in action, 1st August, 1917. Age 24. Son of Henry and Mary Ann Wells, of Main Street, Wolston, Coventry. Native of Rugby. Enlisted Rugby. Resided Coventry. Commemorated Wolston Memorial. Grave Ref. IXA. B. 2. Hooge Crater Cemetery, Ieper, West-Vlaanderen, Belgium.

WELLS, Corporal, W. 1st Bn., Royal Warwickshire Regiment. Ryton and Stretton District.

WELLS, Private, William Henry. 10752, 1st Bn., Royal Scots Fusiliers. Killed in action, Loos, 25th September, 1915 when a shell fell in the dug-out. Age 21. Son of William and Clara Wells. Born 25th November, 1893 at Coventry. Enlisted Coventry. Resided Berkswell. Memorial Ref. Panel 19 and 33. Ypres (Menin Gate) Memorial, Belgium.

WELTON, Private, Frank. 41233, 1st Bn., Worcestershire Regiment. Killed in action, Ypres, 31st July, 1917. Age 31. Husband of Lillie Beatrice Welton, of 45, Sir Thomas White's Road, Coventry. Born 9th October, 1883 at 133, Spon Street, Coventry. Enlisted Coventry. Butcher. Enlisted March, 1917. Memorial Ref. Panel 34. Ypres (Menin Gate) Memorial, Ieper, West-Vlaanderen, Belgium.

WEST, Private, Frederick. 4663, 1/7th Bn., Royal Warwickshire Regiment. Killed in action, 1st July, 1916. Born 7th May, 1894 in St. John Street, Coventry. Enlisted Coventry. Resided Little Park Street. Machinist. Enlisted December, 1915. Grave Ref. I. F. 11. Hebuterne Military Cemetery, France.

WEST, Rifleman, Henry. R/9153, 11th Bn., King's Royal Rifle Corps. Killed in action, 20th September, 1917. Age 34. Son of John and Elizabeth West, of Fillongley. Husband of Sarah Jane West, of Fillongley, Coventry. Enlisted Coventry. Memorial Ref. Panel 115 to 119 and 162A and 163A. Tyne Cot Memorial, Zonnebeke, West-Vlaanderen, Belgium.

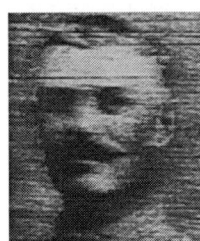
WEST, Lance Corporal, Philip. 201327, 2nd /4th Bn., Hampshire Regiment. Killed in action, 12th September, 1918. Age 41. Son of Thomas and Mary West, of Waterfall Cottage, Meriden, Coventry. Grave Ref. II. A. 5. Hermies Hill British Cemetery, Pas de Calais, France.

WEST, Private, Philip Gray. 30075, 2nd /5th Bn., East Lancashire Regiment. 9th October, 1917. Age 33. Son of Marston and Mary West, of Newbold Verdon, Leicester. Husband of Eleanor West, of 365, Stoney Stanton Rd., Coventry. Memorial Ref. Panel 77 to 79 and 163A. Tyne Cot Memorial, Zonnebeke, West-Vlaanderen, Belgium.

WEST, Private, Walter. G/74860, 23rd Bn., Royal Fusiliers formerly SPTS/3574, Royal Fusiliers. Killed in action, 8th October, 1918. Born Birmingham. Enlisted London. Resided Coventry. Grave Ref. II. B. 19. Masnieres British Cemetery, Marcoing, France.

WESTLEY, Private, Frederick William. 28629, 11th Bn., Royal Warwickshire Regiment. Killed in action, Ypres, 10th August, 1917. Age 19. Son of Mrs. Sarah Ann Westley, of 23, Welland Road, Stoke, Coventry. Born 18th March, 1898 at Warwick. Resided Welland Road. Signwriter. Enlisted December, 1916 at Coventry. Grave Ref. II. B. 5. Oosttaverne Wood Cemetery, Heuvelland, West-Vlaanderen, Belgium.

WESTLEY, Private, William John. 5102, 6th Bn.,. Royal Warwickshire Regiment. Killed in action, Somme, 18th August, 1916. Born 9th February, 1885 at Derby. Enlisted Warwick. Resided 90, The Butts, Coventry. Iron Polisher. Enlisted March, 1916. Grave Ref. IV. G. 25. Pozieres British Cemetery, Ovillers-La Boisselle, France.

WESTON, Acting Corporal, George. 12000, 1st Bn., Duke of Cornwall's Light Infantry. Killed in action, Mericourt, 31st August, 1915. Age 20. Son of James and Jane Weston, of 19, Parkfield Road, Alum Rock, Birmingham. Born 25th September, 1894 at 5, Leicester Terrace, Station Street, Coventry. Enlisted August, 1914 at Birmingham. Resided Saltley, Birmingham. Clerk. Grave Ref. II. M. 11. Cerisy-Gailly Military Cemetery, France.

WESTWOOD, Sergeant, John. 23109, 4th Bn., Worcestershire Regiment. 19th February, 1916. Husband of E. Westwood, of 15, George Terrace, Walsgrave. Born Blackheath, Staffs. Enlisted Coventry. Resided Wyken. Grave Ref. Binley (St. Bartholomew) Churchyard.

WETTON, Private, James Henry. 40408, 6th Bn., East Yorkshire Regiment, formerly 230535, Royal Engineers. Died of wounds, Langemarck, 10th October, 1917. Age 23. Son of John and Mary Annie Wetton, of 31, Adelaide Street, Coventry. Born 19th October, 1893 at Coventry. Enlisted January, 1917 at Whitehall. Resided London. Police Constable. Grave Ref. IX. J. 7. Dozinghem Military Cemetery, Poperinge, West-Vlaanderen, Belgium.

WHATLEY, Private, Joseph Edward. 268082, 2/7th Bn., Royal Warwickshire Regiment. Killed in action, 22nd March, 1918. Age 30. Born 5th April, 1888 at Coventry. Enlisted Coventry. Resided 55a, Hill Street. Spinner, Courtaulds Ltd. Eldest son of Mr. and Mrs. J. Whatley of 53, Seven Road, Stoke, Coventry. Leaves a widow and one child. Memorial Ref. Panel 18 and 19. Pozieres Memorial, France.

WHEAT, Rifleman, James. 10491, "D" Coy. 4th Bn., King's Royal Rifle Corps. Died of wounds, near Bohain, 6th November, 1918. Age 24. Son of James and Ellen Wheat, of 24, Princess Street, Coventry. Born 17th March, 1894 at Foleshill. Resided Coventry. Enlisted Coventry. Soldier. Grave Ref. III. B. 12. Premont British Cemetery, Aisne, France.

WHEAT, Rifleman, William. R/21397, 9th Bn., King's Royal Rifle Corps. Killed in action, 21st March, 1918. Age 27. Son of James and Ellen Wheat, of 24, Princess Street, Coventry. Husband of Sarah Wheat, of 164, Station Street East, Coventry. Born 6th February, 1891 at Foleshill, Coventry. Enlisted April, 1916 at Coventry. Artificial Silk Spinner, Messrs Courtaulds. Leaves a widow and three children. Memorial Ref. Panel 61 to 64. Pozieres Memorial, Somme, France.

WHEATLEY, Private, Charles Henry. 24125, 1st Bn., Royal Warwickshire Regiment. Died of wounds received in France (gas), Ipswich Hospital, 5th September, 1918. Born 4th October, 1884 at Coates near Peterborough. Resided at 1, Cope Street. Coachbuilder. Enlisted February, 1917 at Coventry. Leaves a wife and two children. Grave Ref. West of Church. Coates (Holy Trinity) Churchyard.

WHEATLEY, Private, James. 16413, 8th Bn., Duke of Cornwall's Light Infantry formerly 6612, Royal Warwickshire Regiment. Died whilst prisoner of war, Bulgarian hands, Balkans, 20th October, 1917. Born Exhall. Enlisted Warwick. Resided Exhall. Employed Coventry. Commemorated Exhall Memorial. Grave Ref. VI. H. 2 Berlin South Western Cemetery, Germany.

WHEELDON, Private, James. 26647, 1st /5th Bn., Duke of Wellington's (West Riding Regiment). Killed in action, 4th January, 1918. Age 19. Son of Thomas and Sarah Ann Passam (formerly Wheeldon), of 793, Foleshill Road, Coventry. Born 1889. Resided Foleshill Road. Grave Ref. IV. A. 17. Ypres Reservoir Cemetery, Ieper, West-Vlaanderen, Belgium.

WHEELER, Colour Sergeant, George Edward. 3rd Bn., Royal Welsh Fusiliers. Died home, 21st December, 1920. Born 31st October, 1873 at Pembroke Dock, South Wales, Resided 82, Far Gosford Street. Clerk. Enlisted August, 1914. Grave Ref. Buried Coventry.

WHEELER, Lance Corporal, William. 9743, 9th Bn., Royal Warwickshire Regiment. Died of wounds, Mesopotamia, 6th April, 1916. Born Stratford-on-Avon. Enlisted Coventry. Resided Birmingham. Memorial Ref. Panel 9. Basra Memorial, Iraq.

WHELAN, Private, Thomas Lynch. 8721, 2nd Bn., Worcestershire Regiment. Killed in action, 24th October, 1914. Age 28. Husband of Mary Ada Whelan, of 2, Brookfield Road, Brookfields, Birmingham. Born Coventry. Enlisted Birmingham. Resided Birmingham. Memorial Ref. Panel 34. Ypres (Menin Gate) Memorial, Belgium.

WHETSTONE, Private, Andrew. 4572, 7th Bn., Royal Warwickshire Regiment. Died of wounds, 31st July, 1916. Age 24. Son of Andrew and Emma Whetstone, of Coventry. Husband of Amy Whetstone, of 4, Lime Terrace, Lockhurst Lane, Coventry. Born 20th February, 1893 in Red Lane. Resided 39, Ransom Road. Painter, Mr. J. G. Gray, Builder. Enlisted November, 1915 at Coventry. Leaves a wife and two children. Grave Ref. B. 32. 18. St. Sever Cemetery, Rouen, Seine-Maritime, France.

WHEWELL, Corporal, John James. M2/079423, Army Service Corps attached Mobile Anti-Aircraft Bty., Royal Garrison Artillery. Died, 3rd November, 1918. Age 28. Son of James William and Mary Ann Whewell of Radcliffe, Manchester. Husband of Primrose Jones (formerly Whewell) of 6, Madoc Street, Llandudno. Enlisted Coventry. Resided Llandudno. Grave Ref. S. III. L. 26. St. Sever Cemetery Extension, Rouen, France.

WHINFREY, Gunner, Arthur. 107303, 256th Siege Battery, Royal Garrison Artillery. Killed in action, Broodseinde, 4th October, 1917. Age 21. Son of Frank and Annie Whinfrey of Brandock Marsh, Hampton In Arden. Educated Bablake School. Born 2nd April 1896 at Berkswell. Resided Berkswell. Engineers Apprentice. Enlisted July, 1916 at Coventry. Commemorated Bablake School Memorial. Grave Ref. E. 5. Buffs Road Cemetery, France.

WHITAKER, Private, Frederick Bernard. M2/204353, P Siege Park, Army Service Corps. Killed in action, 10th July, 1917. Age 26. Son of Francis and Emily Ann Whitaker of London. Born Kent. Enlisted Coventry. Resided Eltham. Grave Ref. I. E. 51. Coxyde Military Cemetery, Belgium.

WHITCROFT, Private, Tom. 266485, 2/7th Bn., Royal Warwickshire Regiment. Killed in action, 19th July, 1916. Enlisted Coventry. Resided Bedworth. Memorial Ref. Panel 22 to 25. Loos Memorial, France.

WHITE, Corporal, Dudley Nevill. 200865, D Bn., Tank Corps formerly 32209, Machine Gun Corps. Killed in action by a shell which struck his tank, 9th October, 1917. Age 20. Son of Frederick Charles and Lucy White, of Castle Road, Kenilworth. Born 1897 at Coventry. Enlisted Kenilworth. Resided Coventry. Memorial Ref. Panel 159 to 160. Tyne Cot Memorial, Belgium.

WHITE, Private, Ernest Leonard. 1318, 2nd Bn., Royal Warwickshire Regiment. Killed in action, La Bassee, 19th December, 1914. Age 19. Son of Thomas and Clara White, of 11, East Street, Coventry. Born 1st January, 1896 at 2c. 2h. Whitefriars Street. Enlisted Coventry. Resided 62, Day's Lane. Hardener. Reservist. Memorial Ref. Panel 2 and 3. Ploegsteert Memorial, Comines-Warneton, Hainaut, Belgium.

WHITE, Ordinary Seaman, Horace Stanley. Wales Z/5107, HMS Pembroke, Royal Naval Volunteer Reserve. Torpedoed at sea, 26th October, 1918. Age 18. Son of Thomas W. White, of Stalls Farm, Bartestree, Hereford. Born at Corley, Coventry. Grave Ref. Naval. 4. 208. Gillingham (Woodlands) Cemetery, Kent.

WHITE, J. A. Killed in action. Educated at Bablake School. Commemorated Bablake School Memorial.

WHITE, William. Commemorated Holy Trinity Panels.

WHITE, Private, William. 144191, 18th Bn., Machine Gun Corps (Infantry) formerly Royal Warwickshire Regiment. Killed in action, 21st October, 1918. Born 26th May, 184 in Spon Street, Coventry. Resided at 5c. 13h. Far Gosford Street. Greengrocer's Carter. Enlisted Coventry. Grave Ref. I. A. 8. Highland Cemetery, Le Cateau, France.

WHITE, Sergeant, William Harvey. 2497, 2/7th Bn., Royal Warwickshire Regiment. Died, 19th July, 1916. Age 19. Son of George and Mary Amelia White of The Forge, Dunchurch. Born Frankton, Rugby. Enlisted Coventry. Resided Rugby. Memorial Ref. Panel 22 to 25. Loos Memorial, France.

WHITE, Private, William Henry. 11357, 2nd Bn., Royal Warwickshire Regiment. Died of wounds, 8th May, 1916. Age 30. Husband of Charlotte White, of 4, Irlam St., South Wigston, Leicester. Born 9th October, 1884 in Freeth Street. Resided in Little Park Street. Miner, Binley Colliery. Enlisted September, 1914 at Coventry. Mother resided, 19, St. Peter's Street. Leaves a widow and four children. Grave Ref. III. G. 14. Abbeville Communal Cemetery, France.

WHITEHEAD, Private, David Lancelot. 130022, 50th Bn., Machine Gun Corps (Infantry) formerly 26205, Royal Warwicks Regiment. Killed in action, 27th May, 1918. Born 1890 in Mill Street. Coventry. Enlisted Coventry. Resided Alliance Way. Sheet metal worker. Memorial Ref. Soissons Memorial, France.

WHITEHEAD, Private, Henry Moses. 202582, 10th Bn., Gloucestershire Regiment formerly 15793, Worcestershire Regiment. Killed in action, 20th August, 1917. Born 22nd May, 1880 at Birmingham. Resided Earlsdon Avenue. Labourer, Coventry Corporation Gas works. Enlisted August, 1914 at Coventry. Commemorated Gas Department Memorial, Coventry Corporation. Grave Ref. II. C. 28. Potijze Chateau Grounds Cemetery, Belgium.

WHITEHOUSE, Sergeant, Alfred Ernest. 5857, 1st Bn., King's Royal Rifle Corps. Died of wounds, 24th June, 1915. Age 28. Son of Alfred and Elizabeth Whitehouse. Husband of Ada Whitehouse, of 59, Lowther Street, Stoke, Coventry. Native of Small Heath, Birmingham. Enlisted Birmingham. Grave Ref. I. D. 14. Chocques Military Cemetery, Pas de Calais, France.

WHITEHOUSE, Private, Daniel. 9701, Royal Warwickshire Regiment transf. to (311821), Labour Corps. Died of pneumonia, 31st October, 1918. Age 24. Son of Daniel Whitehouse, of 2A, Queen Street, Coventry. Husband of Louie Whitehouse. Born 18th April, 1894 in St. Michael's Parish. Resided Stockton Road. Mechanic. Enlisted September, 1914. Grave Ref. 199. 195. Coventry (London Road) Cemetery.

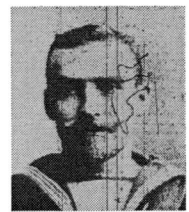
WHITEHOUSE, 1st Class Stoker, Rowland. SS/101037, (RFR/PO/B/3360), HMS Ghurkha. Killed by mine in English Channel, 8th February, 1917. Age 37. Son of Abraham and Ann Allsop Whitehouse, of Heath End, Pelsall, Walsall. Born 15th January, 1880 at Persall, Staffordshire. Resided Beech Cottage, Red Lane. Blacksmith. Reservist. Commemorated War Memorial Park. Memorial Ref. 26. Portsmouth Naval Memorial.

WHITING, Private, Arthur. 201175, 2/5th Bn., Sherwood Foresters (Notts and Derby) Regiment. Died of wounds, 9th May, 1917. Age 39. Husband of Martha Whiting, of 17, Bould Street, Mansfield. Born Derby. Enlisted Derby. Resided Coventry. Grave Ref. I. D. 1. La Chapelette British And Indian Cemetery, Peronne, France.

WHITMILL, Gunner, Horace Rubert. Royal Field Artillery. Died home, 17th February, 1921. Born 1st October, 1897 at Kenilworth. Resided at 72, Northfield Road. Shop assistant. Enlisted May, 1915. Commemorated War Memorial Park. Grave Ref. Radford Churchyard.

WHITMORE, Lance Corporal, Arthur. 27416, 17th Bn., Sherwood Foresters (Notts and Derby) Regiment. Killed in action, 19th October, 1916. Age 42. Son of Thomas and Anne Whitmore. Husband of Harriet E. Whitmore, of 39, Forest Street, Hyson Green, Nottingham. Born Coventry. Enlisted Nottingham. Memorial Ref. Pier and Face 10 C 10 D and 11 A. Thiepval Memorial, Somme, France.

WHITMORE, D. Commemorated Triumph & Gloria Memorial.

WHITTAKER, Lance Corporal, James Thomas. 1785, 1/7th Bn., Royal Warwickshire Regiment. Died of wounds, 23rd August, 1916. Age 25. Son of James John and Elizabeth Whittaker. Native of Rugby. Born Lincoln. Resided Rugby. Miller, Rudge Works. Enlisted 1914 at Coventry. Grave Ref. VIII. B. 154. Boulogne Eastern Cemetery, France.

WHITTINGTON, Pioneer, James. 252697, "A" Signal Depot (Bedford), Royal Engineers formerly Royal Garrison Artillery. Died of wounds, received in France, home, 30th October, 1917 at Rubery Hospital. Born Birmingham. Resided 17, Whitefriars Street. Employed Coventry Ordnance Works. Enlisted Coventry. Grave Ref. Screen Wall. 64. 08644. Birmingham (Witton) Cemetery

WICKERS, Private, Arthur James. 17383, 11th Bn., Royal Warwickshire Regiment. Killed in action, 10th April, 1917. Born Coventry. Enlisted Coventry. Memorial Ref. Bay 3. Arras Memorial, France.

WIGGEN, Private, Thomas William. 22815, 2/5th Bn., Lincolnshire Regiment. Killed in action, 15th April, 1918. Age 21. Son of Thomas E. and Frances. S. Wiggen of 56, James Street, Louth, Lincs. Enlisted Coventry. Resided Louth, Lincs. Grave Ref. XXVI. N. 13. Cabaret-Rouge British Cemetery, Souchez, France.

WIGHTMAN, Second Lieutenant, John Francis. 11th Sqdn., Royal Flying Corps. and General List. 4th September, 1917. Age 18. Son of John Mathew Wightman and of Flora Butler (formerly Wightman), of The Poplars, Quinton Road, Coventry. Memorial Ref. Arras Flying Services Memorial, Pas de Calais, France.

WIGNELL, B. Commemorated Coventry Chain Memorial.

WILCOX, Lance Corporal, Albert. 9276, 11th Bn., Royal Warwickshire Regiment. Killed in action, 16th July, 1916. Born 7th December, 1890 in Cromwell Street. Resided at 2, Newnham Road. Stamper, Smith's Stamping Works. Enlisted November, 1914 at Coventry. Grave Ref. III. F. 16. Pozieres British Cemetery, Ovillers-La Boisselle, France.

WILCOX, Private, Arthur. 9913, 2nd Bn., Royal Warwickshire Regiment. Killed in action, 25th September, 1915. Born Foleshill. Resided Longford. Enlisted Coventry. Memorial Ref. Panel 22 to 25. Loos Memorial, France.

WILCOX, Private, Arthur William. Royal Warwickshire Regiment. Killed in action, France, 1916. Resided at 16, Smith Street.

WILCOX, Private, David. 17370, C Coy., 15th Bn., Royal Warwickshire Regiment. Killed in action, 9th May, 1917. Age 35. Born Coventry. Enlisted Coventry. Resided at 16, Smith Street. Memorial Ref. Bay 3. Arras Memorial, France.

WILCOX, Private, James William. 676, 1st /7th Bn., Royal Warwickshire Regiment. Killed in action, Battle of the Somme, 14th July, 1916. Age 27. Brother of Mrs. S. J. Baynes, of "Senyab," Binley Rd., Coventry. Born 17th February, 1890, in old Tower Yard, Cook Street. Resided at 27, Mount Street. Wood Machinist. Enlisted August 1914 at Coventry. Commemorated Coventry Chain Memorial and War Memorial Park. Memorial Ref. Pier and Face 9 A 9 B and 10 B. Thiepval Memorial, Somme, France.

WILDE, Private, Frank Norman. M2/121687, Mechanical Transport, Army Service Corps. Killed in action, 25th February, 1918. Born Birmingham. Enlisted Coventry. Resided Crouch End. Grave Ref. III. C. 6. Ypres Reservoir Cemetery, Belgium.

WILEMAN, Private, Evan. 16845, 15th Bn., Royal Warwickshire Regiment. Killed in action, 9th May, 1917. Born Mersham, Leics. Enlisted Coventry. Memorial Ref. Bay 3. Arras Memorial, France.

WILES, Private, Albert Victor. 17766, 11th Bn., Worcestershire Regiment. Died, Salonika, 5th October, 1918. Son of Sophia Wiles, of 73, Highland Road, Earlsdon, Coventry. Born 27th September, 1896 at Berkswell. Enlisted Coventry. Resided Coventry. Driller. Grave Ref. 236. Kirechkoi-Hortakoi Military Cemetery, Greece.

WILKES, Private, William. 22116, 7th Bn., Gloucestershire Regiment. Killed in action, 23rd September, 1915. Born 1892. Employed Daimler Ltd. Memorial Ref. Panel 101 to 104. Helles Memorial, Turkey.

WILKINS, 1st Class Stoker, Herbert Charles. 301771, HMS Bulwark, Royal Navy. Killed in internal explosion of vessel, 26th November, 1914. Age 28. Son of Mrs. Dixon of Lincoln House, Foleshill Road. Born 28th September, 1889 at Coventry. Resided Coventry. Clerk. Served 12 years in the Navy. Commemorated War Memorial Park. Memorial Ref. Panel 5. Portsmouth Naval Memorial.

WILKINS, Private, Herbert Musgrove. 16531, 1st Bn., Royal Warwickshire Regiment. Killed in action, Battle of the Somme, 12th October, 1916. Age 22. Son of Thomas and Rosina Wilkins, of 34, Princess Street, Coventry. Born 5th November, 1893 at 30, Cromwell Street. Resided 59, Cromwell Street. Driller. Enlisted February, 1916. Memorial Ref. Pier and Face 9 A 9 B and 10 B. Thiepval Memorial, Somme, France.

WILKINS, John. Commemorated Holy Trinity Panels.

WILKINS, Fitter, John. 88894, "C" Bty. 48th Brigade, Royal Field Artillery. Killed in action, Ypres, 30th July, 1915. Age 21. Son of John and Catherine Wilkins, of 18, Springfield Road, Coventry. Enlisted August, 1914 at Maidstone. Born 4th April, 1894 at Coventry. Resided Springfield Road. Fitter, Daimler Co. Memorial Ref. Panel 5 and 9. Ypres (Menin Gate) Memorial, Ieper, West-Vlaanderen, Belgium.

WILKINS, Rifleman, John Thomas. S/32456, 10th Bn., Rifle Brigade formerly M/298983, Royal Army Service Corps. Killed in action, Cambrai, 21st November, 1917. Age 19. Son of James and Elizabeth Wilkins, of 212, Bell Green Road, Coventry. Born 5th August, 1898 at 218, Bell Green Road. Turner. Enlisted March, 1917 at Coventry. Resided Coventry. Memorial Ref. Panel 10 and 11. Cambrai Memorial, Louverval, Nord, France.

WILKINS, Private, Sidney. 7270, 10th Bn., Royal Warwickshire Regiment. Killed in action, Battle of the Somme, 30th July, 1916. Born 14th October, 1892 at Foleshill. Resided at 16, Welford Place. Fitter. Enlisted 1914 at Coventry. Memorial Ref. Pier and Face 9 A 9 B and 10 B. Thiepval Memorial, Somme, France.

**WILKINS**, Private, William. 3515, 1st Bn., Royal Warwickshire Regiment. Died of wounds, 4th May, 1915 at Boulogne Hospital after having a leg amputated. Age 19. Son of Thomas and Rosina Wilkins, of Coventry. Educated Bablake School. Born 22nd March, 1896 at 30, Cromwell Street. Resided 59, Cromwell Street. Fitter, Humber Works. Enlisted August, 1914 at Coventry. Commemorated Bablake School Memorial. Grave Ref. I. F. 30A. Wimereux Communal Cemetery, Pas De Calais, France.

WILKINS, Private, William John. 10723, 1st Bn., Coldstream Guards. Killed in action, 29th October, 1914. Age 20. Son of Mr. G. and Mrs. E. Wilkins of 59, Waterloo Street, Leamington. Born St. Mary's, Leamington. Enlisted Coventry. Resided Leamington. Memorial Ref. Panel 11. Ypres (Menin Gate) Memorial, Belgium.

WILKINSON, B. Educated Bablake School. Killed in action. Commemorated Bablake School Memorial.

WILKINSON, Private, George. 7911, 2nd Bn., Duke of Wellington's (West Riding Regiment). Died, 10th March, 1918. Age 33. Husband of Edith M. Wilkinson, of 6, Holmsdale Road, Coventry. Born Halifax. Enlisted Halifax. Grave Ref. 3. The Hague General Cemetery, Zuid-Holland, Netherlands.

WILKINSON, Private, George. 16429, 11th Bn., Royal Warwickshire Regiment. Killed in action, 15th July, 1916. Age 20. Son of Mr. and Mrs. John Wilkinson, of 29, Broad Street, Foleshill, Coventry. Born Stockingford. Enlisted Coventry. Memorial Ref. Pier and Face 9 A 9 B and 10 B. Thiepval Memorial, Somme, France.

WILKINSON, Private, Jabez. 19114, 1st Bn., Royal Dublin Fusiliers. Killed in action, 29th March 1918. Age 23. Son of Charles and Maria Wilkinson. Born Coventry. Enlisted Tunstall. Memorial Ref. Panel 79 and 80. Pozieres Memorial, France.

WILKINSON, Able Seaman, John. R/257, Drake Bn., Royal Naval Division. Killed in action, 25th March, 1916. Age 24. Son of Thomas Frederick and Jemima Wilkinson, of "Wychcote," Stoney Rd., Coventry. Born 20th October, 1893 at Coventry. Resided Coventry. Loom maker. Enlisted September, 1916. Memorial Ref. Martinpuich German Cem. Mem. Martinpuich Communal Cemetery, France

WILKINSON, Private, John Herbert. 47029, 9th Bn., Royal Inniskilling Fusiliers. Killed in action, 18th May, 1918. Born Wolverhampton. Enlisted Birmingham. Resided Coventry. Memorial Ref. Panel 70 to 72. Tyne Cot Memorial, Belgium.

WILKINSON, Gunner, Josiah. 119037, "A" Bty. 77th Brigade, Royal Field Artillery. Died of wounds, 1st October, 1916. Age 20. Son of William and Annie Wilkinson, of Little Packington, Meriden, Coventry. Born Meriden. Employed Coventry. Enlisted Coventry. Grave Ref. B. 15. 8. St. Sever Cemetery, Rouen, Seine-Maritime, France.

WILKINSON, Private, Maurice Henry. 29466, 8th Bn., Border Regiment. Died, 26th June, 1918. Age 19. Son of Mrs. Isabella Wilkinson of 15, Selby Street, Hull. Resided at 14, Cope Street. Employed by Coventry Swaging Company Ltd. Enlisted April, 1917 at Coventry. Born Skegness. Resided Worksop, Notts. Enlisted Coventry. Grave Ref. I. A. 41. Aulnoye Communal Cemetery, France.

WILLDAY, Private 2nd Class, Charles James. 198630, Recruits' Depot, Royal Air Force. Died of pneumonia, 29th June, 1918. Age 25. Son of Mrs. E. H. Willday, of 174, Allesley Old Road, Coventry. Born 12th November, 1891 in Much Park Street. Resided 34, Allesley Old Road. Enlisted June, 1918. Grave Ref. 90. 168. Coventry (London Road) Cemetery.

WILLETT, Private, Charles. 17434, 3rd Bn., Coldstream Guards. Killed in action, 9th October, 1917. Husband of Mrs. Willett of 100, London Road, Stockton Heath, Warrington. Born Bedford, Beds. Enlisted Coventry. Resided Clitheroe, Lancs. Grave Ref. VII. F. 13. Artillery Wood Cemetery, Belgium.

WILLIAMS, Private, Albert John. 265444, 1/7th Bn., Royal Warwickshire Regiment formerly Worcestershire Regiment. Died, Italy, 26th October, 1918. Age 26. Son of John and Mary Ann Williams, of St. John's, Worcester. Born Worcester. Resided Warwick. Auto machine attendant. Grave Ref. 8. C. 10. Montecchio Precalcino Communal Cemetery Extension, Italy.

WILLIAMS, Private, Alfred Edward. 3, "D" Coy., 1st Bn., Royal Warwickshire Regiment. Killed in action, 13th October, 1914. Age 27. Son of Alfred and Mary Williams, of 83, Widdrington Road, Coventry. Born 3rd June, 1887 at Newcastle-under-Lyme. Resided Widdrington Road. Factory hand. Reservist. Enlisted Coventry. Grave Ref. IV. C. 614. (Buried near this spot). Meteren Military Cemetery, Nord, France.

WILLIAMS, Private, Arthur Harry. 17730, 14th Bn., Royal Warwickshire Regiment. Killed in action, 30th July, 1916. Age 32. Son of Edward and Mary Ann Williams. Husband of Mrs. Williams of 7c. 5h. Chauntry Place. Born Court House Green. Enlisted Coventry. Memorial Ref. Pier and Face 9 A 9 B and 10 B. Thiepval Memorial, Somme, France.

WILLIAMS, Private, Arthur Sidney. 34312, 2nd /4th Bn., Oxfordshire and Buckinghamshire Light Infantry. Killed in action, 12th September, 1918. Age 19. Son of Sidney Edwin and Beatrice Ann Williams, of 24, Crescent Avenue, Stoke, Coventry. Born Walsgrave-on-Sowe. Enlisted Coventry. Resided Walsgrave-on-Sowe. Grave Ref. III. O. 8. Trois Arbres Cemetery, Steenwerck, Nord, France.

WILLIAMS, Private, Charles Hubert. 14199, C Coy., 12th Bn., Gloucestershire Regiment. Killed in action, 4th September, 1916. Only son of Charles Edward and Sarah Ann Williams of Upton Park, London. Commemorated Iliffe & Sons Ltd. Grave Ref. II. B. 49. La Neuvelle British Cemetery, Corbie, France.

WILLIAMS, Lance Corporal, Charles. 12524, 8th Bn., Royal Welsh Fusiliers. Killed in action, 15th February, 1917. Age 24. Son of Thomas and Emily Williams, of 252, Longford Road, Longford, Coventry. Employed Exhall Colliery. Commemorated Saint Thomas the Apostle, Longford. Memorial Ref. Panel 15. Basra Memorial, Iraq.

WILLIAMS, Lance Corporal, Edward George. 200788, D Bn., Tank Corps formerly 2512, Machine Gun Corps. Killed in action, 9th October, 1917. Age 25. Son of Thomas William of Ty-Nant, Penrhys Road, Tylorstown, Rhonda, Glam. Born Ferndale, Glamorgan. Enlisted Coventry. Memorial Ref. Panel 159 to 160. Tyne Cot Memorial, Belgium.

WILLIAMS, Second Lieutenant, Edward Herbert. 2nd Bn., South Wales Borderers. Killed in action, near Ypres, 31st August, 1916. Born in May, 1891 at Hucknall Torkard, Notts. Resided Coventry. Solicitor, Enlisted September, 1914. Grave Ref. III. F. 7. Essex Farm Cemetery, Belgium.

WILLIAMS, Private, Frank. 307883, 1/8th Bn., Royal Warwickshire Regiment. Died, Italy, 19th January, 1918. Born 1st September, 1899 in Spring Street. Resided at 33, St. Margaret's Road. Turner. Enlisted December, 1914 at Coventry. Grave Ref. A. 1. Cremona Town Cemetery, Italy.

WILLIAMS, Gunner, Fred. 1132, 7th Bty., Machine Gun Corps (Motors). Died of wounds, 30th April, 1918. Age 20. Son of Ann Jane Williams of Langtree Cottage, Kirkby, Liverpool. Born Liverpool. Enlisted Coventry. Resided Liverpool. Grave Ref. I. E. 24. Arneke British Cemetery, France.

WILLIAMS, Private, Jack. 28379, D Coy., 15th Bn., Royal Warwickshire Regiment. Killed in action, 9th May, 1917. Age 29. Son of Mrs. Elizabeth Williams, of 70, Freeston Avenue, Snedshill, Wellington, Salop. Information request by Miss J. Watkins, 34a Smithford Street, Coventry. Memorial Ref. Bay 3. Arras Memorial, France.

WILLIAMS, Lance Corporal, James. M2/050366, Army Service Corps attached 47th Ammunition Sub Park. Died of wounds, 16th October, 1917. Age 30. Son of William Charles and Harriet Williams of 15, Cambridge Road, Hammersmith, London. Enlisted Coventry. Resided Hammersmith. Grave Ref. X. I. 7. Dozinghem Military Cemetery, Belgium.

WILLIAMS, J. H. Employed Humber Ltd. Killed in action, Dardanelles.

WILLIAMS, John Victor. Killed in action. Name on Roll of Honour is St. John the Baptist Church.

WILLIAMS, P. Commemorated Central Methodist Hall.

WILLIAMS, Second Lieutenant, Peter. 12th Bn., Royal Welsh Fusiliers. Killed in action, 13th November, 1916. Age 23. Son of Daniel and Hannah Margaret Williams, of 320, Watery Lane, Sutton, St. Helens, Lancs. Born Bangor. Resided Coventry. Electrical Engineer. Enlisted 1915. Memorial Ref. Pier and Face 4 A. Thiepval Memorial, France.

WILLIAMS, Private, Richard Philip. PO/2705, 1st Royal Marine Bn., Royal Naval Division, Royal Marine Light Infantry. Died of wounds, 28th September, 1918. Age 21. Son of Richard and Elizabeth Williams, of 166, Cross Road, Foleshill, Coventry. Native of Woolwich, London. Born 29th July, 18987 at Bermondsey. Resided 166, Cross Road. Brass moulder. Enlisted March, 1918. Grave Ref. IV. B. 21. Bucquoy Road Cemetery, Ficheux, Pas de Calais, France.

WILLIAMS, Rifleman, Robert. 835, 2nd Bn., King's Royal Rifle Corps. Killed, Battle of the Aisne, 14th September, 1914. Born 3rd June, 1880 at Birmingham. Labourer. Enlisted August, 1914. Memorial Ref. La Ferte-Sous-Jouarre Memorial, France.

WILLIAMS, Sidney A. Commemorated Walsgrave-On-Sowe Memorial.

WILLIAMSON, Harold. Name on Roll of Honour in Holy Trinity Church.

WILLOUGHBY, Gunner, Frank. 212791, "D" Bty. 74th Bde., Royal Field Artillery. Killed in action, 2nd June, 1918. Age 32. Husband of Ada Willoughby, of 41, Bath Street, Leamington Spa. Resided Stratford-on-Avon. Employed Coventry. Grave Ref. XIX. C. 11. Bienvillers Military Cemetery, France.

WILLS, Sapper, Abraham. 155824, 173rd Tunnelling Coy., Royal Engineers formerly 94277, Royal Field Artillery. Died of wounds, 21st May, 1916. Husband of L. Wills, of 21, Grange Avenue, Binley, Coventry. Born Nuneaton. Enlisted Coventry. Grave Ref. I. M. 24. Noeux-Les-Mines Communal Cemetery, Pas de Calais, France.

WILLS, Corporal, Thomas Ernest. 9975, 2nd Bn., South Wales Borderers. Killed in action, Monchy-le-Preux, 23rd April, 1917. Age 25. Son of Thomas and Rachael Wills of 9, Church End, Stoke, Coventry. Born 18th October, 1890 at Coventry. Resided Coventry. Cycle machinist, Raglan Works, Raglan Street. Reservist. Commemorated Stoke (St. Michaels) Church. Memorial Ref. Bay 6. Arras Memorial, Pas de Calais, France.

WILLS, Private, William Henry. 965, 2nd Bn., Royal Warwickshire Regiment. Killed in action, Battle of the Marne, 16th November, 1914. Age 22. Son of Henry and Eliza Mills, of 6, Court, 1 House, Cox Street, Coventry. Born 14th February, 1892 at Coventry. Enlisted Warwick. Resided Coventry. Machinist. Memorial Ref. Panel 2 and 3. Ploegsteert Memorial, Comines-Warneton, Hainaut, Belgium.

WILLSON, Private, Arthur. 3606, 9th Bn., Royal Warwickshire Regiment. Killed in action, Gallipoli, 10th August, 1915. Age 26. Cousin of Betram Jenner of 2, Stanhope Cottages, Lingfield, Surrey. Born Hackney, Middx. Enlisted Coventry. Resided Stoneleigh. Memorial Ref. Panel 35 to 37. Helles Memorial, Turkey.

WILSON, Private, Alfred Albert. 15068, 11th Bn., Royal Warwickshire Regiment. Killed in action, 29th April, 1917. Age 28. Employed Daimler Works. Second son to be killed off Mr. and Mrs. Wilson, 5, Jordan's Building, Spon End, Coventry. Memorial Ref. Bay 3. Arras Memorial, France.

WILSON, Bombardier, Arthur. Royal Field Artillery. Died, home. 7th September, 1923. Born 15th October, 1897 at Coventry. Resided 500, Foleshill Road. Labourer. Enlisted November, 1915. Grave Ref. Colchester.

WILSON, Private, Arthur. 9755, 2nd Bn., Coldstream Guards. Killed in action, 19th September, 1914. Age 24. Born 1890 in Well Street. Resided at 5, Jordan Buildings, Spon End. Machinist. First son to be killed of Mr. and Mrs. Wilson, 5, Jordan Buildings. Enlisted Coventry. Grave Ref. III. A. 3. 1. Vailly British Cemetery, France.

WILSON, C. Commemorated Coventry Chain Memorial.

WILSON, Private, Charles Herbert. 44489, 2/5th Bn., Gloucestershire Regiment. Killed in action, 24th April, 1918. Age 18. Son of John B. and Maria Wilson of 24, Camp Hill Road, Nuneaton. Born Hartshill, Warwick. Enlisted Coventry. Memorial Ref. Panel 60 to 64. Loos Memorial, France.

WILSON, Private, Frederick Gerald. 35002, 5th Bn., Royal Berkshire Regiment. Died of wounds, 30th November, 1917. Age 27. Son of Harry and Mary Jane Evelyn Wilson, of The Laurels, Crescent Avenue, Stoke, Coventry. Husband of Winifred Mabel Wilson, of 6, Warwick Street, Earlsdon, Coventry. Born 26th August, 1891 at Northampton. French polisher. Enlisted December, 1916 at Coventry. Commemorated Stoke (St. Michaels) Church. Memorial Ref. Panel 8. Cambrai Memorial, Louverval, Nord, France.

WILSON, Rifleman George. R/8693, 11th Bn., Kings Royal Rifle Corps. Killed in action, 20th September, 1917. Born Coventry. Enlisted Birmingham. Memorial Ref. Panel 115 to 119 and 162A and 163A. Tyne Cot Memorial, Belgium.

WILSON, Private, George Herbert. 18896, 1/5th Bn., Somerset Light Infantry. Died, Egypt, 14th November 1917. Age 20. Son of Chris and Frances E. Wilson, of Elm Place, Tunley Road, Dunkerton, Bath. Born Coventry. Enlisted Butts Frome, Somerset. Resided Peasedown, Somerset. Grave Ref. P. 21. Ramleh War Cemetery, Israel.

WILSON, Private, Harry. 2030, 51st Bn., Australian Infantry, A.I.F. Killed in action, 2nd April, 1917. Age 31. Son of Henry and Maria Wilson. Husband of B. A. Wilson, of 89, Richmond Street, Coventry, England. Born in Norfolk, England. Memorial Ref. Villers-Bretonneux Memorial, Somme, France.

WILSON, Private, Harry. 8871, 11th Bn., Royal Warwickshire Regiment. Killed in action, 1st July, 1916 by a shell. Born 1888 in Trafalgar Street, St. Thomas', Coventry. Enlisted Warwick. Resided Coventry. Son of Mr. Wilson, 5, Gordon Buildings, Spon End. Grave Ref. A. 4. Hannescamps New Military Cemetery, France.

WILSON, Private, Henry Joseph. 44484, 25th Bn., Northumberland Fusiliers formerly West Yorkshire Regiment. Killed in action, 28th April, 1917. Born at Thirsk, Yorkshire. Employed Coventry. Memorial Ref. Bay 2 and 3. Arras Memorial, France.

WILSON, Air Mechanic 2nd Class, Horace James. 162818, "X" Engine Repair Depot, Royal Air Force. Died, 24th January, 1919. Age 20. Son of Bert and Elizabeth Wilson, of 93, Harnall Lane West, Coventry. Born 19th December, 1898 at Coventry. Resided Harnall Lane West. Mechanic. Grave Ref. Q. 262. Cairo War Memorial Cemetery, Egypt.

WILSON, Private, Horace Llewellyn. 2397, 1st /7th Bn., Royal Warwickshire Regiment. Killed in action, 25th July, 1916. Age 23. Son of Henry Eardley Wilson and Alice Wilson, of 42, Coventry Street, Stoke, Coventry, Warwick. Born Stoke. Resided Coventry Street. Employed Premier Cycle Co. Ltd. Enlisted Coventry. Memorial Ref. Pier and Face 9 A 9 B and 10 B. Thiepval Memorial, Somme, France.

WILSON, Hugh. S. Killed in action. Name on Roll of Honour in Cathedral Church of St. Michael.

WILSON, Engine Room Artificer, James. 370EB, HMS Lameroo, Royal Naval Reserve. Killed in action, 14th August, 1916. Age 34. Son of James and Jean Wilson, of Barrow-in-Furness. Husband of Margaret Ann Wilson, of 246, Lockhurst Lane, Foleshill, Coventry. Born 1882. Coppersmith. Royal Naval Reservist. Commemorated St. Paul's Church. Memorial Ref. 19. Plymouth Naval Memorial, Devon.

WILSON, Private, James. 37998, 22nd Bn., Manchester Regiment. Killed in action, 6th March, 1917. Brother of mr. R. Wilson of 44, Ranin Road, Chester. Born Dublin. Enlisted Coventry. Resided Gorton, Manchester. Grave Ref. II. E. 12. Mailly Wood Cemetery, Mailly-Maillet, Somme, France.

WILSON, Sergeant, Samuel, DCM, MM. 39540, 52nd Bty. 15th Bde., Royal Field Artillery. Killed in action, 4th November, 1918. Age 30. Husband of Naomi F. Wilson, of 39, Pascoe Road, Lewisham, London. Born Coventry. Enlisted Liverpool. Grave Ref. B. 1. Ghissignies British Cemetery, France.

WILSON, Private, Tom Fleming. 206134, Machine Gun Corps (Heavy Branch) formerly 2690, Machine Gun Corps. Died of wounds, 22nd September, 1916. Enlisted Coventry. Grave Ref. IV. H. 6. Heilly Station Cemetery, Meri-Court-L'Abbe, France.

WILSON, Private, William. 12474, 3rd Bn., Cheshire Regiment. Died on service, 28th May, 1915. Age 46. Son of George and Elizabeth Wilson of Coventry. Husband of Rose Wilson, of 8, Bayley Lane, Coventry. Born 4th November, 1868 at Coventry. Resided 36, Alma Street. Employed Coventry Corporation Gas Department. Enlisted January, 1915 at Coventry. Commemorated Gas Department Memorial, Coventry Corporation. Grave Ref. 207. 131. Coventry (London Road) Cemetery.

WILSON, Private, William Henry. 43401, 2nd/8th Battalion, Royal Warwickshire Regiment. Killed in action, 1st November, 1918. Resided at Bilton Hall, Warwicks. Employed by Armstrong Siddeley Motors Limited. Enlisted Coventry. Commemorated Siddeley Roll of Honour. Grave Ref. C. 19. Preseau Communal Cemetery Extension, France.

WINCOTT, Private, Percy. 5811, 2nd Bn., East Lancashire Regiment. Died of wounds, Nueve Chappelle, 2nd July, 1915. Born 17th November, 1892 at Coventry. Resided Coventry. Carpenter. Enlisted August, 1914. Commemorated King Henry VIII School. Grave Ref. II. G. 147. Sailly-Sur-La-Lys Canadian Cemetery, France.

WINCOTT, Percy. Commemorated Holy Trinity Panels.

WINDRIDGE, Private, Matthew Lawrence. 2805, 2nd Battalion, Royal Warwickshire Regiment. Killed in action, 9th October 1917. Born 25th September 1895, at 8, Radford Road. Resided at 3, Hill Cross. Butcher. Enlisted August, 1914 at Coventry. Memorial Ref. Panel 23 to 28 and 163A. Tyne Cot Memorial, Belgium.

WINDRIDGE, Private, Thomas. 361442, transf. to 804th Area Employment Coy., Labour Corps formerly 3379, Duke of Lancaster's Yeomanry. Died, Egypt, 5th July 1918. Age 36. Son of Thomas and Mary Walsh (formerly Windridge). Husband of Anna Windridge, of Kaser El Lulua, 8, Faggala, Cairo. Born Coventry. Enlisted Manchester. Resided Mumps, Egypt. Grave Ref. M. 168. Cairo War Memorial Cemetery, Egypt.

WINFIELD, Sergeant, Alfred Henry. 14855, "C" Coy, 1st Bn., Royal Berkshire Regiment. Died of wounds, 29th April, 1917. Age 37. Son of John and Sarah Ann Winfield, of Beeston, Notts. Employed Humber Ltd. Born Beeston, Notts. Enlisted Coventry. Grave Ref. II. E. 6. Orchard Dump Cemetery, Arleux-En-Gohelle, France.

WING, Private, Herbert John. 11164, 2nd Bn., Oxfordshire and Buckinghamshire Light Infantry. Killed in action, Festubert, 16th May, 1915. Born 7th January, 1887 at Stoke Aldermoor. Resided at Ryton-on-Dunsmore. Gardener, Messrs Webb & Son, Stoke Park. Mother, Mrs. Wing of 3, Owen Street, Coventry. Enlisted August, 1914 at Coventry. He leaves a widow. Commemorated Holy Trinity Panels and Ryton Memorial. Memorial Ref. Panel 26. Le Touret Memorial, France.

WING, Private, Raymond Walter. 132690, 35th Bn., Machine Gun Corps formerly 331276, Royal Warwickshire Regiment. Killed in action, 24th April, 1918. Born in 1899 at Hillmorton. Resided 6, Red Lane. Clerk. Born New Bilton, Warwick. Enlisted Coventry. Grave Ref. II. G. 2. Varennes Military Cemetery, France.

WING, Private, Walter. 266583, 1/7th Bn., Royal Warwickshire Regiment. Killed in action, 27th March, 1917. Born Princethorpe. Employed Coventry. Enlisted Coventry. Grave Ref. IX. A. XIII. Tincourt New British Cemetery, France.

WING, Private, William Francis. 265828, 1st /7th Bn., Royal Warwickshire Regiment. Killed in action, by a sniper's bullet, 15th June, 1918. Age 31. Son of Matthew John and Rebecca Wing of 3, Queen Street, Coventry. Born 25th April, 1888 at Stoke Aldermoor. Resided 3, Queen Street. Gardener. Enlisted September, 1914 at Coventry. Commemorated Holy Trinity Panels. Grave Ref. Plot 1. Row C. Grave 4. Magnaboschi British Cemetery, Italy.

WINSCOMBE, Private, Arthur. 242771, 2/6th Bn., Royal Warwickshire Regiment. Killed in action, 3rd April, 1918. Enlisted Warwicks. Resided Coventry. Memorial Ref. Panel 18 and 19. Pozieres Memorial, France.

WINTERBOTTOM, Private, Charles. CH/2507(S), 1st Bn., Royal Marine Light Infantry. Killed in action, 25th August, 1918. Born 25th December, 1887 at Droylsden near Manchester. Resided at 90, Station Street West. Labourer. Enlisted February, 1918. Grave Ref. IX. G. 8. A.I.F. Burial Ground, Flers, France.

WISDOM, Sapper, Charles. 92847, 213th Army Troops Coy., Royal Engineers. Killed in action, 30th March, 1918 Born 2nd November, 1886 at Woolwich, Kent. Enlisted Leamington Spa. Resided 6, Vauxhall Street, Coventry. Plasterer. Enlisted March, 1915. Memorial Ref. Panel 10 to 13. Pozieres Memorial, France.

WITHERS, Private, George Frederick. 2198, 1st Bn., Royal Warwickshire Regiment. Died of wounds, 13th October, 1918. Son of William Henry and Ellen Withers, of Coventry. Born St. Johns, Coventry. Enlisted Warwick. Resided Coventry. Grave Ref. VIII. B. 7. Berlin South-Western Cemetery, Berlin, Brandenburg, Germany.

WOLFE, Lieutenant, Sidney George. 18th Bn., Lancashire Fusiliers. Killed in action, by a shell after advancing seventy five yards, 22nd October, 1917. Educated Bablake School. Born 14th February, 1890 at Rugby. Resided at 45, Berkeley Road. School teacher. Son of George Wolfe of 45, Berkeley Road. Enlisted September, 1914. Leaves a wife and one child. Commemorated Bablake School Memorial and St. Barbara's Church. Memorial Ref. Tyne Cot Memorial, Belgium.

WOLLEN, Private, A. Royal Warwickshire Regiment. Commemorated Dunlop Memorial.

WOOD, Private, A. J. Killed in action, Neuve Chapelle. Resided Canley/Tile Hill. Commemorated St. Barbara's Memorial.

WOOD, Lance Corporal, Albert. 78673, 15th (The King's) Hussars. Died, home, 9th May, 1920. Age 19. Son of Charles and Jane Wood, of 21, Hollick Crescent, Arley, Coventry. Born Tamworth. Grave Ref. 9453. Tamworth Cemetery, Staffordshire.

WOOD, Private, Albert Thomas. 12799, 1st Bn., Worcestershire Regiment. Killed in action, 13th March 1915. Born Stoneleigh, Warwicks. Enlisted Coventry. Resided Coventry. Memorial Ref. Panel 17 and 18. Le Touret Memorial, France.

WOOD, Barry. Commemorated Saint Thomas the Apostle, Longford.

WOOD, Private, Francis Ernest. CMT/363, 155th (Army) Bde. Royal Field Artillery. Killed in action, 27th May, 1918. Age 28. Son of Richard Ernest and Mary Wood, of Bradmore, Wolverhampton. Husband of Dorothy Elizabeth Wood, of 11, Rudgeheath, Pattingham, Wolverhampton. Born Coventry. Enlisted Wolverhampton. Resided Claverley, Wolverhampton. Grave Ref. XII. B. 13. Warlincourt Halte British Cemetery, Saulty, France.

WOOD, Private, George. 68154, 105th Field Ambulance, Royal Army Medical Corps. Died, 25th October, 1917. Husband of Sarah Elizabeth Wood, of 67, Dibble Road, Smethwick, Staffs. Born Coventry. Enlisted Lichfield. Panel 160. Tyne Cot Memorial, Belgium.

WOOD, Private, George Edward. 16755, 14th Bn., Royal Warwickshire Regiment. Killed in action by shell fire, 8th May 1917. Age 25. Son of John and Helen Wood. Born Kettering. Enlisted Rugby, Warwicks. Resided Coventry. Born June, 1893 at Burton Latimer. Resided 3c. 13h. Spon End. Grinder. Enlisted February, 1916. Grave Ref. IX. A. 21. Orchard Dump Cemetery, Arleux-En-Gohelle, France.

WOOD, Private, Harry. G/69061, 20th Bn., Royal Fusiliers formerly 4904, 4th Buffs Regt. Died of wounds, 30th November, 1917. Age 32. Son of Mr. and Mrs. Thomas Wood, of Northallerton. Husband of Elizabeth Wood, of 129, Aldermans Green, Foleshill, Coventry. Born in 1885 at Kirby Sigston. Enlisted Coventry. Resided Coventry. Grave Ref. IX. C. 20. Nine Elms British Cemetery, Poperinge, West-Vlaanderen, Belgium.

WOOD, Bombardier, Herbert John. 840566, "A" Bty. 307th Brigade, Royal Field Artillery. Killed in action, 15th August, 1917. Age 19. Son of Herbert and Harriet Wood, of 2, Sackville Street, Coventry. Born 3rd October, 1897 at 30, George Street. Resided Sackville Street. Motor cycle fitter. Enlisted 1916. Commemorated Triumph and Gloria Memorial. Grave Ref. III. E. 13. White House Cemetery, St. Jean-Les-Ypres, Ieper, West-Vlaanderen, Belgium.

WOOD, Private, James. 1672, 2nd Bn., Royal Warwickshire Regiment. Killed, 21st July, 1915. Born 25th December, 1888 at St. Michael's, Coventry. Resided at 47, Gordon Street. Iron polisher. Enlisted Coventry. Memorial Ref. 6. Le Touret Memorial, France.

WOOD, Private, Richard. 202347, 2nd /6th Bn., Royal Warwickshire Regiment. Killed, 11th April, 1918 - 12th April, 1918. Age 19. Son of Richard Wood, of 50, Princess Street, Coventry. Born 3rd November, 1898 at West Bromwich. Resided 37, Harnall Lane West. Machinist. Enlisted October, 1916 at Coventry. Memorial Ref. Panel 2 and 3. Ploegsteert Memorial, Comines-Warneton, Hainaut, Belgium.

WOOD, Private, Richard David. G/18292, 8th Bn., Royal Sussex Regiment. Died of wounds, 1st June, 1917. Son of Richard Abraham and Annie Louisa Wood. Age 29. Born Greenwich. Employed Coventry. Enlisted Coventry. Grave Ref. I. E. 7. Sunken Road Cemetery, Boisleux-St. Marc, France.

WOOD, Private, W. R. 9779, 1st Bn., South Staffordshire Regiment. Killed in action, 11th October, 1915. Age 39. Brother of Henry Wood, of "Blenheim," Lythalls Lane, Foleshill, Coventry. Native of Birmingham. Grave Ref. I. G. 1. Woburn Abbey Cemetery, Cuinchy, Pas de Calais, France.

WOOD, Private, William. 11484, 20th Hussars. Killed in action, 21st February 1915. Born St. Thomas, Coventry. Enlisted Coventry. Resided Coventry. Memorial Ref. Panel 5. Ypres (Menin Gate) Memorial, Belgium.

WOOD, Company Sergeant Major, William Henry Croft. 8, 1st /7th Bn., Royal Warwickshire Regiment. Died of wounds, 24th July, 1916. Age 31. Son of George and Annie Wood, of 19, Stanley Road, Earlsdon, Coventry. Born 28th February, 1886 at St. Giles, Kensington, London. Cashier. Enlisted August, 1914 at Coventry. Resided Kensington. Commemorated Bablake School Memorial, St. Barbara's Church and Earlsdon Working Mens Club. Grave Ref. II. C. 3. Heilly Station Cemetery, Mericourt-L'abbe, Somme, France.

WOODALL, Corporal, Albert Edwin. 24997, 14th Bn., Gloucestershire Regiment. Died of wounds, 14th July, 1917 injured through the bursting of a shell, 29th June. Age 31. Son of John and Ann Selina Woodall, of 35, Peel Street, Coventry. Born 2nd December, 1885 at 27c. 4h. Much Park Street, Coventry. Moulder, Foundry Department, Humber Works. Enlisted Coventry. Grave Ref. I. E. 7. Etretat Churchyard Extension, Seine-Maritime, France.

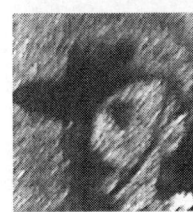

WOODFIELD, Company Quarter Master Sergeant, Thomas. 5243, 2nd Bn., Royal Scots Fusiliers. Killed in action, 24th October, 1914. Born Coventry. Enlisted Leeds. Resided Coventry. Grave Ref. IX. A. 7. Perth Cemetery (China Wall), Belgium.

WOODFORD, Private, Percy Henry. 26526, 10th Bn., Royal Warwickshire Regiment. Died of wounds, at a Casualty Clearing Station, 23rd October, 1918. Born 4th November, 1896 at Budbrooke, Warwicks. Resided 12, Widdrington Road. Grinder, Daimler Works. Enlisted August, 1917 at Coventry. Parents resided Wolverton, Stratford on Avon. Grave Ref. I. H. 16. Delsaux Farm Cemetery, Beugny, France.

WOODHEAD, Private, Thomas. 1619, 2nd Bn., Royal Warwickshire Regiment. Killed in action, 18th December, 1914. Born 27th February, 1874 at Coventry. Resided Warwick. Storekeeper. Enlisted August, 1914. Memorial Ref. 2 and 3. Ploegsteert Memorial, Belgium.

WOODHOUSE, Private, George. 40720, 8th Bn., North Staffordshire Regiment. Killed in action, 10th June, 1917. Born 1879. Resided Coventry. Scrap dealer's assistant. Enlisted May, 1916. Commemorated Saint Thomas the Apostle, Longford. Memorial Ref. 55. Ypres (Menin Gate) Memorial, Belgium.

WOODIER, Private, Albert. 14468, "B" Coy. 8th Bn., Royal Berkshire Regiment. Killed in action, 13th October, 1915. Age 22. Son of Albert and Lizzie Woodier, of 5, St. John Street, Coventry. Born Coventry. Enlisted Rugby at the outbreak of war. Resided Coventry. Employed Rover Company. Memorial Ref. Panel 93 to 95. Loos Memorial, Pas de Calais, France.

WOODINGS, Lance Sergeant, Charles. 9903, 8th Bn., North Staffordshire Regiment. Killed in action, 6th July, 1916. Born Burton-on-Trent. Enlisted Coventry. Resided Wolston. Commemorated Wolston Memorial.Memorial Ref. Pier and Face 14 B and 14C. Thiepval Memorial, France.

WOODMAN, Private, William. 4527, 1/7th Bn., Royal Warwickshire Regiment. Killed in action, 25th July, 1916. Born Cox Street. Resided 23, Gordon Street. Polisher, Humber Works. Brother in law of Mrs. Woodman of 3c. 5h. Leicester Street. Enlisted Coventry. Memorial Ref. Pier and Face 9 A 9 B and 10 B. Thiepval Memorial, Somme, France.

WOODWARD, Driver, Cecil David Charles. Royal Horse Artillery. Died, Home, 19th March, 1920. Born 13th April, 1894 at Barston. Resided at Rosedale, Tile Hill Lane. Labourer. Enlisted May, 1915. Grave Ref. Westwood Heath.

WOODWARD, Private, Edwin. 512809, "C" Coy. 1st/14th Bn., London Regiment (London Scottish). Killed in action, Arras, 5th April, 1917. Son of John and Delilah Ann Woodward, of Leamington. Enlisted Coventry. Resided Coventry. Born 30th January, 1894 at Leamington. Resided at 38, Foleshill Road. Progress clerk. Enlisted February, 1915. Grave Ref. B. 7. Achicourt Road Cemetery, Achicourt, France.

WOODWARD, Private, Frank. 61184, 23rd Bn., Lancashire Fusiliers. Died, home, 3rd December, 1918. Age 22. Resided at 28c. 1h. Spon Street. Son of George and Ada Woodward of Northampton. Grave Ref. Q. 414. (Screen Wall). Manchester Southern Cemetery.

WOODWARD, Private, Herbert Briggs. 13279, 12th Bn., Hampshire Regiment. Killed, 25th April, 1917. Born 1891 at Leamington. Resided at 32, Stoney Stanton Road. Enlisted August, 1914. Employed Gaskell and Chambers, Birmingham. Father, A. Woodward resided at 32, Stoney Stanton Road. Memorial Ref. Doiran Memorial, Greece.

WOODWARD, Private, Richard. 1715, 11th Bn., Royal Warwickshire Regiment. Accidentally killed, 16th September, 1915. Husband of M. L. Woodward, of 3 Court, 1 House, Upper Well St., Coventry. Born 19th May, 1877 at Horniton, Staffs. Polisher, Rudge Works. Enlisted August, 1914 at Coventry. Grave Ref. I. A. 58. Bienvillers Military Cemetery, Pas de Calais, France.

WOODWARD, Gunner, Thomas Alfred. 261457, 108th Brigade, Royal Field Artillery. Died of wounds, 30th September, 1918. Age 21. Son of Thomas and Jenny Woodward. Husband of Lilian Woodward, of 52, Canterbury Street, Coventry. Born 1897 at Birmingham. Resided Ryton-on-Dunsmore. Drop forger. Enlisted February, 1918 at Coventry. Commemorated Ryton Memorial. Grave Ref. III. C. 8. Doingt Communal Cemetery Extension, Somme, France.

WOODWARD, Trooper, Walter. 2739, "D" Sqdn., 1st Life Guards. Killed in action, 1st November, 1914. Age 24. Son of Mrs. Delilah Ann Woodward, of 38, Foleshill Road, Coventry. Born 27th May, 1891 at St. Mary's, Leamington. Resided 33, Foleshill Road. Soldier. Enlisted Coventry. Memorial Ref. Panel 3. Ypres (Menin Gate) Memorial, Leper, West-Vlaanderen, Belgium.

WOODWARD, Private, William Henry. 16911, 1st Bn., Royal Warwickshire Regiment. Died of wounds, received at Arras, 29th November, 1918. Age 27. Son of Frank and Alice Woodward, of Stoke, Coventry. Husband of Ellen M. Woodward, of 59, Villiers Street, Stoke, Coventry. Born 27th July, 1892 at Coventry. Enlisted February, 1916 at Coventry. Grocer's assistant. Commemorated Stoke (St. Michael's) Church. Grave Ref. XI. F. 6. Cologne Southern Cemetery, Koln(Cologne), Nordrhein-Westfal, Germany.

WOOLASTON, Gunner, Frank. 163710, Royal Field Artillery. Died home, 8th January, 1918. Born Baginton. Employed Coventry. Son of Samuel and Mary Ann Woolaston, of 6, Watermoor Villas, Cirencester. Born at Baginton. Enlisted Coventry. Commemorated Baginton Memorial. Grave Ref. North of west end of church. Baginton (St. John the Baptist) Churchyard.

WOOLGAR, Able Seaman, A H. J/5454(PO), HMS Rattlesnake, Royal Navy. Died, home, 5th November, 1918. Age 24. Son of Mrs. M. A. Woolgar, of 17, Sackville Street, Coventry. Grave Ref. 184. 27. Coventry (London Road) Cemetery.

WOOLLEY, Private, Ernest Thomas. 9375, 2nd Bn., Worcestershire Regiment. Killed in action, 24th October, 1914. Age 27. Brother of Mrs. A. M. Sutton, of 85, Cromwell Street, Red Lane, Coventry. Born Dudley. Enlisted Dudley. Memorial Ref. Panel 34. Ypres (Menin Gate) Memorial, Ieper, West-Vlaanderen, Belgium.

WOOLRICH, Private, Williams. 8204, 1st Bn., Royal Welsh Fusiliers. Killed in action, 13th March, 1915. Born Wolverhampton. Enlisted Coventry. Memorial Ref. Panel 13 and 14. Le Touret Memorial, France.

WOOTTON, Private, Thomas. 9162, 1st Bn., Northumberland Fusiliers. Killed in action, 10th January, 1916. Born 16th May, 1884 at Coventry. Enlisted Coventry. Resided at 10, Cope Street. Turner, Gear shop, Daimler Works. Reservist. Memorial Ref. Panel 8 and 12. Ypres (Menin Gate) Memorial, Belgium.

WOOTTON, Sapper, William. 18665, 5th Field Coy., Royal Engineers. Killed in action, 15th November, 1914. Born Coventry. Enlisted Coventry. Born 16th April, 1886 at Coventry. Resided 10, Cope Street, Coventry. Soldier. Memorial Ref. Panel 9. Ypres (Menin Gate) Memorial, Belgium.

WOOTTON, Private, Herbert. CH/2370(S), 2nd Bn., Royal Marine Light Infantry. Killed in action, 22nd March, 1918. Born 18th May, 1896 in Far Gosford Street. Resided at 39, Castle Street. Machinist. Memorial Ref. Bay 1. Arras Memorial, France.

WORKER, Pioneer, Roland Lionel Thomas. 42619, 67th Field Coy., Royal Engineers. Killed in action, Gallipoli, 9th August, 1915. Born Oxford. Enlisted Coventry. Memorial Ref. Panel 23 to 25. Helles Memorial, Turkey.

WORMALD, Private, Samuel. 47042, 15th Bn., Lancashire Fusiliers formerly 22006, Somerset Light Infantry. Killed in action, 10th August, 1918. Born Birmingham. Resided Coventry. Carter. Memorial Ref. Panel 5 and 6. Vis-En-Artois Memorial, France.

WORRALL, Private, Alfred Thomas. 4573, 1st /7th Bn., Royal Warwickshire Regiment. Killed in action, Pozieres, 14th July, 1916. Age 21. Son of Dorothea Maria Darvill (formerly Worrall), of 106, Newcombe Rd., Earlsdon, Coventry. Born 22nd May, 1895 at 5, Much Park Street. Resided at 67, Whitefriars Street. Postman. Enlisted 11th November, 1915 at Coventry. Commemorated Post Office Memorial. Memorial Ref. Pier and Face 9 A 9 B and 10 B. Thiepval Memorial, Somme, France.

WORRALL, Private, Charles Thomas. 20894, 1st /6th Bn., Royal Warwickshire Regiment. Killed in action, 29th November, 1916. Age 25. Son of Charles and Ellen Worrall, of 23, Gordon Street, Butts, Coventry. Born 4th May, 1891 at 9c. 4h., Chauntry Place. Resided at 39, Cook Street. Barman. Enlisted Coventry April 1916. Commemorated Holy Trinity Panels and War Memorial Park. Memorial Ref. Pier and Face 9 A 9 B and 10 B. Thiepval Memorial, Somme, France.

WORRALL, Private, Frank. 28583, 15th Bn., Royal Warwickshire Regiment. Died of wounds, 10th April, 1917. Age 25. Son of Walter Worrall, of Coventry. Husband of Jess Worrall (nee Lester). Born Coventry. Enlisted Coventry. Grave Ref. III. B. 16. Lapugnoy Military Cemetery, Pas de Calais, France.

WORRALL, Sergeant, Leonard Joseph. 14102, 8th Bn., South Staffordshire Regt. Killed in action, Battle of the Somme 10th July 1916. Born 26th August 1896 at Coventry. Resided at Birmingham. Electrical Engineer, GEC, Switchgear Department, Witton works. Enlisted September, 1914. Commemorated War Memorial Park. Memorial Ref. Pier and Face 7B. Thiepval Memorial, Somme, France.

WORRALL, Private, O. L. 30505, 17th Bn., Sherwood Foresters (Notts and Derby Regiment). attd. 254th Tunnelling Coy., Royal Engineers. 6th July, 1917. Age 24. Son of William and Selina Worrall, of 50, Bentinck Street, Hucknall Torkard, Notts. Born Sowe, nr Coventry. Grave Ref. II. B. 24. Poperinghe New Military Cemetery, Poperinge, West-Vlaanderen, Belgium.

WORRALL, Sergeant, William Henry. 2839, 2nd Bn., Royal Warwickshire Regiment. 3rd September, 1916. Age 43. Husband of Clara E. Worrall, of 20, Freehold Street, Coventry. Born 20th March, 1873 in East Street. Labourer. Enlisted August, 1914 at Coventry. Memorial Ref. Pier and Face 9 A 9 B and 10 B. Thiepval Memorial, Somme, France. (Possibly buried Bazentin-le-Petit Communal Cemetery).

WORTHINGTON, Private, Herbert John. S4/122918, 41st Field Bakery, Army Service Corps. Died 3rd September 1915 . Born 16th December, 1889 in Fleet Street, Coventry. Enlisted July, 1915 at Coventry. Resided 92, East Street, Coventry. Silk spinner. Grave Ref. II. L. 205. East Mudros Military Cemetery, Greece.

WORTHINGTON, Lance Corporal, T. 17826, 9th Royal North Lancashire Regiment. Killed in action, 9th November, 1915. Parents resided 53, Spring Road, Coventry. Husband of E. Hinchcliffe (formerly Worthington), of 13, Primet Street, Colne, Lancs. Left a wife and two children. Employed loop line near Coventry. Grave Ref. E. 5. Gunners Farm Military Cemetery, Belgium.

WORWOOD, Private, Bertram. 50758, 10th Bn., Royal Warwickshire Regiment. Died of wounds, 6th June, 1918. Age 18. Son of Thomas Henry Worwood, of Garrick House, Albany Road, Coventry. Born 7th November, 1899 at Exhall. Resided at 6, Ford Street. Ironmongers apprentice. Enlisted November, 1917 at Coventry. Grave Ref. VIII. G. 9. Marfaux British Cemetery, Marne, France.

WORWOOD, Private, John Thomas. PO/17613, 1st Royal Marine Bn., Royal Naval Division, Royal Marine Light Infantry. Killed in action, 25th August, 1918. Age 21. Son of Mr. and Mrs. J. Worwood, of 12, Alexandra Terrace, Lythall Lane, Foleshill, Coventry. Employed Coventry. Memorial Ref. Panel 1. Vis-En-Artois Memorial, Pas de Calais, France.

WRIGGLESWORTH, Private, Theodore Rymer. 7179, 1st Bn., Devonshire Regiment. 18th November, 1914. Age 30. Son of Sarah Wrigglesworth, of 10, Sticklepath Hill, Barnstaple, Devon. Husband of Bessie Liggins (formerly Wrigglesworth), of 626, Stoney Stanton Road, Coventry. Memorial Ref. Panel 21. Ypres (Menin Gate) Memorial, Ieper, West-Vlaanderen, Belgium.

WRIGHT, Private, Albert. 11628, 2/4th Bn., Oxfordshire and Buckinghamshire Light Infantry. Died, 26th July, 1918. Born Foleshill. Resided Bulkington. Grave Ref. VI. H. 8. Berlin South-Western Cemetery, Germany.

WRIGHT, Sergeant, Arthur Tyne. 86361, Machine Gun Corps (Motors). Mesopotamia, Died, 8th October, 1918. Born 15th January, 1898, in Ash Grove. Resided at 77, Ransom Road. Machine tool fitter. Enlisted May, 1918. Commemorated War Memorial Park. Grave Ref. V. E. 3. Tehran War Cemetery, Iran.

WRIGHT, Private, Bertie Leonard. 2631, 11th Bn., Royal Warwickshire Regiment. Died of wounds, 1st August, 1916. Age 20. Son of Mr. and Mrs. W. Wright, of Coventry. Born 24th February, 1896 in Longford Road. Resided at 6, Ash Grove. Labourer, Webster brickyard. Enlisted July, 1914 at Coventry. Grave Ref. VII. E. 12. Warloy-Baillon Communal Cemetery Extension, Somme, France.

WRIGHT, C. Employed Rover Company Ltd. Killed in action.

WRIGHT, Private, David. RMA/3339(S), H.Q. (Eastney), Royal Marine Artillery. Died of influenza, 19th July, 1918. Age 24. Son of Mrs. Catherine Mary Wright, of 9, Grange Terrace, Walsgrave Road, Coventry. Born at Wyken. Grave Ref. In South-West part. Wyken (St. Mary Magdalene) Churchyard.

WRIGHT, Private Edgar Charles. L/16770 9th Bn., Royal Fusiliers formerly 11524, 3rd Hussars. Killed in action, Somme, 19th October, 1916. Born 18th March, 1897 at Leicester. Enlisted Coventry. Resided Coventry. Butcher. Enlisted August, 1914. Commemorated St. John's Church. Memorial Ref. Pier and Face 8 C 9 A and 16 A. Thiepval Memorial, Somme, France.

WRIGHT, Private, Ernest. 17489, 14th Bn., Royal Warwickshire Regiment. Killed in action, 3rd September, 1916. Age 42. Brother of Mr. F. Wright of Brook House, Cheadle, Staffs. Born Cheadle, Staffs. Enlisted Coventry. Memorial Ref. Pier and Face 9A 9B and 10B. Thiepval Memorial, France.

WRIGHT, Private, Frederick John. 32792, 9th Bn., Durham Light Infantry. Died of wounds, 21st July, 1918. Age 20. Son of John and Ann Maria Wright, of 3, Egremont Gardens, Sheriff Hill, Gateshead, Co. Durham. Born at Birmingham. Born Coventry. Enlisted Gateshead. Resided Sherriff Hill, Co. Durham. Grave Ref. III. H. 11. Tournai Communal Cemetery Allied Extension, Belgium.

WRIGHT, Private, George Henry. G/20498, 7th Bn., Royal Sussex Regiment. Killed in action, 3rd May, 1917. Age 25. Son of George and Mary Ann Wright, of Top Road, Barnacle. Employed Coventry. Born Barnacle. Enlisted Coventry. Memorial Ref. Bay 6. Arras Memorial, Pas de Calais, France.

WRIGHT, Private, Herbert George. 4481, 1st /7th Bn., Royal Warwickshire Regiment. Died of wounds, 15th November, 1916. Age 38. Son of George and Rebecca Wright, of Coventry. Husband of Lilly Blood (formerly Wright), of 2, Leigh Buildings, Stoney Stanton Road, Coventry. Born 27th December, 1877 at Stoke, Coventry. Resided at 2 Leigh Buildings, Stoney Stanton Road. Gardener. Enlisted September, 1915 at Coventry. Commemorated Stoke (St. Michaels) Church, War Memorial Park and Parks and Cemeteries Memorial, Coventry Corporation. Grave Ref. I. C. 23. Contalmaison Chateau Cemetery, Somme, France.

WRIGHT, Rifleman, Joseph Castell. B/200885, 8th Bn., Rifle Brigade. Killed in action, 4th April, 1918. Age 27. Son of Mr. A. H. Wright, of 66, Butts, Coventry. Husband of A. Wright. Enlisted Coventry. Resided 32, Meadow Street, Coventry. Machine hand. Enlisted October, 1916. Born 1891 at Coventry. Memorial Ref. Panel 81 to 84. Pozieres Memorial, Somme, France.

WRIGHT, Private, 1st Class, Percy James. 286991, 1st School of Navigation and Bomb Dropping, Royal Air Force. 28th October, 1918. Age 38. Husband of Florence Elizabeth Wright, of 11, Park Gate Road, Holbrooks, Foleshill, Coventry. Grave Ref. 324. Durrington Cemetery, Wiltshire.

WRIGHT, Corporal, Thomas. 10017, 1st Bn., Coldstream Guards. Posted as missing, 23rd December, 1914. Last seen Battle of Givenchy. Age 23. Son of Mrs. Catherine Mary Wright, of 9, Grange Terrace, Walsgrave Rd., Coventry. Born Chadsmoor, Stafford. Enlisted Nuneaton. Resided Coventry. Memorial Ref. Panels 2 and 3. Le Touret Memorial, Pas de Calais, France.

WRIGHT, Private, Walter John. 260032, B Coy., 6th Bn., Duke of Cornwall's Light Infantry formerly Royal Warwickshire Regiment. Killed in action, 17th October, 1917. Aged 19. Born 1898. Resided Coventry. Printers apprentice. Enlisted 1916 at Coventry. Memorial Ref. Panel 80 to 82 and 163A. Tyne Cot Memorial, Belgium.

WYATT, Private, Frederick. 201742, 5th Bn., Oxfordshire and Buckinghamshire Light Infantry. Died of wounds, 6th May, 1917. Age 19. Son of Mrs. Bowerman, of Marston Junction, Nuneaton. Resided Marston Junction, Warwickshire. Employed Coventry. Grave Ref. IX. G. 12. Warlincourt Halte British Cemetery, Saulty, France.

WYKES, Private, Albert. 17908, 16th Bn., Royal Warwickshire Regiment. Killed in action, 23rd April, 1917. Age 22. Husband of Ada I. Wykes, of 65, White Friars Lane, Coventry. Born 5th June, 1895 at 26, Gosford Street, Painter. Coventry. Enlisted April, 1916 at Coventry. Grave Ref. III. F. 10. La Chaudiere Military Cemetery, Vimy, Pas de Calais, France.

WYKES, Company Sergeant Major, Percy. 9135, 1st Bn., Royal Scots Fusiliers. Died of wounds, 3rd September, 1918. Husband of Catherine Wykes, of 36, Captain Street, Greenock. Born 21st September, 1887 at Coventry. Enlisted August, 1914 at Coventry. Resided Greenock. Machinist. Grave Ref. III. F. 11. Bac-Du-Sud British Cemetery, Bailleulval, France.

WYLEY, Lieutenant, William Reginald Fitzthomas. Royal Field Artillery. Killed in action by a shell, Ovillers, 19th September, 1916. Age 24. Son of Colonel William Fitzthomas Wyley and Clara Margaret Wyley, of Charterhouse, Coventry. Born 23rd January, 1892. Resided at Charterhouse. Educated at Oxford University (Balliol College). Enlisted August, 1914. Commemorated War Memorial Park. Grave Ref. G. 44. Aveluy Communal Cemetery Extension, Somme, France.

YAPP, Private, Allen. 3035, 1st Bn., Royal Warwickshire Regiment. Accidentally killed, 8th February, 1915 by a passing train at a railway, Steenwerck. Born 17th December, 1876 at Dudley. Resided at 42, Hope Street. Cycle finisher, Machine Shop, Rudge Works. Enlisted September, 1914. Leaves a widow and a child. Grave Ref. 3. La Creche Communal Cemetery, France.

YARDLEY, Second Lieutenant, Frank. 246th Coy., Machine Gun Corps (Infantry). Killed in action, Ypres, 7th August, 1917. Age 29. Son of Walter and Laura E. Yardley, of 77, New George Street, Coventry. Born 18th June, 1888 in Brewery Street. Resided at 83, Somerset Road. School teacher. Enlisted September, 1914. Commemorated Bablake School Memorial, Education Department Memorial, Coventry Corporation and Holy Trinity Panels. Memorial Ref. Panel 56. Ypres (Menin Gate) Memorial, Ieper, West-Vlaanderen, Belgium. (Possibly buried Oosttaverne Wood Cemetery).

YARDLEY, Private, Frederick Charles. 22298, 20th Bn., The King's Liverpool Regiment. Died of wounds, caused by shrapnel, 22nd February 1916. Born Coventry. Enlisted Liverpool. Resided Liverpool. Born 22nd December, 1897 in Craven Street. Clerk. Enlisted October, 1914. Youngest son of Mr. Thomas. W. Yardley and Mrs. Yardley (nee Evitts) of Craven Street. Commemorated St. Barbara's Church. Grave Ref. I. D. 13. Corbie Communal Cemetery, France.

YARDLEY, Private, William Edgar. 28595, 15th Bn., Royal Warwickshire Regiment. Killed in action, 4th October, 1917. Age 25. Born St. Thomas Parish. Son of William and Elizabeth Yardley. Memorial Ref. Panel 23 to 28 and 163A. Tyne Cot Memorial, Belgium.

YARDLEY, Private, William Gamble. G/11238, 23rd Bn., Middlesex Regiment. Died of wounds, 17th September, 1916. Born 21st November, 1896 at Coventry. Enlisted Coventry. Resided 10 College Square, Cook Street. Carter. Enlisted 1915. Grave Ref. D. 13. Longueval Road Cemetery, France.

YARNEY, James. Commemorated Holy Trinity Panels.

YATES, Corporal, Charles Burdett. CH/19287, 8th Bn. HMS Coventry, Royal Marine Light Infantry. Died of wounds received in Ireland, 24th July, 1920. Age 24. Son of Beatrice Eveline Cleaver (formerly Yates), of Myrtle Villa, 51, Hugh Road, Coventry, and of Frederick Cleaver (stepfather). Grave Ref. 191. 187. Coventry (London Road) Cemetery.

YATES, Sergeant, Thomas, MM. 4876, 11th Battalion, Royal Warwickshire Regiment. 9th July, 1916. Employed by Armstrong Siddeley Motors, Ltd. Born Holborn, Middlesex. Enlisted Warley, Middlesex. Commemorated War Memorial Park and Siddeley Roll of Honour. Memorial Ref. Pier and Face 9 A 9 B and 10 B, Thiepval Memorial, Somme, France

YATES, Lance Corporal, William. C/1069, 16th Bn., King's Royal Rifle Corps. Killed in action, 14th April, 1918. Age 30. Husband of F. G. Yates, of 214, Stoney Stanton Road, Coventry. Employed Coventry. Memorial Ref. Panel 8. Ploegsteert Memorial, Comines-Warneton, Hainaut, Belgium.

YEATES, Driver, Harold. 114582, "D" Bty. 149th Bde., Royal Field Artillery. Killed in action, 18th July 1917. Born Coventry. Enlisted Coventry. Grave Ref. III. E. 10. Reninghelst New Military Cemetery, Belgium.

YEOMANS, George. Commemorated Wolston Memorial.

YOUNG, Sergeant, Alfred. 33711, 1st Bn., Loyal North Lancashire Regiment. Killed in action, 18th September, 1918. Born Droylsden, Lancashire. Resided Coventry. Grave Ref. IV. I. 6. Bellicourt British Cemetery, France.

YOUNG, Private, Henry. 48521, 19th Bn., Manchester Regiment. 22nd June, 1917. Husband of Margaret Young, of 7 Court, 8 House, Back Park Street, Coventry. Grave Ref. Durham Cem. Mem. 72. Perth Cemetery (China Wall), Ieper, West-Vlaanderen, Belgium.

YOUNG, Lance Corporal, John. 37337, 2nd Bn., South Lancashire Regiment. Killed in action, 11th February, 1917. Age 34. Son of William and Sarah Jane Young. Husband of Elizabeth Young, of 39, Church Road, Bell Green, Foleshill, Coventry. Born 1st April, 1883 at Northampton. Labourer, Mr. Buers, Bell Green. Enlisted June, 1916. Leaves a widow and five children. Grave Ref. II. E. 48. London Rifle Brigade Cemetery, Comines-Warneton, Hainaut, Belgium.

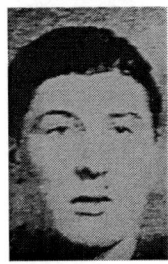

YOUNG, Bombardier, Leonard. 840772, "D" Bty. 307th Bde., Royal Field Artillery. Killed in action, Arras, 16th April 1918 during a heavy bombardment. Born 6th April, 1894 in Vernon Street, Coventry. Resided Paynes Lane. Butcher. Enlisted May, 1915 at Coventry. Leaves a widow and one child. Memorial Ref. Panel 7 to 10. Pozieres Memorial, France. (Possibly buried Gentelles Communal Cemetery).

YOUNG, Private, Roland James. 60727, 27th Bn., Machine Gun Corps (Infantry) formerly Royal Fusiliers. Killed in action, 9th April 1917. Born Coventry. Enlisted Coventry. Grave Ref. B. 14. Bailleul Road West Cemetery, St. Laurent-Blangy, France.